THE JEWS: THEIR RELIGION AND CULTURE

The original preparation of this book was made possible by funds generously made available by the American Jewish Committee.

This is the second volume of a three-volume work. Its companion volumes are:

THE JEWS:

THEIR RELIGION
AND CULTURE

FOURTH EDITION

Edited by

Louis Finkelstein

CHANCELLOR
THE JEWISH THEOLOGICAL SEMINARY OF AMERICA

SCHOCKEN BOOKS · NEW YORK

Second Printing, 1973

First SCHOCKEN PAPERBACK edition 1971

Published by arrangement with Harper & Row, Publishers
Copyright © 1949, 1955, 1960, 1971 by Louis Finkelstein
Library of Congress Catalog Card No. 74–107615
Manufactured in the United States of America

To

IRVING LEHMAN

(1876–1945)

Who in life and precept
integrated the ancient tradition
of the Hebrew prophets with the
spirit of American democracy

CONTRIBUTORS AND MEMBERS OF
THE PLANNING COMMITTEE[1]

William Foxwell Albright, *The Johns Hopkins University*, Emeritus Professor of Semitic Languages

Alexander Altmann, *Brandeis University*, Philip W. Lown Professor of Jewish Philosophy

Hillel Bavli, *The Jewish Theological Seminary of America*, Seminary Professor of Hebrew Literature[2]

Itzhak Ben-Zvi, *The State of Israel*, President (December 8, 1952–April 23, 1963)[2]

Elias J. Bickerman, *Columbia University*, Professor Emeritus of Ancient History

Arturo Castiglioni, *Yale University*, Professor of the History of Medicine[2]

David Daiches, *University of Sussex*, Dean, School of English and American Studies

Moshe Davis, *The Jewish Theological Seminary of America*, Research Professor of American Jewish History

Ben Zion Dinur, *The Hebrew University*, Professor Emeritus of Modern Jewish History

Jessica Feingold, *The Jewish Theological Seminary of America*, Director, The Institute for Religious and Social Studies

Louis Finkelstein, *The Jewish Theological Seminary of America*, Chancellor, Solomon Schechter Professor of Theology

Eli Ginzberg, *Columbia University*, Hepburn Professor of Economics

Nahum N. Glatzer, *Brandeis University*, Professor of Jewish History

Judah Goldin, *Yale University*, Assistant Professor of Classical Judaica, Advisor in Jewish Literature in the University Library, and Fellow of Davenport College

Bernard R. Goldstein, *Yale University*, Assistant Professor of the History of Science

Robert Gordis, *The Jewish Theological Seminary of America*, Seminary Professor of Bible

Simon Greenberg, *The Jewish Theological Seminary of America*, Vice-Chancellor, Vice-President of the Faculties, Professor of Homiletics and Education

Abraham S. Halkin, *The Jewish Theological Seminary of America*, Stuart E. Rosenberg Professor of History

Israel Halpern, *The Hebrew University*, Rosenbloom Professor of Jewish History

Abraham J. Heschel, *The Jewish Theological Seminary of America*, Professor of Jewish Ethics and Mysticism

[1] As of July 1970
[2] Deceased

Oscar I. Janowsky, *City College of The City University of New York*, Professor of History, and Director, New York Area Studies

Mordecai M. Kaplan, *The Jewish Theological Seminary of America*, Professor Emeritus of Philosophies of Religion

Milton R. Konvitz, *Cornell University*, Professor of Industrial and Labor Relations and Professor of Law

Anita Libman Lebeson, formerly Instructor in History, *University of Illinois*, College of Jewish Studies

Frederick Lehner, *West Virginia State College*, Professor of German and French[2]

Shmuel Leiter, *The Jewish Theological Seminary of America*, Associate Professor of Modern Hebrew Literature

Saul Lieberman, *The Jewish Theological Seminary of America*, Rector, Distinguished Service Research Professor of Talmud, and Louis Ginzberg Professor of Palestinian Institutions

R. M. MacIver, *Columbia University*, Lieber Professor Emeritus of Political Philosophy and Sociology

Ralph Marcus, *The University of Chicago*, Professor of Hellenistic Culture[2]

Yudel Mark, *Jewish Education Committee of New York*, Consultant for Yiddish Schools; *YIVO Institute for Jewish Research*, Chief Editor, *"Yiddishe Sprakh"*

Alexander Marx, *The Jewish Theological Seminary of America*, Jacob H. Schiff Professor of History[2]

Abraham Menes, *Zukunft*, Coeditor; *Jewish Daily Forward*, Columnist

Jacob J. Rabinowitz, *The Hebrew University*, Associate Professor of Jewish Law

Cecil Roth, *University of Oxford*, Reader Emeritus in Jewish Studies; Editor-in-Chief, *Encyclopaedia Judaica*[2]

Harry A. Savitz, M.D., *Hebrew Rehabilitation Center*, Physician-in-Chief Emeritus; *Beth Israel Hospital*, Boston, Staff Member

Charles Singer, *University of London*, Professor Emeritus; *University College*, London, Fellow; *Oxford University*, Magdalen College, Honorary Fellow; *History of Technology*, Joint Editor; *American Philosophical Society*, member[2]

Shalom Spiegel, *The Jewish Theological Seminary of America*, William Prager Professor of Medieval Hebrew Literature

Bernard D. Weinryb, *Dropsie College*, Professor of History and Middle East Economics

Eric Werner, *Hebrew Union College*, Professor Emeritus; Chairman, Department of Musicology, *University of Tel-Aviv*, Israel

Rachel Wischnitzer, *Yeshiva University*, Stern College, Professor Emeritus of Fine Arts

CONTENTS

INTRODUCTORY NOTE

This book is the first comprehensive description of Judaism and the Jews. While avoiding the anatomical structure and purely alphabetical organization of an encyclopedia, it is designed as a readable and unified sketch of a singular human phenomenon. The principal relevant facts concerning the people of Israel and its faith are summarized in a succession of essays, which form an ordered whole and afford penetrating glimpses into particular aspects of the subject. This book includes the first compact history of the Jews written by scholars specializing in the several fields; an appreciation of the role of Judaism in world culture, seen from a wide variety of disciplines and skills; an initial effort toward a demography of the Jews in America; and a brief outline of the Jewish religion.

The complexity of the work, despite all efforts to achieve simplicity and uniformity, indicates the difficulty and intricacy of the subject. The history of Israel opens with the birth of Abraham, some 120 generations ago in the Mesopotamian bronze age, the period of Hammurabi, and since that time there has been scarcely a civilized dialect which does not contain some record bearing on the chronicle of this ancient people and its faith. One might almost say that no inhabited land but has witnessed Jewish heroism and martyrdom.

To compose a history of the Jews requires erudition and command of method, rarely, if ever, combined in one individual. It is one thing to reconstruct a living record of prebiblical and biblical Judaism from archaeological and literary records, and quite another to discern in an inexhaustible mass of documents, record books, living monuments or institutions, the pattern of modern Jewish life. Few scholars could master both techniques. And the sort of research that enables a man to interpret a prolix medieval work (its confusion of fact and legend, its reliance on hearsay evidence, its extravagance and vagueness) is completely different from that required for the exegesis of an obscure, but pregnant, biblical or talmudic or philosophical text.

In the course of its long, tortuous history, Judaism has profoundly affected, and been deeply affected by, cultural phenomena covering the whole range of human experience. To understand fully the place of Judaism in civilization it would be necessary to master philosophies and mental outlooks of cultures as varied as those of the ancient Canaanites, the Egypt of the Pharaohs, the Mesopotamia of the Assyrians, the Baby-

xii INTRODUCTORY NOTE

lonians, and the Persians, the Seleucid and the Ptolemaic empires of the Greeks, the world empire of the Romans, the deserts of the Arabs, pre-Christian and Christian Europe, as well as the chaotic and complex world of our own day.

In turn, the faith and tradition of the Jews have left an indelible stamp on Western music, art, science, mathematics, medicine, philosophy, letters, education, philanthropy, law, public administration, manners, morals, and religion. The extent of this influence is not yet fully understood, for there are few scholars who know Jewish lore and, at the same time, enough of any field in Western culture to discover mutual relationships. Histories and anthologies of Western philosophy are still necessarily written with scant reference to such towering figures as Maimonides and Crescas, and none at all to the penetrating insights of the Talmud. The reconstruction of talmudic mathematics, and the analysis of its influence on that of the medieval period, are still in their initial stages; only the merest beginning has been made in the study of the relation of talmudic legal principles to the Canon Law and through it to later norms. The educational technique of the ancient Rabbinic schools, which might be of great practical value today, remains unknown except to the preoccupied, completely dedicated talmudic scholar. Students have still to describe the literary forms of Rabbinic Judaism that directly—and indirectly, through the Gospels—exerted so profound an influence on later composition. The Jewish conception of the whole of life as a work of art, a pageant of worship, in which every action must follow the score set down in the codes, yet may reflect individual ingenuity and piety, is only now beginning to be expounded. The essays in the present volumes can but suggest vast areas of research in these and other fields.

The three paperback volumes are being issued for distribution separately and in one set. Therefore certain material will be repeated in each, such as the introductory note, the list of contributors and member of the planning committee, the contents of all three volumes, and the list of abbreviations. An index will apply only to the volume in which it appears.

The physical size of the present paperback edition was determined by practical problems of manufacture and binding. The difficult choice of chapters from the hardcover edition was made by representatives of the respective publishers, Harper & Row and Schocken Books, necessarily on the basis of the material most needed by a mass audience. Ten excellent chapters had to be omitted; perhaps some readers of this paperback edition will be encouraged to seek that information in previous editions.

The paperback edition contains new material in several areas. "The Modern Renaissance of Hebrew Literature" by the late Hillel Bavli has been expanded by Shmuel Leiter. The contribution of the Jews to medicine described by the late Arturo Castiglioni has been expanded by Harry A.

Savitz, M.D. The chapter on science and Judaism by the late Charles Singer has been expanded by Bernard R. Goldstein. Authors in the original edition who have generously brought their chapters up to date are Moshe Davis, Simon Greenberg, Yudel Mark, Cecil Roth, and Eric Werner. Previous bibliographies have also been enriched by William F. Albright, Alexander Altmann, Elias J. Bickerman, David Daiches, Judah Goldin, Abraham S. Halkin, Israel Halpern, Mordecai M. Kaplan, Milton Konvitz, Anita Libman Lebeson, Bernard Weinryb, and Rachel Wischnitzer.

The bibliographies are not uniform either in their comprehensiveness or in their selectivity. Similarly, the various writers are by no means uniform in their use of footnotes for detailed discussion. In some chapters the notes are numbered by sections of the chapter, notably in the articles by Judah Goldin and Alexander Altmann. In others, the numbering is continuous for the whole chapter.

While grateful for the material provided in the current volume, and realizing that the authors are pre-eminent, the editor can take no responsibility for the views expressed, and is indeed in actual disagreement with a number of them. Some authors disagree with others. Each was invited to write his own chapter because of the special contribution he had to make, regardless of whether it would contradict the views of others or of the editor.

Despite all efforts to bring about common approaches and common standards, a collection of essays inevitably remains an assembly of differing styles, as well as points of view. The editor has made no effort to overcome inconsistencies among the authors; on the contrary, he has drawn attention to them. He has also made no effort to persuade writers to address themselves, necessarily, to the same audience. Some essays are technical; others, without diminution of scholarly integrity and insight, are popular in presentation. Some writers have considered it their task to present merely the consensus of present scholarship, and have avoided reference to their own theories and hypotheses. In other essays, the student will find bold insights and theories, together with references to the commonly accepted views.

The problem of anti-Semitism is dealt with only tangentially in this edition. The editor was persuaded to omit the chapters intended to cover that subject in detail. A number of studies, specifically dedicated to this problem, are now being conducted by various institutions; and the comprehensive works to emanate from them would doubtless make superfluous any summary statement in these volumes.

The English translation of the Hebrew Scriptures issued by the Jewish Publication Society of America (1943) has been used, in general, for quotations from the Bible. However, several authors, for example, Dr. Robert

Gordis, were permitted to substitute their own renderings, because these seemed basic to their argument. Similarly, in specialized articles, such as that by Professor Shalom Spiegel, diacritical marks and technical forms of transliteration have been used, whereas in the book generally transliteration has followed the system set up for popular works by the Jewish Publication Society of America. The names of modern settlements in Palestine have been cited in the spelling commonly used in Zionist English publications, though that may be out of accord with the transliteration system employed in the rest of the book. Hebrew words which have become part of the English language are spelled according to the standard English dictionaries and encyclopedias, as *Cabbala* instead of *Kabbalah*. Because of the fact that the papers were prepared at different times and in different countries, it has been impossible to achieve real consistency in spelling or transliteration. Because of the difference in pronunciation, no effort has been made to reconcile the transliteration of Hebrew with that of Yiddish. In some cases popular pronunciation has determined the transliteration, as in *Agudas* (for *Agudat*) and *kosher* (for *kasher*).

Foreign words and transliterations of foreign phrases are italicized. However, the titles of talmudic treatises are printed in Roman letters in the text, notes, and bibliographies. The abbreviation "R." is used for Rabbinic Sages, who bore the title Rabbi or Rab, and lived in talmudic times. Those who lived after the close of the Talmud are described as "Rabbi."

The notes in brackets, further distinguished by the use of letters of the alphabet, were added by the editor and his associates to guide the reader, particularly where a subject mentioned in one passage is more fully discussed in another essay. The reader will find a number of individuals and organizations mentioned in more than one place. This duplication has been allowed because each of the various authors treats a given subject differently, and the repetition seemed valuable. Sometimes chapters overlap considerably, such as those of Dr. Arturo Castiglioni and Professor Charles Singer, or those of Dr. Moshe Davis and Mrs. Anita Libman Lebeson. However, the reader should find the overlapping helpful to a complete study of the subject.

All royalties will continue to be earmarked for subsequent improved editions, in hopes that the work may become a classic worthy of its subject and useful to generations yet unborn.

And now, having ended this task, I follow the example of R. Nehuniah be Hakkanah, great Sage of the first century, who when he entered the House of Study prayed that no error should occur through him, and when he left gave thanks for his portion.

Louis Finkelstein

The Jewish Theological Seminary of America
New York City, July 1969

THE JEWS: THEIR RELIGION AND CULTURE

CHAPTER I

THE BIBLE AS A CULTURAL MONUMENT

By Robert Gordis

I. ATTITUDES TOWARD THE BIBLE—OLD AND NEW

The observation made almost two centuries ago by Voltaire that *"La Bible est plus célèbre que connue"* is as true today as ever before. Many factors have conspired to produce this unfortunate situation, some superficial, others more fundamental. Many a prospective reader is deterred by the form in which the Bible is generally presented—the columns closely printed, the verses numbered as in a catalogue, with no distinction indicated between prose and poetry, between genealogical tables and exalted poetic utterances. A more basic hindrance to the widespread appreciation of the Bible today is, strangely enough, the veneration in which it is held as the Word of God. As a result, most readers turn to it with more devoutness than alertness and expect to be edified rather than stimulated by its contents.

The most important factor, however, leading to the neglect of the Book of Books in modern times is the confusion prevalent in men's attitude toward the Bible. In this respect, as in so many others, our age is a period of transition, with "one world dying, another powerless to be born." Two conceptions are to be met with today, one steadily losing ground, the other possessing implications as yet imperfectly understood. These contemporary attitudes reflect two stages in the development of Western thought.

For the greater part of its history, until the eighteenth century, Western civilization approached the Bible dogmatically through the theory of verbal inspiration. For nearly two millennia the Bible was regarded as the repository of God's messages to the human race, literal transcripts of His will revealed to worthy men through the ages. The role of the biblical authors was fundamentally passive. Their distinction lay in their moral and spiritual greatness, which made them worthy of receiving the Divine Revelation. Thus, in dealing with the closing verses of Deuteronomy, which describe the death and burial of Moses, the Talmud declares: "The Holy One, blessed be He, was dictating and Moses was writing with a tear."[1]

As will be noted below, this conception of the literal inspiration of the Bible began undergoing reinterpretation as soon as it was subjected to scrutiny by talmudists, theologians and philosophers. But for the masses of the people it remained the regnant view. In large measure it has retained its hold upon devout believers in both Judaism and Christianity to the present day.

This attitude has several important implications. If Scripture is a literal transcript of God's Word, everything in it is of equal importance. As Maimonides quite rightly insisted, the genealogies of Esau in Genesis are no less sacred than the Ten Commandments or the *Shema*.

Moreover, everything within it is forever binding, being an emanation of the Eternal. Hence, many centuries after the composition of the Bible, the Puritans could adopt the Old Testament as the basis of their polity in the New World without the slightest doubt as to its relevance to their problems. At the same time, without any sense of anachronism, they could validate the burning of the witches in Salem by a reference to Ex. 22:17 which declares: "Thou shalt not suffer a witch to live."

The drawbacks inherent in this second implication were largely overcome in Judaism because of a third. Since the Bible is the Word of God, every apparently unimportant word and insignificant incident must have a deeper meaning. In order that the true intent of the Bible be revealed, the text is therefore in need of interpretation. Thus there developed various schools of biblical interpretation, which sought to reveal this hidden meaning of the text by finding important implications in the repetition of words and phrases, and by drawing deductions from each particle and copula, often from each syllable. The imposing development of the Talmud rests upon this method of textual interpretation. Given the premise, the conclusion was inescapably logical—a message coming directly from the Divine could have nothing accidental or superfluous, either in its content or in its form.

Whatever our attitude toward this approach to the Bible, it should be noted that the modern world owes it an incalculable debt, all too often ignored. In the first instance, it meant that the Bible remained a living and evolving law, keeping pace with new conditions and growing insights. Thus, to cite a few instances at random, almost two thousand years ago the rabbis had, by a process of biblical interpretation, virtually eliminated capital punishment, in spite of its frequent mention in the Pentateuch, and interpreted "an eye for an eye" to mean monetary compensation for damages. Similarly, talmudic law abolished the execution of "a stubborn and rebellious son," enjoined in Scripture (Deut. 21:18-21). It also modified the biblical prohibition of interest in order to meet the needs of commercial credit in an advanced society. Particularly noteworthy is the extension of the rights of women beyond the narrow limits of the ancient

Orient. This was accomplished very simply. All the biblical passages which speak of a *na'arah*, or "girl," as being in the power of her father, who could sell her into slavery or marriage, were referred to a girl between the ages of twelve and twelve and a half! Before that age, she was a *ketanah*, or a "minor," and entitled to special protection. Above that age she was a *bogeret*, or "mature" woman and hence free from the *patria potestas*.

Moreover, this conception of the verbal inspiration of the Bible is to be credited with the creation of a fascinating literature in its own right. The vast nonlegal material in the Talmud and in the independent compilations of the Midrash called the Haggada[2a] consists of ethics, legends and folk wisdom of incomparable value and scope. Most of this literature takes the form of interpretations of biblical passages.

This conception of the literal inspiration of Scripture not only produced an evolving law and a rich ethical and religious literature. It also made possible the creation of religious philosophy in Judaism and in Christianity. In two periods, the traditional religion of the Western world came into contact with Greek philosophy. The first was at the beginning of the Common Era, when Alexandria was the cultural center of the world. The second came some eight or nine hundred years later. First in Bagdad and then in Spain, Arab scholars and thinkers, together with their Jewish confrères, were engaged in preserving and expounding the writings of the Greek philosophers, which were neglected and forgotten in Christian Europe. In addition, new discoveries in mathematics and the sciences were enriching and modifying the ideas to be found in these philosophic classics. From this vast and far-flung intellectual activity, there emerged a world view greatly at variance with traditional concepts found in the Bible.

The conflict was resolved by the allegorical interpretation of Scripture, which had been previously utilized with great skill by Philo of Alexandria in the first century. A great line of philosophically trained thinkers arose during the Middle Ages, who interpreted the biblical text so as to bring it into harmony with the "modern" thought of their age. In the process they broadened immeasurably the horizons of traditional religion, besides making many fruitful contributions to philosophy. It is paradoxical but true that the apparently naïve conception of the Bible as the direct dictation of God was the basis for the great medieval philosophical systems of Saadia, Maimonides, Crescas, and their associates.[3a]

The most important debt owing to this dogmatic attitude still remains to be noted: to it we owe the preservation of the Bible. At a time when the great classics of Greek and Latin literature were being neglected and in many instances lost in the West, the Bible was being preserved with loving care, both in the Hebrew original by Jewish scribes and in the Greek and Latin translations by Christian monks. The achievement of these Hebrew scribes, called *masoretes* or "preservers of tradition," has not been sufficiently appreciated.These nameless scribes copied the Sacred Book with meticulous and loving care. Carefully they noted every letter and every detail of spelling, accentuation and musical notation, in order to prevent errors or changes in the text which they had received from earlier ages. They did not hesitate to count the letters and verses in each book, and noted every exceptional form in spelling or usage. The extent of their veneration for the Bible can be judged by their observation that the middle word of the entire Pentateuch was *darash* in Lev. 10:16 and that the middle letter of the entire Bible was the *yod* in the word *bayyir* in Jer. 6:7!

The development of talmudic law, the creation of the religio-ethical literature of the Rabbis, and the growth of medieval Jewish philosophy, as well as the physical preservation of the Bible, all rested upon the theory of literal inspiration. But the detailed study and analysis of the biblical text led to a recognition that there were differences within the Bible which could be explained only in terms of the human factor. The prophets and poets of the Bible were not mere passive vessels for the Divine, or their messages would have been identical in form and content. They were active participants in the process of Revelation, reflecting or refracting the Divine Light in accordance with the depth of their insight and their spiritual capacity. Thus the Talmud noted the differences in the theophanies described by the prophets Isaiah and Ezekiel. It explained that Isaiah's simple and majestic vision of God (ch. 6) was like the reaction of a city dweller accustomed to the proximity of the royal court, while Ezekiel's circumstantial and elaborate picture of the heavenly chariot (2:8) reflected the attitude of a rustic dazzled by the unwonted spectacle of royal splendor.[4] Similarly, Moses' pre-eminence over the later prophets was graphically expressed by comparing him to a stargazer with a clear telescope while they had blurred instruments of vision.[5]

The talmudic Sages could not overlook the obvious fact that, while the Torah and the prophets seemed to be citing the words of the Deity ("The Lord spake to Moses saying," "Thus saith the Lord"), there were other books in the Bible which made no such claim and were obviously human in origin. The beloved Book of Psalms consisted of hymns addressed by men to their Maker. Job was a flaming protest against the apparent miscarriage of justice in Divine Government. The Book of Esther does not so much as mention the Divine Name.

Hence, it was recognized early that there were different levels of inspiration in the Bible. The highest was represented by the Torah, the second by the Prophets, and the lowest by the Hagiographa. This distinction became a principle of talmudic jurisprudence: "Matters of Law [Torah] are not deducible from other biblical books."[6] Similarly in its provisions for the handling and exchange of scrolls of the Torah and the

[טור מרכזי — מקרא]

את־שבתתי תשמרו ומקדשי
תיראו אני יהוה׃
אל־תפנו אל־האלילם ואלהי
מסכה לא־תעשו לכם אני יהוה אלהיכם׃
מפני שיבה תקום והדרת פני זקן
ויראת מאלהיך אני יהוה׃ ס
וכי־יגור אתך גר בארצכם לא תונו
אתו׃ כאזרח מכם יהיה לכם הגר
הגר אתכם ואהבת לו כמוך כי־גרים
הייתם בארץ מצרים אני יהוה
אלהיכם׃ לא־תעשו עול במשפט
במדה במשקל ובמשורה׃ מאזני־
צדק אבני־צדק איפת צדק והין צדק
יהיה לכם אני יהוה אלהיכם אשר־
הוצאתי אתכם מארץ מצרים׃
ושמרתם את־כל־חקתי ואת־כל־
משפטי ועשיתם אתם אני יהוה׃
פ
וידבר יהוה אל־
משה לאמר׃ ואל־בני ישראל
תאמר איש איש מבני ישראל ומן־
הגר הגר בישראל אשר יתן מזרעו
למלך מות יומת עם הארץ ירגמהו
באבן׃ ואני אתן את־פני באיש
ההוא והכרתי אתו מקרב עמו כי
מזרעו נתן למלך למען טמא את־
מקדשי ולחלל את־שם קדשי׃
ואם העלם יעלימו עם הארץ את־
עיניהם מן־האיש ההוא בתתו
מזרעו למלך לבלתי המית אתו׃
ושמתי אני את־פני באיש
ההוא ובמשפחתו והכרתי אתו

A PAGE FROM THE RABBINICAL BIBLE
Leviticus (19.30-20.5)

Bomberg edition, Venice, 1524-1525

Commentary of Abraham ibn Ezra, Italy (1092-1167)

Commentary of Rashi, France (1040-1105)

Massoretic notes

Massoretic notes

Massoretic notes

Targum Onkelos (authoritative Aramaic translation of the Pentateuch)

Massoretic notes

Hebrew text

Massoretic notes on the spelling and other details of the text (handed down by tradition, compiled 7th century)

Prophets, as well as in other legal enactments, the Mishna recognized the higher sanctity of the Torah.

Some influential teachers in the mishnaic period opposed the extremely painful forms of biblical interpretations which made elaborate deductions from particles or stylistic repetitions. Thus the school of Rabbi Ishmael laid down the principle that was destined to become very fruitful in later days, that "The Torah speaks in the language of man."[7] For all its fondness for homiletic and allegorical interpretations, the Talmud recognized that the literal meaning of a text must take precedence over its figurative interpretation, declaring, "The literal meaning of a verse may not be disregarded."[8]

Moreover, the masoretes, whose principal activity followed the compilation of the Talmud, amassed a good deal of sound grammatical material during their ceaseless labors to protect the biblical text. In the tenth century the Gaon, Saadia ben Joseph noticed the similarities of biblical and Rabbinic Hebrew. His contemporary, Judah ibn Koreish, recognized the resemblances of Hebrew to its sister tongues Aramaic and Arabic. Between them, these two scholars laid the foundations of comparative Semitic philology.

The scattered and unsystematic linguistic observations of the masoretes were replaced by the scientific grammatical studies of brilliant philologists like Judah Hayyuj and Abulwalid ibn Janah and by the notable commentaries of gifted exegetes like Rashi, the Kimhis, Abraham ibn Ezra, and a host of others. Their scientific works attained a level of achievement that bears favorable comparison with those of our own day.

Thus, imperceptibly, the basis was laid for a human approach to the Bible that would regard it not as the dictation of God to men, but as the record of man's aspiration to God. Religious thinkers might still regard the Bible as the inspired Word of God, but man now became the agent and not merely the recipient of the Divine Revelation.

This revolutionary attitude toward the Bible began to dominate the thinking of most modern men in the eighteenth century. In the past the Bible had been regarded as great because it was holy. It was now regarded as holy because it was great. The lectures of Bishop Robert Lowth of Oxford on *The Sacred Poetry of the Hebrews* and on Isaiah, and the rhapsodic discourses of Johann Gottfried Herder in Germany on *The Oldest Sources of Humanity*, led to a new aesthetic appreciation of the Bible as literature, as the expression of the national spirit of Israel during its most creative period.

Resting upon the foundations of medieval learning, the modern age has built the imposing structure of biblical scholarship, which today includes a score of disciplines. Comparative philology has revealed the relation of Hebrew to other members of the Semitic group, the vocabulary and grammatical structure of which have shed light upon the biblical idiom. The text-critical study of the Bible has often revealed the true meaning of the text and in many instances faulty passages have been corrected. The higher critical study of the Bible has revealed a great deal concerning the sources, composition and mutual relationship of the various books and helped us understand the message of the biblical authors against the background of their times. Ancient civilizations have been brought to light whose literary and material remains have re-created the history of the ancient Orient and illumined almost every page of the Bible. Above all, archaeology and the allied sciences of comparative religion and anthropology have enlarged the frame within which the Bible is to be set.

Our conceptions regarding the development of biblical civilization and its literature are still in flux, to be sure. There are untold variations of attitude among contemporary scholars, varying all the way from the extremes of traditionalism to ultraradical criticism. Yet modern biblical research is beginning to achieve a new synthesis of critical approach and respect for tradition. In large measure this emerging point of view is the result of the extensive and fruitful excavations in the lands of the Fertile Crescent—Egypt, Palestine, Syria, and Iraq. The discoveries made there have offered welcome evidence of the essential credibility of the biblical writers and corrected the vagaries of some critics, who possess more acumen than sympathy and more analytical method than constructive imagination.

Our understanding of biblical tradition, history, law, ethics, poetry, prophecy and wisdom has been completely revolutionized by modern biblical and Semitic scholarship. But our debt to the past remains imponderable. If today a modern reader possesses the means for comprehending the Bible better than the greatest mind in medieval times, it is because we are dwarfs standing on the shoulders of giants.

What is the significance of the Bible for the modern age? On the most obvious level, the Bible is *literature*. Within its covers repose some of the world's greatest masterpieces in poetry and prose. There is scarcely one branch of literary art not represented by a noble example.

But the importance of the Bible goes deeper. It is an indispensable element in the *religious* and *moral* education of the human race. The Bible is the immortal record of God's Revelation through its various stages and forms, as embodied in the life and thought of the chosen spirits of Israel, who sought after God and the good life. Even this is not all. The importance of the Bible is more than historical—it is living religion. It contains the profound and ever-fruitful insights of lawgivers, prophets, poets, and sages who looked deep into the heart of man and the universe and recognized both as the handiwork of God. The modern religious spirit finds God revealed far more impressively in the majestic harmony and order of the universe than in the miracles which earlier generations delighted to chronicle. Similarly, the Bible as the achievement of man bears impressive testimony to the divine inspiration that is its source.

Finally the Bible is *history*, vivid, revealing, unforgettable. It is the thrilling record of the tragic yet glorious experience of the Jewish people during its most vigorous period. Though Israel has always been politically weak and physically negligible, the world has recognized its unique religious genius and moral power. As Santayana has said, "He who does not know the past is doomed to repeat it." A knowledge of this basic aspect of the world's spiritual development is crucial today. One may well doubt whether mankind will have many more chances to repeat the mistakes of yesterday. Hence, understanding the Bible means not merely excavating the past, but laying the foundations of the future.

2. THE BACKGROUND OF THE BIBLE[9a]

A true appreciation of the Bible as literature, religion and history is predicated upon the recognition that it is not an anthology of sacred texts or a collection of edifying tracts written by the like-minded believers of a religious sect. It is, in the words of an acute twentieth-century scholar, "a national literature upon a religious foundation." The Bible reveals all the varied and even contradictory intellectual currents and spiritual tendencies that characterized the life of Israel during the first fifteen hundred years of its collective experience. The biblical period begins with the emergence of the Hebrew tribes upon the stage of history during the middle of the second millennium B.C.E. and continues until the persecutions of Antiochus, which preceded the Maccabean revolt (168 B.C.E.). Radical, conservative and moderate, rationalist and mystic, believer and skeptic, all have found their place within the canon of Scripture. The stimulating variety of attitudes and contents in the Bible is heightened by the colorful influences of the older, neighboring cultures of Egypt, Syria and Mesopotamia. The roots of the Bible are to be sought throughout the Near East as surely as its fruits belong to the world.

A clue to the lively intellectual ferment within Israel that produced the Bible is supplied by the traditional division of the Hebrew Bible into three parts: the Torah, or Law, the Nebiim, or Prophets, and the Ketubim, or Sacred Writings. This tripartite arrangement, which is very ancient, recalls the three principal cultural elements in biblical thought: the priest, or custodian of Torah, the prophet, or speaker of the Word, and the sage, the teacher of Wisdom. These groups are clearly delineated in two biblical passages. Jeremiah declares: "For instruction shall not perish from the priest, nor counsel from the wise, nor the word from the prophet" (18:18). Ezekiel utters his warning: "They shall seek a vision of the prophet, and

instruction shall perish from the priest, and counsel from the elders"
(7:26).

Each of these three elements must be understood in terms of its individual development, its relationship to the other two strands, and its ultimate incorporation into the common heritage of Israel.

3. TORAH—THE LAW[10a]

The Torah was the particular province of the priest. The Hebrew word *kohen*, "priest," and its Arabic cognate *kahin*, "seer of a spirit, diviner," bear witness to the earliest period of Semitic history. This stage of religion may have preceded the successive eruptions from the Arabian desert into the lands of the Fertile Crescent and Egypt that produced the different Semitic and Hamitic peoples. At all events, in this primitive period, whether before or after the emergence of distinct ethnic groups, there was only one functionary who met all the religious requirements of the clan. He was the diviner, consulted on all individual and group problems, as well as the custodian of the religious cult and the officiant at sacrifices.

With the growth of a more complex social system, and particularly with the transfer from a nomadic or seminomadic life to a settled agricultural economy, the functions of this dignitary were divided. The free spirit of the god, which ancient men believed was most evident and potent in hypnotic trances and similar transports, became the particular province of wandering seers or dervishes, who eked out a precarious existence from the bounty of those who consulted them on the future, particularly with reference to personal problems. On the other hand, more and more elaborate shrines, altars and temples now arose, which were ministered to by priests. The emoluments of the priests were more substantial and their position in society was more respected than that of the wandering seers. As a result, the priesthood early became a hereditary caste, jealously protecting its prerogatives as guardians of the sanctuary. As a matter of fact, the functions of divining the future and revealing the will of the god or gods were never completely surrendered by the priest, yet more and more his activities tended to become formalized through ritual associated with the sacred objects of the shrine.

These priests naturally created and preserved the rituals connected with their sanctuaries. Being the only educated group, they became the custodians of culture. The literature and science of ancient Egypt and Mesopotamia was almost exclusively the work of the priesthood. In Israel during the days of the First Temple, the priests were the medical authorities, the judges in civil and criminal cases, and the arbiters on all religious problems, as well as the custodians of the ancient historical traditions.

The center of all this priestly activity lay in shrines and temples like those at Shiloh, Beth-el, Gilgal, and, pre-eminently, the Temple of Solomon in Jerusalem, which took precedence over these older and lesser sanctuaries, but never succeeded in superseding them completely. In these sanctuaries, ancient historical records and manuals of law were preserved, both for the practical guidance of the priests and for the instruction of their youth.

The Bible contains many of these briefer *torot*, or legal manuals, necessary to the functioning of the priesthood. Such is the torah of the leper, forbidden foods, and the various sacrifices, all in Leviticus. There were also more extensive legal and moral codes of hoary antiquity, often combining ritual enactment, civil and criminal law, moral exhortation and legal procedure. Such is the Book of the Covenant (Ex. 21-23) and the Holiness Code (Lev. 17-26).

In II Kings 24, we read of an even more elaborate code discovered during the reign of King Josiah (621 B.C.E.). Repairs had been undertaken of the Temple buildings and this Torah was found buried in the foundations or hidden in the walls of the sanctuary, as was common in the ancient world. This code is generally identified today, in whole or in part, with Deuteronomy, the fifth book of the Torah. Doubtless, there were many other *torot* of briefer or more extensive compass which have not reached us, especially those of the local sanctuaries. The prophet Hosea seems to refer to such codes when he says, "Though I write him ten thousand *torot*, they are foreign to him" (8:12).[11]

What is the origin of the Five Books, or Pentateuch? To this question tradition gave a very definite answer. It was Moses, the great liberator of Israel, who had bestowed upon his people the Torah he had received from God.

There were, of course, manifest difficulties connected with this view. That Moses could have written the last verses of Deuteronomy, describing his own death, was a problem the Rabbis solved homiletically. Other passages, like Gen. 12:6 and 36:31, for example, which seemed to infer a post-Mosaic date, were noted by medieval Jewish exegetes. Their observations were repeated and reflected by Spinoza in his *Tractatus Theologico-Politicus*, which was the direct stimulus to the modern Higher Criticism of the Pentateuch. Scholars found many repetitions and inconsistencies in the text and were led to the hypothesis of multiple sources embedded in the Torah. Once set in motion, the process of source analysis gained momentum. More and more contradictions in the text were being discovered which could be resolved only by the hypothesis of new sources, subsources, redactors, and redactional schools.

With the assumption that the Pentateuch consisted of multiple documents combined more or less skillfully by redactors, came the tendency to assign increasingly later dates both to the individual sources and to the composite product, many centuries after the Mosaic age. Moses became a legendary, if not mythical, figure and any resemblance between him and the traditional portrait was purely a matter of accident. The Priestly Code, the largest Pentateuchal source, was generally assigned to the days of the Second Temple, and its narratives and legislation were described as an artificial "*Rueckbildung*," or throwback, of Second Temple conditions into earlier ages.

It should be noted that the higher-critical study of the Torah has made important and enduring contributions to our understanding of biblical law and thought. These values need to be salvaged from the exaggerations and errors into which the critics were all too often betrayed. They cannot be dismissed as wholly insignificant, a procedure often advocated today, particularly in nonscientific publications intended for the general reader.

Archaeological discoveries throughout the Near East brought to light law codes of high antiquity. The most important of these, the Babylonian Code of Hammurabi (twentieth century, B.C.E.), and the Assyrian, Hittite and Hurrian codes, possess many elements that shed light upon Pentateuchal law and tradition. Thus, aside from its many points of contact with the Code of Hammurabi, the Book of the Covenant (Ex. 21-23) contains much of the customary law of the Semitic peoples, and is, therefore, in part at least older than the Exodus from Egypt.

A similar situation obtains with regard to the most famous code of all, the Decalogue (Ex. 20; Deut. 5). It is, to be sure, unique in its simplicity and comprehensiveness and bears the unmistakable stamp of Israel's faith in one God, Whose likeness is not to be pictured by man. Nonetheless, the moral standards ordained in the Ten Commandments have their parallels in the Egyptian *Book of the Dead*, which describes the cross-examination that the dead undergo in the nether world.

For reasons of this kind, as well as larger historical considerations, scholars are recognizing increasingly that if there had been no tradition of a legislator like Moses it would have been necessary to invent one. Without such a dominating personality, it remains inconceivable how a band of slaves could have engineered a mass escape from a powerful country like Egypt. What is more, this group of cowed and oppressed helots were transformed into a mighty people, fired with the resolution to brave the hazards of the desert and carry on a long drawn-out struggle for the conquest of the strongly defended Promised Land. Moreover, this aggregation of clans possessed a strong sense of unity, a common historical memory and, underlying both, the worship of the same God. All this presupposed a Liberator who was also a Lawgiver. In order to impress upon the people the way of life they were to follow, what was required was not only the exalted principles of the Decalogue, but the more mundane and tangible details of ritual, civil and criminal law.

The great prophets of later times also bore testimony to the existence of an exalted religious and ethical tradition in Israel. Even Amos, the earliest among them, who spoke in the name of one living and universal God, enforcing His law of righteousness throughout the world, did not speak of himself as an innovator. On the contrary, the prophets called upon the people to "return" to their God and His law. Their denunciations of the people would be as pointless as they would be unfair, if the "Knowledge of the Lord" which they demanded were not already part of the heritage of the people, however misunderstood or violated.

Many other features of the Pentateuch, in both its historical and legal sections, which had previously been dismissed as inventions of Second Temple writers, were seen to have very old parallels. This is true of the Tabernacle and the Ark in the wilderness, which have their analogies in the *mahmal* and the *'otfe*, sacred tentlike structures borne in the religious processions of various Arab tribes. So, too, with regard to the elaborate system of sacrifices described in Leviticus, the technical terms of which are known to us from Syrian and Punic documents. Another example, the *'edah* or *kahal*, inadequately rendered "congregation" in our current Bible translations, is discussed below.

Thus the conviction has been gaining ground among scholars that the tradition of the Mosaic authorship of the Pentateuch is not an invention. It may never be possible to establish the precise extent of legal material emanating from his period, but that the Torah contains the work of Moses appears certain.[11a]

The sanctuaries naturally served as the libraries for the legal codes that were necessary to the priest in carrying on his ritual and judicial duties. They would also be the natural locale for collecting the historical traditions of the people, especially since the lives of Abraham, Isaac, Jacob, Joseph, and Moses were bound up with the sacred sites and thus served to validate their sanctity. In addition to these national traditions there were others of even greater antiquity that Israel shared with its kinsmen, as part of their common Semitic heritage. Such were the narratives of Creation, the first human pair, the rise of sin, and the Flood. These tales, retold in Israel, were imperceptibly transformed by the alchemy of the Hebrew spirit to reflect the higher and profounder insights of Israelite religion.

All these traditions were originally repeated orally and probably were chanted in verse form. As time went on, however, poetry gave way to prose, and oral transmission to written forms. It is by no means easy to recapitulate the literary history of these historical traditions or to trace the origin and order of composition of the law codes now incorporated in our Torah. The process was undoubtedly long and complex. Yet for the reasons indicated, a new respect for the credibility of the biblical narratives and the antiquity of biblical law has developed.

In part, the difficulty that modern scholars have in reconstructing the steps leading to the compilation of the Torah stems from the fact that the composition and redaction of these codes and traditions proceeded slowly and anonymously over a period of centuries. Their final editing and integration into a single continuous work is most plausibly to be attributed to the impact of the destruction of the First Temple by the Babylonians and the exile of the people in 586 B.C.E.[12a] This catastrophe constituted a major threat to Jewish survival. Six centuries later, when the Second Temple was destroyed by the Romans, a similar crisis confronted Jewish leaders. At that time the traditions governing the Temple and its services were carefully collected in the mishnaic treatise *Middot*, lest they be forgotten in time. In very much the same spirit, the traditions and laws preserved by the priests of the First Temple seem now to have been assembled and codified in the Torah par excellence, the Five Books of Moses.

The collapse of the Babylonian Empire and the rise of Persia in its stead gave the Jewish people a new lease on life.[13a] Cyrus was magnanimous and farsighted in his policy toward subject peoples. He permitted those Jews who so desired to reconstitute their community life in Palestine, granting them religious and cultural autonomy. The Torah proved an incomparable instrument for uniting and governing the Jewish community. Three-quarters of a century after the Return, Ezra, who was a priest by birth and a *sofer*, or "scribe," by calling, persuaded the struggling Jewish settlement in Jerusalem to accept the Torah as its constitution for all time. Nor was this all. Though himself a priest, Ezra carried through a unique peaceful revolution, which stripped the priesthood of its position of religious and intellectual leadership, leaving it only the conduct of the Temple ritual as prescribed by law. The spectacle of moral corruption and degeneracy that a hereditary priesthood exhibited led Ezra to transfer the spiritual leadership of the people from the priests to the scholars, who represented a nonhereditary, democratic element recruited from all classes. The ritual ministrations of the priests in the Temple went on unimpaired, but the dynamic creative impulse in Judaism was henceforth centered in a less pretentious institution, the synagogue, at once a house of prayer, study and communal assembly.

The importance of this revolution, unparalleled in ancient religion, can scarcely be exaggerated. The Talmud gives Ezra little more than his due when it declares, "Ezra was worthy of giving the Torah had not Moses preceded him."[14] Ezra and his scholarly successors are to be credited, in large measure, with the progressive, evolving and democratic character of normative, traditional Judaism.[15a]

The *Soferim* and the Rabbis not only preserved the Torah, they gave it new life. Their activity made the Bible relevant to the needs of new generations and thus prepared it to serve as the eternal charter of humanity. They gave the Jewish tradition some of its most noteworthy characteristics, its protean capacity for adjustment, and its fusing of realistic understanding and idealistic aspiration. These nameless scribes thus contributed in no small measure to the survival of the Jewish people. But their significance is not limited to the household of Israel. The Christian world, too, owes them a debt of gratitude. As founders of Rabbinic Judaism they helped create the background from which Christianity arose, formulating many of the basic teachings that both religions share in common.

Henceforth, the written Torah was complete, with nothing to be added or removed. The oral Torah would carry the growth and development of the Jewish religion forward to its new phase.

4. THE PROPHETS OF ISRAEL

The second great division of the Bible is called "the Prophets." Like so many other aspects of Israelite life, the prophets represent a unique Hebrew development of elements common to all the Semitic peoples. Reference has been made above to the single official of the primitive Semites who exercised all religious functions which were later divided between the priest and the prophet. We have briefly traced the role of the priest, the custodian of Torah, who represents one line of development. The other is represented at its highest by the Hebrew prophet, the revealer of the Divine Word. In its origins, the institution was infinitely less exalted.

Side by side with the formalized role of the priesthood, with its emphasis upon ritual, there arose a considerably more informal type of religious leadership, the diviner, soothsayer, or "seer," familiar today in the Arab dervish. Not being attached to a sanctuary, he had no fixed locale. He therefore had to depend upon the resources of his own personality for his maintenance and position. He functioned through trances or ecstatic spells, under the influence of which he would mutter or shout his message derived from his god. Self-hypnosis would be induced through dances, rhythmic swaying, music, ceaseless repetitions of the Divine Name, or self-laceration. The diviner was both feared because of his connection with the Divine and despised as a cross between beggar and lunatic. Throughout history, Semitic soothsayers remained on this low level and unquestionably had their counterparts in ancient Israel.

In the Bible, however, this type of functionary is not to be met, except for a few stray allusions during the earlier period of the Judges and the Monarchy. This is due to two factors. In the first instance, the Bible is written from the incomparably higher vantage point of the great prophets, who despised these lowly practitioners of doubtful arts. In the second instance, in the biblical period this functionary had already evolved into a higher type, the *nabi*, or prophet. Other titles by which the prophet was known were *roeh* or *hozeh*, "seer," and *ish haelōhim*, "man of God." The etymology of the word *nabi* is uncertain, being derived by some authorities from the meaning "mutter" and by others from the meaning "announce, proclaim." Probably both derivations are correct, reflecting different stages in the development of prophecy, which began as hypnotic utterances and became the respected announcement of the will of God.

The prophet was not merely the revealer of God to man; he was also man's intercessor before God. In his role as a prophet, Abraham prays for the recovery of Abimelech, the king of Gerar, exactly as, in later periods Moses pleads for Miriam and Aaron, and Samuel prays for Saul. So, too, the sinful king Jeroboam implores "the man of God" to intercede for him, and Elijah and Elisha pray for humbler folk in distress (Gen. 20:7, 17; Num. 12:13; Deut. 9:20; I Sam. 15:11; I Kings 13:6; 17:21; II Kings 4:33).

When prophecy became national in scope, we find such diverse figures as Moses, Samuel, Amos, Isaiah and Jeremiah interceding for Israel (Ex. 15:25; 32:11; Deut. 9-18, 26 and elsewhere; I Sam. 7:5-9; 12:19; Jer. 42:2, 20; Amos 7:2, 5; Is. 37:4). Time and again, Jeremiah is commanded not to pray for his people (Jer. 7:16, 11:14, 14:11), proof positive that Israel's doom is sealed.

According to the Rabbis of the Talmud, the ritual of prayer was ordained as a substitute for the Temple sacrifices after the destruction of the sanctuary. But before prayer became fixed in form, "the service of the heart" was spontaneous and individual. In this sense, prayer may be traced back to the prophets as well as to the priests.

In general, the differentiation of function between prophet and priest was never absolute, each continuing to influence the other throughout the history of Israel.

Thus the Hebrew priest remained the custodian of the *Urim ve-Tumim* which were used as oracles to foretell the future. On the other hand, prophets like Samuel, especially in the earlier period, officiated at sacrifices. Moreover, several of the prophets were priests by descent and vocation. It should be added that the fixed ritual of the priesthood kept it within narrow limits. On the one hand, it prevented the priesthood's sinking to the level of irrationality and charlatanism that often characterized the soothsayer. On the other hand, it lacked the dynamic, personal character of the "seer," which reached its apogee in the great Hebrew prophets.

These great-souled teachers of humanity rejected with scorn the suggestion that they had anything in common with the soothsayers or their successors. Yet the techniques of the great prophets testify to their link with these lowly types. Many of the devices used to induce religious ecstasy are to be found among the greatest of the prophets. Frequently, the prophet would produce a sign as evidence of the truth of his message, or dramatize his theme by strange behavior. Nonetheless, these methods continued to lose ground among the great prophets. As time went on, the conviction among them grew that the truth of their revelation was evident in its content, and did not require buttressing through ecstatic states or hypnotic seizures.

The successive stages of prophecy among the Hebrews may be reconstructed with tolerable completeness. The most primitive soothsayer or dervish is not described in the Bible, except by indirection. Doubtless, these wonder-working mendicants continued to ply their trade, side by side with the higher types of prophet, exactly as astrologists and fortunetellers are contemporaries of Freud and Einstein. Their activity, however, was limited to personal problems and their influence was almost surely local in extent.

From the ranks of the diviners, some individuals were evolving into leaders of tribal and national importance. These were prophets who spoke in the name of the God of Israel and proclaimed His Will to the people. An example is the prophetess Deborah (twelfth century B.C.E.). It was she who nerved a spineless and disunited aggregate of tribes to unite against their common Canaanite foe in the north, inspiring the Hebrew leader Barak to his great victory at the Kishon River (Judg. 4-5). Another was Samuel (eleventh century) who still carried on the personal activities of a diviner, being consulted on matters as petty as the loss of a farmer's asses (I Sam. 9). But Samuel's functions far transcended this lowly role. Like Deborah, he served to unite the tribes against a dangerous enemy, this time the Philistines in the southwest (I Sam. 4:1). He also functioned as a judge and officiant at the rituals conducted at the principal sacred sites (I Sam. 7:15 ff.; 9). His greatest national role was as kingmaker and kingbreaker, a basic factor in the rise and fall of Saul and the ascendancy of David.[16a] Such dominating personalities tended to attract followers, who formed guilds called *Bnai Nebiim* (Sons of the Prophets). These schools of disciples traveled with their master and sought to learn his ways. The most gifted among them ultimately became leaders in their own right.

As the monarchy became a fixed institution, a king would attach a prophet to his court, so that he could be conveniently consulted on matters of state. In the very nature of things, these prophets would tend to be subservient to their masters, proclaiming the messages their overlords wanted to hear. The biblical historians have not transmitted the names of these typical court prophets for posterity. Only the memory of a heroic exception to the rule, a member of this group who proclaimed the truth to his royal master without fear, has been preserved to us. It is

Nathan, who in his deeply moving parable dared to rebuke King David for his adulterous union with Bath-sheba, which he had sealed with the murder of her husband, Uriah (II Sam. 12:1 ff.).

Playing a role similar to that of the court prophets were others who were not attached to the royal court but remained independent figures. Some of them enjoyed great influence, like Ahiah (I Kings 11:31-9, 14:6-16), who set up Jeroboam's dynasty and later announced its doom. Not being completely dependent on the favor of an individual, these leaders could often be independent in attitude.

Incomparably the greatest of these independent figures was Elijah. Emerging suddenly from the wilderness and disappearing in a heavenly chariot, his meteoric career symbolized the two greatest Jewish contributions to civilization, two that really are one: the faith in the One God and the passion for righteousness. In his contest with the priests of Baal on Mt. Carmel, he battled uncompromisingly against the degradation of the God-idea in Israel. In his encounter with the weak-willed King Ahab, whose greed had led him to murder, Elijah stood forth as the courageous champion of social justice. Elijah left no writings behind him. His dramatic actions were far more effective than words in recalling the erring people to the Living God and His teaching. For twenty-seven centuries the awesome figure of the prophet of Gilead has fired the imagination of men.

Such intrepidity of spirit was naturally rare. By and large, even the unattached prophets were responsive to the royal will or the pressure of mass opinion. They were the purveyors of popular religion, highly esteemed, well remunerated, and doubtless attracting many disciples. The prophet Elisha began his career as a follower of Elijah, and some of the latter's intransigence and truth-speaking clung to him. Before long, however, his path diverged from that of his great master. He was a wonder-worker, enjoying the gifts of the populace and the adulation of his followers. He fulfilled all too literally the curse pronounced by Elijah on Ahab's house, by anointing Jehu as king. It is true that Jehu's cold-blooded massacre of Ahab's family and followers may have been carried out without Elisha's knowledge or approval. Nonetheless, the prophet's career shows how easily even the personally independent seer tended to accommodate himself to the *status quo*.

Lacking any pretension to spiritual independence were men of the stamp of Zedekiah ben Kenaanah (I Kings 22:11), who was consulted by the kings of Israel and Judah as to the outcome of their projected war against Syria. For reply he fashioned two iron horns and unhesitatingly proclaimed, "Thus saith the Lord, with these you will gore the Arameans to destruction." Nearly two centuries later, Hananiah ben Azzur triumphantly proclaimed, "I have broken the yoke of the king of Babylonia" (Jer. 28:1 ff.). When Jeremiah, who saw the imminent ruin of the Judean kingdom, placed a yoke on his neck to underscore the need for political submission to the Babylonian Empire, Hananiah unhesitatingly smashed the symbol, doubtless to the resounding applause of the mob.

These enormously popular and, by their lights, influential prophets, have gone down to infamy because they are described in the Bible as "false prophets," a judgment which not only they but virtually all their contemporaries would indignantly have rejected. This unflattering designation has attached to these well meaning preachers of conventional attitudes only because the Bible is written from the standpoint of a few rebels, who were disliked and despised in their own generation.

Almost from the very beginning of prophecy, there was a tradition of nonconformity in Israel. While the priests traced their functions and prerogatives back to Moses and Aaron, the High Priest, there were some spirits who saw in Moses the great prophet whose life was a flaming protest against slavery, tyranny and immorality. Deborah, Samuel, Nathan and Elijah stood in the same great line of opposition to the supineness, lust and greed of the people and its rulers.

These opponents of the *status quo* became especially articulate in the eighth century, the high-water mark of the kingdoms of Israel and Judah. During almost fifty years, the Northern Kingdom was ruled by perhaps its most capable king, Jeroboam II, while Judah enjoyed the presence of an equally able monarch in Azariah or Uzziah.[17a] Between them these kings restored the boundaries of the Solomonic kingdom by successful campaigns to the east, southeast and southwest. The fortifications of Jerusalem were strengthened and the country grew rich because of the spoils of victory, the tolls levied on the great trade routes linking Egypt and the Mesopotamian Valley, and the growing international trade. Luxury grew apace. Winter palaces, summer homes, elaborate furniture and expensive feminine attire became general. A strong sense of national confidence followed in the wake of prosperity. The present was secure; the future would be even more glorious.

The practical leaders, kings, generals, diplomats and merchants alike, did not recognize that the military victories were due to a brief interlude in the international scene, after the Syrian kingdom had fallen and before the new Assyrian power had risen to world dominion. Nor were these realistic observers interested to note that the prosperity was superficial, limited only to the upper levels of society. For the masses, there was ever growing insecurity and outright want. More and more, the independent farmers were being crowded out, their land foreclosed, their children sold into slavery for debt, and they themselves working as tenants on the fields they once had called their own. Moreover, international trade and diplomacy had introduced fashionable foreign cults. Their licentious rites were sapping the moral stamina of the people as surely as economic exploitation was undermining their stake in the country.

These portents of decline, political, social and religious, were so slight that they were noticed by only a few observers, and these, men of little standing or power in their day. In earlier and simpler days, the influence of the prophets had been widely felt. From Moses, through Deborah and Samuel, to Elijah and Elisha, they had been leaders in action. In later times, however, the prophets were looked upon as traitors and enemies of the people, or, more charitably, were dismissed as insane visionaries. As the national decline gathered momentum, the freedom of action of the prophets was restricted, though their freedom of speech could not be denied. Some were driven out, like Amos, or tried for treason, like Micah, or imprisoned, like Jeremiah. Some were killed through lynch law by hired thugs, as was the fate of Jeremiah's colleague, Urijah (Jer. 26:20-24). In rare instances, a member of this group might still influence the course of events. Such was the case with Isaiah, whose efforts were aided both by his aristocratic birth and connections and by the spiritual sensitivity of King Hezekiah. In general, however, these prophets found the door to effective action closed against them.

The period of literary prophecy now began. Several factors conspired to produce this change. The hostility or indifference of the people could not prevent the prophets from expressing God's truth. In Amos's words: "If a trumpet is blown in the city, will not the people tremble? The Lord has spoken, who can but prophesy?" (Amos 3:8).

Jeremiah has left a poignant description of the spiritual compulsion that drove him and his fellows to court men's hatred and even to face death:

> O Lord, Thou hast enticed me, and I was enticed,
> Thou hast overcome me, and hast prevailed;
> I am become a laughing stock all the day,
> Every one mocketh me.
> For as often as I speak, I must cry out,
> "Violence and spoil" do I shout,
> Because the word of the Lord is made a reproach unto me,
> A derision, all the day.
> If I say: "I will not make mention of Him,
> Nor speak any more in His name,"
> Then there is in my heart a burning fire,
> Shut up in my bones,
> Which I weary myself to hold in, but cannot (Jer. 20:7-9).

There were other motives for literary prophecy. Because the prophets exerted little influence on their contemporaries, they or their disciples began writing down their striking utterances out of the very human desire for vindication in the future (Is. 8:16; *cf.* Job 19:23). Doubtless, too, there was the wish to instruct young disciples to carry on the Lord's work, as well as the fear of reprisals for publicly proclaiming the unpopular truth.

It required extraordinary courage for these men, generally despised or ignored, to stigmatize the popular and influential prophets of their day as "false." That position was not reached overnight. In the earlier period, the rebel prophets did not deny the inspiration of their opponents. In the ninth century, Micaiah ben Imlah bravely contradicts Zedekiah's optimistic prophecy, but he explains that his opponent spoke as he did because God Himself has sent a lying spirit to confuse and mislead the king (I Kings 22:19 ff.). A century later, the Judean prophet Micah had outgrown this concept. For him, the false prophets are hirelings, selling their wares to the highest bidder. "When their maw is fed, they proclaim peace, but against him who does not feed them, they declare war" (3:5). A hundred years later, Jeremiah also denies their claim to divine inspiration and stigmatizes his opponent as a liar (28:15).

The free prophets had no professional stake in their calling; theirs was not the kind of message for which men paid. They therefore resented any identification with the conventional prophets. When Amos was called a *nabi* by the priest at Beth-el, he said: "I am neither a prophet nor a member of the prophetic guild" (7:14). Yet poles apart as the free prophets and their conventional rivals were in the content of their message, their techniques, vocabulary and style were similar. Their greatest divergence lay in their destiny. History, the inexorable judge, consigned the conventional prophets to oblivion, and raised the free prophets to immortality as transcendent spiritual teachers of the human race. As critics of society and as heralds of a nobler day, they remain perennially alive.

5. THE MESSAGE OF THE PROPHETS[18a]

The sources of prophetic thought, in both its negative and positive aspects, are of genuine interest today. In attacking the evils of a complex and decadent civilization, the prophets were convinced that they were not innovators, but rather restorers of the pristine tradition of Israel, which had fallen upon evil days. This conviction was fundamentally correct. Two great experiences had come to the Hebrews at the very inception of their history. As time passed by they would have receded in the national consciousness and ultimately been forgotten. That they have not become vague memories was basically the achievement of the prophets and their disciples.

The first great experience was the bondage in Egypt. The experience of common enslavement and liberation of the Hebrew tribes created a sense of the solidarity of Israel. But that was not all. Ever afterward, Hebrew tradition recalled the period of humiliation and suffering in Egypt, and utilized it to develop in the Hebrews a sense of community with the downtrodden and the oppressed. The prophets could count on this ready sense of identification with the underprivileged and the weak.

The second great factor in molding the life and thought of Israel was the desert period, the age of nomadism. Briefly put, the desert played as significant a role in Hebrew history as did the frontier in American history. Professor Turner has pointed out how the existence of untamed and unclaimed land in the United States throughout the eighteenth century influenced the psychology and institutions of the American people. Equally significant in its effect upon Hebrew ideals was the desert, which lies to the east and south of Palestine.

The influence of the desert, however, was complex, for it bore both a real and an ideal character. First and foremost, there was a period of wandering in the wilderness after the escape from Egypt. The well known biblical tradition places the period of wandering at forty years. Modern scholarship is disposed, however, to assume a much longer period before the settlement in Palestine. Whatever the duration, that period was remembered ever after, and as often happens with memory, was idealized by later generations, under the tutelage of the prophets.

The desert was more than a memory of the past. It was also a present reality to the Hebrews, even after the bulk of the tribes had settled in Palestine and progressed to an agricultural and even an urban economy. In Trans-Jordan and southern Palestine, nomadic conditions prevailed throughout the days of the Hebrew kingdoms and long beyond; in fact, down to the present. In describing the allocation of the territory among the twelve tribes, the Bible states that two or three clans at least remained as shepherds on the eastern banks of the Jordan. Thus the memories of nomadic life in the past were reinforced by the existence of similar conditions in the present. It was in the desert at Sinai that the God of Israel had revealed Himself to His people. His power was limitless, but His favorite abode was still the wilderness, vast and terrifying. Centuries after the Israelites had settled in Palestine, it was to the desert that the prophet Elijah fled, not only to seek escape from persecution but to rekindle his ardor for the God of Israel at His mountain.

The desert life, past and present, in both its real and its ideal aspect, exerted an enduring influence upon Hebraic ideals. The life of the Semitic shepherd, by no means lacking in crudity, possesses some noteworthy traits. Nomadic society is fiercely egalitarian. Within the tribe, complete social equality prevails; there are no kings or nobility, no ranks or classes. When a crisis or war threatens, the individual of superior sagacity or prowess emerges as a leader, but he is emphatically *primus inter pares*. When the emergency is over, he reverts to his normal place. The Book of

Judges in the Bible is largely concerned with this type of leadership. It tells, too, of the attempt of an ambitious leader, Abimelech, to establish a hereditary kingship in its stead, an attempt which ended in ignominious failure.

Recent research has demonstrated that this type of primitive democracy was characteristic of all early Semitic societies, indeed of Indo-European groups as well. Under this system, authority is vested in the entire adult male population, which decides questions of war and peace, chooses its leaders and deposes them, and is the supreme legislative and judicial power. In brief, it exercises all the functions of government. Unmistakable traces of this people's assembly (Akkadian *puhrum*, Syrian *mo'ed*) have been discovered in Babylonian epics and Assyrian legal documents, as well as in the Egyptian narrative of Wen-Amon which describes conditions in Syria in the twelfth century B.C.E.

With the evolution of more complex social and economic patterns, and the establishment of a monarchy, the democratic institution of the assembly disappeared, giving way to absolutism in the Babylonian and Assyrian Empires.

The existence of the people's assembly in Israel was overlooked. The terms by which it is referred to in the Bible, *'edah* and, secondarily, *kahal* were erroneously translated "congregation," and thus suggested ecclesiastical connotations wide of the mark. These terms are better translated as "commonalty" or "people's assembly." When a monarchy was established in Palestine, its power was never absolute. During the days of the kingdom the "people's assembly" fought a slowly losing battle to retain its prerogatives. In many respects, which cannot be detailed here, the powers of the *'edah* remained effective to the end; in others, its role became largely symbolic. But the democratic impulse, which gave it birth and which in turn it nurtured, was never wiped out in Israel.

As significant as this primitive democracy is the fact that in the nomadic stage there is virtually no private ownership of wealth. The flocks are owned in common, and rights to wells and pasture grounds are vested in the tribe as a whole. Even after nomadism had given way to settled agricultural life and private ownership of land had become the norm in ancient Israel, as everywhere else, the recollection of the earlier conditions of social equality and common ownership persisted among the Hebrews.

Finally, nomadic society is marked by a strong sense of mutual responsibility. "All for one and one for all" is the law of the tribe. Avenging a crime against any individual member is the duty of the entire tribe. The long-standing feuds among Arab tribes described in the chronicles represent the negative aspect of this conception of tribal brotherhood. The moral code did not extend beyond the tribe, but within the tribe it was all-powerful. Injustice, deception and dishonesty were hotly resented, and indignation found passionate expression in a society where every man was conscious of being the equal of everyone else.

Of themselves these factors—the period of the Egyptian bondage, the nomadic age and the old Semitic inheritance of a primitive democracy—could not have created the basic characteristics of biblical thought. Many peoples have had lowly origins, but most have preferred to forget their past or, better still, to distort it. As for nomadism, it represents a normal stage in social evolution, preceding an agricultural and commercial economy. Among most groups, the end of nomadism meant the surrender of nomadic ideals, and the democracy of the early period disappeared, leaving scarcely a trace

That the same process did not take place in Israel was due to the activity of the prophets. Their role, as will be noted, is not limited to their own activity and writings. Their influence permeated the biblical historians, who recounted the national past from the prophetic standpoint. It also deeply affected the legal codes by which Israelite society was governed. Through history, law and exhortation the Hebrew prophets made it impossible for their fellow countrymen ever to forget that they had been slaves and shepherds. The prophets utilized the Egyptian bondage to inspire the hearts of the people with humanitarian sympathies. Contemporaries of an advanced and often corrupt culture, they recalled the simple laws of justice, freedom and equality by which their nomadic ancestors had lived, and declared those days to have been the most glorious. "I remember for thee the kindness of thy youth, the love of thy bridal state, when thou didst go after Me in the wilderness, in a land unsown" (Jer. 2:1).

In the face of an effete and morally corrupt civilization, nostalgic advocates of the past were not lacking in ancient Israel. There was a clan or guild called the Rechabites, who sought mechanically to revert to a simpler culture, by living only in tents and abstaining from wine, the building of houses, the sowing of seed and the planting of vineyards. Somewhat similar was the institution of the Nazirites, "consecrated to the Lord," who took a vow not to cut their hair, and to abstain from wine, besides avoiding defilement by contact with the dead.

At one with these groups in regarding the nomadic period as a glorious tradition, the prophets were no such ineffectual romantics. On the contrary, they were creative geniuses of the first order, who knew how to utilize the past for the vital needs of the present. Part of the past was dead beyond recall, some of it could be retained, much of it needed to be extended and deepened, while in other respects it had to be transcended completely. The prophets did not urge a return to nomadic conditions, nor did they forbid wine, the dwelling in houses, or the practice of agriculture. They accepted the inevitable social transformation of a settled life. But they demanded the practice of those ideals of nomadism which are valid in every system of society: its concrete sense of mutual responsibility, its passionate attachment to freedom, its instinct for human equality. As Hosea put it, "Sow to yourselves according to righteousness, reap according to mercy, break up your fallow ground. For it is time to seek the Lord, till He come and cause righteousness to rain upon you" (10:12). How the prophets treated the various elements of the nomadic way of life is of more than historical interest. Their procedure points the way to the creative adjustment of tradition to the contemporary scene.

In a nomadic society the strict moral system rested ultimately on the principle of vengeance. When a murder was committed, the relatives of the dead man were enjoined and empowered to exact retribution from the killer and his kinsmen. The prophets transformed vengeance into justice and then proceeded to deepen its meaning to include mercy and loving-kindness. These, they taught, were the attributes of God and must govern the relations of men. More concretely, the Torah limited clan vengeance to cases of premeditated killing and established "the cities of refuge" for accidental murderers (Num. 33:9-34; Josh. 20:1-9). Thus began the long process, still incomplete today, as the tragic incidence of lynchings in America testifies, of bringing human passions and self-interest under the sway of law.

In another direction, also, the prophets transcended nomadic ideals. In the wilderness the clan or tribe is the largest recognized unit, beyond which morality does not apply. Doubtless, there were objective political and economic factors constantly at work breaking down the tribal distinctions in Israel, which were traced back to the twelve sons of the patriarch Jacob. But the process of creating a sense of national solidarity was not easy. Again and again centrifugal forces were in evidence, the most disastrous of which was the division of the Kingdom after the death of Solomon. So powerful were these divisive factors that some scholars doubt whether there ever was a United Kingdom. They regard the reigns of Saul, David and Solomon as a dual monarchy with a single head.

Whatever the truth of this view, it is undeniable that in stimulating the national spirit that ultimately emerged, the prophets played a significant role. They seldom refer to the individual tribes, and even the prime divisions into north and south they regard as a sin and a catastrophe. Amos was a Judean whose principal activity was in Israel, Hosea an Ephraimite who recalled the Davidic dynasty with affection. Jeremiah, who lived long after the destruction of Samaria, looked forward to the restoration of Ephraim to Divine favor, while Ezekiel foretold of a reunion of Judah with their kinsmen from the house of Joseph. The prophets broke the tribal barriers that hemmed Israel in and were therefore the fathers of Jewish nationalism.

In this process of extending the frontiers of solidarity, the Hebrew prophets went beyond the nation to a vision of a united humanity. Unity did not mean uniformity. For the prophets nations were integral elements of God's plan, but their relationship to each other must be governed by His law—justice and mutual co-operation were binding upon all. To use a terminology they themselves would not have recognized, the prophets were the fathers of ethicocultural nationalism. They pointed a way out for mankind between the Scylla of bloodthirsty chauvinism and the Charybdis of lifeless cosmopolitanism, which is sometimes suggested as its remedy. For they demonstrated in their life and thought that national loyalty, properly conceived, is the gateway, not a barrier, to human brotherhood.

It is impossible within the confines of this paper to discuss adequately the insights of Hebrew prophecy in general and the particular contributions of individual figures to such eternal issues as the relationship of God and man, the meaning of history, Israel's role among the nations, the future of society and the character of faith. On these and other problems the prophets have profound contemporary significance, which is all too often ignored through the combination of adulation and neglect which has overtaken the Bible as a whole.

Of the stirring activity of the great prophets, the Bible has preserved only magnificent fragments. It is certain that the prophets whose words have survived must have produced much more than the few hundred verses that have come down to us. There are, moreover, good grounds for assuming that others, less fortunate but perhaps equally worthy, have been completely forgotten. All that has reached us are four books containing prophetic addresses: Isaiah, Jeremiah, Ezekiel, and the Twelve, or Minor, Prophets.

The first three prophetic books follow a broad chronological order. Isaiah belongs to the late eighth century, Jeremiah to the late seventh and early sixth, while Ezekiel is a somewhat younger contemporary of Jeremiah.

Nonetheless, the internal arrangement of these books is not based on historical grounds. Scholars diverge greatly in their views as to the extent of interpolation undergone by each book, Ezekiel in particular being the subject of acute controversy at present. It is, however, universally recognized that beginning with Chapter 40, the Book of Isaiah contains the work of one (and possibly more than one) unknown prophet, who lived nearly two hundred years later, during the Babylonian Exile. In profundity of thought and grandeur of style, this unknown prophet, often called Deutero-Isaiah, eminently deserves his place by the side of Isaiah ben Amoz, who was probably the mightiest intellect among the prophets of Israel. The closing chapters of the Book of Jeremiah consist of oracles against the neighboring nations, which are probably from another hand. The bulk of the book, however, reveals the soul of Jeremiah with a poignant clarity unmatched by any other biblical author.

That historical considerations were not the guiding principle in the arrangement of the prophetic books becomes especially clear in the fourth book of this group. The Hebrew title, the Twelve, is apter than the common English designation, the Minor Prophets. For several of these are minor only in point of size, not significance. The Talmud correctly indicates the reason for joining the work of these twelve prophets, "because each is small, it might have been lost."[19]

This statement is a clue to a principle which has not been adequately evaluated in the arrangement of biblical writings. Since each document was preserved on a scroll, the scribe's tendency was to write the longer text first and then append, often on the remaining section of the same scroll, shorter material, whether or not related in theme. Thus also in the Koran, the longer suras, recognized as later, come first, and the shorter chapters, indubitably the oldest visions of Mohammed, come last. This principle, which sheds light on the organization of material within each biblical book, may explain the position of the Minor Prophets after Isaiah, Jeremiah, and Ezekiel.

The Twelve Prophets include the two earliest literary prophets, Amos and Hosea (middle of the eighth century), and Micah, a younger contemporary of Isaiah. These prophets are among the greatest of the immortal company. The Book of Jonah is an acute satire on the attitude of the popular chauvinist prophets which takes the historical figure of Jonah ben Amittai as its hero to drive home a profound and lasting truth.[20a] Others, like Joel, Obadiah, Nahum, Habakkuk, and Zephaniah, belong to the middle period, while Haggai, Zechariah, and Malachi are representative of the last stage of prophecy in the Persian period, shortly before its disappearance.

These four books, containing the addresses and writings of the prophets, are preceded in the Hebrew Bible by four historical books, Joshua, Judges, Samuel, and Kings, called the Former Prophets. Together, these eight books constitute the second section of the Bible, *Nebiim*, or Prophets. The four historical books contain the history of the Jewish people from their entrance into Palestine until the Babylonian Exile. Superb examples of historical narrative, these works interpret the past experience of Israel in terms of prophetic ideals. They are far more concerned with the religious conditions and the activity of the prophets than with political and economic factors or military and diplomatic events. Thus, the two greatest kings of Judah and Israel, Uzziah and Jeroboam the Second, are dismissed in fourteen verses (II Kings 14:23-15:7), while the prophet Elijah receives more than five chapters (I Kings 17-21) and Elisha eight (II Kings 2-9).

The anonymous historians who created these works, from still older sources now lost, were, on the one hand, disciples of the prophets. On the other, they were deeply influenced by the Torah and its norms for national life, as will be noted below. Hence the historical books, or Former Prophets, which continue the history of Israel begun in the Torah and supply the background for the activity of the prophets, are an ideal link between these two spiritual tendencies.

Both Torah and prophecy find their foil and their complement in the third strand of Hebrew thought, called *Wisdom*.

6. THE VOICE OF WISDOM

The Hebrew priests and prophets have their analogues among all the Semitic peoples, as we have seen. Fundamentally, however, their work was concerned with the life of Israel and therefore it reflects specific national characteristics. Wisdom, on the other hand, is broadly human, dealing with the individual as such. It is therefore even more closely linked to the culture pattern of the ancient Orient.

The connotations of the Hebrew *Hokmah* are far wider than the English rendering "Wisdom" would imply. *Hokmah* may be defined as a realistic approach to the problems of life, including all the practical skills and the technical arts of civilization. The term *hakam*, "sage, wise man," is accordingly applied to the artist, the musician, the singer. Bezalel, the skilled craftsman who built the Tabernacle and its appointments in the wilderness, as well as all his associates, are called "wise of heart" (Ex. 28:3; 35:31; 36:1). Weavers (Ex. 35:25), goldsmiths (Jer. 10:9), and sailors (Ez. 27:8; Ps. 107:27) are *hakamim*.

Above all, the term is applied to the arts of poetry and song, vocal and instrumental. The song in ancient Israel was coextensive with life itself. Harvest and vintage, the royal coronation and the conqueror's return, courtship and marriage, were all accompanied by song and dance. The earliest traditions dealing with the exploits of tribal and national heroes were embodied in song. Snatches of these poems are preserved in the later prose narratives, some being explicitly quoted from older collections, like *The Book of the Wars of the Lord* (Num. 21:14) and *The Book of the Just* (Josh. 10:13; II Sam. 1:18; I Kings 8:53 in the Greek).

The guilds of singers in the Temple, the women skilled in lamentation (Jer. 9:16), the magicians and soothsayers with all their occult arts, are described by the same epithet, "wise" (Gen. 40:8; I Kings 5:10-12; Is. 44:25; Jer. 9:16). Skill in the conduct of war and in the administration of the state (Is. 10:13; 29:14; Jer. 49:7) is also an integral aspect of Wisdom.

All these phases have disappeared with the destruction of the material substratum of ancient Hebrew life. What has remained of Wisdom is its literary incarnation, concerned not so much with the arts of living as with developing a sane, workable attitude toward life. To convey its truths, Wisdom created an educational method and a literature generally couched in the form of the *mashal*, the parable or proverb, brief, picturesque, unforgettable.

It is now clear that the third section of the Bible, called *Ketubim*, the Sacred Writings or Hagiographa, is not a miscellaneous collection, but, on the contrary, has an underlying unity. Basically, it is the repository of Wisdom. The Book of Psalms is a great collection of religious poetry, most of which was chanted at the Temple service with musical accompaniment. Both the composition and the rendition of the Psalms required a high degree of that technical skill which is *Hokmah*. Moreover, in point of content, many Psalms (like 37, 49, 112, 128) have close affinities with the proverbial lore of the Wisdom teachers.

Three other books, Proverbs, Job and Ecclesiastes obviously belong in a Wisdom collection. So does Ben Sira,[21a] or Ecclesiasticus, which was not included in the canon of Scripture, because it clearly betrayed its late origin. Lamentations is a product of *Hokmah* in its technical sense. The Song of Songs is included, not merely because it is traditionally ascribed to King Solomon, the symbol and traditional source of Hebrew Wisdom, but because these songs, whether sung at weddings or at other celebrations, were also a branch of technical song. It has also been suggested that the Song of Songs entered the Wisdom collection because it was regarded as an allegory of the relationship of love subsisting between God and Israel. From this point of view, it would be a *mashal*, which means "allegory" or "fable" as well as "proverb." The Book of Daniel, the wise interpreter of dreams, obviously is in place among the Wisdom books.

The reason for the inclusion of Ruth and Esther is not quite as evident. Perhaps they were included here because both reveal practical sagacity, Esther in saving her people from destruction and Ruth in securing a desirable husband! The three closing books of the Bible, which survey history from Adam to the Persian period, are really parts of one larger work, Chronicles-Ezra-Nehemiah.[22a] It is possible that they may have been included in the Wisdom section merely because they were placed at the end as an appendix to the Bible as a whole. The place of these last-named books in *Ketubim* has also been explained differently. It has been suggested that Chronicles (with its adjuncts) is really an appendix to Psalms, since one of its principal concerns is to describe in detail the establishment of the Temple ritual. Ruth may then have been a supplement to the Psalms, since it concludes with the genealogy of David, the traditional author of the Psalter. Esther may be an appendix to Chronicles, the style of which it seeks to imitate. These links, however tenuous they may appear to the Western mind, will not seem farfetched to anyone familiar with the Semitic logic of association, evidence for which is plentiful in the redaction of the Bible and in the organization of the Mishna and the Talmud.

Wisdom literature in its narrower sense, as it appears in Proverbs or Ecclesiastes, for example, impresses the modern reader as the most secular element in the Bible, being based on clear, realistic observation and logical inference and deduction, rather than on tradition and revelation. Yet in an age permeated by the religious consciousness, the devotee of Wisdom was both unable and unwilling to surrender his claim to Divine inspiration. Thus the *hakam* took his place by the side of the *kohen*, who derived his authority from the Divine Law revealed by Moses, and the *nabi* who spoke out under the direct impact of the Divine. Hence the "wise man," in all the ramifications of the term, could be described, as was Bezalel the craftsman. as "filled with the spirit of God, with wisdom, understanding, knowledge and all manner of skill" (Ex. 31:3).

This conception was given a metaphysical form as well. Each cultivator of Wisdom is endowed with a portion of the transcendental, Divine Wisdom, dwelling in Heaven. This supernal *Hokmah* is described in various poetic figures. Wisdom is the instrument by which God has created the world, or the pattern He has followed in fashioning the universe. She is the beloved playmate of His leisure hours, or the gracious hostess inviting men on the highway to enter her seven-pillared palace (Pr. 8:1 ff.; 8:22 ff.; 9:1 ff.; Ecclus. 1:8 ff. and *passim*). This Hebrew conception of Wisdom as a semidivine figure doubtless draws upon ancient Oriental ideas. In turn it has had wide influence upon such varied elements of thought as Philonian philosophy, Rabbinic speculation, Christian theology, and Gnosticism.

Biblical Wisdom itself was a true Oriental product that had been cultivated for centuries throughout the lands of the Fertile Crescent, Egypt, Palestine, Syria and Babylonia. Everywhere its purposes were similar: the preparation of youth for success in government, agriculture and commerce. Thus Wisdom was part of the cultural inheritance of the Semitic-Hamitic world, which the Hebrews shared with their neighbors and kinsmen.

The tradition that King Solomon was "the wisest of men" and the author of the Song of Songs, Proverbs and Ecclesiastes is no longer airily dismissed by scholars as a mere figment of the folk imagination.[23a] It is seen to reflect the historical fact that the intensive cultivation of Wisdom goes back to his reign, when wide international contacts and internal prosperity contributed to the flowering of culture. Its origins are even more ancient. Embedded in the historical books are gems of Wisdom literature older than Solomon: Jotham's biting fable of the trees and the thornbush (Judg. 9:7), Nathan's parable of the poor man's lamb (II Sam. 12:1), the melancholy comment on the transitoriness of life by the "wise woman of Tekoa" (II Sam. 14:14), not to speak of the later parable of King Joash (II Kings 14:9). Moreover, it is increasingly recognized that the Books of Psalms, Proverbs, and the Song of Songs are anthologies containing a great deal of pre-exilic material, for which parallels of considerable antiquity have been discovered in Babylonia, Syria and Egypt.

Nonetheless, the Golden Age of Hebrew Wisdom literature is the first half of the Second Temple period, roughly between the fifth and the second century B.C.E. This flowering was fostered by both positive and negative factors. After the Babylonian Exile, a far reaching change had taken place in the spirit of the people. It was a chastened folk that returned to Jerusalem after the Proclamation of Cyrus, to rebuild the shattered foundations of the national life. The tragedy of exile had convinced them of the truth of the prophetic message and had imbued them with the desire to fulfil the will of God as revealed in the Torah. Hence, one of the first concerns of the returning settlers was the rebuilding of the Temple. Here, as has been noted, the priests resumed their function as officiants at the ritual, but the spiritual hegemony passed to the scholars, the expounders of the Law.

Prophecy, like the written Torah, had passed its creative phase. It declined and finally ceased to function in the days of the Second Temple. Ultimately the impulse reasserted itself in a strange, scarcely recognizable form, to produce the apocalyptic writings. Various factors contributed to the disappearance of prophecy. The postexilic period as a whole was well described as "an age of small things," with little to stir men's hearts to ecstasy or to wrath. There was neither stimulus nor need for the grand prophetic vision. The Jews were a struggling community under the domination of successive foreign rulers, Persian, Greek, Egyptian and Syrian. The unyielding insistence of the prophets upon national righteousness as the basic premise of national well-being was now an accepted element of Jewish thought, but it was neither particularly novel nor especially relevant to the problems of the hour. For there was little prospect of national greatness and power for Jewish life either in the present or in the recognizable future.

A fundamental revolution in men's thinking now took place. The ancient Semitic outlook, which was shared by the Hebrews, had placed the well-being or decline of the group, the family, tribe or nation in the center of men's thoughts. This collective viewpoint now gave way to a heightened interest in the individual. Prosperity and freedom for a tiny weak people was not likely to be achieved in a world of mighty empires. All that remained was for each human being to strive to attain his personal happiness. What qualities were needed, what pitfalls had to be avoided by a man seeking to achieve success and a respectable place in society? To these perennially modern and recurrent questions, Wisdom now addressed itself with zeal and skill.

The Wisdom literature of the First Temple was sedulously collected and augmented. All signs point to its cultivation by the conservative, upper classes in society, just as the Oral Law was the particular province of the lower and middle classes. These upper strata of society, even the high priestly families among them, whose position and income derived from their services in the Temple, were concerned less with the Will of God than with the way of the world. Their goal in education was utilitarian, the training of youth for careers as merchant princes, landed gentry or government officials. To satisfy this need, a special type of preceptor arose, principally if not exclusively, in Jerusalem, the capital. Like the Sophists in classical Greek, who performed a similar function for the upper class youth of Greek society, these teachers taught "Wisdom" (Hebrew *Hokmah*, Greek *Sophia*).

The Hebrew Wisdom teachers sought to inculcate the virtues of hard work, zeal, prudence, sexual moderation, sobriety, loyalty to authority, and religious conformity—all the elements of a morality making for worldly success. What is more, they did not hesitate to urge less positive virtues on their youthful charges, such as holding one's tongue, and even bribery, as aids in making one's way:

> Where words abound, sin is not wanting,
> But he that controls his tongue is a wise man. (Prov. 10:19)

> A man's gift makes room for him,
> It brings him before great men. (Prov. 18:16)

In brief, this practical Wisdom represented a hardheaded, matter-of-fact, "safe and sane" approach to the problems of living. Of this practical Wisdom the literary repositories are Proverbs in the Bible and Ben Sira or Ecclesiasticus, in the Apocrypha. Both works contain aphorisms and injunctions and observations on life designed to direct youth. Proverbs is more original in style; Ben Sira more derivative. On the other hand, while the literary unit in Proverbs is generally a single verse, Ben Sira has expanded it to a larger form, bordering on our essay.

Among the many preceptors of Wisdom, however, were some whose restless minds refused to be satisfied with these practical goals of what may be termed the lower Wisdom. They sought to penetrate to the great abiding issues: the meaning of life, the purpose of creation, the nature of death, the mystery of evil. In grappling with these ultimate problems they insisted on using the same instruments of observation and common sense that they applied to daily concerns, rather than religious authority and conventional doctrines. Like so many rationalist minds since their day, however, they found unaided human reason incapable of solving these issues. Some, no doubt, finally made their peace with the traditional religion of their day. But others, more tough minded, refused to take on faith what their reason could not demonstrate. Hence their writings reveal various degrees and types of skepticism and heterodoxy.

Several of these devotees of the higher or speculative Wisdom were highly fortunate, for it was given them to transmute the frustration and pain of their quest into some of the world's greatest masterpieces, notably Job and Kohelet. Job is the immortal protest of man against the mystery of suffering. Kohelet expresses the tragic recognition that the basic truth of the universe is beyond men's ken, so that all that remains in life is the achievement of happiness, itself illusory and fleeting. Thus, Wisdom, which began with practical and down-to-earth matters, ended by grappling with the profoundest and most abiding issues of life.

7. The Higher Unity of the Bible

The three principal types of religious and cultural activity in ancient Israel were obviously distinct in purpose, emphasis, and technique. Torah and prophecy were principally concerned with the group; Wisdom almost exclusively with the individual. On the other hand, Torah and Wisdom had their gaze fixed on the present, while the prophets used their vision of the ideal world of the future as a touchstone for evaluating the real world of today.

For the priests, ritual was the central feature of the religious life. The Wisdom teachers regarded the Temple service as part of the accepted order of things, but not as especially significant. The prophets, on the other hand, saw righteousness as the goal of religion, and differed among themselves in their attitudes toward ritual. In the brief Book of Amos no favorable reference to sacrifice is to be found. On the other hand, the prophet Ezekiel, himself a priest, drew up a manual on Temple worship after the destruction of the sanctuary. Midway between them stood Isaiah and probably most of the prophets. Isaiah sharply criticized the unholy alliance of piety and plunder in his day. On the other hand, he recognized the Temple in Jerusalem as the seat of God's glory, where he himself had experienced his inaugural vision (ch. 6). In the critical hour when Sennacherib besieged Jerusalem, Isaiah boldly declared that the city of God was inviolate. For the moderate Prophets, ritual was not an end in itself; if it proved a gateway to righteousness, it was acceptable; otherwise it was a snare and a delusion.

It is clear that the activities of priest, prophet, and sage were not carried on in mutual isolation or antagonism. On the contrary, there was a very lively intellectual interchange among them. As a result, the Bible is pervaded by a higher unity, all the more striking because it rests upon the diversity of its component elements.

Doubtless, there were priests in Israel whose interests were purely professional, and for whom religious duty was exhausted in the punctilious fulfillment of the ritual. But the Torah is not the work of priests of this character. On the contrary, it is deeply impregnated with the prophetic spirit. It is profoundly significant that the Torah bears the name of Moses, who is the first of the prophets, "trusted in God's house" beyond any of his successors (Num. 12:7, 8). The great moment of Moses' life is the Divine Revelation on Sinai. His hope for his people is "would that all the Lord's peoples were prophets" (Num. 11:29)!

Moreover, the Torah goes beyond the abstract ethical and religious demands of the prophets and translates these ideals into concrete institutions. The Sabbath law for the protection of the slaves, the six-year period of bond service, the sabbatical year of release from debt, the Jubilee Year for the restoration of real property, the ordinances regarding poor relief, these and countless other elements of biblical legislation are a signal contribution to righteousness in human affairs. All these are explicitly or implicitly motivated by the memories of Egyptian bondage and by the ideals of equality and justice inherited from the wilderness period, the recollection of which the prophets kept alive in the consciousness of the people.

The Ten Commandments are proclaimed in the name of God, who is described as the Redeemer of Israel from the land of bondage, and not as the Creator of heaven and earth, a fact that the medieval philosopher Judah Ha-Levi noted in another connection. The Sabbath rest was enjoined not only upon the Jew, but also upon the slave, "for thou wast a slave in the land of Egypt." The stranger, who in those days, even more than today, had no rights, was not to be oppressed, nor his life embittered, "for ye know the soul of the stranger, for ye were strangers in the land of Egypt" (Ex. 23:9). On the contrary, as is emphasized no less than thirty-six times in the Torah, one law was to be binding upon the alien and the citizen alike. The Golden Rule, "Thou shalt love thy neighbor as thyself" (Lev. 19:18), has its even nobler counterpart in the same chapter, which commands: "And if a stranger sojourn with thee in your land, ye shall not do him wrong. The stranger that sojourneth with you shall be unto you as the home-born among you, and thou shalt love him as thyself; for ye were strangers in the land of Egypt: I am the Lord your God" (Lev. 19:33 f.). Undoubtedly, the persistent effort to limit slavery and the hostility toward the institution manifested by biblical law are the end products of the Hebrews' experience with Egyptian slavery. With extraordinary courage, one biblical code goes further and demands that the Hebrew should not hate the Egyptian, "for thou wast a stranger in his land" (Deut. 23:8). As the Bible became accepted as sacred, these doctrines exerted a continuous educative influence upon the people, giving them a sympathy for the oppressed and a passionate attachment to liberty which was intensified by their later tribulations.

Obviously, these exalted ideals were never universally realized and were often flouted in life. But their enunciation is itself a great achievement. We have only to contrast the Bible with such exalted writings as Plato's *Republic*, which pictures the ideal state of the future as protected by a standing army perpetually on guard against the non-Greek barbarians, or Aristotle's *Politics*, with its reasoned defense of human slavery.

In sum, the spirit of the Torah is best described as "priestly-prophetic." The world's most categorical ethical ideals are to be found in the Decalogue, side by side with ritual enactments. Within the Book of Leviticus, which contains the priestly regulations, the Holiness Code (chs. 17-26) is embedded. Aside from countless ritual ordinances, this code contains the Golden Rule, the demand for loving the stranger and the Jubilee legislation to prevent monopoly in land.

The interplay of both prophetic and priestly elements is particularly evident in Deuteronomy. The insistence upon a single sanctuary (ch. 12 and *passim*) doubtless harmonized with the interests of the Jerusalemite priesthood, though it had obvious religious and moral advantages. On the other hand, the highly varied legislation throughout the book (as *e.g.*, 15, 20, 21, 27) reflects a sympathy for the poor, a hatred of tyranny, and a compassion for the weak, the underprivileged and the alien that is genuinely prophetic in spirit.

Prophecy likewise reveals an intimate relationship with both Torah and Wisdom. The fundamental emphasis of the biblical historians is on the prophetic doctrine that disaster is the inescapable consequence of sin and that national well-being rests upon national righteousness. Interestingly enough, this doctrine is formulated most clearly in Wisdom literature: "Righteousness exalts a people but sin is the shame of a nation" (Prov. 14:34). In retelling the history of Israel in the spirit of the prophets, the Books of Joshua, Judges, Samuel and Kings continue the historical narratives in the Torah. Hence, many scholars refer to the Pentateuch and Joshua as the Hexateuch, while some go even further and include all the historical books under the name Octateuch.

The predilection of the prophets for the techniques of Wisdom needs no elaborate demonstration. The prophets used parables and apothegms with telling effect. Most of their oracles and other addresses are poetic in structure and much of it must have been chanted to musical accompaniment. Prayers and psalms are by no means uncommon in the prophetic books. Moreover, the searching issues that troubled the unconventional Wisdom teachers could not have been overlooked by the profound spirit of the prophets. Jeremiah, Ezekiel and Deutero-Isaiah, in particular, grappled with the agonizing problem of the undeserved suffering of the righteous, both individually and in the collective experience of Israel.

The attitude of Wisdom to the Torah and prophets has already been indicated. Doubtless the Sages looked askance at the emotional basis of prophetic activity, and were skeptical about the prophets' extravagant hopes for the future. Nevertheless, prophetic attitudes penetrated even into their rationalistic circles. Witness the hatred of injustice in Ecclesiastes and Job, the emphasis upon morality as the heart of religion in Psalms 50 and 81, the triumphant affirmation of the coming Divine Judgment on evil in Psalms 75 and 82, and the passionate yearning for purity and freedom from sin throughout the Book of Psalms.

The Bible possesses a unity fashioned out of every current of Hebrew thought and action. It is inexhaustible in the wealth and variety of its contents. Priest, prophet, historian, poet and sage rub shoulders with one another within its covers, as they actually did in their own lifetimes, differing, arguing and influencing one another and unconsciously collaborating in producing the greatest spiritual force in the history of mankind. The prophets' magnificent faith in God's justice, and Job's equally noble protest against undeserved suffering, the Psalmists' mystical absorption in God, and the practical counsel of the Sages in Proverbs, the love of life and the life of love hymned in the Song of Songs and the melancholy reflections of Ecclesiastes—all were authentic expressions of the genius of Israel.

8. THE BIBLE AS LITERATURE

The nobility and eternal relevance of the Bible is heightened by its superb literary form. The Bible is a library of masterpieces written by men who are artists not for art's sake, a conception which they would not have favored had they known it, but for life's sake. They were impelled by a single purpose, to tell their message as directly and effectively as possible. With the sure instinct of genius, they utilized the literary techniques and forms of their day and developed them to perfection. Unbeknown to themselves, they produced a gallery of classics in which deceptive simplicity conceals the highest art.

Tolstoy has called the Joseph saga in Genesis the greatest narrative in the world, unrivaled for dramatic power and psychological finesse. Throughout the four books of the Torah in which Moses is the guiding spirit, no formal description of the great leader is to be met with, except for one brief passage where he is described as the "humblest of men" (Num. 12:3). Nonetheless, the character of Moses is one of the most vivid ever drawn. The trajectory of his career is traced through mounting trials and crises with an art as consummate as it is unconscious, an art that Boswell might well have envied but could not surpass.

Over and beyond the sheer perfection of its elements is the architectural structure of Genesis. The majestic opening verse, "In the beginning, God created the heaven and the earth," takes the cosmos as its background. Immediately thereafter, with characteristic Jewish realism, heaven is let alone and the narrative turns to the earth. Concerning itself with the human race, it traces the origin of mankind, its trials and sins culminating in the Flood, from which only Noah and his family survive (2-9). The offspring of two of his sons, Ham and Japhet, are briefly listed and dismissed (10:1-20), so that the descendants of Shem may be treated at greater length (10:21 ff; 11:10 ff.). This serves as a preface to the career of Abraham, with whom the history of Israel begins (12-24). Of his two sons, Ishmael's descendants are briefly noted (25:12 ff.), and the narrative concentrates on Isaac (25:19-27). He, too, has two sons, Esau whose stock is dismissed in one chapter (36), and Jacob, whose personal fortunes and family misfortunes become the fundamental theme of the rest of the book. The Joseph saga then prepares the way for the bondage in Egypt, the liberation by Moses and the giving of the Law at Sinai. With unsurpassed literary art, the Book of Genesis has thus linked Creation and Revelation.

The historian-author of Samuel has painted an unforgettable portrait in the life story of Saul, with its bright early promise and the cloud of mental instability and ruin later descending upon him. At least equally notable is the vivid narrative of David's life with its bright ascendancy, its glorious noonday and its tragic dusk. Surrounding these two principal figures stands an immortal gallery of human nature, Samuel and Jonathan, Michael and Bath-Sheba, Nathan and Solomon, Absalom and Barzillai. Ruth has been described as the most perfect short story ever written. Jonah has been justly called by C. H. Cornill the "noblest book in the Old Testament." For sheer storytelling art, it belongs with the Elijah cycle and Esther. The memoirs of Nehemiah are a revealing picture of the period of the Restoration, with the problems strikingly similar to our own. Oratory has suffered in esteem in modern times, but the tenderness of Deuteronomy, the majesty of Isaiah, and the heartrending pathos of Jeremiah will never lose their power, because they speak from the heart and deep calls to deep.

The poetry of the Bible is perhaps its crowning glory. The moral fervor of the prophets, the passionate tenderness of the love lyrics in the Song of Songs, the grief of Lamentations, and all the human impulses reflected in the Book of Psalms have never been surpassed and rarely equaled. Faith and doubt, victory and defeat, hatred and doom, rebellion and submission, all find matchless expression in the Psalter, the world's most beloved songster. The nature poetry in Psalms (19 and 104) and the great God-speeches in Job have been acclaimed by figures as various as Herder and von Humboldt. The common sense of Proverbs will never cease to charm as well as to instruct young and old, while mature minds grappling with the mystery of life and the existence of evil will find both comradeship and comfort in Ecclesiastes and Job. The one was called by Renan "the most charming book ever written by a Jew." The other was pronounced by Carlyle "the grandest book ever written with pen."

Earlier generations were admonished with regard to the Bible, "turn it over and over, for everything is in it, and grow old and gray with it, but do not swerve from it."[24] That judgment is vindicated anew, as men penetrate ever more deeply into its spirit. For the Bible's goal is righteousness, its weapon is truth, and its achievement is beauty.

NOTES

[1] Baba Batra 15a.

[2a] Cf. Judah Goldin, "The Period of the Talmud (135 B.C.E.-1035 C.E.)," this work, Vol. I, pp. 165-168.]

[3a] Cf. Alexander Altmann, "Judaism and World Philosophy: From Philo to Spinoza," this work, Vol. III, Chap. 3, *passim*.]

[4] Hagigah 13b.

[5] Yebamot 49b.

[6] Baba Kamma 2b and parallel passages.

[7] Berakot 31b and parallel passages.

[8] Shabbat 63a and parallel passages.

[9a] Cf. William Foxwell Albright, "The Biblical Period," this work, Vol. I, Chap. 1.]

[10a] Cf. below, Louis Finkelstein, "The Jewish Religion: Its Beliefs and Practices," pp. 473 ff. See also Mordecai M. Kaplan, "A Philosophy of Jewish Ethics," this work, Vol. III, p. 42.]

[11] Reading with the Kethib *ribbo' torothai*.

[11a] Cf. Albright, *op. cit.*, pp. 13-14.]

[12a] Cf. *ibid.*, pp. 47 ff., and Goldin, *op. cit.*, pp. 181-183.]

[13a] Cf. Albright, *op. cit.*, pp. 50 ff.]

[14] Sanhedrin 21b.

[15a] Cf. Albright, *op. cit.*, pp. 55 ff.]

[16a] On Samuel, David and Saul, cf. *ibid.*, pp. 25-31.]

[17a] Cf. *ibid.*, pp. 39-42.]

[18a] Cf. Kaplan, *op. cit.*, pp. 54 ff.]

[19] Baba Batra 15b.

[20a] Cf. Elias J. Bickerman, "The Historical Foundations of Postbiblical Judaism," this work, Vol. I, pp. 106-107.]

[21a] Cf. *ibid.*, pp. 97-98, 100-101.]

[22a] Cf. *ibid.*, pp. 79 ff., and Albright, *op. cit.*, pp. 52 ff.]

[23a] Cf. below, Ralph Marcus, "Hellenistic Jewish Literature," pp. 67-69.]

[24] Cf. Abot 5:22.

BIBLIOGRAPHY

In a field in which the literature is enormous, this bibliography makes no pretense to completeness. It consists largely of works in English and is intended to serve as a guide for further reading. Philological studies, detailed commentaries and other technical works beyond the purview of the general reader are generally not included.

A. *Bible Translations and One-Volume Commentaries*

The Authorized and Revised Versions.

The Holy Scriptures—Jewish Version. Philadelphia, 1917.

EISELEN, F. C., *Abingdon Bible Commentary*. New York, Cincinnati, 1929.

MARGOLIS, MAX L., *The Story of Bible Translations*. Philadelphia, 1917.

MOFFATT, JAMES, *A New Translation of the Bible*. New York and London, 1935.

MOULTON, RICHARD G., *The Modern Reader's Bible*. New York and London, 1926.

PEAKE, ARTHUR S. (ed.), *A Commentary on the Bible*. London and New York, 1936.

SMITH, JOHN M. P. (ed.), *The Complete Bible—An American Translation*. Chicago, 1945.

B. *Biblical Criticism*

DRIVER, S. R., *An Introduction to the Literature of the Old Testament* (12th ed.). New York, 1906.

EISSFELDT, OTTO, *Einleitung in das Alte Testament*. Tuebingen, 1934.

MARGOLIS, MAX L., *The Hebrew Scriptures in the Making*. Philadelphia, 1922.

PFEIFFER, ROBERT H., *Introduction to the Old Testament*. New York, 1941.

Driver's classic work is a balanced presentation of the critical position as maintained a generation ago. Eissfeldt's work incorporates the results of the past four decades of Bible study. Pfeiffer's work, which generally adopts radical critical positions, is invaluable because of its succinct summaries of all important views and its rich bibliographical references, especially to recent literature. Margolis's small work presents in popular form a great conservative scholar's views on the composition and canonization of Scripture.

CHEYNE, T. K., *Founders of Old Testament Criticism*. London, 1893.

RUBASCHEFF, S., and SOLOWÉITSCHIK, M., *Toledot Bikoret Hamikra*. Berlin, 1925.

Studies in the history of biblical criticism and the progress of investigation.

HOOKE, S. H. (ed.), *Myth and Ritual*. London, 1933.

PEAKE, ARTHUR S. (ed.), *The People and the Book; Essays on the Old Testament*. Oxford, 1925.

ROBINSON, H. WHEELER (ed.), *Record and Revelation, Essays on the Old Testament*. Oxford, 1938.

Collected papers on various phases of Bible studies from the critical point of view.

CASSUTO, U., *La Questione Della Genesi*. Florence, 1934.

——, *Torat Hateudot Ve'Sidduram Shel Sifrei Hatorah*. Jerusalem, 1941.

——, *Me'adam 'ad Noah*. Jerusalem, 1944.

COPPENS, J., *The Old Testament and the Critics* (trans. from the French by Ryan and Tribbe). Paterson, N. J., 1941.

HOFFMANN, DAVID, *Die Wichtigsten Instanzen gegen die Graf-Wellhausensche Hypothese*. Berlin, 1904-1916.

ORR, JAMES, *The Problem of the Old Testament*. New York. 1906.

Cassuto's works in Italian and Hebrew subject the Documentary Hypothesis to the criticism of a leading scholar of our day. Hoffmann's and Orr's works are thoroughgoing critiques of the higher critical position, as expounded a generation ago by a traditionalist Jewish and Protestant scholar, respectively. Coppens's work, translated from the French, is the fair-minded and valuable survey of the various critical theories by a Belgian Catholic scholar.

C. History and Archaeology

BERTHOLET, A., *A History of Hebrew Civilization*. London, 1926.

BEVAN, E. R., and SINGER, C., *The Legacy of Israel*. Oxford, 1927.

CAUSSE, A., *Du Groupe Ethnique à la Communauté Religieuse*, Paris, 1937.

FINEGAN, JACK, *Light from the Ancient Past*. Princeton, 1946.

GORDIS, ROBERT, "The Edah—Primitive Democracy in Ancient Israel," in *Professor Alexander Marx Jubilee Volume* (English section). New York, 1949.

GRAHAM, W. C. and MAY, H. G., *Culture and Conscience*. Chicago, 1936.

KAUFMAN, J., *Toledot Ha'Emunah Ha'Israelit*. 7 vols. Tel-Aviv, 1937-1942.

LODS, ADOLPHE, *Israel, from its beginnings to the middle of the eighth century*. New York, 1932.

MAISLER, B., *Toledot Eretz Israel*, Tel-Aviv, 1938.

OESTERLEY, W. O. E., and ROBINSON, T. H., *Hebrew Religion, its Origin and Development* (2nd ed.). London, 1937.

——, *A History of Israel*. Oxford, 1932.

OLMSTEAD, A. T., *A History of Palestine and Syria to the Macedonian Conquest*. New York and London, 1931.

PEDERSEN, J., *Israel: Its Life and Culture*. London, 1926.

SMITH, G. A., *Historical Geography of the Holy Land* (25th ed.), 1932.

SMITH, W. ROBERTSON, *Lectures on the Religion of the Semites*. London, 1927.

WRIGHT, G. E., and FILSON, F. V., *Westminster Historical Atlas to the Bible*. Philadelphia, 1945.

These works deal with the history of the Hebrew people and its religion and civilization in terms of the background of the ancient Orient and in the light of archaeology.

ALBRIGHT, WILLIAM FOXWELL, *Archaeology and the Religion of Israel*. Baltimore, 1942.

————, *The Archaeology of Palestine and the Bible* (3rd ed.). New York, 1935.

————, *From the Stone Age to Christianity*. Baltimore, 1940.

BAILEY, ALBERT EDWARD, *Daily Life in Bible Times*. New York, 1943.

BARTON, G. A., *Archaeology and the Bible* (7th ed.). Philadelphia, 1937.

BURROWS, MILLAR, *What Mean These Stones?* New Haven, 1941.

FRAZER, J. G., *Folk-Lore in the Old Testament*. London, 1918.

GARSTANG, JOHN, *The Foundations of Bible History: Joshua, Judges*. New York, 1931.

GLUECK, NELSON, *The River Jordan*. Philadelphia, 1946.

GRANT, ELIHU (ed.), *The Haverford Symposium on Archaeology and the Bible*. New Haven, 1938.

The Heritage of Solomon. London, 1934.

JACOBSON, DAVID, *The Social Background of the Old Testament*. Cincinnati, 1942.

These works are concerned largely with the bearing of archaeology on the various phases of biblical life and thought.

SMITH, ROY L., *It All Happened Once Before*. New York and Nashville, 1944.

WALLIS, LOUIS, *The Bible Is Human; a study in secular history*. New York, 1942.

————, *God and the Social Process*. Chicago, 1935.

————, *Sociological Study of the Bible*. Chicago, 1927.

WEBER, MAX, *Das antike Judentum*. Tuebingen, 1921.

Works stressing the social and economic aspects of biblical thought.

D. *Torah*

GREENSTONE, JULIUS H., *Numbers With Commentary*. Philadelphia, 1939.

HERTZ, J. H., *The Pentateuch and Haftorahs*. London, 1938.

REIDER, J., *Deuteronomy With Commentary*. Philadelphia, 1937.

E. *The Prophets*

BUBER, MARTIN, *Torat Ha'Nebiim*. Tel-Aviv, 1942.

BUTTENWIESER, MOSES, *The Prophets of Israel*. New York, 1914.

DRIVER, S. R., *Isaiah: His Life and Times*. New York, 1888.

FINKELSTEIN, LOUIS, *The Pharisees*. Philadelphia, 1938.

HAMILTON, EDITH, *The Prophets of Israel*. London, 1936.

HOSCHANDER, JACOB, *The Priests and Prophets*. New York, 1938.

MARGOLIS, M. L., *The Holy Scriptures with Commentary: Micah*. Philadelphia, 1908.

MORGENSTERN, JULIAN, *Amos Studies*. Cincinnati, 1941.

SMITH, GEORGE A., *The Book of the Twelve Prophets*. Garden City, N. Y., 1929.

SMITH, W. ROBERTSON, *The Prophets of Israel*. London, 1907.

Buber approaches the problems in a characteristically philosophical fashion. Finkelstein's study contains three chapters (15-17) dealing with the religious and ethical teachings of the prophets. Edith Hamilton's work is a well-written, deeply personal approach to the prophets. The third book of Morgenstern's study, which is called *The Antecedents of Amos' Prophecy* traces the background of Hebrew prophecy by a highly original biblical scholar of our day. W. Robertson Smith's and Buttenwieser's works are based on the "classic" form of the higher critical theory.

F. *Wisdom*

BUTTENWIESER, MOSES, *The Psalms*. Chicago, 1938.

CHEYNE, T. K., *Job and Solomon; or, The Wisdom of the Old Testament*. New York, 1887.

FICHTNER, JOHANNES, *Die altorientalische Weisheit in ihrer Israelitisch-juedischen Auspraegung*. Giessen, 1933.

FREEHOF, SOLOMON, *The Book of Psalms*. Cincinnati, 1938.

GORDIS, ROBERT, "Mabo Le'Safrut Ha'Hokmah," in *Sefer Hashanah*. New York, 1942.

———, "The Social Background of Wisdom Literature," in *Hebrew Union College Annual*. Cincinnati, 1944.

———, *The Wisdom of Ecclesiastes*. New York, 1945.

———, "Introduction to the Book of Job," in *Morris Raphael Cohen Memorial Volume*. New York, 1950.

JAMES, FLEMING, *Thirty Psalmists*. New York, 1938.

KIRKPATRICK, A. F., *Cambridge Commentary on Psalms*. Cambridge, 1921.

MACDONALD, DUNCAN BLACK, *The Hebrew Philosophical Genius*. Princeton, 1936.

OESTERLEY, W. O. E., *A Fresh Approach to the Psalms*. New York, 1937.

RANKIN, O. S., *Israel's Wisdom Literature*. Edinburgh, 1936.

RANSTON, H., *The Old Testament Wisdom Books and Their Teaching*. London, 1930.

G. *Literary and Religious Appreciation*

BEWER, JULIUS A., *The Literature of the Old Testament* (2nd ed.). New York, 1933.

CHASE, MARY ELLEN, *The Bible and the Common Reader*. New York, 1944.

FOSDICK, HARRY EMERSON, *A Guide to Understanding the Bible*. New York and London, 1938.

MACDONALD, DUNCAN BLACK, *The Hebrew Literary Genius*. Princeton, 1933.

MOULTON, RICHARD G., *The Literary Study of the Bible*. Boston, 1899.

PEAKE, ARTHUR S., *The Bible, Its Origin, Its Significance, and Its Abiding Worth*. London and New York, 1914.

CHAPTER 2

HELLENISTIC JEWISH LITERATURE

By Ralph Marcus

I. INTRODUCTION

The name "Hellenistic" is given by students of classical civilization to the period of about three centuries following the conquests of Alexander the Great in the Near East. The Greek noun *hellenistes* commonly meant a non-Greek speaker of Greek or imitator of Greek fashion; "Hellenistic" is therefore an appropriate term for an age in which Jews, Egyptians, Syrians, Iranians and other Oriental peoples were united—so far, at least, as their wealthier urban classes were concerned—in a common pattern of Greek-Oriental culture with more or less important variations of local color.

Students of European history usually consider the lower limit of the Hellenistic period to be 30 B.C.E. because by that time the Roman Empire under Augustus had consolidated its control over the Greek-Oriental kingdoms of Egypt, Syria and Asia Minor. But the orientalist and the historian of Western culture are inclined to extend the lower limit another few centuries because the official and educated classes in the large cities of the Near East continued to be Greek rather than Roman in speech and culture long after the Hellenistic kingdoms had been incorporated as provinces of the Roman Empire. In the case of the Jews this is true even of the Diaspora communities in Italy and other parts of Europe.

While each age has, of course, its peculiar significance in the perspective of world history even for those who assume that historical development is continuous in most spheres of social activity, that significance may seem to later ages to be clearer in one form of culture than in others. Thus, the Hellenistic age is especially interesting to us because it saw the birth and early nurturing of a world-consciousness in philosophy, law, religion and politics. This cosmopolitanism, to use a term coined by the Stoic philosophers or possibly by the Jewish philosopher Philo under Stoic influence, was only partially realized in such forms as Jewish-Christian ethics, Roman law, Greek ethnography, pagan astrology and Gnosticism; but these forms of universalism or cosmopolitanism were sufficiently developed in the Hellenistic age to provide thought and impulse to action for many centuries afterwards.

2. THE SEPTUAGINT

While the scribes of the Second Commonwealth were collecting and ordering the sacred books, many Jews both in Palestine and in the Diaspora were circulating didactic or historical or apocalyptic writings, some of them under the names of patriarchs or prophets, in order to obtain greater authority for their works. These books, even those written in Hebrew or Aramaic, were not admitted into the canon of Sacred Scripture by the Rabbinic scholars of the early talmudic period for one of two reasons: either the Rabbis thought that they had been written after the close of the Persian period, when prophetic inspiration was supposed to have ceased, or else they regarded them as unorthodox in content. In a few cases, however, such postprophetic books were admitted into the canon; for example, the Book of Daniel, which represents itself as a work of the Babylonian period, and perhaps the Book of Ecclesiastes, ascribed to Solomon.

But the noncanonical Hebrew and Aramaic writings were translated into Greek and circulated among the Jews of the Diaspora. Some of these writings in their Greek version were included in manuscripts of the Greek Bible, and were preserved either as sacred or as edifying books by the Christian church. In a few cases the original Hebrew or Aramaic text, or one based on the original, has been preserved by Jewish scribes, for example, the Wisdom of Ben Sira and the Book of Tobit. But in the case of most of these so-called apocryphal or pseudepigraphic books, we have only the Greek version, handed down by Christian scribes.

Although this chapter does not discuss the apocryphal writings composed by Palestinian Jews in Hebrew or Aramaic, they have been mentioned because of their being preserved in Greek and included in manuscripts of the Greek Bible. We must now turn our attention to this translation, which is extremely important and interesting in its own right.[1a]

This great monument of Hellenistic Jewish literature is called the Septuagint, meaning "seventy" in Latin, because there was current among early Christian scholars of Western Europe the story, first told by a Hellenistic Jewish writer (see below on the Letter of Aristeas), that seventy-two elders were sent from Palestine to Alexandria in Egypt to translate the Law of Moses from Hebrew into Greek. In the course of time the title "Translation of the Seventy-two" was simplified into "the Seventy" and was extended to include the translation of the prophetic and hagiographic portions of the Hebrew Bible.

The Septuagint is of great importance for several reasons. In the first place, it is a valuable control of the traditional Hebrew text of the Bible, known as the Masora. The earliest complete Hebrew manuscript of the Bible dates from the tenth century C.E., whereas the principal manuscripts of the Greek Bible date from the fourth and fifth centuries c.e. (There are considerable papyrus fragments written still earlier but they agree very closely with the chief manuscript, *Codex Vaticanus*.) Moreover, the Greek translations of the various books of Scripture were made from unvocalized Hebrew texts. Thus they sometimes yield a reading of a form or the meaning of a root which makes better sense than that of the masoretic text.

In the second place, this early translation, having been made by competent scholars with some knowledge of early Palestinian exegesis, is of great aid in interpreting some obscure passages in the Hebrew. There is also a strong probability that in some passages the Hebrew text was altered by the Palestinian scholars for theological or legalistic reasons, and since the Greek version was made from an earlier text than that handed down to us by the Palestinian authorities, it sometimes enables us to recover the original meaning of the biblical passage.

In the third place, the Septuagint was the source of a number of secondary versions made for the early Christian churches in Europe and the Near East such as the Coptic, Ethiopic, Armenian, Slavonic, Gothic and Old Latin. (The Old Latin has not been entirely replaced by Jerome's translation, called the Vulgate, which became the official Bible of the Roman Catholic Church by decree of the Council of Trent in 1546.) Thus through the Septuagint the contents of the Hebrew Bible became known to the peoples of Europe and Western Asia and contributed greatly to the forming of their beliefs and institutions.

In the fourth place, the Greek Bible played a considerable part in the gradual transformation of Greek philosophy into the theology of the Church Fathers and into the influential body of thought known as Neoplatonism. These in turn exerted an immeasurably great influence on medieval Scholasticism, Christian, Jewish and Moslem. For example, it would be difficult to overrate the importance for following centuries of the synthesis effected between the Platonic theory of the creation of the world by a beneficent spirit, the Demiurge, as described in the *Timaeus*, and the account of the creation given in the first two chapters of the Greek Genesis. Such syntheses are presented by the Jewish philosopher Philo and by the Christian philosopher Chalcidius in his Commentary on Plato's *Timaeus*.

As we shall deal with Philo below, it may suffice to remark here that his great work of harmonizing Greek philosophy with Judaism, which deeply influenced Christian theologians, perhaps all the way down to Dante, would have been almost impossible if he had not had at his disposal an official Greek translation of the Hebrew Bible, which he regarded as no less inspired than the original text.

The most important fact about the Septuagint for those who are interested in the history of European civilization, as well as in Judaism, is that the existence of this version was indispensable to the rise of Christianity. The earliest Christian apostles to the Gentiles would probably have had much less success in converting Jews of the Diaspora and "God-fearing" Gentiles to Christianity if they had not had an authoritative Greek text of the Jewish Scriptures with which to support their claim that Jesus of Nazareth, whom they called the Lord Christ, was the Messiah whose coming had been predicted by the Hebrew prophets. The quotations from the Old Testament found in the writings of Paul and the Apostolic Fathers agree closely with the text of the Septuagint, although in some cases, of course, the Christian writers quote from memory or alter the wording to suit their apologetic purposes.

For the several reasons given above we may fairly say that the Greek translation of the Bible by the Jewish scholars of Alexandria was one of the most important translations ever made.

Before turning to the original Hellenistic Jewish writings, let us briefly consider some of the stylistic aspects of the Septuagint. Its vocabulary and inflections were not very different from those of contemporary pagan writings composed in the language used by the vast majority of people in the Hellenistic period, the so-called "common" Greek dialect or *Koiné*. But because the Septuagint was a translation from Hebrew and dealt with concepts and ways of living and speaking peculiar to Jewish Palestine, its Hebraic style and special usages of many terms must have made it seem a strange and un-Greek book to such Gentiles as may have chanced to read it or hear it quoted. Many Hebrew idioms, to be sure, were adapted to Greek usage, but most of them were taken over literally, with curious results to the Greek style. The various books of the Bible differ in this respect. Some of the narratives in the Greek versions of Samuel and Kings, for example, read fairly smoothly, while the Greek Book of Ecclesiastes is so literal as to be almost unintelligible to one ignorant of the Hebrew original.

On the whole, the Greek Bible is a poor specimen of literary Greek, not because of the linguistic incompetence of the translators but because their primary concern was to produce a faithful rendering of the Hebrew for Greek-speaking Jews. There are occasional surface Hellenizations, such as allusions to well-known mythological figures and the use of Greek metrical forms in parts of the Book of Proverbs. But beneath these superficial adaptations there is a thoroughly Jewish, even Hebraic, spirit in the Septuagint. Those Jews in the Diaspora whose reading was confined to the Greek Bible were in no danger of being seduced by the charm of Greek literature.

3. HISTORICAL LITERATURE

When we turn to the historical literature of the Jews originally written in Greek, we must not expect to find anything like the relatively scientific spirit of inquiry and concern for factual accuracy that we admire in such Greek historians as Thucydides and Polybius. Rather we shall find that most of the historical writing preserved to us is heavily weighted with self-conscious pride in Jewish cultural achievements and might more justly be called apologetic or hortatory than historical. Some of it is merely historical fiction.

1. *Demetrius, Eupolemus and Artapanus*

Let us begin by briefly discussing three (probably) Alexandrian writers of whose works we have only fragments preserved in the ninth book of the Evangelical Preparation of the Church Father Eusebius, written about 300 C.E. Eusebius took these excerpts from a *Universal History* compiled by Alexander Polyhistor, a Greek encyclopedist of the first century B.C.E.

Some time near the end of the third century B.C.E. a Jew named Demetrius wrote a history of Israel in brief chronological form. The extant fragments deal with some of the events in the lives of Jacob and Moses and with the number of years that elapsed between the Israelite deportation to Assyria and the writer's own date, the reign of Ptolemy IV. Although Josephus held Demetrius to be a Gentile, the author's painstaking attempt to fix the exact dates of Jewish history makes it more likely that he was a Jew. Neither the style nor the content of the remaining fragments is of exceptional interest.

More promising are the fragments of Eupolemus, who wrote a *History of the Jews* about the middle of the second century B.C.E. Whether he lived in Egypt or Palestine is not known. Some scholars identify him with the Eupolemus mentioned in I Macc. 8:17 as an envoy sent to Rome by Judas Maccabeus; they do so partly on the ground that Eupolemus the historian seems to have used a Hebrew as well as a Greek text of Scripture. But there is no reason why an Alexandrian Jew should not have known Hebrew in addition to Greek. On the whole, it is more probable that Eupolemus wrote in Egypt than in Palestine.

Like most of the Hellenistic Jewish historians known to us Eupolemus embellished his work with legendary material showing the Jews in the most favorable light. He tells us, among other things, that Moses was the first Sage and the first to introduce writing among the Jews; the Phoenicians took it from the Jews and the Greeks took it from the Phoenicians. The most extensive fragment preserved by Eusebius tells of the building of Solomon's Temple and includes the imaginary correspondence between

Solomon and Vaphres (biblical Hophra). We may cite from this the reply made by the Egyptian king to Solomon's request for assistance, which was obviously designed to impress Gentile readers with the greatness of the Hebrew king.

King Vaphres to the great king, Solomon, greeting. I have read your letter with great pleasure, and I and all my court regard as memorable the day of your accession to the throne, for you are a worthy man and one favored by a very great god. In accordance with your request I have sent you eighty thousand men from the following districts, etc.

Eupolemus, as we can see from this brief excerpt, was not an impartial historian of the Jews. But his partiality was moderate in comparison with that of his near-contemporary Artapanus.

On internal evidence it is clear that Artapanus wrote in Alexandria, but when he lived is more difficult to determine further than that he was active before the first century B.C.E., since he was known to Alexander Polyhistor, who flourished about 100 B.C.E.

Artapanus bettered the example of rationalistic Greek historians who taught that the popular gods were only deified men who had made useful discoveries in art and science. He went so far as to assert that Moses was none other than the Greek Museus and the Egyptian Hermes (Thoth). Not only were the Jews a distinguished people of Syrian origin, and not the descendants of plague-carrying outcasts from Egypt, as their enemies charged, but Moses had even given the Egyptians the elements of their culture. It seems strange to us that a Jewish writer should have attributed the origin of Egyptian idolatry to Moses, but perhaps, as some scholars have suggested, Artapanus meant to pass off his work as that of an Egyptian priest (some of whom, like Artapanus himself, bore Persian names after the conquest of Egypt by Cambyses). It is probable that Josephus in his narrative of Moses in the *Antiquities* used the writings of Artapanus, thinking him to be a pagan author.

A translation of part of the longest extant fragment of Artapanus may serve to show his inventive powers.

After the death of Abraham [a slip for "Jacob"] and his son and also Mempsasthenoth, the king of Egypt, the latter's son Palmenoth succeeded to the throne, but he proved to be unfriendly to the Jews. He first built Kessan and erected a temple there, and then built a temple in Heliopolis. He had a daughter named Merris, whom he married to a certain Khenephres, king of the region above Memphis; at that time there were several kings in Egypt. Merris, being childless, secretly adopted a Hebrew child whom she called Moses. By the Greeks he was called Museus. This Moses was the teacher of Orpheus. When he reached manhood he devised many things useful to mankind; he invented boats and stone-laying machines and Egyptian weapons and instruments for irrigation and war. He was also the founder of philosophy.

Moreover, he divided the country into thirty-six nomes, and to each of these he assigned the worship of a particular god. To the priests he gave the sacred writing [hieroglyphs]. Now these gods were cats and dogs and ibises. He also assigned to the priests separate estates. All these things he did in order to make Khenephres's rule more secure, for before that time the unruly populace had expelled some of their kings and installed others in their places or reinstalled the dethroned ones. Because of all these achievements Moses was loved by the common people and was granted divine honors by the priests under the name of Hermes ["interpreter"] because he had interpreted the sacred writings.

2. *II Maccabees*

The Second Book of Maccabees is no mere variant of the First Book of Maccabees even though their contents are in part the same. The differences between them are more interesting and significant than the similarities. I Maccabees was originally written in Hebrew; II Maccabees is a Greek epitome of an original Greek work in five books composed by an otherwise unknown Jason of Cyrene (in North Africa). I Maccabees covers a period of forty years, 175-135 B.C.E., from the persecution of Antiochus Epiphanes to the death of Simon and the winning of Judea's political independence; II Maccabees covers a period of only fifteen years, 175-161 B.C.E., from the persecution of Antiochus Epiphanes (or a little earlier) to the victory of Judas Maccabeus over Nicanor. I Maccabees is a rather matter-of-fact account of the military achievements of the Hasmonean family; II Maccabees is a partly legendary account of the Jewish heroes and martyrs whose noble deeds were achieved with the miraculous help of God. It is largely because of the exalted tone and picturesque marvels of II Maccabees that it has won a more favored place in biblical literature than the more sober and historical I Maccabees. The heroic loyalty to ancestral tradition of the old man Eleazar and the mother with seven sons, in spite of the tortures inflicted on them by the Syrian king, became a classical example of martyrdom that was imitated in the vast literature of persecution of both Jews and Christians.

To the historian of Judaism and Christianity the book is especially important because in addition to various statements about the observance of the Sabbath and other practices that may be said to reveal a Pharisaic point of view, it contains what are probably the earliest explicit references to the resurrection of the body. This particular belief became one of the few cardinal dogmas of Pharisaism. It is stated in several passages of the book. In 7:9 one of the martyred youths says to the king before dying under torture:

You braggart, you release us from this present life, but the King of the world will resurrect us to an eternal new life because we have died for His laws.

Again in 12:43-44 we are told that Judas made a sin-offering in Jerusalem because of his belief in resurrection.

For if he had not expected that those who had fallen would rise again, it would have been superfluous and foolish to pray for the dead.

Incidentally, this last passage is one of several which have made II Maccabees one of the biblical writings most esteemed by Roman Catholic theologians.

As a characteristic example of the author's (or perhaps epitomator's) love of the marvelous and his rhetorical inventions we may select the following passage, 3:24-28, concerning the Divine punishment visited on the Syrian official Heliodorus for attempting to rob the treasury of the Temple in Jerusalem.

But no sooner had he and his guards arrived before the treasury than the Lord of our fathers and Master of all authority gave a great manifestation, so that all those who had come with him in their recklessness were smitten by the power of God and paralyzed and routed in terror. For there appeared to them a horse bearing a terrible rider and adorned with most handsome trappings, which rushed swiftly on Heliodorus and struck him with its forefeet. And its rider appeared in golden armor. And two youths also appeared to him, remarkably strong and most handsome in form and splendid in dress. These stood on either side of him and flogged him continually, showering many blows upon him. Suddenly he fell to the ground and was overwhelmed by great darkness, and so his men seized him and placed him on a litter—the same man indeed who had just entered the treasury we mentioned before, with such pomp and so great a retinue they now carried off because he was unable to help himself. Thus did they clearly recognize the sovereign power of God.

The author's ability to use simpler but more effective rhetoric is illustrated by his account of the death of the aged martyr Eleazar, 6:30-31:

As he was about to die under the blows, he said with a groan, "The Lord with His holy knowledge knows that though I might have escaped death, I endure dreadful pains in my body, being flogged, but in my soul I am glad to suffer this through fear of Him." And so he died, leaving in his death an example of nobility and a memorial of virtue not only to the young but also to the greatest part of his nation.

3. *III Maccabees*

The Third Book of Maccabees is found in most manuscripts of the Septuagint and in the Greek editions of the Apocrypha but it is not included in the Vulgate version or in the King James version, and is therefore less known to English readers than are I and II Maccabees. The word "Maccabees" in its title is misleading since the book is concerned with the Jews of Egypt and has nothing to do with the Hasmoneans; still there is a certain appropriateness in connecting this book with the two books of the Maccabees since it bears an obvious resemblance to II Maccabees in conception and style and also to some extent in the incidents related.

III Maccabees supposedly dates from the reign of the Macedonian king of Egypt, Ptolemy IV Philopator, 221-203 B.C.E. It relates that Ptolemy, after defeating the Seleucid king Antiochus III at Raphia on the Egyptian-Palestine border in 217 B.C.E., attempted to enter the Temple of Jerusalem and was miraculously kept therefrom (like Heliodorus in II Maccabees). On his return to Egypt the wrathful king decreed that his Jewish subjects were to suffer the loss of some of their religious and political privileges unless they should register as worshipers of the Ptolemies' patron god Dionysos. On seeing that the vast majority of Jews remained loyal to their religion, he had Jews brought from the country to Alexandria and imprisoned in the Hippodrome to be trampled to death by intoxicated elephants. Through Divine intervention the elephants turned against the persecutors of the Jews, and King Ptolemy, being convinced that the Jews enjoyed Divine protection, repented of his hostility and allowed them to return home safely and to take vengeance, not on Greek or Egyptian persecutors, be it noted, but on Jewish apostates. The story and atmosphere of the book remind one strongly of II Maccabees, the Letter of Aristeas and the Book of Esther.

When the book was actually written and to what incident in Jewish history it refers is difficult to determine. The incident of the exposure to trampling by drunken elephants is practically the same as that described by Josephus in his *Against Apion* as having taken place in the reign of Ptolemy VII Physcon, almost a century after the time of Ptolemy IV Philopator; moreover, the political troubles of the Jews hinted at in the book seem to belong to the time of Ptolemy Physcon rather than to that of Ptolemy Philopator. On the other hand, the description of the battle of Raphia and other details of the official acts of Ptolemy Philopator indicate that the author had a good knowledge of the events of his reign. The various problems of date and composition are best solved by assuming that an Egyptian Jewish writer of the first century B.C.E. has combined events of the reigns of two different kings and has added picturesque details suggested by the Book of Esther and II Maccabees to make up a well-knit piece of historical fiction. Several scholars have argued that III Maccabees was written in the Roman period and really alludes to the persecution of the Jews in Alexandria (and Palestine) by the Roman emperor Caligula, but, for reasons which cannot be given here, the present writer believes that the book was written in the first century B.C.E. to encourage the Jews of Palestine and Egypt to hope for Divine intervention in the face of an invasion of Palestine by the Ptolemaic sovereigns Cleopatra and Ptolemy VIII Lathyrus during the reign of Alexander Janneus.

The book is written in quite respectable and sometimes rather polished

Greek. As a story it is continuously interesting and even exciting. Not the least skillful device of the author is the succession of pointed references to God's power to save the Jews from their enemies. As a whole the work has less of the miraculous than II Maccabees but is no less orthodox in doctrine. The following brief passage illustrates its style and theology:

6:16-21. And just as Eleazar was ending his prayer, the king came to the Hippodrome with the beasts and his whole insolent force. And when the Jews beheld this, they cried out to heaven so that the adjacent hollows re-echoed their cry and caused an uncontrollable wailing among all the host. Then the greatly glorious, almighty and true God manifested His holy countenance and opened the gates of heaven, from which two glorious angels of terrible aspect descended, being visible to all except the Jews. And these stood over against them and filled the army of their adversaries with confusion and fear and bound them with immovable fetters. And a trembling fell upon the king's body, and forgetfulness of his heavy-handed arrogance came upon him. And the beasts turned round against the forces that followed them and began trampling on them and destroying them.

4. Josephus

The late Henry St. John Thackeray began his discussion of Josephus in his admirable Stroock Lectures on the historian by reminding his audience that there was a time in his country (England) when almost every house possessed two books, a Bible and a Josephus in the old eighteenth-century version of William Whiston. The same thing might be said of Presbyterian Scotland and Puritan New England and of other Protestant countries of Europe with their various vernacular translations of Josephus. But translations and paraphrases of Josephus were popular long before Whiston's English translation was made. Great numbers of Jews from the early Middle Ages down to recent times have eagerly read the Hebrew *Yosippon*, which is to a large extent a paraphrase of Josephus's *Jewish War*, while the Latin paraphrase ascribed to Hegesippus found great favor among Christian Latinists. Few pagan historians of classical antiquity have been more widely read or quoted than Flavius Josephus, the Palestinian Jew, whose Greek works on the history of his people and their war with Rome and eloquent apology for Judaism have done much to atone for his adherence to the Roman cause when his country was conquered by Vespasian and Titus.

Joseph, son of Matthias, later called Flavius Josephus, claims, in his *Life*, to have been of priestly and Hasmonean descent. He was born in 37 or 38 c.e. in the year when Caligula became emperor. He tells us that he was so precocious a student of the Jewish law that learned Rabbis consulted him when he was only fourteen. He studied the doctrines of the various Jewish schools and even retired to the wilderness for three years of ascetic training with a certain Bannus.

At the age of nineteen Josephus became a member of the Pharisaic party. In 64 C.E. he sailed to Rome and succeeded, with the help of a Jewish actor and the Empress Poppea, in liberating some priests who had been sent to Nero for trial. Josephus's visit to Rome impressed him with the hopelessness of a Jewish revolt against Rome which the extremists were planning. However, during the interval between the defeat of the Twelfth Legion under Cestius in the autumn of 66 and Vespasian's arrival in Palestine in the spring of 67 Josephus became an important figure in the revolt.

What his private attitude was toward the Romans and the exact nature of the commission entrusted to him by the authorities in Jerusalem are matters of doubt. In his earliest work, the *Jewish War*, Josephus states that the responsible leaders appointed him commander of the Jewish forces in Galilee.[2a] In the *Life*, written some thirty years later, he writes that he and two other priests were chosen to induce the rebels in Galilee to lay down their arms and to leave the decision of war to the authorities in Jerusalem; only afterwards was he made supreme commander of the forces in Galilee. Those scholars are probably right who prefer the later account and hold that in the *Jewish War* Josephus has exaggerated the importance of his appointment in order to impress Roman readers. At any rate, it appears from both works that he fought without conviction though he may have shown resourcefulness and military skill.

After the fall of the town of Jotapata, which had held out against the Romans for more than a month, Josephus with a few companions escaped to a cave, and persuaded them not to kill him to prevent his capture or surrender but to draw lots to determine the order of their mutual self-destruction. "He, however—" the evasive writer tells us, "should one say by fortune or by the providence of God?—was left alone with one other, and anxious neither to be condemned by lot nor, should he be left to the last, to stain his hand with his countryman's blood, he persuaded this man also under a pledge to remain alive." Brought before Vespasian, Josephus predicted that the Roman general would become emperor (as the Roman historian Suetonius also attests) and thanks to this prediction was liberated from bonds when Vespasian was acclaimed emperor by his troops in July, 69 C.E. During the last two years of the war Josephus served as interpreter and mediator. At the end of the war he was given a piece of land outside Jerusalem and some sacred books; he also obtained the liberation of several of his friends.

The last thirty years or so of his life the Jewish careerist spent in Rome, enjoying for about a third of this time the patronage of the imperial family. But life was not wholly pleasant for him during his residence in Rome, for he was constantly subject to the criticism of his coreligionists as a deserter or as a falsifier of his part in the war. Whatever the justice of these charges, we must be sincerely grateful to Josephus for having left us the four works which have so greatly enriched our knowledge of Jewish and Greco-Roman history.

The earliest extant work, the *Jewish War* or *Capture* (of Jerusalem) as Josephus himself probably meant it to be called, was clearly written soon after 70 C.E. at the suggestion of the Roman government in order to discourage further opposition by the Jews and other peoples living in Parthian territory. Our Greek text is apparently a second edition of the book, the first presumably being closer to the original draft, now lost, written in Aramaic. Parenthetically I may say that it is a very doubtful assumption that the Slavonic version is a translation of the original Aramaic text rather than a secondary translation of the Greek. Various references to Christianity or Jewish prophecies of the Roman period, which are found in the Slavonic version, are probably additions made by Byzantine scribes.

The *Jewish War* has a rapid survey of Jewish history in the Hellenistic-Roman period in the first book, largely based on the *Life of Herod* by Nicholas of Damascus, and in the remaining six books dramatically narrates the course of the Jewish war against Rome and its aftermath. Josephus not only drew on his personal experience but also used the military journals of the Roman commanders Titus and Vespasian and other official Roman documents. For these reasons the work has the greatest value as a historical source. At the same time, like most ancient histories, it contains a number of rhetorical embellishments, especially in the speeches attributed to the leading actors, and various echoes of Greek writers, notably the tragic poet Sophocles. Also it naturally reflects the prejudices and private interests of Josephus himself. With the help of a well-trained Greek collaborator the Jewish historian was able to produce a work of considerable literary skill both in construction and in style. We may safely conjecture that educated Romans found considerable pleasure in reading it.

Of even greater interest to students of Judaism and Christianity is Josephus's second great work, the *Jewish Antiquities*, divided into twenty books like its partial prototype, the *Roman Antiquities* of Dionysius of Halicarnassus. The *Jewish Antiquities*, written during the reign of Domitian after Josephus had lost his royal patrons, was put out with a different motive from that which prompted him to publish the *Jewish War*. The later work was designed not to celebrate the achievements of the Romans but to acquaint them with the history of the conquered Jewish people and to show that the Jews had a glorious past worthy of the respect of their Roman conquerors.

The first ten books of the *Jewish Antiquities*, covering the history of the Jews from the patriarchal period to the Babylonian Exile are in the main a paraphrase of the Greek version of the biblical narratives from Genesis to Daniel. Josephus's paraphrase of the Septuagint is no mere stylistic variation of the biblical text. He has incorporated numerous legendary and homiletic additions, most of them from Alexandrian writers (including Philo) and Palestinian tradition. Recent studies have shown that in addition to the Greek Bible Josephus used the Hebrew original and an Aramaic version closely resembling the extant Targums of Onkelos and Jonathan. The *Jewish Antiquities* is, of course, a valuable check on the Septuagint text, but more than that, it is of great importance as one of the earliest specimens of Jewish biblical exegesis.

The second half of the *Jewish Antiquities* covers the period from the return of the exiles to Judea in the reign of Cyrus to the term of the last procurator before the outbreak of the war against Rome. For the history of the Persian period and the Hellenistic period down to the reign of Hyrcanus, Josephus has used as his chief sources the Books of Ezra and Nehemiah, Esther, the Letter of Aristeas and I Maccabees, supplemented by handbooks of Greek history written by Gentile historians. For the Hasmonean, Herodian and procuratorial periods he is chiefly dependent on Jewish tradition and on the works of the Greek historians Nicholas of Damascus and Strabo and some unknown Roman historians. His quotations and paraphrases of Nicholas and Strabo make up a considerable part of the fragments preserved of their lost works.

The *Jewish Antiquities* is not only our chief and in part our only source for the history of the Jews in Palestine and in the Diaspora during the Hellenistic and Roman periods but it is also a valuable source for some otherwise poorly documented episodes of Seleucid and Roman history; for example, it gives us the most detailed account we possess of the assassination of the Emperor Caligula and the accession of Claudius. Where the *Jewish War* and the *Jewish Antiquities* overlap, as in the reign of Herod the Great, a comparison of the two accounts reveals significant differences of arrangement and political attitude, and thus throws light on Josephus's methods and motives. Not the least interesting portions of the parallel passages in the *Jewish War* and the *Jewish Antiquities* are those dealing with the Jewish schools or parties, Pharisees, Sadducees and Essenes.[3a] Although Josephus, following the example of Nicholas of Damascus, who wrote for Gentile readers, has converted social and theological differences among the Jewish parties into matters of philosophy, his discussion of their doctrines and controversies must be recognized as one of our principal sources for the history of Judaism in the early talmudic period.

There is another reason why the *Jewish Antiquities* was studied and prized by Christian scholars after the time of Eusebius; in Book XVIII there occurs a brief passage about the life and death of Jesus, the so-called *Testimonium Flavianum*, which is the only extant explicit mention of the founder of Christianity, outside the New Testament of course, dating from the first century of the Common Era. A vast literature exists dealing with the problem of the genuineness of this passage. Almost no modern scholar regards the testimony to Jesus's miraculous powers and resurrection as genuine in its present form; a few scholars believe that it is a Christian revision of an original reference to Jesus that was quite neutral in tone; most scholars believe, with greater justice, that the entire passage is a Christian interpolation.

We have already mentioned the *Life*, published as an appendix to the second edition of the *Jewish Antiquities*. It was probably written to answer the criticisms of the *Jewish War* made by a rival Jewish historian, Justus of Tiberias. Besides being valuable as an account of Josephus's activities as commander of the Jewish forces in Galilee (see above), it provides us with our only though sketchy account of Josephus's entire career.

The latest work of Josephus, *Against Apion*, in two books, has a greater scope than the title indicates, since Apion was only one of several Greek writers whose calumnies against the Jews Josephus undertakes to refute. This little treatise is not only a persuasive and eloquent refutation of the various charges, some of them patently absurd, some more insidious, which were brought against the Jews by Egyptian and Greek anti-Semites and sometimes by more impartial Gentile historians, but it is also an inspired defense of the Mosaic Law and a triumphant vindication of Jewish morality and culture. Few champions of Judaism have more successfully presented their case; and so, this earliest reply to literary anti-Semitism must be regarded as ample atonement for any sins Josephus may have committed against his people as a military leader.

There are far too many quotable passages in Josephus's four works to make it easy to choose any single one in this brief sketch, but I cannot resist quoting part of the conclusion of the *Against Apion* in Thackeray's translation:

I would therefore boldly maintain that we have introduced to the rest of the world a very large number of very beautiful ideas. What greater beauty than inviolable piety? What higher justice than obedience to the laws? What more beneficial than to be in harmony with one another, to be a prey neither to disunion in adversity nor to arrogance and faction in prosperity; in war to despise death, in peace to devote oneself to crafts or agriculture, and to be convinced that everything in the whole universe is under the eye and direction of God? Had these precepts been either committed to writing or more consistently observed by others before us, we should have owed them a debt of gratitude as their disciples. If, however, it is seen that no one observes them better than ourselves, and if we have shown that we were the first to discover them, then the Apions and Molons and all who delight in lies and abuse may be left to their own confusion.

4. JEWISH PROPAGANDA IN GENTILE GUISE

The basic instincts and broad patterns of social behavior were not very different, whether among Jews or Gentiles, in the Hellenistic age from those of present-day peoples, but some of their conventions were dissimilar enough from our own to evoke surprise in a modern person when first he learns of them. The ancient attitude toward plagiarism and literary borrowing, for example, was much less proprietary than it is today. The same is true of their attitude toward the practice of foisting one's own work on the great names of classical tradition. Bearing this in mind, we should not be too greatly scandalized by the fact that some Jewish apologists composed works in prose or verse designed to show Jews in a favorable light, and published them as the writings of real or imaginary Gentile authors, just as Christian writers of the fourth or fifth century forged a correspondence between the Roman philosopher Seneca and the Apostle Paul. The present section deals with the best known works or fragments of this kind which have come down to us. In all probability they are only a small part of the entire body of this literature.

1. *Pseudo-Hecateus*

Among the Gentile historians of the time of Alexander the Great and his immediate successors whose works have been preserved only in excerpts by later writers of antiquity was a certain Hecateus who wrote, among other things, a *History of Egypt* including passages on the Jews. Some portions of this book have been preserved by the Greek historian Diodorus Siculus, who flourished under Augustus. There is no reason to doubt the genuineness of these passages. But there are other passages cited by Josephus and early Christian writers, supposedly from Hecateus's book *On the Jews* or *On Abraham*, which are generally regarded as extracts from a Jewish work passed off as Hecateus's and therefore known today as excerpts from Pseudo-Hecateus. Recently, however, some scholars have convincingly argued that the suspected passages in Josephus's *Against Apion* are really from the genuine Hecateus, and it is likely that as our knowledge increases through the discovery of new evidence, the extent of the assumed pseudepigraphic material will have to be considerably reduced. But the strong probability remains that other fragments from "Hecateus," for example, in Clement of Alexandria and Eusebius, are from Pseudo-Hecateus, the Jewish apologist, whose real name and date are unknown to us. That even in antiquity there was some suspicion of the supposititious character of passages quoted from Hecateus's book *On the Jews* is indicated by a statement in Origen that

the author is so attached to this nation because of its wisdom that Herennius
Philo [a Hellenized Phoenician, who flourished about 100 c.e.] in his work
On the Jews in the first place expresses doubt whether the work is by the historian, and in the second place says, if it really is his work, that he has been
ravished by Jewish persuasiveness and won over by their doctrines.

It is perhaps Pseudo-Hecateus, not the genuine Hecateus, who is quoted
in the Letter of Aristeas (§5) as saying that pagan writers have refrained
from discussing Jewish history because of the great sacredness attaching
to it.

2. *The Letter of Aristeas*

Although the Letter of Aristeas was highly esteemed and used by such
early Jewish writers as Philo and Josephus (and, of course, by Christian
theologians), it was not until the sixteenth century that the liberal Italian
Jewish scholar Azariah de'Rossi rescued it from the neglect into which,
because it was written in Greek, it had fallen among his coreligionists. De'-
Rossi's Hebrew translation and discussion of the Letter of Aristeas are
included in his critical history of Jewish tradition, called *Meor Eynayim*.

The Letter of Aristeas purports to be a letter written to a certain
Philocrates by his brother, a court official of Ptolemy II Philadelphus
(285-247 B.C.E.). It narrates the events leading up to the translation of
the Hebrew Pentateuch into Greek made by the Palestinian scholars whom
the king invited to Alexandria at the suggestion of the royal librarian,
Demetrius of Phalerum. The account of the translators' methods takes
up only the last twelfth of the book; the preceding sections describe the
emancipation of Jewish captives in Egypt by royal command, the invitation to Eleazar, the High Priest in Jerusalem, to send scholars to Alexandria for the work of translation, the presents sent to the Temple in
Jerusalem by Ptolemy, the impressions made on Aristeas by the Temple
and the city, and the splendid reception given to the Palestinian scholars
on their arrival in Alexandria; then comes a long philosophical discussion,
in the form of question and answer, between the king and the Jewish
Sages on matters of politics and morality.

Even a casual reading of this fascinating book reveals that the author
was not, as he pretends, a Ptolemaic official narrating a series of historical
events but a Hellenistic Jew writing a sort of historical novel (or novel-
ette) about the translation of the Law and embellishing it with apologetic
passages skillfully employing the devices of Greek philosophical literature.

The problem of the date has long exercised the ingenuity of scholars
but the weight of learned opinion today favors a date not long after 200
B.C.E. Such a date would account for some slight errors about the history
and court etiquette of Ptolemy II's reign made by the generally well-
informed author as well as for his use of certain forms and phrases known

to be current in Egypt in the early part of the second century B.C.E. It may be conjectured, though it would be difficult to prove, that in addition to giving a laudatory description of Jewish customs for the edification of Gentiles, the author had the more specific purpose of alleviating any suspicions entertained by the Ptolemaic ruler of his time that the friendly relations between the Jewish communities of Alexandria and Jerusalem might trouble the political situation in Egypt.

To the Jewish and Christian historians of antiquity the most important part of the Letter of Aristeas was that which told how the Law was translated into Greek. Josephus was content to paraphrase this account but other ancient writers, like the Christian Fathers, Ireneus, Clement and Epiphanius, repeat the picturesque invention of Pseudo-Justin that the seventy-two translators mentioned by Aristeas were placed in thirty-six cells and by Divine inspiration separately produced versions that were found to be in absolute agreement. The original account (§§301-309) reads in part as follows.

Three days later Demetrius [the royal librarian] took the men and passing along the sea wall of seven stadia to the island, crossed the bridge and went to the northern part. Here he called them together in session in a house built on the seashore; it was very splendid and located in a quiet place. He then encouraged them to carry out the work of translation, for everything had been well provided that was needed for this purpose. So they began their task, making their results agree by comparing them, and what was agreed upon was duly written down with the approval of Demetrius. The session lasted until the ninth hour [3:00 P.M.] After this they were dismissed to attend to their bodily needs, and everything they wanted was freely supplied to them. In addition they were given the same daily provisions as the king; Demetrius attended to this, having been ordered by the king so to do. Early every day they appeared at court and paid their respects to the king, after which they went back to their own place. And, as is the custom among the Jews, they washed their hands in the sea in order to pray to God and then began to read and translate the passages given to each. . . . And it so happened that the work of translation was completed in seventy-two days, as though this had been arranged of set purpose. When the work had been completed, Demetrius called the Jewish populace to the place where the translation had been made, and read it to all in the presence of the translators, who received a great ovation from the populace on the strength of the great benefits for which they had been responsible.

To a modern reader there are other equally interesting passages that deserve quotation, but lack of space forbids giving more than a part of the section (§§ 128-171) that contains the earliest moral allegory of some of the ritual prescriptions of Mosaic Law, such as was later richly developed by Philo.

For though in general all things are alike in their physical principles, being governed by the same power, in every case there is a deep reason why we abstain from the use of some things and enjoy the use of others. This I will summarily explain by one or two examples. For you must not get the degrading notion that it was out of respect for mice and weasels and such creatures that Moses showed such care in his legislation. Rather did he draw up all these solemn prescriptions for the sake of righteousness and to aid in attaining holiness and the perfecting of character. For all the birds we use [for food] are tame and distinguished by their cleanliness and feed on grain and pulse, such as pigeons, turtledoves, moorfowls, partridges, geese and other such birds. But the birds that are forbidden you will find to be wild and carnivorous and to dominate others by their strength and wrongfully prey on the tame birds mentioned above. . . . He therefore used them as examples, calling them "unclean," to show that those for whom the Law was ordained should practice righteousness in their souls and not dominate anyone in reliance upon their own strength nor deprive others of anything, but steer their lives by what is right, just as the tame birds mentioned above consume various kinds of pulse growing in the earth, and do not dominate their kindred species in order to destroy them.

3. *Pseudo-Phocylides*

Among the Greek moralistic poets of whose works only a few fragments have come down to us was a certain Phocylides of Miletus who lived in the sixth century B.C.E. Evidently he was a writer of considerable authority in later times, for a Jew of the Hellenistic period chose Phocylides as the pagan poet on whom to foist his own composition consisting of 230 hexametric verses in classical Greek style and with a content chiefly based on the moral prescriptions of Mosaic Law.

This crypto-Jewish work in Greek form is the more interesting for its failure to denounce pagan idolatry or to praise specific Jewish customs, as did outspoken Jewish Hellenists like Philo and the author of III Maccabees. Pseudo-Phocylides is so careful to conceal his Jewish origin that he presents only the most universalistic features of biblical morality and piety. This concealment, it is safe to say, is due to his technique of propaganda and not to expediency or timidity. Of course, there is a bare possibility that the author was not a Jew but a pagan admirer of the Greek Bible, or even a crypto-Christian. But in view of the assured Jewish character of similar works, it is far more probable that the author was Jewish. A few specimen lines (8-11, 84-85) are here translated in rough approximation of the Greek style and dactylic meter:

First honor God, and next after Him honor those who begot thee.
Deal out justice to all men, and twist not judgment to favor.
Turn not away the poor without right, and respect not men's persons.
Be not a wicked judge lest God in turn some day condemn thee.

Flee from false witness, and justice alone be what thou desirest.
Let no one take from the nest all the birds that are sheltered within it,
But set the mother bird free, and some other day thou'lt have her fledglings.

4. *The Wise Menander*

Most famous of the writers of the comedy of manners in the Hellenistic world was the Attic poet Menander, who flourished in the generation after Alexander the Great. His numerous plays were not only imitated and adapted by the two great Roman comedy writers Plautus and Terence but continued to influence Roman satirists of the imperial age, and like the plays of Shakespeare, became a part of the general culture of the Western world after their author had died. Echoes of Menander's informal philosophy are found even in the New Testament, for example, "evil communications corrupt good manners" in I Cor. 15:33. Moreover, wise and witty sayings were culled from the numerous works of Menander (of which, unfortunately, only fragments have survived) and included in anthologies of maxims from the Greek poets and philosophers.

It was probably the Attic Menander who was in the mind of the author or editor of a collection of gnomic sayings, probably in the iambic meter of six feet used for this purpose in Greek literature, of which a Syriac translation was found in a seventh-century manuscript of the British Museum, bearing the title *The Wise Menander Said*. Thirty years after its publication by J. Land in 1862, another scholar, Frankenberg, showed that these verses, about a hundred and fifty in number, closely resembled sayings in biblical Wisdom literature, and thus, he argued, they represent the work of a Jewish writer of the Roman period. But since the collection contains a number of genuine sayings of Menander and other pagan writers, it is probable that the Greek original of this Syriac translation was a Jewish pseudepigraph, designed to convey Jewish ideas in a form that would appeal to Greek readers, particularly because of the prestige that was attached to the name of Menander. The following few verses are given in a translation that attempts to suggest the meter probably used in the lost Greek original of the Syriac text.

> Fear God, and honor too thy father and thy mother.
> Mock not old age, for thou thyself wilt come to it.
> If from his youth thy son emerge both meek and wise,
> Teach him the scribal art and wisdom; these two things
> Are good to learn and bring clear eyes and flowing tongue.
> What's hateful to thee, unto friends seek not to do.

In the expression "scribal art and wisdom" the reader will immediately recognize an allusion to Dan. 1:17.

5. The Sibylline Oracles

Among the ancient legendary givers of oracles and prophecies the mysterious women called Sibyls enjoyed great prestige in the Hellenistic-Roman period. Most high school boys of past generations were familiar with the story, told by Virgil in the sixth book of the *Aeneid*, of Aeneas's visit to the Cumean sibyl who foretold to him the future trials and triumphs of the Roman people and prepared him for his descent into the nether world. But the Cumean sibyl was only one of several whose prophecies, recorded in Greek hexameters, were widely circulated in the early days of the Roman Empire. Besides the Greco-Roman sibyls of Cumae in Italy, of Erythrae in Asia Minor, of Libya, of Delphi in Greece, there were also Oriental sibyls, Hebrew, Persian and Chaldean. Sometimes they were considered separate figures, sometimes the Persian and Chaldean sibyls were identified with the Jewish sibyl, Sabbe or Sambathe, the daughter of Berossus (Berossus actually having been a Babylonian historian of the third century B.C.E. who translated cuneiform records into Greek).

The extant manuscripts of Sibylline Oracles represent a collection made in the fifth or sixth century C.E., which contains several thousand verses, divided into fourteen or fifteen books. They are ostensibly pagan prophecies of the dire calamities about to overtake the Gentile world, but actually they are in large part Jewish and Christian compositions in pagan disguise, meant to warn their readers to repent of their sins and to recognize the truth of Jewish or Christian teaching. Some of the Jewish oracles probably date from the second century B.C.E. It is hardly necessary to state that they were not genuine predictions of things to come but, like many apocalyptic writings, were prophecies after the event.

It is not always easy to distinguish the Jewish from the Christian portions because the original Jewish prophecies were imitated or revised by Christian writers. However, there is general agreement that we have basically Jewish material in most of Books III, IV and V and in parts of later books. Many events of Jewish history in the Hellenistic-Roman period are alluded to in these supposed prophecies, but the language is often so poetically obscure and the symbolism so vague that it is not always possible for modern scholars to be certain of the exact incidents described. From the less ambiguous passages we can be fairly sure that the Jewish author or authors included a rapid survey of Jewish history from the reign of Antiochus Epiphanes to the decades following the destruction of the Temple of Jerusalem by the Romans in 70 C.E. Clearly Jewish is the tone of those passages in which the sibyl denounces pagan idolatry and immorality, announces the coming of a Messianic age and the punishment of the godless, and consoles the righteous with promise of Divine help.

Unfortunately there is not sufficient material to enable us to estimate how deep an impression was made upon pagan readers by these crypto-Jewish Sibylline Oracles, but it is safe to say that Virgil was influenced by them in writing his *Fourth Eclogue*, which describes the coming golden age of Roman imperialism. Occasional echoes of Messianic imagery in later Greek and Latin literature suggest that these Jewish verses in Greek form had considerable effect in forming certain types of pagan literature during the early centuries of the Roman Empire. Whether they had a more practical effect in winning pagan converts to Judaism can only be conjectured.

Of the large number of verses of undoubted Jewish origin, the following few are selected as representative; they are given in metrical translation suggesting the form of the Greek meter employed (Book III, 36-39, 46-52).

> O generation delighting in blood, crafty, evil and godless,
> Men who lie and are double-tongued and evil of nature,
> Stealing other men's wives, idolators, craftily plotting;
> Evil lurks in your breasts, like a maddening gadfly pursues you.
> But that day will come when Rome will rule over Egypt,
> Though it be still delayed, and then the almighty kingdom
> Of the eternal King will appear to mankind in glory.
> Then will the holy prince come and on earth bear the scepter
> Throughout all aeons forever, as time hurries onward.
> Then shall the wrath inexorably descend on the Latins,
> And by a pitiful fate Three will bring Rome into ruin.

5. EPIC AND DRAMA

Until quite recent times it was generally thought that the Jews of the Greek-speaking Diaspora were almost completely unaffected by the artistic impulses of their Greek neighbors. However, the excavations of synagogues decorated with mosaic and painted representations of human, animal and floral figures have caused us to revise our opinions concerning the lack of pictorial art among the Jews of the Hellenistic-Roman period. By contrast, philologists have long been aware that among Greek-speaking Jews there were persons of literary talent who showed skill in adapting the language and style of Greek epic and dramatic poetry to biblical themes. Unfortunately the works of all but three of such writers have been completely lost, and of the three whose poetry has escaped oblivion only scant fragments have survived in the ninth book of the *Evangelical Preparation* of Eusebius, the same writer who has preserved fragments of the Hellenistic Jewish prose writers mentioned above. For this reason it may be something of a surprise to the general reader that in the Hellenistic age there were Jews who wrote epics and dramas in Greek about the sacred history of Israel.

1. *Philo the Elder* (*Philo Epicus*)

The Jewish epic poet Philo was not, of course, the philosopher Philo of Alexandria (on whom see below) but was probably the same person whom Josephus, in his *Against Apion*, refers to as Philo the Elder and couples with the Hellenistic Jewish historians Demetrius and Eupolemus. Since Josephus and Eusebius depend for their information about Philo the Elder upon Alexander Polyhistor, who flourished about 100 B.C.E., it is clear that the poet must have written as early as the second century B.C.E.

According to Eusebius, Philo wrote an epic called *On Jerusalem*, but the learned Church Father has seen fit to quote only three fragments amounting in all to twenty-four lines. It is also unfortunate that the few extant verses are written in the recondite and labored style of Alexandrian epic poets and are somewhat difficult to understand. The following is a verse-translation of a five-line fragment on Joseph, quoted by Eusebius from the fourth book (we must amend ms. "fourteenth" to "fourth"). From the position of this fragment and the statement of Clement of Alexandria that Philo wrote about the kings of Israel, we may conjecture that the epic covered twenty-four books, like the *Iliad* and the *Odyssey*.

> For them a blessed abode did the great world leader establish,
> He, the Most High, of old for the children of Abram and Isaac
> And of the child-blessed Jacob. Thence came Joseph the dreamer,
> Prophet of God, who wielded the scepter over all Egypt,
> And revolved in his mind the secrets of time in the floodtide of fortune.

2. *Theodotus*

About Theodotus, the author of an epic *On the Jews*, we know as little as about his contemporary Philo Epicus. The forty-seven hexameter verses cited by Eusebius in the ninth book of his *Evangelical Preparation* from Alexander Polyhistor are concerned with the Israelites' conquest of Shechem and the revenge taken by Simeon and Levi for the seduction of Dinah. From the fact that the extant fragments narrate only this episode and that Shechem is called a "holy city" some scholars have inferred that Theodotus was a Samaritan rather than a Jew. But "holy city" is a stock epithet in Greek epic poetry, and there is no trace of anti-Jewish feeling in the poem, such as one would expect in a Samaritan work; moreover, the poem stresses the impiety of the Shechemites. We shall therefore probably be right in considering Theodotus a Jewish writer.

Theodotus writes in a simpler and more Homeric style than Philo Epicus, who, as we saw, preferred the artificial manner of contemporary

Alexandrian poets. In respect of the Hellenistic elements in this Jewish work it is interesting that Eusebius reports the author as saying that the city got its name from "Shechem son of Hermes." But in spite of Theodotus's use of the language of Greek mythology we must, I think, agree with the German editor Ludwich in regarding "Hermes" as a corruption of *Hamor* (Greek *Emor*), since Shechem is so designated in the poem itself as in the Greek version of Genesis, on which the extant fragments are based (ch. 34).

The following few lines from the passage describing Jacob's coming from Mesopotamia to Palestine (here called Syria) may suffice to give an idea of the style:

> Then Jacob made his way to the kine-bearing land of Syria,
> Leaving behind the stream of the wide, onrushing Euphrates,
> For he had come from there, leaving the bitter reproaches
> Made by his very own kin, though gladly had Laban received him
> Into his home, who was cousin to him, and sole ruler
> Over all Syria . . .

3. *Ezekiel the Tragic Poet*

Epic poetry was not the only field of Greek literature cultivated by the Jewish writers of Alexandria. Centuries before Christian monks and clerics produced dramas based on biblical themes, a Jewish poet named Ezekiel wrote tragedies on these subjects. Considerable fragments, amounting to over two hundred lines, from one of his dramas on the Exodus have been preserved by Eusebius in that precious ninth book of his *Evangelical Preparation*, again from the lost compilation of Alexander Polyhistor.

Ezekiel has taken the story of Moses and the Israelites' flight from Egypt from the Greek version of the Book of Exodus, and has given it dramatic form on the lines of classical Greek tragedy, especially under the influence of Euripides. There are, however, some deviations from the pattern of Attic drama, such as more frequent changes of scene and the omission of choral passages. Unity of action is obtained by making Moses the central figure in all the scenes. The meter used in the extant fragments is the iambic trimeter, regularly employed in the dialogue of Attic plays.

Modern scholars disagree on the question whether Ezekiel's *Exodus* was meant to be presented in an Alexandrian theater or merely to be read as a closet drama. The latter is more likely, not merely because of the technical problems presented by frequent changes of scene but also because it is difficult to believe that Jews would have attended a theatrical performance of a sacred legend in which God Himself was one of the actors. Nor is it much more likely that there would have been a Gentile audience for such a play. But it would be foolish to speak dogmatically on this

subject in the present state of our knowledge about the everyday life of
Jews in the Hellenistic Diaspora.

It is also probable that Ezekiel wrote this drama about Moses and the
Exodus not merely for the instruction or encouragement of Jews who had
a Greek secular education but also for Gentiles whom he might hope to
impress with the power of Israel's God to save His people from persecution. For translation I have selected part of the dialogue between God and
Moses concerning the miracles which God wishes Moses to perform with
his staff (based on Ex. 4:2-7). The language here is simple, rapid and
almost prosaic:

GOD: What is this thing in thy two hands? Speak quickly now.
MOSES: It is a staff with which to strike both beasts and men.
GOD: Cast it upon the ground and quickly move away.
            For 'twill become a serpent dreadful to behold.
MOSES: See, I have thrown it down. O Lord, be gracious now.
            How dreadful! What a monster! Do Thou pity me!
            I shudder at the sight and tremble in every limb.
GOD: Fear naught, but stretch thy hand and take its tail,
            And once more it will be a staff just as before.
            Now thrust thy hand into thy bosom and draw it out.
MOSES: Thy bidding I have done. My hand is white as snow.
GOD: Now thrust it back again. 'Twill be just as before.

6. WISDOM LITERATURE AND PHILOSOPHY

Like the other nations of the ancient Near East the Israelites treasured
the admonitions and counsels of their wise men concerning right behavior
toward God and fellow man. These sayings, though written in language
more prosaic, more reflective and less emotional than that used by the
prophets, were no less religious in content, if we give to the word "religion"
the more inclusive meaning that it had in antiquity. Sometime during the
early part of the period of the Second Commonwealth, a collection of
such wise sayings was published under the title the Proverbs of Solomon,
though in fact a large part of the collection dates from a period after
Solomon, and a few of the thirty-one chapters are actually a translation
of Egyptian Wisdom literature written long before Solomon's time.

This Book of Proverbs became the model for Palestinian writers of the
Hellenistic period, like the authors of the Book of Ecclesiastes and the
Wisdom of Ben Sira,[4a] who further developed the ancient theme that "the
beginning of wisdom is the reverence of God." In their choice of subjects
to moralize about and their concern to identify *Hokmah* (Wisdom)[5a] with
Torah (Revealed Law), they closely followed traditional lines of moral
and religious speculation.

Among the Jewish thinkers of the Greek Diaspora, however, the contact with Greek philosophy and theology, however superficial it may have been in some cases, led them to give a more logical or systematic or metaphysical form to their expositions of Judaism. This is not to imply that the talmudists of Palestine were less acute in argument or less rational in ethics than the Greek philosophers or Hellenistic Jewish theologians. It is only to state the innocuous truism that the formal aspects of our Western intellectual traditions go back to the Greeks, and that it was the Greek philosophers, particularly those of the Hellenistic period, who created the terminology and methodology of our scientific thinking.

1. *The Wisdom of Solomon*

Of the three Hellenistic Jewish philosophical works that have survived in addition to the extensive remains of Philo, only the Wisdom of Solomon (which is also, of course, apologetic and eschatological in content) adheres to the pattern of Wisdom literature established by the Book of Proverbs. What distinguishes it most conspicuously from this and other Hebrew books of like nature, such as Ecclesiastes and Ben Sira, is its occasional use of Greek philosophical terms and forms of argument and its partial adoption of Greek notions of the pre-existence and immortality of the soul and of the Divine powers. In some passages, as in the catalogues of virtues and sins, its rhetoric reminds one of that of the Stoic diatribe, a kind of streetcorner sermon.

On the other hand, it is clear from the frequent use made of biblical doctrines, imagery and phrases that the author must have been familiar with the Scriptures, probably with the Hebrew text as well as with the Greek translation. In this connection we are reminded that the book was well known to the apostle Paul whose own teaching was an even more subtle blend of Jewish and Hellenistic ideas and turns of expression. Perhaps it was Paul's admiration for the Wisdom of Solomon that caused the early Christian church to regard it as one of the most important books in the Apocrypha.

While there is an undeniable unity of tone and vocabulary throughout the nineteen chapters of the book, the subject matter is rather obviously divisible into three parts. Chapters 1-5 deal with future rewards and punishments for good and evil conduct and briefly allude to the part played by Wisdom in promoting righteousness. Chapters 6-10 form an eloquent dissertation on Wisdom which, as an effluence of God's power, has preserved the righteous throughout Israel's history. This section takes as its point of departure the famous passage in the Book of Kings in which Solomon prays for wisdom rather than riches and power, at least according to later tradition. In this part of the book Wisdom corresponds fairly closely to the Rabbinic personification of Torah as well as to the Stoic *Pronoia*, or Providence. Chapters 11-19 sketch Israel's earlier history and in Rabbinic fashion demonstrate how Israel's enemies have been punished on the principle of "measure for measure"; for example, the various plagues that afflicted the Egyptians were appropriate to the injuries they had done the Israelites. These chapters also present a well-reasoned argument against idolatry, having especially the Egyptians in mind, and give a quasi-anthropological account of the origins of this practice, which though more tolerant is not less effective than the prophetic denunciations of idol worship.

With the technical problems of the date, composition, authorship and original language of the Wisdom of Solomon we have not space to deal at length. It must suffice to say that the weight of evidence supports those scholars who believe that most if not all the book was composed in Greek by an Alexandrian Jew who probably spoke or at least read Hebrew as well as Greek. Though several distinct subjects are treated, perhaps based on different sources, the writer has combined them in such a way as to give the work the stamp of single authorship. The date of composition or final editing cannot be fixed exactly but was probably near the beginning of the Common Era. Some scholars of an earlier period conjectured that the philosopher Philo was the author of this apocryphal book, but this conjecture is no longer taken seriously.

With many interesting and eloquent passages to serve as quotations from a book which has had so great an influence on Christian thought, it is an ungrateful task to select a very few as illustrative of its doctrine and style. It is hoped that the following three passages are sufficiently representative.

In 3:1-5 we have, in answer to the age-old query of why "the good die young," a testament of faith that the righteous do not die but pass on to eternal life. This belief is found also in Philo and Rabbinic literature but there it is perhaps less poetically expressed.

> The souls of the righteous are in the hand of God,
> And no torment will touch them.
> In the eyes of the thoughtless they seem to have died,
> And their departure is reckoned as an evil,
> And their going hence as a disaster.
> But they are at peace.
> For if in the sight of men they have been punished,
> Their hope is full of immortality.
> Being chastised a little, greatly will they be rewarded.
> For God has tested them and found them worthy of Him.

When, in 6:17-20, the author commends to earthly rulers the study and practice of Wisdom, he attempts to show that Wisdom alone leads to kingship by using the *sorites*, or chain argument, favored by the Stoics. Thus he combines Stoic logic with the spirit of Judaism to make the point, central in the teachings of Plato and later Greek political thinkers, that kings should be philosophers.

> For her [Wisdom's] beginning is the most sincere desire for instruction,
> And the concern for instruction is love.
> Love is the keeping of her laws,
> And observance of the laws is assurance of incorruption.
> Incorruption brings men close to God.
> Thus does the desire for Wisdom lead men to kingship.

The last passage for which there is room here is part of a breathless catalogue, in 7:22-23, of the various beneficent aspects of versatile Wisdom. In this catalogue some commentators have found a striking similarity to a list of the attributes of wisdom or virtue made by the Stoic philosopher Cleanthes.

> For in her there is a spirit intellectual and holy,
> Only-begotten, of many parts, subtle,
> Mobile, delicate, undefiled,
> Clear, harmless, loving good, keen,
> Undeterred, beneficent, humane,
> Firm, sure, without care,
> All-powerful, all-seeing,
> Pervading all spirits
> That are intellectual, pure and subtle.

This spirit of Wisdom, the chapter continues, is a breath of God's power and a reflection of eternal light, which has passed into the holy souls of all generations and made them friends of God and prophets. Nowhere in Jewish literature except in Philo, who is more elaborate and sophisticated, does one find so appealing a fusion of Greek and Jewish teaching concerning the part played by Wisdom in human affairs.

2. *Aristobulus*

We have seen, in the brief discussion of the Letter of Aristeas, that that book contains some passages of a philosophical nature, but as they are merely incidental to the book's apologetic purpose, the author is hardly to be classed as a professional philosopher. Among the Alexandrian philosophers who preceded Philo, however, there is one writer of whose work extensive enough fragments have been preserved to enable us to form some notion of the more strictly philosophical literature produced by Philo's coreligionists.

This writer was Aristobulus who was, according to the Church Father Clement of Alexandria, a contemporary of Ptolemy VI Philometor who reigned 181-145 B.C.E. Some scholars place Aristobulus in the Roman period and some hold him to have been a Christian, but so far no convincing evidence has been offered to refute the traditional date. More doubtful is the accuracy of Clement's statement, echoed by Eusebius, that Aristobulus belonged to the Peripatetic, or Aristotelian, school of philosophy. What is clear from the extant fragments is that he attempted to harmonize the Law of Moses with the teachings of Greek philosophy in a work which bore the title *Interpretation of the Law of Moses,* or *Interpretation of the Sacred Laws.*

This harmonization Aristobulus sought to achieve partly through an allegorical explanation of the anthropomorphic allusions to God in the Pentateuch (that is, allusions to the eyes, arms, countenance, walking, etc., of God); partly by quoting Greek verses falsely attributed to Homer, Hesiod and other real and mythical poets who supposedly supported the statements of Scripture; and partly by attempting to show that Pythagoras, Plato and other Greek thinkers drew their theological doctrines from Moses. From these passages it appears, on the plausible assumption that Christian tradition correctly placed Aristobulus in the second century B.C.E., that he was a forerunner of Philo with respect to harmonizing Greek philosophy with Judaism. Whether he was Philo's equal in learning, subtlety and literary skill it would not be fair to decide, in view of the little we have from his pen compared with the extensive Philonic literature that has come down to us. From the few fragments that we have, however, it does seem that he was inferior to Philo in all three respects.

The following selections from the excerpts found in the ninth and thirteenth books of Eusebius's *Evangelical Preparation* may give some idea of the peculiar combination of ingenious interpretation and elusive phrasing that seems to characterize Aristobulus's writing.

For often what our lawgiver Moses wishes to convey when he is using language proper to other matters, by which I mean their appearances, he expresses by physical qualities and the forms of great things[?]. Now those who are able to think clearly admire the wisdom and divine inspiration for which the prophet is celebrated. To their number belong the philosophers we have mentioned and many others, especially poets who have taken notable arguments from him, for which they are admired. But to those who do not share his power and understanding and attend only to what is literally set down, he does not seem to be interpreting anything of great import. I will begin by taking each of the passages in question and explaining it so far as I am able. And if I do not find the truth or convince you, do not attribute the lack of sense to the lawgiver, but to me who am unable to make clear exactly what was in his mind. Now the arms are something that is clearly and commonly understood by us. And when you as king send out your forces with the intention of achieving something, we say that the king has a "great arm," for the word used is referred to the force which you possess. This is the very thing alluded to in our law by Moses when he says, "God brought you out of Egypt with a mighty arm."

The second fragment explains the passage in Genesis that describes how God rested on the seventh day after creating the world.

It is consistent with this that God created the whole world and, because daily life is a difficult experience for all, gave us the seventh day as a day of rest. Thus it may physically [*i.e.*, philosophically] be called the genesis of light, since by this all things are perceived. The same metaphor may be applied to Wisdom, for all light comes from her. And some of the Peripatetic school have said that she fills the part of a lantern, for those who steadily follow her will remain unconfused throughout the whole of life. But still more clearly and beautifully did one of our ancestors, Solomon, say that she existed before heaven and earth. And this is in harmony with what has been said before. For the interpretation of the statement in the Law that God rested on this day is not, as some have understood it, that God no longer continued to create but that He made an end of ordering things so that they were ordered as they were for all time. For [Scripture] indicates that in six days He made heaven and earth and all things in them that He might reveal what the various times were and foretell the order of their precedence. For once having ordered them, He preserves them and does not alter their positions. This He has made clear to us in the Law in order that we may have the principle of the number seven before us, and through this have knowledge of things human and divine. For the whole world of things that are born and grow revolves through periods of seven. And this seventh day is called the Sabbath which translated means "rest." Both Homer and Hesiod, who used our [sacred] writings as a source, have indicated that it is holy.

At this point Aristobulus introduces a number of spurious verses from Homer, Hesiod and the mythical Linos to show that the ancient Greeks also held the seventh day to be holy.

3. *IV Maccabees*

It was probably sometime near the beginning of the Common Era that an Alexandrian Jew with an intimate knowledge of Greek philosophy, especially that of the Stoic Posidonius (early part of the first century B.C.E.), and a formidable Greek vocabulary composed a sort of sermon or lecture on the theme: reason can control passion. This argument is illustrated by examples taken from Jewish history, especially of the Maccabean period.

Though this book, commonly known as IV Maccabees, is included in three of the oldest and most important manuscripts of the Greek Bible, it was (mistakenly) regarded by Eusebius, Jerome and other early Church Fathers as the work of Flavius Josephus; for this reason it is not found in the Latin Bible and consequently is not counted among the apocryphal books of the English and other modern versions of the Bible. IV Maccabees seems to have been entirely unknown to the Jews until modern times but it is not impossible that it was used, perhaps at second hand by the author of the medieval Hebrew work *Yosippon*. Christian writers, on the other hand, greatly admired the book, and the famous Erasmus made a revision of the Latin version.

Like Aristobulus and Philo, the author of IV Maccabees is chiefly concerned to show that the great virtues of the Platonic-Stoic tradition are to be attained by observing the Law of Moses. The larger part of the book, chapters 4-18, is a glorification of the triumph of reason over passion achieved by the martyrs of the Maccabean period, Eleazar, and the mother and her seven sons, whose defiance of Antiochus Epiphanes had earlier been told in II Maccabees.

Chapter 1 is a philosophical introduction that reminds one forcefully of the treatises on reason and passion that are found in the writings of Cicero and Seneca, who, like the writer of IV Maccabees, were greatly influenced by Posidonius. The theme of the book is admirably announced in verses 13-17 of this chapter.

We are inquiring, then, whether reason is sovereign master ["autocrat" in Greek] of the passions. But let us define what reason is and what passion is, and how many forms of passion there are, and whether reason has power over all of these. Reason, then, is thought [or "mind"] based on correct principles, which chooses above all else a life of wisdom. Wisdom, moreover, is the knowledge of things human and divine and their causes. And this is education [or "culture"] acquired from the Law, through which we religiously learn things divine, and for our profit learn things human.

As historical examples of self-control in the face of great provocation or desire the author, in chapters 2 and 3, cites the cases of Moses when angered by Dathan and Abiram, of Jacob when incensed with Simeon and Levi at their cruel treatment of the Shechemites, and of David when his soldiers risked their lives to bring him water after an all-day battle with the Philistines (here our book considerably alters the account given in II Samuel and I Chronicles). In this last instance it gives a vivid impression of David's thirst and of the bravery of the soldiers who sought to bring him water.

But he [David], although burning with thirst, considered that the drink, being equivalent to blood, was a great danger to his soul. He therefore opposed his reason to his desire and poured the drink as a libation to God. For the temperate mind is able to conquer the constraint of passion and to quench the fires of goading desire and to wrestle victoriously with the pains of the body, however overpowering they may be, and by the excellence of reason to spurn the bid for power made by the passions. But now the opportune moment calls us to narrate the story of temperate reason.

With this introduction the narrator launches into the story of the persecution of the Jews by Seleucus IV and his brother (here called son)

Antiochus Epiphanes. In general the narrative follows the contents and order of II Maccabees, but there are many variations in detail and a more extended and philosophical treatment of the martyr episodes. In II Maccabees, for example, the aged Eleazar nobly meets death under torture with a comparatively few defiant words; in IV Maccabees, however, he makes a longer and more didactic speech. Though here the details of the torture and his suffering are realistically and horrifyingly described, the author does not hesitate to represent the aged martyr as taking time to make a philosophical defense of the Mosaic Laws. With a quotation of part of his eloquent address (5:33-38) this brief account of IV Maccabees may fittingly be concluded.

I will not belie thee, O Law, that wast my teacher, nor will I abjure thee, dear Continence, nor will I bring shame upon thee, O wisdom loving Reason, nor deny thee, honored Priesthood and knowledge of the Law. Neither shalt thou, O mouth, defile my revered old age or the years I have spent in living according to the Law. Pure shall my fathers receive me, nor do I fear thy [Antiochus's] torments even unto death. For over impious men thou mayest tyrannize, but neither by words nor by deeds shalt thou be master over my pious reason.

4. *Philo*

Of the Hellenistic Jewish writers whose works have come down to us in part or whole none is so intrinsically worthy of study or, with the possible exception of Josephus, so important in the Western tradition of learning as Philo of Alexandria. Throughout the whole period of scholarship since the Renaissance there has been a continuous and intensive study of his writings by theologians and exegetes. But it has been only during the past few decades that Philo has begun to achieve recognition as a creative or at least historically productive philosopher,[6a] and there has been an ever-increasing number of books and monographs devoted to this aspect of his work. Some indication of the attitude that prevailed half a century ago among historians of ideas is given by the fact that the great German historian of Greek philosophy, Eduard Zeller, in the fourth edition of his magisterial *Philosophie der Griechen* (1903) gives only half as much space to Philo as to Plotinus, and treats Philo as a theologian rather than as a philosopher. By the time this chapter has been published there will have appeared two substantial volumes from the pen of Professor Harry A. Wolfson of Harvard University which will seek to rehabilitate Philo as an original philosophical thinker and to give him his rightful place in the history of that discipline.[7a]

We are not concerned here, however, with the problem of whether Philo was primarily a theologian or a philosopher, since the distinction between theology and philosophy had far less, if any, meaning for the intellectuals of Philo's time than for us. What is of greater importance in this connection is the fact that his writings have a threefold value in the study of philosophy. In the first place, they furnish us with a body of thought with which to compare the theology and ethics of Paul and of the Rabbis of Palestine and thus enable us to arrive at a more just estimate of the intellectual climate in which Christianity arose. Second, on closer scrutiny they are revealed as the source of a great part of the synthesis of Hellenism and Judeo-Christian tradition that was effected by the Greek Church Fathers (many of whom liberally quoted or paraphrased Philo's interpretations of Scripture). Third, it was Philo more than any single predecessor of Plotinus who, as Zeller admits (iii. 2.89), gave the first powerful impetus to that fusion of Greek and Oriental thought known as Neoplatonism, which in turn became the inspiration of one of the chief currents of medieval Scholasticism and even of some modern idealistic philosophies.

Apart from the philosophical aspects of Philo's works one must notice the gratifying fact that among religious historians of today there has arisen a new appreciation of the poetry and mystical insights of Philo, which are so pervasive an element in his writings that some scholars have gone so far as to argue that he was primarily a mystic who used Judaism merely as an outer form in which to clothe an esoteric personal religion. Such a view, however, is a distortion of his whole manner of thought and expression and does not correspond to what we know of his practical activity. It is far more reasonable to regard Philo as the most gifted and versatile of those pious Hellenistic Jews who sought to find the highest truths of Greek philosophy, science and religion in the laws of Moses. Like Aristobulus, Pseudo-Aristeas and others, Philo tried to show that a life lived in accordance with the Jewish tradition was not incompatible with the attainment of Greek culture but that Judaism was as full and rich a doctrine as Platonism or Stoicism or Orphism or any combination of pagan beliefs. He further tried to prove that even the rigorous discipline and ceremonial requirements of the Mosaic Law might lead to a devout and unworldly inner life of piety and contemplation.

The little we know of Philo's life is based on a brief paragraph in Josephus and occasional personal remarks in his own writings. He was a resident of Alexandria and must have been born about 20 B.C.E., since he speaks of himself as "an elderly man" at the time of his mission to Rome in 40 C.E. The wealth and prestige of his family are indicated by the facts that his brother Alexander was an important tax official of the Roman government and that one of his nephews, a son of Alexander, was married to a daughter of King Agrippa I, while another nephew, named Tiberius Julius Alexander, was at one time Roman procurator of Judea and later a Roman prefect of Egypt and one of the leading Roman generals who took part in the siege of Jerusalem. Whether Philo quarreled with his brother's son because of his completely anti-Jewish attitude we do not know. Neither do we know whether Philo was throughout his life as active a political figure in the Alexandrian Jewish community as was his apostate nephew in the Roman government. We do know, however, that Philo was head of the Jewish legation sent from Alexandria to Rome in 40 C.E. to protest to the mad Emperor Caligula against the pogrom instigated by Egyptian and Greek anti-Semites and abetted by Roman officials. Incidentally, there is no trustworthy evidence to support the Christian story that while in Rome Philo met the Apostle Peter.

From incidental statements in his writings we learn that, though Philo scrupulously observed Jewish ritual, he attended the Greek theater, athletic contests and chariot races. Moreover, in addition to his firsthand knowledge of the more external aspects of Greek culture, Philo had a wide and deep knowledge, which would have been remarkable even in a Gentile scholar, of Greek poetry and philosophy.

Though we no longer possess the whole of Philo's work, to judge from the catalogue of his writings given by Eusebius we do have a large part of it, amounting to some thirty complete treatises and a large number of fragments. His writings have been variously classified by modern scholars on the bases of chronology, content and motivation (whether addressed primarily to Jews or to Gentiles). The following classification closely follows that made by Leopold Cohn, one of the greatest Philonic scholars of modern times.

I. Writings of Purely Philosophical Content.

These include four treatises: *On the Eternity of the World; That Every Good Man is Free; On Providence* (preserved partly in Greek, wholly in Armenian); *Alexander,* or *That Animals Have Reason* (preserved only in Armenian).

II. Interpretation of the Pentateuch (chiefly Genesis and Exodus).

This body of work is subdivided into three classes.

A. The Allegorical Commentary on Genesis. This is a running commentary on Gen. 2-41, consisting of sixteen treatises, concerned chiefly with the first half of the biblical book.

B. Questions and Answers on Genesis and Exodus. This is a briefer running commentary, preserved only fragmentarily in Greek and much more fully in Armenian. The Armenian version has preserved most of the original six books on Genesis and two of the original five on Exodus.

C. A Historical-Exegetical Commentary on the Mosaic Law. This is not a running commentary, except on the biblical narrative of the Creation, but a systematic treatment of the ethics of the Pentateuch, partly arranged under types of morality symbolized by the Patriarchs and Moses. This systematic work contains the following treatises: *On the Creation of the*

World; On Abraham; On Joseph or *The Statesman; On the Special Laws* (of the Decalogue) in four books with various subtitles.

III. Historical-Apologetic Writings. These include: *On the Life of Moses* in three (originally two) books; *Hypothetica* (preserved only in fragments); *Apology for the Jews* (preserved only in fragments); *On the Contemplative Life* (of the Therapeuts); *Against Flaccus* (the anti-Jewish governor of Egypt); *The Legation to Gaius.* The last two treatises once formed part of a larger work in five books dealing with the Divine punishments visited upon the persecutors of the Jews.

It would be foolish to try to give in the limited space at our disposal even an outline of Philo's metaphysical and ethical and theological doctrines, to say nothing of his views on education and politics. It must suffice to state summarily that Philo, like some of his Alexandrian Jewish predecessors, used whatever Greek philosophical theories were convenient for adaptation to his allegorical interpretation of the Bible, of which the Greek text was regarded by him as no less inspired than the Hebrew original. Thus, to give a few obvious examples, he makes consistent use of the Platonic doctrine that the immaterial ideas are superior to sense-perceived matter, that the world was created as a perfect thing by a benevolent God, and that the ills of human life arise from the victory of sense and passion over reason. From Plato and the Stoics he borrowed the formulation of the idea (though not the idea itself) that reason must control the senses and that through reason, which is a spark of the Divine in man, we can come closer to God. Philo was the first philosopher known to us who achieved any degree of success in harmonizing the idea of an eternal immaterial God with the God of Jewish history, and in showing how a transcendent God came into contact with a material world subject to the changes of time and with the human personality. Philo solves these problems, to his satisfaction and that of many of his Neoplatonic and Christian readers, by assuming that there were intermediaries between God and the world, these being hypostatized physical and moral powers emanating from God Himself. The first intermediary power was the *Logos*, which Philo poetically describes as the eldest son of God (but not in the sense that the Gospel of John has in making the pre-existent Word of God identical with Jesus). The *Logos* in turn produced from itself other powers of God, the royal power and the beneficent power, which remind us of the two *Middot* or attributes of God in Rabbinic theology, the attribute of mercy and the attribute of justice. Like the Rabbis, Philo connects one power with the name "Lord" and the other with the name "God," but differs from them in connecting mercy with "God" and royalty with "Lord" instead of the reverse. The history of the idea of a *Logos*, or immaterial principle, pervading the material world is too complex to be more than mentioned here. But it may be of interest to note that the

Logos plays somewhat the same role in Philo's theology that Torah does in Rabbinic theology.

What is probably of more interest to a casual reader is the ingenuity of Philo's allegorical interpretation of Scripture and his amazingly consistent use of biblical symbols to describe the unresting pilgrimage of the soul to the eternal truth of a God beyond space and time. His great allegory of the patriarchal history and the Mosaic Law is a kind of *Divine Comedy*. Though it is written in prose and without formal literary unity, it has the architectonic quality of Dante's great poetic synthesis of medieval theology and history.

Not only do the more obvious "properties," to borrow a theatrical term, such as the Patriarchs and the sacred cult objects serve Philo as symbols of moral and religious ideas, but even the most neutral and common things mentioned in the Pentateuch, such as rivers, mountains, plants and animals, are all made to play a meaningful part in this dramatic composition. His ability to create a consistent theological pattern out of bits of natural lore, folklore, Pythagorean number-mysticism and a vast assortment of materials constantly astonishes and sometimes wearies the faithful reader of his works.

Just as there is something Dantesque in the sustained dramatic intention of his allegory, so there is something Proustian in the psychological acuteness of his observation of human actions and in the overrich complexity of his discourses on morality and history. Some fifty years ago Claude Montefiore published in the *Jewish Quarterly Review* a delightful anthology of choice passages from Philo that deserves reprinting in more convenient form. The reader who has access to the files of that periodical is urged to read the whole of Montefiore's *Florilegium Philonis*. The following few passages, chosen independently by the present writer, are given not with a view to making a miniature anthology of the most appealing passages in Philo but merely to illustrate some of his characteristics.

The first selection is from Philo's later and briefer commentary on Genesis and Exodus, called *Questions and Answers* (preserved only in Armenian except for a few score incomplete paragraphs). This particular passage, from Book II:42, takes the biblical verse, Genesis 8:11, part of the story of the flood, and draws from it, as a magician might from a plain hat, a variety of colorful interpretations. The verse reads, "And the dove returned again to him at eventide; holding an olive-leaf, a dry branch" ("dry branch" is Philo's interpretation of the "plucked branch" of Scripture). Let us see how Philo skilfully transforms each of these simple words into complex symbols.

All these are chosen symbols and tests: The "returning again," the "at evening," the "bearing an olive-leaf," the "dry branch," the "oil" and the "in its mouth." But the several symbols must be studied in detail. Now the return is distinguished from the earlier flight. For the latter brought the report of a nature altogether corrupt and rebellious and one destroyed by the flood, that is, by great ignorance and lack of education. But the other repents of its beginning. And to find repentence is not easy but a very difficult and laborious task. For these reasons it comes at evening, having passed the whole day from early morning until evening in inspection, in word by passing through various places, but in actuality by looking over and inspecting the parts of its nature and in seeing these clearly from beginning to end. And the third symbol is "bearing a leaf." The leaf is a small part of a plant. However, it does not come into being without the plant. And similar to this it is to begin to repent. For the beginning of improvement gives a slight indication, as if it were a leaf, that it is to be guarded and can also be shaken off. But there is great hope that it will attain correction of its ways. The fourth symbol is that the leaf was of no other tree than the olive. And oil is the material of light. For evil, as I have said, is profound darkness, but virtue is a most radiant splendor. And repentance is the beginning of light. But do not think that the beginning of repentance is already in blossoming and growing things, but only while they are still dry and arid do they have a seminal principle. Wherefore the fifth symbol is that when it [the dove] came, it bore a "dry branch." And the sixth symbol is that the dry branch was "in its mouth," since six is the first perfect number. For virtue bears in its mouth, that is, in its speech, the seeds of wisdom and justice and altogether goodness of soul. And not only does it bear these gifts but it also gives a share in them to outsiders, offering water to their souls, and watering with repentance their desire for sin.

An aspect of Philo's thought which has no parallel in extant Hellenistic Jewish literature is his frequent use of the terms and ideas used in the pagan mystery-cults which professed to enable the initiate to be reborn and by divesting himself of earthly encumbrances to come into ecstatic union with a savior-god such as Dionysos or Osiris or Mithra. Philo's conception of mystical union with the Divine was less physical and emotionally primitive than that found in even the most spiritualized pagan mysteries, partly because Philo's God was less personal and more transcendent than Greek-Oriental gods, and partly because his healthy Jewish instinct or training kept him from too exalted or irrational a flight into unreality. The dangers of substituting pure symbolism for a life of active and traditional piety enriched by symbolism are pointed out in one of the more frequently quoted passages from Philo, *On the Migration of Abraham* (89 ff.), which reads in part:

There are some who take the literal laws as symbols of intellectual matters, and while they are overscrupulous about the latter, they carelessly neglect the former. Such men I for my part would blame for their offhandedness. They ought to give attention to both things . . . We should have to neglect the holy service of the temple and a thousand other things if we gave thought only to the things revealed in their deeper sense. Rather should we look on these [outward] things as resembling the body, and the other [inner] things as resembling the soul. Now just as we have to take thought for the body as the dwelling-place of the soul, so we have to pay attention to the letter of the laws, for if we keep them we shall have a clearer notion of the things which they symbolize, and at the same time we shall escape the blame and reproach of the multitude.

What seems to a modern reader most salutary in his writing is his adherence to a doctrine that while the senses are not to be completely suppressed they are to be constantly controlled by reason and that through this same reason the soul can be possessed by a mystical rapture. It is no mere use of picturesque quotation but sober truth to say that long before Spinoza the unique beauty of "the intellectual love of God" was celebrated by Philo. The following passage, from the *Sacred Allegories* (i. 39 ff.), illustrates Philo's belief that the soul achieves mystical rapture not by intoxication or other disturbances of normal behavior, as in the pagan mysteries, but by submerging the senses in a flood of reason, a flood that wells up from the hidden sources of the Mosaic Law rightly understood and practiced. The passage is a commentary on Gen. 2:7, "And God formed man by taking clay from the earth and breathed into his face the breath of life; and the man became a living soul."

Philo comments as follows:

There are two kinds of men, one the heavenly man, the other earthly . . . We must account the man made of earth to be mind in the process of being mixed with body but not already mixed. This earthly mind is in reality corruptible except that God breathes into it a power of true life . . . God projects the power that comes from Him through the mediating breath [or wind] till it reaches the subject. And for what other purpose is this than that we may obtain a conception of Him, for how could the soul have conceived of God if He had not breathed into it and seized it through His power? . . . For the mind imparts to the irrational part of the soul a share of that which it has received from God, so that the mind is besouled by God while the irrational part is besouled by the mind. For the mind is, as it were, the God of the irrational part, just as Scripture does not hesitate to speak of Moses as "a God to Pharaoh."

Of Philo's poetic metaphysics we have a good example in the treatise *On Creation* (20 ff.), where he compares the creation of the world through the instrumentality of the *Logos* with the planning of a city by an architect using charts which set down the ideal city he has in mind and from which he proceeds to build the actual city. The same idea of the divine architect is found in Plato's *Timaeus* and in the Rabbinic work *Bereshit Rabbah*, but Philo's metaphor is more sustained and more vivid. A part of the passage in Philo reads as follows:

Similarly one must think about God, that when He was minded to found the great city [*i.e.*, the world], He first conceived of the types of its parts, and from these He wrought an intelligible [*i.e.*, ideal] world, which He used as a model for the sensible [*i.e.*, visible] world. And just as the city formed within [the mind of] the architect has no place outside him but has been engraved in his soul as by a seal, so also the world of ideas would have had no other place than the Divine *Logos* which made this ordered world.

It is a great pity that lack of space makes it impossible to comment on many other aspects of Philo's work and to illustrate these by quotations. Perhaps this brief study can best be concluded with a quotation from the treatise *On the Change of Names* (39 ff.), which shows that this mystical thinker was not concerned solely with his own salvation but was also constantly mindful of his fellow man.

These men are possessed by a divine madness and live a wild and solitary life. But there are others who are familiars of a gentle and tame wisdom. They practice piety eminently and do not despise human things. This is attested by the oracle in which it is said to Abraham out of the mouth of God (Gen. 17:1), "Be well-pleasing before Me." "This means 'not to Me only but to My works also [*i.e.*, other human beings], while I as judge watch and oversee thee' " . . . And so Moses in his exhortations gives this charge (Deut. 12:28), "Thou shalt do what is well-pleasing before the Lord thy God," which means that you should do such things as shall be worthy to appear before God and which he will see and approve; such deeds are likely to be well-pleasing to our fellows as well.

NOTES

[1a Cf. Elias J. Bickerman, "The Historical Foundations of Postbiblical Judaism," this work, Vol. I, pp. 99-103.]

[2a Cf. Judah Goldin, "The Period of the Talmud (135 B.C.E.-1035 C.E.)," this work, Vol. I, p. 147.]

[3a Cf. *ibid.*, pp. 120-121.]

[4a Cf. Bickerman, *op. cit.*, pp. 97-98, 99-101.]

[5a Cf. above, Robert Gordis, "The Bible as a Cultural Monument," pp. 28-33.]

[6a Cf. Alexander Altmann, "Judaism and World Philosophy: From Philo to Spinoza," this work, Vol. III, pp. 66 ff.]

[7a In 1948 the Harvard University Press published Professor Wolfson's two volumes, *Philo: Foundations of Religious Philosophy in Judaism, Christianity, and Islam.*]

BIBLIOGRAPHICAL NOTE

A

The English reader will find the books here discussed most conveniently edited and translated in the following works:

The apocryphal and pseudepigraphic books are well translated and provided with instructive introductions and notes by various scholars in R. H.

Charles (ed.), *The Apocrypha and Pseudepigrapha of the Old Testament.* 2 vols. Oxford, 1913.

The best English translation of Josephus is that in the Loeb Classical Library, London, of which seven volumes have appeared to the present time: Vols. 1-4 were translated by the late Henry St. John Thackeray. Vols. 5-7 by Ralph Marcus.

The best English translation of Philo is also that in the Loeb Classical Library, of which nine volumes have appeared: Vols. 1-5 were translated by F. H. Colson and G. H. Whitaker; Vols. 6-9 by F. H. Colson; Vols. 11-12 by Ralph Marcus.

The fragments of the Hellenistic Jewish writers will be found in the work of Wallace N. Stearns, *Fragments from Graeco-Jewish Writers.* Chicago, 1908.

B

The following books will be of interest to those wishing to have more detailed discussions of some of the writers here treated.

NORMAN BENTWICH, *Philo Judaeus of Alexandria.* Philadelphia, 1910. Though now antiquated in some respects, this book is still useful because of its abundance of information and its excellent judgment. Moreover, it is written in attractive style.

ERWIN R. GOODENOUGH, *Introduction to Philo Judaeus.* New Haven, 1940. The author, a well-known Philonist of Yale University, always writes in a stimulating and illuminating way though not all of his views are to be accepted.

CLAUDE G. MONTEFIORE, "Florilegium Philonis, in *Jewish Quarterly Review,* VII, pp. 481-545. London, 1894-1895. The excellence of this anthology has already been mentioned.

ROBERT H. PFEIFFER, *Introduction to the Old Testament.* New York, 1941. A comprehensive and authoritative, though somewhat technical, study of Old Testament literature with valuable chapters on versions of the Bible and excellent bibliographies, including apocryphal literature.

HARRY A. WOLFSON, *Philo: Foundations of Religious Philosophy, Judaism, Christianity and Islam.* 2 vols. Cambridge, 1947.

Since this bibliography was prepared in 1946, Professor Harry A. Wolfson's monumental work on Philo has appeared. It should therefore be added to this original list.

CHAPTER 3

ON MEDIEVAL HEBREW POETRY

By Shalom Spiegel

I.

To some the mere notion of postbiblical Hebrew poetry will seem a presumption. As if the Bible could have a sequel, or as if at the end of the Psalter one could promise: To be continued. The objection will sometimes be stated in purely aesthetic categories. After the heights ascended by Second Isaiah, or the depths plumbed by Job, can aught be said or sung in the Hebrew language, and not be a poor or pitiable anticlimax? It is true, all great poetry leaves us with a sense of discouragement or defeat, diffident to exercise again the craft of the poet. Awed by extraordinary accomplishment, men are prone to invoke the miraculous and to speak of inspiration. Still, poets in every age and culture will pray and strive for the miracle to happen again.

Could a Hebrew poet in postbiblical times expect a similar grace of Heaven, or did the canonization of Scripture forbid it?

The conception of a canon attests and implies a feeling and a belief that the age of direct communication with God is past, and that with the death of the latter prophets, the holy spirit departed from Israel. This doctrine of the sealing of prophecy would appear to put a ceiling to the aspiration of even the most gifted poet ever to rise in postbiblical Hebrew. To be sure, though God may hide His face, His hand is stretched lovingly over Israel, and hints of His revelation may still be disclosed in dreams.[1] Moreover, there persists in all the ages the hope of the ultimate renewal of prophecy in the end of days.[2] But in the concrete here and now, after the completion of the canon, all one could hope for, at best was *bat kol*, the "daughter of the voice," an echo of the glories of the past.[3]

With the expiration of prophecy, Israel was to incline its ear to the words of the Sages.[4] In fact, some took it to apply already to the entire period of the Second Temple in which the Divine Presence, the source of all prophecy, no longer resided.[5] The reliance on the Torah and its scholars became more urgent and insistent after the loss of state and sanctuary, when the very future of Judaism seemed imperiled. Jerusalem lay in ashes, her gates sunk to the ground. Was one still to believe that "the Lord loveth the gates of Zion more than all the dwellings of Jacob" (Ps. 87:2)? If the Holy Writ was to retain any meaning, and Jewish life any hope, was one not driven to conclude, in the face of the disasters that had overtaken the nation, that the gates of Zion (*ziyyon*) henceforth must mean gates marked (*ziyyun*) or distinguished in the Law? "Ever since the Temple was destroyed, the Holy One, blessed is He, has nothing else in His world but the four cubits of *halaka*."[6] To these four cubits of the law the people clung desperately as to its only remnant of freedom and insurance of restoration. All that mattered from now on was the preservation of the Torah, little else was permitted to weigh as much in the scales of Israel. "The elders have ceased from the gate, the young men from their music" (Lam. 5:14): when the elders ceased from the San-hedrin, the highest seat of Jewish learning and the supreme court of Jewish law, how could the young be allowed to make music or to indulge in song?[7] One was in no mood to encourage the arts or "to rejoice in mirth as other peoples."[8] This, too, like the renewal of prophecy, must wait until God's own good time: Then only will our mouth be filled with laughter, and our tongue with singing, when it will be said among the nations: the Lord hath done great things with Israel![9] Embattled by a hostile world, often reduced to mere subsistence, the synagogue had to maintain an austere economy of spiritual resources and to huddle all its strength for its prime task of keeping the light of the Torah aflame.

The Jewish Middle Ages build upon this twofold legacy of the Rabbinic age. Divine inspiration is relegated to the remote past or the distant future, and the word of the Lord is sought in the present from the disciples of the wise, the scholars of *halaka*.[9a] Certain critical remarks of the Rabbis against prophecy are retained and elaborated, no doubt, to strengthen the hold of the Torah upon the people. A poet as devoted to his calling as Moses ibn Ezra (d. after 1135) writes in his *ars poetica*:[10]

When our sins increased, and we were scattered among the nations because of our evil doings, and God (exalted is He) allowed the period of prophecy to come to a standstill, the Almighty was gracious unto us and sustained us with His servants who transmitted to us His Torah and the words of the prophets from generation to generation. It is from them that we have inherited our faith and institutions. The prophet Zechariah (peace be unto him) whose prophecy was late, foresaw this succession of sages (their memory be blessed) when he said (Zech. 9:12): "Return to the stronghold, ye prisoners of hope; even today do I declare that I will render double unto thee." The words allude to the company of illustrious scholars upon whom the holy spirit has rested. They are the luminaries of the Torah who lead us to goodness in this world and to bliss in the world to come. In this verse the prophet announced to the children of Israel that they will return from Babylon to their homeland, and that there will rise among them, in place of the prophets who will have ceased, men whose wisdom will be double that of the prophets, as was said: "A sage is superior to a prophet."[11] For the prophet delivers his message as it was given to him, and the prophecy as made known to him by God, whereas the Sage hands down what he received from the prophets, and draws one thing from another in accordance with the powers granted to him by the Torah, and contributes from his own mind in conformity to the laws of reason. His is therefore the excellence of originality. This is evident and indicated, I believe, in Scripture (Jer. 18:18): "Instruction shall not perish from the priest, nor counsel from the wise, nor the word from the prophet." Thus Scripture, making three distinctions, awards to the prophet merely "the word," i. e., the word which he is to make known in the name of God. The entire matter was summed up in a wonderful adage of the sage (peace be unto him): "Where there is no vision, the people perish." (Pr. 29:18), hence he immediately exhorted the people to hold on to the words of the wise, when prophecy and prophets will have ended, saying: "But he that keepeth the law, happy is he."

A compatriot and contemporary of this Spanish poet, the great talmudic scholar and head of the academy at Lucena, Joseph ibn Migas (d. 1141) words it more tersely:

A sage is superior to a prophet, because the prophet reports only what he heard and what was put in his mouth to be said, while the sage reports what was said to Moses from Mt. Sinai, although he did not hear it.[12]

The gift of inspiration is disparaged for the greater glory of the wisdom in the holy Law. This doctrine adhered to by artist and rabbi alike in the period of the highest flowering of the poetic genius in Spain, is characteristic of the whole of the Jewish Middle Ages. In agreement with talmudic teaching, the Sage is accorded what is denied to the seer, continued possession of the holy spirit. "From the day the Temple was destroyed, although prophecy was withdrawn from the prophet, it has not been withdrawn from the wise,"[13] the custodians and interpreters of the law in each age.

Modesty naturally forbade the medieval scholar to boast of or lay claim to inspiration, at least, not openly. But there were exceptions to the rule, and men famed for their learning and piety, dropping all restraint, admit receiving missives from heaven. Rabbi Abraham son of David of Posquières (d. 1198), the keen critic of the code of Maimonides, is audacious or outspoken enough to avow that "the holy spirit appeared in our school."[14] There may be sin of pride in such assertions, but not heresy. "Saintliness leads to the holy spirit"[15] and "God's secret is with them that fear Him" (Ps. 25:14).[16] In reply to some knotty question in the law, a medieval Rabbi will write: "This is what I was shown in heaven,"[17] a legal locution not hackneyed, but not improper. A scholar's faith or fidelity is not impugned because of such revelations.

Nothing of the sort is ever permitted to the medieval poet. To be sure, he had often enough to blow his own bugle (in absence of the modern art of the paid advertisement), but however frivolous or extravagant his self-praise, he never dared to include in it the faintest pretension to the holy spirit. It would have had the effect of a bad joke. There are sundry varieties of religious delusion in the Middle Ages, but we never hear of a poet to have come forward unreservedly as a prophet, as did in Arabic letters Mutanabbi, *i.e.*, "the pretender to prophecy" (d. 965), in the estimate of his countrymen the most famous of all the poets born or made in Islam.[18]

Of course, a true poet will always await and witness anew the miracle of inspiration and sing of its ecstasies. Hebrew literature, also, has some magnificent examples of poetry quivering with the excitement of the un-accountable but unmistaken event. Invariably, however, there is a chaste reticence about such visitations of the Divinity. The experience is stated almost impersonally, in the traditional imagery, as if to hide the new rapture of the poet in the ancient and familiar memories of his people. Hence the ease with which the medieval synagogue could turn these intimate revelations of the individual into collective prayers of Israel. Take for example the lovely nocturne of Judah'Ha-Levi (d. after 1140):

> My thought awaked me with Thy Name,
>> Upon Thy boundless love to meditate;
>>> Whereby I came
> The fullness of the wonder to perceive,
>> That Thou a soul immortal shouldst create
> To be embound in this, my mortal frame.
>> Then did my mind, elate,
> Behold Thee and believe;
>> As though I stood among
>> That hushed and awe-swept throng
> And heard the Voice and gazed on Sinai's flame!
>
>> I seek Thee in my dreams,
>> And lo, Thy glory seems
> To pass before me, as of old, the cloud
>> Descended in his sight, who heard
>> The music of Thy spoken word.
> Then from my couch I spring, and cry aloud,
> "Blest be the glory of Thy Name, O Lord!"[19]

Quite fittingly, the poem is included in the liturgy of Shabuot, the holiday of revelation, commemorating the covenant established at Sinai. Originally, however, it is the record of a very personal encounter. In answer to long probings into the riddle of soul and body, the poet experiences, half awake and half in a dream, how into the clouds of his soul there descends the glory of God as into a tabernacle: "My heart beheld Thee and believed Thee, as though I were standing at Sinai." Purged of vanity by such undeserved favor of heaven, the poet's lips murmur a benediction, not a boast. The individual experience loses itself in the event basic to all Israel, the inspiration of today reaffirms the dawn of the historic faith, and the new seeks humbly to bring home the old revelation.

The same poet, as others before and after him, is also familiar with some of the formal aspects of inspiration: the feeling of being but a passive tool and mouthpiece, of being "carried away and overpowered" (Jer. 20:7), of saying not what one pleases, but what one cannot help saying. He knows also the sense of exhilaration, when the halting tongue is quickened of a sudden by the onrush of words, heaven born, pouring in effortlessly, infallible in their felicity, so convincing and compelling as to leave simply no other choice. "The speech of a prophet at the time when he is en-wrapped by the holy spirit is in every part directed by the divine influence, the prophet himself being powerless to alter one word."[20] The description has personal accents, as has in the same book the impassioned and insistent inquiry into the state of the prophet and the secret of prophecy, but there is a self-imposed censorship and discipline of silence about any such adventures or aspirations of the poet. The restraint reflects a climate of opinion reared on a doctrine which stressed the pathos of distance separating the present from the ancient days when holy men still walked and talked with God.

In the medieval world one was ready to exercise patience and forbearance even with inordinate claims when made in the name of religion, not poetry. Saadia Gaon (d. 942), perhaps under the influence of certain Moslem ideas, evolved a remarkable doctrine that God never fails to provide His people with a "scholar" in each age whom He enlightens and inspires to guide his generation and make them prosper through him. Significantly, the Gaon adds that such was his own experience, having witnessed "what God in His grace has done for me and for the people."[21] The word used is *talmid*, or disciple (of the wise) or scholar in the law, and thus the claim is advanced on behalf of the Torah and its foremost exponent in every age. But since Saadia was also a prolific poet, and his contemporaries could not help being apprised of the opinions he entertained about himself, we hear the resentment voiced that his poetic compositions were written in verse units and supplied with accents and vowel points. Such resemblance to the Sacred Writ was seized upon by his opponents, who denounced it as a pretense to prophecy.[22] The last such instance, on the threshold of the modern era, is that of Moses Hayyim Luzzatto (d. 1747). Under the spell of inspiration, he believed himself to be receiving revelations from a mentor-angel and to write a second *Zohar*, a sequel to the classic book of Jewish mysticism.[22a] But since he was also a gifted poet, he had to contend with the rumor that he had written one hundred and fifty poems to supplant the Psalms of David. In vain did the poet disavow any such claim or comparison, his devout teacher aiding him by testifying that the poems were the product of toil and skill, not inspiration, as could clearly be seen from the many corrections and deletions, in the handwriting of the author, "such as occur in the natural process of composition, when one writes and crosses out and writes again."[23] The suspected manuscript had to be surrendered to a Rabbinic court, a portion was burned and the remainder buried in the ground, and so lost to posterity.[24] It is true, those were the days of the Sabbatian heresies when the guardians of the law may have thought it their duty to be especially severe.

Not only in times of crisis or peril to religion, but throughout the Middle Ages one can detect a latent or patent hostility to the craft of the poet. On second and serious thought, it must have appeared to be dangerous folly for a scattered and threatened community to dissipate its meager resources in toying with verse or enjoying poesy. Nor is it strange that the philosophic spirits in medieval Judaism were just as inimical to the poets, and particularly to the religious poets. Unrestrained fancy and loose talk, so the philosophers contended, could not but offend against the true precepts of an enlightened faith and breed crude or corrupt notions about God.[25] Rationalists and traditionalists alike seemed to concur that the cause of religion is best served, and error best eschewed, by banning poetry altogether from the worship of the synagogue. If piety prompts one to add or amplify praises to God, there is always inspired Scripture to draw upon with profit, or one can at all times safely turn to the Psalter.[26]

2

The advice was heeded. The Psalter served throughout the ages as a primer of prayer and praise, and handbook of devotion. It became the hymnal of the synagogue and the common man's household book of poetry. It would be difficult to overrate the effect of this most widely circulated anthology of Hebrew verse on the language of faith and the habits of piety of countless generations. Multitudes of men at every period of history discovered in the Psalms the stirrings and strivings of their hearts, and clothed in the venerable words of the book their own penitence and hope. This power of the Psalter stems from the belief that it is not merely a collection of priceless poetry, or a formulary of edifying prayers, but that it is part and parcel of the Holy Writ.

There is nothing more precious than the Book of the Psalms which contains everything. Therein are many praises to His Name, hallowed is He, and many a summons to repentance as well as many supplications for forgiveness and

mercy . . . By reciting the Psalms, we at once offer prayer and study Holy
Scripture, for King David, peace be unto him, long ago beseeched heaven that
whoever will read the Psalter should receive as much reward as he who delves
in the depths of the Torah.[1]

This, then, was the unique distinction of the Psalter, that it combined the
two fundamental elements of all Jewish worship: it served as a pattern
of *prayer* and as a repository of guidance and *instruction* in holy living.
The two functions are inseparable, of course, and yet it is the latter that
carried most weight in the eyes of the believer. His standards of value are
succinctly stated in a maxim current in the Middle Ages:

He who prays, speaks to God; but he who reads the Writ, God speaks to
him, as it is said (Ps. 119:99): "Thy statutes are (Thy) converse with me."[2]

It is in this double capacity of the Psalter to furnish both request and
reply, search and solution, the cry of human want and the answer of
Divine bounty, that one must seek the secret of the unrivaled influence
exercised by the book in all ages.

Being a part of Scripture, the Psalms share the fate of that widely read
Book: they are subject to ever-new and ever-changing rereading by new
generations of men. Each period pours its own inner life into the patient
and pliant texts of old which engagingly oblige new inquirers with new
answers. Devout centuries extract or extort from the familiar documents
messages undreamt of or unsuspected by the original writers. Such fresh
and fanciful embroidering upon the ancient design is properly called
legend, as the Latin *legenda* literally means: that *which will be read* by
successive ages into the events or records of the past. The more a book is
used, the more it will be abused, fiction prevailing over fact, or—to vary
Aristotle[3]—poetry outlasting history.

The Bible, too, had such a posthumous adventure in its passage through
the centuries, its text becoming disengaged from the original intention and
enriched by the faith and fantasy of innumerable readers. We can follow
this afterlife of the Bible in scattered comments or orderly commentaries
which mirror the temper and the trends of the Jewish Middle Ages.
Moreover, the centrality of Scripture in the medieval scene accounts not
only for the natural and unconscious metamorphosis of the biblical legacy
in the course of time, but also for the frequency with which so much of the
original creation of the Middle Ages was sunk into biblical exegesis. To
gain foothold in medieval Israel, every spiritual endeavor had to be related
to the chief concern of the people, Torah. Hence medieval expression is
so often cast in the form of a commentary on Scripture. Even dissent and
revolt are clothed in what is in name or shape but a commentary. The
form succeeded in disguising and preserving a great deal of the independent achievement of the Middle Ages. Whatever their usefulness for the

study of the Bible itself, the medieval Bible commentaries are invaluable and indispensable for the revelation of the internal life of the Jew in the Middle Ages.

An example from the Psalter will illustrate the vigor and variety of this invisible creativeness passing unchallenged as biblical interpretation.

Psalm 29 is probably a very old hymn, voicing the dread and the wonder of ancient man before the fury of the elements. A storm is gathering out at sea, "upon many waters," and breaks upon the land, tossing the cedars of Lebanon and rocking the snow-capped Hermon to its foundations. The massive mountains seem to shake helplessly like frightened animals. The storm and the winds, the peals of thunder and the "flames of fire" or the lightning flash herald the power of "the God of glory" as He sets out to strike at the insurgent foes. When the tempest dies away in the desert, all rebellion is quelled, and the conqueror can return to His celestial palace, built "upon the flood" or the upper waters above the firmament, there to receive the tribute and honor due to a "king for ever." The heavenly ceremony is pictured after the fashion of earthly courts, or rather in images borrowed from prebiblical myths.[4] We see the lesser divinities, the *bene elim*, or "the sons of the gods," assemble to pay homage to the victorious godhead. With such "praise on high" the Psalm opens, and it ends with a prayer for "peace on earth."

Quite appropriately we find the earliest use of the Psalm in the liturgy of the festival of Sukkot, when prayers for rain were offered.

Already in the age of the *Tannaim*,[4a] the meaning of the Psalm was thoroughly overhauled:

Rabbi Eleazer of Modaim said: When the Holy One, blessed be He, appeared to give the Torah to Israel, the earth shook and the mountains quaked, and all the sons of the mighty (*bene elim*) trembled in their palaces, as it is said: "And in his palace every one says 'Glory' " (Ps. 29:9). Whereupon the kings of the world assembled and came to Balaam, saying: What is the uproar that we heard? Is a flood to come to destroy the earth? Said he to them: "The Lord sitteth upon the flood" (*ibid.*, 10). The Holy One, blessed be He, swore long ago that He would not bring a flood upon the world for ever. They then said to him: He will not bring a flood of water, but He may bring a flood of fire as it is said: "For by fire will the Lord contend" (Is. 66:16). But he said to them: He is going to bring neither a flood of water, nor a flood of fire. However, He possesses in His storehouse a priceless treasure, the Torah which He is to present to His sons, as it is said: "The Lord will give strength unto His people" (Ps. 29:11). As soon as the kings heard that from him, they joined in the benediction: "The Lord will bless His people with peace" (*Ibid.*).[5]

Rabbi Eleazar of Modaim died during the siege of Bethar (*c.* 135 c.e.) and taught in days when it became clear that the natural base of the

Hebrew polity, the state and the sanctuary, were lost. However impoverished, Israel still possessed a priceless treasure from God's storehouse, the Torah. Hence the new stress on the gift of revelation, and on God's power in history rather than nature. Transposed, as it were, into a new key, the Psalm was employed in the liturgy of the Feast of Weeks, which commemorates the covenant at Sinai, when the Torah was given to Israel.[6] In medieval Spain[7] the custom seems to have originated of reciting the Psalm on the Sabbath, the traditional day of Revelation,[8] as the Torah is being returned to the Ark, or the treasure brought back to His storehouse, a practice still observed in our synagogues.

Echoes of darker centuries survive in the *Midrash to the Psalms*, a collection of homilies from various times, some perhaps going back to days of Roman or Byzantine rule and oppression:[9]

Bene elim or "the sons of the gods"—what does that mean? The sons of the dumb *(bene ilmim)* and of the deaf *(i. e.,* the sons of Israel) who could answer back the Holy One, blessed be He, but they refrain from answering back, and suffer the yoke of the nations for the sanctification of His name. This is what Isaiah said (42:19): "Who is blind, but my servant, or deaf, as my messenger that I sent?"

Bene elim—what else can that mean? The sons of those who are slain like rams *(elim)*. Abraham said: I slay; Isaac said: I am (ready to be) slain.[10]

Pained and puzzled by the triumph of the wicked, the religious conscience sought solace and support in the examples of patriarchal piety or the songs of the suffering servant. The ways of God were inscrutable. Abraham did not comprehend how a father could be commanded to slay his only son, but he did not refuse or reproach God, he obeyed instead, to be rewarded and relieved in the end. Silently also the servant of the Lord must bear his martyrdom, a spoil and sport of all mankind, and yet it is with his stripes that the world will be healed. It was in the light of such memories or monition that Psalm 29 was reread in the early Middle Ages.

When the swift victories of Islam and the vast realm conquered by the new faith seemed to make the hopes of Jewish repatriation impracticable or illusory, the troubled heart turned again to the Psalter for courage and comfort. Psalm 29 was rendered as summoning the children of Israel to be *bene elim*, sons of might or men of valor, and to persevere in the faith as there was hope in their future. Verse 10 was understood to contain the solemn assurance that just as the Lord guards the universe against the flood, so He remains His people's king forever: "For as I have sworn that the waters of Noah should no more go over the earth, so have I sworn that I would not be wroth with thee, nor rebuke thee. For the mountains shall depart, and the hills be removed, but my kindness shall not depart from thee, neither shall the covenant of my peace be removed, saith the

Lord that hath mercy on thee" (Isa. 54:9 f.). The Psalm was so translated by Saadia, and his version is still current among Arabic-speaking Jews.[11]

In the lands of medieval Christendom, the Psalm was construed as a prophecy about the days of Messianic deliverance, when "the cedars of Lebanon," the proud kingdoms of the earth will be humbled. The Lord will thunder "upon many waters"; these are the rich and rapacious that grab the goods of this world as greedily as waters cover the sea. But in the end, justice will be enthroned for ever, and in His temple all will say "Glory," as it is said: "Then will I turn to the peoples a pure language, that they may all call upon the Name of the Lord, to serve Him with one consent" (Zeph. 3:9).[12]

After the banishment from Spain (1492),[12a] which uprooted the most populous and prosperous community of the Middle Ages, mystical tendencies gained the ascendancy. The Psalter was read fervently as an apocalypse in which every word is infused with references to the events of the imminently expected Messianic catastrophe or redemption. In fact, the Psalms themselves were discovered to be a book of war songs, an arsenal of mystic or magic weapons, "a sharp sword in Israel's hand"[13] to strike at the root of evil and thus precipitate the end. When the crack of doom failed to come, and the Messianic fever wore away, there spread from Safed, a town in northern Galilee, audacious new doctrines such as the cabbala of Isaac Luria (d. 1572), which gave a new answer to the basic and baffling facts of the historic experience of the Jew and a new meaning to his acts of worship.[14, 14a]

The homelessness of the Jewish people was conceived to be but a detail in the general dislocation of the whole of existence due to a primordial flaw or fracture of all creation which the new cabbala called "the breaking of the vessels." Because of it, all realms of being were unhinged and deranged, thrown out of their proper and purposed station, everything in the order of creation was displaced, all were in exile, including God. Supernal lights fell in the abyss of darkness, and sparks of holiness became imprisoned in shells of evil. The unity of the Divine Name was shattered (the new cabbala speaks of the letters YH being torn away from WH in the name YHWH). It was the mission of man and the purpose of religion to restore the broken name of God and so heal the original blemish of all the visible and invisible worlds. By observing the commandments of the Torah and the ordained discipline of worship, every Jew could become a partner in the work of redemption: he could help to lift the fallen lights of God and set free the holy sparks from the powers of evil.

With ardent precision every detail in form and language of the Psalms was instilled with mystic meaning and function. Concretely, in Psalm 29, three times it was said "Give unto the Lord," seven times "the voice of the Lord," eighteen times the Divine Name is spelled, making seventy-two letters or the numerical value of *hesed*, or mercy. The eleven verses of the Psalm equal WH in the tetragram, while the ninety-one words in the whole Psalm correspond to the sum total of YHWH and Adonai.[15] By means of each of these mysteries of prayer, the worshiper who knew the secrets of the holy letters and was capable of utter inwardness (*kavvanah*) in his devotions, could work miracles of *tikkun* or restitution by which sparks scattered in the lower depths could be reassembled, and "the Holy One, praised be He, reunited with His exiled *Shekinah*." Acts of religion determine the fate of the world, and it is the essential distinction and dignity of man that without his free choice the breach of creation could not be mended. Feeble as man is, unlike the angels, he alone knows, in every breath of his, about the struggle of good and evil, and can influence it by his freedom of action. Hence only man, and not any of the celestial beings, can lead the banished glory of God back to the Master, and thus literally "give unto the Lord glory and strength," thereby completing His enthronement as "king for ever."

In this new myth, which burst forth in the heart of Judaism at so late a stage of the historic faith, mystic notions verge on magic, or perhaps revert to the origins of all worship in which prayer and spell commingle. As if the wheel had come full circle, and the new cabbala had recovered, on another plane, the prebiblical rudiments of magic, residual in the Psalms and perhaps irreducible from man's vocabulary of prayer.

These few examples of Rabbinic and cabbalistic interpretation of Scripture will suffice to indicate the amazing freedom with which the Middle Ages were able to make the words of an old text yield new meaning. Even though the syllables and sentences of the Bible remained intact, a new sentiment infused them with new significance, and transformed the Psalm, far beyond the purposes of the first author, into an untrammeled expression of a new religious attitude and outlook. Often it is an original conception that asserts itself in, or despite, the ancient and venerable vocables, which suffer no outward change through the centuries. The new creation escapes notice (also by the historians of literature), for it is deposited invisibly in the same old words of the Writ.

Above all, even a hurried glimpse into biblical lore of the Middle Ages will prove how futile was the endeavor to exorcise error and heresy from the synagogue by advising the faithful to turn with a safe conscience only to inspired Scripture, particularly the Psalms. We saw traditionalists and rationalists agreeing that it would be best to praise God with the songs of King David alone.[16] Little did either of them dream what dangerously novel ideas could nest in the innocent and time-honored words. The letter is too feeble to imprison the spirit. It is useless to try to freeze the tides of spiritual life into permanent retrospection. Ancient meanings cannot be perpetuated through the ages. At best, the sounds may be reproduced, or perhaps only the symbols of script, but a new spirit will transfigure them in each age.

Fortunately, the synagogue discovered quite early how hopeless it would be to invite the great poetry of biblical antiquity to keep new expression suppressed in Judaism. It was better insight to make room in the synagogue, along with the classical heritage, also for new creative endeavor, and thus enlist the genius of the poets to lend freshness and vigor to the religious quest of medieval Jewry.

3

The beginnings of poetry in the synagogue may well go back to the dawn of public prayer, or to the very origin of the synagogue. The Jews were the only people of antiquity who succeeded in divorcing prayer from sacrifice, and so were the first to evolve the modes and manners of public worship as the world knows them now. The new institution of the synagogue was to grapple first with the two basal needs of all congregational service: conformity and nonconformity. Untutored or undisciplined prayer may grow haphazard and slipshod, self-seeking or disreputable, anarchical and antisocial. Regulated for public propriety, or legislated for the good of society, it may become a stale and spiritless convention. The synagogue strove to retain and reconcile both the requirement of agreement and informality. The oldest order of services includes, along with instruction in the Writ meant for the whole congregation, private devotions or confessions. These elements of spontaneous or subjective piety (called *debarim*, words, or *tahanunim*, supplications) originally followed the recitation of the *Shema*, or the creed of Judaism, and thus hark back to a time before the eighteen benedictions or the principal prayer became an established order of the synagogue.[1] Moreover, even when the eighteen benedictions were finally agreed upon, toward the close of the first century c.e., only their sequence was settled, the wording remaining in flux for centuries. As a matter of fact, there continues for generations the deliberate tendency to keep the prayer fresh and fluid, modified with something new each day, to quote a Rabbi of the fourth century.[2]

Probably there was here at work a rejection of the heathen notion of piety which rigidly forbade any deviation from the hallowed formulary of ancestral ritual. Even the slightest change would only weaken the potency of the prayers, believed by the ancients to be missives from the gods themselves and hence especially efficacious and inviolable.

To prevent the confusion of religion with magic, the Rabbis emphasize that there are no set or sacred spells certain to force down the blessing from heaven. On the contrary, prayer must not be fixed,[3] but free, welling out of the depths of a contrite heart and reaching out entreatingly for the unpredictable grace and goodness of God.

Whatever the motives of the Rabbis, the religious and aesthetic benefit was indisputable. By asking with variety of circumstance also variety of words, the synagogue admitted or even invited into its midst the craftsmen of words, or the poets. As a result the common prayers of Judaism gained increasingly in richness of inspiration and beauty of expression.

The Middle Ages followed the Rabbinic age in the endeavor to preserve both obedience to tradition and individual assertion. The standard prayers, the oldest nucleus of the liturgy, always and everywhere became the center of Jewish worship, a bond of union despite geographic dispersal, and a bridge across the ages linking the present to the past. At the same time, each period and place was left free, if not encouraged, to speak its own mind in new compositions added to, or inserted within, the ancient prayers. These additions, called *piyyut*, or poetry, constitute—in contrast to the stable and stationary standard prayers—an ever-changing and restless element in the Jewish liturgy. They enliven with personal accent or local color the established and universal order of services, and unlike the latter, frankly bespeak the soil and sun, season or situation, which nurtured or ripened them. In fact, it was the vigorous and abundant growth of the *piyyut* that was responsible for the development within medieval Judaism of about half a hundred different rites.[4] Within the larger brotherhood of Israel, and the stock of prayers common to all generations, the medieval synagogue attempts and attains both a contemporary note and regional differentiation. The religious expression varies in the Byzantine age and in the era of Islam; in the same century, Franco-German Judaism differs from Spanish Judaism, as do the rites of Aleppo and Yemen, Prague and Amsterdam. Yet there underlies them all, despite the dissimilar and distinctive body of their poetry, the core of ecumenic prayer invariable in all Jewries.

In fine, before the invention of printing slackened or congealed its growth, medieval Judaism essayed and effected a conciliation and concordance of two contrary but complementary necessities of all spiritual life, arriving at a remarkable synthesis of liberty and order, unity and diversity, permanence and change. The old and the new, the recent and the remote, the casual and the constant, blend to enrich and to reinforce each other. It is this peculiar and pregnant amalgam of opposites, of pattern and freedom, system and vitality which imparts to medieval utterance both strength and suppleness, the discipline of a consistent doctrine and accord with the tune of the times.

A few examples of religious verse may serve as illustration, and help to point out some of the forms and functions of medieval Hebrew poetry.

The heart of the Jewish service is the *Shema*, the Jew's acceptance of the

Kingship of Heaven. It begins with a summons to the worshipers: "Bless ye (*bareku*) the Lord!" It is here, before the call is sounded, that the medieval poet asks "leave" (*reshut*) to intersperse the hallowed prayers with his own effort. Such introductions usually strike the note of preparation for the actual prayer. For example, the poet meditates upon what is to be affirmed in the *Shema*. The first words, after the avowal of faith, command to love God "with all thy heart and all thy might" (Deut. 6:5), that is to love Him "in truth" (cf. Jer. 32:41). For in the holy tongue, God's name is Truth (Jer. 10:10), and in the view of the Rabbis, His seal is truth.[5] These are, also, the very last words of the *Shema*: "I am the Lord your God—Truth," in prayer the immediately following word being joined to the last of recited Scripture (Num. 15:41). The beginning and the end of the *Shema* set the theme of one of the magnificent preludes by Judah Ha-Levi:

> With all my heart, O Truth, with all my might
>   I love Thee; in transparency, or night,
> Thy Name is with me; how then walk alone?
>   He is my Love; how shall I sit alone?
> He is my Brightness; what can choke my flame?
>   While He holds fast my hand, shall I be lame?
> Let folk despise me: they have never known
>   My shame for Thy sake is my glorious crown.
> O Source of Life, let my life tell thy praise,
>   My song to Thee be sung in all my days![6]

When promptly thereafter the congregation is summoned to praise or bless the Lord, the familiar *bareku* of the prayer book seems now immeasurably widened in its meaning, or perhaps restored to its real meaning. For what is required cannot be the mere mouthing of pious words, but the truth of a whole life given in service to the Truth that is God. Given? Gained is the better word, for what speaks here is not renunciation, nor even resentment over the world's scorn and hate, but the glad surrender of the failing self to the "source of life" wherefrom every breath is borrowed and all our strength supplied.

The first of the benedictions preceding the *Shema* voices gratitude for the gift of light. It is probably a very old practice, going back to the ancient mystics of Palestine, the Essenes,[6a] who, as Josephus records, would not speak before daybreak about profane matters, but would first greet the dawn with prayers that had come down to them from their forefathers, "as if praying for the sun to rise."[7] Adopted into the synagogue, the morning prayer grew to include the glorious words of Second Isaiah (45:7) about the One God "Who formeth (*yozer*) light and createth darkness." The *piyyut* which is here inserted is called *yozer* and usually hymns the wonders of creation. But sometimes, as in the following example, the poet

ponders over the darker might of God which the medieval community had
so often to experience. Bewildered by the ways of God with men and His
incomprehensible neutrality or apparent assent to evil, the distressed heart
seeks in the Holy Writ a clue to the uncanny power and purpose of darkness. Four Scriptural passages on the theme of darkness voice the complaint
and the comfort, and form the final line and rhyme of each stanza:

> O silent Dove, pour out thy whispered prayer,
> Stricken amid the tents of Meshekh;
> And lift thy soul unto God—
> Thy banner, thy chariot and thy horseman—
> Who kindleth the light of thy sun:

Is. 45:7   *Who formeth light and createth darkness.*

> To the whole He called with His word,
> And it arose in a moment, at His bidding,
> To show unto all the strength of His glory
> In the world which unto life, not waste, He had formed,
> When from the east, unto His light

Ex. 10:21   *He called and moved the darkness.*

> And the host of His heavens heard
> The word: "Let there be Light"; and learned to know
> That there is a Rock by whom are cleft
> The firmaments, and the earth's foundations laid.
> And they gave thanks to their Maker, now understanding

Eccl. 2:13   *The excellency of light over darkness.*

> So will He yet light up my gloom,
> And help to raise my fallen estate,
> And shed radiance over mine assembly.
> Then His people shall yet rejoice:
> "Behold the light of the Rock of my praise

Mic. 7:8   *Is mine, though I sit in darkness.*"[8]

One must read in Hebrew the assurance of the ancient seer broken off
suddenly, in the middle, as if to indicate the yet unfinished processes of
history, to understand the triumph of trust which amidst all the terrors of
medieval darkness never despairs of a new dawn: "As for me, I will look
unto the Lord; I will wait for the God of my salvation: my God will
hear me. Rejoice not against me, O mine enemy: though I am fallen, I
shall arise; *though I sit in darkness*, the Lord is a light unto me" (Mic.
7:7-8). When the worshiper is returned to the prayer book, the innocent
blessing at sunrise of the ancient mystics does not seem innocent at all: it
is heavy with the sighs and salted with the tears of yesterday and today.

Toward its close, the benediction of light contains a prayer for the
renewal of the light of Zion. On logical grounds, some schoolmen (notably

Saadia) objected to having the praise of creation and the prayer for redemption rolled into one.[9] In vain: the homeless people clung in fervent
hope precisely to this correlation between the first wonders of light and
the last wonders of the new day of the Lord. Here the poets of the
synagogue interpose a composition called *meora*, for it precedes the praise
of the Creator of the luminaries (*meorot*). Sometimes the grief and faith
of the captivity is worded in a poignant dialogue, as in the selection here
presented, between the "curtains of Solomon" and a pilgrim. He remem-
bers them in their former glory, the pride of a palace, and barely believes
his eyes to find them now, faded and frayed, in a Bedouin tent:

Ye curtains of Solomon, how, amid the tents of Kedar,
Are ye changed? Ye have no form, no beauty!

"The multitudes which dwelt aforetime in our midst,
Have left us a desolation, a broken ruin, unprotected—
The holy vessels have gone into exile and become profane,
And how can ye ask for beauty of a lily among thorns?"

Rejected of their neighbors, but sought of their Lord,
He will call them each by name, not one shall be missing.
Their beauty, as in the beginning, He shall restore in the end,
And shall illume as the sevenfold light their lamp which is darkened.[10]

The rebuff of the world is forgotten in knowing oneself befriended by
God Who, in the language of the great Unknown of the first captivity,
forgets none among His hosts, calling each by his first name, the faithful on
earth as His stars in heaven. "Why sayest thou, O Israel: my way is hid
from the Lord, my right is passed over from my God?" (Is. 40:26-31).
Again, one comes back to the accustomed prayers with a heart revived
through proud memories and new hope.

The second benediction before the *Shema* turns from nature to history,
or from creation to revelation. It renders thanks for the gift of the Torah,
"the statutes of life," which in His everlasting love God chose to com-
municate to Israel, and it asks for divine aid properly to understand the
commandments and to fulfill them in love. The *piyyut* here ingrafted
is called *ahaba* (love), and as its name and place implies, has for its theme
the love of God for Israel and of Israel for God. Medieval piety spoke its
inmost soul in some of these poems:

Let my sweet song be pleasing unto Thee—
The incense of my praise—
O my Beloved that are flown from me,
Far from mine errant ways!
But I have held the garment of His love,
Seeing the wonder and the might thereof.

The glory of Thy name is my full store—
My portion for the toil wherein I strove:
Increase the sorrow:—I shall love but more!
Wonderful is Thy love![11]

Amid all degradation, Israel knows herself borne and sustained by God's boundless love: "Enough for me the glory of Thy Name!" Clinging to the fringe of His love gives bliss and strength enough to endure all the taunt and torment of the world. If the price of mere knowledge be sorrow (Eccl. 1:18), what would not one readily brave for the love of God?

In another *ahaba*, such love is driven to an even bolder extreme:

Since Thou hast been the abode of love,
My love hath camped wherever Thou hast camped.
The reproaches of mine enemies have been pleasant to me for Thy sake:
Leave them, let them afflict him whom Thou dost afflict!
My foes learned Thy wrath, and I loved them,
For they pursued the victim whom Thou didst smite.
From the day that Thou didst despise me, I despised myself,
For I shall not honor what Thou hast despised.
Until the indignation be overpast, and Thou send redemption,
To this, Thine inheritance that Thou didst once redeem.[12]

Divorced from power, unable to retaliate, how was one to remain free from the corrosions of hate in a dark and cruel age? The medieval Jew won such internal freedom in external bondage through his unconditional trust in God: it was His inscrutable will that redemption should be preceded by penance in exile. The evil forces of the world do unknowingly the will of God. The Jew's love for God enables him to recognize in the enemy the instrument of Divine Judgment, "the rod of His anger," and compels the incredible or impossible: love for one's enemy.

But though love is the willing obedience of all wills to the Will of God, the poet never confuses the remediable ills of society with Divine Purpose. He will not acquiesce in injustice, nor suffer the unworldliness of the saints to benefit tyranny. He knows that lazy opportunism and religious perfectionism may alike cripple the attempts at self-liberation.

In an *ahaba* which must have offended the leadership of its day, our poet warns sternly against the perils of political expediency. These were the times when the charities and welfare funds of Jewish Spain were engaged in aiding the refugees from the Moslem south to establish themselves in the Christian north. The kings of Christian Spain welcomed the influx of Jewish commerce and capital for reasons of statecraft and strategy: such exodus could not but weaken the Moslem provinces and facilitate their reconquest. Was it safe, the poet seems to ask, to put confidence in transitory interests of the crown, and disregard the growing enmity of the populace, the lawless independence of the nobility, the unrelenting opposition of the Church? Will not the Jewish confidants of the king see that they build the future of their people upon a smoldering volcano? Will not the Jewish philanthropists recognize the futility of the endeavors to solve the Jewish question through a policy of new migrations in the lands of dispersion?

> The hand of my rescuers is short,
> It cannot save.
> O that my ways were straight before God,
> Maybe He would see how powerless
> Are all my would-be-redeemers . . .
>
> Weary am I to tread
> The old itinerary of woe,
> Find anew the foe cast his greedy eye
> Upon the remnant of my survivors . . .[13]

Piety and political realism prompt this disagreement with the notables of Jewish Spain, and will ultimately influence the poet to leave his home and journey to the Holy Land. But what interests us momentarily is the fact that the current issues and controversies of the times often found their way and vehicle in the *piyyut*.

After the *Shema* there follows in our prayer book the assurance by the congregation that the Divine behest is cherished in the present as it was in the past, and that it will forever endure in the hearts of Israel, for "there is no God *beside* (*zulat*) Thee." Here a poem may be installed, called *zulat* because of its location in this passage of the liturgy. Often it echoes the strife of the environment against the Jew, the subtle or coarse coercion to make him renounce his faith:

> They reproach me
>   When I seek to serve Him,
> And revile me
>   When I give glory to His Name.
> They seek to set me far,
>   O God, from Thy service:
> But my suffering and oppression
>   Are better than Thine estrangement;
> My portion and my pleasure,
>   The sweet fruit of Thy law.
>
> Let my right hand forget—
>   If I stand not before Thee;
> Let my tongue cleave—
>   If I desire aught but Thy law.

> My heart and mine eyes
> > Will not suffer my feet to slip,
> For He, the Lord, is One,
> > There is none beside Him.[14]

The concluding benediction of the *Shema* strikes the third chord of the Jewish faith, redemption, the previous blessings being devoted to creation and revelation, respectively. Here a poem may be embedded named *geulla*, or redemption. Its frequent theme is the pain and plight of the present which seeks relief or redress from the Rock of Israel:

> Let Thy favor flow over me,
> Even as Thy wrath hath overflowed.
> Shall mine failings for ever
> Stand between me and Thee?
> How long shall I search
> For Thee beside me, and find Thee not? . . .
> My Redeemer! to redeem my multitudes
> Rise and look forth from Thine abiding place.[15]

There are yet other poetic additions to the morning prayer, but the above are in the main the typical. Perhaps mention should be made also of the *ofan* (wheel), a poem deriving its name from the passage in the prayer book that describes the heavenly host, winged and wheeled (as in the visions of Isaiah and Ezekiel), chanting the praises of God on high, as Israel does on earth. Here the poet has occasion to delve into the labyrinth of heaven or the music of the spheres, or the mysteries of the Divine Name, or the very secret of prayer. Sometimes stress is laid on the daily experience of God's ubiquity, which is more wondrous than even the celestial chariot:

> O Lord, where shall I find Thee?
> Hid is Thy lofty place;
> And where shall I not find Thee,
> Whose glory fills all space?[16]

The paradoxes of God are then itemized: All-hidden, He is revealed everywhere; transcendent, and enclosed in the breast of lowly man; a God afar off, and yet near at hand (Jer. 23:23); exalted above all praise, He inhabits the praises of Israel (Ps. 22:4).

> Oh, how shall mortals praise Thee
> When angels strive in vain—
> Or build for Thee a dwelling,
> Whom worlds cannot contain?
>
> Yet when they bow in worship
> Before Thy throne, most high,
> Closer than flesh or spirit
> They feel Thy Presence nigh.[16]

Such is the miracle of prayer that we forget to think of the very presumption of all prayer. For in the inwardness of the act, the offering of man and the gift of God are indistinguishable. With the Psalmist, one experiences "my prayer" to be "His mercy" (Ps. 66:20). He already answered us, when He prompted our heart to pray. Hence the sense of surprise and gratitude voiced by the medieval poet when he finds that God is invariably ahead of His children in the game of hide and seek:

> I have sought Thy nearness,
> With all my heart have I called Thee,
> And going out to meet Thee
> I found Thee coming toward me.[17]

It is by such disclosure of fresh exploration and adventuring away from the beaten track that the poets of the Middle Ages kept the windows in the house of prayer open to the breezes of the green outdoors. Spontaneous piety continually interrupts the order of established service and quickens it with a breath of fragrant life. New expression adds relevance to the legacy of ages, and the timeless is enhanced by the timely.

The poetic embellishments of the standard prayers were, of course, not restricted to the morning service, or to the benedictions of the *Shema*. The *Amidah*, or the prayer proper of the synagogue, is copiously adorned by the poets, especially on distinguished Sabbaths and holidays. Every event of the Jewish liturgical calendar is enriched by poetic compositions which vary in form and structure and show steady growth and intricate development through the centuries. In the course of time the *piyyut* penetrated into every part of the religious life and every portion of the service. Nor was it confined to public worship in the synagogue.[18] It entered the Jewish home, cheered the family at meals, welcoming the Sabbath and bidding it farewell, partaking in the jollities as well as in the trials of the house from birth to death.

4

At least 35,000 poems by 2,836 poets are listed by Israel Davidson in his *Thesaurus of Medieval Hebrew Poetry*,[1] an indispensable reference book for all study of the subject. New discoveries have added to our knowledge of medieval letters, however a vast amount of medieval creation still lies buried in unpublished manuscripts.

The discovery of the Genizah in Cairo[2] brought to light the forgotten remains of the ancient *payyetanim*, or poets, of Palestine. Their activity spans the centuries between the compilation of the Palestinian Talmud, toward the end of the fourth century, and the havoc wrought to Jewish Palestine by the Crusades. We have now the evidence of literary endeavor in the Holy Land and its environs that extends for more than twenty generations. Slowly there emerges the outline of recognizable growth from the artless prayers of the earlier talmudic age to the more stately and studied diction of the first poet known to us by name, Yose ben Yose (c. 400 c.e.?), down to the more intricate and involved patterns of speech and poetry characteristic of the Palestinian school of *payyetanim* and their imitators in other lands. The most important single find in that period of literature is the recovery of the lost poetic work of Yannai (c. 550 c.e.), the first poet consistently to employ rhyme in Hebrew. It is he, also, who loaded his verses with the lore of the Midrash, so that his *Kerobah*, or poetic elaboration of the *Amidah*, is in fact a rhymed homily on the portion of the Writ read that week in the synagogue.[3] His disciple is said to be Eleazar ben Killir, the most fertile and influential among the early *payyetanim*. There is no season of the sacred year which he did not supply with prolific compositions some of which are still recited on the major holidays. For long generations, late into the Middle Ages, he remained the model and legislator of synagogal poetry. He is remembered especially for his bold or bizarre word formations some of which were criticized by medieval or modern biblical purists. However, we know now that his was not wholly a private idiom, and that many of his forms and locutions occur in other, both earlier and later, poets of the Palestinian school, or even in the nonpoetic remains of Palestinian literature. All of this tends to prove that the Palestinian *piyyut* is also valuable as a surviving witness of the postbiblical Hebrew vernacular.[4]

There are extant fragments of literary production by a score of poets living in the Holy Land or its vicinity, all of them new surprises of the Genizah, *e.g.*, Joseph ben Nisan of Shaveh-Kiriathaim or Nawe in Trans-Jordan, or Pinehas ben Jacob of Kefar, a suburb of Tiberias (c. 800 c.e.), or Samuel ben Hoshana whom we encounter in Egypt in 1011, or Solomon ben Amr al-Singari, named so probably from his native town in Kurdistan, a fecund versifier who wrote *Yozerot* and *Kerobot* for all the sabbaths and festivals, his compositions mirroring the mind and mood of Near Eastern Jewry on the eve of the Crusades.[5]

Saadia Gaon (882-942), reared in Egypt and head of the academy in Sura, old seat of Babylonian learning,[5a] is a versatile writer who used Hebrew verse for a variety of purposes. We have from his pen polemical[6] and didactic,[7] liturgic[8] or even philosophic[9] compositions, some facile and fluent, others dark and difficult. An adept student of the Palestinian *piyyut*, he outdid all *payyetanim* by his audacious innovations and playful artificialities of language. The poems of his elder contemporary, the blind and saintly Nissi Nahrawani[10] win by their simplicity and sincerity. The poets of the house of al-Baradani for two or three generations serve as chief *hazzanim* in Bagdad and as supervisors of all the *hazzanim* in Iraq: it is through them that the Palestinian *piyyut* as well as their own creations spread in the East, or even to northern Africa. We can trace such channels of transmission thanks to a letter in the Genizah written in 1106 to Kairuan by the Gaon Hai (d. 1038)[10a] who is also a poet of considerable stature. Some of his *selihot* voice stirringly the sense of homelessness, and hence the helplessness of the medieval Jew.[11]

Recent yields of scholarship permit us to trace poetic development in both Egypt and Babylonia down to the thirteenth century. In the first half of that century, Eleazar Hababli,[12] poet of wealthy patrons in Bagdad, records the conditions of the closing period of the Abbassid caliphate, while in the second half of the century, Joseph ben Tanhum Yerushalmi,[13] house poet of the Nagid in Cairo, sheds light on Jewish ways and worthies in Egypt under the Mamelukes.

From Palestine *piyyut* spread not only to the east and south, but also to the west and north, to Byzantium, Italy, and the German lands. Southern Italy is the first center of Hebrew culture in Europe and several of its poets, such as Shefatiah (d. 886) and his son Amittai, contributed fine lyrics to our prayer book, some recited in the most solemn part of the service on the Day of Atonement.[14] The ritual for the same day preserves a *keroba* by the son of Kalonymos of Lucca, Meshullam. He died in Mayence in the beginning of the eleventh century. Both the style and the structure betoken the influence of the Palestinian *piyyut*, like most creations of the *payyetanim* in Frankish and German territories, from Simon bar Isaac bar Abun in Mayence in the tenth century, and his younger contemporary Gershom the Light of the Exile (d. 1028), to Rabbenu Tam of Rameru (d. 1171) and Ephraim of Regensburg (d. 1175) foremost *payyetan* of medieval Germany, the last two showing acquaintance with elements of meter as developed in Spain.[15]

The first to adapt the Arabian quantitive or metrical scansion to Hebrew verse was Dunash ben Labrat,[16] a disciple of Saadia, active in Cordova in the middle of the tenth century. The first great poet of Hebrew Spain is Samuel Ha-Nagid (993-1056),[16a] the vizier of the Berber kings of Granada, equally distinguished as statesman, grammarian, and talmudic scholar. He is the outstanding representative if not the founder of the knightly and courtly taste and tradition in Hebrew secular poesy. For nearly two decades he used to accompany the armies of his state on their yearly campaigns and to write in his bivouac poetic reports to his family, describing in detail his military exploits or political feuds, the intrigues at the court or the designs of the rival city-states of Andalusia, appending prayers before battle or songs of victory which breathe a robust, almost antique faith. In decisive crises on the battlefield, or dire danger to his very life, he never despairs, firmly convinced that even on the brink of disaster a vow or prayer, and the intercession of his ancestors in the cave of Machpelah, will summon help from heaven, and the stars in their

courses will fight against the enemy as in the days of Sisera. Intermingled
with such martial verse are solicitous inquiries about the health of his sons
or the progress of their education, exhortation and counsel how to win
favor in heaven and friends on earth, and what or how best to study, and
moving lyrical outbursts of love and longing for Zion, where he would
rather be a humble Levite in the courts of God than retain rank and rule
among the great on earth. In short, his *diwan,* or collected poetry, is a
diary in verse of a scholar-father turned warrior-statesman, a rare and
revealing human document which bares the private cares and the public
career of an altogether remarkable man of affairs and man of letters in
eleventh-century Spain.[17]

His younger contemporary is Solomon ibn Gabirol (b. 1021), who
died early in his thirties and yet won immortal fame as one of the foremost
thinkers and poets of the Middle Ages. Known as Avicebron to the scho-
lastics, his *Fons Vitae* is a landmark in medieval philosophy,[17a] and he is
equally distinguished as one of the most gifted poets in the Hebrew
language. The conflict of the genius with his environment, his being forever nettled and lacerated by "the thorns and thistles of the earth,"[18] the
mass of the uncreative who set themselves up as "the norm" and dismiss
as "abnormal" the endeavor or the behavior of the creative individuality,
this perpetual martyrdom of the spirit is unforgettably uttered in his
sorrowful lyrics, or impassioned invective, or his landscape pictures of
night and storm, the comrades and symbols of his somber and restless
soul. Conscious of his gifts, proud of his calling, ascetically devoted to the
search of truth, he was constitutionally unable to serve men or stoop
before the mighty "like the priest of Edom before his icons."[19] Hence
the inevitable misunderstandings and untoward setbacks of his life which
must have sowed the seeds of his early disease and death. Pure and chaste
are his sacred songs, the finest fruit of medieval devotion. Discontent and
discord die away, and rid of resentment and resistance, "humble of spirit,
lowly of knee and stature,"[20] he bows before the throne of glory, "like
the beggar who cries at the door for grace."[21] But when he rises from
prayer, the knowledge of being loved by God gives him such peace and
power that nothing can bow him down. Restored to His favor, the lowly
self knows itself restored to lordliness, capable again to recollect and
redeem the innate kingliness of the soul and her kinship with God:

> Thy life to God's life is akin,
>   Concealed like His beneath a veil,
> Since He is free of flaw or sin,
> Like purity thou too canst win,
>   To reach perfection wherefore fail?[22]

His religious verse, notably *The Royal Crown,* a lofty poem charting the
solar system of medieval science, entered the rites of many Jewries, bring-

ing to humble houses of worship in distant lands glimpses of vision and insights of contemplation which immeasurably enhanced the sense of wonder at the mystery and vastness of the universe, and in the same breath increased the spirit of magnanimity for all that share the sight of the stars and the warmth of the sun:

Thou art God, and all creatures are Thy witnesses and Thy worshipers.
Yet is not Thy glory diminished by reason of those that adore aught beside
    Thee,
For the intention of them all is to reach Thee . . .[23]

The sun-kissed summit of Hebrew poetry is Judah Ha-Levi (d. after 1140), the heart and harp of medieval Judaism.[23a] His is the most beloved name among his people who feel that he voiced and embodied the best in Israel. Wittily but reverently, they apply to him the Scripture (Deut. 12:19): "Take heed to thyself that thou forsake not Ha-Levi (the Levite)," and heartily endorse the homage of his contemporary,[24] *kol Jaakob mityahadim*, "the entire household of Jacob keeps faith with *Judah.*" Because he is an authentic mouthpiece of his people and representative of the genius of its faith and art, all the selections from medieval verse in the foregoing chapters were drawn from his poetry, and yet they give no adequate notion of his grandeur. Every translator of his advises in the end: "Dear reader, study Hebrew, and throw my version in the fire!"[25] For no rendering can recapture the music and magic of his Hebrew, abounding in perfect miracles of sense and sound.

He started as a prodigy in the literary salons of Andalusia. A lively lad and singer born, he showed uncanny skill in adapting Hebrew words to the strains and stanzas of the Arabian love ballads then in vogue. He could match with amazing ease the lightsome lilt or the licentious lines of any of the song hits of the day, as a comparison with the *muwassah* by the popular poet of Seville, al-Abyad, will show:

barrid ġalīl	rakīk belīl
ṣabb al-ʿalīl	nofeth kelīl
lā yastaḥīl	yōfī we-lyl-
fīhi ʿan ʿahdi	-ʾoth sefath maddi
wa lā yazāl	hatter we-gal
fī kulli ḥāl	shad kam ke-gal
yarǧū ʾl-wiṣāl	ki-shdē shegal
wa-hwa fī ʾṣ-ṣaddi[26]	hēn we- ʿas daddi[27]

Such amatory verses unexpectedly turn panegyrical, including a toast or tribute to the patron or benefactor whose name and fame they spread abroad on the wings of a favorite tune. The praise or dispraise of song writers could thus make or mar the reputation of their friends or clients.

No wonder that our poet soon became the darling of polite society and the despair of his fellow minstrels, as he facilely mingled frolic with flattery to his hosts or backers, and gaily caroled the delights of the body and the merriments of youth with a seductiveness in the holy language which perhaps a few regretted, and all the others relished. "Why not fill my *kad* (the Hebrew for a *jug* of wine), while my years are not full *kad* (*i.e.*, twenty-four)!"[28] With such inborn gift of mirth and wit and pun, one wonders what would have become of him in another environment or tradition. The poet himself later rued his celebrity as the acknowledged master of the exquisite trifle. But that was the mood of the changed and harsh realities of the Spanish scene, when the *reconquista* and the counter-attacks of Islam plunged the Peninsula into turmoil and strife.

> They fight in their frays,
> And we fall in defeat,
>   As is the custom in Israel.[29]

The poet found a theme for his tongue, touched with the live coals of the ancient altar. At first, the poems that welled out of his new heart were dark and penitential, unsparing in remorse and reproof, austere and ascetic. His friends shook their heads, or began inquiring about his health. A few scholars nodded assent. The spokesmen for religion were delighted. Only the poet felt more and more ashamed, precisely for being a religious poet. Was not that the burden of his message that since men cannot save, the Will of God must be done? Done, not sung. So he decides to put lived life behind his written lines. He turns his back on the Jewish court society, its Arabian meters and melodies, its culture of the senses and its Grecian wisdom, its trust in princes and its worship of men, and in obedient servant-ship of his Lord, seeks a threefold return to the holy language, the holy law and—hardest of all—the Holy Land. Such resolve is not easy, and the poet does not conceal his lapses, love of life, irresolution. But when he braved all and risked all in utter surrender to his God, he came to his own at last. The wintry mind of the aging poet experienced a belated Indian summer of poetic exultation. Never before had all the wells of inspiration burst in such jubilant and masterly song as on the eve of his departure from Spain, or his voyage on the sea, or in Egypt where he falters and nerves himself anew to go whence there is no return. In these last years of his life, he left some of the finest bits of poetry written by the hand of men.[30]

The days of Judah Ha-Levi are the golden age of Spanish literature. We know about fifty names of contemporary Hebrew poets in Spain,[31] among them writers of renown such as Moses and Abraham ibn Ezra.[32] No Hebrew poet in subsequent generations was able to recapture the glories of this classical epoch. Some excellent verse is still written, and some new patterns of literature are adopted from the Arabic, *e.g.*, the *maqamah* ("assembly," often rendered as "miscellany"), a picaresque genre in rhymed prose intersected by verse, a rather curious blend of mime and satire, tract and tale, farce and homily. Its best known examples in Spain are *The Book of Delight* by Joseph Zabara (written *c.* 1190) and the *Tahkemoni* by Judah al-Harizi (d. before 1235).[33]

Of the poets of the thirteenth century Meshullam de Piera deserves to be singled out for his originality and integrity. Rooted in the mystic faith of the circle of Gerona, center of Spanish cabbalism, he writes with mordant scorn of the pedantries and platitudes of both grammarians and philosophers to whom Writ and Prophecy were but a playground for linguistic or allegorical exercises. A proud and independent spirit, un-bribable alike in his blame and praise, he walked his own ways with men or even with the Hebrew language. He sets it free from the pinfold of the biblical vocabulary, resolutely employing all its resources from Midrash and Talmud or even medieval science.[34] His most admired friend and compatriot was the illustrious Moses ben Nahman (1194-*c.* 1270), one of the master minds of medieval *halaka*. In his poems one finds the first intimations of mystic ideas in Spanish Hebrew sacred poetry, and his hymn on the descent of the soul, its sojourn as a stranger on earth, and its home-ward journey to God, entered the liturgy of the New Year.[35] The *diwan* of Todros (son of Jehudah) Abulafia (d. after 1300) is a kind of poetic diary, containing the memoirs and fragments of autobiography in verse by a courtier in thirteenth century Castile. It mirrors the light and gay mores of the upper stratum of Jewish society, and the inroads of Aver-roistic enlightenment[35a] which the mystic revival and the classic books of the Spanish cabbala sought to counteract.[36] Little is known about the poet Nahum, whose *meorot* and *geullot* have the fragrance and radiance of dew. Ecstatic faith blends with a delicate feeling for nature: a blossom-ing twig in the garden stirs the hope for the branch out of the stem of Jesse, and the sunrise, or the spring, whisper in the ear prospects of free-dom and deliverance.[37]

The political decline and spiritual breakdown of the Jewish society in its last century in Spain, the tragic chapter of Marranism and defection since the pogroms of 1391 and the disputation at Tortosa in 1414, are reflected in the verses of Solomon de Piera (*c.* 1340-1420), mentor and minstrel of the Jewish aristocrats and apostates in Saragossa.[38] Proud of his historic faith, though contemptuous of its plebeian new leaders, is Solomon Bonafed (d. *c.* 1450), humanist, polemist, satirist who pleaded with the renegades, heartened the vacillating, rebutted the assailants, and generally voiced the conviction, the consternation, and the confidence of the faithful remnant resolved to persevere in the path of their ancestors.[39]

Provence, a bridge and intermediary between the Arabic culture in

Spain and the lands of Christian Europe,[40] saw flowering of Hebrew
poetry in the thirteenth century. Preciosity and artificial fanciness seems to
be characteristic of this school of poets who delight in toying with language,
in ingenious grammar games and all manner of whimsicality to parade
their prowess in Hebrew. Abraham Bedershi (*i.e.*, of Béziers) wrote a
piece for the Day of Atonement in which only the first half of the letters of
the Hebrew alphabet is used, while another of his devotional poems consists of a thousand words each beginning with the same letter.[41] Similar
feats of virtuosity are exhibited in the poetic efforts of his son Yedaiah
Penini (*c.* 1270-1340) who is best known for his *Behinat Olam* (Scrutiny of the World), one of the most popular and frequently reprinted
moral tracts of the Middle Ages.[42] A genuine poet who versed, vaga-
bonded and vilified like a true Provençal troubadour is Isaac Gorni (*i.e.*,
of Aire): impecunious and impudent, he never came to good, either in his
own time or in the memory of posterity.[43]

A kindred spirit is Immanuel of Rome (*c.* 1270-1330), the greatest poet
of medieval Italy.[44] A delightful rogue with an uproarious sense of humor
and irrepressible relish for mischief, he can make the holy language utter
the naughtiest improprieties, for which he was placed on the list of prohibited authors.[45] Of course, he keeps assuring the reader, as have all poets
since Ovid (*crede mihi lasciva est nobis pagina, vita proba est*) that lasciv-
ious is only his lay, not life, and that far from being dissolute, he is devout.
But there is something to his protestations. Flippant and frivolous, he has
his graver moods, and there runs through his poetry a serious strain of religion and asceticism, nourished from native founts of Jewish piety and reinforced by kindred currents in contemporary Christendom.[46] Immanuel
introduced into Hebrew the form of the *sonnet* which had just been transferred into Italian from Provençal; otherwise his diction discloses the
impact of the Hispano-Arabic patterns of song and scansion. His vision of
hell and heaven, the last of his *maqamat*, or miscellanies, is the first attempt
at an imitation of Dante in Hebrew letters. It was followed, almost a century later, by the more ambitious effort of Moses da Rieti (1388-d. after
1460), rabbi, physician, and philosopher who in his *Little Shrine*[47] achieved
hardly more than a versified survey of the Jewish Sages and the principal
philosophers of the past. But his use of the *terza rima* was deft and in his
decasyllabic lines (with the *shewa mobile* counted as a vowel) he follows
the Italian syllabic-tonic (rather than the Arabian quantitive) meter.[48] No
wonder that the Italian Jewish communities were so proud of this Hebrew
disciple of Dante that they adopted one of his cantos into the ritual,
dividing it into seven parts, one for each day of the week.

Exiles from Spain enrich Hebrew writing in Italy. Judah Abrabanel,
known also as *Leone Ebreo*, the celebrated author of the *Dialoghi di
Amore*,[48a] excelled in Hebrew verse as well. In a moving elegy, written in
Naples in 1503, he depicts the vicissitudes of his life and his sorrow of

separation from his firstborn son who was snatched away from his parents in Portugal and forcibly baptized: paternal affection and fidelity to his faith are voiced with fiery passion of feeling and almost frosty perfection of form.[49] The most engaging poet of the Italian Renaissance is Joseph Sarphati (d. 1527), known in his professional life as Giuseppe Gallo, a physician and son of an eminent physician to Pope Julius II and the Medici. He wrote satirical, humorous and erotic verse full of salt and sparkle, small pieces as a rule, since he took delight and pride in brevity. He seems to have been the first to introduce into Hebrew poetry the *ottava rima*, as he was the first to translate a play into Hebrew, the famous Spanish tragicomedy *La Celestina*, of which only his own introductory poem survived.[50] The earliest original attempt at Hebrew drama seems to be the comedy by Judah Sommo (1527-1592), playwright and producer at the court of Mantua who wrote in Italian a dozen or so theatrical pieces, and a pioneering treatise on stagecraft. He also engaged in the favorite fashion of the times of interchanging poems in commendation or condemnation of the female sex, of course gallantly chiming a paean of praise to the noble lady of his heart in his *Magen Nashim* (Shield or Defense of Women).[51]

One will look in vain for such uses or examples of Hebrew poetry in the northern lands of Europe. Massacres by the Crusaders,[52] persecutions and expulsions (from England in 1290, from France in 1306, 1322, and 1394, from Austria in 1421, from Bavaria in 1452), successive waves of pogroms in which during the frightful year of the "Black Death" alone, in 1348-1349, some three hundred Jewish communities were drowned in blood and fire, left their traces in the poetry of the synagogue, in *selihot*, or penitential verse, and *kinot*, or dirges. The sacrifice of Isaac, the *akeda*, or the story of the *ten martyrs* of antiquity,[53] a prefiguration of Israel's passion and pilgrimage of pain through the centuries, is the recurrent theme of the poets in these lands who mingle recent with ancient grief, and draw new hope from the timeless tale. Poets they are sometimes not by choice or inclination, but perforce, under the lash of brute facts or fate. Often it is the scholar in Rabbinic law who feels the duty to appeal to heaven and to report to posterity the plight of his people or the cruelties of hatred and superstition in his day. Accusations of ritual murder (such as wiped out the community of Blois in 1171, and found expression by several poets, among them Rabbi Ephraim of Bonn[54] and Rabbi Barukh of Mayence[55]), the burning of the Talmud (*e.g.*, in Paris in 1244, bewailed by Rabbi Meir of Rothenburg[56]), the charges of poisoning the wells or of desecrating the Host by which mobs were incited to slaughter the Jews (*e.g.*, on the Easter Sunday of 1389 in Prague, mourned by Rabbi Abigdor Kara[57]), such are the topics and pursuits of poetry in these dark centuries and countries.

Poland, where the persecuted found shelter, became in the sixteenth century a stronghold of talmudic studies so that its *payyetanim* are as a rule its leading rabbinic authorities as, for instance, Solomon Luria (d. 1573).[58] In the next century, the bloody Cossack revolts in 1648 in which several hundred communities were wiped out, shook East European Jewry to its depth, taking such heavy toll in lives that altogether the Jewish population in the world sank to its smallest number in history.[59] Again it was the foremost talmudists in their time who believed they were called upon to be the tongue and the graving tool which would keep alive in the memory of the after ages the anguished shrieks of the murdered multitudes and the atrocious details of the carnage: hence the lamentations or chronicles by rabbinic scholars such as Rabbi Yomtob Lipman Heller (d. 1654) and Sabbetai Cohen (d. 1663).[60]

The shores of the Mediterranean, in both Africa and the Balkans, as well as in other Jewish centers of the Ottoman Empire, witnessed a revival of Hebrew poetry in the sixteenth century as a result of the influx of Spanish refugees. Much of the classical heritage of the Middle Ages was preserved, and some good new poetry written in the literary circles that sprang up in Constantinople (*e.g.*, the poet Solomon ben Mazaltob), in Salonica (Saadia Longo, and especially the splendid poet David Onkeneyra), on the islands of the Aegean (Judah Zarko at Rhodes), in Oran, Tlemcen, and Algiers (Abraham and Isaac Mandil Abi Zimra and Abraham Gavison).[61] But it was particularly Safed in Galilee, a city of legists and mystics,[62] which decisively determined the spiritual outlook and also the poetic utterance of the closing centuries of the Jewish Middle Ages. The new cabbala which spread from there over all the scattered communities was the last religious movement in Judaism to reach and affect every country of the Diaspora without exception.[63] This mystic revival influenced the rites and usages of the synagogue, pervaded the liturgy and the prayer book,[64] and imbued Hebrew expression with new fervor and urgency. The hymn *Lekha dodi* (Come, my beloved) by Solomon Alkabez, the teacher and brother-in-law of the famous Safed cabbalist Moses Cordovero (d. 1570), entered all rituals and is sung all over the Jewish world, when Queen Sabbath is welcomed to the tents of Jacob.[65] In almost all the prayer books of Eastern Jewry there will be found also the hymns for the Sabbath meals of Isaac Luria (d. 1572), the inspired visionary of the new cabbala.[66] The sweetest of all mystic singers and the most significant poet of his century is Israel Najera (*c.* 1542-1619) who in over a thousand songs gave utterance to the new temper of devotion and to the feverish Messianic urge of his times. Set to various Turkish, Armenian, Spanish, and new Greek airs, which the wandering minstrel picked up in his younger and gayer life of the road, and suffused with erotic-mystic imagery, these hymns and elegies treat—in alternating mood and melody, now tender, now tearful, now triumphant—of the quarrel and conciliation of the lovers, of estrangement, forgiveness, and renewal of the covenant between the heavenly bridegroom and His earthly spouse, the community of Israel. The stark sensuality at places met with censure. To some such love songs to the *Shekinah* seemed to speak "the language of adulterers,"[67] especially when suited to strains or reminiscent of sounds known to be flagrantly culpable in a carnal way. But all such misgivings were silenced, when Isaac Luria himself endorsed the *piyyutim*, saying that they were listened to with delight in heaven.[68] The liturgy of the Oriental Jews abounds with his poetry, which spread far and wide not only in the Near East and the Balkan Peninsula, but even to Aden, Calcutta, and Cochin-China. His literary influence was likewise far reaching and pervasive,[69] as attested, among others, by the poetry of Shalom Shebesi (d. after 1677), foremost poet of the remote and remarkable tribe of the Jews of Yemen.[70]

The Messianic ardor of the Lurianic cabbala was bound to erupt in movements such as were precipitated by the appearance of Sabbatai Zevi[70a] as the Messiah and Nathan of Gaza as his prophet (1665-1666), and the kindred mystical heresies of that century. One can study the literary reflections of that convulsion best in Italy again. There earlier than anywhere else, within two decades after the death of Luria, a self-styled disciple of his carried on lively propaganda on behalf of the new school.[71] The struggle for or against cabbalism and Sabbatianism is mirrored in the literature and poetry of seventeenth-century Italy which produced such colorful and contradictory personalities as Leon Modena (1617-1648) and the gifted pair of poets and brothers, Jacob (1615-1667) and Immanuel (1618-d. after 1703) Frances, intrepid fighters against all mystic or Messianic delusions.[72] An eager votary of the new cabbala was Moses Zacuto (1625-1697), rabbi in Venice and Mantua, whose secular verse and dramatic works prove that he was sensitive also to other winds of doctrine. His first drama betrays the Spanish background in Amsterdam from where he stems, for its theme—Abraham shattering the idols of his father —carries overtones of the contemporary conflict of the Marranos who sought to return to Judaism.[73] His mystery play on life beyond life[74] is a remarkable artistic attainment. Gifted beyond all others, as well as comprehensive, is Moses Hayyim Luzzatto (1707-1747), poet, dramatist, mystic, and moralist, in all alike distinguished, a self-confessed Messiah in the days of Voltaire, and the reputed father or forerunner of modern Hebrew literature.[75] He still belongs to an age that did not know, nor would have approved, our new compartments and labels: secular and religious. He wrote secular dramas to gladden friends at their wedding which he considered a religious commandment. This was as little ruse on his part as the inclusion of erotic verse as nuptial songs in the prayer books especially of Oriental Jewries. Both are rather the outcome of that all-embracing unity of the Middle Ages in which what is termed the religious included all that was to be found in the nonreligious, and much else besides. Anyhow, the new and the old fuse imperceptibly even in nineteenth-century Italy, as can be seen in the devotional verse of Samuel David Luzzatto (1800-1865), the last of the *payyetanim* to write an *Aboda* or a poetic description of the ritual of the Day of Atonement.[76]

It was also S. D. Luzzatto who toiled most to retrieve for the new age the lost classics of the Middle Ages. For when the poets of the *Haskala* or the era of Enlightenment set about reviving Hebrew,[76a] they found for their endeavors, in Berlin or Vienna, in Zolkiew or Vilna, no usable past. The masters of medieval song had long sunk in oblivion, and even their names faded from memory. "Who is Yannai?" asks in 1829 the best informed scholar of the times.[77] The choicest lyrics of Judah Ha-Levi were clean forgotten until his *diwan* was recovered and parts thereof printed in 1840 and 1864 by S. D. Luzzatto.[78] The bulk of the poetry of Samuel Ha-Nagid remained unknown until our day, and was published for the first time in 1934.[79] Other admirable poets of the Middle Ages are still hidden in the dust of libraries.

NOTES

I

[1] Hagigah 5b, citing Deut. 31:17 f. and Is. 51:16.

[2] Tanhuma, Behaalotka 6.

[3] Tosefta Sotah, 13, 2. Cf. Sotah 48b; Yoma 9b; Sanhedrin 11a.

[4] Seder Olam R. c. 6.

[5] Yer. Taanit II, 1 f. 65a; b. Yoma 21b and parallel passages.

[6] Berakot 8a.

[7] Cf. Mishna Sotah 9, 11; Sotah 48a; Yer. *ibid.*, IX, 12 f. 24b.

[8] Hos. 9:1 and Gittin 7a; Yer. Megillah III, 2 f. 74a.

[9] Ps. 126:2 f. and Berakot 31a.

[9a] Cf. Judah Goldin, "The Period of the Talmud," this work, Vol. I, pp. 160, 163, 164.]

[10] Transl. by B. Halper, *Shirat Yisrael* (Leipzig, 1924), pp. 51 f.

[11] Baba Batra 12a.

[12] Shita mekubbezet on Baba Batra 12a. See Abraham J. Heschel, in *Alexander Marx Jubilee Volume* (New York, 1949).

[13] Baba Batra, 12a.

[14] Hasagot on Hilkhot Lulab 8, 5.

[15] Mishna Sotah 9, 15 end.

[16] Sotah 4b.

[17] Examples from the age of the Geonim, see Aptowitzer, in *Tarbiz* 1, 4 (1930), pp. 82 f. In Spain, see Louis Ginzberg, *Genizah Studies*, II, 273; R. Gershom "the Light of the Exile," see S. Assaf, in *Ziyyunim* (Berlin, 1929), p. 119.

[18] R. A. Nicholson, *A Literary History of the Arabs* (Cambridge, 1930), pp. 304 ff.

[19] *Diwan of Jehudah Halevi*, ed. H. Brody, III, 65. Transl. by Solomon Solis-Cohen, in *United Synagogue Recorder*, I, 1921, No. 3.

[20] Judah Ha-Levi, *Kitab al Khazari*, transl. by H. Hirschfeld (London, 1931), p. 251 (ch. 5, 20).

[21] A. Harkavy, *Zikron la-Rishonim* (St. Petersburg, 1891), pt. 5, pp. 166 f.

[22] *Ibid.*, pp. 160 f.

[22a Cf. below the chapter by Abraham J. Heschel, "The Mystical Element in Judaism."]

[23] *The Letters of M. H. Luzzatto and his Contemporaries*, ed. by S. Ginzburg (Tel-Aviv, 1937), p. 357.

[24] *Ibid.*, pp. 381, 397.

[25] *e.g.*, Maimonides, *Guide for the Perplexed*, I, ch. 59.

[26] Cf. Jonah of Gerona (d. 1263) and Aaron Ha-Levi (*c.* 1300) quoted by Joseph Caro, *Bet Joseph*, Orah Hayyim 113. See also Shem Tob Falaquera, *Sefer ha-Mebhakkesh*, Haag, 1779, f. 27b.

2

[1] Isaiah Horovitz, *Shne Luhot ha-Berit* (Wilhelmsdorf, 1686), f. 185b.

[2] *Yosippon*, ed. D. Guenzburg (Berditchev, 1913), p. 22; *Iggeret Musar* by Kalonymos b. Kalonymos, ed. Isaiah Sonne, in *Kobez al Yad* I, 1936, p. 103. See A. M. Habermann, in *Tarbiz*, 13, 1941, p. 55.

[3] Poetics, ch. 9 (1451b).

[4] H. L. Ginsberg, *The Ugarit Texts* (Jerusalem, 1936), pp. 129 ff., and Th. H. Gaster, JQR 37, 1946, 55 ff.

[4a Cf. Goldin, *op. cit.*, pp. 172-173.]

[5] Mekilta, ed. Lauterbach, II, 162, 198, 233 f. Sifre Deut. 343, ed. Friedmann p. 142b. Zebahim 116a.

[6] Mas. Soferim, ed. Higger, p. 314.

[7] Jacob b. Asher, *Tur Orah Hayyim*, 284 end.

[8] Shabbat 86b.

[9] Cf. Ch. Albeck in the Hebrew edition of Zunz, *Die gottesdienstlichen Vortraege* (Jerusalem, 1947), pp. 132 f.

[10] Midrash Tehillim, ed. Buber, p. 231.

[11] Saadia's Arabic transl. of the Psalms with Commentary, ed. S. Lehmann (Berlin, 1901), pp. 10 and 32 f.

[12] See the commentaries of David Kimhi (d. 1232) and Menahem Meiri (d. *c.* 1315), ed. J. Cohn (Jerusalem, 1936), pp. 63 f.

[12a Cf. Cecil Roth, "The European Age in Jewish History (to 1648)," this work, Vol. I, pp. 246 ff.]

[13] *Kaf ha-Ketoret* on Ps. 29, quoted from Ms. Paris by Gershom G. Scholem, *Major Trends in Jewish Mysticism* (New York, 1946), p. 408, n. 9, and p. 248.

[14] On the Cabbala of Luria and his school see the excellent chapter by Scholem, *loc. cit.*, pp. 253 ff.

[14a Cf. also Heschel, *op. cit.*]

¹⁵ *Siddur Ozar ha-Tefillot* (Vilna, 1923), p. 586. Cf. *Siddur ha-ARI* (Zolkiew, 1781), f. 108 b ff. and *Shaar ha-Kavvanot* (Jerusalem, 1873), f. 64c ff.
¹⁶ See above I, n. 26.

3

¹ Tosefta Berakot 3, 6. See Louis Ginzberg, *A Commentary on the Palestinian Talmud* (New York, 1941), I, p. 68-73.
² R. Aha (*c.* 325 C.E.): Yer. Berakot IV, 3f. 8a; cf. also Berakot 29b: Rabba (d. 331) and R. Joseph (d. 333).
³ Berakot 4, 4, and Abot 2, 13. See Louis Ginzberg, *loc. cit.*, III, 333.
⁴ See Israel Davidson in *Festskrift* in honor of Dr. Simonsen (Copenhagen, 1923), pp. 89 ff.
⁵ Yer. Sanhedrin I, 1 f. 18a.
⁶ Ed. Brody, II, p. 221. Transl. by Judah Goldin in *Menorah Journal*, 33, 1945, p. 196.
[^{6a} Cf. Goldin, *op. cit.*, p. 120.]
⁷ Josephus *Jewish War* II, 8, 5. See S. J. Rapoport. *Toledoth R. Eleazar ha-Killir*, n. 20.
⁸ *Selected Poems of Jehudah Halevi,* ed. H. Brody, transl. by Nina Salaman (Philadelphia, 1924), p. 130. Here, as elsewhere, I have occasionally revised the translation, to bring it closer to the Hebrew.
⁹ See *Siddur R. Saadia Gaon*, ed. Davidson-Assaf-Joel (Jerusalem, 1941), p. 37, and Ismar Elbogen. *Der juedische Gottesdienst*, 3 ed., (Frankfort, a. M., 1931), p. 19. See also N. Wieder, in *Saadya Studies* (Manchester, 1943), pp. 254 ff.
¹⁰ *Selected Poems of Jeh. Halevi*, p. 116.
¹¹ *Ibid.*, 117 and 165.
¹² *Diwan*, ed. Brody, IV, 232.
¹³ *Ibid.*, III, 18 f., and I. F. Baer, in *Zion* 1, 1935, p. 23.
¹⁴ *Selected Poems*, p. 97 f.
¹⁵ *Ibid.*, p. 109.
¹⁶ *Ibid.*, p. 134, transl. by Solomon Solis-Cohen, *Judaism and Science* (Philadelphia, 1940), pp. 174 ff.
¹⁷ *Selected Poems*, pp. 134 ff.
¹⁸ Zunz, *Die synagogale Poesie des Mittelalters* (Berlin, 1855), p. 70.

4

¹ 4 vols. (New York, 1924-1933). See also the *Supplement* in *Hebrew Union College Annual*, 12-13, 1937-38, pp. 715 ff.
² See S. Schechter, *"A Hoard of Hebrew Manuscripts"* (1897), repr. in his *Studies in Judaism* (Philadelphia, 1908), II, 1-30.
³ Fragments of Yannai were first identified by Israel Davidson and published in his *Mahzor Yannai* (New York, 1919). All extant compositions were edited by Menahem Zulay, *Piyyute Yannai* (Berlin, 1938). Cf. also his valuable monograph in *Studies of the Research Institute for Hebrew Poetry* (*SI*) (Berlin, 1936), II, 213 ff. The Institute, founded by Salmann Schocken, has in Jerusalem an unrivalled collection of photostats of the scattered remains of

poetry in the Genizah, and its publications have greatly advanced the study of medieval poetry. New fragments of Yannai were found by P. Vidor (in *Jubilee Volume in Honor of Bernhard Heller* [Budapest, 1941], pp. 32 ff.), and Isaiah Sonne, in HUCA, 18, 1944, pp. 199 ff. See also Zulay, in *Haaretz* (Tel-Aviv, February 8, 1947), release No. 100 of the Schocken Institute, and in *Semitic Studies in Memory of Immanuel Loew* (Budapest, 1947), pp. 147 f. On historic and halakic aspects in the research of Yannai, cf. Saul Lieberman, in *Sinai* (Jerusalem, 1939), II, 221 ff.

[4] Some historical and critical problems of this *payyetan* are discussed by the writer in SI, 5, 1939, 269 ff., also in *Encyclopaedia Judaica*, vol. 9, col. 816-820.

[5] See Menahem Zulay, in SI, 3, 1936, pp. 164 ff., and 5, 1939, pp. 109 ff., and in *Sinai*, 9, 1945, pp. 296 ff.

[[5a] Cf. Goldin, *op. cit.*, p. 202.]

[6] I. Davidson, *Saadya's Polemic against Hiwi Albalki* (New York, 1915); *Esa meshali*, ed. B. M. Lewin, in J. L. Fishman's collection *Rav Saadia Gaon* (Jerusalem, 1943), pp. 481 ff. Cf. B. Klar, in *Tarbiz*, 14, 1943, pp. 156 ff. and 15, 1944, pp. 36 ff.

[7] *E. g.*, "Saadia's Piyyut on the Alphabet," ed. by S. Stein, in *Saadya Studies*, (Manchester, 1943), pp. 206 ff.; cf. Zulay, in *Melilah* (Manchester, 1946), II, 162 ff.

[8] The sacred poetry is ed. by Israel Davidson, *Siddur R. Saadia Gaon*, (Jerusalem, 1941). See also Zulay, in *Tarbiz*, 16, 1945, pp. 57 ff.

[9] Parts of a philosophical poem were published anonymously by Joseph Marcus, *Ginze Shirah u-piyyut* (New York, 1933), pp. 81 ff., now identified by Zulay, *Haaretz*, March 9, 1945, release No. 78.

[10] See Zulay, *Haaretz*, September 25, 1946, release No. 96.

[[10a] Cf. below, Abraham S. Halkin, "Judeo-Arabic Literature," p. 137.]

[11] On Joseph and Nahum al-Baradani see J. Mann, *Texts and Studies in Jewish History and Literature* (Cincinnati, 1931), I, 122, and Spiegel, in SI, 5, 1939, p. 272. The poems of Hai Gaon were edited by H. Brody, in SI, 3, 1936, pp. 5 ff.

[12] *Diwan*, ed. H. Brody (Jerusalem, 1935). On his sacred poetry cf. S. Bernstein, in *Sinai* 9, 1945, No. 104, pp. 8 ff.

[13] See J. Mann, *Texts and Studies*, I, 435 ff.; J. Schirmann, in *Kobez al Yad*, 3, 1939, pp. 40 ff.; A. M. Habermann, *Inbe-hen* (Tel-Aviv, 1943), pp. 31 ff.

[14] Ed. by Benjamin Klar, in his *Megillat Ahimaaz* (Jerusalem, 1943), pp. 71 ff. Cf. J. Schirmann, in SI, 1, 1933, pp. 96 ff.

[15] A. M. Habermann edited the *Liturgical Poems* of Simon bar Isaac (Berlin, Jerusalem, 1938), of R. Gershom (Jerusalem, 1944), and of Ephraim of Regensburg in SI, 4, 1938, pp. 119 ff.

[16] Ed. Nehemiah Allony (Jerusalem, 1947).

[[16a] Cf. Halkin, *op. cit.*, p. 138.]

[17] *Diwan*, ed. D. S. Sassoon (Oxford, 1934); a vocalized ed. by A. M. Habermann (Tel-Aviv, 1945-1947). For a full bibliography see J. Schirmann, *Kirjat Sefer*, 13, 1936, pp. 373 ff., and cf. *idem. Ziyyon*, 1, 1936, pp. 261 ff. and 357 ff., and *Keneset*, 2, 1936, pp. 393 ff. See also Joseph Weiss, preliminary announcement of a contemplated study, *Tarbut hasranit veshirah hasranit* (Jerusalem, 1947).

[17a Cf. Alexander Altmann, "Judaism and World Philosophy: From Philo to Spinoza," this work, Vol. III, pp. 81 f.; also Halkin, *op. cit.*, pp. 144-145.]

18 *Shire Shelomo b. Jehudah Ibn Gabirol,* ed. Bialik-Ravnitzky (Berlin, 1924), I, 29, 1.42.

19 *Ibid.,* I, 9, 1.33, and correction, III, 3, pp. 115 and 31.

20 *Selected Religious Poems of Solomon Ibn Gabirol,* ed. I. Davidson, transl. into English verse by Israel Zangwill (Philadelphia, 1923), p. 17.

21 *Ibid.,* p. 16.

22 *Ibid.,* p. 69.

23 *Ibid.,* p. 86. A selected bibliography is appended to J. Schirmann, *Shlomo Ibn Gabirol Shirim nivharim* (Tel-Aviv, 1944), pp. 161 f., to which his recent study in *Keneset,* 10, 1946, pp. 244 ff., and José M. Millás Vallicrosa, *S. Ibn Gabirol como poeta y filósofo* (Madrid-Barcelona, 1945), may be added.

[23a On Judah Ha-Levi as philosopher, cf. Altmann, *op. cit.*, pp. 83-84.]

24 Jehudah ben Abun of Seville, cf. Brody-Albrecht, *Shaar ha-Shir* (Leipzig, 1905), p. 129, No. 115, line 3.

25 Franz Rosenzweig, *Jehuda Halewi, Zweiundneunzig Hymnen und Gedichte,* p. 153. See also S. Solis-Cohen, "Judah Halevi," in his *Judaism and Science* (Philadelphia, 1940), p. 174.

26 A. R. Nykl, *Hispano-Arabic Poetry* (Baltimore, 1946), p. 246: about the sweet lips of the beloved, "may they refresh the thirsty one, the lover in pain," etc.

27 *Diwan of Jehudah Halevi,* ed. Brody, I, 136: the last lines parody Ez. 23:21. Cf. now S. M. Stern, in *Tarbiz,* 18, 1947, pp. 168 ff.

28 *Diwan,* ed. Brody, II, 309.

29 *Ibid.,* IV, 131, lines 9 f.

30 The best study on the life of Judah Ha-Levi is by J. Schirmann, in *Tarbiz,* 9, 1938, pp. 35 ff., 219 ff.; 10, 1939, pp. 237 ff.; on his age by I. F. Baer, in *Zion,* 1, 1935, pp. 6 ff.; cf. also his paper in *Schocken Almanach 5699* (1939), pp. 74 ff., and his Hebrew book on the *History of the Jews in Christian Spain* (Tel-Aviv, 1945), p. 49 ff. See also Salo W. Baron, in *Jewish Social Studies,* 3, 1941, pp. 243 ff.

31 J. Schirmann, in SI, 2, 1936, pp. 119 ff.; 3, 1938, pp. 249 ff., and 6, 1946, pp. 253 ff.

32 *The Diwan of Moses b. Ezra,* ed. H. Brody (Berlin, 1935), and the *Commentary* (Jerusalem, 1941). *Selected Poems,* ed. H. Brody, transl. by S. Solis-Cohen (Philadelphia, 1934). Cf. also Brody, *JQR,* 24, 1934, pp. 309 ff. *The Diwan of Abraham b. Ezra,* ed. Jacob Egers (Berlin, 1886); *Reime und Gedichte,* ed. D. Rosin (Breslau, 1885-1894); *Kobez hokmat RABE,* ed. D. Kahana (Warsaw, 1894). See also Simon Bernstein, in *Tarbiz,* 5, 1934, pp. 61 ff., and 10, 1939, pp. 8 ff., and H. Brody, in SI, 6, 1945, pp. 1 ff. On his life cf. the various papers by J. L. Fleischer and the recent literature surveyed by Alexander Marx, in *Essays and Studies in Memory of Linda R. Miller,* ed. by I. Davidson (New York, 1938), pp. 135 f.

33 Zabara's *Sepher Shaashuim,* ed. Israel Davidson (New York, 1914), rev. Hebrew ed. (Berlin, 1925). An English transl. by Moses Hadas (New York, 1932) (Records of Civilization, v. 16). Cf. Hadas, *JQR,* 27, 1936, pp. 151 ff. Harizi's work, ed. P. de Lagarde (Goettingen, 1883); ed. A. Kaminka (Warsaw,

1899). See J. Schirmann, *Die hebr. Uebersetzung der Maqamen des Hariri* (Frankfort a.M., 1930), pp. 113 ff. (full bibliography) and in *Moznayim*, 11, 1940, pp. 101 ff. Cf. also S. M. Stern, in *Tarbiz*, 17, 1946, pp. 87 ff.

[34] Ed. Brody, in SI, 4, 1938, pp. 12 ff. See Joseph Patai, *Misefune ha-Shirah* (Jerusalem), pp. 44 ff. Cf. Schirmann, in *Haaretz*, Jan. 1, 1940, and J. N. Epstein, in *Tarbiz*, 11, 1940, pp. 218 f.

[35] M. Sachs, *Die religioese Poesie der Juden in Spanien* (Berlin, 1901), Hebrew section p. 50, and the transl. p. 135. See also G. G. Scholem, in *Schocken Almanach 5696* (1935), pp. 86 ff. Another example of his religious verse, A. M. Habermann. *Be-ron yahad* (Jerusalem, 1945), p. 79.

[35a Cf. Altmann, *op. cit.*, pp. 85-86.]

[36] *Gan ha-meshalim we-ha-hidot*, ed. David Yellin (Jerusalem, 1932-1936); cf. Brody, SI, 1, 1933, pp. 2 ff. On the poet and his age see I. F. Baer, in *Zion*, 2, 1937, pp. 19 ff.

[37] Brody-Wiener, *Anthologia Hebraica* (Leipzig, 1922), pp. 299 ff., and Habermann, *Be-ron yahad*, p. 83. Cf. D. H. Mueller-Schlosser, *Die Haggadah von Serajevo* (1896), pp. 59 and 64. See J. Schirmann, *Kirjat Sepher*, 22, 1945, p. 128.

[38] *Diwan*, ed. Simon Bernstein (New York, 1942), and sacred verse *HUCA*, 19, 1946, pp. 1-74. Cf. also Brody. *Leket shirim u-piyyutim* (Jerusalem, 1936), pp. 3 ff., whose author is de Piera, and not Bonafed. See next note.

[39] See J. Schirmann, in *Kobez al-yad*, 14, 1946, p. 11, where the literature is summarized. Cf. also *Haaretz*, Aug. 12, 1938, release No. 13, and July 19, 1946, release No. 93.

[40] Zunz, *Zur Geschichte und Literatur*, pp. 439 ff.

[41] *Bakasha beth-El*, cf. Davidson, *Thesaurus*, III, 37, No. 800, and *Eleph alphin* (Dan. 7:11) in *Kerem Hemed*, 4, pp. 59 ff. See I. Davidson, "Eccentric Forms of Hebrew Verse," in *Students Annual*, Jewish Theol. Seminary (New York, 1914), p. 82.

[42] The *mem* prayer, Davidson, *Thesaurus*, III, 178, No. 2353, also the *rehuta, ibid.*, I, 271, No. 5957. See also *Zunz Jubelschrift* (Berlin, 1884), Hebrew section 1-19.

[43] Ed. H. Gross, in *Monat. Ges. Wiss. Judentums* (*MGWJ*) 31, 1882, 510 ff. (cf. *ibid.*, 27, 1878, 476 f.); Steinschneider, in G. J. Polak's edition of Bedershi, *Hotem tokhnit* (Amsterdam, 1865), p. 4; Schirmann, in *Haaretz*, April 4, 1944, release No. 69.

[44] For editions and literature cf. Schirmann, *Die hebr. Uebersetzungen der Maqamen des Hariri*, pp. 121 ff. Cf. also H. S. Lewis, in *Proc. Amer. Academy for Jewish Research*, 6, 1935, pp. 277 ff.

[45] Joseph Caro, *Shulhan Arukh*, Orah Hayyim 307:16.

[46] Cf. Isaiah Sonne, in *Tarbiz*, 5, 1934, pp. 324 ff.

[47] *Mikdash meat*, ed. J. Goldenthal (Vienna, 1851). Selections in J. Schirmann's *Mivhar ha-Shirah ha-Ivrit beitalia* (Berlin, 1934), pp. 195 ff.

[48] Rhine, JQR, n. S. 1, 1911, pp. 349 ff., and especially M. Hack, in *Tarbiz*, 11, 1939, pp. 91 ff.

[48a Cf. Altmann, *op. cit.*, pp. 87-88.]

[49] Schirmann, *Mivhar*, pp. 217 ff.

[50] Schirmann, *ibid.*, pp. 223 ff., and in *Haaretz*, Sept. 25, 1942, release No. 57,

and Oct. 8, 1944, release No. 75; Umberto Cassuto, in *Jewish Studies in Memory of G. A. Kohut* (New York, 1935), Hebrew section pp. 121 ff., and in *Gaster Anniversary Volume* (London, 1936), pp. 58 ff. Cf. Cecil Roth, *The History of the Jews in Italy* (Philadelphia, 1946), p. 220.

[51] *Zahot bedihuta de-kiddushin*, ed. Schirmann (Jerusalem, 1946); *Magen Nashim, ibid.*, pp. 149 ff.; cf. *idem*, MGWJ, 75, 1931, pp. 97 ff., and *Keneset*, I, 1935, pp. 430 ff.

[52] See A. M. Habermann, *Sefer gezerot Ashkenaz VeZarephat* (Jerusalem, 1946), with an introduction on the age by I. F. Baer.

[53] See Louis Finkelstein, in *Essays and Studies in Memory of Linda R. Miller* (New York, 1938), pp. 29 ff., and Solomon Zeitlin, JQR, 36, 1945, pp. 1 ff. and 209 ff.

[54] S. Bernfeld, *Sefer ha-Demaot* (Berlin, 1924), I, 225 ff., and Habermann, *Sefer gezerot*, pp. 133 ff.

[55] Ed. Habermann, in SI, 6, 1945, pp. 133 ff.

[56] Brody-Wiener, *loc. cit.*, pp. 295 ff.; Habermann, *Be-ron yahad*, p. 169, and *Sefer gezerot*, pp. 183 ff.

[57] S. Bernfeld, *loc. cit.*, II, 159 ff.

[58] Habermann, *Be-ron yahad*, pp. 175 ff. Cf. Davidson, *Thesaurus*, IV, 475.

[59] Salo W. Baron, *A Social and Religious History of the Jews* (New York, 1937), II, 165, and III, 129 f.

[60] Bernfeld, *loc. cit.*, (Berlin, 1926), III, 173 ff. and 169 ff. On the chronicles cf. M. Steinschneider, *Die Geschichtsliteratur der Juden* (Frankfort a.M., 1905), pp. 120 ff. Cf. Simon Bernstein, in *Ha-toren*, 10, 1923, pp. 83 ff.

[61] Sol. b. Mazaltob, in *Shirim u-zemirot* (Constantinople, 1545); cf. I. Zinberg, *Hist. of Jewish Literature* (in Yiddish) (Vilna, 1933), vol. 4, p. 353, n. 7, and p. 492. On the Society of Poets in Salonica cf. J. Patai, pp. 86 ff., who also published the poetry of Onkeneyra, in *Kobez al Yad*, 2, 1937, pp. 77 ff. On Saadia Longo cf. also H. Brody, in *Minha le-David* (Yellin) (Jerusalem, 1935), pp. 205 ff. Jehudah ben Abraham Zarko, *Sefer Lehem Yehudah* (Constantinople, 1560); cf. Schirmann, in *Haaretz*, May 17, 1945, release No. 81. Abraham, and Jacob, and Abraham (Jr.) Gavison, see *Omer ha-Shikhah* (Leghorn, 1748), where also verses by Abraham Abi Zimra (f. 135b, see also 134a, 138a and 106a) and by Mandil (122b, 138b f. and 4b preface) are printed. See also Habermann. *Be-ron yahad*, p. 192. Generally on the state of research in this epoch cf. Schirmann, *Kirjat Sefer*, 12, 1935, pp. 389 ff.

[62] See S. Schechter, *Studies in Judaism* (Philadelphia, 1908), II, 202 ff.

[63] G. G. Scholem, Hebrew lecture on the *Idea of Redemption in the Cabbala* (Jerusalem, 1941), p. 13; and *Major Trends*, pp. 285 f.

[64] Abraham I. Schechter, *Lectures on Jewish Liturgy* (Philadelphia, 1933), pp. 40 ff.

[65] A. Berliner, *Randbemerkungen zum taegl. Gebetbuch* (Berlin, 1909), I, 43 ff. Cf. Simon Bernstein, *Shomere ha-homot* (Tel-Aviv, 1938), pp. 83 ff.

[66] G. G. Scholem, *Major Trends*, pp. 271 f. Cf. Meir Wiener, *Die Lyrik der Kabbalah* (Vienna, 1920), pp. 75 ff. (reviewed by Scholem, in *Der Jude*, 6, 1921, pp. 55 ff.)

[67] See Menahem Lonzano, *Shte Yadot* (Venice, 1618), f. 142ab.

[68] Najera's *Zemirot Yisrael* were recently edited by Judah Fries-Horeb (Tel-Aviv, 1946). See also David Yellin in *Jewish Studies in Memory of G. A. Kohut*, (New York, 1935), Hebrew section pp. 59 ff.; I. Davidson in *Jubilee Volume* in honor of *Samuel Krauss* (Jerusalem, 1937), pp. 193 ff. and in *Sefer ha-Shanah liyhude Amerika* (New York, 1939), pp. 282 ff.; Isaac Mendelsohn, in *Horeb*, 9, 1946, pp. 53 ff., and A. Mirsky, in *Sefer Ish ha-Torah Vehamaaseh* in honor of Rabbi M. Ostrowski, (Jerusalem, 1946), pp. 125 ff. On the data of his life cf. S. A. Rosanes (Hebrew), *Hist. of the Jews in Turkey* (Husiatyn, 1914), Pt. III, pp. 173 ff. and 309 ff., and M. D. Gaon, in *Mizrah u-maarab*, 5, 1930, pp. 145 ff.

[69] On the influence of Najera on Joseph Ganso in Brusa, see Simon Bernstein, *Shomere ha-homot*, pp. 114 ff., on Solomon Molkho II, *ibid.*, pp. 163 ff., on the rite of Corfu, see *idem*, in *Horeb*, 5, 1939, pp. 46, 48 ff.

[70] *Kobez shire kodesh* (Jaffa, 1931). See A. Z. Idelsohn and H. Torczyner, *Diwan of Hebrew and Arabic Poetry of the Yemenite Jews* (Cincinnati, 1930), pp. 88 ff. Older literature listed by R. Levy, in *I. Abrahams Mem. Volume* (Vienna, 1927), p. 266, n. 1. See recently on the Yemenite *piyyut* Y. Ratzaby in *Kirjat Sefer*, 19, 1942, pp. 65 ff. and the list *ibid.*, 22, 1946, pp. 247 ff.

[70a] Cf. Cecil Roth, "The Jews of Western Europe (from 1648)," this work, Vol. I, p. 269.]

[71] G. G. Scholem, in *Ziyyon*, 5, 1940, pp. 215 ff., and briefly also in his *Major Trends*, p. 257.

[72] Dr. Simon Bernstein edited *The Diwan of Leo de Modena* (Philadelphia, 1932) and *Immanuel Frances* (Tel-Aviv, 1932) (cf. *M. Wilensky*, HUCA, 18, 1944); also poems by Jacob Frances in his *Mishire Yisrael beitalia* (Jerusalem, 1939), pp. 73 ff.

[73] Cf. A. Berliner, in his ed. of Zacuto's *Yesod Olam* (Berlin, 1874), and J. Schirmann, in *Moznayim*, 4, 1936, pp. 625 ff.

[74] *Tofteh Arukh* (Venice, 1715). See the introduction by D. A. Friedmann to his edition of the play (Berlin, 1922).

[75] Cf. my *Hebrew Reborn* (New York, 1930), pp. 29 ff. and 441 f., where the literature is listed. Add now S. Ginzburg, *The Life and Works of M. H. Luzzatto* (Philadelphia, 1931); Isaiah Sonne, in *Sefer ha-Shanah liyhude Amerika*, 1935, pp. 218 ff., and 1938, pp. 154 ff., and *Horeb*, 6, 1941, pp. 76 ff.; F. Lachower, in *Keneset*, 4, 1939, pp. 365 ff., and Benjamin Klar, in his introd. to Luzzatto's *Sefer ha-Shirim* (Jerusalem, 1945).

[76] Published in *Bikkure halttim*, 1825, pp. 29 ff. See I. Elbogen, *Studien zur Geschichte des jued. Gottesdienstes* (Berlin, 1907), p. 95.

[76a] Cf. below, Hillel Bavli, "The Modern Renaissance of Hebrew Literature," pp. 228-230.]

[77] S. J. Rapoport, in his biography of Killiri, n. 19.

[78] *Betulat Bat Yehudah* (Prague, 1840), and *Diwan R. Yehudah Halevi* (Lyck, 1864).

[79] Ed. D. S. Sassoon (Oxford, 1934).

BIBLIOGRAPHY

DELITZSCH, FRANZ, *Zur Geschichte der juedischen Poesie.* Leipzig, 1836.

DUKES, L., *Zur Kenntnis der neuhebraeischen religioesen Poesie.* Frankfort a.M., 1842.

(Both these works are rather antiquated.)

Still basic and by far the best are the works of

ZUNZ, LEOPOLD, *Die synagogale Poesie des Mittelalters.* Berlin, 1855.

———, *Der Ritus des synagogalen Gottesdienstes.* Berlin, 1859.

———, *Literaturgeschichte der synagogalen Poesie.* Berlin, 1865.

A survey of the major *payyetanim* will be found also in

ELBOGEN, ISMAR, *Der juedische Gottesdienst,* pp. 280-353. Frankfort a.M. 1931.

For an introduction to Spanish poetry, see

YELLIN, DAVID, *Ketabim nibharim* II, pp. 165-352. Jerusalem, 1939.

———, *Torat ha-Shirah ha-Sepharadit.* Jerusalem, 1940.

MILLÁS VALLICROSA, JOSÉ M., *La Poesía sagrada hebraicoespañola.* Madrid, 1940.

See also the relevant chapters in

ZINBERG, ISRAEL, *Die Geschichte fun der Literatur bei Yiden.* Vilna, 1929-1937.

WAXMAN, MEYER, *A History of Jewish Literature.* New York, 1930-1941.

CHAPTER 4

JUDEO-ARABIC LITERATURE

By Abraham S. Halkin

Judeo-Arabic literature comprises works composed in Arabic, almost always in Hebrew script, by Jewish authors who lived in lands where Arabic was the dominant language. More specifically the title is applied to the output of authors from, roughly, the ninth to the thirteenth century. But if one were to write a comprehensive history of Judeo-Arabic literature, one would extend the limits at both ends, to the sixth century and to our own time, respectively.

The most striking aspect of this literary activity is its variety of subject matter and its novel approach. Jewish creativity, which for centuries had confined itself to religious themes, so that even purely literary material was clothed in a religious garb, developed a catholicity of expression which included medicine, mathematics and other sciences, philosophy, history. Under the same impetus, secular poetry and belles-lettres appeared in Hebrew. Even within the field of religion new disciplines were introduced. Investigation of Hebrew grammar was pursued far more seriously than at any time in the past, commentaries were written to explain the Bible text and systematic codification of the law occupied the minds of great talmudists.

Before we undertake to account for this efflorescence it is important to know something of the environment within which the literature developed, to appreciate the economic, political and cultural conditions under which the Jews labored. They lived in a world which was predominantly Moslem in religion and Arabic in vernacular. Judged by any standard and, particularly, by the conditions prevailing in non-Moslem regions, this world was quite comfortable.[1a] Upon the payment of a special tax, collected from all *Dhimmis* (non-Moslems who were permitted to live by their faith), they were not harassed on religious grounds, nor did they, save for isolated occasions, suffer from any serious disability. They were privileged to engage in all economic activities, including services in the administration. They were not segregated and thus came in contact with the non-Jewish population. Moreover, politically they benefited from the characteristic concept of the state in medieval times, especially in Moslem lands. The Islamic state was a theocracy, and its head a representative or successor (caliph) of the prophet. The Koran, which is the revealed Book of the followers of Mohammed, was the source of all Islamic law. Like Judaism, it did not distinguish between a civil and an ecclesiastical law, different from each other in origin. Both were derived from the same religious sources. To be a member of the Moslem body politic was a privilege which only adherents of that faith could enjoy. Non-Moslems lived under the protection of the dominant group as a result of a special agreement between the sovereign church-state and them. The state was organized along religious lines. The dominant group possessed the right to administer the state and to regulate its affairs. But the tolerated religious minorities, in addition to the guarantee of the right of domicile, of earning a liveli-hood, and of the safeguarding of life and limb, were also granted internal autonomy. All matters in which the state had no direct interest would be regulated within these units by their duly authorized administrators, in conformity with the laws of the particular group. As a result, it was possible for a non-Moslem individual not only to share in the rights and privileges that belong inherently to a human being, but also to identify himself with his own group and participate in its life and functions.

Undoubtedly, the political theory of the Islamic state, or even its appli-cation, did not eliminate difficulties or friction among the several sections of the population. We know of a considerable amount of animosity, of literary polemics, of religious persecutions, and of occasional outbreaks of violence. In Jewish writings we read complaints of the state of exile, and yearnings for the restoration of Zion and the realization of Messianic hopes. While such themes were to some extent conventional, they cer-tainly indicate some dissatisfaction with conditions as they were. The pathetic terms in which the highly placed and wealthy Jewish public official, Hasdai ben Shaprut, expresses his readiness to come and kneel before the distant Jewish king of the Khazars, or the pitiful plaints of oppression by Christians and Moslems which resound so loudly in the writings of the Jewish poets of Spain, certainly reveal an awareness of being alien and the existence of difficulty and trouble. Yet, in general, life under Moslem rule was as comfortable a one as the Jews have ever had under foreign domination, and the average individual probably found little to complain of on religious grounds.

The Arab-speaking world within which the Jews lived was the most cultured center of medieval times. Having absorbed through conquest the civilized centers of Christianity and Zoroastrianism—within which Greek culture, in modified form, no doubt, had previously continued its existence after the classical period—the Arabs became disciples, and set about learn-ing what the two civilizations of East and West had to offer. A wave of translations marks the ninth and tenth centuries, in the course of which scientific and philosophic writings of the ancients were rendered into

Arabic. Thanks to the interest of enlightened caliphs, the efforts of zealous translators, and the gratitude of a substantial body of readers and students, the Arabic-reading public fell heir to the scientific and philosophic thought of the Greeks, the Syrians, the Persians and the Hindus. The new cultural possessions served as the groundwork for a ramified and intensive pursuit of study and enlightenment among the Moslems. In the wake of the translated texts, original works in Arabic followed in the same fields, and thus the Greek cultural tradition, with all its modifications, found its redeemer and heir in the lively activity in which the Moslems were now engaged. In all this literary productivity neither ethnic nor religious boundaries interfered. Although literary polemics abounded along both national and religious lines, the efforts of the numerous men of letters, of diverse national and religious origin, all contributed to the enhancement and enrichment of Arabic literature. As a result, during the centuries when Western, and even Eastern, Christendom passed through the so-called Dark Ages, the vast Moslem empire, particularly after its decentralization into several states, housed learning and enlightenment. Indeed, the eventual awakening of Christian Europe, the age of Scholasticism, and the subsequent Renaissance are indebted to the impetus given by Islam.

The Jewish communities in the Moslem countries had, of course, a long cultural history behind them. In Mesopotamia, Palestine, Egypt, North Africa and Spain, all now dominated by rulers who professed Islam, the Jews possessed, to a greater or lesser degree, the Rabbinic literature produced over the many centuries from the beginning of the Common Era or earlier to the rise of Islam. With all allowance made for external influences in the centers where this literature was created, it cannot be denied that it bears a native Jewish stamp. It is Jewish in spirit, in emphasis, in form. The successive additions to the cultural treasures, visible as the effect of foreign ideas and environments may be, are all—with the possible exception of the esoteric literature of that period—genuinely Jewish, natural and logical outgrowths of the earlier strata to which they are added.

As time passed, these Jewish communities found themselves increasingly within a milieu which, religiously, was akin to their own and, culturally, challenged their self-sufficiency. As no hard and fast social, economic or political boundary lines separated them from their Moslem countrymen, they responded to the lure and challenge of the larger world within which they were continuing their Jewish existence. They gradually abandoned Aramaic, which had been their vernacular, and became speakers of Arabic; they studied works in Arabic; nor did they limit themselves to translations from other languages into it. They also read and learned original writings in poetry, history and grammar. They even studied the Koran. In a word, they went through a profound process of adaptation to the environments.

As a result, the cultural history of the Jews in Moslem countries necessarily followed new paths. New interests and problems engaged the intellectuals, and they found expression in a multitude of works written in Arabic and Hebrew. The Moslem world is not the only instance in Jewish history where the Jewish way of life encountered another which it regarded with interest and was impelled to emulate. Both before and after there were occasions when Jews came in contact with a civilization which had much to offer and from which they gladly took. There have been environmental conditions other than the Moslem where Jews looked to the environment with respect and felt themselves called upon to defend and justify their adherence and loyalty to their way of life before themselves and the larger world. Yet, if we exclude modern Hebrew and Yiddish literatures, which have their own causes and explanations,[2a] and cannot therefore figure in this generalization, the Arabic period is the only one where this contact resulted in a lasting and positive contribution to the Jewish cultural heritage, and produced works which have been recognized and revered by Jews of other days and other lands.

For an explanation of this phenomenon it is necessary to dwell briefly on the character of the civilization that developed within Islam. It has already been stated that Greek culture came into this world from the outside. Its presence confronted the adherents of Islam with the problem of adjustment. Greek ideas of God, of man, of the world, and of their relation to one another, were not at all like the basic conceptions in the Koran or the subsequent literature that elaborated upon it. And while the majority of Moslems knew little about the imported ideas and cared less, and, on the other hand, some individuals may have been so completely captivated by them as to divorce themselves entirely from the traditional faith, a large number of intelligent and honest people found themselves in the throes of an inner conflict. The situation paralleled to an extent that which existed for Hellenistic Jewry.[3a] This section in Islam was driven by the philosophic discussions and doctrines of Greek origin not only to ponder and analyze religious dogmas and problems which were either nonexistent in the native Moslem world or definitely stated and put beyond question but also to agree with a good deal of what was taught by the ancient philosophers. But when this happened, a reconciliation was made necessary between what was rationally acceptable to them and what they received on faith. The result was a theology which made some concessions to philosophic method and discipline, and a philosophy which nominally paid homage to religion, but essentially adhered to the truths it inherited from the classical environment. It cannot be truthfully said that the compromise was a success, when objectively studied; it may even be doubted whether a compromise is possible. But it worked for a time, and in one form or another it won adherents.

The experiences of the Moslems were an inestimable boon to the Jewish communities in that world. The issues they later had to face were almost identical with those confronting the dominant group of that time. The problem that both groups were called upon to solve was to establish peace and harmony between two truths: the truth of religion and the truth of philosophy. The product of the peace was not a real synthesis in which the two components were integrated. Whether religion was the core and philosophy the veneer, or *vice versa*, it was not difficult to discern the dichotomy, the dualism that remained, although the two were seemingly poured into one mold. Moreover, the compromise was not one which was adopted by all adherents of Islam. Many remained the same simple believers their forefathers had been, hostile to the encroachment of philosophy on their precious holdings. But some saw clearly the logical conclusions to which philosophic speculation led, and remained faithful to them, even if they were ready to pay lip service to the accepted tenets of the faith, and appreciated the benefits it bestowed on the uninitiated. All this facilitated the problem of the Jews. The dominant civilization remained a religious one. This naturally made the Jewish religion secure among its followers. There was no group with which one could have identified oneself without involving one's religion. There was no trend away from the religious outlook to a secular point of view which left religion, or the lack of it, to the conscience of the individual. As for that section of Jewry which, like its counterpart in Islam, was faced by a problem of reconciliation, it, too, profited by the discernible dichotomy in the Moslem compromise. All that it was necessary to do was to replace the Moslem component in the theology with the Jewish one. For better or worse, whatever fate the Moslem achievement would enjoy within its domain would be shared by the Jewish one within its realm. In this way a guarantee of survival and vitality was provided for the Jewish way of life by the experiences of the Moslem way of life.

Thus it happened that the encounter of Judaism within the world of Islam with the Greek tradition was a positive beneficial influence. It acted as a leaven, stimulating activity in fields not hitherto cultivated and suggesting new directions and points of view in previously pursued activities. It opened the eyes of Jewish students to secular subjects: to medicine, to mathematics, to history. It aroused Jewish interest in secular poetry and in literary prose. It fostered a rational approach to religious prescriptions, whether of creed or of deed. It instilled a love of style and form, of systematization and organization. It added much, very much that was new to Jewish culture, but it did not shake the foundations of Judaism. Jewish civilization became much more variegated, much more diverse, but it remained Jewish. Not only were the authors and creators of that culture thoroughly Jewish in their background and in their knowledge of

Jewish literature, or in their profession of their Jewish faith and in their observance of its commandments, but they also exhibited their Jewishness in their writings. Even in books which were totally devoid of Jewish content, such as books on medicine or on some other science, an introduction was included in which the gratitude to God and other items testified to the author's group and religious affiliation. In addition, an occasional reference to a biblical or talmudic matter indicated the religion of the author.

The adaptation, beneficial as it was, also produced some negative effects. Of necessity it failed to discriminate between emulation and imitation. The positive gains also showed an obverse side which was not so commendable. The new vistas that opened before them through the acquisition of Arabic led to an attitude toward Hebrew which was not quite wholesome. One writer actually seeks to justify the composition by Saadia Gaon of a work in Hebrew. Another keeps harping on the relative poverty of Hebrew as compared with Arabic. The admiration of Moslem achievements or, perhaps more correctly, the trend of assimilation, led to some surprising and distasteful manifestations. The Koran was transcribed in Hebrew characters, evidently for people who could not read Arabic script. A fortune book exists in Hebrew which lists Mohammed as one of the Prophets. Other strange facts indicate similarly the relaxation of the Jewish way of life, sometimes all the way to "the dogmatic barrier between Judaism and Islam," and occasionally even beyond that.

The tensions and strains within Islam in its process of adjustment, the rationalism that penetrated from without and was so disturbing yet so persuasive, the individual investigations and interpretations of religion that, in this realm, are very significant, marking as they do the assertion of the individual in the face of sacred tradition, even if nominally it is within the framework of that tradition—all these found their parallels within Judaism in thought and in literature as well as in deed. The condition generated a sectarianism which produced little and insignificant schisms, and also a large and threatening party like the Karaites. It gave rise to many questionings, doubts and perplexities to which the works of medieval Jewish philosophers bear witness, and an intellectualism which at least in some cases was tantamount to a rejection of the cardinal principles of Judaism. At any rate, this intellectualism is potentially at least always a threat to the wholehearted, sincere and unquestioning faith of the simple believers. It may even be that the behavior of the Jews of Spain some centuries later, in the catastrophes of 1391 and subsequently,[4a] so strikingly different from the martyrdom of the Franco-German Jews in 1096 or 1348, has its explanation in this "liberalism." These and other alarming signs and effects are true enough; but they do not alter the fact of the rich and ramified productivity that is the subject of this chapter.

In their writings, the Jewish authors who lived in Islamic lands employed two languages. Poetry and a small part of their prose were composed in Hebrew. But the bulk of the prose and a little of the poetry were written in Arabic. The quality of the language is generally colloquial. It becomes apparent, from a study of the work, that the authors paid but little attention to the artistic aspect of their composition, and did not strive to imitate models in style and eloquence, as did their Moslem contemporaries. Their language is clearly akin to the speech of the environment, except for the peculiarly Jewish expressions and the Hebrew words and phrases that found their way into Arabic as they have into every other language spoken by Jews. By the use of the vernacular even in tracts on law or commentaries on the Bible the Jews in Moslem countries distinguish themselves from their contemporaries in Christian lands who did not employ their daily language for writing, and resemble Jews in modern times in Western countries who likewise utilize the language of the land for specifically Jewish works. (It may be said in passing that the similarity between the two civilizations manifests itself in other aspects as well, as any comparison will show.) This unhesitating readiness to write in a language other than Hebrew demonstrates of course an identification with environment which was not reached in other lands, and a rather remarkable lack of consciousness of the importance of the medium of expression. That the problem presented itself to them is evident from the regrets and protests over the neglect of Hebrew voiced by individuals who themselves composed works in Arabic. They were also undoubtedly familiar with a Rabbinic word of praise for the Jews in ancient Egypt who were redeemed because they had not abandoned their language. Yet they continued to use Arabic. Reasons have of course been advanced, such as, for example, the desire of the author to reach the widest audience possible. This may be true in one instance or another, but we ought not to exaggerate its applicability. There is no reason to assume that the masses in Islamic countries were more interested in matters intellectual than in other centers at other times, or that the authors were so democratically minded or so unaware of the cultural gradations as to strive to reach everyone. Maimonides specifically declares in the introduction to his *Guide* that he does not desire to have his work on philosophy fall into the hands of the masses, or even of the whole intellectual group within them. Moreover, one may venture the assertion that the readers who were mature and sufficiently interested to read and study these books could read Hebrew with the same fluency as Arabic. Another reason which has been offered may again be partly true though it is not cogent. The inadequacy of Hebrew for expressing what they had to, allegedly prompted authors to fall back on Arabic. But this argument, too, is not strong. Had the desire existed, the way would have been found. It was found by translators into Arabic who had to adapt their language to the logic and the syntax of

Greek and had to coin a new vocabulary. It was found by later translators from Arabic into Hebrew who succeeded in developing a terminology and a style to meet the exigencies of the undertaking, and it could have been found by the authors themselves. Again Maimonides may be cited, who, in the first part of his major Hebrew work on Jewish law, gives an eloquent example of his facility in Hebrew, a facility which is unquestionably superior to that of his subsequent translators. The most probable explanation is that they did it because it was the most natural and the most effortless thing to do. Furthermore, they probably did not feel that in compositions on science the language selected preserved an ideological importance as in the case of artistic creations.

The almost consistent use of Hebrew in poetry also is an interesting problem. The naturalness of which we spoke should certainly have asserted itself in their poetic writings, in which the individuality of the writer comes to the fore. It is hardly correct, however, to suggest, as has been done, that the lyric character of poetry made the use of Hebrew imperative because the poet was compelled to sing in the language with which he felt himself most intimate. It simply goes against the facts to assume that Arabic, which they spoke from birth and used in all situations, was less their most intimate vehicle than Hebrew, which was an externally acquired medium. The explanation is to be sought more plausibly in the character of their poetry. It was considered by the people of the time as an art which approached perfection in proportion to its excellence in externals: rhythm, rhyme, language and various skills in the handling of the language. Technique, in other words, was the most important endowment of the artist, and his poetic talent an additional gift. It is to be remembered that, unlike their prose, the poetry of the Jews was grounded in an old tradition, much older than the impact of Islam. The origins of medieval poetry[5a] are to be sought in the liturgical compositions of earlier days. Since those were all written in Hebrew, a precedent was established which was maintained in later days not only in sacred but also in secular compositions. Furthermore, Moslem poetry, more perhaps than any other genre of their literature, was regarded by Moslems as a national expression, a genuinely Arab creation. It was the preferred vehicle for showing off the glory of Arabic and singing the praises of the Arabs. Jews very likely reacted by displaying a pride in their language, in its glories, its antiquity and its tradition. There may also have been involved a religious issue. The Koran was accepted by Moslems as a literary masterpiece, and although the models were pre-Islamic poets, the holy book was neverthless respected as an ideal. One of the dogmas of orthodox Islam is that the Koran is a miracle, both because of its revelation and because of its inimitable style. It provoked among the Jews a natural desire to lean on their greatest literary masterpiece, to draw on the Hebrew Bible, and to benefit from its perfection.

Among the basic productions in Judeo-Arabic literature we must undoubtedly include the translation of the Bible. Apart from its significance as a barometer of the conquest of Arabic, to the loss of Hebrew and Aramaic, comparable to a similar phenomenon in other countries—Hellenistic Egypt or the English-speaking communities—it is further important as evidence of the interest in the Bible which led to a large output of studies connected with it and the Hebrew language. The written translations were probably an outgrowth of oral traditions with their local variations. Hence the similarity in terminology among several translations which otherwise show some divergences. The best known version is that of the great and many-sided scholar Saadia ben Joseph al-Fayyumi (882-942),[6a] who, though actively participating in Jewish affairs of his day and even assuming leadership, nevertheless wrote on many subjects. He seems to have rendered almost all, if not all, of the Bible into Arabic, even if to date a comparatively small portion of his work is known. While he may have been prompted by certain apologetic motives, such as the desire to display proudly before the non-Jewish world the grandeur of Jewish Scriptures—achieved by the apparent employment of Arabic script in his version—or the wish to make the Bible palatable to intellectuals who might have objected to some rationally unacceptable items in the Sacred Text, his primary goal seems to have been to render this necessary service to a public which had no access to the Bible other than through Arabic. In his work he strove consistently to present a smooth-reading, logically arranged text. With this in mind, he took certain liberties with the original, inserting words and phrases, eliminating repetitions, and occasionally offering somewhat free renderings. He was particularly aware of the need of modifying all references to God which might hurt the sensibilities of a rationally minded person, such as himself, who conceived of God in a highly philosophic and abstract manner. And while he believed that the chief duty of a translator or a commentator was to adhere to the literal text, he asserted unequivocally that a free translation or interpretation was required whenever the literal text appeared contrary to sensual experience or to reason, to another specific statement in the Bible or to authoritative tradition. Besides Saadia's we possess remnants or complete versions by other translators, both Rabbanite and Karaite, but there is little point in either listing or characterizing them.

However, a bare translation provides only a meager understanding of biblical literature. Apart from the need for an interpretation of difficult passages, which should be fuller and longer than a translation, there were other factors which made commentary writing on the Bible a necessity.

The Bible, which was accepted by Judaism as its guide in life, was, as is known, interpreted and thus expanded by the Rabbis in order to yield that vast harvest which is termed the Oral Law. While no commentator could venture to include in his commentary all the Oral Law that he believed to be implicit in the Bible, he undoubtedly regarded it as his duty to interpret biblical passages in the spirit of Rabbinic Judaism, particularly where the failure to do so might lead to a wrong conclusion. Care also had to be exerted to take note of and refute unorthodox explanations that were circulated in large quantity by the Karaite sect, which was virile and aggressive in the ninth and tenth centuries.[7a] One may cite in illustration a discussion between Saadia and a Karaite regarding the meaning of "an eye for an eye." Saadia not only renders it "the value of an eye for an eye," as expected—since this is Rabbinic—but seeks to demonstrate that it is the only rationally tenable interpretation. The Karaite, on the contrary, disputes his rendering. The celebrated medieval polygraph, Abraham ibn Ezra, who reports this debate, realizing that no rational proof is possible, concludes with this comment: "We are unable to explain the laws of the Torah correctly unless we depend on the words of the Sages. For in the same way that we have received the Written Law from the ancients we have also received the Oral Law. There is no difference between them." This point of view necessitated a reinterpretation of the Bible in at least its prescriptive portions. The need of commentaries was felt on still another ground. The Bible, which is central in Jewish life, and regarded as the last word in truth, was not unnaturally viewed by each age as the repository of whatever it accepted as valid. In other words, as the scientific and philosophic truths developed and changed from age to age, the adherents of these evolving truths were always intent on finding them in the Bible. Since the period during which Judeo-Arabic literature was written was strongly under the influence of Greek thought in its medieval garb, it strove to read its beliefs and doctrines into the Bible. This, too, made commentary writing a basic need.

The outstanding commentator who wrote in Arabic is the previously mentioned Saadia. He composed either complete commentaries or selected notes probably on the whole Bible. These products, to the extent to which they are known to us, are masterpieces in their field. It is evident that Saadia's chief aim was to clarify. With this in mind he appended introductions to the various books, in which, from a philosophic point of view, he undertook to elucidate the purpose of the book, its method, its teachings and its plan. In his commentaries on the first half of the Five Books of Moses (it was completed by Samuel ben Hofni, see below) he is much more prolix than in the other books. The reason for it lies in the central position of the Torah in Jewish life and the consequent need for elaboration. In addition to the obvious task of explaining what is not clear, he also supplied grammatical notes whenever a knotty language problem arose, he sought to rationalize incidents and events which taxed men's credulity, and endeavored to raise the level of what sounds mythical to a philosophic plane. He is particularly ardent, in his Pentateuch commentary, in his defense of Rabbinic tradition, and in its counterpart, the attack on the Karaites, the opponents and critics of that tradition. In his commentaries on the other books he is noticeably briefer and sparser so that his explanations are in the form of occasional notes and not of a full commentary.

Another important commentator who lived in the Orient is Samuel ben Hofni, head of the Sura Academy (d. 1013).[8a] He prepared an Arabic translation of the Pentateuch, generally more literal than Saadia's, completed Saadia's commentary on the Pentateuch and wrote a commentary on it, and perhaps also on other books of the Bible. He was lengthy in his explanations, giving little attention to linguistic matters, but elaborating on various topics related to the verse or subject under discussion. He was an exponent of rationalism in his exegesis, but he accepted the halakic interpretation of the Bible and believed, contrary to Saadia's view, that all laws could be arrived at rationally. Unlike his critical attitude to the wonders related in the Talmud, he conceded the literal truth of the biblical miracles. But his rationalism forced him to approach certain biblical matters in a manner which aroused opposition. He rejected astrology and necromancy, and hence considered the success of the Witch of Endor a clever trick, and the performance of Joseph's cup the result of some mechanism with which it was equipped. He explained all dreams naturally, even those which were prophetic in character. By the same sober reasoning, however, he also shunned the discovery of the philosophy of his day in the words of the Bible.

Moslem Spain from the eleventh century on overshadows the Orient as a center of Jewish activities, and the Bible commentators of that period were almost all residents of Spain. Judah ibn Balam (c. 1080) wrote commentaries on most if not all of the Bible. An interesting light is shed on his conception of the function of a commentator by this statement of his: "I acceded to his request [i.e., of the man who asked him for an explanation of the ambiguous and difficult words which occur in the Bible], knowing that this undertaking involves three requisites: (1) that I render each word by the most approximate equivalent which Arabic furnishes; (2) that I cite in evidence other texts in the Bible where the same root is employed or, if such are not available, support from the ancients or from Aramaic or Arabic; (3) that I explain the inflection and syntax of the word. . . . As an additional favor to him I shall mention, besides, some interpretations which belong there and which come to mind, whether they are taken from others or derived from my own reasoning." While he does not display much originality in his explanations, his commentaries are valuable because of their eclectic character. We find numerous grammatical notes as well as exegetic comments. He had a faculty for conciseness and organization of his material. He was critical of Saadia, whom he accuses of violence to the Arabic in his translations. He was rather free in condemnation of others, and was not restrained in his remarks. He sometimes attacked his master, Jonah ibn Janah to whom he is indebted for a great deal, much of it without due acknowledgment. His chief target was his contemporary Moses ibn Chiquitilla, whom he criticized for his excessive rationalism. But it is his merit that he did not hesitate to admit his inability to give an adequate explanation of a word or phrase when such was the case.

Moses Ha-Cohan ibn Chiquitilla is unfortunately represented to modern scholarship by relatively few remnants culled from others who cited his explanations. He seems to have written commentaries on the bulk of the Bible, but unlike those of his younger contemporary, ibn Balam, whose works have survived in large part, ibn Chiquitilla's seem to have perished. From the little that remains it is possible to draw certain conclusions regarding his method. He attempted to apply all prophetic predictions to the immediate time of the Prophet rather than to a distant Messianic future. Accordingly, not only general prophecies but apparently Messianic sayings were related to the time of the Prophet who spoke them. The oracles of Isaiah, for example, in which he looks forward to an age of universal peace, refer, according to ibn Chiquitilla, to the time of King Hezekiah. He also made every effort to explain miracles rationally. In an apparently oral dialogue between himself and ibn Balam he denied that at Joshua's bidding the sun and moon ceased their revolutions, "for it is impossible for perpetual motion ever to be interrupted," and explained that the miracle consisted in the continued reflection of the sun even after its setting. By virtue of his enlightened approach to his work he did not hesitate to assign to sections of the Bible dates which run contrary to tradition. He believed that the chapters in Isaiah from 40 on form a separate section. While it may not be warranted to credit him with the recognition of a "Second Isaiah," he sensed the difference between the two portions of the book. He recognized a number of psalms to be of exilic date. In short, it may be stated that ibn Chiquitilla is a clear example of the rational, enlightened spirit of the Jewish-Arabic age as it manifested itself in exegesis.

But the rationalism that characterizes the commentaries of Saadia or ibn Chiquitilla was carried much further by a school of exegetes which adopted the views of Aristotelian philosophy. The beginnings of this extreme intellectualism were made by men who wrote in Arabic. Indeed, the Nestor of this school was the great Maimonides, who, without devoting much of his time and energy to the field of exegesis, indicated the lines it was to follow. The method employed by this school is that known as allegory, *i.e.*, the presumption that the Bible stated abstract truths and concepts in the form of stories, of personalities or of other figures of speech. Its tradition is old and venerable, going back to Rabbinic times, but its consistent application and, perhaps, the assumption that it is the real purport of the Bible, is the contribution of the disciples of Maimonides. The master himself is wrongly credited with an interpretation of Psalm 45, originally apparently a wedding song, which converts the entire chapter into a philosophic discourse. A few remarks by him on some verses in the Song of Songs make it clear that this booklet was conceived by him as a highly philosophic allegory of the Soul and the Active Intellect. The latter interpretation was executed in detail in the lengthy Arabic commentary on the book by Maimonides's contemporary, Joseph ibn Aknin. However, the full results of this method of exegesis became evident in a series of commentaries written in Hebrew by admirers of Maimonides who lived in Provence or in Italy.

The Orient likewise produced a commentator who was an ardent disciple of Maimonides, but his exegesis was by no means one-sidedly allegorical. Joseph ben Tanhum of Jerusalem (d. after 1260) wrote a commentary probably on the entire Bible, and his work is still extant, in whole or in part, or is at least attested for all the books except Ezra and Nehemiah. Besides the expected aid that it offers toward an understanding of the text, his exegesis is rich in discussions of realia, medicine and physics, geography, chronology and philosophy. He displays independence of mind remarkable for his age. In chronological matters he occasionally disagrees with the calculations of the universally accepted Seder Olam and suggests that the Bible sometimes gives round numbers rather than the exact extent. He recognizes copyists' errors in the transmission of names or numbers, and introduces emendations, although not explicitly. He treats the Aggada[9a] more critically than most of his colleagues. The attention he pays to the aesthetic beauty of the biblical rhetoric and to its stylistic traits is a marked feature of his approach. In this he was probably influenced by Moses ben Ezra (see below). Notwithstanding his rationalism, he nevertheless indulges in allegorical interpretation to a considerable degree. His commentary was preceded by a comprehensive introduction, with a separate title, in which he discoursed on grammar, and on other matters such as the relation of the Aggada to the literal meaning, the attitude toward Midrash[10a] and philosophical and ethical problems.

The desire to understand the Bible led to a necessary interest in Hebrew grammar, and its study resulted in notable advances. Its importance was appreciated by those who undertook to elucidate the Scriptures, as is illustrated by the large quantity of grammatical discussion and analysis in the works of the commentators, and also by those who, noting the increasing employment of Hebrew in liturgical and secular poetry, were ardent in their desire to see the language used correctly.

Like the study of the Bible, the investigation of grammar commenced in the Orient. Saadia made his contribution to this as to other fields. There were many who wrote on it, Karaites as well as Rabbanites, mostly in Arabic and some in Hebrew, but in this necessarily sketchy analysis we shall confine ourselves to three men, each of whom made a distinguished and specific contribution. Judah ibn Kuraish of North Africa, who apparently flourished during the first half of the tenth century, addressed an Epistle to the community of Fez in which he reprimanded them for neglecting to read the Aramaic version of the Pentateuch and the Prophets. He relates that when he pointed out to them how many obscure words and passages in the biblical text could be elucidated through Aramaic, and how closely related the two were, they realized the importance of the study of Targum. This experience impelled ibn Kuraish to compose his Epistle in which he would give a list of the numerous biblical and mishnaic words that have Arabic and Aramaic cognates. Of the latter about one-half has survived, but the comparisons with Arabic are lost. He attempted to account for the similarity by the physical proximity of the speakers of these languages and the common ancestry of the people who spoke them. We thus have in his Epistle the first recognition of the importance of comparative study in language, a fundamental of philological research in our day. It is noteworthy that, although the Jewish interest in Hebrew received an impetus from Arabic, the emphasis on comparative linguistics is original with them. Unlike the Arabs whose needs were adequately filled by their one language, the Jews utilized all the three and eventually came to realize their interrelation.

The man who laid the foundation of Hebrew grammar as we know it today, a veritable genius in philology, is Judah ben David Hayyuj of Fez. He was born about the middle of the tenth century and came to Spain early in life, spending the rest of it in Cordova, where he passed away early in the eleventh century. In two basic works on verbs containing weak and double letters, he established the principle that *all* Hebrew verb roots are composed of three radicals, whether they appear in every inflected form of the root or not. Before him, scholars had been inclined to argue from forms in which only one or two of the root letters appeared that such roots consisted of only one or two radicals. Hayyuj discovered both the triliteral scheme and the morphological changes that govern the "irregular" verbs. In his introduction he relates that he was pained to discover wrong verbal forms in the works of poets. He realized that if this procedure were not checked it would lead to a complete breakdown of the linguistic structure of Hebrew. He undertook, therefore, through a systematic analysis of the classes of weak verbs, followed by an alphabetic arrangement of them according to their classes, to fix and regulate the proper treatment of each root both in the interpretation of the biblical text and in the creation of new forms in contemporary compositions.

After Hayyuj discovered the principles underlying the Hebrew verb and noun, his achievements were summarized and further developed by his outstanding disciple, Jonah ibn Janah, who flourished in the first half of the eleventh century. In a comprehensive work, called *al-Tankih*, which comprises a grammar and a lexicon, he covers the various questions pertinent to Hebrew grammar, and also lists most of the roots with their definitions and illustrations of their forms as they occur in the Bible. He explains that he resented the supercilious attitude to Hebrew and to its proper use, and was annoyed to find that, whereas the Arabs devoted so much energy to the study of their language, the Jews paid but little attention to theirs. His grammar, called *Sefer Ha-Rikmah* (*Florilegium*), reviews the principles of the organs of speech, the distinction between radicals, auxiliary letters and affixes, the laws of mutation of letters, inflection of nouns and verbs and numerous other topics. It also includes valuable material on the syntax of the language. Although Janah did not deal with the subjects discussed by Hayyuj, his grammar, together with two or three of his minor works, can well serve as textbooks even for the modern scholar. His work marks the pinnacle of grammatical achievement. His successors, whose writing was almost entirely in Hebrew, not only failed to surpass him but lost ground by comparison with him by introducing views which were wrong yet were adopted for centuries. His dictionary also is exceedingly helpful. Assuming a general knowledge on the part of his readers as well as an acquaintance with his earlier contributions, he did not compile as complete a lexicon as modern standards require. But it is valuable for the light it sheds on vague and doubtful points, and the attention it pays to shades of meaning.

Other Hebrew-Arabic dictionaries were compiled, both before and after Janah's time. Hai Gaon (see below) wrote *al-Hawi* (the Compendium), a dictionary of biblical and Rabbinic Hebrew. Only fragments of it have been recovered thus far. From these we learn that he discussed under one heading words made up of similar groups of letters even if the order of the letters differed. His definitions were brief, but he seems to have elaborated where he felt it necessary. An early lexicographer, his etymologies are often faulty. The Karaite David ben Abraham al-Fasi (tenth century) composed a biblical dictionary which is really a concordance. Following a strictly alphabetical order—vitiated, however, by his belief in the existence of one- or two-letter roots—he gives the meaning of the vocables, often adding explanatory comments of grammatical, philosophical or other nature. Three centuries later, the commentator Tanhum of Jerusalem issued his *Adequate Guide*, which was designed to serve as a convenient handbook in Arabic for the vocabulary of Maimonides's Hebrew code, *Mishne Torah*, and for that section of the mishnaic terminology which was not utilized by the codifier. He felt that notwithstanding the existence of the *Aruk*, an eleventh-century talmudical dictionary, his work was needed because the former was rare, too compendious and of defective arrangement, due to its faulty understanding of grammar. Although Tanhum did not carry out his program fully, his work is useful because of the Arabic translation of the words, and also because by applying the triliteral system it accomplished for mishnaic Hebrew what Hayyuj and Janah did for its biblical phase.

Unlike the fields of biblical exegesis and philology, which were comparatively recent developments and, directly or indirectly, owed their existence to the stimulus received from Islam, the study of Talmud does not seem to have been interrupted from the time when it was first initiated. When the talmudic text was compiled, edited and declared closed, its study continued, although little material is traceable to the years 500-750. At any rate, the earlier works in Halaka during the Moslem period—responsa and codifications—were written in the Aramaic dialect which we find in the Talmud. But Arabic encroached on this field as well and challenged the supremacy of the former, and actually almost superseded it. Both the language and the method of presentation eventually attest the influence of the environment. A greater interest in systemization, in summaries, introductions and lexicography characterizes many of the halakic works in Arabic.

Once again the first outstanding author is Saadia. He enjoyed an illustrious reputation throughout the Middle Ages when his works were better known. From his extant writings, from fragments and from quotations found in books by later authorities, it is clear that he was an absolute master in Rabbinics, which he conceived to be not something additional and posterior to the Bible but an integral part of the one great unity, of Judaism, which dates from the time of Moses. His output was voluminous. He compiled compendia on legal subjects such as ritual slaughter, incest, documents and inheritance. He may have written an Introduction to the Talmud, of which, if the conjecture is correct, we still have his discussion of the thirteen hermeneutic principles for the study and expansion of the biblical law. He is also credited with either a commentary on, or a translation of the Mishna, or both. He seems to have compiled a Book of Commandments which, to judge from a recently discovered fragment, was a comprehensive list and analysis of the precepts of Jewish law. He is also the author of Responsa on various subjects. All the surviving halakic writing, and doubtless also the lost material exhibit the same system, logical order and comprehensive treatment that characterize his output in other fields. It is indeed unfortunate that so little of his contributions to Halaka has been preserved, probably because it was not translated into Hebrew.

Another Oriental talmudist who wrote in Arabic was Hefes ben Yasliah.

He probably lived after Saadia, but like those of the latter, his works also suffered a sad fate. Only fragments have survived. He compiled a comprehensive compendium of Jewish law called *Book of Precepts*, which he organized according to some plan into at least thirty-six sections. His method was to state the biblical source of the law and follow it with development and ramification in Rabbinic literature. But, ambitious and comprehensive as this program was, he went beyond it. He wrote a lengthy introduction in which, among other things, he expounded his plan and criticized the method and arrangement used by predecessors. In the body of the book he often digressed into lexicographic, philosophic and other fields, all of which undoubtedly enhanced both the quantity and the quality of the book. The extant portion includes about fifty precepts of probably 613, if, as appears probable, he followed the traditional pattern of listing that number. His influence was widespread, his book having been utilized by philologists like ibn Janah, exegetes like ibn Balam and halakists and philosophers like Bahya ben Pakudah and Maimonides.

Samuel ben Hofni (d. 1013), the most important Gaon of the Sura Academy after Saadia, seems to have employed Arabic in all his halakic writings. His output was so voluminous that a mere list of his works occupied two notebooks. He composed an Introduction to the Talmud in 145 chapters of which considerable fragments have survived. It included the history of the Talmud as well as an analysis of its method and terminology. In addition to a Book of the Laws, which may have presented a philosophic treatment of rational and traditional law and their sources, he wrote a large number of tracts on legal subjects, such as contracts, partnership, agency, court procedure, marriage and others. He seems to have participated in the lively religious polemic of his time, contributing a work which apparently dealt with the disputed problem of whether the Mosaic dispensation could be abrogated, as the Moslems contended.

Samuel's son-in-law, Hai Gaon (d. 1038), who became head of the Academy of Pumbedita after his father, the equally renowned Sherira (d. 1006), author of the famous epistle on the history of the Oral Law, wrote a number of volumes in Arabic on subjects of Jewish law. Of these, which included discussions on oaths, judges, pledges, loans and others, only fragments, if anything, have remained, either in Arabic or in Hebrew translation. The only complete item extant—in a Hebrew recension—is on purchase and sale. He is further credited with commentaries in several talmudic tractates. He also corresponded extensively, as did his predecessors and successors, replying to inquiries in the Bible, Talmud, law, prayer and worship, faith and reason and other subjects. From his responsa it can be concluded that he sought to interpret the Aggada rationally, eliminating the anthropomorphisms, and characterizing some miraculous incidents as dreams or visions of the mind's eye. He emphasized that one cannot rely on Aggada alone. His comparative broad-mindedness is illustrated by his request of aid from a Christian patriarch in the explanation of some biblical words.

By the end of the tenth century the Orient, generally speaking, yielded to the Spanish-Jewish center and the Franco-German Jewish communities, and the stream of halakic compositions continued in the West. However, on our way from the older to the newer homes of Jewish culture, we must linger with the North African settlement of Kairouan where, since the tenth century, a prosperous and intellectually alert Jewish community was in existence. Home of scholars in various fields, such as medicine, astronomy, philosophy and philology, its renown rests on its great Talmudists. Outstanding among them was Nissim ben Jacob, who flourished in the eleventh century. One of his major works, written in Arabic, is *The Key to the Locks of the Talmud*. Covering the entire Talmud, its aim was to shed light on indefinite and unsupported statements in this vast compendium by quoting the support and proof from where it may be found and by citing the *locus classicus* of all the Halakas that are stated elsewhere in the Talmud as accepted truths. A considerable portion of this voluminous work is still extant. His other major work, *A Secret Scroll,* is a compilation in Hebrew and Arabic of discussions of halakic and aggadic matter in Rabbinic literature. This work enjoyed wide circulation. Nissim also left us an interesting work which plainly ascribes its origin to the influence of Arabic literature. Its probable title was *Stories of the Sages, Being a Worthy Compilation for Comfort*. In the Introduction we are told that it was written for his father-in-law when the latter lost a son. Its purpose was to provide a book of Jewish content in place of the writings of "heretics," that is, Moslems, which his father-in-law would have read. It belongs to a type of literature which is known in Arabic by the name of "Comfort After Distress," and was calculated to distract people in their hour of sorrow. It is the popular counterpart of a more serious class of consolation literature which was produced by Jews, Christians and Moslems alike in the Middle Ages.

In Spain, the versatile Samuel Ha-Nagid (d. 1056),[11a] son-in-law of the preceding, statesman, poet and philologist, also excelled in talmudic studies. He is the author of an Arabic *Introduction to the Talmud* of which a considerable fragment is available in a Hebrew version. In this section he defines various technical terms and their implications and also establishes principles to determine whose opinion is to be accepted in case of controversy. It is evident that the Introduction was marked by a systematic and scientific approach. He also compiled a Code, which he called *Major Laws*, as a token of gratitude to God for having delivered him from his hostile captor. Too little is known of the work to enable us to characterize it, but in his poem, in which he tells us of his resolve to undertake this labor, he declares that it is his purpose to confound the Karaites. He also states there that Hai Gaon's works will be his chief guide.

The outstanding eleventh-century scholar is Isaac ben Jacob al-Fasi (d. 1103), but his main work is in Hebrew and Aramaic. His legacy in Arabic consists of some responsa and elucidations. The same is true of Joseph ibn Migas, for, although he also achieved great fame, his Arabic writings consist only of some responsa.

However, all these men are overshadowed by the truly gigantic achievements in Halaka[12a] of Moses ben Maimon, or Maimonides (d. 1204). Possessed of a vast erudition and an extraordinarily logical mind, he made an inestimably great contribution to Halaka. His first major work, chronologically, is a commentary on the complete Mishna, which he compiled while still a young man. His method of explanation is by the use of paraphrase. In each small unit—or Mishna, as it is called—he defines the difficult words and then summarizes its contents. Sometimes the definitions are woven into the paraphrase. In addition to the lucidity of the interpretation, evident throughout, and particularly in the order of *Toharot* (Laws of Cleanliness), his work is remarkable for the introductions and digressions of which there are several. It begins with a lengthy preface on the place of the Mishna in the Oral Law and on the plan followed by Rabbi Judah, the compiler of the Mishna, in the arrangement of the material. Besides this relevant matter it contains a statement on the author's views regarding the objectives of the world's creation and his assumption that all creation was meant to serve the intellectually and morally superior. He has brief introductions to the various tractates, and occasional notes within the body of the tractate in which he strives to put the reader in a position to understand the discussion in the text, a very helpful device in view of the practice of the Mishna to plunge into a subject in the belief that the reader is equipped to follow. To the ethical tractate of *Abot*, Maimonides wrote a lengthier preface in which he stated his views of the soul, its aspects, and the ethical and psychological principles that ought to guide an individual's life. Sometimes, as in the case of the chapter in the tractate of Sanhedrin which lists those who are and those who are not deserving of a portion in the world to come, he also prefaced an introduction on the subject, and, in the course of it, stated the thirteen articles of faith that are incumbent on the Jew. These, despite vigorous opposition, became virtually the accepted creed of the Jewish people.

Maimonides's greatest work in Halaka is his *Mishne Torah*, a compendium of the entire body of Jewish Law, both the part that is always operative and applicable and the part that is pertinent only in a Jewish state, or in Palestine, or when the Temple is in existence. This work, however, was written in Hebrew, the only one of his major works in that language. But he prepared a kind of outline of it in Arabic, which is known by its Hebrew name of *Sefer Ha-Mizvot*. Its purpose is to list the 613 laws that are traditionally regarded as Sinai-given. Before listing them, he enters into a lengthy discussion of the correct method in selecting the laws that properly form part of the 613. He points out errors and inconsistencies in the lists of his predecessors, stressing particularly the need to discriminate between a Mosaic and a Rabbinic ordinance. The work is characterized by the same strict logic that is evident in all his writings.

From the sketch of Maimonides's halakic writings we turn to consider important epistles left by him and by his father. The latter is the author of a pious and warm *Letter of Comfort* to the many Jews in the Moslem world who, as a result of the grievous persecutions by the Almohades in the middle of the twelfth century, were troubled and almost despaired of redemption. In the epistle, Maimon emphasizes that the promise which God made, supported as it is by the Bible and, notably, by the prophecy of Moses, whom the author characterizes in the most glorifying and adulatory terms, will most certainly be fulfilled. In connection with his exhortation he offers an edifying interpretation of Psalm 90, and recommends it as reading for those who are in difficulty.

From Maimonides's pen we possess a letter addressed to the same circle of readers, but more practical in its purpose and significance. He was deeply angered by the verdict of a contemporary Rabbi who ruled that crypto-Jews were apostates from Judaism. He felt rightly that the psychological effect of this ruling on the victims of the persecution would be disastrous, and he undertook to refute it. In his tract he makes a fine distinction between genuine and apparent conversion, and between the outward acceptance of Christianity and that of Islam. He offers the Jews sound advice to do everything possible to rid themselves of the duplicity by leaving the country, but at the same time he is passionate in his encouragement to the Marranos and in his desire to allay their fears.

Another writing, known as the *Epistle to Yemen*, also deals with persecution, this time in Arabia Felix. The contention of a converted Jew that Islam superseded the Mosaic dispensation, and the claim of another individual that he was the Messiah confused the Yemenite Jews and made a difficult life more difficult. Again Maimonides stepped in to bolster up failing spirits, to restore reason to well-meaning enthusiasts, and to keep alive in every Jew's heart the faith that he was following the right road, and the hope that salvation was not far.

Family talent was not exhausted by Maimon and his illustrious son. Abraham, the son of Moses, wrote a commentary on the Pentateuch, and a compendious work on Judaism, its principles, character, requirements and rewards. David, the son of Abraham, compiled a very readable commentary on the *Ethics of the Fathers*.

At least passing notice should be taken of a prayer book arranged by the indefatigable Saadia Gaon. In his usual manner he converted even this task into an important contribution. It comprises the laws of prayer in general, the regulations for the special occasions of the year, the ordinary prayers for private and public recitation, and a considerable body of liturgical poetry by him and by others. All this adds up to a very impressive performance, which is enhanced by the independence of mind that Saadia displays here as elsewhere.

A unique representative in Jewish literature of a genre which is extremely common in Arabic is found in a work produced by the renowned poet Moses ibn Ezra. As its florid Arabic title is a little hard to render, we may identify it by the title given it in its recent Hebrew translation: *The Poetry of Israel.* In response to a request for information, the author discusses such topics as the natural propensity of the Arabs toward poetry, the reason for the superiority of Spanish-Jewish poetry to that of other Jews, and the history of Hebrew poetry. His longest chapter is devoted to a discussion of the art of Hebrew poetry. In it he lists the various devices for enhancing the aesthetic appeal of verse and illustrates them by example from the Bible and later works. In this manner, as indicated previously, ibn Ezra displays an appreciation of the literary beauty of the Bible, which was generally overlooked until modern times. The charm of the work lies in its rambling, informal and intimate style, which puts the reader at ease. Ibn Ezra does not hesitate to digress, whether for the length of a chapter, as in his essay on the credibility of dreams, or for shorter stretches. This style of writing, generally known as *Adab,* is a very prominent feature of Arabic literature.

It is in the field of philosophy or, more correctly, religious philosophy or theology that the spirit of Judeo-Arabic literature reveals itself most fully. For one thing, the concern with the problems that form the substance of theological speculation marks a new departure. There was, it is true, Philo in Alexandria who wrote on philosophy. There are, it is true, numerous questions touched on in Rabbinic literature which properly belong to the realm of theology. But Philo's work and conclusions were not directly absorbed into the stream of Jewish thinking even if its influence may be discovered in one Rabbinic statement or another. Philo's work was not sufficiently rooted in Jewish lore, for his knowledge of that lore was deficient, so that extrinsically, let alone intrinsically, it had the appearance of an alien product.[13a] And the Rabbinic manner of dealing with its problems, by finding its support in a biblical verse, or reconciling two seemingly contradictory verses, however definitely it may represent an earnest desire to understand a certain problem or to solve a certain difficulty, cannot be called formal theology. Nor can the mystical speculations that were influenced by Gnosticism be regarded as theology, even if they concerned themselves with the celestial sphere, God and His throne, or the angels. The theological literature that was produced in the period under consideration is the effect of factors which played a major role in that period, characterized by qualities inherent in it, and permeated by an attitude peculiar to it.

Basically the impact that brought about this theological activity came from Greek and Oriental philosophy. The Jews, however, became conscious of this influence in the Moslem milieu and in an Arabic version. Within this milieu they discovered not only some of the original writings of Plato and Aristotle with their Neoplatonic commentators, but also the clash and the consequent compromise evolved in the Christian church; the polemics between the Christians and the Moslems, or between Oriental religions and the Moslems; the questionings and the doubts within the Moslem world; the rational, antireligious challenge and attacks by various people; the anti-Jewish arguments from several quarters; and certain centrifugal, disruptive tendencies which had developed in the Jewish community under these several influences. As a result, the theological or philosophical inquiries and analyses that abound in Judeo-Arabic may be reasonably regarded not as a luxury but as a necessity. Of course, it may not have been a necessity for those who remained entirely unaffected by the lively discussions and disputations, but it was a necessity for those who felt the challenge, either in their own lives or in the lives of fellow Jews whom they wished to set aright.

For purpose of simplification it is best to classify the Jewish philosophic writings, like their Moslem parallels, into three categories. One of these is known as Kalam.[14a] Its underlying physical premise is that all existence is composed of atoms, which form the substance, characterized by certain properties, which are called accidents. The latter are constantly changing since their duration is only momentary. As no object can be conceived without its properties and these are constantly created, it follows that all existence must have been created, and in this way it establishes creation. It further argues that this created world must have been fashioned by an outside force, namely, God. Among the Jewish philosophers who employed the system of Kalam, not all adopt the atomic theory. The most notable among them, Saadia Gaon, does not incline to it, preferring a variety of the Aristotelian conception of matter and form. They all, however, share in common the view that God's existence is proved by establishing the fact of creation and thus necessitating a creator. The Jewish philosophers, following the Mutazilites, one of the two schools of Moslem Kalam, are inclined to deny that God possesses attributes which stand in the same relation to Him as do properties to substances. Again, like their Moslem models, they devote much attention and space to God's justice, discussing under this heading revelation and prophecy, reward and punishment, good and evil, freedom of the will, the problem of the suffering of the righteous, and so forth. The best known work of this type is the *Book of Beliefs and Doctrines* by Saadia Gaon. He accounts for his composition of the book by explaining that as a result of the philosophic currents, doubts and perplexities and criticism have been engendered in the minds of many Jews, which threaten their loyalty to the faith. He defines our sources of knowledge, counting, in addition to the three channels of perceptual, conceptual and rationally necessary, also historical, or information reported from others. This last means, by the aid of which, as is known, so much of our knowledge is attained, serves Saadia to confirm the other source of truth, revelation. For, although he is convinced of the divine character of the Bible, and also of the complete identity of true revelation and reason, he is scientist enough to seek to demonstrate the veracity of the tradition regarding revelation, so that it might not be challenged on the basis of method. Moreover, he is rationalist enough, despite his unshaken faith in the truth of the Bible, to concede that whenever the biblical text contradicts reason the text is to be interpreted so as to obviate that contradiction.

His method in elucidating the verities of the Jewish faith in the light of reason is on two levels. In the case of a large part of the Jewish creed, he works on the assumption that it is rationally demonstrable. In this manner he proves, for example, that reason compels the belief in creation, in the existence and unity of God, in revelation, in reward and punishment, and in freedom of the will. In the case of some specifically religious articles of faith, such as the purely traditional laws, the graphic description of the procedure in the world beyond, the resurrection, Messianic times and the like, he feels it his task to prove that they are not contrary to reason. It is interesting to note that Saadia succeeds in preserving the entire religious legacy, even to details which are really incidental, from the attack of rationalism.

There were other able Kalam theologians among both Rabbanites and Karaites, with more or less original contributions. But while among the latter Kalam remained the accepted system to the end of the philosophic writing activity, Rabbanite philosophers turned from it to other systems, to Neoplatonism and to Aristotelianism with Neoplatonic coloring.

In the view of Neoplatonic philosophy, the cardinal difficulty is that of reconciling the composite, corruptible world, in which evil and wickedness inhere, with its Creator, the perfect and unique God. Its basic principle, formulated in order to resolve that difficulty, is emanation, that is, the doctrine that the entire universe, including the sublunar world, stems from God not by an act of creation but by a series of evolutions. God, as it were, separated part of Himself from Himself, without however, diminishing Himself in any way, and this part, in turn, evolved another from itself, and the next as well, and the next, until the celestial, as well

as the terrestrial, world came into being. Taken over by some Jewish philosophers, it confronted them with the task of integrating this conception
with the Jewish doctrine. The work of Philo, the first-century Neoplatonist, who, in his Greek writings, sought to identify the Jewish and the
philosophic teachings, left little or no effect on Jewish thinking except,
perhaps, through indirect channels. Medieval thinkers who favored this
view were compelled to find their own solutions. The celebrated Jewish
physician Isaac ben Solomon Israeli (d. *c.* 950), for example, made room
for the belief in creation by apparently excluding the terrestrial world
from the system of emanations and regarding it as an outcome of a *fiat*
by God.

On the other hand, the most important and profound Jewish Neoplatonist, Solomon ben Judah ibn Gabirol (d. *c.* 1050),[15a] the renowned
poet and ethical writer, whose philosophic work *The Fountain of Life,*
originally written in Arabic, is extant only in a Latin translation, was
evidently so firmly convinced of his view of the universe that he made
almost no concession to Jewish beliefs, but chose rather to write philosophy
pure and simple with no effort at reconciliation and no utilization of
alleged proof from biblical or Rabbinic texts. Believing that matter,
which he defined as that aspect of an object on which the form is impressed,
underlies every existing thing, he assumed the existence of Universal
Matter. Parallel to it, he postulated the existence of Universal Form,
which is what distinguishes one object from another. This dualism which,
in his view, extends from the lowest to the highest entities in the universe,
could not be accounted for by the usual Neoplatonic explanation that as the
emanations receded further from their source they became more composite,
coarser, more material and corruptible. Since, in his opinion, matter is at
least as noble as form, and is found in the celestial and in the intellectual
worlds, he was obliged to trace both to God, their primary source. As he
did not resort to creation, he endeavored to obviate the difficulty by
assuming an intermediate force between God and the world. This force,
which he calls the Will, he defines but vaguely (perhaps, as a statement
in his *Fountain of Life* has been understood, because he discussed it
separately in a no longer existing work), and students are perplexed as
to its nature and to its capacity to serve as the source of both matter and
form. However, notwithstanding some difficulties in his system he is
acknowledged by modern scholars as an original and deep thinker.
Although among Jewish philosophers his theories did not spread widely,
owing to the domination of Aristotelianism among them, he exerted a
far-reaching influence on Christian theologians such as William of
Auvergne and Duns Scotus, who adhered to his views, and even on
opponents such as Albertus Magnus and Thomas Aquinas.

Ibn Gabirol is also the author of a popular and none too profound ethical work, *On the Improvement of the Qualities of the Soul*. Starting with the assumption that physically man is the most harmonious of all creatures, and intellectually he is on a par with the angels, he teaches that man, a microcosm, should strive to preserve in the exercise of his qualities the same harmony which is so evident in his counterpart, the macrocosm. In an original, if forced, distribution of ten cardinal virtues and ten cardinal faults among the five senses, four to each, he urges control and discipline of these, counseling the practice of the Aristotelian golden mean. The work abounds in biblical citations, as also in sayings of Greek philosophers. Of the latter, ibn Gabirol compiled a collection called *The Choice of Pearls*, which enjoyed much popularity.

Bahya ben Joseph ibn Pakudah (d. *c.* 1100), author of the *Duties of the Heart*, is correctly described as a religious thinker rather than as a philosopher. Philosophically, as evident from his proof of the existence of God, he stands on Kalam ground. In his ideals, however, and the means to attain them, he is firmly rooted in Jewish tradition, although he is also beholden to Neoplatonism and to Moslem asceticism, which is itself deeply colored by the latter. The ideal he urges is the attainment of the stage in which the individual experiences a love of God. It is reached when man has realized God's greatness and providence, on the one hand, and man's insignificance and helplessness, on the other. The means required to reach that are given in the chapters of the book and their contents can be surmised from the headings, which include God's unity, consideration of creation, trust in God, humility, penitence, love of God and others. Bahya's work in its Hebrew version has become one of the most popular Jewish books and was studied by Jews even in cultural centers where philosophy did not gain a foothold.

Although certain Neoplatonic influences may be discovered in his system of philosophy, the most beloved medieval Jewish poet, Judah Ha-Levi (d. *c.* 1140), is the most independent and original thinker of the Jewish-Arabic period.[16a] Like his older contemporary in the Moslem world, Abu Hamid al-Ghazali, he was aware of the inadequacy of metaphysical reasoning, and, in his book called *Al Khazar* with its subtitle, the "Arguments and Proofs in Behalf of the Disparaged Religion," he followed another road. Ha-Levi was far from being an antirationalist. On the contrary, to the extent to which he believed its reasoning valid, he utilized the method and conclusions of philosophy. Moreover, it was his purpose to make his own doctrine rationally demonstrable. But he objected to the position taken by philosophy on matters which, in his mind, were within the domain of religion and hence superrational. He did not feel that its evidence for the existence of God was adequate. He resented its conception of God as an inactive, disinterested force, and its indifference to religious works or to the relative validity of one religion as over against another. He disagreed entirely with the conceit of philosophers that by their efforts or methods they could attain the rank of prophecy, or the true knowledge of God, and the bliss which that elevated state bestows on man. The precious gifts that living with God brings to man are acquired not by man's intellect but by knowing and doing what God has taught. The basic capacity to lead such a life is bestowed by Him. It is "a Divine matter," as Ha-Levi calls it, a special talent or quality which God grants. Historically, Ha-Levi finds, following the story of the Bible, the "Divine matter" became the heritage of Israel. Moreover, Ha-Levi, alone among medieval Jewish philosophers, regards Palestine as an essential factor in the destiny of Israel. It is the only land where Israel, endowed with the Divine matter, can, in an almost biological sense, grow and prosper, in the same way as fruits and vegetables will grow only in the appropriate soil and climate. This special quality of the Jewish people is what gained for them the revelation of God and the rank of prophecy. The revelation on Mt. Sinai, an undoubted fact, as judged by medieval standards of historical knowledge, is at once the firmest proof of the existence of God, the most valid evidence of the election of Israel, and the clearest statement of the correct and only method of attaining the coveted degree of God's favor and love. Thus, in Ha-Levi's view, the Jewish religion as it was developed and practiced by the Rabbis, rather than any philosophy, is the proved way to follow, and the Jewish people, rather than any self-appointed group of elect individuals, are humanity's most privileged species. Their present sad state is due to their sins and, particularly, to their failure to return to the appropriate soil when the opportunity was afforded. It is significant that the Jewish spokesman (the book is in the form of a dialogue between a pagan king who is eventually converted to Judaism and a representative of the Jewish faith) concludes the discussion with the decision to settle in Palestine, so as to find for himself the proper place in which he can best live the fullest Jewish life. Because of its religious fervor and its passionate defense of Israel and its Law, the book enjoyed tremendous popularity among the Jews.

Medieval Aristotelianism and Neoplatonism were not so sharply divided as in ancient times. The latter, though it postulated the emanation of the entire universe from God, recognized a dualism of matter and form in the sublunar world and, in the philosophy of ibn Gabirol, this dualism is evident in the entire universe. Aristotle's teachings, on the contrary, were suffused with a strong Neoplatonic coloring because, through a bibliographic error, part of a work by the Neoplatonist Plotinus was accepted as a writing of Aristotle. As a result, medieval Aristotelianism also speaks of emanation, and the dualism that is so fundamental in the master's teachings is at first confined to the terrestrial world, and is no longer a universal principle. It also considers the bliss that comes from a union with God rather than from a knowledge of God, as the goal of man.

Yet certain differences remained or became more emphasized. The dualism of matter and form, as the two extreme poles of existence, was much more prominent in Aristotelianism, and eventually matter was excluded from the process of emanation. Not only God, pure form, and the source of all form, is eternal and pre-existent, but also pure, formless matter. In Aristotelianism, one could talk with even less justice than in Neoplatonism of an act of creation, in view of the eternal coexistence of both matter and form. Aristotelianism further taught that God is Thought thinking Itself, creating the problem of what God knows of the world. The soul was regarded by it as the form of the body rather than an emanation of the Universal soul of Neoplatonism, and immortality became a more difficult problem. The theory of knowledge, too, although influenced by the Neoplatonist view of the action of the Active Intellect on a passive human mind, regained much of Aristotle's contention that it is dependent on perceptual knowledge and the abstraction of the latter, giving a new importance to logic and to natural philosophy.

Moreover, in the problem facing medieval Moslem and Jewish philosophers, the reconciliation of philosophy and religion, Aristotelianism proved to be a formidable system to bend and adapt. For despite the apparent similarity between reason and faith in their recognition of God, of purpose in the Universe, of a variety of immortality, of a discipline to which man must subject himself, the divergences nevertheless remained distinct. The God of Aristotle, even in his medieval definition, is most impersonal and inactive; the philosopher's purpose of the Universe is the result of a natural order which necessarily proceeds from certain eternally functioning laws, and is not subject to any direct control or voluntary regulation; its immortality a vague abstraction in place of the richly colored belief of religion; its discipline an intellectual rather than a moral system. It left little room for prophecy or revelation; it had no need of what were called traditional, or revealed, laws. In general, it was intellectual, rational, rigid and antagonistic to the irrational, romantic and intuitive, which religion brings with it.

Of the two outstanding Jewish Aristotelians, Abraham ibn Daud (d. c. 1180) did not achieve great importance because he was justly overshadowed by his superior successor Maimonides. Although ibn Daud justified the composition of the book *The Noble Faith* as a solution to the issue of the freedom of the will, he does not treat the latter more prominently than other philosophic problems. He gives a lengthy exposition of the physical world in preparation for the proof of the existence of God, and of the psychological world as background for the proof of the belief in immortality. He adopts the Aristotelian argument in proof of the existence of the First Cause, but for him, as for Moslem Aristotelians, it is not only the first cause of motion, but also the first cause of existence, and God the Creator. The contradiction between this and the theory of universal emanation, superimposed upon Aristotelianism, he solves by rejecting the latter, because it does not fit his Judaism; yet he adopts some of the teachings of emanation, such as the development of the terrestrial world out of the superlunar. In his teachings regarding the soul, he argues, like his Moslem predecessor ibn Sina, that, although it may be regarded as the form of the human body, the postulate that the form perishes with the object does not apply to it. It is obviously an independent, immaterial force in the body, and as such, immortal even if the body is mortal. This immortality, however, is limited to the intellectual part of the soul, which receives its knowledge from the Active Intellect. Its highest degree is prophecy, but it is unique in that it receives knowledge concerning the future. He goes even further and sees in prophecy, contrary to its apparently natural origin, a mission from God by which He instructs the less gifted, and even limits this gift to Israel and to Palestine. He predicates complete freedom of the will for man, and obviates the difficulty of accepting this freedom in the light of God's omniscience by limiting God's foreknowledge just as His omnipotence is limited from including human actions. In his ethical teachings, he naturally identifies the doctrines of Plato and Aristotle, which were joined by medieval philosophers, with the teachings of the Torah. While, in Aristotelian fashion, the knowledge of the celestial world is the goal of man, his main ideal is to know God, and through knowledge to gain the love of God, which is the highest happiness of man.

By his comprehensive work in philosophy called *Guide for the Perplexed*, and by the dominant position he held in Jewish and in general philosophy for the three centuries following his, Maimonides came to be recognized as the outstanding medieval Jewish thinker.[17a] While he assumed as fully as his predecessor that philosophy and religion teach the same truth, he was far more conscious than ibn Daud of the disagreements of the two sources of truth, much more conscientious in threshing the difficulties out, and much more desirous of arriving at a valid synthesis. He opens his work, which is divided into three parts, with a penetrating analysis of words and phrases in the Bible which at first glance are anthropomorphic and anthropopathic. He disposes of them by predicating that such expressions, when applied to God, have a different meaning, and that their purport is to indicate the effect of God's work or providence in the Universe. From this he proceeds to a keen study of the vexing question of God's attributes, and takes the position that whereas we have the right to describe God by adjectives which indicate our reactions to Him, such as merciful, sovereign and the like, we have no right to apply to God any term which will imply that a certain characteristic is inherent in Him. He is so singularly One, so uniquely Himself, that any statement regarding His essence impugns His Oneness. The best we can do is to speak of Him negatively or to

understand that when we say anything positive of Him we merely mean to
imply that He is not the opposite. When we say, for example, that He is
existent, we assert that He is not nonexistent, not that His essence possesses
the attribute of existence. What it really amounts to is that all of God's
attributes are really He, and not distinguishable from Himself. The
concept, however, is so difficult to understand that Maimonides justly
admits that we have no way of knowing God except in a moment of
illumination.

Only after the author has stated his views of God's attributes, and
critically refuted the philosophy of Kalam, does he turn to the question
of God's existence. His purpose is to make the proof of the existence of
God independent of the problem of the world's creation, so that if the
latter should prove to be nondemonstrable, the belief in the existence of
God would not thereby be affected. With this in view, he utilizes the
Aristotelian argument of the First Mover, Who is the cause of all motion
in the Universe, and is God. He also employs an argument from Moslem
Aristotelians, distinguishing between the universe which is possibly existent, that is, might or might not exist, and God, Who is necessarily
existent, implying that God is not only the Prime Mover, but also the
First Cause of the Universe. By these proofs Maimonides establishes
God's existence, simplicity and eternity. After developing the system
of emanations which came into Aristotelianism, he turns to the problem of
creation versus eternity. After a lengthy and intricate examination of the
pros and cons of both, he concludes that neither is demonstrably certain,
and therefore decides in favor of creation by bringing the religious belief
as an arbiter.

In his interpretation of prophecy, Maimonides shares with Aristotelian
philosophy the view that it results from the close natural relation between
the potential prophet and the Active Intellect. However, he recognizes
that a naturally endowed prophet requires God's Will before he can
prophesy, and that the figurative form in which prophecies are delivered
is the result of the imaginative faculty of the soul in addition to the intellectual. The prophet, although he is necessarily a philosopher, is
superior to the latter in that he succeeds in acquiring that knowledge of
God which comes through illumination alone. Maimonides also makes
an exception for Moses, declaring him to have been a prophet *sui generis*.
In this way he makes Moses unique and similarly his revelation or the
Torah. They are not higher degrees of certain types but single examples in
their fields. The purpose of prophecy is to bring a certain amount of
necessary information to the masses who are not equipped to acquire it
by their own initiative.

Maimonides, as we have seen, diverges from strict Aristotelianism in
the problems of creation and of prophecy. He also shows his independence
in the assertion that the miracles related in the Bible are true and that

they formed from eternity part of God's plan of the universe, and that God knows every human action. Maimonides at the same time preserves the freedom of the will by arguing that God's foreknowledge is essentially different from the human, and the apparent contradiction between freedom of the will and knowledge is not true of God. There are, however, important religious principles regarding which Maimonides follows the Aristotelian view more closely. He defines the rational soul as the part that acquires knowledge from the Active Intellect, and limits immortality to it alone. He relates providence to the same Active Intellect and man's share in providence in proportion to his share in the knowledge which can be acquired from it. Although he recognizes the importance of moral living, it is only a means to a higher end, the intellectual perfection toward which man should strive. This makes Torah and religious living not ends in themselves but means to a loftier goal. Maimonides makes a strong effort to find a rational explanation for the laws of the Torah, and endeavors to show that traditional laws whose reasons are not apparent are either pedagogical in aim, in that they strengthen certain moral qualities within us, or a reaction to the habits and practices of the times when the Torah was revealed, whether as a concession to them or a rejection of them. The highest perfection is that which can be reached by the philosopher. In a famous example of Maimonides in which he likens the Object of human striving, as he conceives it, to a king within a palace, and the several classes of people to groups who seek to stand before the king, the talmudists are not successful in entering the palace. It is the philosopher who comes closest to Him. It should be noted that this highest bliss is not a union with God in any mystical sense but a supreme state of knowledge and the love that results from it.

After the departure of Maimonides from Spain in 1148, as a result of the religious persecutions instituted by the fanatical Moslem sect known as the al-Muwahhidun (Almohades), he lived in the Orient and produced his greatest works there. His son Abraham compiled an ethical work called by the translator of a part of it *The Highway to Perfection,* and his disciple Joseph ibn Aknin is similarly the author of an ethical treatise *The Hygiene of the Soul.* From his grandson's pen we have an interesting commentary on the *Ethics of the Fathers.* Since then, down to the present, Judeo-Arabic literature has continued in lands where Arabic has remained the spoken and written language, but its significance, save for some few exceptions, is minor, and its importance is local.

In Spain, Arabic writing practically ceased among the Jews after Maimonides. The period of intense religious zeal was finally succeeded by sweeping victories celebrated by the Spanish Christians, who were bent on freeing their land from Moslem hold. The thirteenth century saw the almost complete liberation of Spain. With the fall of Islam and the domination of Latin and Spanish, Judeo-Arabic production virtually came to an end. Subsequent creations were usually written in Hebrew. It may be added in passing that Hebrew played a significant role at this stage in the transmission of Moslem lore to the Western world. Many works were rendered into Latin not from their original Arabic but from the Hebrew version, either prepared for Jewish consumption and utilized by a Latin translator, or deliberately made for retranslation by a man who did not know Latin for a man who did not know Arabic.

But the gradual elimination of Arabic as the vernacular of the Jews in Spain did not simultaneously result in the elimination of the written monuments from Jewish life in Christian countries, not to speak of the Moslem world. Even before that time came, an interest in Judeo-Arabic literature was aroused among the Jews in neighboring Provence and Italy. Already in the twelfth century we find Judah ibn Tibbon busily engaged in Provence in translating grammatical and philosophical books into Hebrew at the request of Jewish intellectuals. This activity was maintained in succeeding generations by members of his family and others in Spain, Provence and Italy, until a considerable portion of the Judeo-Arabic legacy became available in Hebrew. Many works were unfortunately neglected, and of these some were preserved in libraries as silent witnesses of an outlived era in Jewish life, and others irretrievably lost. We should not, however, overlook the numerous Hebrew works written by men who were still conversant with Arabic, in which more or less of the lore of the ancients is preserved. Several of the translations, particularly in philosophy and ethics, made their way even into the German-Polish center, which knew little of, and was interested even less in, the diversified Jewish productivity that had flourished in the Moslem environment. Indeed, it is an irony of fate that some originally Arabic works enjoyed a far better fortune than many, if not most, of the originally Hebrew works which did not deal with Halaka or exegesis. The reaction against secular literature that was especially prevalent in northern Europe and Poland hit belles-lettres hardest, and it is remarkable to record that poets and storytellers who deliberately preferred to write in Hebrew even when the vogue was to employ Arabic were the men whose creations were the least sought after, so that they became the easiest prey of the ravages of time and bookworms.

The work pursued so actively in Moslem Spain was taken up in the Hebrew language in Spain, Provence and Italy. In the first two centers until the expulsion, and in Italy even after, individuals continued to write poetry and literary prose and to study science and philosophy. This work maintained the tradition so nobly begun under the Moslems, and although, as was the case of the authors who functioned in Italy, the Renaissance that was experienced by that land unquestionably left its mark on Jewish creativity, the activity was the continuation of the literary life begun under Judeo-Arabic stimulation and, what is just as important, the subject-matter and even the artistic devices were clearly modeled after the products of that period. Above all, however, the noteworthy fact is that the interest in belles-lettres, in science, in philosophical and theological problems, and the general concern with the world beyond their own kept alive and furthered a stimulus begun in Spain and bequeathed to these lands. And just as in its day Jewish Spain was distinguished from other European Jewries by this diversity of culture,[18a] so Italian Jewry was alone in Europe in the cultivation and preservation of the secular studies. Northern and eastern Europe remained virtually as unaffected by either the legacy of Spain or its extension in Italy as it had been centuries before when southwestern Europe went through a rich development. Only when the European Enlightenment began to show its effects in central and eastern Europe, and Jews were stirred to ask more of life politically as well as culturally, did they develop an interest in secular literature.

On the threshold of this transformation stands the great eighteenth-century Italian-Jewish poet and mystic Moses Hayyim Luzzatto.[19a] Scholars are divided on whether to consider him the father of the new wave of cultural creativity, which was imminent in Germany, Austria and Russia, or the last of the era in Italy, whose beginnings go back to the twelfth century. This uncertainty regarding the individual carries a symbolic significance. One is hardly entitled to claim that modern Hebrew literature is indebted to Judeo-Arabic writings, but one can say with full justice that it is a link in the golden chain that was first forged in biblical times, and, after a long interruption, resumed in the Moslem world, whence it has continued steadily to our day. Indeed the contribution of the Judeo-Arabic period lies not alone in the rich legacy of works which exerted a profound influence on subsequent Jewish thought, but in that it kindled a light which, sometimes glowing brilliantly, sometimes merely flickering, continued to burn until it gained a new brilliance in modern Hebrew literature. Traveling by way of Provence, Italy and Holland, medieval literature found a fertile soil in eastern Europe, where Jewish life pulsated at its strongest in the nineteenth century, and there it once again began a rich and variegated activity which continues right to the present in several Jewish centers and, most notably, in Palestine.

NOTES

[1a Cf. Judah Goldin, "The Period of the Talmud (135 B.C.E.-1035 C.E.)," this work, Vol. I, pp. 189 ff.]

[2a Cf. below, Chap. 7, Hillel Bavli, "The Modern Renaissance of Hebrew Literature"; also below, Chap. 10, Yudel Mark, "Yiddish Literature."]

[³ᵃ Cf. Elias J. Bickerman, "The Historical Foundations of Postbiblical Judaism," this work, Vol. I, pp. 95 ff.]

[⁴ᵃ Cf. Cecil Roth, "The European Age in Jewish History (to 1648)," this work, Vol. I, pp. 242 f.]

[⁵ᵃ Cf. above, Chap. 3, Shalom Spiegel, "On Medieval Hebrew Poetry."]

[⁶ᵃ Cf. Goldin, *op. cit.*, pp. 205 f.]

[⁷ᵃ Cf. *ibid.*, pp. 199 f.]

[⁸ᵃ On the Sura Academy, cf. *ibid.*, pp. 183-184.]

[⁹ᵃ Cf. *ibid.*, pp. 165 f.]

[¹⁰ᵃ Cf. *ibid.*, pp. 152-153.]

[¹¹ᵃ Cf. Spiegel, *op. cit.*, pp. 103-104.]

[¹²ᵃ Cf. Goldin, *op. cit.*, pp. 163-164.]

[¹³ᵃ Cf. Alexander Altmann, "Judaism and World Philosophy: From Philo to Spinoza," this work, Vol. III, pp. 68 ff.; also above, Chap. 2, Ralph Marcus, "Hellenistic Jewish Literature," pp. 73 ff.]

[¹⁴ᵃ Cf. Altmann, *op. cit.*, pp. 79-80.]

[¹⁵ᵃ Cf. Spiegel, *op. cit.*, pp. 104-105.]

[¹⁶ᵃ Cf. Altmann, *op. cit.*, pp. 83-84; for his poetry see Spiegel, *op. cit.*, pp. 105-107.]

[¹⁷ᵃ Cf. Altmann, *op. cit.*, pp. 84 f.]

[¹⁸ᵃ Cf. Roth, *op. cit.*, pp. 232-233, 243.]

[¹⁹ᵃ Cf. Spiegel, *op. cit.*, pp. 111-112.]

BIBLIOGRAPHY

HALPER, BEN-ZION, "Jewish Literature in the Arabic Language" (Hebrew), in *Ha-Tekufah*, XXIII (Warsaw, 1925), 262-275; XXIV (Berlin, 1928), 359-388.

KARPELES, GUSTAV, *Geschichte der juedischen Literatur*. 3d ed. Berlin, 1920-1921. Vol. I, 398-448.

STEINSCHNEIDER, MORITZ, *Die arabische Literatur der Juden*. Frankfort a.M., 1902.

———, *Jewish Literature from the Eighth to the Eighteenth Century*. London, 1857. Pp. 59-203.

WAXMAN, MEYER, *A History of Jewish Literature from the Close of the Bible to Our Own Days*. New York, 1930-1941. Vol. I, pp. 155-375.

ZINBERG, ISRAEL, *Geschichte fun der literature bei Yiden* (Yiddish) (History of Literature among the Jews). Wilna, 1929, Vol. I.

ARNOLD, SIR THOMAS, and GUILLAUME, ALFRED (eds.), *The Legacy of Islam*. Oxford, 1931.

FRIEDLAENDER, ISRAEL, "Jewish Arabic Studies," in *Jewish Quarterly Review*, new series, I, pp. 183-215; II, pp. 481-516; III, pp. 235-300. Philadelphia, 1910-1912.

O'LEARY, DE LACY, *Arabic Thought and its Place in History*. London, 1922.

TRITTON, A. S., *The Caliphs and Their Non-Muslim Subjects*. London, 1930.

ADDENDUM

BLAU, J., *The Emergence and Linguistic Background of Judaeo-Arabic*. Oxford, 1965.

GOITEIN, S. D., *Jews and Arabs, Their Contacts Through the Ages*. New York, 1955.

GUTTMANN, J., *Philosophies of Judaism*. Translated by David W. Silverman. New York, 1964, pp. 47-208.

HALKIN, A. S., "The Judeo-Islamic Age," in *Great Ages and Ideas of the Jewish People*. Edited by Leo Schwarz. New York, 1956, pp. 215-263.

1949

CHAPTER 5

THE MYSTICAL ELEMENT IN JUDAISM

By Abraham J. Heschel

1. THE MEANING OF JEWISH MYSTICISM

There are people who take great care to keep away from the mists produced by fads and phrases. They refuse to convert realities into opinions, mysteries into dogmas, and ideas into a multitude of words, for they realize that all concepts are but glittering motes in a sunbeam. They want to see the sun itself. Confined to our study rooms, our knowledge seems to us a pillar of light; but when we stand at the door that opens out to the Infinite, we see how insubstantial is our knowledge. Even when we shut the door to the Infinite and retire to the narrow limits of notions our minds cannot remain confined. Again, to some people explanations and opinions are a token of wonder's departure, like a curfew after which they may not come abroad. In the cabbalists, the drive and the fire and the light are never put out.

Like the vital power in ourselves that gives us the ability to fight and to endure, to dare and to conquer, which drives us to experience the bitter and the perilous, there is an urge in wistful souls to starve rather than be fed on sham and distortion. To the cabbalists God is as real as life, and as nobody would be satisfied with mere knowing or reading about life, so they are not content to suppose or to prove logically that there is a God; they want to feel and to enjoy Him; not only to obey, but to approach Him. They want to taste the whole wheat of spirit before it is ground by the millstones of reason. They would rather be overwhelmed by the symbols of the inconceivable than wield the definitions of the superficial.

Stirred by a yearning after the unattainable, they want to make the distant near, the abstract concrete, to transform the soul into a vessel for the transcendent, to grasp with the senses what is hidden from the mind, to express in symbols what the tongue cannot speak, what the reason cannot conceive, to experience as a reality what vaguely dawns in intuitions. "Wise is he who by the power of his own contemplation attains to the perception of the profound mysteries which cannot be expressed in words."[1]

The cabbalist is not content with being confined to what he is. His desire is not only to *know* more than what ordinary reason has to offer, but to *be* more than what he is; not only to comprehend the Beyond but to concur with it. He aims at the elevation and expansion of existence. Such expansion goes hand in hand with the exaltation of all being.

The universe, exposed to the violence of our analytical mind, is being broken apart. It is split into the known and unknown, into the seen and unseen. In mystic contemplation all things are seen as one.[2] The mystic mind tends to hold the world together: to behold the seen in conjunction with the unseen, to keep the fellowship with the unknown through the revolving door of the known, "to learn the higher supernal wisdom from all" that the Lord has created and to regain the knowledge that once was in the possession of men and "that has perished from them."[3] What our senses perceive is but the jutting edge of what is deeply hidden. Extending over into the invisible, the things of this world stand in a secret contact with that which no eye has ever perceived. Everything certifies to the sublime, the unapparent working jointly with the apparent. There is always a reverberation in the Beyond to every action here: "The Lord made this world corresponding to the world above, and everything which is above has its counterpart below . . . and yet they all constitute a unity";[4] "there being no object, however small, in this world, but what is subordinate to its counterpart above which has charge over it; and so whenever the thing below bestirs itself, there is a simultaneous stimulation of its counterpart above, as the two realms form one interconnected whole."[5]

Opposed to the idea that the world of perception is the bottom of reality, the mystics plunge into what is beneath the perceptible. What they attain in their quest is more than a vague impression or a spotty knowledge of the imperceptible. "Penetrating to the real essence of wisdom . . . they are resplendent with the radiance of supernal wisdom."[6] Their eyes perceive things of this world, while their hearts reverberate to the throbbing of the hidden. To them the secret is the core of the apparent; the known is but an aspect of the unknown. "All things below are symbols of that which is above."[7] They are sustained by the forces that flow from hidden worlds. There is no particular that is detached from universal meaning. What appears to be a center to the eye is but a point on the periphery around another center. Nothing here is final. The worldly is subservient to the otherworldly. You grasp the essence of the here by conceiving its beyond. For this world is the reality of the spirit in a state of trance. The manifestation of the mystery is partly suspended, with ourselves living in lethargy. Our normal consciousness is a state of stupor, in which our sensibility to the wholly real and our responsiveness to the stimuli of the spirit are reduced. The mystics, knowing that we are involved in a hidden history of the cosmos, endeavor to awake from the drowsiness and apathy and to regain the state of wakefulness for our enchanted souls.

It is a bold attitude of the soul, a steadfast quality of consciousness, that lends mystic character to a human being. A man who feels that he is closely enfolded by a power that is both lasting and holy will come to know that the spiritual is not an idea to which one can relate his will, but a realm which can even be affected by our deeds. What distinguishes the cabbalist is the attachment of his entire personality to a hidden spiritual realm. Intensifying this attachment by means of active devotion to it, by meditation upon its secrets, or even by perception of its reality, he becomes allied with the dynamics of hidden worlds. Sensitive to the imperceptible, he is stirred by its secret happenings.

Attachment to hidden worlds holds the cabbalist in the spell of things more basic than the things that dominate the interest of the common mind. The mystery is not beyond and away from us. It is our destiny. "The fate of the world depends upon the mystery."[7]* Our task is to adjust the details to the whole, the apparent to the hidden, the near to the distant. The passionate concern of the cabbalist for final goals endows him with the experience of surpassing all human limitations and powers. With all he is doing he is crossing the borders, breaking the surfaces, approaching the lasting sources of all things. Yet his living with the infinite does not make him alien to the finite.

2. THE EXALTATION OF MAN

In this exalted world man's position is unique. God has instilled in him something of Himself. Likeness to God is the essence of man. The Hebrew word for man, *adam*, usually associated with the word for earth, *adamah*,[8] was homiletically related by some cabbalists to the expression, "I will ascend above the heights of the clouds; I will be like (*eddamme*) the Most High" (Is. 14:14). Man's privilege is, as it were, to augment the Divine in the world, as it is said, "ascribe ye strength unto God" (Ps. 68:35).

Jewish mystics are inspired by a bold and dangerously paradoxical idea that not only is God necessary to man but that man is also necessary to God, to the unfolding of His plans in this world. Thoughts of this kind are indicated and even expressed in various Rabbinic sources. "When Israel performs the will of the Omnipresent, they add strength to the heavenly power; as it is said, 'To God we render strength!'" When, however, Israel does not perform the will of the Omnipresent, they weaken—if it is possible to say so—the great power of Him Who is above; as it is written "Thou didst weaken the Rock that begot thee"[9] (Deut. 32:18). In the *Zohar* this idea is formulated in a more specific way. Commenting on the passage in Ex. 17:8, "Then came Amalek and fought with Israel in Rephidim," R. Simeon said: "There is a deep allusion in the name 'Rephidim.' This war emanated from the attribute of Severe Judgment and it was a war above and a war below . . . The Holy One, as it were, said:

'When Israel is worthy below, My power prevails in the universe; but
when Israel is found to be unworthy, she weakens My power above, and
the power of severe judgment predominates in the world.' So here,
'Amalek came and fought with Israel in Rephidim,' because the Israelites
were 'weak' [in Hebrew: *raphe*, which the *Zohar* finds in the name
'Rephidim'] in the study of the Torah, as we have explained on another
occasion."[10] Thus man's relationship to God should not be that of passive
reliance upon His Omnipotence but that of active assistance. "The impious
rely on their gods . . . the righteous are the support of God."[11] The
Patriarchs are therefore called "the chariot of the Lord."[12] The belief in
the greatness of man, in the metaphysical effectiveness of his physical acts,
is an ancient motif of Jewish thinking.

Man himself is a mystery. He is the symbol of all that exists. His life
is the image of universal life. Everything was created in the spiritual
image of the mystical man. "When the Holy One created man, He set in
him all the images of the supernal mysteries of the world above, and all
the images of the lower mysteries of the world below, and all are designed
in man, who stands in the image of God."[13] Even the human body is full of
symbolic significance. The skin, flesh, bones and sinews are but an outward
covering, mere garments,[14] even though "the substances composing man's
body belong to two worlds, namely, the world below and the world
above."[15] The 248 limbs and 365 sinews are symbols of the 613 parts of
the universe as well as of the 248 positive and 365 negative precepts of
the Torah. Man's soul emanates from an upper region where it has a
spiritual father and a spiritual mother, just as the body has a father and
mother in this world.[16] The souls that abide in our bodies are a weak
reflection of our upper souls, the seat of which is in heaven. Yet, though
detached from that soul, we are capable of being in contact with it. When
we pray we turn toward the upper soul as though we were to abandon
the body and join our source.

Man is not detached from the realm of the unseen. He is wholly involved in it. Whether he is conscious of it or not, his actions are vital to
all worlds, and affect the course of transcendent events. In a sense, by
means of the Torah, man is the constant architect of the hidden universe.
"This world was formed in the pattern of the world above, and whatever
takes place in this earthly realm occurs also in the realm above."[17] One
of the principles of the *Zohar* is that every move below calls forth a corresponding movement above.[18] Not only things, even periods of time are
conceived as concrete entities. "Thus over every day below is appointed a
day above, and a man should take heed not to impair that day. Now the
act below stimulates a corresponding activity above. Thus if a man does
kindness on earth, he awakens lovingkindness above, and it rests upon
that day which is crowned therewith through him. Similarly, if he per-

forms a deed of mercy, he crowns that day with mercy and it becomes his protector in the hour of need. So, too, if he performs a cruel action, he has a corresponding effect on that day and impairs it, so that subsequently it becomes cruel to him and tries to destroy him, giving him measure for measure."[19] Even what we consider potential is regarded as real and we may be held accountable for it: ". . . just as a man is punished for uttering an evil word, so is he punished for not uttering a good word when he had the opportunity, because he harms that speaking spirit which was prepared to speak above and below in holiness."[20]

The significance of great works done on earth is valued by their cosmic effects. Thus, e.g., "When the first Temple was completed another Temple was erected at the same time, which was a center for all the worlds, shedding radiance upon all things and giving light to all the spheres. Then the worlds were firmly established, and all the supernal casements were opened to pour forth light, and all the worlds experienced such joys as had never been known to them before, and celestial and terrestrial beings alike broke forth in song. And the song which they sang is the Song of Songs."[21]

Endowed with metaphysical powers man's life is a most serious affair; "if a man's lips and tongue speak evil words, those words mount aloft and all proclaim 'keep away from the evil word of so-and-so, leave the path clear for the mighty serpent.' Then the holy soul leaves him and is not able to speak: it is in shame and distress, and is not given a place as before . . . Then many spirits bestir themselves, and one spirit comes down from that side and finds the man who uttered the evil word, and lights upon him and defiles him, and he becomes leprous."[22]

Man's life is full of peril. It can easily upset the balance and order of the universe. "A voice goes forth and proclaims: 'O ye people of the world, take heed unto yourselves, close the gates of sin, keep away from the perilous net before your feet are caught in it!' A certain wheel is ever whirling continuously round and round. Woe to those whose feet lose their hold on the wheel, for then they fall into the Deep which is predestined for the evildoers of the world! Woe to those who fall, never to rise and enjoy the light that is stored up for the righteous in the world to come!"[23]

3. THE EN SOF AND HIS MANIFESTATIONS

Mystic intuition occurs at an outpost of the mind, dangerously detached from the main substance of the intellect. Operating as it were in no-mind's land, its place is hard to name, its communications with critical thinking often difficult and uncertain and the accounts of its discoveries not easy to decode. In its main representatives, the cabbala teaches that man's life can be a rallying point of the forces that tend toward God, that this world is charged with His presence and every object is a cue to His qualities. To the cabbalist, God is not a concept, a generalization, but a most specific reality; his thinking about Him full of forceful directness. But He who is "the Soul of all souls"[24] is "the mystery of all mysteries." While the cabbalists speak of God as if they commanded a view of the Beyond, and were in possession of knowledge about the inner life of God, they also assure us that all notions fail when applied to Him, that He is beyond the grasp of the human mind and inaccessible to meditation.[25] He is the *En Sof*, the Infinite, "the most Hidden of all Hidden."[26] While there is an abysmal distance between Him and the world, He is also called All. "For all things are in Him and He is in all things . . . He is both manifest and concealed. Manifest in order to uphold the all and concealed, for He is found nowhere. When He becomes manifest He projects nine brilliant lights that throw light in all directions. So, too, does a lamp throw brilliance in all directions, but when we approach the brilliance we find there is nothing outside the lamp. So is the Holy ancient One, the Light of all Lights, the most Hidden of all Hidden. We can only find the light which He spreads and which appears and disappears. This light is called the Holy Name, and therefore All is One."[27]

Thus, the "Most Recondite One Who is beyond cognition does reveal of Himself a tenuous and veiled brightness shining only along a narrow path which extends from Him. This is the brightness that irradiates all."[28] The *En Sof* has granted us manifestations of His hidden life: He had descended to become the universe; He has revealed Himself to become the Lord of Israel. The ways in which the Infinite assumes the form of finite existence are called *Sefirot*.[29] These are various aspects or forms of Divine action, spheres of Divine emanation. They are, as it were, the garments in which the Hidden God reveals Himself and acts in the universe, the channels through which His light is issued forth.

The names of the ten *Sefirot* are *Keter, Hokmah, Binah, Hesed, Geburah, Tiferet, Netsah, Hod, Yesod, Malkut*. The transition from Divine latency to activity takes place in *Keter*, the "supreme crown" of God. This stage is inconceivable, absolute unity and beyond description. In the following *Sefirot, Hogmah* and *Binah*, the building and creation of the cosmos as well as that which divides things begins. They are parallel emanations from *Keter*, representing the active and the receptive principle.

While the first triad represents the transition from the Divine to the spiritual reality, the second triad is the source of the moral order. *Hesed* stands for the love of God; *Geburah* for the power of justice manifested as severity or punishment. From the union of these emanates *Tiferet*, compassion or beauty of God, mediating between *Hesed* and *Geburah*, between the life-giving power and the contrary power, holding in check what would otherwise prove to be the excesses of love.

The next triad is the source of the psychic and physical existences—*Netsah* is the lasting endurance of God, *Hod* His majesty, and *Yesod* the stability of the universe, the seat of life and vitality. *Malkut* is the kingdom, the presence of the Divine in the world. It is not a source of its own but the outflow of the other *Sefirot*; "of itself lightless, it looks up to the others and reflects them as a lamp reflects the sun."[30] It is the point at which the external world comes in contact with the upper spheres, the final manifestations of the Divine, the *Shekinah*, "the Mother of all Living."[31]

The recondite and unapproachable Self of God is usually thought of as transcendent to the *Sefirot*. There is only a diffusion of His light into the *Sefirot*. The *En Sof* and the realm of His manifestations are "linked together like the flame and the coal," the flame being a manifestation of what is latent in the coal. In the process of the emanation, the transition from the Divine to the spiritual, from the spiritual to the moral, from the moral to the physical, reality takes place. The product of this manifestation is not only the visible universe but an endless number of spiritual worlds which exist beyond the physical universe in which we live. These worlds, the hidden cosmos, constitute a most complex structure, divided into various grades and forms which can only be described in symbols. These symbols are found in the Torah, which is the constitution of the cosmos. Every letter, word or phrase in the Bible not only describes an event in the history of our world but also represents a symbol of some stage in the hidden cosmos. These are the so-called *Raze Torah*, the mysteries, that can be discovered by the mystical method of interpretation.

The system of *Sefirot* can be visualized as a tree or a man or a circle, in three triads or in three columns. According to the last image the *Sefirot* are divided into a *right* column, signifying Mercy, or light, a *left* column, signifying Severity, the absence of light, and a *central* column, signifying the synthesis of the right and left. Each *Sefirah* is a world in itself, dynamic and full of complicated mutual relations with other *Sefirot*. There are many symbols by which each *Sefirah* can be expressed, *e.g.*, the second triad is symbolized in the lives of each of the three Patriarchs. The doctrine of *Sefirot* enables the cabbalists to perceive the bearings of God upon this world, to identify the Divine substance of all objects and events. It offers the principles by means of which all things and events can be interpreted as Divine manifestations.

The various parts of the day represent various aspects of Divine manifestation. "From sunrise until the sun declines westward it is called 'day,' and the attribute of Mercy is in the ascendant; after that it is called 'evening,' which is the time for the attribute of Severity . . . It is for this reason that Isaac instituted the afternoon prayer (*Minhah*), namely, to mitigate the severity of the approaching evening; whereas Abraham instituted morning prayer, corresponding to the attribute of mercy."[32]

The plurality into which the one Divine manifestation is split symbolizes the state of imperfection into which God's relation to the world was thrown. Every good deed serves to restore the original unity of the *Sefirot*, while on the other hand, "Sinners impair the supernal world by causing a separation between the 'Right' and the 'Left.' They really cause harm only to themselves, . . . as they prevent the descent of blessings from above . . . and the heaven keeps the blessings to itself." Thus the sinner's separation of the good inclination from the evil one by consciously cleaving to evil separates, as it were, the Divine attribute of Grace from that of Judgment, the Right from the Left.[33]

4. The Doctrine of the Shekinah

Originally there was harmony between God and His final manifestations, between the upper *Sefirot* and the tenth *Sefirah*. All things were attached to God and His power surged unhampered throughout all stages of being. Following the trespass of Adam, however, barriers evolved thwarting the emanation of His power. The creature became detached from the Creator, the fruit from the tree, the tree of knowledge from the tree of life, the male from the female, our universe from the world of unity, even the *Shekinah* or the tenth *Sefirah* from the upper *Sefirot*. Owing to that separation the world was thrown into disorder, the power of strict judgment increased, the power of love diminished and the forces of evil released. Man who was to exist in pure spiritual form as light in constant communication with the Divine was sunk into his present inferior state.

In spite of this separation, however, God has not withdrawn entirely from this world. Metaphorically, when Adam was driven out of Eden, an aspect of the Divine, the *Shekinah*, followed him into captivity.[34] Thus there is a Divine power that dwells in this world. It is the Divine Presence that went before Israel while they were going through the wilderness, that protects the virtuous man, that abides in his house and goes forth with him on his journeys, that dwells between a man and his wife.[35] The *Shekinah* "continually accompanies a man and leaves him not so long as he keeps the precepts of the Torah. Hence a man should be careful not to go on the road alone, that is to say, he should diligently keep the precepts of the Torah in order that he may not be deserted by the *Shekinah*, and so be forced to go alone without the accompaniment of the *Shekinah*."[36] The *Shekinah* follows Israel into exile and "always hovers over Israel like a mother over her children."[37] Moreover, it is because of Israel and its observance of the Torah that the *Shekinah* dwells on earth. Were they to corrupt their way, they would thrust the *Shekinah* out of this world and the earth would be left in a degenerate state.[38]

The doctrine of the *Shekinah* occupies a central place in the cabbala.

While emphasizing that in His essence "the Holy One and the *Shekinah* are One,"[39] it speaks of a cleavage, as it were, in the reality of the Divine. The *Shekinah* is called figuratively the *Matrona* (symbolized by the Divine Name *Elohim*) that is separated from the King (symbolized by the ineffable Name *Hashem*) and it signifies that God is, so to speak, involved in the tragic state of this world. In the light of this doctrine the suffering of Israel assumed new meaning. Not only Israel but the whole universe, even the *Shekinah*, "lies in dust"[40] and is in exile. Man's task is to bring about the restitution of the original state of the universe and the reunion of the *Shekinah* and the *En Sof*. This is the meaning of Messianic salvation, the goal of all efforts.

"In time to come God will restore the *Shekinah* to its place and there will be a complete union. 'In that day shall the Lord be One and His Name One' (Zech. 14:9). It may be said: Is He not now One? no; for now through sinners He is not really One. For the Matrona is removed from the King . . . and the King without the Matrona is not invested with His crown as before. But when He joins the Matrona, who crowns Him with many resplendent crowns, then the supernal Mother will also crown Him in a fitting manner. But now that the King is not with the Matrona, the supernal Mother keeps her crowns and withholds from Him the waters of the stream and He is not joined with her. Therefore, as it were, He is not one. But when the Matrona shall return to the place of the Temple and the King shall be wedded with her, then all will be joined together, without separation and regarding this it is written, 'In that day shall the Lord be One and His Name One.' Then there shall be such perfection in the world as had not been for all generations before, for then shall be completeness above and below, and all worlds shall be united in one bond."[41]

The restoration of unity is a constant process. It takes place through the study of the Torah, through prayer and through the fulfillment of the commandments. "The only aim and object of the Holy One in sending man into this world is that he may know and understand that *Hashem* (God), signifying the *En Sof*, is *Elohim* (*Shekinah*). This is the sum of the whole mystery of the faith, of the whole Torah, of all that is above and below, of the written and the oral Torah, all together forming one unity."[42] "When a man sins it is as though he strips the *Shekinah* of her vestments, and that is why he is punished; and when he carries out the precepts of the law, it is as though he clothes the *Shekinah* in her vestments. Hence we say that the fringes worn by the Israelites are, to the *Shekinah* in captivity, like the poor man's garments of which it is said, 'For that is his only covering, it is his garment for his skin, wherein he shall sleep.' "[43]

5. MYSTIC EXPERIENCE

The ultimate goal of the cabbalist is not his own union with the Absolute but the union of all reality with God; one's own bliss is subordinated to the redemption of all: "we have to put all our being, all the members of our body, our complete devotion, into that thought so as to rise and attach ourselves to the *En Sof,* and thus achieve the oneness of the upper and lower worlds."[44]

What this service means in terms of personal living is described in the following way:

Happy is the portion of whoever can penetrate into the mysteries of his Master and become absorbed into Him, as it were. Especially does a man achieve this when he offers up his prayer to his Master in intense devotion, his will then becoming as the flame inseparable from the coal, and his mind concentrated on the unity of the lower firmaments, to unify them by means of a lower name, then on the unity of the higher firmaments, and finally on the absorption of them all into that most high firmament. Whilst a man's mouth and lips are moving, his heart and will must soar to the height of heights, so as to acknowledge the unity of the whole in virtue of the mystery of mysteries in which all ideas, all wills and all thoughts find their goal, to wit, the mystery of *En Sof.*[45]

The thirst for God is colored by the awareness of His holiness, of the endless distance that separates man from the Eternal One. Yet, he who craves for God is not only a mortal being, but also a part of the Community of Israel, that is, the bride of God, endowed with a soul that is "a part of God." Shy in using endearing terms in his own name, the Jewish mystic feels and speaks in the plural. The allegory of the Song of Songs would be impertinent as an individual utterance, but as an expression of Israel's love for God it is among the finest of all expressions. "God is the soul and spirit of all, and Israel calls Him so and says: (My soul), I desire Thee in order to cleave to Thee and I seek Thee early to find Thy favor."[46]

Israel lives in mystic union with God and the purpose of all its service is to strengthen this union: "O my dove that art in the clefts of the rock, in the covert of the cliff" (Song of Sol. 2:14). The "dove" here is the Community of Israel, which like a dove never forsakes her mate, the Holy One, blessed be He. "In the clefts of the rock": these are the students of the Torah, who have no ease in this world. "In the covert of the steep place": these are the specially pious among them, the saintly and God-fearing, from whom the Divine Presence never departs. The Holy One, blessed be He, inquires concerning them of the Community of Israel, saying, "Let me see thy countenance, let me hear thy voice, for sweet is thy voice"; "for above only the voice of those who study the Torah is heard. We have learned that the likeness of all such is graven above before the Holy One, blessed be He, Who delights Himself with them every day and watches them and that voice rises and pierces its way through all firmaments until it stands before the Holy One, blessed be He."[47]

The concepts of the cabbala cannot always be clearly defined and consistently interrelated. As the name of Jewish mysticism, "cabbala" (lit.: "received lore"), indicates, it is a tradition of wisdom, supposed to have been revealed to elect Sages in ancient times and preserved throughout the generations by an initiated few. The cabbalists accept at the outset the ideas on authority, not on the basis of analytical understanding.

Yet the lips of the teachers and the pages of the books are not the only sources of knowledge. The great cabbalists claimed to have received wisdom directly from the Beyond. Inspiration and Vision were as much a part of their life as contemplation and study. The prayer of Moses: "Show me, I pray Thee, Thy glory" (Ex. 33:18) has never died in the hearts of the cabbalists. The conception of the goal has changed but the quest for immediate cognition remained. The Merkaba-mystics, following perhaps late prophetic traditions about the mysteries of the Divine Throne, were striving to behold the celestial sphere in which the secrets of creation and man's destiny are contained. In the course of the centuries the scope of such esoteric experiences embraced a variety of objectives. The awareness of the cabbalists that the place whereon they stood was holy ground kept them mostly silent about the wonder that was granted to them. Yet we possess sufficient evidence to justify the assumption that mystic events, particularly in the form of inner experiences, of spiritual communications rather than that of sense perceptions, were elements of their living. According to old Rabbinic teachings, there have always been Sages and saints upon whom the Holy Spirit rested, to whom wisdom was communicated from heaven by a Voice, through the appearance of the spirit of Elijah or in dreams. According to the *Zohar*, God reveals to the saints "profound secrets of the Holy Name which He does not reveal to the angels."[48] The disciples of Rabbi Simeon ben Yohai are called prophets, "before whom both supernal and terrestrial beings tremble in awe."[48a] Others pray that the inspiration of the Holy Spirit should come upon them.[49] The perception of the unearthly is recorded as an ordinary feature in the life of certain Rabbis. "When R. Hamnuna the Ancient used to come out from the river on a Friday afternoon, he was wont to rest a little on the bank, and raising his eyes in gladness, he would say that he sat there in order to behold the joyous sight of the heavenly angels ascending and descending. At each arrival of the Sabbath, he said, man is caught up into the world of souls."[50] Not only may the human mind receive spiritual illuminations; the soul also may be bestowed upon higher powers. "Corresponding to the impulses of a man here are the influences which he attracts to himself from above. Should his impulse be toward holiness, he attracts to himself holiness from on high and so he becomes holy; but if this tendency is toward the side of impurity, he draws down toward himself the unclean spirit and so becomes polluted."[51]

Since the time of the prophet Joel the Jews have expected that at the end of days the Lord would "pour out His spirit upon all flesh" and all men would prophesy. In later times, it is believed, the light of that revelation of mysteries could already be perceived.

The mystics absorb even in this world "something of the odor of these secrets and mysteries."[52] Significantly, the Torah itself is conceived as a living source of inspiration, not as a fixed book. The Torah is a voice that "calls aloud" to men;[53] she calls them day by day to herself in love . . . "The Torah lets out a word and emerges for a little from her sheath, and then hides herself again. But she does this only for those who understand and obey her. She is like unto a beautiful and stately damsel, who is hidden in a secluded chamber of a palace and who has a lover of whom no one knows but she. Out of his love for her he constantly passes by her gate, turning his eyes toward all sides to find her. Knowing that he is always haunting the palace, what does she do? She opens a little door in her hidden palace, discloses for a moment her face to her lover, then swiftly hides it again. None but he notices it; but his heart and soul, and all that is in him are drawn to her, knowing as he does that she has revealed herself to him for a moment because she loves him. It is the same with the Torah, which reveals her hidden secrets only to those who love her. She knows that he who is wise of heart daily haunts the gates of her house. What does she do? She shows her face to him from her palace, making a sign of love to him, and straightaway returns to her hiding place again. No one understands her message save he alone, and he is drawn to her with heart and soul and all his being. Thus the Torah reveals herself momentarily in love to her lovers in order to awaken fresh love in them."[54]

6. THE TORAH—A MYSTIC REALITY

The Torah is an inexhaustible esoteric reality. To enter into its deep, hidden strata is in itself a mystic goal. The Universe is an image of the Torah and the Torah is an image of God. For the Torah is "the Holy of Holies"; "it consists entirely of the name of the Holy One, blessed be He. Every letter in it is bound up with that Name."[55]

The Torah[55a] is the main source from which man can draw the secret wisdom and power of insight into the essence of things. "It is called Torah (lit.: showing) because it shows and reveals that which is hidden and unknown; and all life from above is comprised in it and issues from it."[56] "The Torah contains all the deepest and most recondite mysteries; all sublime doctrines both disclosed and undisclosed; all essences both of the

higher and the lower grades, of this world and of the world to come
are to be found there."[57] The source of wisdom is accessible to all, yet
only few resort to it. "How stupid are men that they take no pains to know
the ways of the Almighty by which the world is maintained. What prevents
them? Their stupidity, because they do not study the Torah; for if they
were to study the Torah they would know the ways of the Holy One,
blessed be He."[58]

The Torah has a double significance: literal and symbolic. Besides their
plain, literal meaning, which is important, valid and never to be overlooked, the verses of the Torah possess an esoteric significance, "compre-
hensible only to the wise who are familiar with the ways of the Torah."[59]
"Happy is Israel to whom was given the sublime Torah, the Torah of
truth. Perdition take anyone who maintains that any narrative in the
Torah comes merely to tell us a piece of history and nothing more! If
that were so, the Torah would not be what it assuredly is, to wit, the
supernal Law, the Law of truth. Now if it is not dignified for a king of
flesh and blood to engage in common talk, much less to write it down, is it
conceivable that the most high King, the Holy One, blessed be He, was
short of sacred subjects with which to fill the Torah, so that He had to
collect such commonplace topics as the anecdotes of Esau, and Hagar,
Laban's talks to Jacob, the words of Balaam and his ass, those of Balak,
and of Zimri, and such-like, and make of them a Torah? If so, why is it
called the 'Law of Truth?' Why do we read 'The Law of the Lord is
perfect . . . The testimony of the Lord is sure . . . The Ordinances of the
Lord are true . . . More to be desired are they than gold, yea, than much
fine gold' (Ps. 19:8-11). But assuredly each word of the Torah signifies
sublime things, so that this or that narrative, besides its meaning in and for
itself, throws light on the all-comprehensive Rule of the Torah."[60]

"Said R. Simeon: 'Alas for the man who regards the Torah as a mere
book of tales and everyday matters! If that were so, we, even we, could
compose a torah dealing with everyday affairs, and of even greater excellence. Nay, even the princes of the world possess books of greater worth
which we could use as a model for composing some such torah. The Torah,
however, contains in all its words supernal truths and sublime mysteries.
Observe the perfect balancing of the upper and lower worlds. Israel here
below is balanced by the angels on high, of whom it says: 'who makest
thine angels into winds' (Ps. 104:4). For the angels in descending on
earth put on themselves earthly garments, as otherwise they could not
stay in this world, nor could the world endure them.

"Now, if thus it is with the angels, how much more so must it be with the
Torah—the Torah that created them, that created all the worlds and is
the means by which these are sustained. Thus had the Torah not clothed
herself in garments of this world the world could not endure it. The

stories of the Torah are thus only her outer garments, and whoever looks upon that garment as being Torah itself, woe to that man—such a one will have no portion in the next world. David thus said: 'Open thou mine eyes, that I may behold wondrous things out of Thy law' (Ps. 119:18), to wit, the things that are beneath the garment. Observe this. The garments worn by a man are the most visible part of him, and senseless people looking at the man do not seem to see more in him than the garments. But in truth the pride of the garments is the body of the man, and the pride of the body is the soul. Similarly the Torah has a body made up of the precepts of the Torah, called *gufe torah* (bodies, main principles of the Torah), and that body is enveloped in garments made up of worldly narratives. The senseless people only see the garment, the mere narrations; those who are somewhat wise penetrate as far as the body. But the really wise, the servants of the most high King, those who stood on Mt. Sinai, penetrate right through to the soul, the root principle of all, namely to the real Torah. In the future the same are destined to penetrate even to the super-soul (soul of the soul) of the Torah . . ."[61]

How assiduously should one ponder over each word of the Torah, for there is not a single word in it which does not contain allusions to the Supernal Holy Name, not a word which does not contain many mysteries, many aspects, many roots, many branches! Where now is this "book of the wars of the Lord"? What is meant, of course, is the Torah, for as the members of the Fellowship have pointed out, he who is engaged in the battle of the Torah, struggling to penetrate into her mysteries, will wrest from his struggles an abundance of peace.[62]

7. THE MYSTIC WAY OF LIFE

A longing for the unearthly, a yearning for purity, the will to holiness, connected the conscience of the cabbalists with the strange current of mystic living. Being puzzled or inquisitive will not make a person mystery stricken. The cabbalists were not set upon exploring, or upon compelling the unseen to become visible. Their intention was to integrate their thoughts and deeds into the secret order, to assist God in undoing the evil, in redeeming the light that was concealed. Though working with fragile tools for a mighty end, they were sure of bringing about at the end the salvation of the universe and of this tormented world.

A new form of living was the consequence of the cabbala. Everything was so replete with symbolic significance as to make it the potential heart of the spiritual universe. How carefully must all be approached. A moral rigorism that hardly leaves any room for waste or respite resulted in making the cabbalist more meticulous in studying and fulfilling the precepts of the Torah, in refining his moral conduct, in endowing every-day actions with solemn significance. For man represents God in this world. Even the parts of his body signify Divine mysteries.

Everything a man does leaves its imprint on the world. "The Supernal Holy King does not permit anything to perish, not even the breath of the mouth. He has a place for everything, and makes it what He wills. Even a human word, yes, even the voice, is not void, but has its place and destination in the universe."[63] Every action here below, if it is done with the intention of serving the Holy King, produces a "breath" in the world above, and there is no breath which has no voice; and this voice ascends and crowns itself in the supernal world and becomes an intercessor before the Holy One, blessed be He. Contrariwise, every action which is not done with this purpose becomes a "breath" which floats about the world, and when the soul of the doer leaves his body, this "breath" rolls about like a stone in a sling, and it "breaks the spirit." The act done and the word spoken in the service of the Holy One, however, ascend high above the sun and become a holy breath, which is the seed sown by man in that world and is called *Zedakah* (righteousness) or (loving-kindness), as it is written: "Sow to yourselves according to righteousness" (Hos. 10:12). This "breath" guides the departed soul and brings it into the region of the supernal glory, so that it is "bound in the bundle of life with the Lord thy God" (I Sam. 25:29). It is concerning this that it is written: "Thy righteousness shall go before thee; the glory of the Lord shall be thy reward" (Is. 58:8). That which is called "the glory of the Lord" gathers up the souls of that holy breath, and this is indeed ease and comfort for them; but the other is called "breaking of spirit." Blessed are the righteous whose works are "above the sun" and who sow a seed of righteousness which makes them worthy to enter the world to come.[64]

Everything a man does leaves its imprint upon the world: his breath, thought, speech. If it is evil, the air is defiled and he who comes close to that trace may be affected by it and led to do evil. By fulfilling the Divine precepts man purifies the air and turns the "evil spirits" into "holy spirits." He should strive to spiritualize the body and to make it identical with the soul by fulfilling the 248 positive and 365 negative precepts which correspond to the 248 limbs and the 365 sinews of the human body. The precepts of the Torah contain "manifold sublime recondite teachings and radiances and resplendences,"[65] and can lift man to the supreme level of existence.

The purpose of man's service is to "give strength to God," not to attain one's own individual perfection. Man is able to stir the supernal spheres. "The terrestrial world is connected with the heavenly world, as the heavenly world is connected with the terrestrial one."[66] In fulfilling the good the corresponding sphere on high is strengthened; in balking it, the sphere is weakened. This connection or correspondence can be made to operate in a creative manner by means of *kawwanah* or contemplation of the mysteries of which the words and precepts of the Torah are the symbols. In order to grasp the meaning of those words or to fulfill the purpose of those precepts one has to resort to the Divine Names and Qualities which are invested in those words and precepts, the mystic issues to which they refer, or, metaphorically, the gates of the celestial mansion which the spiritual content of their fulfillment has to enter. Thus, all deeds—study, prayer and ceremonies—have to be performed not mechanically but while meditating upon their mystic significance.

Prayer is a powerful force in this service and a venture full of peril. He who prays is a priest at the temple that is the cosmos. With good prayer he may "build worlds," with improper prayer he may "destroy worlds." "It is a miracle that a man survives the hour of worship," the Baal Shem said. "The significance of all our prayers and praises is that by means of them the upper fountain may be filled; and when it is so filled and attains completeness, then the universe below, and all that appertains thereto, is filled also and receives completeness from the completion which has been consummated in the upper sphere. The world below cannot, indeed, be in a state of harmony unless it receives that peace and perfection from above, even as the moon has no light in herself but shines with the reflected radiance of the sun. All our prayers and intercessions have this purpose, namely, that the region from whence light issues may be invigorated; for then from its reflection all below is supplied."[67] "Every word of prayer that issues from a man's mouth ascends aloft through all firmaments to a place where it is tested. If it is genuine, it is taken up before the Holy King to be fulfilled, but if not it is rejected, and an alien spirit is evoked by it."[68] For example, "it is obligatory for every Israelite to relate the story of the Exodus on the Passover night. He who does so fervently and joyously, telling the tale with a high heart, shall be found worthy to rejoice in the *Shekinah* in the world to come, for rejoicing brings forth rejoicing; and the joy of Israel causes the Holy One Himself to be glad, so that He calls together all the Family above and says unto them: 'Come ye and hearken unto the praises which My children bring unto Me! Behold how they rejoice in My redemption!' Then all the angels and supernal beings gather round and observe Israel, how she sings and rejoices because of her Lord's own Redemption—and seeing the rejoicings below, the supernal beings also break into jubilation for that the Holy One possesses on earth a people so holy, whose joy in the Redemption of their Lord is so great and powerful. For all that terrestrial rejoicing increases the power of the Lord and His hosts in the regions above, just as an earthly king gains strength from the praises of his subjects, the fame of his glory being thus spread throughout the world."[69]

Worship came to be regarded as a pilgrimage into the supernal spheres, with the prayerbook as an itinerary, containing the course of the gradual ascent of the spirit. The essential goal of man's service is to bring about the lost unity of all that exists. To render praise unto Him is not the final purpose. "Does the God of Abraham need an exaltation? Is He not already exalted high above our comprehension? . . . Yet man can and must exalt Him in the sense of uniting in his mind all the attributes in the Holy Name, for this is the supremest form of worship."[70] By meditating upon the mysteries while performing the Divine precepts, we act toward unifying all the supernal potencies in one will and bringing about the union of the Master and the Matrona.

Concerning the verse in Ps. 145:18, "The Lord is nigh to all them that call upon Him, to all that call upon Him in truth," the *Zohar* remarks that the words "in truth" mean in possession of the full knowledge which enables the worshiper perfectly "to unite the letters of the Holy Name in prayer . . . On the achievement of that unity hangs both celestial and terrestrial worship . . . If a man comes to unify the Holy Name, but without proper concentration of mind and devotion of heart, to the end that the supernal and terrestrial hosts should be blessed thereby, then his prayer is rejected and all beings denounce him, and he is numbered with those of whom the Holy One said, 'When ye come to see my countenance, who hath required this from your hand, to tread my courts?' All the 'countenances' of the King are hidden in the depths of darkness, but for those who know how perfectly to unite the Holy Name, all the walls of darkness are burst asunder, and the diverse 'countenances' of the King are made manifest, and shine upon all, bringing blessing to heavenly and earthly beings."[71]

The lower things are apparent, the higher things remain unrevealed. The higher an essence is, the greater is the degree of its concealment. To pray is "to draw blessings from the depth of the 'Cistern,' from the source of all life . . . Prayer is the drawing of this blessing from above to below; for when the Ancient One, the All-hidden, wishes to bless the universe, He lets His gifts of Grace collect in that supernal depth, from whence they are to be drawn, through human prayer, into the 'Cistern,' so that all the streams and brooks may be filled therefrom." The verse in Psalm 130:1, "Out of the depths have I called Thee," is said to mean not only that he who prays should do so from the depths of his soul; he must also invoke the blessing from the source of all sources.[72]

8. THE CONCERN FOR GOD

The yearning for mystic living, the awareness of the ubiquitous mystery, the noble nostalgia for the nameless nucleus, have rarely subsided in the Jewish soul. This longing for the mystical has found many and varied expressions in ideas and doctrines, in customs and songs, in visions and aspirations. It is a part of the heritage of the psalmists and prophets.

There were Divine commandments to fulfill, rituals to perform, laws to obey—but the psalmist did not feel as if he carried a yoke: "Thy statutes have been my songs" (119:54). The fulfillment of the *mitzvot* was felt to be not a mechanical compliance but a personal service in the palace of the King of Kings. Is mysticism alien to the spirit of Judaism? Listen to the psalmist: "As the hart panteth after the water brooks, so panteth my soul after Thee, O Lord. My soul thirsteth for God, for the Living God; when shall I come and appear before God?" (42:2-3). "My soul yearneth, yea even pineth for the courts of the Lord; my heart and my flesh sing for joy unto the Living God" (84:3). "For a day in Thy courts is better than a thousand" (84:11). "In Thy presence is fulness of joy" (16:11).

It has often been said that Judaism is an earthly religion, yet the psalmist states, "I am a sojourner in the earth" (119:19). "Whom have I in heaven but Thee? And beside thee I desire none upon earth" (73:25). "My flesh and my heart faileth; but God is the rock of my heart and my portion forever" (73:26). "But as for me, the nearness of God is my good" (73:28). "O God, Thou art my God; earnestly will I seek Thee; my soul thirsteth for Thee, my flesh longeth for Thee in a dry and weary land, where no water is . . . for Thy lovingkindness is better than life. My soul is satisfied as with marrow and fatness; . . . I remember Thee upon my couch and meditate on Thee in the nightwatches . . . My soul cleaveth unto Thee, Thy right hand holdeth me fast" (63:2, 4, 6, 7, 9).

In their efforts to say what God is and wills, the prophets sought to imbue Israel with two impulses: to realize that God is holy, different and apart from all that exists, and to bring into man's focus the dynamics that prevail between God and man. The first impulse placed the mind in the restful light of the knowledge of unity, omnipotence, and superiority of God to all other beings, while the second impulse turned the hearts toward the inexhaustible heavens of God's concern for man, at times brightened by His mercy, at times darkened by His anger. He is both transcendent, beyond human understanding, and at the same time full of love, compassion, grief, or anger. The prophets did not intend to afford man a view of heaven, to report about secret things they saw and heard but to disclose what happened in God in reference to Israel. What they preached was more than a concept of Divine might and wisdom. They spoke of an inner life of God, of His love or anger, His mercy or disappointment, His interest or participation in the fate of Israel and other nations. God revealed Himself to the prophets in a specific state, in an emotional or passionate relationship to Israel. He not only demanded obedience but He was personally concerned and even stirred by the conduct of His people. Their actions aroused His joy, grief or disappointment. His attitude was not objective but subjective. He was not only a Judge but also a Father. He is the lover, engaged to His people, who reacts to human life with a specific *pathos,* signified in the language of the prophets, in love, mercy or anger. The Divine pathos which the prophets tried to express in many ways was not a name for His essence but rather for the modes of this reaction to Israel's conduct which could be changed by a change in Israel's conduct. Such a change was often the object of the prophetic ministry.

The prophets discovered the holy dimension of living by which our right to live and to survive is measured. However, the holy dimension was not a mechanical magnitude, measurable by the yardstick of deed and reward, of crime and punishment, by a cold law of justice. They did not proclaim a universal moral mechanism but a spiritual order in which justice was the course but not the source. To them justice was not a static principle but a surge sweeping from the inwardness of God, in which the deeds of man find, as it were, approval or disapproval, joy or sorrow. There was a surge of Divine pathos, which came to the souls of the prophets like a fierce passion, startling, shaking, burning, and led them forth to the perilous defiance of people's self-assurance and contentment. Beneath all songs and sermons they held conference with God's concern for the people, with the well out of which the tides of anger raged.

There is always a correspondence between what man is and what he knows about God. To a man of the *vita activa,* omnipotence is the most striking attribute of God. A man with an inner life, to whom thoughts and intuitions are not less real than things and deeds, will search for a concept of the inner life of God. The concept of inner life in the Divine Being is an idea upon which the mystic doctrines of Judaism hinge. The significance of prophetic revelation lies not in the inner experience of the prophet but in its character as a manifestation of what is in God. Prophetic revelation is primarily an event in the life of God. This is the outstanding difference between prophetic revelation and all other types of inspiration as reported by many mystics and poets. To the prophet it is not a psychic event, but first of all a transcendent act, something that happens to God. The actual reality of revelation takes place outside the consciousness of the prophet. He experiences revelation, so to speak, as an ecstasy of God, who comes out of His imperceivable distance to reveal His will to man. Essentially, the act of revelation takes place in the Beyond; it is merely directed upon the prophet.

The knowledge about the inner state of the Divine in its relationship to Israel determined the inner life of the prophets, engendering a passion for God, a *sympathy* for the Divine pathos in their hearts. They loved Israel because God loved Israel, and they frowned upon Israel when they knew that such was the attitude of God. Thus the marriage of Hosea was an act of sympathy; the prophet had to go through the experience of being betrayed as Israel had betrayed God. He had to experience in his own life what it meant to be betrayed by a person whom he loved in order to gain an understanding of the inner life of God. In a similar way the sympathy for God was in the heart of Jeremiah like a "burning fire, shut up in my bones and I weary myself to hold it in, but cannot" (20:9).

The main doctrine of the prophets can be called *pathetic theology*. Their attitude toward what they knew about God can be described as religion of sympathy. The Divine pathos, or as it was later called, the *Middot*, stood in the center of their consciousness. The life of the prophet revolved around the life of God. The prophets were not indifferent to whether God was in a state of anger or a state of mercy. They were most sensitive to what was going on in God.[73]

This is the pattern of Jewish mysticism: to have an open heart for the inner life of God. It is based on two assumptions: that there is an inner life in God and that the existence of man ought to revolve in a spiritual dynamic course around the life of God.[73a]

NOTES

[1] *Zohar* (to which all unspecified references in the following notes relate. The translation used is that mentioned in the Bibliography.) II, 23a.

[2] I 241a.

[3] II 15b.

[4] II 20a.

[5] I 156b.

[6] II 2a.

[7] II 15b.

[7*] III 128a.

[8] Cf. *Midrash Rabbah* (Soncino Press Edition. London, 1939), Gen. XVII; Mid. Hag. Gn. 2, 7.

[9] *Pesik,* ed. Buber, XXVI, 166b.

[10] III 65b.

[11] Gen. R., *op. cit.,* LXIX. 3; Cf. Louis Ginzberg, *Cabala,* JE, v. 3.

[12] Gen. R., *op. cit.,* XLVII. 6; LXXXII, 6.

[13] II 75a.

[14] II 76a.

[15] II 23b.

[16] II 12a.

[17] II 144a.

[18] I 164a.

[19] III 92a-92b.

[20] III 64b.

[21] II 143a.

[22] III 64a.

[23] II 220b.

[24] III 109b.

[25] II 42b.

[26] I 21a.

[27] III 288a.

[28] II 146b.

[29] *Tikkune Zohar*, 1.

[30] II 23a; cf. I, 27a; II 158a.

[31] On the concept of *Shekinah* in rabbinic literature cf. J. Abelson, *The Immanence of God in Rabbinical Literature*. London, 1912.

[32] II 21a-21b.

[33] II 26b.

[34] I 22b.

[35] I 76a.

[36] I 230a.

[37] II 120b.

[38] I 61a.

[39] II 118b.

[40] II 9b.

[41] III 77b.

[42] II 161b.

[43] I 23b.

[44] II 216a-b.

[45] II 213b.

[46] III 67a.

[47] III 61a.

[48] III 78b.

[48*] II 144b.

[49] II 154a.

[50] II 136b.

[51] I 125b; cf. I 99b.

[52] *Sefer Hassidin,* ed. Wistinetzki (Frankfort, 1924). Cf. *Zohar* I 105b.

[53] III 58a; III 23a.

[54] II 99a.

[55] III 73a.

[[55a] Cf. above, Robert Gordis, "The Bible as a Cultural Monument" (Chap. 1); also below, Louis Finkelstein, "The Jewish Religion: Its Beliefs and Practices" (Chap. 11).]

[56] III 53b.

[57] I 134b-135a.

[58] III 75b.

[59] II 95a.

[60] III 52a.

[61] III 152a.

[62] III 55b-56a.

[63] II 100b.
[64] III 59a.
[65] II 218b.
[66] I 70b.
[67] II 145b.
[68] III 55a.
[69] III 40b.
[70] II 55b.
[71] II 57a.
[72] III 63a.
[73] Cf. Abraham Heschel, *Die Prophetie* (Cracow, 1936), pp. 56-87; 127-180.
[[73a] For the influence of cabbala on the philosophic thought of the Renaissance, see Alexander Altmann, "Judaism and World Philosophy: From Philo to Spinoza," this work, Vol. III, pp. 91-92.]

BIBLIOGRAPHY

Only an inkling of the vast literature of Jewish mysticism can be offered in the limits of a single chapter. It was considered proper to dwell primarily upon one phase of the Cabbala, the history of which abounds in thoughts and events. The *Zohar,* the authoritative book of the movement, was chosen as the basis of our chapter.

GINZBERG, LOUIS, "Cabala," in *The Jewish Encyclopedia,* III, 456-479. New York and London, 1902.
SCHOLEM, GERSHOM, *Major Trends in Jewish Mysticism.* Jerusalem, 1941; 3d rev. ed., New York, 1954.
WAITE, ARTHUR E., *The Holy Kabbalah.* London, 1929.
The Zohar. Translated by Harry Sperling and Maurice Simon. 4 vols. London, 1931-1934.

CHAPTER 6

PATTERNS OF JEWISH SCHOLARSHIP IN EASTERN EUROPE

By Abraham Menes

Introduction

Jewish history in the past 1,000 years has been, primarily, a history of Jewish life in Europe. There were, as indicated in previous chapters, a number of Jewish settlements there much earlier, even as far back as the time of the Second Temple. Their role in Jewish life as a whole was, however, quite modest. Up until the tenth century Jewish history mainly hinged on the large Jewish centers of the East: Palestine, Egypt, and Babylonia.

The general decline of the Roman Empire from the third century on led also to a decline of the Jewish settlements in the countries under Roman rule. The status of the Jewish population in the Roman world, including Palestine, became particularly difficult after the triumph of the Church during the reign of Constantine (beginning of the fourth century). The center of gravity of Jewish life gradually shifted eastward (to the countries of the Persian Empire), primarily to Babylonia. For the next seven hundred years the Babylonian academies played a leading role in the spiritual history of the Jews, and the Babylonian Talmud became increasingly respected and followed in Jewish settlements the world over.

Babylonia preserved the heritage of Palestine. The large settlement in the east managed to develop a distinctive and rich cultural life unparalleled in any other community in the Diaspora. The fact that Babylonian and Palestinian Jews spoke the same language (Aramaic), despite certain dialectal divergences, undoubtedly played an important role in the successful and complete maintenance of continuity in Jewish cultural life.

After the beginning of Arab-Islam expansion in the seventh century, the Jewish communities in Mesopotamia became a center of emigration. Babylonian Jews settled in Palestine, North Africa, and a number of localities in Europe. The decline of the Bagdad Caliphate, which began in the ninth century, and the continuous disturbances in the country, increased the stream of Jewish emigration from east to west. At the same time, the revival of the urban centers of Western Europe created favorable conditions for Jewish immigration. Before long the Jewish communities in Western Europe had established themselves. Babylonia no longer played the role of a spiritual center, and the beginning of the eleventh century can, without doubt, be considered the beginning of the European or Western era in Jewish history.

Until the end of the Middle Ages the West European communities were the most prominent in the Jewish world. After the expulsion from Spain (1492), the center of gravity of Jewish life shifted eastward, and the sixteenth century brings us to the East European era in Jewish history.

General conditions in Western Europe were very different from those in Babylonia. The Jews in Europe were mainly an urban element. They were less concentrated and therefore felt the pressures of the non-Jewish surroundings more acutely. There was another important difference. The language of everyday life and the language of study were, in Babylonia, one and the same: Aramaic. (This condition changed slowly after the rise of Islam.) Moreover, it was not too difficult for the student who knew Aramaic to learn to understand a Hebrew text. In Europe, on the other hand, a split was created between the language of everyday life and that of study. The student had to overcome the considerable difficulties of studying texts in language that was totally unfamiliar. Of course, translations could have been used, as in Egypt during Hellenistic times, when the Bible was translated into Greek. The new communities in Europe, however, held on to the Babylonian tradition. True, Palestinian and Babylonian Jews had also, to some extent, made use of an Aramaic translation of the Bible. The Bible in Hebrew, however, continued as the foundation of Jewish education. This particular Babylonian tradition—under much more exacting conditions—was now adopted by the Jewish settlements in Europe.

The development in Europe itself was not uniform. The differences between the Sephardim (the Jews in Spain) and the Ashkenazim (the communities in northern France and Germany) were particularly important. While Spain was almost completely under Arab rule (from the eighth to the twelfth centuries), the Jewish community there was very strongly influenced by the then blossoming Arabic culture. A considerable number of learned Sephardim held their own with the times, even as far as secular knowledge was concerned, being well versed in scientific and philosophical literature in Arabic. Thus there was close spiritual contact between Jews and the non-Jewish environment. The state of the Ashkenazic communities was very different. The Church did everything in its power to maintain the division between Jews and non-Jews. At best the Jews were "tolerated." The Ashkenazim were, therefore, to a lesser extent "men of the world," and secluded themselves more within the confines of Judaism. The study of the Talmud assumed a central position; talmudic law reigned over the totality of Jewish life. The well-known Ashkenazic authority, Rabbi Jacob ben Asher, who early in the fourteenth century moved from Germany to Spain with his father, Rabbi Asher ben Jehiel, characterized the difference between the Ashkenazim and Sephardim as follows: "The custom of the former was to observe the commandments and to like them. . . . It was also the custom in Ashkenaz for the leaders in the community to be the first in observance . . . which is not the case in Sepharad. . . ."[1]

Small wonder, then, that while Maimonides began his *Mishne Tora* with a religio-philosophical introduction explaining and proving the principles of the existence and the oneness of the Creator, Rabbi Jacob ben Asher, on the other hand, began the first part of his *Arbaa Turim* with the order of procedure to be followed upon rising in the morning. The Sephardic thinkers began with the question, "What must a Jew know?" The Ashkenazic asked, "What must a Jew do?"

The Ashkenazic Jews were secure in their faith, and were not in need of a *Guide to the Perplexed*, such as Maimonides attempted to create for the doubters of his time. Education in the Ashkenazic communities was, first and foremost, aimed at teaching deeds, at the raising of generations of Jews who would be ready to offer maximum resistance in times of overwhelming temptation. Surely this was also the aim of education among the Sephardim. In the Ashkenazic communities, however, the notion of Torah and Commandments was the exclusive content of Jewish education and the main theme of Jewish life. The Ashkenazic Jew was therefore better prepared in times of trial, and during periods of danger the number of Jews who left their faith was incomparably smaller in the Ashkenazic communities than had been the case in Spain.

THE JEWISH COMMUNITY IN POLAND

The Jewish settlements of Eastern Europe also have a history of some two thousand years. Until the close of the Middle Ages, however, the Jewish communities in the Slavic countries were far from the mainstream of Jewish life. After the Crusades, when Jewish emigration from Western Europe increased, this gradually changed. In a controlled and regimented economy, characteristic of the end of the Middle Ages, the status of the Jews in Western Europe became more and more precarious.

The battle of the guilds of Christian artisans and merchants against the competition of the "foreigners" became steadily more acute, and the hatred of Jews continually rose. In 1290, the Jews were expelled from England. Shortly thereafter, in 1306, the large Jewish community in France met with the same fate. During the fourteenth and fifteenth centuries the majority of Jewish communities in the German countries was destroyed. The tragic chain of persecutions and catastrophes culminated at the close of the fifteenth century (1492) with the downfall of the proud and creative community in Spain.

The expulsion from Spain was a particularly great shock to the Jewish world, representing the greatest crisis in Jewish history since the destruction of the Second Temple. The large Jewish communities in Western Europe as a whole ceased to exist.[1a] Thousands upon thousands died the death of martyrs, while others were forced, at least nominally, to give up the religion of their parents. Even of those who managed to survive, even of those who had the opportunity to emigrate, only a fraction achieved their goal. A considerable number of the exiles died en route. Fortunately, the gates of several countries remained open to Jewish refugees. The large majority of those who had escaped from Spain and Portugal found new homes in the provinces of the then powerful Ottoman Empire (Turkey), while Poland became the most important haven for the refugees from Germany. The road of Jewish migration now went from west to east. The exiles received hospitable treatment precisely in those countries that were least developed economically and where there was dire need for an urban population.

At the beginning of the sixteenth century, the Sephardim doubtless still were pre-eminent in the Jewish world. With the passage of time, this role of the Sephardic communities in Jewish life as a whole steadily diminished. The refugees from Spain and Portugal had not found appropriate conditions for normal continued development.

A very different fate was in store for the Jewish community of Poland, where refugees from the German persecutions found an opportunity to become integrated into a rising economy. The cities were only beginning to develop, and there was more than enough place for Jewish work and Jewish initiative. Poland and the other Slavic countries were, it is true, still very poor compared to Western Europe. However, the general trend was upward. This explains the optimism prevalent among the Jews in Poland. In this respect a letter by Rabbi Moses Isserles (*c.* 1525-1572), the famous rabbi and head of the Cracow *Yeshiva*, to a student traveling to Germany in search of a rabbinical position, proves instructive. When the young scholar quickly returned to Poland, the Rabbi of Cracow wrote him:

> I was happy to learn that you have safely returned, although I had hoped that you would remain to become a rabbi and guide in one of the communities. But perhaps a piece of dry bread and a tranquil life in our countries . . . where their hatred toward us is not as great as in Germany, is better, after all. If it could only stay this way until the Messiah's arrival.[2]

Since the golden age of Jewish life in Babylonia, Jews had not felt as much at home in a country as they now did in Poland. The general situation of the Jewish population with regard to security of life and property was incomparably better than in the German countries. The Polish Jew felt greater security because he was fully integrated into the economic life of the country. Jews were represented in the most varied branches of com-

merce and crafts, both in the cities and in the villages. And the more differentiated and ramified the Jewish economy became, the more compact
the Jewish communities, the more the Jews lived together as a separate
group. In the seventeenth and eighteenth centuries Poland already had
numerous cities and towns in which Jews were a majority of the total population. For this reason the Jew felt more secure with respect to his own
future and the fate of his children. The East European Jew lived hopefully. Even during difficult times he rarely despaired: with God's help one
would find a solution; as long as one lived among Jews one would not be
abandoned! This optimism created appropriate conditions not only for the
flowering of Torah study in the sixteenth century but also for the development of a ramified network of Jewish autonomous institutions in the form
of local communal and social organizations, culminating in the central
organization for Jewish autonomy, the *Vaad arba arazot* (Council of the
Four Lands).[2a]

The path of Torah and of Commandments in the Ashkenazic version
attained its greatest development in Poland. Jews felt relatively freer there,
and relations with the non-Jewish population were much friendlier than in
the German lands. At the same time, Jews lived more among their own
kind, and the Jewish world was a separate world. Only in Poland did
Judeo-German become the Yiddish language, while the remnants of an
older Jewish population that had been settled there for hundreds of years
and had spoken a Slavic language were also gradually assimilated to the
Ashkenazic newcomers and began speaking Yiddish. The Jews in Poland
usually lived in separate sections of the cities. There was, however, no trace
of a ghetto life, as in many communities of Western Europe. The Jew in
Eastern Europe thus had more opportunity to be a Jew at home and a Jew
outside his home: "The Jews here did not know what being ashamed of
Jewishness meant. . . . It did not even occur to them that their non-Jewish
neighbors might laugh at them."[3]

A special role was played by the synagogue (Yiddish, *bes-medresh*;
Hebrew, *bet hamidrash*). One can say, without exaggeration, that a considerable portion of the Jews spent more of their time in the synagogue
than in the market place. It was in the synagogue that the Jew began his
day, and it was there that he said his prayers, met his friends, and occupied
himself with public affairs. There were synagogues whose doors were never
closed: night and day men studied and prayed. They studied both alone
and in groups. There was a widespread custom of "appointments" (Hebrew,
keviot), according to which each man pledged himself to study an appointed page of the Talmud, a chapter of the Mishna, a portion of the
Pentateuch, etc., each day. Merchants would frequently take along a book
while on the road, to be able to keep up with the daily portion. Rabbi

Abraham Danzig, the author of *Hayye Adam,* who remained a merchant
until the last years of his life, wrote about himself as follows:

And the merchants will bear witness that it was always my custom to take
along copies of the Talmud, Bible, and Mishna with me on the road, and
that even during trade fairs I would study one and a half pages of the Talmud,
in addition to the Mishna, every day.

Should a merchant have to miss his daily lesson, he would "repay" his debt
on his return home. There were also some who would learn a certain section
of the Talmud by heart and repeat it on the road, lest they violate the Commandment to study, even when they had no books with them. Collective
study was also very popular. The talmudic sentence, "Learning is achieved
only in company" (*Berakot,* 63), was always highly thought of, and it was
not particularly difficult to find friends with whom to study in the cities and
towns of Eastern Europe. Indeed, the Jewish communities were full of
study societies. In a description of the small town of Kroz in 1887, nine
study societies were listed. Among them the Talmud Society, which was
"full of scholars well-versed in the Law," occupied the highest prestige
position. The town of Kroz at that time had a total of 200 Jewish families.
Yet this small, poor town supported by its own means as many as ten male
teachers, two women (who probably taught girls), a rabbi, two slaughterers
(of *kosher* cattle), three sextons, and—what is perhaps exceptionally important to note—two bookbinders. (It was customary then to buy books
unbound. Moreover, from time to time sacred books were rebound, particularly in the synagogue, where they were used a good deal.) In addition
there were, of course, also a considerable number of scholars who studied
alone, both at home and in the synagogues.

In his autobiographical work, *Shloyme Reb Khayims* the well-known
Yiddish and Hebrew writer, Mendel Moieher Sforim,[3a] gives a description
of the synagogue in his native town of Kapulye:

The synagogue is full of householders and young married men who are
engaged in study, and also of *yeshiva* students and men from other towns
who have abandoned their wives and children . . . as they receive charitable
board. Every evening, between afternoon and evening prayers, artisans and
others in the crowd gather around separate tables to catch a "good word"
from the reciters: at one table of the Midrash, at another of *En Yakob,* at
a third *posuk* [Bible], at a fourth *Hobat ha-Lebabot* and similar philosophical
and edifying books.[4]

THE YESHIBOT IN POLAND IN THE SIXTEENTH AND SEVENTEENTH CENTURIES

The founder of the Polish system of study was Rabbi Jacob Polak (*c.*
1460-1530), the *Baal ha-Hilukim.* Rabbi Jacob was educated in Germany;

he was, however, not satisfied with contemporary methods of studying the Law. The persecutions at the end of the Middle Ages had led to a decline in talmudic learning. The Jew no longer had the peace of mind necessary for profound study. Because there was little time for studying for its own sake, efforts were made to study at least the fundamentals, so that one would know the laws covering everyday conduct. Even the great scholars in Germany at the end of the Middle Ages felt they were living in an orphaned generation. They therefore saw as their objective the preservation of the heritage bequeathed them by previous generations. It was a time for collecting rather than for creating. And there was good reason behind this, for the French-German period had introduced into Jewish life the profoundest changes since the completion of the Talmud. On the other hand, there was peril in this concentration on practical problems and on local customs. The practical needs varied from country to country, and each community had its own customs. There was therefore increased danger of atomization in the Jewish world. Moreover, a deep spiritual crisis had been created by the expulsions and the migrations. Would it be possible, it was asked with anxiety, to preserve the unity of the Jewish people in such difficult times?

Rabbi Jacob Polak saw the answer to this problem in a novel way of studying the Law. There must be a return to the tradition of the *yeshibot* in France and Germany as they had functioned during the time of Rashi and the *Baale ha-Tosefot* (eleventh to twelfth centuries), and that involved a *return to the Talmud*. The function of the *yeshibot* must be not only to educate rabbis able to consult an authority in interpreting a law, but above all to raise a generation of scholars who could find their own way through the maze of the Talmud. Thus it would be possible to introduce more unity in the way of life of the various Jewish communities.

Rabbi Solomon Luria, one of the greatest scholars in sixteenth-century Poland, motivated the necessity for a return to the Talmud as follows:

And the Torah became not two doctrines, but 613 of them; everyone built his own platform—the Sephardi justifying the Sephardic books, while the Zarfatim [the French] their own, each one choosing his own, just as each people has its own language and considers the Law a family heirloom. But this is the wrong means to the wrong end. For since the days of Rabina and Rab Ashi no one has the authority to make judgments like one of the Gaonim or Aharonim [Latin scholars] unless these opinions can be demonstrably based on the Babylonian or Palestinian Talmud or on the Tosafot—where the Talmud is not decisive.[5]

The central idea was: one people, one Law. A return to the source of the Law, i.e., to the Talmud, was essential. This, however, was far from a simple task. The Halakic literature that was collected in the Mishna and in the Talmud had taken several centuries to create, and is a meeting place of authorities of various eras and of various schools. In addition, the Talmud lacks clear-cut organization. A great many laws are scattered throughout its six orders, and only one who is thoroughly versed in talmudic literature knows where to look for a given legal text. It was therefore necessary to teach students to think independently, to be able to compare one legal text with another, and—above all—to understand the spirit of the text. This could best be achieved, according to the great scholars of Poland, by the dialectic method (*pilpul*), because "dialectics reveal the spirit of things." It was this new method of study which Rabbi Jacob Polak introduced in his *yeshiva* in Cracow.

The dialectic method evoked great dissatisfaction from a number of scholars of the day. Modern historians of Jewish life in Eastern Europe also often speak contemptuously of it. Without doubt, the dialectic method can be misleading; it can become a game of questions and answers. It should, on the other hand, be remembered that it was the old method of the legal texts themselves. It was precisely this old and now renewed dialectic method that endowed Rabbi Jacob's *yeshiva* with such extraordinary prestige, and which enabled the upsurge of scholarship in Poland.

Rabbi Shalom Shakna, a student of Rabbi Jacob, continued the tradition of his teacher. His *yeshiva* in Lublin attracted students "from the ends of the earth." Among them were such scholars as Rabbi Moses Isserles and Rabbi Hayyim ben Bezaleel, brother of the Maharal of Prague. It is important to note that neither Rabbi Jacob Polak nor Rabbi Shalom Shakna left any written works. That this was not accidental we know from the testimony of the son of Rabbi Shalom Shakna, who wrote in a letter to Rabbi Moses Isserles:

On my word of honor, many scholars and I asked him to compile his decisions. His reply, because of his great piety and modesty, which was unparalleled in the world, was: I know that in the future people would base their judgments on my writings; I don't want the world to rely on me. And for this reason, too, his teacher, Rabbi Jacob Polak, did not write any book. Nor did these scholars make copies of any of their responsa to be sent abroad, for the same reason.[6]

Rabbi Jacob Polak and his pupil, Rabbi Shalom Shakna, thus remained true to their method of study. Their aim was to raise a generation of scholars who could pass legal judgments according to their own interpretations of talmudic texts. In this way the spirit of the great *yeshibot* of Babylonia was reborn in Poland. The study of the Law became the outlet for all the spiritual energies of the Jewish community in Poland. In the Law the scholar sought the answer to all questions relating to life, and in the Law he found joy, consolation, and encouragement. Those who could not devote themselves to study did all in their power to help others to do so. The greatest joy was for one's children to become scholars, or to take a scholar as son-in-law. An entire people lived for scholarship; each, according to his

own means, studied the Law. Jews the world over, therefore, admired the
Jewish community in Poland. The well known mystic, Aaron Berechiah
of Modena, Italy (died 1639), cites in the Introduction to his *Seder Ash-
moret ha-Boker* the testimony of a "dependable man" about the "Ashkenazic
communities in Poland: where the entire community consists of holy persons. There they are engaged in the discussions and argumentations of
Abayye and Raba, and they do not rest night or day." And this certainly was
not mere exaggeration. The Law here became the property of the entire
people. Thanks to the relatively rich religious literature in Yiddish, e.g.,
the *Tsene-rene* (the so-called "women's Bible," first published about 1600),
the *Kab ha-Yashar* (1706), etc., women also became partners in the Law.
Suffice it to record the fact that up until 1732 as many as thirty-four editions of the *Tsene-rene* appeared. Yiddish in Poland, incidentally, was unrelated to the language of the country, contrary to the case in Germany.
Thus the Jews in Eastern Europe became trilingual. Polish (or another
Slavic language) was spoken to non-Jewish neighbors; Yiddish was the
language of the home and the synagogue; while Hebrew was the language
of the Law and of prayer. Yiddish, in time, absorbed more and more
words of Hebrew origin, and also a good deal of the sacred atmosphere
of the *heder*, synagogue, and *yeshiva*.

Study of the Talmud with children was started very early—usually at
eight or nine, and often even earlier than that. At thirteen to fourteen a
student was expected to be able to study a page of the Talmud "on his
own." That meant that he ought to find his way through a relatively
complicated talmudic text without the help of his teacher. There were
a number of rabbis and scholars who believed that the method of study
in Poland and in the Ashkenazic communities in general was not proper,
who pointed rather to the example of the Sephardic communities, where
much more time was devoted to the Bible and to Hebrew grammar. One
of the sharpest critics of the Polish Ashkenazic system of education was the
Maharal of Prague. How could one begin, he asked, to teach the Talmud
to a child of six or seven? The methods of the past must be restored: "In
the early generations they set limits and periods to educating a boy in a
natural way: at five he was taught the Bible, at ten—the Mishna, at
fifteen—the Talmud. And it is harmful to give a boy a heavier load than
he can naturally lift."[7]

Mere erudition and false dialectics were too much pursued, and the result
that was achieved, complained the famous rabbi of Prague, was just the
opposite: little of what he learned was retained by the pupil, who, at the
end, would abandon his studies altogether. The Maharal wrote a good
deal on the necessity of improving the education of the young, and on
the method of teaching, in general. He also addressed the communities
of Poland and the Ukraine on these matters. He did not, however, find
any response to his plans. There were very important reasons for this.

The Jews in Poland were "Talmud Jews." Their ramified system of administrative autonomy offered favorable opportunities for the practical application of talmudic law. Moreover, it should be borne in mind that the world of the Bible was far removed from the realities of Jewish life in the sixteenth century. A large portion of the Biblical injunctions could not be observed under Diaspora conditions. On the other hand, many new customs and laws which are not mentioned in the Bible had been gradually introduced. For example, the Bible offers very little on prayers and benedictions. The same holds true for laws related to family life and to commerce. All of this is, however, given elaborate treatment in the talmudic literature. One of the defenders of the Polish method of education, Rabbi Solomon of Mezritsh, in fact, pointed to the practical importance of the Talmud as a subject of study.

> Even a bit of the Talmud will do more to produce piety than a great deal of other study, and consequently it has been said that the Talmud is great, because it leads to action, and it also leads to insight into all the sacred and philosophical books. . . . But the Bible students, upon my soul, do not even know the ritual of putting on *tephillin* as required.[8]

It should also be remembered that Jews in Poland were largely simple working people, artisans, and poor tradesmen. Allowing a child to study until the age of thirteen or fourteen was a great economic strain. To accept the Maharal's plans for reform would, in effect, have led most of the students to leave the *heder* with very little knowledge. The alternative method of beginning the Talmud as early as at the age of eight or nine had the great advantage of offering the pupil the key to the entire Jewish literature. Those who could handle a page of the Talmud could easily manage a chapter of the Bible, but not vice versa. Actually, for the student of the Talmud the door was open to everything written in Hebrew and Aramaic. The study of the Talmud put the young student on his own. This was the greatest merit of the Polish way of studying.

Moreover, the study of the Talmud gave the student exceptional intellectual satisfaction. Most of the students in the *yeshibot* did not aspire to be rabbis. The cities and towns of Eastern Europe were, as we have seen, full of learned householders, who studied not only for the sake of studying, i.e., to fulfill the commandment to study, but because they actually felt an urge to study. They sang their studies; they sang them fervently, and felt transported to a higher world. There was a certain enchantment to studying a page of the Talmud. The great poet Hayyim Nahman Bialik in an autobiographical note described, in classic fashion, the uplift of the soul experienced by the student of the Talmud:

> At midnight I was sitting alone in the synagogue, as always, and I was completely absorbed in the Talmud. The fierce snowstorm that night drove even the last two or three stragglers from the synagogue to their homes

earlier than usual, and I was left alone. . . . On nights like these I would suddenly be seized by a spasm of diligence and piety, and would dive in completely, with all my 248 limbs and five senses, into the sea of the Talmud, and immersed in it up to my neck, I would descend down to its depths, and my soul would be filled with nameless delights unlike anything else. These were wonderous hours of an uplifted soul, of ecstasy, of barriers and curtains transcended. Study turned to prayer. Its rules became songs to me.[9]

The Talmud is notable for allowing the student many possibilities for searching and for thinking. Herein lies a basic difference between the Bible and the Talmud. In studying the Bible the student is confronted with the word of God; "the written Law" thus does not admit any discussion, only differences of interpretation. The Talmud—"the oral Law"—on the other hand, confronts the student with human beings—great men, to be sure, Tannaim and Amoraim, but only men. The Talmud not only enables the student to interpret the Law but also to introduce innovations. The creators of the Talmud brought the Law down from heaven to earth, and presented it to man. The fact that the Talmud offers many differences of opinion has been particularly exciting to the imaginations of young students, for this meant that one could choose between one opinion and another, and, furthermore, that everyone had a chance to be creative. And if there could have been several schools of thought in the *yeshibot* of Sura and Nehardea, the same might then be applied to the *yeshibot* of Cracow and Lublin. It is therefore not surprising that the scholars felt so fully at home in the world of the legal texts. It was only necessary to learn the art of "swimming in the sea of the Talmud." For this reason the study of the Talmud was particularly capable of introducing so much life and movement into the minds and hearts of the students.

However, even study of the Law in Poland could not remain merely an oral process. The introduction of printing in the middle of the fifteenth century, which doubtless greatly stimulated the dissemination of the study of the Law in Poland, at the same time served as a stimulus for a number of scholars to put their talmudic innovations into writing. The Jewish population of Poland had grown substantially, as had the number of students within and outside of the *yeshibot*. A need was therefore felt for new compilations, and particularly for a summation of talmudic law.

This task was taken up by Rabbi Solomon Luria (also known by the initials Maharshal or Rashal, 1510-1573), who was one of the greatest scholars of the sixteenth century. His work *Yam shel Shlomo* is an attempt to treat talmudic law systematically, not in the form of a codex such as Maimonides' *Mishne Tora*, but as an exhaustive commentary on the talmudic text. The Maharshal felt that it was not enough merely to list the final decisions; that definitive solutions were not always possible, and authorities had, from time to time, fallen into error. Therefore, he felt, the scholar must be given opportunity to rely on his own wisdom in interpreting the talmudic sources, although, of course, he must be cognizant of what other scholars had thought on these matters. This gigantic task, however, was too much for even so great a scholar as Rabbi Solomon Luria. The vast and courageous undertaking of the Maharshal, unequaled in Polish rabbinical literature, was never completed.

At the beginning of the sixteenth century appeared the first printed editions of the Talmud. (Individual sections had been published even earlier.) Many errors crept into these printed editions, both from mistakes in the manuscripts and printers' errors. Rabbi Solomon Luria therefore felt it necessary, in the first place, to investigate the talmudic text. His commentary *Hokmat Shlomo*, which is included in all larger editions of the Talmud, was the result of this difficult and strenuous critical work. The commentaries and novellae of Rabbi Samuel Eliezer Edels (Maharsha, 1555-1631) and Rabbi Meir of Lublin (Maharam, 1558-1616) are usually published together with *Hokmat Shlomo*. Both the Maharam and the Maharsha dwelled at length on the explanation of the difficult passages in Tosafot. In their commentaries on the Talmud, the Maharsha and the Maharam were little concerned with practical legal problems. The commentaries were not meant for rabbis but rather for students. In time the commentaries of the Polish scholars (the Maharshal, the Maharsha, and the Maharam) came to occupy a position in the *yeshibot* similar to that of the commentaries of the Tosafists.

It was, however, impossible to do without a systematization of the legal texts in the form of a codex. This applied not only to Poland, but to the Jewish world in general. After all, 1,000 years had passed since the Babylonian Talmud had been completed. Over the years, profound changes had taken place in Jewish life. A number of new regulations and customs had been introduced, and it was, in effect, no longer possible for even the great scholars to pass legal judgments on the basis of the Talmud alone. In the *yeshibot* it was therefore also necessary to study the post-talmudic authorities. Even these authorities, however, were no longer suited to the times, especially as there were many differences of opinion among them and "doctrines without number" were arising.

The task of introducing unity and organization into the legal material that had accumulated in the West European era was shouldered by the Sephardic scholar Rabbi Joseph Karo (1488-1575). Of Spanish or Portuguese origin, he went to Turkey as a child, along with his family and many other exiles. Later he settled in Safed, then an important center for scholarship and, incidentally, the place where the famous Sephardic scholar, Rabbi Jacob Berab, had attempted the creation of a Sanhedrin. At this time Sephardim still played the leading role in the spiritual life of the Jews. Poland was already an important center of learning, but the Polish scholars had not yet done much writing. At that time Rabbi Joseph Karo began writing his commentary, entitled *Bet Yosef*, on the *Turim*, the code of Rabbi Jacob ben Asher. In fact it was more than a mere commentary; in his introduction to *Bet Yosef* he explained his purpose, as follows:

> As time went on, we were thrown from and dispersed from vessel to vessel, and many heavy trials and tribulations descended upon us. The Law became not two Laws, but doctrines without number, because of the many existing books that explain its judgments and regulations. . . . In view of this, I conceived the idea of compiling a book which would include all the customary regulations, with an explanation of their origin and their derivation from the *Gemara* along with the discussions of the post-talmudic authorities.

On the basis of *Bet Yosef*, the Sephardic scholar then drew up a condensation of the Laws entitled *Shulhan Aruk* (*The Set Table*). The *Shulhan Aruk* was, initially, intended as an auxiliary book for handy reference by those unable to look up the laws in primary sources. As it developed, however, this was precisely the kind of book that was needed by his generation.

The *Bet Yosef* was sharply opposed by the Polish scholars, mainly because the author showed preference for the Sephardic tradition. (There were also some scholars who felt that a new authority was not necessary.) It was for this reason that Rabbi Moses Isserles (Rama), rabbi and director of the *yeshiva* in Cracow, wrote his work, *Darke Moshe*, likewise in the form of a commentary to the *Turim*, in which he defended the Ashkenazic tradition. Later, after the *Shulhan Aruk* had appeared, the Rama became even more aware of the necessity of allowing the Ashkenazic authorities to be heard, in view of the fact that the *Shulhan Aruk* merely listed laws without their justification and without their sources. The Rabbi of Cracow then wrote his *Mappa* (*Tablecloth*) for *The Set Table* of the Sephardic authority.

In this way the *Shulhan Aruk* became a joint work, in which both the Sephardic and Ashkenazic traditions were properly represented. This fact did much to help raise the prestige of the new authority. On the other hand, an authority without the justifications and without references to talmudic sources was not enough for the East European scholars. Eventually, in the first half of the seventeenth century, commentaries to the *Shulhan Aruk* were prepared by some of the most prominent Polish scholars. Thanks to these commentaries, the so-called *Nose Kelim*, the *Shulhan Aruk* became the recognized and accepted authority in the Jewish world.

THE 1648-1649 MASSACRES AND THE SPIRITUAL CRISIS

At the beginning of the seventeenth century Poland had achieved its pinnacle of power and influence. Internally, however, signs of decline were beginning to appear. The rebellion of the Cossacks in the Ukraine in 1648 made its internal weakness evident to the world, and Poland never re-covered after that. Unfortunately, as is often the case during revolutions and wars, the Jews were exposed to particular suffering also during the Cossack uprising. A wave of terrible pogroms swept the country. Hundreds of Jewish communities were destroyed and tens of thousands of Jews martyred. Not quite five years after the pogrom of 1648-1649, the invasion of Byelorussia and Lithuania by the Russian armies began, again accom-panied by a series of pogroms. In 1656, during the Swedish-Polish War, a number of Jewish communities were destroyed by Polish forces. To make things worse, the general poverty and the epidemics sweeping the country threw the Jewish population into despair and helplessness. Rabbi Nathan ben Moses Hannover, author of *Yeven Metzulah* (1653), ends his descrip-tion of the 1648-1649 persecutions, as follows: "To this day there is in Poland devastation and hunger and great pestilence throughout the land, and other common troubles in addition. In the evening they say: If it were only morning, and in the morning they say: Would that it were evening."

The destruction in Poland shocked the entire Jewish world. Over one-third of the Jewish population was wiped out; tens of thousands of families were dismembered: parents lost their children, children their parents. Not quite 200,000 Jews remained in Poland. A large number of the com-munities were destroyed; the entire settlement was impoverished. It is not surprising that mystical messianic moods gained strength at this time. After so tragically experiencing the pains of the Messiah, the birth pangs of salvation, it was not difficult to believe that the Redeemer was about to arrive.

The uprising and wars ruined the entire country. The process of economic and political decline ended, at the close of the eighteenth century, with the total collapse of the Polish state. And the worse the situation became in Poland generally, the more difficult and insecure became the situation of the Jews. Persecutions and pogroms became frequent, and the competitive war by Christian townsmen more acute. Even so-called protectors and friends —the state officials and the gentry—made things worse for the Jews by pressing more and more money from them at every opportunity. The Jew had to pay for everything: not only for a trading or artisan's license, but even for the right to be a Jew. When a community was in need of a rabbi, it was necessary to offer an appropriate "gift" to the local squire or governor. Feelings of helplessness were heightened by the general reign of anarchy and corruption, and it was no longer possible to study in a peaceful atmos-phere.

After the great national disaster, the Jew in Poland was dejected. His thoughts turned to theological problems and to the fate of the Jewish people. The old books were examined more deeply, with an eye to determin-ing the date of salvation, the time when all troubles would cease.

The trend toward mysticism and asceticism increased, while the approach to life became more stringent. "How can I forget the destruction of the Temple and of the sacred sheep who died a martyr's death?" cried out a mystic of those days. "May God, blessed be He, say 'enough!'" In this atmosphere the Cabbala of Rabbi Isaac Luria (1534-1572), with its doctrine of *tikkun*, met with the strongest response. The Sabbatai Zevi movement likewise had a great following, and even after this messianic pretender had accepted the Mohammedan religion (1666), many remained faithful to him. Secret societies of his followers, who continued to wait for the return of their messiah, continued to function in Poland for two or three generations.

To be sure, these were only small groups; yet the messianic tensions enveloped much larger numbers. The legal tradition based on the talmudic texts taught the people how to live in the Diaspora, and how to preserve its Jewishness there. This, however, was no longer sufficient. Many asked: How much longer could one wait? Hence the reaction against the implied pro-Diaspora nature, so to speak, of the talmudic texts. It is not enough merely to wait for the Messiah. The students of Rabbi Isaac Luria were taught that each generation can bring on salvation, if only it desires it with all its heart. Repentance, fasting, and an entire system of mystical rituals can help hasten the time of salvation. For this reason the mystics were disgruntled at the overemphasis on personal problems and the lack of concern for the anguish of the Divine Presence in exile. They felt it to be the mission of man to do all in his power to hasten salvation.

In 1699 Rabbi Judah Hasid of Siedlce (or Szydlow) set out from Poland to Palestine.[9a] A considerable number of his followers—men, women, and children—went with him. This was the first case of mass migration from Eastern Europe to Palestine. A strict ascetic and a great preacher, Rabbi Judah called upon his people to repent, pray, and fast because the time of Redemption was at hand. Rabbi Hayyim Malak, who did not think highly of Rabbi Judah's ascetic doctrine, nevertheless joined this group gone forth to meet the Anointed King. With this we now approach the second stage in messianic mysticism.

From time immemorial, militant messianic movements have been critical of the Commandments. There is a well-known dictum in the Talmud which says, "Commandments will be void in the future world." Naturally, this is no more than theory: when the Messiah arrives, man will become morally pure and the strict discipline of Commandments will no longer be necessary. There were, however, messianic visionaries who felt that the "burden of Law and Commandments" should be cast off immediately. This, incidentally, was simpler than casting off the burden of the Diaspora. The messianic expectations provoked profound spiritual unrest, and people tended to accept extreme doctrines, particularly in view of the fact that the messianic dream was generally tied in with the longing for *temporal prestige, for power and splender.* It was a protest against resigned acceptance of life in the Diaspora and therefore, to a certain degree, also against Talmudic law.

It is no coincidence that the regal behavior of Sabbatai Zevi greatly impressed his followers. Delegates from Poland who met him reported enthusiastically "on the reverence, and the abundance of silver and gold, and the regal clothes which he would wear every day, and the large crowds who came there, and the honors which the Gentiles bestowed on him."[10] Not surprisingly, the idealized figure of the Anointed King overshadowed the authority of scholars, and even of the sacred books. Moreover, the messianic mystics often referred to the authority of direct divine revelations in the form of prophecy or divine inspiration, and therefore needed no moral support from the rabbis.

For the first time Polish Jewry encountered sharp opposition, in principle, to the whole pattern of talmudic law and the authority of the rabbis. The ideological crisis took on serious dimensions because the central institution of Jewish autonomy, the *Vaad arba arazot*, for a long time the pride and joy of the Jewish community in Poland, had gone through a long process of continuous decline as a result of general developments in the country. The same holds true for the local institutions of Jewish autonomy. The communities could no longer manage on their small budgets during the difficult times when persecutions were rampant. The more necessary it became to use ransom money to escape persecution and libel, the deeper the communities sank into debt, and the heavier became their tax burden. At the same time, the general rule of anarchy in the country led very often to the selection of unqualified persons as the heads of the communal organizations. The only point in their favor was that they were on good terms with the gentry and government officials. Moreover, the moral prestige of the rabbinate fell. The rabbi was, in many cases, helpless. It was difficult for him to pass over the wrongs in silence, and equally difficult to oppose them. Arguments occurred frequently in the communal organizations from time to time—even between the community leaders and the rabbis.

In 1764 the Polish government completely abolished the central organization for Jewish autonomy, the Council of the Four Lands, and the Council of Lithuania. Less than eight years later came the first partition of Poland.

It was the messianic adventurer, Jacob Frank (1726-1791), who openly declared war on the Talmud. His followers called themselves "counter-talmudists" or "Zoharists." Copies of the Talmud were burned at the order of the Kamenets Bishop Dembowski after the tragic dispute between the Frankists and the rabbis of Kamenets (Podolia) in 1757. It was no longer possible for the Frankists to remain a Jewish sect, and in 1759 Frank and a number of his followers adopted Catholicism. It is, nevertheless, important to note that for several generations the Frankist families, though nominally

Catholic, continued to marry within their own group and to observe the Frankist tradition.

In the Frankist movement anti-Talmudism assumed extreme forms. The mere fact that the crude and ignorant Jacob Frank was able to enchant men superior to him culturally is symptomatic of the profound confusion in Jewish life. This messianic adventurer symbolized, in grotesque form, the protest against generations of strict, ascetic piety, of fasts and repentance, of mourning and mortification. The Frankist movement went so far as to create an ideology of "Gentileness" (paganism). The Jews, it was felt, must become like other peoples, emphasizing the pleasures and interests of this world rather than the hereafter. Despite the fact that Frank and some of his followers adopted Catholicism, he tried to retain a certain independence. He called his doctrine the faith of Edom. By this he meant not the Christian faith, but rather the Christian secularity, the splendors of statehood, military might, wealth, and all worldly pleasures. Frank had visions of a Jewish state, not in Palestine, but in an autonomous region of Poland. This striving for the pleasures of the world in the Frankist movement at times led to forms of moral irresponsibility and depravity. "I have come," he declared to his followers, "to nullify all faiths and all mores, and my intention is to bring life into the world." He particularly protested against Jewish concentration on books. The time has come, he taught his followers, for the Jews to become a military nation. Children six years of age should be taught military craft. Jews should begin to follow in the footsteps of Esau, because "even the Resurrection will be by the sword, and it will be appropriate that women, too, bear arms."

Jewish community life had been shaken to its very roots, and the individual Jew felt lonely and abandoned. Hence this strong longing for leadership, for a messianic personality.

Rabbi Israel Baal Shem Tob and the Gaon of Vilna

A search began for a new approach, rather than for a renewal of the old patterns of Jewish tradition. The search was not for a new Law, but for new things within the Law, for new reformulations of old truths. Never before were Jews in Poland so in need of undaunted thinkers and spiritual guides. Fortunately, there were such teachers and guides. In the southern districts of Poland, where spiritual unrest had enveloped the broadest masses, Rabbi Israel baal Shem Tob[10a] (Besht, *c.* 1700-1760), founder of the Hasidic movement, again found an approach to the people; at about the same time, in the northern region of Poland, Rabbi Elijah ben Rabbi Solomon (the Gaon of Vilna, 1720-1797) redirected the people onto the road of the Law.

Neither the Besht nor the Gaon were associated with the traditional institutions of Jewish community life. They were neither rabbis nor leaders in communal affairs. No organization or institution backed them; but precisely because of this, their influence on their own generation and on generations to come was extraordinary.

In various ways and employing different methods the Besht and the Gaon managed to give a new look to Jewish tradition. Both were messianic visionaries, strongly influenced by the mysticism of salvation; both made the attempt to migrate to Palestine: "however, they were prevented by heaven because their generation was not worthy of it."

To understand the development of the Jewish communities in Eastern Europe during the eighteenth and nineteenth centuries, it is essential to consider the Jewish *shtetel* (small town). At the same time that the situation in larger communities was continually worsening, the number of Jews in Poland as a whole greatly increased, especially in the villages and small towns. This fact changed radically the whole face of East European Jewry and created the appropriate conditions for a renaissance of Jewish cultural life.

In Western Europe the centuries-long battle of Christian burghers against Jews had culminated in their expulsion from England, France, and Spain and the destruction of the majority of Jewish communities in Germany. In Poland, too, the battle against the Jews was fought with particular venom in those cities where Christian craftsmen and tradesmen were organized in guilds, and where, following the German model, the "Magdeburg Laws"[11a] were in effect. The Christian guilds fought for their monopolistic privileges, and in some cities managed to bar entry to Jews as early as the fifteenth and sixteenth centuries (*Privilegium de non tolerandis Judaeis*). On the other hand, there were many private markets and trading points in Poland that had been founded by the gentry, and where Christian craftsmen and tradesmen could not claim old privileges and reserved rights. In many cases these private market places had actually been established by Jews, naturally with the approval of the gentry, for whom these private towns were a source of income. Here greater opportunities for work and economic initiative were open to the Jews. For the first time in their history, Jews tried to establish their own towns in Europe. They were able to succeed in Eastern Europe because the larger urban centers were, at the time, completely incapable of satisfying the demands of the poorest consumer—the peasant. This explains the rise of the small towns in the eighteenth century.

For the very same reasons, many Jewish merchants and craftsmen left the cities for the villages. It is remarkable that Jews often felt more secure in village communities than in large cities. At the close of the eighteenth century, about 80 per cent of the Jewish population in Poland lived in small towns and villages.

The *shtetel* gradually became the center of Jewish spiritual life. The old centers of learning, such as Lublin, Cracow, and Lemberg, continuously lost their importance. The great centers of learning in the nineteenth century were associated with the names of such small communities as Volozhin, Mir, Eyshishok, Slobodka, Telz, etc. Similarly, the centers of Hasidism were almost exclusively in small towns: Mezhbizh, Lyubavitsh, Ger, Talne, etc. In a large number of towns Jews comprised a majority of the population and were the only craftsmen and tradesmen. Thus the Jew enjoyed more freedom and security precisely in the smaller towns. Relations with non-Jewish neighbors were generally friendly, and embittered competition between the guilds and the Jews was lacking.

As is well known, the *shtetel* has been given an exceptional place in modern Yiddish and Hebrew literature. This is no mere coincidence. It is hardly possible for us, today, to appreciate the role played by the *shtetel* in East European Jewish life. The situation of the village Jews, on the other hand, was more difficult. Although relations with the peasant population were generally friendly, Jewish villagers often suffered from the whims of the gentry, on whom they were totally dependent for their livelihood. It was particularly hard to give children a proper Jewish education in the village. Nevertheless, the village contributed much to Jewish cultural life in Eastern Europe.

Rabbi Israel baal Shem Tob lived in the Ukraine and Galicia, where the number of village Jews was particularly large. The Baal Shem Tob himself lived in a village for a long time. There, in the southern regions of old Poland, the influence of the messianic adventurers and the opposition to talmudic law were still strong. It is therefore understandable that the Jewish villager felt especially lonely there. It was in the Ukrainian village that the founder of Hasidism discovered the individual Jew living in tragic solitude and spiritual helplessness. In the small towns, on the other hand, Jews lived together, and the Divine Presence was with them. The *shtetel* had a rabbi, a synagogue, and people could study and pray together. Pressures emanating from the outside world were not felt as keenly. But in the villages, could a single Jewish family, without a praying quorum, without a synagogue, preserve its Jewishness?

Of course it could, Rabbi Israel replied. "The entire earth is full of His glory." God is omnipresent, and can be served everywhere. In this way the Besht introduced the Divine Presence, as it were, right into the Jewish villager's home: no matter where a man happens to be, he is never alone; everywhere and at all times the Presence is with him.

Thus ancient Jewish monotheism received new emphasis. Jews understood the meaning of "the entire earth is full of His glory" very clearly. The belief in a single God, the Creator of the universe, supplied them with the strength to withstand the greatest of temptations offered by life in the Diaspora, because wherever they migrated the Divine Presence was with them. At the same time, however, Jewish tradition continually emphasized the immense difference between the world of impurity and the sacred world, between the world of evil and the world of justice. The ascetic mystics went further still. They constantly called upon man to wage war against the powers of impurity, in order to redeem the Jewish people from living in the Diaspora and the Divine Presence from its exile. The mystics argued that precisely because the Divine Presence is with the Jews in the Diaspora it is their duty to mourn, since the sorrow of the people in their wanderings is compounded by the sorrow of the Divine Presence.

This was too much of a burden for the simple man. The Besht believed that it was impossible and also unnecessary to burden him with so much sorrow. On the contrary, the way to serve God is through joy and faith, and there are grounds for joy and faith. We are never alone. God is also with us in our solitude, even in the Diaspora. There is therefore no cause to despair. God will not foresake His people.

The author of *Seder ha-Dorot he-Hadash* formulated the difference between Rabbi Isaac Luria's Cabbala[12a] and the Besht's doctrine, as follows:

All that Rabbi Isaac revealed pertains to heaven, beyond the uppermost sphere, and it is not every mind that is capable of comprehending these lofty matters. But the Besht revealed the Divinity here on earth, especially in earthly man, who has no limb and no power that is not clothed with the Divine Power contained and concealed in him. And of all the things that exist in the world, there is literally none that is removed from the Divine Power.

There is therefore no absolute line between evil and good: "Evil is the chair on which rests the good," for nothing can happen without Divine Providence: "And this is the secret of the dictum, 'And Thou givest life to all'—that even when man commits a sin, God forbid, even then Divine Providence is with him. And this, as it were, is the exile of Shekinah [Divine Presence]."[13]

Clearly Hasidism could not assume the ascetic approach to life on earth. The Besht taught that sorrow, indeed, causes man to stray from the Jewish path. God can be served through simple, everyday deeds, even through conversation and social customs. A Hasidic leader stated that even when two Hasidim clink glasses, it is as if they were engaged in studying a page of the Talmud.

Sharp polemics against scholars and rabbis are frequently found in the older Hasidic literature. Not study, but prayer, was first in importance in the Hasidic movement. "God sees the heart," is a central motif in the doctrine of the Besht and his followers. The right intention is the main thing. Hasidic folk literature is replete with stories of untutored men who did not even know their prayers. In their own mute tongue, they poured out their hearts to their Father in heaven. And the helpless, unlearned man's silent prayer was better received by God, blessed be He, than the prayer of the greatest scholar, because "God sees the heart."

This brings us to that tendency in the early period of the Hasidic movement which was in opposition to the prevalent rabbinic tradition. Hasidism brought about a re-evaluation of traditional Jewish values. It is mainly a question of emphasis. Hasidism did not negate learning, nor was there any direct argument with the pattern of the Commandments. Rather, special emphasis was laid upon intention, prayer, and on serving God in joy.

Weeping is very bad. For man should serve [God] in joy. But if the tears are those of joy, then weeping is very good. And let not man burden his deeds with excessive pedantry, for it is the intention of [Evil] Inclination to make man worry that his actions are insufficient in order to bring him to sorrow, and sorrow is a great obstacle to the service of the Creator, blessed be He. And even he who has stumbled into sin ought not to be too sorrowful, for his devotion will be nullified; let him be sorrowful over the sin, but rejoice in the Creator, blessed be He, precisely because his repentance is complete.[14]

Hasidism also created a new type of leader; in this respect it was greatly influenced by the prevalent longing for a messianic figure, an intermediary between man and his Creator. Talmudic law had replaced the crown of Priesthood by the crown of Learning, the rabbi functioning mainly as a learned man to whom questions were referred. Contrariwise, the *rebe* or the *zaddik* (saintly man) is not only a teacher and guide; he is in the category of a priest (or even of a high priest), who brings requests made by the plain folk to the heavenly Father. The *rebe's* court is in the category of the Temple and the *rebe's* table is in that of its altar.

The *zaddik* is the focus of the Hasidic community. Hasidic leadership is founded on the principles of authority and heredity. Hasidism teaches that the *zaddik* cannot be approached with ordinary human measures; even when it appears that the *zaddik* committed some sin, no evil should be thought of him. Even his sinfulness may have profound meaning. For it is written, "Seven times the saint falls; yet he rises."

Consequently, visiting the *zaddik* takes on great importance. It is comparable to undertaking a pilgrimage to Jerusalem. *To a certain degree* the *zaddik*, thus, also replaces the sacred book. One of the students of Rabbi Dov Ber of Mezritsh once said, "I did not visit the preacher of Mezritsh to study the Law with him, but to observe how he tied his shoelaces." Every movement of the *zaddik* is of the greatest significance. His entire conduct, even in simple day-to-day living, is worthy of study.

The road of Hasidism was full of perils, especially after Hasidim began isolating themselves, creating their own *shtiblekh* (prayer houses), and replacing the Ashkenazic with the Sephardic tradition of prayers. It is not surprising, therefore, that the most prominent rabbis and scholars of that time showed concern. They were fearful lest the Besht's methods lead to a new schism in the Jewish world. The Gaon of Vilna headed the Opponents of Hasidism (Mitnagdim).[15a] At the end of the eighteenth century, sharp and embittered conflicts raged. After long-drawn-out quarrels, a *rapprochement* was achieved between the two parties at the beginning of the nineteenth century, and the pattern of Law and Commandments remained accepted by both Hasidim and their opponents. The efforts of the Gaon and his students to restore the status of learning had its effects on the Hasidic world.

According to a widely held view, the rise of Hasidism was principally a result of social conflicts within the Jewish community in Poland. The protests of the wronged masses against the leadership of the rabbis and the wealthy members in communal organizations and in Jewish life generally are alleged to have received their expression in Hasidism. There is a grain of truth to this. On the other hand, one should be wary of exaggerations. As noted earlier, the Gaon of Vilna was associated neither with the institution of the rabbinate nor, to be sure, with the leaders of the communal organizations. It is also worth mentioning that the Gaon's doctrine was well and widely received in impoverished Lithuania, while the doctrine of Hasidism found its following among the more well-to-do Ukrainian villagers and townsmen. The conflict between Hasidism and its opposition was first and foremost an ideological one, although social factors undoubtedly played some role, too.

The tendency of Hasidism to create separate prayer houses and its polemics against scholars, which naturally led to a denigration of learning, caused the Gaon the greatest anxiety. While the Besht was so concerned with the problems of the individual, the Gaon concentrated more on the group as a whole. The Besht focused on the Jew in the Diaspora, while the Gaon was deeply concerned with the fate of Jewishness in the Diaspora. Both were actually striving toward a single goal, although their methods diverged. The Besht attempted to bring the Divine Presence down to earth; the Gaon, on the contrary, tried to raise man to heaven. The way of achieving this, according to the Gaon, was not through weakening but, on the contrary, through strengthening the talmudic legal tradition. With an eye on the classic era of scholarship in Poland, the Gaon called for a *return to the Talmud*. At the same time, however, the strong influence of messianic mysticism can be observed in the writings of the Gaon and his followers. The longing for the unification of the people made itself felt with particular strength. Messianic tensions are given further expression in the Gaon's method of studying the Law. *One people, one Law* meant to

him *an undivided people and an undivided Law.* The Law must therefore
embody all that the people have created over the many generations. No
part of the Law may be deleted, since the totality of the Law and the
totality of the people are one and the same thing. Consequently, the Gaon
and his followers studied not only those subjects related to the Commandments that could be observed in the Diaspora but also paid particular attention to those parts of the Mishna and Talmud (including the Palestinian
Talmud) that are exclusively concerned with the Commandments pertain-
ing to the Holy Land. The Law and the Commandments are the path to
redemption and restoration, and as long as the Law is in exile the people
of the Law will be in exile and the world will be in exile, too.

To observe the Law in its entirety, however, clearly implies abiding by
the talmudic ruling, "the Law is no longer in heaven." The Law was
given to man and it is his duty and his privilege to study, interpret, and
amend it. This can only come about through great effort. Every attempt
at making innovations in the Law through direct revelation can lead astray.
Therein lies the danger of coining a new Law which might break away
from the existing tradition.

Stories about people who had the privilege of studying the Law with
angels are frequent in Hasidic literature. The Gaon and his followers likewise believed that angels sometimes visited man to reveal secrets of the
Law. Yet this possibility did not hold particular interest for the great anti-
Hasidic scholar.

One of the most prominent disciples of the Gaon reported the following
extraordinary tale about his master:

> I heard from the saintly man himself that many times there came to his
> door numerous heralds from heaven, asking and praying for permission to
> transmit to him secrets of the Law without any effort. . . . And he said . . .
> I don't want my understanding of the Law of the Lord to be based on any
> contrivances whatsoever. My eyes are raised to Him; let Him reveal to me
> whatever He wants, and impart to me my portion of the Law with the
> effort which I have given it, with all my strength. . . . But I have no desire
> for insights conveyed by angels and heralds and heavenly masters of the Law
> over which I have not labored nor cogitated.[16]

The Gaon definitely harbored no ambitions for creating a new philosophy
of Judaism. Nor did he ever formulate his doctrine in systematic fashion.
On the other hand, on the basis of his own works and of the various biographical notes in his disciples' works, it is possible to delineate in its general
characteristics his approach to the problems of the Law and the Commandments.

The Gaon's doctrine represents a synthesis of Jewish thought from
Biblical times to his own day, with the exception of the philosophical inquiries of Maimonides and of several other philosophical thinkers to which
he did not subscribe. He did, on the other hand, include the Cabbala along

with the mystical deliberations of Rabbi Isaac Luria. The secret of man, the Gaon taught, is that he was created in God's image. His disciple, Rabbi Hayyim of Volozhin, gave a particularly detailed treatment of the subject of the secret of man in the first chapter of his *Nefesh he-Hayyim.*

The subject of "God's image," he explained, belongs among the "highest things in the world." We cannot take these words literally, since it is explicitly stated, "What likeness will you compare unto Him?" (Isaiah 40: 18). The true meaning is entirely different. The Creator made man a partner to the world's continued existence: "Because by his good deeds, words, and thoughts, he gives reality and potency to many powers and sacred upper spheres . . . and, on the contrary, God forbid, by his evil deeds, words, and thoughts he immeasurably damages, heaven forbid, many powers and sacred upper spheres."

The Law and the Commandments are the instruments by which man becomes partners with the Creator in the process of creating and supporting the world. The Law and the Commandments are also the roads to restoration and perfection. No one can, therefore, ask, "What can I achieve by my acts and what difference does it make what I do?"

And this is the Law of man: Let no man of Israel think, heaven forbid, "What am I, and what power do I possess to achieve anything in the world with my lowly deeds?" Rather, let him understand and know and resolve in his mind that every detail of his deeds and words and thoughts are not lost at any time, God forbid. And how numerous are his deeds and how great and lofty in that each rises to its [sacred] roots to have an impact in the heights above, in the clarities of the upper light.[17]

The responsibility of man, of every man, is therefore very great, and great demands must be put on man. It is no mean task to be the partner of the Creator, to bear God's image in oneself. It is a great honor, a difficult mission, and a tremendous responsibility.

The Gaon and his disciples therefore have another attitude toward the problems of intention and deeds. Of course intention is very important, but it is not everything.

And although it is man's thought that ascends upward to cleave to his root, it is not thought which is the essence, but deed which is the essence in our serving [God], and a good thought attaches itself to the deed. . . . Because just as a man cannot get up on the upper rungs of the ladder if he misses the lower steps, so, too, it is the duty of us, men, whose houses in our lifetime are in the world, to fulfill the deeds. The more sincerely one performs the deeds, the better it is.[18]

The anti-Hasidic thinkers understood the meaning of intention, of the principle that "God sees the heart," very well. They were aware, however, of the immense pitfalls of mere intentions, of good wishes that are not accompanied by deeds. They felt, therefore, that men should be judged not only by their intentions but also by their deeds.

In the Gaon's doctrine there is therefore no place at all for the *zaddik*, for an intermediary between man and the Creator. Every man is rather in the category of a *zaddik*. God did not create any superhumans. The privilege of being a human being, and of fulfilling the functions God has appointed for man, should more than suffice.

Rabbi Hayyim of Volozhin also strongly argued against the Hasidic interpretation of the principle, "The earth is filled with His glory," as if there was no evil on earth. Unfortunately, forces of evil do exist, and man must wage war against them. Man is not merely a partner to the creation and preservation of the world; he is also a partner to the creation of both heaven and hell: "The truth is that the future world is made by man himself, who, by his deeds, expands and enlarges and perfects a portion for himself . . . and the point of the penalty of Hell, too, is that the sin itself is the penalty."[19]

The Gaon and his disciples also were in favor of serving God in joy. Can there, however, be a greater joy than that of studying the Law and observing the Commandments? Moreover, the Gaon was afraid that the road taken by Hasidism would lead to contempt for the Law. Man, after all, has so much to do in the world and so little time in which to do it. This concern led the Gaon to a strict, ascetic approach to life. It is the asceticism of the pioneer who knows he has much to accomplish during the short period that he is ordained to spend in the *world of deeds*, and must therefore be very sparing with his time, which is his greatest treasure. It is told that, before his death, the Gaon placed his *sisit* in his hands, burst into tears, and said, "How difficult it is to part with the world of deeds, where man, by observing so simple a Commandment as the wearing of *sisit* earns the privilege of seeing the Divine Presence. How shall we achieve this level in the world of souls?"[20]

It is clear from this that the Gaon's longing for redemption was not related to the idea that "the Commandments would be nullified in the future." What, then, is the purpose of life without the Commandments? The problem of statehood likewise held little interest for him. The Gaon waited for redemption so that Jews, once freed from the yoke of the Diaspora, would be able to devote themselves more to the Law and the Commandments, so that they would grow firmer as Jews, and more saintly. The purpose of salvation is the perfection of the world and of the Law, and the road to salvation is the road of the Law.

Volozhin

The first partition of Poland took place in 1772. Not long thereafter Poland ceased to exist as an independent state (1795). Russia received the largest portion of land and population, and for more than a century, until the First World War, the history of Jewish life in Eastern Europe is mainly associated with the large Jewish settlement in the Czarist empire.

The Jewish settlement in Russia took over the Polish and Lithuanian heritage. The first sproutings of the Jewish Enlightenment (*Haskala*)[20a] began to appear in Eastern Europe at the threshold of the nineteenth century. The secular tendencies of the Enlightenment were often supported by the Czarist government, which, however, had another purpose in mind, namely, assimilation. In spite of this, the nineteenth century brought with it a remarkable revival of traditional learning. The founding of the large *yeshiva* in Volozhin played a very large role in this.

The most important task now was to *revive the prestige of learning*. East European Jews never ceased studying, even in the most difficult times. The problem was, however, as we have already seen, the position of learning in the scale of moral values.

A life based on studying the Law was always difficult. The *yeshiva* students were mostly young sons of poor parents, and the community organizations had to assume responsibility for them. Widespread was the custom of "eating days" (*esn teg*). Every day of the week the student would eat in a different house. In most cases, the communities also had to assume the salary of the head of the *yeshiva*, and this was often more difficult than arranging eating days for the pupils. The purchase of necessary books for *yeshibot* and synagogues represented a particularly large expenditure. A set of the Talmud cost a small fortune (about $3,000 at current rates). The fact that learning had lost much of its earlier prestige made its support difficult, as the need for special efforts to preserve the *yeshibot* was not felt strongly. In his last chapter of *Nefesh he-Hayyim*, Rabbi Hayyim of Volozhin complained:

And now in the present generations . . . many people concentrate their studies, on most days, on books of devotion and edification, saying that it is of the essence for every man in his world to be concerned with them always. . . . And I saw, with my own eyes, in a certain region that this had become so widespread among them that most synagogues had only edifying books in abundance, but not a single complete Talmud was in them. . . . Should this continue, it may come to pass, heaven forbid, that there will be no scholar any more, and then what is going to happen to Learning?

The disciple of the Gaon felt that the time was ripe for searching the answer to the question, "What will happen to our Learning?" The great prestige of his master helped him greatly, but it was in no small measure to his own credit that the Volozhin *Yeshiva*, founded in 1802, rapidly became a center of learning for all of Russia.

It is not an exaggeration to state that the Volozhin *Yeshiva* marks the beginning of a new epoch in the history of learning in Lithuania and

Poland. The mere fact that the *yeshiva* was founded not in Vilna, capital of Lithuania, but in a small town, little known until then, is characteristic, and undoubtedly was intentional. In the small towns Jewish life was freer; outside pressures and influences were felt less poignantly. Furthermore, in the small town the *yeshiva* could make itself felt. It became the pride of the town. In the large city of Vilna the *yeshiva* could not have occupied so prominent a position.

The main task was, after all, to raise the prestige of learning and of the scholars. Rabbi Hayyim therefore immediately abolished the old custom of eating days. Pupils received assistance directly from the *yeshiva* treasury. It was a very modest amount, but the social position of the *yeshiva* students was greatly enhanced by the changed system. The *yeshiva* was totally independent of the town in a financial sense, and was actually a source of income to the town. In Volozhin the student was no longer called "*yeshiva* boy" (*yeshive bokher*) but "*yeshiva* man." The mere change in name is representative of the new pattern of scholarship.

Volozhin revived the tradition of learning for learning's sake. The *yeshiva* man was not preparing for the rabbinate; his ambition was, rather, to be a scholar. The methods of study were established with this in mind. No differentiation was made between those sections of the Talmud that had practical value for contemporary times and those that dealt mainly with the Commandments applicable to the Holy Land. In Volozhin the entire Talmud was studied, page by page, from the beginning, *Berakot*, to the end of *Niddak*, day after day excepting the Sabbath, the holidays, and the ninth of *Ab*. The daily lesson was a kind of "daily sacrifice."[21]

The study of the Law here became a kind of service, like the divine service in the Temple of old. In the Volozhin Temple of Learning men studied night and day, even during the Sabbath and holiday nights. The sound of study was continuous all twenty-four hours of the day.

In Volozhin it became clear what the prestige and love of learning could mean. This explains the extraordinary influence of Volozhin and the other great *yeshibot* in Lithuania. Even the admirers of the Enlightenment, who often criticized the old forms of Jewish life so carpingly, felt it their duty to offer wholehearted recognition to the students in the *yeshibot*. It was not only the diligence of the *yeshiva* men that was so impressive but also their passionate desire for knowledge, their desire to immerse themselves in study and to seek truth—characteristics which called forth feelings of reverence among writers such as Peretz Smolenskin, Judah Loeb Gordon, Hayyim Nahman Bialik, etc.

At the death of the founder of Volozhin, the leadership of the *yeshiva* went to his son, Rabbi Isaac of Volozhin, who possessed his father's positive traits. After his demise, in turn, the leadership passed on to his sons-in-law. In this way a dynasty was established, which continued to the last days of Volozhin.

It should not be imagined that giving the daily lecture in this Temple of Learning, filled with accomplished scholars, was an easy task. For this reason the directorship of the *yeshiva* was often handed down not from father to son, but rather from father-in-law to son-in-law. To choose a scholar as son-in-law was at times simpler than to raise a son to be an outstanding scholar, worthy of the directorship in a *yeshiva* such as Volozhin.

Volozhin reached its peak in the size of its student body and in prestige under the leadership of Rabbi Naftali Zevi Judah Berlin (known also as Nzib, 1817-1892), son-in-law of Rabbi Isaac of Volozhin. For forty years he headed the largest Jewish center of learning in the nineteenth century. The number of students exceeded 400; they came from various countries. The Nzib carried on the tradition of the Gaon and of Rabbi Hayyim of Volozhin. In the first place, he always emphasized the importance of "toiling" as one studies. In his lectures he put particular store by "immediate" comprehension of the problem. The lecture was given every day but Saturday, from 12:30 to 2 P.M., three times a week by the director of the *yeshiva* and three times by his deputy, who was also customarily a member of the Volozhin dynasty. In the 1880's Rabbi Hayyim Soloveytshik (later rabbi of Brisk, known also as Rabbi Hayyim of Brisk) was deputy director. His lectures were particularly popular. Rabbi Hayyim's method of teaching was distinguished by his logical analysis of the legal texts. Great weight was placed, in Volozhin, on independent work by the student. Even attendance at the lectures was optional. There were no formal examinations. The head of the *yeshiva* occasionally interviewed the students or joined them in their studies, thus deriving a good idea as to their achievements. Moreover, there were no separate divisions or classes, although the differences among students, both with respect to age and knowledge, were considerable. Despite differences, the spirit of a single *yeshiva* family prevailed. The custom of studying together in teams of two was widespread. At times a younger student would seek out an older *yeshiva* man and compensate him for his tutorship. This was a small source of income for the older students. Larger groups used to get together for "conversational study." Usually they discussed the director's lecture, and this gave them opportunity for dialectic exercises, for original observations, and for clarifying certain matters that had remained obscure.

In this fashion each student studied alone and yet all studied together. Each *yeshiva* man depended primarily on himself, on his own abilities and his own diligence; at the same time all were imbued with the spirit of the *yeshiva*, of complete spiritual partnership. And the partnership extended to material things as well. They helped one another. The *yeshiva* men had their own "Society for the Support of Scholarship," whose function was to help students in times of need, and a "Student Loan Fund." The main responsibility for the maintenance of the *yeshiva*, however, lodged with the director of the *yeshiva*, and the responsibility was great indeed.

Fund-raising emissaries from Volozhin traveled all over Russia, while contributions came from other European countries as well. In the 1880's, the United States contributed relatively substantial sums for the great *yeshiva* in Russia.

Some of the *yeshiva* men came from wealthy families, and were not in need of support. These, however, represented a relatively small minority. Most students had to resort to the stipend of the *yeshiva* treasury, between half a ruble and a ruble a week. Thus the life of scholarship in Volozhin was also rather difficult. Most of the students had to be satisfied with "bread and tea for breakfast and supper, bread and some warm dish for luncheon, and meat once a week—on the Sabbath." The budget of a *yeshiva* man amounted only to 1.50 rubles a week. Of this, about 30 to 40 kopeks went for rent. Ordinarily two or three *yeshiva* men shared a room. A student did not even dream of the luxury of having a room to himself. The student's landlady also took care of buying and preparing his food.

The trends of the times, however, also found their way to Volozhin. There were *yeshiva* men who would leaf through a *Haskala* book or a Hebrew newspaper. The Hebrew press of that day often discussed the question of introducing secular subjects and Russian-language instruction into Volozhin and other *yeshibot*. In the 1880's, after the south-Russian pogroms, the "Lovers of Zion" movement met with strong response from the students of Volozhin. The secret society "Nes Ziona" (A Banner Toward Zion) was founded, and counted among its members a number of the most prominent *yeshiva* men. The very existence of such a group, basically secular in its nature, tended to weaken the internal discipline of the *yeshiva,* even though the director himself favored efforts for settling the Holy Land.

External pressures, particularly the government's decision to introduce Russian as obligatory, also added to this tendency at the time. The *yeshiva* administration finally was forced to submit. Secular subjects were, however, not included in the *yeshiva's* regular program of study. A teacher was hired, a separate room assigned him, and those students who wanted to study Russian were able to. The number of *yeshiva* men who attended his courses was very small. Naturally this did not satisfy the government. In the winter of 1892 the police suddenly appeared on the scene. They forced all the students to evacuate the *yeshiva* building, and ordered them to leave Volozhin within three days.

For several years the *yeshiva* was closed. When it reopened (in 1895), Rabbi Berlin was no longer alive, and the renewed *yeshiva* never regained its former prestige.

The Volozhin *Yeshiva* existed for almost 140 years. Founded in 1802, shortly after Poland had disintegrated, it closed in 1939, at the outbreak of the Second World War. Throughout its existence, the Volozhin *yeshiva* observed times of prosperity and times of decline. Until 1892, Volozhin had been the most prominent center of Jewish learning. From all corners of Russia and from many Jewish communities in other lands, young Jewish scholars were drawn to the source of learning. But even later, when the *Musar yeshibot* of Rabbi Israel Salanter's school occupied first place, the name of the Volozhin *yeshiva* was sanctified and beloved by the entire Jewish world.

THE YESHIBOT IN MIR AND EYSHISHOK

The large *yeshibot* of Mir and Eyshishok had also been founded at the start of the nineteenth century. The Mir *Yeshiva* was set up like Volozhin, yet did not enjoy the same prestige and was poorer financially. Some of the poorer students had to resort to eating days, while it was even more common to eat the Sabbath meal at the home of a benefactor. In the second half of the nineteenth century, when Rabbi Hayyim Leyb Tiktinski headed the Mir *yeshiva*, about three hundred students were studying there. His lectures were outstanding for their simplicity and lucidity. His strong point was his "immediate comprehension" without dialectics. "Anyone who wants to understand a page of the Talmud," said Rabbi Israel Salanter, "ought to hear a lecture given by Rabbi Hayyim Leyb." A new era began in Mir in 1900, when Rabbi Elijah Barukh Kamay became its director. In 1907 Rabbi Eliezer Judah Finkel, the son-in-law of Rabbi Kamay, became deputy director. Mir achieved the height of its success in the period between the two World Wars, when it occupied first place among the *yeshibot* of Poland. (See pages 415-422 on the *Musar yeshibot.*)

The *yeshiva* in Eyshishok, a small town in impoverished Lithuania, needs a chapter in itself. Little was known about Eyshishok, and for the simple reason that Eyshishok sent no fund raisers abroad, although its great scholars made it worthy of a place among the great *yeshibot* of the world. This small town in Lithuania supported over one hundred students, unmarried boys and particularly young men preparing for the rabbinate, by its own modest means, and very respectably at that.

The *yeshiva* in Eyshishok also managed to preserve the dignity of learning and of the students in its unique and modest way. The tradition of the Gaon of Vilna and his disciples influenced this *yeshiva* as much as it had that of Volozhin. The students did not go out for meals to local townspeople. In Eyshishok the townspeople brought the meals to the students.

In the proclamation *Ez Pri*, issued by Rabbi Israel Salanter and other leading personalities in 1881, for the purpose of arousing the public to establish and support *yeshibot*, Eyshishok was set up as an example:

Why do you not emulate in piety the small town of Eyshishok, where they have taken it upon themselves—rich and poor alike—not to eat their bread

themselves unless they have first given food to the students of the Law who
sit there before the Lord; in joy they bring their food, like the first crops,
each one at a specified time, to his house of study.

In addition to food for the students, the townsmen also took care of
the other expenses of the *yeshiva:* fuel, light, books, and all other needs.
This was the concern of special societies, and the sums that they collected
were relatively large. It is therefore not surprising that this poor town in
Lithuania became the symbol of "love of learning."

THE SMALLER AND MEDIUM-SIZED YESHIBOT

The number of students able to travel to the large *yeshibot* was relatively
small. The greater number of students were in the smaller and medium-
sized *yeshibot*, which, although lesser known, nevertheless played no lesser
role than the large *yeshibot* in the diffusion of scholarship in Eastern
Europe.

The smaller and medium-sized *yeshibot* employed no fund raisers, and it
was therefore necessary to collect on the spot the funds necessary to support
the institutions of learning. Consequently, it was impossible to renounce
the old system of eating days. Of course it was difficult for the young students, often no more than children, to live away from home and to eat at
unfamiliar tables. We must remember, however, that eating days were
common until the beginning of the twentieth century. The student who was
enjoying an eating day at a strange house knew very well that at his own
parents' table there also sat an out-of-town student, enjoying a similar
privilege, and therefore had no feelings of degradation. Those householders
who offered eating days to students usually knew how to preserve the students' sense of pride.

In the smaller *yeshibot* most of the students were local boys and men.
Parents of means would, in many cases, pay the tuition of their sons. In
the medium-sized *yeshibot* the number of out-of-town students was con-
siderable, and here poverty was much more obvious. The well-known
Yiddish and Hebrew writer, Mendel Meicher Sforim, in his memoirs,
Shloyme Reb Khayims, offers the following description of the *yeshiva* in
Slutsk, where he studied in the late forties of the past century:

One of the cities in Lithuania which God has blessed with a *yeshiva* is a
certain city called S——k. No other thing does it possess, aside from the
yeshiva which is known far and wide, to give it a mark of distinction and
a name in the world. . . . Its professors are common people, needy teachers,
even if they are called "directors of *yeshibot*"; the students there—poor boys,
without a groshn [penny] to their name, who mostly hike to school on foot,
empty-handed and bare. No sooner does the student cast off his bundle—some
two old patched shirts and a pair of mended socks that have been worn

through, brought from home—than the city assumes the burden of caring for this out-of-towner, supporting him in every possible way, despite its own impoverished circumstances and the claims of its own paupers upon it. The poorest man is prepared to share such food as he may have, for the sake of scholarship.[22]

There were smaller and medium-sized *yeshibot* in many communities in Lithuania, and also in a number of communities in Poland and the Ukraine. There were also *yeshibot* supported by individual synagogues, societies, or even by individuals. In Vilna, for example, at the close of the past century, there was a *yeshiva* in the butchers' synagogue where about eighty students studied. Another such *yeshiva* existed in the furriers' synagogue of Minsk.

In the memoirs of Israel Isser Katsovitsh we find the following description of the Minsk *yeshiva:*

Our *yeshiva* was built and supported by furriers, i.e., by poor people. . . . The head of our *yeshiva* has a yard-goods store. The store is run by his wife. He is in the shop only for a few hours, and devotes all of his time to studying alone and to teaching. All week he studies with us, the *yeshiva* students, and on Saturday with the furriers. . . .[23]

The founders of the well known *yeshiva* in the Ramayles Synagogue in Vilna also were simple artisans. In the forties of the past century such prominent personalities as Rabbi Israel Salanter and Rabbi Mordecai Meltzer headed it. Most of the students had eating days assigned to them. Those students who were short an eating day received bread and a warm dish at the *yeshiva*. In the nineties these conditions even led to a strike of students, who complained that they were not getting enough bread.

THE SYNAGOGUE STUDENTS

It is very likely that the large majority of young students in Eastern Europe belonged to the category of so-called synagogue students (*kloyz-nikes*). The entire system of scholarship was founded on the principle of "independent study." Even the large *yeshibot* could not have existed, from the financial point of view, but for the method of independent work on the part of the students; therefore generally there was no division into classes according to age or previous knowledge. All the students heard the same lecture; all studied the same section— although they were completely free to study additional sections—and each one tried to achieve as much as his powers allowed. Thus even so large a *yeshiva* as the one in Volozhin was able to manage with only two directors.

Ordinarily, independent study was begun at the age of thirteen or fourteen. Parents of means, however, used to keep a teacher for their children even after this. Very poor but capable children sometimes started on their own even before their thirteenth year because their parents did not have the means to pay for tuition.

If the young student did not travel to a *yeshiva*, he might take up study in a synagogue—sometimes in his home town—where there were books aplenty and where he also had opportunity for "conversational study," to discuss things with friends of his age or with older scholars. The well known scholar and author, Simeon Bernfeld, for example, tells of his father:

> My father began his studies with his maternal grandfather, Rabbi Zevi Hirsh. Thereafter he may have had another teacher who tutored him until he was eleven. From then on he sat in the synagogue of his native town and studied on his own. The frequenters of the synagogue loved this upright boy who was very industrious and worked hard at his studies. For this reason they helped him with all their means, but my father studied primarily on his own.[24]

No less characteristic is the education of the great thinker, Ahad Ha-Am (Asher Ginzberg), who came from a rather well-to-do family, his father being a pious Hasid, a merchant in the Ukraine. When young Ginzberg reached the age of twelve, his family moved to a village where, in the solitude of rural life, Ahad Ha-Am spent his school years.

> Coming to the village far from other children and the amusements of childhood, my soul came to long for learning. I spent night and day on the Talmud and subsequent authorities, at first with the help of a teacher and later, when I was fifteen, on my own. My labors bore fruit in a remarkable way. . . . Along with this, I applied myself to Hebrew grammar and the Bible and I also read chapters in the philosophical books of the Sephardim, but all these readings were scattered and random, a bit here and a bit there, without instruction or assistance.[25]

This, incidentally, had been the method of study for generations. Personalities such as Rabbi Israel baal Shem Tob, the Gaon of Vilna, and Solomon Maimon had never studied in a *yeshiva* at all. Early in their lives they had set out to study independently. This was made possible by a system of education which helped even the very young student to work on his own.

There were, of course, also dangers in this system of independent study. Not every student is capable at the age of thirteen or fourteen of finding his way independently through the sea of the Talmud. There were, as a result, a considerable number of failures. Not all who started out became scholars. All things considered, however, the method of studying independently was actually the only one possible in view of the economic level of the Jewish population in Eastern Europe.

Ordinarily a young boy would seek out a synagogue where there were other students, young and old. Many cities and towns had a large synagogue or study house which served as a center of learning. Older scholars and younger men who lived and studied at their parents-in-laws' expense, would engage in discussions, and the younger boys would listen and interrupt with questions or individual opinions. Frequently the young boys would study in groups of two or three, which was more congenial and enabled them to converse on scholarly subjects.

The custom of studying in a synagogue or study house was particularly widespread in Poland, where there were relatively few *yeshibot*. Polish synagogues and study houses were filled with students, and although there was no set discipline for the students who worked independently, the sound of study was usually heard in the synagogues and the study houses from early morning on.

At 5 A.M. on a frosty winter day, when the city of Warsaw was still engrossed in slumber, hundreds of young men were already seated around tables in the study houses of Ger, Ostrowce, Sochaczow, and Radzyn, engaged in the study of the Law. This was the early morning lesson before prayers. The best preparation for prayers, it was said in these study houses, is a page of the Talmud.[26]

In the synagogues and study houses of Poland there were large numbers of young married men who boarded with their in-laws. The younger boys were also mainly from the locality. The reverse was true in Lithuania, where it was customary to travel to another city for one's studies. Among the synagogue students in Lithuania there were many out-of-towners, young boys and also married men, so-called *prushim*. In a description of the tiny town of Kapule in the middle of the past century, we read:

The Kapule synagogue served at the same time as a college, where young boys . . . supplemented their knowledge of the Talmud and the later authorities. In addition to the local boys, there also studied in the Kapule synagogue young married and unmarried out-of-towners. The inhabitants of Kapule treated these newcomers, with their tremendous thirst for study, very hospitably. No sooner did such a boy appear in the synagogue, carrying a walking stick in his hand and a bundle on his shoulders, than everyone surrounded him, greeted him, and immediately began supplying him with eating days. . . . Food—he had; books and candles—all that his heart desired; a royal shelter—the synagogue; a bed and pillow—he had no need of, since he slept on a bench with his coat as his pillow.[27]

There were several synagogues and study houses with a long tradition of learning, such as, for example, the Gaon's study house in Vilna. Except for the Sabbath meals, those students did not resort to eating days. The synagogue used to supply them with very modest financial assistance.

Independent study in a synagogue had the great advantage of allowing the student freedom to consult various books in the fields of Cabbala, philosophy, etc. He was able, himself, to decide on the order of his studies; and his knowledge, provided that he possessed the proper ability and diligence, was often more extensive than the knowledge of the students in the *yeshibot*. A large portion of the *yeshiva* students, incidentally, had earlier been synagogue students for varying periods of time. There were also cases where a young student would purposely choose a desolate synagogue so that he could be alone more, and study and think independently. This independence placed a certain stamp on the life and thinking of the *yeshiva* boys and synagogue students. In Yiddish and Hebrew literature we still hear, from time to time, the echo of such years of loneliness and isolation. The following autobiographical note by Bialik about his synagogue years (before he went to Volozhin) proves instructive in this respect:

When I was thirteen, I passed from the jurisdiction of the teachers to my own, and began to study in the synagogue alone. Alone—because I was the only boy in the whole suburb who sat and studied in the synagogue except for the *dayyan* [rabbi's assistant], who bent over the Torah and prayers until midday. Otherwise there was no teacher there. This solitary sitting in the synagogue became one of the most important channels of influence on my spiritual development, and on my inner world. Alone with my old and new thoughts, my doubts and suppressed meditations, I sat there many days, near the bookcase, interrupting my study to sink into a mass of dreams and visions, contemplating relations and calculating the structure of the world, seeking meaning for myself and humanity.[28]

In this creative loneliness many other young students worked out their relations to themselves and to the world. These ruminations and reckonings not infrequently led to tangential courses. It was precisely among the synagogue students that the Enlightenment found many enthusiastic followers. The ideological crisis that arose, even in a center of learning such as Volozhin, was felt even more keenly among the scattered synagogue students. Once again it became necessary to introduce novelty into the pattern of study, so that the student might be able to resist the currents of secularity which were becoming ever stronger. This task was taken up by Rabbi Israel Salanter Lipkin (1810-1883), founder of the Musar (Ethical) Movement.

THE MUSAR MOVEMENT

The nineteenth century was, for the Jews in Russia and in Europe in general, a period of spiritual searchings. Until the second half of the eighteenth century, Jews in Europe, and above all in Eastern Europe, had lived completely in a world of their own. There were very few opportunities for social contacts and cultural exchanges between Jews and non-Jews. For this reason the Jewish "apartness" was not obvious. The rise of a capitalistic economy, the great French Revolution, the gradual introduction of universal military service and universal education, introduced profound changes in this respect. The problem of integrating the Jewish population into the general social, political, and spiritual life of the land was posed. More favorable conditions tended to further such an integration. The modern bourgeois culture strongly appealed to the Jewish intelligentsia. The Jewish student always had had tremendous respect for reason, and because of this he was enchanted by the modern, thoroughly rationalistic, culture.

The Enlightenment in Europe was replete with optimism and faith in man, and it was this faith in man that was also characteristic of the Jewish Enlightenment movement. Not only did men feel drawn to the rich world outside, but there was also a profound belief that the world keeps improving, and it was felt to be the duty of young men to get to know the world and to be in closer touch with it. Sproutings of the Enlightenment were found in Eastern Europe as early as the end of the eighteenth century; however, it was not until the nineteenth century that it became an important factor in Jewish life.

The center of the Enlightenment in Lithuania was Vilna. In the early forties Rabbi Israel Salanter reached Vilna, where he became the head of the *yeshiva* in Ramayles Synagogue. Here the founder of the Musar movement discovered more than the Enlightenment. In 1847 the Czarist government opened a rabbinical school in Vilna, whose function it was to educate "progressive" rabbis. Since the young man heading the Ramayles *Yeshiva* was held in great esteem in Enlightened circles, he was offered the directorship of the rabbinical school. Rabbi Israel, however, categorically refused, and when the offer was made official by the government, he left Vilna.

Rabbi Israel was no less aware of the ways of the world than any of the naïve and optimistic Enlightened men who did not see the true motivation behind the Czarist policy of "civilizing" the Jews. Rabbi Israel also took into account the problems of the new era; yet he at the same time realized the great perils connected with the trends of the Enlightenment and reform.

There were a number of religious leaders who, in principle, were opposed to secular education. Yet the first question that required answering was: Is it possible to manage to offer both a general and a Jewish education to children in the relatively short time they spend in *heder* and *yeshiva*? Even more serious was another problem: experience taught that general education often led away from the traditional path of Jewishness. It was difficult to find a harmonious adjustment between tradition and modern secular culture, and Rabbi Israel also was unable to find the harmonious solution, although he did look for it. Thus throughout all of the nineteenth century there was no *rapprochement* between the rising stream of secular culture and religious Jewishness in Eastern Europe.

The strong impression made by the Enlightenment on *yeshiva* youth can be explained, to a large extent, by its *new* approach to the world and to contemporary problems. After going through a popular book on natural science, the young student often saw new vistas opening before him. He became aware of a *new* world, a large, bright, and beautiful world. Compared to this, Jewish life seemed old, perhaps too old. For this reason a *new* approach to Jewish life, a *new* interpretation of Jewish philosophy, as Rabbi Israel put it, was so important. To the slogan of the Enlightenment, "Know the world," Rabbi Israel replied, "Know yourself; comprehend the meaning of Jewishness"; and he also tried to demonstrate that there was, indeed, something to know and to understand in Jewishness.

The Enlightenment was naïvely optimistic. It believed in man and was hardly aware of his evil inclinations. For this reason, men of the Enlightenment held knowledge in great esteem and set great store by education. On the contrary, Rabbi Israel felt it important to stress the role of the human will, of actions, because "the distance between knowledge and actions is even greater than the distance between knowledge and ignorance." The same idea was expressed in another aphorism, frequently quoted in Musar circles in the name of Rabbi Israel: "If only the greatest did what the littlest knows."

It is not too easy to control the deeper powers that operate within us, taught the founder of the Musar movement. Nature constantly drags man downhill, and only by very strenuous efforts can he gradually overcome his evil inclination and attain good habits. All of life is a continuous struggle with oneself. "Life is a ladder. One either goes up or down; one cannot stop in the middle." Therefore the greatest sin is casual action and living. Just as the Gaon, less than a century earlier, had strongly emphasized the necessity of effort in study, Rabbi Israel emphasized the importance of effort in attaining good habits. Man must work on himself, and know himself and the world, because "Every man is a Musar book [edifying book], and all the world is a house of Musar."

Rabbi Israel especially emphasized the responsibilities of the leaders. He did not think much of the quiet and hidden saints who seclude themselves from the hubbub of the world. In our days, he said, it is the duty of the higher type of man to take part in the concerns of the generation. And if we see men leaving the path of the Law, it is our fault. *We* will have to answer for this, because *we*, the teachers and guides of the people, have not done our duty. There is even a connection between Jewish communities of various countries. "All Jews are responsible for each other," and Rabbi Israel formulated this mutual responsibility in classic form: "If people gossip in the Kovno synagogue, the Sabbath is desecrated in Paris." Consequently, the leaders upon whom such weighty responsibilities rest must also have a good deal of courage. When he was once asked why he had not accepted the offer to direct the rabbinical school, he replied that the education of rabbis called for a very special approach.

We see from experience, from daily events, that if a rabbi receives an inquiry from a poor man, he hastens to issue a decision, even in the middle of his meal. He makes an effort and properly consults authoritative books, and seeks grounds for a favorable answer. But if an inquiry comes to him from a rich man, he makes no corresponding effort to find the best solution. However, among doctors one knows the opposite from experience. When he is summoned to a rich patient, he hastens to run to him to treat him with extreme devotion, whereas he does not hurry so much to a poor patient, and tries to avoid visiting him.[29]

The reason for this, explained Rabbi Israel, is simple. From his youth onward, the rabbi studies for the study's sake, so that the morality of the Law becomes ingrained in his nature; while the doctor does not study medicine at first as a mission, but rather as a skill that is to bring him a respectable and sizable income. The doctor therefore apportions his work according to the income he can count on. The rabbinical position, however, cannot be properly fulfilled unless the rabbi is permeated with the idea of a mission and pursues his path regardless of all obstacles. If we want to educate rabbis to become worthy of being leaders of their generation, it is necessary to conform to the *yeshiva* tradition. Rabbi Israel was once asked whether preparation for the rabbinate could be considered study for its own sake. His response was that there could be no better example of this than studying the Law in order to become worthy of a position as responsible as that of rabbi. The student had to realize, however, that the path of the rabbinate is difficult. Not everyone could be pleased, and a spiritual leader of a community ought not to feel intimidated by opposition. "A rabbi that is not threatened by expulsion from town," Rabbi Israel once said, "is no rabbi; and if he is, in fact, driven out, he is no man."

There are certain similarities, as has rightly been pointed out by some, between Hasidism and Musar; but even greater are the differences between these two movements. It is therefore a mistake to call the Musar movement the Lithuanian form of Hasidism. On the contrary, a distinguishing feature of the Musar movement is the great demands it placed on man. "I cannot understand," Rabbi Israel once said, "how a Jew can so much as move without the Talmud." For the observance of all matters in human relations it was necessary to know the appropriate laws. This is why the Musar movement never became a folk movement, despite Rabbi Israel's great efforts to disseminate the Musar doctrine among plain folk.

The founder of the movement also realized that merely studying the Law was hardly enough. And this held true for the study of Musar works as well. Merely by reading an edifying book or listening to a moralizing sermon, one could not improve oneself, "for distant is the road between knowledge and action, between words and deeds, as distant as the heavens from the earth." The main question for Rabbi Israel was, therefore, how to study ethics. How could one achieve the gradual transformation of the purified words of Musar into good deeds and good habits? How could the study of ethics be made to help Jews turn into better people?

First of all, *ethics must be studied regularly every day*. Just as a Jew has set hours for prayers and for study, so, too, must he find time for edification. Rabbi Israel was once asked, "What should a person do who can hardly manage an hour a day for study? Ought he to study ethics or a page of the Talmud?" Rabbi Israel answered that he ought to study ethics, for he would then realize that he had more than the one hour to devote to study. Furthermore, Rabbi Israel taught that the study of ethics was everyone's duty, from the greatest scholar down to the simplest man.

In the second place, *ethics must be studied with fervor*. Man's heart is locked and good words do not always find their way to the human mind. One must therefore study so that one is aroused and shaken to the depths of one's soul. Rabbi Isaac Blazer, a disciple of Rabbi Israel, added that one should note the effects of music, which has the power to evoke the strongest emotions in us, of both joy and sadness. Similarly, the edifying words should be said in such a manner as to arouse man and lead him to repentance and self-evaluation.

The third rule is *repetition*. The main task of studying ethics is to reach the stage where correct moral behavior becomes habit, a part of human nature. It is therefore important to repeat the same ethical dictum again and again to engrave it ever more deeply on the soul. The founder of the Musar movement used to refer to the well-known talmudic legend about Rabbi Akiba in this connection. Until he reached the age of forty, it is told, Rabbi Akiba was an ignorant man. Once, while standing near a well, he noticed a hole in a stone below. To his question, "Who made the hole in the stone?" he was given the answer, "The drops of water that continually fell onto it." Rabbi Akiba then said that if soft water had the power to pierce through stone, then surely the words of the Law would be able to penetrate his heart. And he began studying the Law.

Likewise, the words of edification will not fail in their effect if man will continually allow them to work on him. Each individual impression alone is weak, to be sure, but in time they strengthen one another and become inscribed in one's heart. Only through continual repetition do the main ideas of ethics become a part of human nature.

The fourth rule of the Musar doctrine is to *study ethics together*. In a group it is easier to find strength and overcome Evil Inclination. Many rabbis and scholars of the day strongly doubted the wisdom of collective study. Musar had become a movement. Separate Musar circles were founded and the question was posed: Is this a new sect? May it not, God forbid, lead to schisms in Jewish life? If someone wants to study ethics alone there can be no objections; but collectively? Rabbi Israel Salanter, however, insisted on the importance of creating a movement for Musar. Like the Law, ethics is not merely a matter for individuals. Hence a way of arousing the public to the study of ethics must be found.

The Musar movement, too, distinguished itself by its profound faith in man. Of course, Rabbi Israel was far from harboring the naïve view that man is, by nature, good. He believed, however, that each man had the ways and means of achieving a higher stage. Rabbi Israel warned, in particular, against fatalistic approaches to the matter of human sinfulness:

> Let man not say: what God has made cannot be changed; the Lord, blessed be He, has implanted in me the power of evil, and how can I hope to root it out? This is not the way things are. Human powers are capable of suppression and change. Just as our eyes see animals in nature which man has the power to conquer and to impose his will on, to make them harmless and domesticate them . . . so, too, man has it within himself to conquer his evil nature, to prevent it from escaping from human control, and to change his nature for the better through study and practice.[30]

The Musar movement of Rabbi Israel Salanter was for a select group. It was difficult for busy and overtired people to spend so much time on introspection and on delving into the Law. On the other hand, the Musar movement had its greatest influence in the circles of the young students where the Enlightenment had introduced so much anxiety and doubt. The mere fact that Musar called for profound study, that it was a complete doctrine in itself, helped spread it as a subject of study in the *yeshibot*. The men of Musar were not overwhelmed by the wide world, and therefore had the power to stand up to it. They realized that all the material affluence of modern civilization could not compensate for the moral failings of man. The richer our cultural life became, the more confused the individual felt. Rabbi Israel therefore taught his disciples always to keep man in mind, to understand the individual and to help him in his tribulations and gropings.

THE MUSAR YESHIBOT

At the end of the seventies, on the initiative of Rabbi Israel Salanter and Rabbi Isaac Elchanan Spektor (the famous rabbi of Kovno), there was founded in Kovno the *Kolel ha-Perushim*, a center for married students from other towns, to give young married scholars the opportunity to prepare for a rabbinical career. In 1880 Rabbi Isaac Blazer, former rabbi of St. Petersburg and one of the most prominent students of Rabbi Israel Salanter, was appointed manager of the newly established center of learning. In 1881 Rabbi Eliezer Gordon, a disciple of Rabbi Israel, became rabbi in Telz (Kovno province). He became head of the *yeshiva*, which had been founded there several years before, and under his leadership the name Telz became increasingly well known and recognized in the *yeshiva* world. At about the same time, the foundations were laid in Slobodka, a suburb of Kovno, for the later famous Musar *Yeshiva Keneset Yisrael*. Lithuania proper (actually the area of Kovno) now became the most important center of learning in Russia. Many of Rabbi Israel Salanter's friends and disciples lived in Lithuania, so a wide field for Musar activities now opened. With this, the stormy period of the Musar movement in the *yeshibot* was launched.

The Musar doctrine in the first place armed the young student with a philosophy of Jewishness. It raised his own self-respect and his esteem for the Law. And it was precisely this pride of the men of Musar, their belief that they had rediscovered the light of the Law, that was of such great consequence for the revitalization of the *yeshibot*. The *yeshibot* needed Musar even more than the movement needed them.

The pride of the men of Musar and their aggressive method in attempting to disseminate their doctrine, however, caused rabbis and scholars to voice protests. Among the opponents of militant Musar was such an authority as Rabbi Isaac Elchanan Spektor. Sharp quarrels ensued. Rabbi Isaac Blazer was ultimately forced to resign from his post in the *Kolel ha-Perushim*. In the meantime, however, the men of Musar had managed to establish their positions firmly in the *yeshibot*. The leadership of the Musar movement was now taken over by Slobodka.

The founder of the *Yeshiva Keneset Yisrael* in Slobodka was Rabbi Note Hirsh Finkel, an original thinker and an excellent organizer with a profound insight into human nature. Rabbi Finkel had all the characteristics necessary for a teacher and guide of young people with great intellectual demands and ambitions. He was not the head of a *yeshiva*, but merely a supervisor. For forty-odd years he was, however, the heart and soul of Slobodka, and his influence went far beyond the boundaries of this suburb. He was middle-aged when *yeshiva* students began calling him "the old man," and it was under the name of "the old man of Slobodka" that he was known in the *yeshiva* world.

Rabbi Note Hirsh was a disciple of Rabbi Simha Zisl Broyde of Kelem, which held a very special position in the Musar movement. Rabbi Simha Zisl was one of the oldest and most beloved disciples of Rabbi Israel Salanter, and the first to attempt, in systematic fashion, to apply the Musar doctrine to the field of education.

Man must study all his life. Man must work at self-improvement all his life. These are the central motifs of Rabbi Simha Zisl's pedagogic doctrine. What a man studies in his youth is insufficient. No matter how thorough his education at that time, there are many things that cannot be understood by the young student, and this is particularly the case of the Commandments regarding man's relations with his fellows. As a consequence we go through life with the same childish notions that we acquired in our youth. Therefore it is imperative that the mature person begin studying anew, as if he were confronting the world for the first time. Above all, however, a man must study hard to understand himself:

Man lives with his body and his soul all his life as he eats and drinks and sleeps, and does not make a single step without himself, and he knows all his own deeds, his private thoughts, his joys and his sorrows, and he is a partner to his own secret and he cannot separate one hand from another, even for an instant. . . . And after all this he does not know himself on as much as a single point, unless he is a very wise man, who has toiled and labored at it.[31]

Rabbi Simha Zisl liked to say that each man is a Musar book, and it is not at all a simple matter to understand the book called man. The trouble is, however, that we are generally too indolent to make any mental efforts. Our first task is therefore to learn to think: "Not to let a single day pass without practice in thinking, for this is the key to wisdom and the preface to all powers, and that is man." And to think means to be able to concentrate on a specific point, and not permit thoughts to wander to unrelated subjects.

Rabbi Simha Zisl's Talmud Torah in Kelem, which was in the beginning an educational institution for younger students, became in the eighties a Musar *yeshiva* on a higher plane. It was attended mainly by students who aspired to greater perfection in Musar. A number of Rabbi Simha Zisl's students later headed the large *yeshibot* in Lithuania. Kelem thus strongly influenced the entire Musar movement. On the other hand, the pedagogic method of Rabbi Simha Zisl was not completely suited to the *yeshibot*. The *yeshiva* students were accustomed to more freedom, more independence. Of course, they also needed assistance and guidance; yet they were not prepared to turn the *yeshiva* into a *heder*, even a *heder* along the ideal lines of the Talmud Torah in Kelem.

Rabbi Note Hirsh Finkel, founder of the Slobodka *Yeshiva Keneset Yisrael*, therefore had to find his own solution. Slobodka preserved, to the utmost, the principle of the scholar's independence, and it was precisely the study of Musar that enhanced the student's faith in his own powers. Other large *yeshibot* in time copied the example set by *Keneset Yisrael*. They introduced the study of Musar, and the teacher of Musar, the *mashgiah*, took on an increasingly prominent position in the life of the *yeshiva*.

In Slobodka Musar was studied each day, half an hour before evening prayers. It was the daily hour for stocktaking. Each student was able to select the Musar work of his choice, and each made his own self-reckoning.

Saturday, at twilight, they studied even more earnestly, making their accounts for the entire week. The Sabbath-eve longings, the twilight mood that always came over the Jew when the sacred Sabbath was departing, when his "additional soul" was leaving him, were underscored even more strongly here through the earnest stocktaking.

Every day between afternoon and evening prayers, not to speak of Sabbath at twilight, the *yeshiva* resembles a ship about to sink. The holy Sabbath is departing; everyone wants to preserve the tranquillity a little longer. But darkness looms ever closer. Shadows become longer, and more crowded together. The week is approaching. No light can yet be lit. To peruse a book is impossible. This is the time when each man is engaged in thinking edifying thoughts. One bemoans his sins in a loud voice . . . one beats his desk with his hand . . . in order to chase away evil thoughts, and another is carried away on wings by thoughts. . . .
And after evening prayers, all recite, in a chorus of tears, the Psalm *Maskil le-David* [Ps. 142]. One man recites, employing such a heart-rending melody that stones are caused to move from their place. The entire group repeats after him in unison, woefully and in tears. Everyone moans. . . .
Suddenly, there appears on the scene, from among the crowd, "the old man." He performs the end of Sabbath ceremony with utmost sweetness. The atmosphere becomes less dense, and more pleasant. He hastens from bench to bench, wishing everyone an intense *gutvokh* [good week].[32]

The Musar movement held the guiding teacher in great esteem. For this reason the Musar discourses on colloquy by the supervisor were not considered any less important by the students than the lectures given by the head of the *yeshiva*. The purpose of the Musar discourses was mainly to teach the student to consider more deeply problems that at first sight appear simple. The supervisor therefore often reverted to the same matter again and again, to clarify the various aspects of a Musar problem, and to demonstrate that there is much to learn.

The idea of the dignity of man occupied a central position in the school of "the old man" of Slobodka. He taught that man is not merely a book; he is a subject for profound study. This is the meaning of the dictum: Respect for man comes before the Law. "The Law was not given to man as a command and admonition, but it reveals itself through man's personality. . . . " And if we study and understand man, we will understand the Law the better. We must therefore try to reach the point where we are worthy of the name man, and then we will also be worthy of studying the Law.

Man is the crown of God's creation. Hence the importance of preserving the honor and dignity of man. We must watch our conduct lest our acts put the species of man to shame. Self-respect, and therefore the utmost responsibility for one's actions, was an especially important issue in the Slobodka school.

The laws of the Torah, "the old man" taught, are mainly concerned
with preserving man's dignity. It is a mistake, for example, to believe that
the benedictions we make when we have enjoyed something in the world
are a toll that man owes the Creator for his pleasures. The true meaning of
the benedictions is very different. They are God's gift to man to help him
realize the beauty and splendor of God's world.

The ways of the world are such that man is only surprised by new
things. As soon as he becomes accustomed to something, he loses the pleasure of its enjoyment. Man should, however, view the world each day as if
it were created on that day. Each day he should admire anew the greatness
and beauty of God's creation. The benedictions were given man so that
he might approach the world each day as if he were newborn, as if he were
enjoying the creation of God, blessed be He, for the first time in his life.

The following Musar discussion by "the old man" on reverence and joy
is characteristic of the Slobodka school. It is usually held that fear of God
and joy are two concepts that are mutually exclusive. People think that he
who lives in fear does not enjoy himself, and he who is happy has no fears.
But this is erroneous. The Law teaches us that fear and joy are not entirely
different matters. On the contrary, the fear of God includes happiness over
God's Law and His Commandments. Man cannot become God-fearing unless he can become joyous over God's Law. We find proof of this in the
Commandment of "the second tithe." The Law admonished our parents
to take along their tithes to Jerusalem and to consume them there, so that
they might become God-fearing in Jerusalem. It might then appear that
Jews used to come to Jerusalem worried, sad, and frightened because of
their fear of God. Actually, just the reverse is true. In the Law itself it is
written that when one arrives in Jerusalem for a holiday, one should be
joyous, and Jerusalem itself is called the "joy of the world."

The doctrine of "the old man" was far from asceticism. Slobodka did not
deny the world. The Commandments were not given to enslave man but,
on the contrary, to elevate and purify him. The world was created for man,
and the Law was given to man. "And if man is lacking something, the
Law, too, is lacking."

All of this concerns the individual and not the group. The men of Musar,
as we have seen earlier, generally devoted much thought to the problems
of the individual. Rabbi Jeruham Lvovits, head of the great Mir *Yeshiva*
and one of the most prominent thinkers the Musar movement produced,
paid particularly great attention to the matter of the individual versus the
group.

Why did God command the Jews to be counted in the desert? Because
he wanted to set apart, answered Rabbi Jeruham, *each individual, each
individual with his own name and with his own concerns.* Through the process of counting, each individual making up the group became a personality

in his own right, and not merely part of a whole. The Torah, likewise, was given on Mt. Sinai, not only to the group, but to each individual separately; "for each individual received the holy Torah with his interpretation."

In general, it is wrong to give the group one's main consideration. Man is shamed when the Divine Image is reduced to a group. Man was created to be an individual, a personality in his own right. This may be conceit, but a necessary conceit. Man's modesty must not go to such extremes that he totally disappears into the group. "Man needs to be an individual unto himself." Each individual is a world of his own. For this reason the Law so strictly prescribed all Jews to share alike the taxes for the *Ohel Moed* (the tent of meeting). "The rich man shall not exceed and the poor man not fall short of half a shekel." It would have been highly unfair to have allowed the rich man to offer more than half a shekel. This would have meant, after all, that the rich man had a larger share in the House of God. A group of rich people might even have offered to take on the entire expense of the tent of meeting, on condition that it be in their name. Rather, each individual had an equal share in the tent of meeting and an equal share in the community of Israel.

A unique path was taken by Novaredok (Nowogródek). Rabbi Joseph Yozel Hurvits, founder of the Novaredok *yeshiva*, belonged to the first group of scholars in the "Center for Married Students" in Kovno. While he was studying in Kovno, his wife died, and Rabbi Joseph Yozel cut himself off from the world completely. He lived isolated for almost two years, neither leaving his room nor allowing anyone to enter. Rabbi Joseph Yozel was a man of Musar, however, and he realized that his isolation from the world was but a preparation for a higher stage when he would take on the mission of spreading his ideas throughout the Jewish world.

Rabbi Joseph Yozel belonged to the extreme pioneering ascetic wing of the Musar movement. The first and most important task, he believed, must be the dissemination of learning, the founding of *yeshibot* which would raise a generation of scholars with the necessary courage and power to negate the world and oppose the streams of the Enlightenment. After several attempts in various cities, he founded the *yeshiva* of Novaredok in 1896, and within a short time it became one of the most prominent centers of scholarship and Musar in Eastern Europe.

Novaredok was ascetic and militant. The world can be changed, if only one really wants it changed. The students of Novaredok frequently repeated the dictum: "All the world says that if you can't [go] over, you must [go] under; Rabbi Joseph Yozel says that if you can't [go] over, you must [go] over." The following Musar aphorisms of Rabbi Joseph Yozel emphasize the same ideas. "I never ask if it is possible; I ask only if it is necessary. If there is no path, I will blaze one."

The human personality occupies a foremost position in Musar philosophy, including the Novaredok school. Rabbi Joseph Yozel's approach is stated with particular clarity in the first chapter of his work *Madregat ha-Adam*. How did it happen, asks the author, that Adam defied God's injunction and ate of the Tree of Knowledge? Was it only due to weakness, because he was unable to resist Evil Inclination? That is an error, answers Rabbi Joseph Yozel. Eating of the Tree of Knowledge was not the beginning of sinfulness, but the beginning of our human culture; it was man's first attempt to raise himself to a higher level, an attempt that was unsuccessful. In the Garden of Eden Adam was in the category of an angel: "He knew evil and recognized it, and in spite of this he did not do anything but good." He did not even have the desire to do any evil. However, there was one important difference between him and an angel. The first man was given a choice: "If he wished he could cease being an angel, and if he wished to live a life of decision-making and not the life of an angel—it was up to him. . . . This depended on eating of the Tree of Knowledge. If he wanted to live the life of an angel, without any danger to his spiritual properties, then he must take care not to eat of the Tree of Knowledge. But if he wished to choose a life of decision-making, if he wanted the passions and desires to awaken in him so that he would have the possibility of combating and conquering them—then he should eat of the Tree of Knowledge." The first man did not want to remain in angelic state because he wanted to be free to choose between Good and Evil. The privilege of freedom, to be sure, is associated with great perils, since man can rise ever higher only if he is willing to take the risk of sinking ever lower. Adam was not disturbed by the danger, and he ate of the Tree of Knowledge. This was when man's wars against the powers of Sin and Evil began.

This remarkably original and, in fact, revolutionary explanation of the story of Adam offers us the key to the Novaredok school. "Man is the only creature in the world," Rabbi Joseph taught his disciples, "who can commit sins; therein lies his greatness."

Therefore all of man's life is a war. His function is to rise ever higher. And if man, for his part, does all that is necessary and possible, he need not be anxious whether he will succeed. Hence the problems of hope and faith have a particularly important role in the Novaredok doctrine. Man must never lose faith in himself, and Rabbi Joseph Yozel of Novaredok cites Maimonides on this: "All men are worthy of being as saintly as Moses or as evil as Jeroboam."

The Novaredok doctrine therefore also held that the world could be changed. "In order to remedy the present situation we have to begin by the building of *yeshibot* on dependable foundations, and from them the world will gradually be built." The *yeshiva* students are therefore under particular obligation to concern themselves with the group. In the last chapter of *Madregat ha-Adam* Rabbi Joseph Yozel appeals to the "public workers" (by this he meant scholars in general, and particularly his own students), as follows:

Therefore, anyone who has the power to establish learning must not remain aloof. Let him not love restfulness, but gather his strength for wandering from place to place and for founding places of learning and piety. For who will be to blame for the low state of learning and piety? Only the workers who had the possibility of establishing it and of trusting that God would fulfil their wishes.

Can individuals change the world? Certainly, answered Rabbi Joseph Yozel: "Every worker, if only he abandons his family and devotes his strength on behalf of the Truth, can as an individual exert an influence on the whole world. . . . Above all, let the individual be an individual and not look behind him to see if the multitude is following; but let him stand firm on the point of Truth and the multitude will follow."

Rabbi Joseph Yozel's words were properly received by his disciples. The expansion of Novaredok began even before the First World War. During the war years, when the Novaredok *yeshiva* moved to Gomel, Rabbi Joseph Yozel founded *yeshibot* in Kiev, Kharkov, and a number of other cities. In 1920 Rabbi Joseph Yozel died in Kiev. Because of the Soviet persecutions, his disciples were forced to leave Russia. This is when the era of Novaredok's great expansion began. Between the two World Wars over seventy "Bet Joseph" *yeshibot* named for him, with a student body of about 4,000, were founded in Latvia and Poland. Among the *yeshibot* in Poland that merit mention were those in Bialystok, Warsaw, Mezritsh, and Pinsk. The dynamic development of the "Bet Joseph" *yeshibot* is unequalled in the history of the *yeshibot* over the past three centuries.

The doctrine of "the dignity of man," in its various nuances, strengthened the students' belief in themselves and in Jewish tradition. The philosophy of understanding and grasping the Law through efforts at first understanding man, understanding oneself, became the philosophy of the Musar *yeshibot*.

BETWEEN THE TWO WORLD WARS

Between the two World Wars the number of students in the East European *yeshibot* grew considerably. The *yeshibot* drew scholars away from the synagogue houses of study. The economic status of the students in the *yeshibot* was better than that of the students in the synagogues. The old custom of eating days was no longer appropriate to the times. It also became more difficult to study alone after secular trends had so strongly influenced all of Jewish life. Consequently, this was a time for traveling away from home to study. The number of students in the *yeshibot* grew, and along with this the budgets of the large centers of learning also increased in size. A considerable portion of the income came from America, partly via the Joint Distribution Committee, but mostly through independent campaigns for the *yeshibot*.

Since the end of the nineteenth century, since the rise of the great political organizations such as the Zionist movement, the Bund, and so on, Jewish life in Eastern Europe became more organized and centralized. In 1912 the Agudat Israel, the organization for the strictly traditional sector in the Jewish world, was founded in Katowice. The rise of political parties played an important role in the reorganization of the entire educational system in Eastern Europe. The private *heder* all but disappeared. A large number of religious schools for girls (the Bet Jacob schools) were now created; a program of secular studies was introduced in the boys' schools. In 1929 the Agudat Israel founded a central body called Horev which took over the administration of the religious schools, including the *yeshibot*. In the northeastern provinces of Poland, however, where there were centers of learning with long traditions, such as Volozhin, Mir, and Radin, there already existed an organization called the *Vaad ha-Yeshibot* in Vilna, which had been founded in 1924 on the initiative of Rabbi Israel Meir Hacohen, author of *Hafez Hayyim*, and the Vilna rabbi, Hayyim Ozer Grodzenski.

In the Hasidic world, as well, the significance of the *yeshibot* was now better appreciated. And the importance of the rule, "Learning cannot be acquired except collectively," became more evident. In 1897 the Tomeke Temimim *yeshiva* was founded in Lyubavitsh. Shortly thereafter a number of additional Tomeke Temimim *yeshibot* were created in various cities in Russia. After World War I the Lyubavitsh *yeshibot* in Russia continued their work for many years despite Soviet persecution. Between the two World Wars several Tomeke Temimim *yeshibot* were founded in Latvia, Lithuania, and Poland. A good deal of attention was devoted to the study of Hasidism in these institutions. In general the method of study was almost the same as in the Lithuanian *yeshibot*.

Among the large *yeshibot* in Poland, several deserve special mention: *Yeshiva* Hakme Lublin, founded by Rabbi Meir Shapiro; the Metivta in Warsaw; and the Keter Tora *yeshibot*, founded by the Rebe of Radomsk. The number of *yeshibot* in Warsaw and throughout Poland in general increased considerably after the First World War, although in Hasidic regions the number of students in the synagogues and study houses even between the two World Wars was still very considerable. The large Musar *yeshibot* were mainly concentrated in the northeastern provinces of Poland. Of these, the *yeshibot* in the following cities and towns should be mentioned: Mir, Kamieniec, Kletsk, Radin, Grodno, Baranowicze, Lomza, and Bialystok. Tiny Lithuania also managed to preserve its honorable place in the world of the *yeshibot*: Slobodka, Telz, Ponevezh, and Kelem remained important centers of Talmudic study and of Musar up until the catastrophe in Europe.

In all, the *yeshibot* in Poland, Lithuania, and Latvia had a student body of about 25,000. In many *yeshibot* the system of dividing students into classes according to their knowledge had been introduced. On the other hand, the principle of independence was now also preserved to a great extent, both with respect to the study of the Talmud and Musar and to life in the *yeshiva* in general. In the larger *yeshibot* the students had their own mutual aid societies for loans to the needy, and for help to the sick. In several *yeshibot* there were "committees for conversational study" and for Musar.

The tragic years of World War II saw the destruction of the *yeshibot* in Eastern Europe. Only very small remnants of the *yeshiva* teachers and students managed to escape. And the enormous spiritual strength of the *yeshibot* is revealed in the fact that wherever rescued leaders and students have turned up—be it Western Europe, America, or Israel—they have once again built centers of learning that continue the great traditions of Eastern Europe.

NOTES

[1] *Tur Orah Hayyim,* 5585, sec. *Rosh ha-Shanah.*

[1a See Bernard D. Weinryb, "East European Jewry (Since the Partitions of Poland, 1772-1795)," this work, Vol. I, Chap. 7.]

[2] *Responsa of Rabbi Moses Isserles,* 95.

[2a See Israel Halpern, "The Jews in Eastern Europe (From Ancient Times until the Partitions of Poland, 1772-1795)," this work, Vol. I, pp. 320 f.]

[3] Jacob Lifshits, *Zikron Yaakob,* Vol. I, Kaunas, 1924-1930, p. 71.

[3a See below, Chap. 7, Hillel Bavli, "The Modern Renaissance of Hebrew Literature"; also below, Chap. 10, Yudel Mark, "Yiddish Literature."]

[4] Mendele Moicher Sforim, *Shloyme Reb Khayims,* Warsaw, 1928, ch. 2.

[5] Quoted after Hayyim Tschernovits, *Toledot ha-Posekim,* Vol. III, New York, 5708, p. 6.

[6] Rabbi Isserles, *op. cit.,* par. 25.

[7] Quoted after Simhah Assaf, *Mekorot le-Toledot ha-Hinuk be-Yisrael,* Tel-Aviv and Jerusalem, Vol. I, 5685-5703, par. 46.

[8] *Ibid.,* Vol. IV, p. 43.

[9] F. Lahover, *Toledot ha-Sifrut ha-Ivrit ha-Hadashah,* Tel-Aviv, Vol. IV, 5708, p. 47.

[9a See Itzhak Ben-Zvi, "Eretz Yisrael Under Ottoman Rule, 1517-1917," this work, Vol. I.]

[10] Quoted after Gershom Scholem, *"Ha-Tenuah ha-Shabetait be-Polin,"* in *Bet Yisrael be-Polin,* Jerusalem, 5714, Vol. II, p. 43.

[10a See Halpern, *op. cit.;* Ben-Zvi, *op. cit.*]

[^{11a} See Halpern, *op. cit.*, pp. 317 ff.]

[^{12a} See Ben-Zvi, *op. cit.*; see above, Chap. 5, Abraham J. Heschel, "The Mystical Element in Judaism."]

^{13} *Degel Mahaneh Efraim*, sec. *Ki Teze.*

^{14} *Tzvaat ha-Ribash*, Lemberg, 1860, 3.

[^{15a} Ben-Zvi, *op. cit.*, pp. 454-456, 476.]

^{16} Introduction to the *Biur ha-Gra al Sifra de-Zeniuta.*

^{17} *Nefesh he-Hayyim*, Part I, ch. 4.

^{18} Introduction by Rabbi Hayyim Volozhiner to the *Biurha-Gra* on the *Shulhan Aruk.*

^{19} *Nefesh he-Hayyim*, Part I, ch. 12.

^{20} *Aliot Eliyahu*, end.

[^{20a} See Halpern, *op. cit.*; Weinryb, *op. cit.*; Bavli, *op. cit.*; Mark, *op. cit.*]

^{21} Rabbi Meir Berlin, *Fun Volozhin biz Yerusholayim*, New York, 1933, p. 25.

^{22} *Sforim, op. cit.*, Part II, p. 29.

^{23} Abraham Isser Katsovitsh, *Zekhtsik yor lebn*, pp. 83-84.

^{24} Simeon Bernfeld, "*Zikronot*," in *Reshumot*, Vol. IV, p. 149.

^{25} *Kol Kitbe Ahad Ha-Am*, Jerusalem, 5707, p. 467.

^{26} A. Zamba, "*Shtiblakh bevarshe*," in *Mosedot Torah be-Eropah*, New York, 1956, p. 356.

^{27} A. Paperne, *Zikhroynes*, Warsaw, 1923, pp. 16-18.

^{28} Lahover, *op. cit.*, Vol. IV, p. 47.

^{29} Dov Kats, *Tenuat ha-Musar*, Vol. I, Tel-Aviv, 5706-5716, p. 148.

^{30} Isaac Blazer, *Or Yisrael*, Vilna, 5660, p. 80.

^{31} Kats, *op. cit.*, Vol. II.

^{32} M. Gerts, *Musernikes*, Riga, 1936.

BRIEF BIBLIOGRAPHY

ASSAF, SIMHAH, *Mekorot le-Toledot he-Hinuk be-Yisrael.* Vols. I-IV. Tel-Aviv and Jerusalem, 5685-5703.

BERLIN, MEIR, *Fun Volozhin biz Yerusholayim.* Vols. I-II. New York, 1933.

Bet Yisrael be-Polin. Vol. II. Jerusalem, 5714.

BLAZER, ISAAC, *Or Yisrael.* Vilna, 5660.

CARLEBACH, ESRIEL, "*Mussar*," in *Jahrbuch der juedisch-literarischen Gesellschaft,* Vol. XXII. Frankfort-am-Main, 1931-1932.

DUBNOW, SHIMON, *Toledot ha-Hasidut.* Vols. I-III. Tel-Aviv, 5690.

GINZBERG, LOUIS, *Students, Scholars and Saints.* Philadelphia, 1928.

GLENN, MENAHEM G., *Israel Salanter.* New York, 1953.

HORODETSKI, SH. A., *He-Hasidut ve-ha-Hasidim.* Vols. I-IV. Jerusalem, 5683.

———, *Lekorot ha-Rabbanut.* Warsaw, 1914.

KATS, DOV, *Tenuat ha-Mussar*. Vols. I-III. Tel-Aviv, 5706-5716.

LIFSHITS, JACOB, *Zikhron Yaakob*. Vols. I-III. Kaunas, 1924-1930.

Lite. New York, 1951.

MAIMON, Y. L., *Sefer ha-Gra*. Jerusalem, 5714.

Mosedot Torah be-Eropah. New York, 1956.

OVSAY, JOSHUA, *Maamarim ve-Reshimot*. New York, 5707.

SCHARFSTEIN, ZEVI, *Toledot ha-Hinnuk be-Yisrael be-Dorot ha-Aharonim*. Vols. I-III. New York, 5705-5709.

Sefer ha-Yobel li-Kebod Rabbenu ha-Gaon R. Shimon Yehudah ha-Kohen Shkop Shelita. Vilna, 5696.

Sefer ha-Zikkaron shel ha-Yeshibah ha-Gedolah "Keneset bet Ishak," be-Kamenets de-Lite (Polin). Warsaw, 5698.

TSCHERNOVITS, HAYYIM (RAV TSAIR), *Toledot ha-Posekim*, Part III. New York, 5708.

ZAVIN, SHELOMO YOSEF, *Ishim ve-Shitot*. Tel-Aviv, 5712.

CHAPTER 7

THE MODERN RENAISSANCE OF HEBREW LITERATURE

By Hillel Bavli

Foreword

During the past century and a half Hebrew literature has experienced a remarkable transformation. It emerged with newborn power from the obscurity into which it had sunk after the splendid medieval period. Quickened by the Enlightenment of eighteenth-century Western Europe, Hebrew literature soon grew receptive to new ideas and new forms, more sensitive to rising contemporary problems and conscious of its high calling to inspire and to guide the Jewish people.

In spirit, modern Hebrew literature is in close affinity with universal literature. It has drawn strength from many cultures and it bears the imprint of many environments. Italian Renaissance, French rationalism, and pseudoclassicism, German and English romanticism affected its course. This is but natural, since it has flourished in various countries.

Having assimilated the foreign influences that stimulated it, Hebrew literature before long became aware of its own traditions, and was gradually regenerated by the force of its own consciousness. In its totality, modern Hebrew literature embodies a record of the physical and spiritual life of the Jewish people. It expresses the temporal and the eternal, the national and the universal. Through it and with many voices, the social, religious and aesthetic forces that went into the making of our modern age became articulate.

The following pages attempt a summary and an appraisal of the leading tendencies and personalities through whom modern Hebrew literature, in my opinion, is best represented.

1. AIMS OF HASKALA

The predominant characteristic of modern Hebrew literature, from the middle of the eighteenth to the latter part of the nineteenth century, is generally described by the word *Haskala*, that is, Enlightenment. This very name is given to the literature of that entire age. The urge for Haskala brought about a literary revival, first in Germany, where it was short lived, then in Austria, particularly in the province of Galicia, and in Russia, including Poland and Lithuania, in which countries it was more enduring and of great significance.

Haskala aimed primarily at a studied adjustment of Jewish life to the modern world as a prelude to the social and political emancipation of the Ghetto Jew.[1a] Hence it called for drastic change in the curriculum of the Jewish school in Germany and Eastern Europe, where secular studies were completely disregarded. The translation of the Pentateuch into German by Moses Mendelssohn (1729-1786), first fruit of Haskala in Germany, was to provide a stimulus to the study of the German language and an introduction to Western culture. The study of the humanities became the coveted goal of the Haskala movement in Germany and elsewhere. There was nothing revolutionary in this idea, nor anything contrary to Jewish tradition. In fact, the leading rabbinic authority of the age, the Gaon of Vilna (1720-1797), considered the study of "worldly wisdom" essential for a deeper understanding of the Torah. Still, the vigorous effort of the Haskala movement to remove the barrier between religious and worldly culture made the ideal of secularism 'a contributing factor in the Hebrew literary revival.

Haskala meant also a cultivation of the aesthetic sense, a craving for beauty. Poetry above all, as a symbol of the sublime and the beautiful, became a subject of special adoration. The young poet Shlomo Loewisohn (1789-1821), a native of Hungary, gave artistic utterance to the ideal of the age. In an exalted ode, *Poetry Speaks*, written in colorful blank verse, he pictured poetry, "the offspring of beauty," as the guiding and all-dominating spirit of the universe. This majestic ode has in it something of the impassioned sublimity of Shelley's *Defence of Poetry* with its challenging final pronouncement: "The poets are the unacknowledged legislators of mankind."

Synonymous with poetry and with beauty was the Hebrew language. An ecstatic devotion to the Hebrew tongue, a sustained vision of its complete revival, inspired the entire Haskala literature. The love of Hebrew has been the expression of a great faith in the vitality of the Jewish people. The sacred tongue, long associated in the minds of most people with religious culture only, shook off the dust of antiquity and assumed a creative role for the renewal of Jewish life in all its phases.

Haskala strove to normalize Jewish life. It proclaimed the ideal of manual labor, of agricultural pursuit in particular, as a great moral catharsis, a spiritual as well as physical cure for the sorely tried Ghetto Jewry. This ideal was stressed with homiletic skill, supported by numerous quotations from ancient texts, by the pioneer champion of Haskala in Russia, Isaac Baer Levinsohn (1788-1860). Life alone with nature, a life of labor, became the theme song for many a poem, allegory and story.

In its later militant stages, the Haskala movement sought radically to reinterpret traditional Jewish values, to shatter ancient forms and patterns of thought and behavior. In short, Haskala aspired to reform Jewish life socially, religiously and aesthetically, to regenerate Hebrew literature by injecting into it the serum of reality.

The most striking characteristic of Haskala literature is the deep humanity pervading it, its abiding faith in mankind, in the triumph of reason, in human progress. A representative poet of Haskala, Adam Lebenson (1794-1878) of Lithuania, visualized Mercy, "the heavenly daughter," standing at the crossroads pleading with the passers-by to sustain her in healing humanity of its ills due to cruelty, to adversity, to catastrophe. The note of woe and mercy, the common bond of humanity, struck in his poem *Mercy*, is characteristic of the entire age, for while the immediate concern of Haskala was the Jewish people, its outlook was worldly, and its supreme ideal the universal.

2. THE RISE OF THE SCIENCE OF JUDAISM

The Haskala movement was the outgrowth of an idea. But ideas have a way of releasing strange forces, unforeseen by those with whom the ideas are original. Thus Haskala, which aimed to teach the modern Jew to observe the world about him, eventually led the thinking Jew to look more deeply into his own world.

The Age of Enlightenment, which saw a deepening of historical thinking, witnessed the emergence of the "Science of Judaism," whose main purpose was to study the Jewish past critically, with scientific thoroughness, through a systematic examination of the minutest details. The founders of the Science of Judaism, Solomon Judah Loeb (Shir) Rapaport (1790-1867) and Nachman Krochmal (1785-1840) in Galicia, Samuel David Luzzatto (1800-1865) in Italy, and Leopold Zunz (1794-1886) in Germany, the first three in Hebrew and the last one in German, applied the discipline of scholarship to vast unexplored regions of Hebrew literature, ancient and medieval. They, their disciples and followers, brought to light the inner spirit of Judaism manifesting itself in biblical and Rabbinic literature, in liturgy and homily, in the Hebrew language and Hebrew poetry. The achievements of the Science of Judaism in the past century made possible a more proper evaluation of Judaism's civilizing role throughout the ages.

To reveal the historic character of Judaism was the main objective of Nachman Krochmal and Samuel David Luzzatto, two of the boldest spirits of the Haskala age.

In his philosophic work, *Guide for the Perplexed of the Age*, Krochmal brought the history of Judaism within the orbit of world civilizations and applied the laws of change and development governing all peoples and cultures to the study and interpretation of the spiritual values of Israel. Probing into the past, Krochmal performed a twofold task: he traced the points of similarity between the historic course of Israel and that of other peoples and, above all, he indicated the distinctiveness of the Hebrew genius. "In truth," he affirmed, "the individuality of a nation as such is merely the individuality of its spirit."[2] The mark of Jewish individuality, he reasoned, is the absolute spirit, the belief in an incorporeal God Who is not predicated by any material symbolism. Therein, he concluded, is the secret of the eternity of Israel, inasmuch as the Infinite, the Absolute Spirit, is imperishable.

To Krochmal, the disciple of Maimonides and the devotee of German idealism, faith and reason, religion and philosophy complemented one another as manifestations of the spirit. Neither is adequate to retain its loftiness and purity, escaping fanaticism or skeptic materialism without the inspiration and guidance of its counterpart.

A different road was taken by Samuel David Luzzatto, the poet and critic, exegete and interpreter of medieval Hebrew poetry. Intensity of emotion rather than depth of thought was the dominant force of his personality. His writings, in both poetry and prose, are characterized by optimism and human tenderness. Unlike Krochmal, he disclaimed any philosophic, theoretical approach to Judaism and emphasized instead the humanitarian aspect, the quality of mercy, which he regarded as one of the fundamentals of Judaism.

In him faith was stronger than reason. He exalted the religion of the heart above the intellect, the primitive traditional religion with its belief in the supernatural and the miraculous. Like Judah Ha-Levi,[3a] whose poetry he interpreted so beautifully, he believed that the intuitive grasp, the ecstatic emotion could open gates of Divine Revelation which no philosophic system could. With Ha-Levi he could say: "And my heart saw Thee and believed in Thee, as though it had stood at Mount Sinai. I sought Thee in my visions and Thy glory descended and passed through my clouds."

He, too, rejected the "wisdom of the Greeks," with its emphasis upon intellectualism, and extolled Judaism, the Abramitic spirit, as he called it, with its insistence upon moral improvement, upon training of character. Challenging the rationalist views of the age, Luzzatto called for a rebirth of Judaism from within through a deepening of emotional attachment to tradition, through a heightening of national consciousness.

Krochmal and Luzzatto, for all their differences in outlook and temperament, were at one in some respects. Both saw in the Jewish individuality an emblem of indestructible nationhood. Both analyzed the problems of the past with an eye to the future, convinced that the Hebrew genius still had great contributions to make. Finally, both maintained that only in cultivating the original character of Judaism through the Hebrew language and literature, was there any hope for the spiritual revival of the Jewish people.

3. VOICES FROM THE BIBLE

Nowhere has the Renaissance of Hebrew literature been so pronounced as in the field of poetry. At the beginning of the nineteenth century the Hebrew muse was remarkably inarticulate. The poetic vigor of medieval Spain had long been spent. Whatever there was of Hebrew poetry was stilted, didactic and colorless. In time, however, Hebrew poetry found its voice again. In form, in color, in tone, it grew rich and broad.

There was one great voice heard in Hebrew poetry in the eighteenth century, that of Moses Hayyim Luzzatto (1707-1747) of Padua, Italy.[4a] This Messianic visionary, whose chief work lies in the fields of religious mysticism and ethics, was destined to inject new life into Hebrew literature by his poetry. His two major dramatic poems, the imaginative *Tower of Strength* and the allegorical *Praise to the Righteous,* clearly bear the marks of European pseudoclassicism. In fact the first is, in part, borrowed from the popular pastoral drama, *Il Pastor Fido,* by the sixteenth-century Italian, Guarini. Nevertheless, in Luzzatto the minor pseudoclassic strain became a major classic voice, austere and strong and melodious. Luzzatto's two love stories, with their recurring moralism in the triumph of the simple, pure heart endowed with natural piety over the cunning of the wicked and blind cruelty of the mob, combine to a rare degree romantic imagery with classic severity of composition. The occult and rational qualities of man, dreamlike vision and intellectual observation, are fused in these works. Their sublimation of nature, of simple life, their deep sense of the ethical and the aesthetic alike re-echoed strongly in later Haskala literature. The exalted blank verse of Luzzatto, couched in purest biblical style, turned renascent Hebrew literature to the Bible itself.

Literary revival very often implies the power to lend new meaning and importance to ancient lore, to revitalize the inherited and make it function again. The Haskala poets, in their quest for humanism and classic beauty, rediscovered the Bible as a source of poetic inspiration, as an instrument of cultural and social progress. Characteristically enough, the above-mentioned Shlomo Loewisohn made the first attempt in modern Hebrew literature at a literary, aesthetic appreciation of the Scriptures, in a volume on the rhetoric of the Bible.

In an introduction to his long and tedious epic on the life of Moses, Napthali Herz Wessely (1725-1805), chief spokesman of Haskala in Germany, spoke about the need for poetic commentary on the Bible. Such a commentary indeed was written by numerous gifted poets; it was, however, not merely a commentary on the Bible but also on their own lives and on the age in which they lived. Many searched deeply in the ancient Book for the elixir of creative life. From the Bible, dramatic and narrative poems borrowed characters in ancient dress—kings, prophets, peasants, shepherds—who were nevertheless sufficiently European in manner to befit the modern age. Voices from the Bible mingled with echoes from French and German poets. Collectively, this poetry constitutes a cultural phenomenon. To the Ghetto Jew, removed from nature, it brought both a glorious vision and contact with the soil.

Occasionally biblical scenes and characters reflected the poet's own personality and his inner struggles. A notable example is Micah Joseph Lebensohn (1828-1852) of Vilna. In him epic serenity and lyric ecstasy were equally strong. His short and tragic life is compressed in his noble poetry.

Romantic melancholy, worldly illusion, a passion for life, and the bitterness of approaching death, fill his verse. The search for truth and beauty and the tragedy of unfulfillment, the antinomies of reason and emotion, are the leitmotifs of his lyric poetry. They are also the very heart of his biblical epics. The striking image of youthful King Solomon drunk with love, with poetry, with faith, is a stirring image of romantic youth and high idealism. The somber figure of Kohelet, Solomon in his declining years, seared by delusions and doubts and frustrations, is, in its symbolic allusions, the poet's mocking criticism of the rationalistic trend of his age. With tense feeling, in soulful, musical lines, the poet portrays the tragic beauty of ancient characters: Moses at Mt. Abarim breathing his last while "his eye is turned toward Jerusalem"; Jael, torn between love of country and deep compassion as she is about to slay Sisera; blind and furious Samson avenging himself on the Philistines in his last heroic act; and the medieval poet Judah Ha-Levi, struck by a marauder's hand as he prays at the gates of Jerusalem. The remote past envisioned by the poet becomes an intimate personal experience.

Bible-inspired poetry reached its peak in the works of Abraham Mapu (1808-1867), a native of Lithuania. His two major historical novels, *The Love of Zion* and *The Guilt of Samaria*, the first novels in modern Hebrew literature, have in them much of the intensity and ardor of true poetry. In Mapu, the romantic novel found an accomplished artist, the biblical epic its great master.

The novels of Mapu are fantastic love stories, intricate in plot, rich in action, in intrigue and adventure, in the tradition of the romantic school. The great and magnanimous lover, the virtuous and the wicked, the nobleman and the simple peasant—all these inevitable characters are here. The righteous come to their reward, of course, and the lovers triumph over all obstacles.

The great popularity of these tales in their day was due to the many fascinating surprises in the narratives. But the real value and significance of Mapu lie in his *ars Hebraica*. Mapu transplanted the romanticism of the Occident into the soil of ancient Palestine; he saturated that romanticism with the living waters of the prophetic fountain, and raised it to a splendor and originality all its own.

Amid the squalor and horrors of Ghetto life in czarist Russia, Mapu projected a vision of ancient Judea and presented a pageant of wholesome Hebrew life rooted in its own soil, nurtured by its own culture. Jerusalem with its environs, its landscape and its populace; the countryside with its peasantry; prince, priest, prophet and plain people, customs and ritual—all assumed an illusory reality. Mapu was able to make his vision vivid by his unusual insight, by his genius for the primitive, and above all, by his marvelous sense of the rhythm and spirit of the Bible.

Reading Mapu one gets the feeling that here is not a mere studied imitation of biblical style but rather a complete self-identification with the temper and speech and outlook of biblical days. Therein, in his intuitive, creative penetration into the very accent of the Bible, lies his great cultural significance.

More than any of his contemporaries, Mapu symbolized the deep, newborn consciousness of nature and the spirit of Jewish regeneration through contact with the soil of Palestine.

4. SEEING THE PRESENT

Modern Hebrew literature was not confined merely to classic beauty and idyllic aestheticism. The scholarly and imaginative treatment of the past constituted but one phase of that literature. Another phase, predominant in the latter half of the nineteenth century, was the realistic portrayal of the present. The entire structure of Jewish life in the Ghetto was exposed to critical scrutiny. The ideal of change and revision permeated much of Hebrew prose and poetry. Finally, literature became critical of itself and examined its own character, its functions and its ideals.

One of the severe critics of the age was its most representative poet, Judah Loeb Gordon (1830-1892), a native of Vilna.

The poetry of Gordon is distinguished by its epic quality; occasionally it is colored by lyrical soliloquy. The minor romantic strain of his early poetry is the least characteristic of it. It has little of the rapture and sweet melancholy of impassioned youth. It is rational, forceful and incisive. Satirical invective is its strongest weapon.

In a series of powerful narratives Gordon portrayed Jewish society, holding up to ridicule all that seemed ugly, stagnant and unworldly. He fought the phantoms of the past: rigorous traditions, stifling prejudices, bigotry and ignorance. In historical epic, biblical monologue and contemporary tale, he inveighed against the ills and follies of the present, and called for a more liberal outlook on life, in consonance with the spirit of the time.

His epic, *Between the Lion's Teeth*, is a striking portrayal of the loss of the Judean state and the heroism of one of its defenders who met a martyr's death at the arena in Rome. The tragedy of a people is compressed in stirring scenes. Out of the past rises the piercing voice of the poet, scorning the ancient Jewish leaders and, by innuendo, the leaders of his day who, in their preoccupation with spiritual matters, failed to prepare their people for the day of trial, and have taught Israel "to be dead on earth, alive in the heavens."

A similar note is struck in the dramatic monologue, *Zedekiah in Prison*. Blinded King Zedekiah, in captivity contemplating his fate, appears as a progressive leader of the state, an advocate of labor and agriculture, in opposition to the superspiritual views of the prophet Jeremiah. But Zedekiah is merely the poet's mouthpiece. Gordon challenges those of his contemporaries who would divorce Judaism from worldly interests and activities and would confine it mainly to the archives of ancient glory.

His *Epics of the Present* are stirring narratives of tragic episodes in Jewish life resulting from a lack of adjustment of the ancient tradition to the modern environment. These "Epics" storm with protest, with indignation against the severity of Jewish orthodoxy, the static state of Jewish society, the shortsightedness of its leaders.

The influence of Gordon's poetry on Hebrew literature was far reaching. It was a dynamic factor in rousing the creative forces in Jewry to self-renewal through a deeper attachment to the soil and the world, and through a stronger faith in the future destiny of the Jewish people.

The ideal of social and religious reform was the motivating force of the best work of Moshe Leib Lilienblum (1843-1910), a notable figure in Haskala literature.

His most colorful work, *Sins of Youth*, unfolds the ghastliest pictures of Ghetto life in Lithuania. The author's experiences are drawn with the pain and joy of self-revelation in a series of oppressive scenes: his gloomy childhood in an environment of ugly fanaticism and melancholy asceticism, his rabbinic training and youthful piety, the rising doubts and passions of adolescence, his struggles for Haskala and the fury of persecution unleashed against him. Lilienblum himself characterized his work as "a Hebrew drama without theatrical effect and unfinished, but rich in misfortune."[5] It is, in essence, a book of revolt against obsolete forms, against an ascetic tradition, against indolence and ignorance.

To Lilienblum the need for the liberalization of Judaism was prior to any social reform. Consequently, he advocated that the principle of change and inner development which once influenced talmudic literature be recognized again by the Rabbinic authorities. The legal abolition of out-dated customs and inhibitions would, he believed, strengthen Judaism from within and open the road for social and economic progress.

In the persistent call for realism, for the adjustment of religion to life, Lilienblum and many of his contemporaries showed little understanding of the emotional and romantic aspect of religion. Any mystic or legendary strain was damned by them as reactionary. Hasidism, with its imaginative, emotional approach to life, they regarded as a source of all evil; to them folklore was sheer nonsense and superstition.

The vision of the poet and the polemic of the publicist were made lively by the story of the novelist. In fact, the Haskala novel combined poetic lyricism, publicistic moralizing, and plain, realistic storytelling. Those traits are particularly evident in the works of Perez Smolenskin (1842-1885), a native of White Russia who spent his creative years in Vienna, where he founded and edited the influential Hebrew monthly *Hashahar*.

Smolenskin attempted to portray the totality of Jewish life, the various strata of society in and outside the Ghetto with a naturalness and broad sweep unknown before in Hebrew literature. Out of his rich picture gallery three collective types come to the fore.

First the forlorn souls who, like the hero in his leading novel are *lost in the ways of life*. These are the budding intellectuals, uprooted from the soil of their own traditions and maladjusted to any other milieu; they wander aimlessly like spiritual gypsies.

Next come the "pillars of society," the men of might and influence, community elders who despise and crush the poor, the exploiters, wicked obscurantists and hypocrites who attack Haskala, adventurers and scoundrels.

Alongside these characters stand the men of truth and high idealism, the torchbearers of Haskala; with them are the saintly men of deep faith and religious ecstasy.

The novels of Smolenskin are volatile and dramatic. They suffer from overmoralizing and loquacity, from an overabundance of the bizarre and extravagant. Nevertheless, for all their artistic imperfections, they contain magnificent portraits and caricatures of the age. They did for Hebrew literature what the novels of Dickens did for English literature. They are charged with the reformer's zeal and the idealist's passion, and their love is reserved for the weak, the humble, the oppressed.

The weakness of the Haskala novel lies in its inability to describe natural objects accurately, or to perceive the elements of character dis-tinctly. Vague generalization prevented the novelist from recognizing reality.

The great master of Hebrew realism was Mendele Mocher Seforim (1836-1916), *i.e.*, Mendele the Bookseller, pseudonym of S. J. Abramowitz, a native of White Russia who spent a major part of his life in Odessa.[6a] An artist in both Hebrew and Yiddish literature, Mendele is unique as a novelist. He is the type of author whom only a rich, indigenous Jewish life and culture could have produced.

Mendele the Bookseller, his leading character, is a typical Jew who, following his calling, roams the Ghetto far and wide. He is the observant eye describing all he sees. In truth, the author assures us, there are two Mendeles struggling within him. One is simple and naïve and the other critical and satirical. And we see Ghetto life through the eyes of both. The external ugliness of the Ghetto, depicted so mercilessly by Mendele, is mellowed by the spiritual grandeur and nobility of Jewish traditional life. An unrivaled painter of Jewish poverty and Jewish tragedy, Mendele is, equally, the fierce critic who satirizes the provincial backwardness of the Ghetto Jew, his rootlessness, his detachment from the soil.

Mendele is distinguished alike as interpreter of human character and painter of the visible world. His gloomy pictures of Ghetto misery are set within a framework of quiet, natural scenery.

The descriptive art of Mendele is matched by the magnificence of his style. Mendele revitalized classical Hebrew, gave it new color and marked it with the reality of a spoken, pungent vernacular. He merged biblical and Rabbinic diction, spiced it with elements of popular colloquialism, and created an instrument of powerful expression.

The acute critical sense which Hebrew literature displayed in the last decades of the nineteenth century was in time directed against literature itself. Hebrew literature became critical of its own functions and accomplishments. Style, motif, plot, craftsmanship, were subjected to critical analysis. The most representative critic of his age was David Frishman (1860-1922), a native of Poland.

Frishman made his critical debut in 1883, at the decline of the Haskala age, but the spirit of Haskala lived on in him to the end. His activities covered a number of fields—poetry, short story, essay—but it is chiefly as a critic that he is to be remembered. He detected in Hebrew literature the very faults that Gordon and Mendele exposed in Ghetto life: provincialism, ignorance, lack of perspective and good taste. In a musical biblical style approaching poetic prose, he preached the doctrine of aestheticism and universalism. "To create gradually through the good a feeling and taste for the good"—this dictum of Goethe which he repeatedly quoted served him as guide in his work. He was the inspired herald and interpreter of classic European literature and the charming translator of many masterpieces from the works of Shakespeare and Byron, Goethe and Heine and Nietzsche.

Frishman was one of the last knights-errant of Haskala; a firm believer
in the ideals of humanism, and above all in the power of poetry and pure
art to guide and elevate mankind.

5. THE FORCE OF NATIONALISM

In 1880 Gordon, poet of Haskala, elegized: "I am distressed for you,
unfortunate poet of mine. You, too, I know, are as sick as I am. Your perfume is fouled here by stench and mud, ånd no wide spaces have you for
the wandering of the spirit."[7] Thus the saddened poet heard the departing
Shekinah, fugitive inspiration, speak to him. A disenchanted age was
speaking through the voice of the poet.

By the end of the century, Haskala as a creative force had spent itself.
The overemphasis which Haskala laid upon Western culture as a pattern
of Jewish life, upon secularism and universalism as supreme ideals, inevitably brought about a shrinkage of Jewish individuality, a weakening of
its moral fiber. A reaction was bound to set in. The current of assimilation
that swept many of the "enlightened" Jewish youth, the rise of anti-
Semitism in Germany, the outburst of pogroms in Russia, disillusioned
the most ardent champions of Haskala, who had failed to realize sufficiently that the growth of a people comes primarily from within, from its
own spiritual source.

A new force was emerging, shaping the course of Hebrew literature;
it was the force of national orientation. Emphasis was now being laid upon
the nationhood of the Jewish people, upon the uniqueness of its culture
and traditions.

Perez Smolenskin, one of the chief exponents of Haskala, was among
the first to expose and criticize its failures. Smolenskin charged the
Haskala movement, particularly in its German phase, with a disruptive
influence upon Jewish life, due mainly to its servile imitation of Western
ways, without regard for Jewish individuality. The Reform movement,
which denied the Messianic hope of Israel's restoration on the assumption
that Israel was merely a religious community, not a nation, was an outgrowth, Smolenskin asserted, of this self-effacing imitation, leading to
national suicide. The survival of Judaism as a creative force, he proclaimed,
is dependent on the recognition of the Jewish people as a national entity.

The concept of nationhood, argued Smolenskin, has always been primary
in Jewish consciousness. Israel never ceased regarding itself as a people.
It is national consciousness that served to unify all elements in Israel, even
the wayward sons, as long as they regarded themselves members of the
Jewish people. The religious idea and the national concept are inseparable
in Jewish history. Torah is a national as well as religious covenant. The
religious precepts also attest to the national will and spring therefrom.

Nationalism, Smolenskin pleaded as did Moses Hess in his *Rome and Jerusalem*, is not in opposition to the spirit of universal progress. It is a rung in the ladder of humanity leading to its very top which is universal brotherhood.

In expounding his theories, Smolenskin laid stress upon the spiritual character of Jewish nationalism which was founded upon three basic principles: (1) Torah, the very essence of true spirituality, (2) the ideal of Israel's restoration as a people in Eretz Yisrael, and (3) the Hebrew language. But spiritual nationalism must remain pale and ineffective without a national soil. The abstract theories of Smolenskin and his contemporaries eventually were transformed into the vigorous affirmations of *Hibbat Zion*, the movement for Jewish colonization of Palestine. The rebuilding of Palestine along with Hebrew cultural renaissance became the driving forces of modern Hebrew literature.

In the peaceful quarters of Haskala, with their bright universal illusions, a dark, foreboding figure made its appearance—Jewish tragedy. Its horrible features cast their menacing shadows over story and essay and poem alike.

Leon (Judah Loeb) Pinsker's *Autoemancipation*, with its keen analysis of the Jewish problem and its diagnosis of Judophobia as a hereditary psychic aberration incurable by Haskala and emancipation, found fertile ground in Hebrew literature.

Pinsker's call for the rise of national self-respect, for a "national decision" to lay the ghost of Jewish homelessness (main cause of anti-Semitism, in his view), was in line with the fiery challenges of Smolenskin and the stern warnings of Lilienblum.

The destructive effect of homelessness, of *Galut* on Jewish character and morale was drawn in bold and dark lines. The Jewish people has to make its choice, exhorted Lilienblum in his eloquent essay *The Revival of Israel on Its Ancestral Soil*, either to live as a minority in the Diaspora, subject to endless persecution and massacre, to dissolve gradually under the corroding influence of assimilation, or to take the only honorable course—to live a normal life on the reconstituted ancestral soil.

With the rise of Hebrew nationalism another ideal emerged: the revival of Hebrew as a spoken tongue. Throughout the ages, even when it ceased to be spoken, Hebrew had been more than a mere literary language. It was and is one of the deep sources of Jewish consciousness. It is the unbroken chain linking the entire religious and cultural tradition of the Jewish people, bearing the indelible imprint of Hebrew individuality. Nevertheless, having been confined for ages to the book primarily, it lost touch with reality. The revival of Hebrew as a vernacular became the very symbol and touchstone of Hebrew Renaissance.

This phenomenal revival was accelerated by numerous factors: the amazing evolution of Hebrew literature during the nineteenth century, the creative ingenuity of such masters as Mapu, Gordon, Mendele, their contemporaries and their followers, the rise of Hebrew dailies, the work of Hebrew educators and pedagogues.

Eliezer Ben Yehuda (1858-1922) stands out as the pioneer of spoken Hebrew. In 1878 he had already formulated his view that Hebrew spiritual revival is futile unless Palestine is established as a national center. He settled in Palestine in 1881 and dedicated his life with singlehearted devotion to the revival of spoken Hebrew. As journalist, editor and philologist he had but one goal: the adjustment of Hebrew to daily life. His monumental encyclopedic *Dictionary of Ancient and Modern Hebrew* comprises the accumulated linguistic wealth of the ages and abounds in words coined by the author, current in Hebrew speech of today.

The miraculous revival of spoken Hebrew in modern Palestine is one of the great testimonies to the reality of the Hebrew Renaissance.

The ideal of national revival found its clearest expositor and interpreter in Ahad Ha-Am (born in the Ukraine 1856, died in Tel-Aviv 1927).

Ahad Ha-Am saw the national movement as the latest stage in the long evolution of the Hebrew spirit. He regarded it as the manifestation of the national will-to-live—the very blind force that asserted itself during crucial periods in Jewish history. The critical position of Judaism in the modern era that called forth the national movement as a saving force was due, in the view of Ahad Ha-Am, no less to internal than to external dangers. Judaism, which in the remote past was in a continuous state of flux and development, in conformity with the needs of each generation, is in danger of becoming atrophied. It is losing contact with life. The Jewish people is on the verge of disintegration. Not that it has lost its creative powers. But Jewish genius is diverted to strange channels and whatever it produces is marked by foreign influence. Judaism can no longer be isolated. "Not only the Jews, but Judaism, too, came out of the Ghetto wherever it came in contact with modern culture. Leaving the Ghetto walls it is in danger of losing its individuality or, at best, its national cohesiveness."[8] Only a great national ideal could save the Jewish people from stagnation. But such an ideal cannot be born in the Diaspora. It can grow only within the historical atmosphere of Judaism, where the Hebrew spirit can assert itself freely, unhampered by foreign influences.

Zionism is therefore synonymous with Judaism itself. Through Zionism, Israel declares itself to be alive. Palestine, rejuvenated by Hebrew culture, would become the mainstay of Judaism and "the true miniature of the Jewish people as it ought to be." Ultimately it would develop "not merely as a state of Jews but as a Jewish state."[9] To the Jews in the Diaspora Palestine would be a "spiritual center" embodying the spirit of Judaism at its highest. It would serve the Diaspora as a "center of imitation," symbolizing a pattern of life to be followed, uplifting Jewish morale, integrating Jewry the world over.

Since it sought the spiritual rehabilitation of Israel, Zionism would be insufficient, reasoned Ahad Ha-Am, as a mere political movement. A small state would be inadequate compensation for two thousand years of agony. The Jewish people was preserved through the ages by two great forces. It was maintained by the exalted ideals of the prophets who placed spiritual values above physical prowess and taught Israel never to be dismayed by brute power. Secondly, it was kept intact by a peculiar genius to assimilate any alien elements which threatened its existence and to utilize them for the enrichment of its own individuality. A political ideal which does not draw its support from the national culture would not be in consonance with Jewish tradition.

Consequently, the national ideal calls for spiritual regeneration, for complete Hebraization of Jewish education, for revival of Hebrew literature and Jewish learning, for activization of the prophetic teachings. Hence, the function of Hebrew literature is to illuminate Jewish past and present, to cultivate Jewish mind and consciousness to the end that national interests shall be placed above the individual good. Like Smolenskin, Ahad Ha-Am said that true nationalism is in no way contrary to the universal spirit. "Nationalism is a concrete form whereby the universal spirit reveals itself in every people in conformity with that people's circumstances, special needs and historic course."[10] Living normally on its own historic soil, engaging in all branches of human culture, developing its own national treasures, the Jewish people will rise to its highest possible level. Israel realizing itself will make its maximum contribution to the civilization of the world as it did in the past.

Rational as the theories of Ahad Ha-Am seem on the surface, they rise ultimately from the deep well of ancient faith. Judaism is viewed by Ahad Ha-Am not merely as a religion but as the sum total of all that the Jewish spirit created. Yet, in discussing the essence and destiny of Judaism, Ahad Ha-Am often assumes an air of mystery akin to religious fervor.

Throughout the same mirror of reason and faith with which he looked upon Judaism, Ahad Ha-Am beheld nationalism not as a lone episode in Jewish history but as the very core of Judaism.

Alongside the stream of clear thought emanating from the essays of Ahad Ha-Am, there was a current flowing in the opposite direction, represented by Micah Joseph Berdichevsky (1865-1922), a native of the Ukraine who spent a great part of his life in Germany.

Berdichevsky was a complex personality ever on the threshold of conflicting ideas, caught in the twilight of thought and emotion. The problem that confronted him in his youth and ever after was disturbing many of his contemporaries. It was the dilemma so magnificently presented by Mordecai Zeeb Feierberg (1874-1899) in his autobiographical story

Whither—to the deep shadows of a strangely fascinating and repelling past or to the alluring lights of European culture? The cry of a torn soul lost in a maze of conflicts is audible in many of the essays, soliloquies, and stories of Berdichevsky.

As a way out of the dilemma, Berdichevsky struggled—unsuccessfully, however—to sever the ties of the past altogether. The entire Jewish cultural history appeared to him as one continuous effort to curb the will of the individual and to impose the discipline of normative Judaism on the unwilling masses. With a touch of pagan heresy, he clamored for a transvaluation of values in Jewish history, for the abrogation of the supreme authority of the Book in Jewish life, for renewal of spirituality through contact with the soil, through life in nature.

Berdichevsky regarded as the supreme purpose of Hebrew renascence the liberation of the individual rather than the fortification of the national will, the obliteration of any prohibitive distinction between the sacred and profane, between the national and universal. Pathetically, he exclaimed: "The great world, life in all its fullness, the manifold passions, desires, instincts—everything concerns us and our own soul as it concerns any human being. We can no longer solve life's problems, nor can we live and act as our fathers did. We are children and grandchildren of the generations that preceded us, but not their coffins. It is up to us: either to be the last Jews or the first of a new people."[11]

Yet, in his wildest rebellion, Berdichevsky was tragically aware of his double loyalty: to the past and the future. Mournfully he confessed: "I would like in my innermost to unify, to create a new nation, new people; but I am torn in my soul."[12]

Berdichevsky's stories present the same ideological background as his essays. They glow with the nostalgic melancholy of afflicted souls, of lone rebels who broke away from old sanctuaries without finding new ones to replace them. Or else they glorify the ecstatic joys and primitive passions of plain people. In their simple unadorned style the tales of Berdichevsky produce a weird romantic atmosphere of ancient chronicles. Even stern reality assumes an almost legendary character. The remote becomes intimately close and a casual event is endowed with vision.

Berdichevsky represented the spirit of revolt, critical self-analysis and inquiry which pervades modern Hebrew literature. In his gropings and in his heresies, he was a spirit of liberation, calling for the reassertion of a vigorous, well-balanced Hebrew individuality as the basis of national revival.

6. POETRY OF REVIVAL

The new spirit that permeated Hebrew literature at the eclipse of Haskala and the rise of the national movement manifested itself with particular power and beauty in the domain of poetry. Within the past half century Hebrew poetry rose to its greatest heights. It became not only more expressive of Jewish life, but also more universal in character and scope.

This new era dawned with Hayyim Nahman Bialik (1873-1934), a native of the Ukraine who spent the last ten years of his life in Palestine. His poetry reads like a confession of a great heart, like the spiritual auto-biography of a generation.

Bialik is a poet of intense emotions, rooted in the soil of his native village, in the "basic visions," as he calls them, of his childhood days and, equally, in the variegated culture and the tragically sublime history of his people. His poetry is a record of recurrent flights from one sphere to another—from his own "self" to nature and to his people's past and present.

The world appeared to Bialik in a state of continuous revelation. His nature poetry has a religious ecstasy. His major nature poem, *The Lake*, is a realistic description of a lake and a neighboring forest. But the lake grows into the living spirit of the universe, the all-seeing eye that absorbs everything, tree and cloud and man, and yet lives its own imperceptible, dreamy life. It is symbolic of Bialik's poetry as a whole, in which the borderland between vision and reality is indeterminate.

Nature showed to the poet not only the path to the Infinite; it also revealed his limitations in this finite world. It accentuated the abject Ghetto life and opened the dark chambers of elegy. The singer of sunshine became the poet of Jewish tragedy. His cycle of poems called forth by the pogroms in czarist Russia, in the first decade of the century, added a horrible chapter to Hebrew poetry of martyrdom. These poems unleash the pent-up furies, the protest and defiance of generations. They contain a modern version of the piercing challenge of Job: "O earth, cover not thou my blood, and let my cry have no resting place!" Jewish tragedy becomes world tragedy. Martyrdom is visualized by Bialik as an elemental force which may upset the equilibrium of the world. God Himself is pictured as being in despair. With biting irony Bialik portrays the defeat of divinity through the downfall of humanity.

Thwarted, disheartened by his people's bitter lot, Bialik took refuge in the House of Study, the Yeshiva, where the spiritual life of Israel has been nourished for generations. In a semilyrical epic, he drew the picture of a saintly Talmud student whose life is consecrated to the study of Torah. The triumph of spirit over matter, of faith over skepticism, gives the epic an inexhaustible beauty.

Bialik's ability to make vivid ancient Hebrew lore and to give it universal significance is best shown in his epic *The Dead of the Wilderness*. The poet utilized an old myth that the Israelites, who died in the wilderness upon leaving Egypt, still lie somewhere, dead in appearance only. Out of this material Bialik drew a series of bold and awesome figures. The vengeful desert, mysterious, like the force of destiny; the creatures of the desert: the eagle, the lion, the serpent and, above all, the dead of the wilderness, giants asleep, gruesome. Whoever approaches them withdraws in terror. The epic moves like a Greek tragedy, leading to inevitable doom. A storm breaks. The dead rise singing in chorus a song of rebellion. But the Supreme Will is not to be forced. The storm passes and the spell of ages remains unbroken.

In grandeur of expression, in the art of delineation and power of suggestion, the epic is as mighty and universal as the Greek *Prometheus*. The historic struggle of the Jewish people is presented against a background of splendid color and imagery that cannot but stir human fancy.

One of the definite contributions of modern Hebrew poetry is the revival of prayer, twin sister of lyric poetry. In this revival Bialik led the way.

Free of all worldly illusions, the poet communes with himself and sinks into meditation—on the visions of his childhood, on his orphanhood, on life's ambitions and frustrations, on the silent tragedies of the soul. Humbly he pays tribute, in one of the noblest of his poems, to "the meek of the world, the mute in soul who weave their lives in secret, modest in thought and in deed." With them he would unite his lot. These "princes of the spirit, who pass through the paths of life on tiptoe," exclaims the poet, "are the faithful guardians of the Divine Image on earth."

The intuitive grace of many of Bialik's poems, the purity of their accent, and their moral loftiness qualify them as high among the prayers of mankind.

The newly acquired world awareness which, alongside deepened national consciousness, is so characteristic of modern Hebrew poetry is manifested with particular effectiveness in the works of Saul Tchernichovsky (1875-1943). Tchernichovsky saw the world as one harmonious entity, a unity in multiple phenomena. He conceived the poet as the seer who envisages the essential affinity between apparently discordant elements in nature, the one who perceives, amidst a confusing multitude of sounds and voices, the intimate notes uniting mankind's remote past with the present. Tchernichovsky lived up to this exalted notion of the poet in his own works. His creative spirit drew its subject matter from many ages, from many lands and cultures, and from varied strata of the animate and the inanimate world.

Tchernichovsky has an eye and feeling for the minutest details, for the remotest scenes of nature. His *Nocturne*, his *Charms of the Forest*, are benedictions to the meanest plant, to the tiniest creature. Nature to Tchernichovsky is not merely a source of aesthetic enjoyment. It is the model, the archpattern for human conduct, a symbol of power ever renewing itself. Man cannot but follow its dictates, be imbued with its dynamic, invincible spirit, for man is "brother to the storm, to rock and to forest."

> I am unto God like hyacinth and mallow,
> Having nothing in the world but this bright sun.

These opening lines of the superb sonnet sequence *To the Sun* are an apt motto for the nature poetry of Tchernichovsky.

As a worshiper of nature and as priest of beauty, Tchernichovsky turned for inspiration to ancient Greece, "the cradle of the beautiful and mighty souls," as he calls it. Greek mythology, the abundant, harmonious life of the ancient Greeks, to whom "beauty was wisdom and wisdom beauty," exerted a deep influence on his poetry.

Tchernichovsky's emphasis on ancient Greece was due not only to his absorption in Greek culture. The poet's return to Apollo symbolized the return to the beauties and bounties of the earth from which his *Galut*-weary forebears and a cruel world had torn him. His Neo-Hellenism actually meant Neo-Hebraism—the regeneration of the Jewish people through a profound attachment to the soil, through cultivation of the aesthetic sense and a keen appreciation of the eternal values of mankind.

The path of beauty and heroism led Tchernichovsky from ancient Greece to ancient Israel. He invoked images and characters from the distant past—bold, rebellious Jewish spirits. Out of the mouths of the ancients he spoke to his contemporaries, bearing the message of revival on the soil of Palestine.

"Man," says Tchernichovsky, "is merely the image of his native environment." The poet-wanderer roaming through the world, ancient and modern, returned ever and again to his native Crimea and painted its mountains, its prairies, its historical monuments and ruins and above all its people. In a series of idylls in dactylic hexameter, he drew, with keen observation and quiet humor, intimate pictures of simple people. His characters are drawn from all walks of life: merchants, laborers, farmers, clergymen, servants, jailbirds. A bond of common humanity unites them all. Frequently, a Jew and non-Jew are paired and presented in the light of spiritual affinity. Elements of native folklore, both Jewish and Slavic, and a background of luxuriant natural scenery add spice and charm to the magnificent human panorama.

The universality of the poet's spirit is evident in his translations no less than in his original works. Among his translations are ancient Babylonian epics, all of Homer, *Oedipus Rex* of Sophocles, Anacreon, the odes of Horace, Shakespeare's *Macbeth* and *Twelfth Night*, Goethe's *Reineke Fuchs*, old Slavic epics, the Finnish *Kalevala*, Longfellow's *Hiawatha* and *Evangeline*.

This singer of the heroic and the beautiful was also the poet of the sad and the cruel. In lyric and epic poetry Tchernichovsky gave powerful expression to medieval Jewish martyrdom and to the horrors of our present age. Still, the close relationship between man and the world of beauty is not broken even in his poetry of martyrdom. Tragedy itself is softened through a portrayal of human courage, by a radiance flowing from natural phenomena. In the epic *Baruch of Mayence*, on Jewish suffering in Germany during the Crusades, some of the most memorable passages are descriptions of idyllic, rural scenes of the beauties of evening, night and dawn before the outbreak of furious persecution.

The broad humanity of Tchernichovsky, his ruggedness, his nature consciousness became more intense after he settled in Palestine in 1932. To his many lovable characters was added the image of a land rising from its ruins, renewed in vigor through toil and suffering and valor. The inborn strength of the poet, his blithe spirit, were invigorated by the soil of Palestine.

In Palestine, shortly before his death, he produced his major epic, *The Golden People*, the locale of which is Crimea and modern Palestine. The main characters are a retired deacon of the Greek Orthodox Church, whose life hobby is the nurture of bees, and a young *Halutz*, an admirer of the deacon who takes up the nurture of bees in Palestine.

The epic is a résumé of the aesthetic and social tendencies of the poet. The beehive becomes the symbol of humanity, with its feuds and class wars and social experiments. Revolting against the beehive system, the poet sings a song of individual freedom concluding with an exalted ode on the symphony of nations in which each member plays its individual instrument.

In Bialik and Tchernichovsky, Hebrew literature presented two figures whose achievements entitle them to be ranked among the foremost poets of the modern age in world literature.

At the turn of the century, Hebrew poetry was enriched by a variety of new talents. It became more diverse in content and in form. It shed new light on the inner life of the individual. It plumbed the depths of man, unraveling his psychic perplexities, exposing the darkest recesses of mind and the obscurest passions.

A poet of striking individuality is Zalman Shneour (born 1886 in White Russia, long a French and until his death in 1959 a U.S. resident). With Walt Whitman, Shneour could readily say: "I celebrate myself and I sing myself." His poetry is refreshingly bold, in utter defiance of established conventions and patterns of thought. It is a lusty hymn to the poet's ego, to the will of man, to intellectual vigor, to physical and spiritual adventure. It sublimates human passions, the blind, dark forces of man, the *fleurs du mal*. His full-blooded eroticism is, in a measure, an outcry against the ascetic traditions of his forebears.

The world appears to Shneour as a giant arena where man is forever wrestling with his own weak self, with hostile elements and with tyrant society. Shneour loves to pit the rebellious self-assertive individual against the colorless, amorphous mass. In dashing verse he exalts the ancient Roman gladiator Spartacus and his followers of all ages, whose watchword was eternal resistance.

The poetry of Shneour explores wide regions of the universe. It abounds in natural scenery of great charm. The epic *Among the Mountains*, for instance, contains marvelous descriptions of the Swiss Alps in all their wild beauty. But man holds the central place in the world of Shneour. Nature itself is deeply humanized by the poet. The very cosmos is the means for the display of man's superior qualities.

The social upheavals within recent decades impressed themselves greatly upon the poetry of Shneour. The poet sees society in dissolution, in spiritual bankruptcy, without God, without ideals. In an elegy, *At the Banks of the Seine*, he pictures modern man as emptyhearted, bored, and scared by ghosts of a dying past. "Culture with all its uproar, its smoke and flash could not drown the whisper of the dying gods." Man, godless and forlorn, is compared by the poet to a lone child who, frightened by the shadows at twilight, plays with wooden toys in order to overcome his fears "while his little heart is beating in the quiet: where is father, where is mother? O, when will they return home?"

Contemptuous fury and bitter irony are the mightiest weapons of Shneour. Their sharpest edges he reserves for the enemies of his people. In an exalted ode, *The Melodies of Israel*, he portrays the historic struggle of disinherited, exiled Israel to retain its individuality, alone among the nations. Anti-Semitism he views as the nemesis of the pagan deities subdued by the Hebraic spirit, subdued but not crushed. Thus, the inner strength of Israel is cause of its martyrdom. An outraged sense of justice, national pride, contemptuous indignation, burn in this poem of challenge to a cruel world which failed Israel, its spiritual benefactor.

The Middle Ages Are Approaching is the name of another remarkable poetic utterance of Shneour. In prophetic vein it predicted, in 1913, the decline of the era of progress ushered in by the Renaissance and the resurgence of medievalism with all its attendant horrors, chief among them the persecution of the Jews. It is a song of doom unequaled in its day for farsightedness.

There is an undertone of deep melancholy in the poetry of Shneour. "Who are you, hangman," asks the poet in his *Song of Grief*, "God, the great world, or my own self?" His is the tragic loneliness of one venturing on majestic flights of vision and thought.

The three representative poets discussed above, together with their contemporaries and successors, made Hebrew poetry the living spirit of

Hebrew revival. Modern Hebrew poetry rose to the highest calling of
poetry in general, which is to expose in fullest measure the very essence
of human life.

7. THE NEW PROSE

The spirit of revival asserted itself also in Hebrew fiction. The master
of Hebrew prose, Mendele Mocher Seforim, whose artistic portrayals
of Jewish life reached their height at the turn of the century, set an
example for a rising generation of prose writers. The Mendele tradition
meant a penetrating observation and minute description of the Jewish
milieu, thorough craftsmanship and a classic robust style. The new realism
gave to Hebrew prose a concentrated power, a precision and vividness
which it lacked in Haskala days. In the wake of this realism with its insistence upon sharp delineation of the material, objective world, there was
to follow a realism of the spirit based on the close observation of the inner,
occult world of man. Particular respect was now paid to the manifestations
and experiences of religious life. Jewish tradition, which heretofore super-
critical Haskala saw in its gloomiest aspect, was viewed now from a bright
angle under the influence of the national renaissance. Hasidism, long the
target of rationalists, came into its own and exerted a salutary influence
upon literature.[13a] This great movement of religious revival with its
optimistic, enthusiastic approach to the world, to God and to the common
man, with its emphasis upon the godliness and sanctity of everyday life,
stirred a new spirit in Hebrew literature, softening and brightening the
somber aspect of Hebrew prose.

Isaac Leibush Peretz[14a] (1851-1915), Judah Steinberg (1863-1908),
Micah Joseph Berdichevsky and their followers discovered divine inspiration and artistic loveliness in ancient rites and ceremonies, in Jewish
folklore in general, and, particularly, in the simple hasidic tales and
miracle stories, in hasidic melodies and folk dances.

The poetic quality of hasidism is caught in the imaginative stories and
monologues of Peretz, who left his mark on Hebrew and Yiddish
literatures. The media of Peretz were many, even as his tendencies were
divergent. In essay and short story, in verse and in prose poetry, in
allegorical fantasy and in dramatic play, he touched upon the boundaries
of Haskala rationalism, of social realism and symbolism. His crowning
achievement, however, was his hasidic lore.

A great solemnity marks the simple characters of his stories, whose
religious ecstasy turns an ordinary occurrence into a lofty spiritual experience. The common, uneducated man and the most revered saint are
joined in a comradeship of piety. Peretz succeeded in reproducing the
emotional climate in which religious ideas grow, in which even the

irrational appears to be a natural phenomenon. His folk stories about plain Jewish people are ethical gems. Through Peretz and his contemporaries, a never-dying past reaches out toward the future.

These sympathetic views of tradition did not alter the course of the younger realists, successors of Mendele, who, with eyes on the present, depicted the less festive side of Jewish life. The small town, nerve center of Jewish life in Russia, was described from close quarters with a greater degree of truthfulness and naturalism than ever before. The average man—the worker, the artisan, the tradesman—became the central figure. The struggle for a livelihood within the Pale of Settlement, the oppressive czarist regime, the dissensions between the young and old, between the pious and young rebels, small-town episodes and character sketches constitute, by and large, the subject matter of renascent Hebrew fiction. Occasionally the dark panorama was brightened by scenic descriptions of Bessarabia, the Ukraine, Lithuania, and other regions.

All in all, a new feeling for the common run of life, a new sensitivity to man and nature, pervaded Hebrew prose. This is evidenced also in the Hebrew language which adopted the rhythm of daily life and the manifold subtleties and nuances of living speech.

Bialik, in his appreciation of the short-story writer S. Ben-Zion (1860-1932), drew the following distinction between Mendele and his disciples: Mendele "is the great artist of small details. But one thing Mendele lacked: there is no alcoholism in his writing, none of the sheer joy of life and its intoxication. Not so Ben-Zion and his colleagues, in most of whose works there is a definite quantity of that alcoholism, something of that intoxication and joy of living, in the sense of 'my heart and my flesh sing for joy.'" This is an apt characterization by one who himself was a master of realistic prose.

The stormy days of the Russian Revolution of 1905 and its aftermath of pogroms had deep repercussions in Hebrew prose as well as poetry. No one expresses the temper of this turbulent age as fully as Joseph Hayyim Brenner (1881-1921).

Brenner's novels and short stories are unpolished. The narrative is frequently broken by lyrical passages. Slight attention is given to externals, to scenic effects. The plot is of little significance. But they abound in profound studies in which the autobiographical element plays a prominent part. They are pageants, so to speak, of acute human suffering and Jewish misery. The locale of Brenner's stories varies: Russia, land of his birth, the Whitechapel Ghetto in London, where he lived from 1904 to 1908, and Palestine, where he settled in 1909 and met a martyr's death at the hands of Arabs. But the leading character in all his novels is the same introspective Ghetto-wearied individual, desperately self-analytical, lashing himself and his environment, clamoring for freedom, for personal salvation. Brenner saw nothing but decay and misery in the Ghetto. With stark realism and deep sympathy he described the wretchedness of the poor and lowly, the agonies and frustrations of a neurotic Jewish intelligentsia, the empty prattle of social reformers, the bitter despair of a maladjusted youth, broken in faith and spirit.

In Brenner's works there is no hope for Jewish life in the Diaspora. "I, the Zionist," says one of his characters in the story *From Here and From There*, "do not speak of renaissance, of spiritual revival, but of the exodus, the ideal of exodus from the Ghetto."[15]

His maturest novel, *Bereavement and Defeat*, written in Palestine, is also his saddest. In the background is old Jerusalem with its winding streets, its hospitals and poorhouses and human wreckage, the driftwood of European Ghettos. We witness the lives of the weak and the meek: forsaken creatures, ascetic scholars, dreamers and mystics, and sick souls whom not even the city of Divine healing could cure. And amidst and above all these is the solitary figure of the leading character, an index of human agony and spiritual derangement. With rare insight Brenner dissects his inner life and portrays the gradual metamorphosis of a broken spirit from hopeless despair to a moderate, philosophic affirmation of life despite its horrors. The road to individual salvation may be symbolic of the larger course of national regeneration. "The passion for redemption," says one of Brenner's unfortunates, "saved me from compromise. This love of the people and the tortures of such love are in no way smaller than the tortures of another love of some Werther."

In the stories of Uri Nisan Gnessin (1880-1913) the spiritual physiognomy of an ultra-individualist is drawn with acumen and fastidious imagery. The plot is often of the flimsiest sort; but by means of most painstaking description the author lays consciousness bare. We look into the inner life of a self-centered, half-somnambulant individual, given to metaphysical obscurities and lyrical hallucinations, completely detached from the environment and from the vexing problems of the day.

A manifold view of reality is presented by Gershom Shofmann (born 1880 in White Russia), an accomplished master of the short story. His compact and suggestive stories are among the finest products of Hebrew narrative.

Shofmann is the interpreter of life and of human character through a studied observation of small incidents and episodes. He is the great observer who explores and sees things from an oblique angle in an original manner. An isolated, trivial action, an evanescent mood, a fleeting moment become under his searching eye all important in determining the mainsprings of human behavior. His subjects represent a cross section of cosmopolitan polyglot society in its upper and lower strata: pious old Jews and young radicals, scholarly professors, and "eternal students," disinherited artists and globe trotters, Russian soldiers and officers of the czarist regime, prisoners and harlots, Viennese damsels and sturdy peasants.

The tragic position of the Jew in a strange and hostile world and, lately, the horrifying Nazi brutalities were recorded by Shofmann in sharp and gruesome pictures. In his recent volume, *Before the All-Quiet*, the stress and agony and heroic behavior of the Jewish community in Palestine are drawn in refreshing sketches that breathe quiet power and faith.

A rounded picture of small-town life, reflecting the idyllic as well as the tragic side, is given by Yitzhok Dov Berkowitz (b. 1885 in White Russia). With clear vision and subdued lyricism, with a fine touch of wholesome humor, Berkowitz projects the image of a Lithuanian small town: austere, melancholic, impoverished, yet abundant in life, verdant amidst poverty, rich in human material and Jewish character. The underprivileged, the forlorn, silent souls are shown with compassionate understanding. A simple Jew vainly tries to express his elation over his boy's admittance to a Russian *Gymnasium*; a lonely working girl is driven by a nostalgic urge from the big city to her native town but is no longer able to adjust herself to her home environment; a country boy is subjected to ridicule and torture by big-town boys on account of his boorish ways. The quiet tragedies of these and similar characters are treated by Berkowitz with discernment and tenderness.

Coming to New York in 1915, Berkowitz became one of the builders of modern Hebrew literature in America. In his American stories and plays the small-town characters of his earlier work flourish with all their peculiarities on American soil. They are either pathetic, completely out of step with the New World, bitterly critical of American Jewish life, or else they are comic in their exaggerated efforts to parade their Americanism by denying their Jewish identity.

In addition to his original work, Berkowitz is famous for his superb translations from the works of Sholem Aleichem, the great Yiddish humorist.[16a] The tales, monologues and plays of Sholem Aleichem, portraying Jewish life in an inimitable style, were transformed by Berkowitz into Hebrew classics.

In his recent works Berkowitz reveals the influence of Palestine, where he now lives. The novel *Messianic Days* depicts modern Palestine in broad outline. Eretz Yisrael is shown through the mature vision of an intellectual physician who spent many years in the United States and through the youthful eyes of an idealistic American Jewish lad. Contemplation and quiet enthusiasm mark the entire novel. The solid, reserved portrayal of the growing Palestinian community is pervaded by a sense of wonder at the miracle that has come to pass.

The works of Brenner, Shofmann, and Berkowitz, aside from their inherent qualities, are indicative also of the changing locale of Hebrew literature.

Modern Hebrew fiction as a whole pictured the weakening and gradual disintegration of the traditional Eastern European Jewish small town under the impact of social and economic changes. In narrative and imagery it recorded Jewish life in transition.

8. DIASPORA AND ERETZ YISRAEL

The past few decades, which brought fateful changes in Jewish life, saw the shift of the main Hebrew literary center from Russia—since the Revolution of 1917 a banned territory for Hebrew culture—to rejuvenated Eretz Yisrael, and the strengthening of Hebrew literary activity in the United States.

In the interval between the two World Wars, the Hebrew center in Poland, long pre-eminent, was gradually dwindling away. Only a few literary figures remained there. Of these, Matithyahu Shoham (1893-1937) deserves special attention.

Shoham is the interpreter of Israel's spiritual history in his four biblical poetic dramas: *Thou Shalt Not Make Thee Iron Gods, Balaam, Jericho, Tyre and Jerusalem.* Through the conflicting characters of Abraham and the legendary Gog, dictatorial chieftain of the Kingdom of the North, through Moses and Balaam, the Prophet Elijah and Queen Jezebel, Shoham presents decisive struggles of Judaism with the pagan world at various stages of biblical history. In the clash of ancient personalities and ideas we hear the wrangling ideologies of our own troubled age. In a number of magnificent scenes, Shoham sublimates the liberating spirit of Judaism destined to ennoble mankind and to unite the family of nations.

During this very period, Hebrew literature formed an important colony on the American continent. Hebrew literary attempts had already been made here in the latter part of the nineteenth century. In 1871 the first Hebrew weekly in the United States made its appearance. An occasional sheaf of verse, a stray scholarly or pseudo-scholarly work, a short-lived periodical sounded the note of Hebrew culture on American soil. It was a melancholy, solitary note, at times a note of bitterness and despair, as that of Menahem Mendel Dolitzky (1856-1931), one of the pioneers of Hebrew poetry in America. During the past few decades [1946], however, Hebrew literary expression in America assumed, both quantitatively and qualitatively, the character of literature. At present, Hebrew letters in America hold the tragic distinction and responsibility of being the only Hebrew literature in the Diaspora. Literary activity is being stimulated by a regular periodic press, the weekly *Hadoar*, edited for over a quarter of a century by Menachem Ribalow, and the monthly *Bitzaron*, founded in 1939 by the Talmudic scholar and essayist Chaim Tchernowitz (1871-1949), besides various other publications.

In general, American Hebrew literature manifests traits common to modern Hebrew literature as a whole, of which it forms an integral part. Its poetry and prose, however, reveal also the impact of the American locale.

American Hebrew poetry, in the main, follows the classic tradition. Aestheticism, moral speculation, the longing for "the sublime and the beautiful" and religious exaltation are voiced in many memorable lyrics. Jewish martyrdom and the revival in the Land of Israel have inspired American Hebrew poets along with all other Hebrew writers. The Hebrew poetry of the New World has turned to the Bible and Jewish history for many of its characters. Abraham Regelson's *Cain and Abel*, *The Love of Hosea* by Simon Ginsburg (1891-1944), Simon Halkin's lyrical monologue, *Baruch, the Son of Neriah*, the odes to the medieval poets Gabirol and Ha-Levi by Eisig Silberschlag and Moses Feinstein's dramatic poem *Abraham Abulafia* are but a few noteworthy examples of this tendency.

The immigrant Jew, perplexed by the new American environment, struggling pathetically to retain his individuality, has found a sympathetic spokesman in the American Hebrew poet. The broad canvas of America, American natural scenery, portraits of American life and character, are woven into the very texture of American Hebrew poetry, notably in the works of Israel Efros, Ephraim E. Lisitzky, Gabriel Preil and A. Z. Halevy.

American folklore had a marked effect on the Hebrew muse. Three Hebrew epics, wide in scope, relate the story of the American Indian: *Facing the Tent of Timora* by Benjamin Nahum Silkiner (1882-1933), *Sinking Bonfires* by Ephraim E. Lisitzky, and *Silent Wigwams* by Israel Efros. Much as these epics vary in artistic achievement, they have this in common: they all depict the heroic life and struggle of the red man in his decline, all draw richly upon Indian lore, and the tragic narratives are set against a background of luxuriant scenery. In singing of the American Indian, the Hebrew poets voiced not only their attachment to American soil and American lore, but also the outcry of a small minority in the struggle for survival.

In prose, too, American Hebrew literature made some important contributions. The historical plays and tales of Harry Sackler, revolving around characters drawn from various periods of Jewish history, dramatize the course and destiny of Judaism and its heroic battle for the supremacy of the spirit. Sackler's stories combine intellectual insight and the fantasy of folklore. The biographical novels of Jochanan Twersky—*Uriel Acosta*, *Alfred Dreyfus*—are rich in descriptive power, pageant-like in effect. They portray character through an abundance of historical details, and accentuate environment and the *Zeitgeist*. The trilogy by Samuel Loeb Blank, a story of a Jewish family on a farm in Bessarabia, is a romantic saga about simple people and their sentimental attachment to the soil. Simon Halkin, in his analytical stories, conveys the spiritual gropings of confused Jewish individuality caught in the maelstrom of American life. Reuben Wallenrod's stories and sketches are vivid pictures of immigrant life in New York City, in the process of gradual adaptation to the American environment.

The essay in its various forms, particularly the critical essay, occupies a place of importance in American Hebrew prose.

In a class by themselves are the achievements of American Hebrew scholars in talmudic and Rabbinic literature, in medieval Hebrew poetry, in philosophy, philology, and pedagogy.

To the credit of Hebrew literature in America should be added the numerous translations in poetry and prose from English and American literature. Among the translations are those of Shakespeare's works.

Thus far Hebrew literature in America has been an immigrant product, though its leading exponents have lived in the United States from their early youth. In a sense, Hebrew literature presents a challenge to American Israel. Whether this literature is to be a permanent, growing expression or merely a transitory episode depends largely upon the cultural and spiritual course American Jewish life will take in the future.

The very center of present-day Hebrew literature is Palestine.

Eretz Yisrael has been one of the great stimuli of modern Hebrew literature, even as it was a mainstay of the Hebrew spirit throughout the ages.

Palestine in the Hebrew literature of preceding ages was principally a coveted vision of religious exaltation. The land was viewed through an ideal veil colored by biblical imagery. Only recently did it become a reality in Jewish life and letters.

The last decades of the nineteenth century were noted largely for the valiant efforts of Ben Yehuda to revive Hebrew as a spoken tongue. But at the turn of the century the growing Palestinian Jewish community became articulate. The new life on the soil of Palestine was described and interpreted romantically in the stories and adventure novels of Moshe Smilansky. He also gave a sympathetic portrait of Arab primitive life in his short stories *Children of Arabia*. The Hebrew press and periodic literature became increasingly important and influential.

The early stages of Hebrew literature in Palestine were guided by the stalwart spirits of Joseph Hayyim Brenner and Aaron David Gordon.

In his publicistic and critical writings no less than in his novels discussed in a previous chapter, Brenner unsparingly laid bare the ills and frustrations of Diaspora Jewish life. *Galut* was to him a malignant disease, a lingering moral evil. For Brenner, the Jewish problem had a very simple solution: the methodical salvation of the Jewish people, collectively and individually, through a life of labor in the Land of Israel.

This ideal of agricultural labor as a moral cure was henceforth to become a creative force in the growing literature of Eretz Yisrael. Its most zealous advocate was Aaron David Gordon (1856-1922). He came to Palestine from Russia in 1904 and by his own life, as a laborer in the fields of Palestine, personified the return of the intellectual Jew to the soil from which he had been estranged for generations. Gordon ascribed mystic qualities to labor. He saw in it an ennobling power capable of bringing man closer to nature, of revealing his higher self. Literature and all cultural activity were of value to him only if they were by-products of life, resulting from communion with nature. With many of his Haskala forerunners Gordon believed that the ideal of labor was "the great human universal ideal" which alone could revitalize the Jewish people. Moreover, the saving influence of labor, he declared, was necessary not merely as a means of becoming attached to the soil but also as the source and mainspring of a truly national culture.

Gordon's ethical personality, stamped upon his ponderous essays and meditations, became a telling factor in the new center of Hebrew literature.

The spirit of modern Palestine is at its best in its poetry. A group of poets, for all their individual differences, have jointly become the voice of a land rising above ruin. The beauty of the country, whose inner character they have perceived and with which they feel a strong kinship, has haunted many of its poets.

A poet of the Palestinian landscape is Jacob Fichman (b. 1881 in Bessarabia; in Palestine after 1912; d. 1958). He painted the weird beauty of Palestinian scenery in sonnet cycles and in the dramatic poems *Ruth* and *Samson in Gaza*. With subdued ecstasy he observes the effect of rain on "the ringing trees of a jubilant garden" and the magnificence of "a vine spreading green-handed on a hillock, embroidering a shadowy inscription with luminous fingers." Quietly he unites austere, multicolored Jerusalem, the picturesque ruins of Jericho and Anatoth, and the flourishing modern settlements of Deganiah and Nahalol.

Remote biblical figures become close to us through the soil of Palestine. Well may the poet apply to himself and to his generation the words he put into the mouth of Ruth: "Each contact with the ground under my feet is a holy covenant with this new home, as if all I knew and loved since my glorious childhood days till now beaconed to this small and blessed land wherein I found myself."

A longing for complete absorption by Eretz Yisrael rises like a prayer from many Palestinian poets. In the doleful, simple lyrics of the poetess Rahel (1890-1931), who as a girl toiled in the fields of Kinnereth in Galilee, the passion for Palestine takes the form of life's greatest fulfillment.

Palestinian poetry was also quickened by the pioneering spirit, *Haluziut*, which has been active in Jewish life at various intervals since 1882 and which reached its height after the First World War.

Haluziut, as a movement of liberation, is an outlet for a variety of forces. It is inspired by ages of longing and praying for Zion, by Jewish tragedy, by an inner protest and revolt against an unjust world where the Jewish people can find no security, by the hope of constructing in Palestine a righteous society, and by a Messianic ideal for human salvation and the restoration of Israel. These forces are expressed with varied emphasis and poetic form by a number of Palestinian poets.

In a series of idylls, David Shimoni (1886-1956), who first visited Palestine in 1909 and settled there in 1921, pictured the regeneration of Palestine from the beginning of the century to our day. He describes Palestine in the making, the transformation of dream and legend into reality, the enthusiastic pilgrimage of the *Halutzim,* the building of settlements and communes, the mounting hardships of daily life, the struggles of acclimatization, the toil and suffering, the bloody Arab disturbances. A host of characters come to the fore: farmers, laborers, watchmen, drivers— all of them observed by the poet-traveler tramping through the country.

The unrest and social turmoil that engulfed Europe after the First World War found strong repercussions in the poetry of Palestine.

Yitzhak Lamdan (1900-1954), who witnessed the pogroms in the Ukraine in 1919, projected in *Massada,* his blank verse epic, the background of horror and utter despair of the ravaged Russian Jewish communities, the former homes of the *Halutzim.* Massada was the last Judean fortress defended with great heroism against the Roman conquerors. Thus, modern Palestine is to the poet the last refuge and citadel of Jewry. Scenes of destruction and gloom alternate with those of renascent life in this work. In shrill, pathetic verse, in touching prayer, in buoyant choral song Lamdan sublimates the tragedy of modern Jewish life, the last hopeful act of which is Eretz Yisrael.

With ingenious metrical effect, the poetry of A. Shlonsky expresses the hurly-burly of the early twenties, the confused, jittery state of war-torn society. His work reflects the mad joy of throwing off the burdens of the past, the intoxication of working in the fields of the Emek (Valley of Jezreel), and of building a new home.

The most characteristic note was struck by Uri Zevi Greenberg (born 1894 in Galicia). His poetry is uneven in temper, as discordant as the tumultuous period in which it was produced. Mockery, blatant bravado, melancholy, passion, and lyrical solemnity—all blend in a medley of forceful expression. Greenberg's poetry flings a mighty challenge to a world that haunted and persecuted him. In stirring apocalyptic visions he predicts the coming of the Messianic age and the restoration of Israel.

A deep religious mood pervades Palestinian poetry. The revival of Eretz Yisrael is seen as a prelude to a new revelation, to the return of the prophetic spirit.

"This is the soil, the soil of madness," exclaims Avigdor Hameiri (born

1886 in Hungary) in a poem-cycle *Sinai Is Seething*: "Each clot here is aglow with bliss divine. Come hither, brother, if your soul be imprisoned, come hither barefoot, a pilgrim, and you shall see open-eyed the God of the wilderness of Sinai."

The miraculous rebuilding of the land gave wing to fancy. As of old, Jerusalem, Zion, became full of mystic significance. The eternal covenant with these hallowed names is renewed in enthralling odes. "And it matters to me," declares Uri Zevi Greenberg, "that I do not enter you, Jerusalem, with a golden prayer shawl, even as a High Priest entering your gates towards evening. And it matters to me that Jews walk in your midst without psalms on their lips and hands uplifted as candelabra." And another poet, Yehuda Karni prays: "Take me with the Jerusalem-stone and place me in the walls, daub me with plaster, and out of the wall's enclosure my pining bones will sing towards the Messiah."

Palestine as a symbol of the resurgence of the Divine Spirit is epitomized by noted poet Jacob Cahan (b. 1881, White Russia; d. 1960) in his *Psalm for the Remnant of Israel*. Its concluding lines are: "Forged by the divine hammer, purged by flames divine we shall stand upon Zion's soil, our psalm in our mouth, the divine psalm, and skies will respond, all the extremes of the world, and all the peoples will respond to us."

The impress of modern Palestine is also in its prose, though to a lesser degree than in poetry. On the whole, Palestinian prose shows a growing tendency to throw off the oppressive yoke of a curbed, maladjusted life which weighs heavily upon much of Diaspora fiction. It is distinguished by a new vigor and a refreshing awareness of reality.

The joy of work in the fields, the thrill of cultivating fallow soil, of redeeming a land in ruins, the adventures and dangers of pioneering, are recurrent themes in Palestinian fiction. The individual with his personal problems and complexities becomes secondary to the larger problems of community welfare.

Immersed in the present, Palestinian prose shows sympathetic understanding not merely of the growing new life but also of old forms of Jewish life in Palestine and elsewhere.

Ancient Jerusalem looms large and inspiring. Its character, partly luminous, partly perplexing, magnificently sketched by the poet-essayist Jacob Steinberg (1887-1947), appears like a protecting genius of the country and its people.

The various communities of Jerusalem, a veritable "gathering of exiles," are pictured by a number of storytellers and novelists against the background of the mother city. The novels of Yehuda Burla (born 1886 in Jerusalem), the first important novelist Palestine produced, portray the life of Orthodox Sephardic Jews and the influence of modernity upon the younger generation, with unaffected simplicity and Oriental charm.

Similarly, the little-known Yemenite Jew has recently come into full view through the work of Haïm Hazaz, a novelist of impressive literary stature. Thus, the literature of Palestine serves as a cultural interpreter and unifier of the tribes of dispersed Israel.

Much of Palestinian Hebrew fiction deals with Jewish life in the Diaspora. The humane stories of Asher Barash, for instance, center primarily around country life in Galicia; the compact short stories of Deborah Baron are small-town epics of Lithuania; while the expansive narratives of Hazaz give masterly pictures of Jewish life in Russia before and after the Revolution of 1917.

In recapturing the spirit of the past, Palestinian literature made notable contributions. A significant figure among these interpreters is Shmuel Yosef Agnon (b. 1888 in Galicia; d. 1970 in Jerusalem).

Agnon depicts Jewish life of yesterday with an uncritical love, with grace and humor, and with something like epic fullness. He takes particular delight in describing the idyllic, harmonious side of that life, its spiritual cohesiveness and moral grandeur. His tales, couched in colorful, ornate style, brocaded with biblical and talmudic allusions, have a legendary character. They are much like old family pictures set in huge antique frames from which look down smiling, patriarchal faces.

Agnon is essentially the poet of Jewish tradition. He seems to be moving in a remote, enchanted world, which to him is very real, miraculously preserved and left altogether intact. The world is the Polish Ghetto of more than a century ago, when Jewish life was self-sufficient and followed its natural course, untouched by influences from without. There is tranquillity and contentment and good cheer in that world, despite poverty and adversity. It is a world illuminated by learning and kept warm by the exuberant spirit of genuine piety.

The Bridal Canopy, one of the major works of Agnon, is on the surface a simple story of quiet adventure—the record of a quixotic journey made through Galician Jewish communities sometime during the early part of the nineteenth century by two amiable God-fearing Jews. The importance of the work, however, lies in the particular art of storytelling which it reveals. Folk tale and anecdote, Rabbinic homily and parable are strung together and fused into one narrative. It is a veritable mine of folklore and learning, a treasure of Jewish customs and ceremonies, manners of speech and thought, superstitions and beliefs.

Another travel narrative of his, *In the Heart of the Seas*, is a profound expression of the deep-seated Jewish love for Palestine. It is a poetic description of the dreamlike adventures of a group of Galician Jews on a journey to Eretz Yisrael. The story is a monument of love to high idealism and all-conquering spirituality.

Agnon approaches the task of storytelling with deep religious ecstasy, with a spirit akin to that of one of his characters, the saintly Raphael the Scribe, who dedicated his life to copying the Scrolls of the Torah. His quaint art invokes the spirit of Jewish tradition with fresh beauty.

A novelist's or poet's interpretation of the past is very often an artistic device to advance definite ideas for the present. To the visionary, past and present are indivisible. Hence, Hebrew literature in Palestine, as elsewhere, has summoned from the past important figures to serve as heralds of the modern revival. The work of Aaron Abraham Kabak (1882-1944) is an excellent illustration of this art.

Kabak was the faithful interpreter of his own age and earlier ages. His novels and stories, whether dealing with the immediate present or with the remote past, are of a piece: they are studies of environment and of human character in its relationship to society; and they are alive with ideas, with psychological and social problems.

The revival of Israel on its own historic soil occupies a central position in Kabak's works. But this theme never stands alone. It is always associated with the ideal of general human and individual welfare. The universal, the personal are inseparable from the national.

In his first novels *Alone* and *Daniel Shaffronov*, written in Russia in the early part of the century, Kabak drew parallel characters—Jewish intellectuals who sacrificed their lives to the cause of the Russian Revolution and, on the other hand, bold idealists who champion Hebrew renaissance and Jewish rehabilitation in Palestine. Zionism becomes stronger and nobler by the juxtaposition of two remote spheres united by the ideal of liberation. Strikingly enough, *Under the Shadow of the Gallows*, the very last work of Kabak, published in Palestine in 1944 as part of his monumental trilogy *The History of a Family*, treats of the Polish insurrection of 1863; and the leading character is a Jewish youth, an enthusiastic advocate of the Polish cause.

The ideal of liberation in its triple form—universal, national, individual —was beautifully expressed by Kabak in his historical trilogy *Shlomo Molcho*. This sixteenth-century Marrano who was under Messianic illusions and who died a martyr's death, becomes in Kabak's hands the embodiment of human struggle for salvation and the symbol of Israel's deep yearning for redemption. We follow the bold dreamer on his strange and devious road through his native Portugal, through Palestine, through Germany, proclaiming the restoration of Israel. We see a lone soul in flight from a contaminating environment, from his past, from his passions and worldly ambitions, consumed by a love of God, of man and of his martyred people.

In *In the Narrow Path*, Kabak's novel on the life of the Founder of Christianity, the crucial problem is individual versus national salvation. Here nature and man vie with equal power. Picturesque Palestinian scenery and intricate human character combine in a magnificent portrayal of Jewish religious and social life at the closing period of the Second Commonwealth.

In sum, Kabak penetrates into the Jewish past and sheds upon it the brilliant light of national and universal ideas.

9. RECENT PHASES

Since the Second World War, Hebrew literature has been strongly influenced by two dominant forces: the catastrophe which overtook Jewry under the Nazi regime of terror and the heroic struggle of the *Yishuv* in Eretz Yisrael culminating in the rise of the State of Israel.

The horrors of Nazi bestialities and the tragedy of Jewish martyrdom pervade much of Hebrew literature of the given period, its poetry in particular.

Mortifying chronicles, tales of despair, lamentations and prayers, challenging defiance and protest commingle in this substantial literature of martyrdom.

Occasionally, an author takes refuge in the past, shedding from distant spheres a reflected light on the present. Thus Saul Tchernichovsky enshrined the horrors of the age in his elegiac "Ballads of Worms" chronicling in the form of folk tales tragic events of the Crusades' period, among them the martyrdom of Rabbi Meir of Rothenberg. Jacob Cahan re-created in dramatic monologue, "The Third Cry," the story of the Ten Martyrs of the ancient Roman period. David Shimoni chose a legendary character of medieval folklore, "The Wicked Armelus," half Satan, half stone, to portray the dehumanized, diabolic figure of Hitler battling the spirit of Divine Providence and human freedom symbolized by the Jewish people. Yitzhak Lamdan invoked the spirit of the Patriarchs to envision the tragic destiny of Israel in his biblical ballads, "The Covenant Between the Parts" and "For the Sun Descended." As Abraham watches the vulture coming down upon the carcasses, he muses and wonders, in the words of the poet:

> And so ever endlessly: vulture and God together
> Both of you forever on one side and I—on the other, alone?

And Jacob, communing with God in the Dream at Beth-el, is made to utter his refusal, forcefully but ineffectually, to be the Chosen One of God, "to be despised by men but beloved by God." This very note of spurning the Election of Israel as a historic target for persecution was voiced with plainspoken irony also by the poet Nathan Alterman during the same period.

Defiance and spiritual exaltation in the face of tragedy are raised to sublime heights by the novelist Asher Barash in his story "He Who Remained
in Toledo." It is the story of a cultured Spanish Jew, a dealer in old manuscripts, a friend of the dignitaries of the Church, to all appearances indifferent to the faith of his fathers, who, upon the expulsion of the Jews from
Spain in 1492, stays on in Toledo refusing to be converted to Christianity
(as have members of his own ostensibly pious family) or to join the mass
of fugitives. The words of the Psalmist "I shall not die, but live!" which
he inscribes on a piece of parchment and carries with him attached to his
body, like "a holy Scroll," become his watchwords and magic symbol.

This lone, proud figure, regarded by the populace as a madman, walking
ghostlike through the streets of Toledo decades after the Jewish expulsion,
with the death-defying words of the Psalmist on his lips, is an enduring
image of moral grandeur.

The picture of an entire community meeting death with firm heart in
a state of worshipful exaltation is presented by the poet Sh. Shalom as a
grim chronicle in his ballad, "A Procession."

Few, if any, expressed the horrors of the age as vividly, as boldly as Uri
Zvi Greenberg. His volume *Streets of the River* may be viewed as a compendium of the various aspects of Hebrew poetry of martyrdom. It contains
the tender elegy, the full-throated, tempestuous lamentation, the fiery
condemnation, the lashing irony, the flamboyant vision.

The very name of the volume is indicative of its character. It envisions
persecution of the Jews as one great historic river with many confluent
streams and the tormentors of the various ages as one many-faceted mon-
ster.

The deep gloom of horrible scenes is invariably lightened by a streak
of light emanating from the consciousness pointing toward the historic
destiny of Israel, heralding its ultimate triumph. "Amen," says the poet,
"ours is the eternal word in the universe."

At this point, special mention should be made of the martyred poet and
playwright Yitzhak Katzenelson (1886-1944). In the prison camp in Vital,
France, where he was incarcerated, he wrote his stirring elegy in Yiddish,
"The Song of the Slain Jewish People," a Hebrew play "Hannibal" and
a number of Hebrew poems which were hidden in the ground and retrieved
after the war. A bare, simple stanza from this martyr's legacy may stand
as his epitaph:

> For no cause lost, destroyed in vain,
> All, all for no cause slain;
> No eye did see, no ear did hark—
> No grave, no mark.

In the dramatic poem "Between Fire and Redemption," a work in three
parts by the American Hebrew poet, Aaron Zeitlin, whcih appeared in 1957,

both the catastrophe and the emergence of the State of Israel are viewed
from a visionary sphere. The hidden meaning of the two, the Fire of Doom
and the miracle of Redemption, is probed and visualized by the poet. And
indeed these two forces were actuating Hebrew literature simultaneously.

The trials and struggles of the *Yishuv*: the Arab terror, the severe
British impositions, Jewish open and underground resistance, the feats of
the *Maapilim*, the daring spirits who defied the British blockade, bringing
in under the cover of night "illegal" immigrants—the various stages which
led to the birth of the State of Israel, including the War of Liberation, are
reflected in recent Hebrew literature.

The spirit of self-sacrifice which animated the *Yishuv*, the steadfastness
of purpose, the resoluteness and valor which characterized the defenders
of Israel—these are the common notes in the odes and prayers, elegies and
ballads of such diverse poets as, for instance, David Shimoni and Nathan
Alterman, Sh. Shalom and Hayyim Guri.

"It is good to live with death at you staring," is the opening line of a
poem by Sh. Shalom. This consciousness of the call of destiny, accompanied
by an unflinching spirit of self-reliance, is characteristic of the war literature
of Israel, of its poetry and prose alike.

The chronicles, reminiscences and realistic tales, the published letters and
diaries of many of the victims of the war, the numerous memorial volumes,
the enormous anthology *Parchments of Fire* edited by Reuben Avinoam
containing "the literary and artistic legacy of those who fell in the War
for Israel's Independence"—these are destined to be documents of great
human value and perennial sources of strength for Hebrew literature.

In recent years a group of native Israelis have come to the fore in Hebrew fiction and drama: Joshua Bar-Yoseph, Moshe Shamir and S. Yizhar;
Yigal Mosenson, Mordecai Tabib and Nathan Shaham, to cite a few out of
many. This group constitutes a creative force of considerable achievement. It grapples with the new reality of modern Israel, with life on the
farm, in the *kibbutzim* and in the *maabarot*, the transistory camps for the
new immigrants, the *olim*. It probes the varied social and cultural problems
presented by the "ingathering of exiles" and shows a keen awareness of the
Oriental Jew. It is marked by a deep consciousness of the soil and landscape
of Israel, as the pictorial stories of S. Yizhar—to single out one of the
group—indicate.

In the past decade [1947-1957], Hebrew fiction has been enriched by a
number of works of high merit. Of great significance is the latest novel
by the old master Shmuel Yosef Agnon, *Yesterday and Before Yesterday*,
which portrays on a broad canvas Eretz Yisrael in the early part of the
century. The old *Yishuv* and the new one meet in this novel in a series of
character representations and in the consummate reproduction of the particular atmosphere and milieu characteristic of the two.

Another work of distinction is the massive novel *Yaish*, by Haïm Hazaz, which pictures with great subtlety Yemenite Jewish life, its primitivism and piety, in Yemen and in Israel. The novel revolves around the main character, Yaish, a unique personality, and we get a clear view of his religious ecstasies and vagaries, his messianic illusions and worldly temptations, his artistic urge and ascetic eccentricities.

Of the numerous recent novels by native Israelis, two in particular stand out prominently. One is the historical novel *King of Flesh and Blood* by Moshe Shamir, a dramatic narrative depicting Judea seething with conflicting ideas and personalities during the Hasmonean period, with King Alexander Yannai as the leading character. The other work is the trilogy *Enchanted City* by Joshua Bar-Yoseph. It is a vivid, colorful portrayal of a Safed family during the course of three generations, from the middle of the nineteenth century to World War I. The guiding spirit of the novel is the "Enchanted City," the ancient city of Safed, renowned center of Cabbala, with its inhabitants, its traditions, its festivities, its scenic beauty and mystic lore.

The literature of Israel is an initial fulfillment of the hopes and visions of the moving spirits of modern Hebrew literature. It is the partial culmination of the great ideal which inspired the Hebrew renaissance: the self-renewal of the Jewish people, individually and collectively, on its own soil, and the continued growth of an indigenous Hebrew culture, in harmony with the highest aspirations of mankind.

NOTES

[1a For the emancipation movement by countries, cf. Cecil Roth, "The Jews of Western Europe (from 1648)," this work, Vol. I, pp. 273-274.]

2 *More Nebukhe Hazeman*, ed. S. Rawidowicz, p. 36.

[3a Cf. above, Shalom Spiegel, "On Medieval Hebrew Poetry," pp. 105-106.]

[4a Cf. *ibid.*, pp. 111-112.]

5 *Collected Works of M. L. Lilienblum*, II, 399.

[6a Cf. below, Yudel Mark, "Yiddish Literature," pp. 433 ff.]

7 In the poem *Siluk Shekinah*.

8 *Al Parashat Derakhim*, II, 28.

9 *Ibid*, p. 29.

10 *Ibid.*, I, p. 87.

11 Collected Works of Berdichevsky, *Baderech*, II, 20.

12 *Ibid.*, I, 74.

[13a Cf. Mark, *op. cit.*, pp. 427 ff.]

[14a *Ibid.*, pp. 439 ff.]

15 *Mikan Umikan*, p. 39.

[16a Cf. Mark, *op. cit.*, pp. 438 ff.]

SELECTED BIBLIOGRAPHY

A

General

HALKIN, SIMON, *Modern Hebrew Literature From the Enlightenment to the Birth of the State of Israel: Trends and Values*. New York, 1950; new edition, 1970. "A study," in the words of the author, "of the socio-historical forces which have motivated Jewish life during the last two centuries" and influenced the course of Hebrew literature.

KLAUSNER, JOSEPH, *A History of Modern Hebrew Literature (1785-1930)*. Translated by H. Danby, London, 1932. A brief survey of the main trends of modern Hebrew literature.

SLOUSCHZ, NAHUM, *The Renascence of Hebrew Literature*. Philadelphia, 1909. Stresses the role of Hebrew literature as a civilizing factor in Jewish life and as an instrument of national emancipation.

SPIEGEL, SHALOM, *Hebrew Reborn*. New York, 1930. A series of essays in historical perspective on leading figures and ideas in modern Hebrew literature.

WAXMAN, MEYER, *A History of Jewish Literature from the close of the Bible to our own Days*. New York, 1936. Vols. III and IV. Very detailed and informative.

B

Special

Studies of distinct periods or authors

BAVLI, HILLEL, *Some Aspects of Modern Hebrew Poetry*. New York, 1958.

EFROS, ISRAEL, *Hayyim Nachman Bialik*. New York, 1940. An essay published by the Hebrew P.E.N. Club of the U.S.A.

GINSBURG, SIMON, *The Life and Works of Moses Hayyim Luzzatto*. Philadelphia, 1931.

GREENBERG, LOUIS S., *A Critical Investigation of the Works of Rabbi Isaac Baer Levinsohn*. New York, 1930.

HALKIN, SIMON, "The Hebrew Literature in Palestine," in *Jewish Review* (New York), 1943, pp. 48-82.

KABAKOFF, JACOB, "Hebrew Culture and Creativity in America," in the Quarterly, *Judaism*. New York, 1954.

LANDAU, J. L., *Short Lectures on Modern Hebrew Literature*. From M. H. Luzzatto to S. D. Luzzatto. London, 1923.

MORAIS, SABATO, *Italian Hebrew Literature*. New York, 1926. Some material about S. D. Luzzatto and a few of his contemporaries noted in Hebrew literature.

RAISIN, JACOB S., *The Haskalah Movement in Russia*. Philadelphia, 1913. A detailed study of the social and literary forces of the period.

RHINE, A. B., *Leon Gordon; an Appreciation.* Philadelphia, 1920. A study of the life and works of the distinguished poet of the *Haskala* period.

SCHECHTER, SOLOMON, "Nachman Krochmal and the Perplexities of his Time," in *Studies in Judaism*, Series I. Philadelphia, 1896.

SILBERSCHLAG, EISIG, "Hebrew Literature in America," in *Jewish Book Annual.* New York, 1955.

SIMON, LEON, *Ahad Ha'am.* Introduction to Selected Essays of Ahad Ha-Am. Philadelphia, 1912. A critical analysis of the teachings of Ahad Ha-Am.

WALLENROD, REUBEN, *The Literature of Modern Israel.* New York, 1956. A study of Hebrew literature in Eretz Yisrael, mainly till the rise of the State of Israel.

C

Translations

The number of *adequate* translations from modern Hebrew literature is, unfortunately, very limited.

AGNON, SHMUEL YOSEF, *The Bridal Canopy.* Translated by I. M. Lask. Garden City, N.Y., 1937; reissued New York, 1967.

AHAD HA-AM, *Selected Essays.* Translated by Leon Simon. Philadelphia, 1912.

——, *Ten Essays on Zionism and Judaism.* Translated by Leon Simon. London, 1922.

BIALIK, HAYYIM NAHMAN, *Complete Poetic Works.* Translated by various translators. Edited with introduction by Israel Efros. New York, 1948.

——, *Aftergrowth and other Stories.* Translated by I. M. Lask. Philadelphia, 1939.

——, *And it Came to Pass: Legends and Stories about King David and King Solomon.* Translated by Herbert Danby. New York, 1938.

GORDON, A. D., *Selected Essays.* Translated by Frances Burnce. Boston, 1938.

GREENBERG, URI ZVI, *Jerusalem.* Translated by Charles A. Cowen. New York, 1939.

HAZAZ, HAYIM, *Moki Sa'id.* Translated by Ben Halpern. New York, 1956. A novel of Yemenite life.

MALETZ, DAVID, *Young Hearts.* Translated by Solomon N. Richards. New York, 1950. A novel of modern Israel.

SHAMIR, MOSHE, *The King of Flesh and Blood.* Translated by David Patterson. London, 1958. An historical novel of the Hasmonean period.

SHIMONI, DAVID, *Idylls.* Three selected idylls, with an essay on the poet, by Joseph Klausner. Translated by I. M. Lask. Jerusalem, 1957.

SNOWMAN, L. V., *Tchernichowsky, S. and his Poetry.* London, 1929. Selections from his poetry with biographical and critical comments by the translator.

STEINBERG, JEHUDA, *In Those Days.* Translated by George Jeshurun. Philadelphia, 1915. A story of a kidnapped Jewish conscript during the reign of Czar Nicholas I.

Tchernichowsky, Saul, "Baruch of Mayence." Translated by Sholom J. Kahn, in *Poet Lore*. Summer, 1948.

Wallenrod, Reuben, *Dusk in the Catskills*. Translated by Mrs. Wallenrod. New York, 1957. A novel of American Jewish life.

Yaari, Yehuda, *When the Candle Was Burning*. Translated by Menahem Horwitz. London, 1947. A novel of Jewish life in Eastern Europe and in Eretz Yisrael during and after the First World War.

Additional translations are to be found in the following collections and anthologies:

Fein, Harry H., *A Harvest of Hebrew Verse*. Boston, 1934. Selections from the poetry of *Haskala* and the modern age.

Fleg, Edmond, *The Jewish Anthology*. Translated by Maurice Samuel, New York, 1925.

Schwarz, Leo W., *A Golden Treasury of Jewish Literature*. New York, 1937.

————, *The Jewish Caravan*. New York, 1925.

Israel Argosy. Edited by Isaac Halevi Levin. Jerusalem, 1952-1956.

Sound the Great Trumpet. Edited by M. Z. Frank. New York, 1955.

Tehilla and other Israeli Stories. London and New York, 1956.

The Literary Review, an International Quarterly of Contemporary Writing, published by Fairleigh Dickinson University, Teaneck, New Jersey. Israeli Number, Spring, 1958. Selections from modern Hebrew poetry and prose, including a play, "Michal, The Daughter of Saul," by A. Ashman.

POSTSCRIPT

By Shmuel Leiter

The development of Hebrew literature has been accelerated in its recent phases by the tensions of contemporary life and by new influences in literary theory and practice. The dynamic nature of the past three decades and the problems of a young society and an uncrystallized cultural tradition have given rise with great rapidity to new voices, thus telescoping the literary history of the period. As a result, four generations of writers have been creating side by side, giving a simultaneous quality to much of Hebrew literature and cautioning us that its history must be comprehended not only sequentially but also in terms of the considerable interaction among the writers themselves.

We are now able to see patterns of evolution that put the work of many writers in better perspective. In 1941 S. Y. Agnon (1888-1970) collected his *Book of Deeds,* surrealistic stories of alienation and terror that he had written during the previous decade. His novel *A Guest for the Night* (1939) portrays the loss of vitality in a representative Jewish town in Europe. Literary motifs of the coming decades—psychological terror, moral decay, and spiritual peril—were very much present in his work. Even his earlier writing appears less sentimental today than it seemed to contemporary readers. We find the six decades of his production bound together by the ironic, complex vision of a thoroughly modern man.

Today the works of Haïm Hazaz and Y. D. Berkowitz still reverberate with spiritual and social vitality. The stories of Isaac Shenhar (1902-1957) display culture and good taste. The poetry of Fichman has endured with a new intricacy and a deeper sadness discovered by today's reader. The stories and poems of Jacob Steinberg provide deep insight into the modern sensibility and have won new appreciation in the past decade.

In retrospect the poems of David Vogel (1891-1944) and Avraham Ben Yitshak (1883-1950) fall into a pattern of modernist poetry that can be traced back to World War I. They appear as forerunners of a tradition that becomes central with the work of Avraham Shlonsky. Lea Goldberg (1911-1970) emerged as a poet of consistently high achievement. *Early and Late* (1959) reflects control, intelligence, and poetic cogency. The collection in 1963 of Yocheved Bat Miriam's poems gives a clearer picture of a rare spiritual sensitivity expressed in a deeply personal, symbolist poetry. The work of A. L. Strauss (1892-1953) is a remarkable record of the intellectual in quest of spiritual meaning (*Hours and Generation,* 1951).

These writers had deep roots in Judaism. They were educated in Europe and learned their Hebrew from the classics. Their ambivalent attitude toward that tradition did not divest them of the cultural values it gave them. There was a sense of mission and a coherence of values that the generation of rebels was able to transfer to its secularized ideologies. Thus the verse of Shlonsky is rich in religious metaphor that lends it depth and a cultural dimension enriching it and joining it dialectically to a tradition.

With the destruction of European Jewry, Hebrew literature became Israeli literature. Palestinian-born writers whose mother tongue was Hebrew had a new sense of place. They did not have to discover the landscape, they were born into it and part of it. They were, on the whole, not raised in the traditions of Judaism. Their senses were open to the present, and their memories were sealed off from the past.

An earlier generation had tried to assimilate the Palestinian landscape and to write of pioneering, of youth, toil, and suffering. Yehudah Yaari (b. 1900), Israel Zarchi (1909-1947), Ever Hadani (b. 1899), Nathan

Agmon (the Hebrew name of Bistritsky, b. 1896), and David Maletz (b. 1899) were inhibited by the ambivalence of a memory that stubbornly invoked the distant landscapes of childhood. An indigenous literature had to wait for writers with a native awareness of place.

The next phase of Hebrew prose is reckoned from publication of the first story of S. Yizhar (Yizhar Smilansky, b. 1916), whose stories are confined to the southern landscapes of the country. His work revolves about the triad of *kibbutz, Palmach,* and the War of Liberation. Those experiences of the 1940's provided an ordeal, a reservoir of deep, personal experience that became a collective biography of the generation, and for thirty years Yizhar's stories have described that eventful decade.

"Ephraim Goes Back to the Alfalfa" (1938) is characteristic of Yizhar's exploration of the experience of people who stand apart from the group, longing to be free of the routine and responsibility imposed by society. External events are minimal: Ephraim appears before the *kibbutz* members to request a change in chores. The rest is convoluted interior monologue.

Yizhar's prose is distinctive. Long, many-layered sentences, enormous resources of vocabulary, inventive combinations of words are fused into a lyrical style that describes the delicate movements of the spirit as well as the gentle contours of the southland.

The war stories written in the shadow of war, "The Captive" (1948) and "The Story of Hirbat Hizah" (1949), evince deep moral commitments in their examination of vacillations of conscience in situations of war. His long war novel *Days of Ziklag* (1958) portrays a week in the life of soldiers battling for a hill which they at first mistake for David's ancient retreat, Ziklag. The rhythms of the scorching days in the open terrain and the fear of death compress their experience into a fragile, exposed present, ironically free of echoes from the biblical past.

The work of Moshe Shamir (b. 1921) is charged with narrative power. A keen eye for detail, a plastic imagination, and a sense of the dramatic have helped him broaden the range of subjects available to the Israeli writer. His narrative appetite carried him beyond the autobiographical concerns which defined the scope of his early novels (*He Walked in the Fields,* 1947; *With His Own Hands,* 1951). Soon his historical novel *A King of Flesh and Blood* (1954) released contemporary Israeli fiction from its narrow limits and initiated a trend of historical fiction.

In order to examine the moral aspects of power and of statehood, Shamir turned to the Hasmonean period. He creates atmosphere and paints the sweep of events in which power crystallizes. Decision, power, and the attempt to build a state offer ready analogues to the problems that confronted the State of Israel in its first decade. The conception of history that shapes the book is pessimistic. In *A Poor Man's Ewe* (1956) Shamir returned to the same theme, tracing David's rise to power through the diary of Uriah.

Shamir incorporated the idioms of the period, elements of Mishnaic and Midrashic Hebrew of the Second Commonwealth into his own style, a feat characteristic of the stylistic versatility of the young writers.

The stories of Mordecai Tabib (b. 1910), which describe the Yemenite community facing the complexities of a modern society, achieve integrity by their rich, traditional style. His novels *Like the Grass of the Field* (1948) and *Like a Willow in the Wilderness* (1957) depict the process of growing up in a distinctive environment. The work of others has not withstood the test of time as well. The stories of Yigal Mossenson (b. 1917) seem too involved with surface strategies of plot, and the fiction of Nathan Shaham (b. 1925) is too tendentious.

A pattern of commitment which changed to doubt and finally to despair is common to most of the young writers whose integrity led them from collective certainties to the absurd. The sense of national and social mission could not replace the absolute values of religious tradition. Once the secularized mission had triumphed in war and the dedication to battle was over, trepidation and alienation ensued.

Eight years after the appearance of Shamir's novel of Elik's education to idealism and self-sacrifice (*With His Own Hands*) his novel *For You Are Naked* (1959) studies a man who lives by impulse, stripped of ideals. Yizhar's *Six Stories of Summer* (1950) were suffused with tenderness, but the *Stories of the Plain* (1964) are rife with disillusion. The early stories of Aaron Megged (b. 1920) delight in the real, in detailed description of fishermen, stevedores, and new immigrants, but in *The Case of the Simpleton* (1960) he pictures the alienation of the individual in a nightmare atmosphere in which reality crumbles. Binyamin Tammuz (b. 1919) has written with rare sensitivity of a childhood (*The Sands of Gold*, 1950) that turned to disillusion (*A Locked Garden*, 1957); his most recent work is a most grotesque, cynical escapade in decadence (*A Castle in Spain*, 1966). David Shachar (b. 1926) writes with insight of the death of old ideals. His stories ("On Dreams," 1956; "Caesar," 1960) describe the vicissitudes of rootless, lonely people. The spiritual homelessness of people without the shelter of a past is portrayed in *A Peg for the Tent* (1960) by Shlomo Nitzan (b. 1922).

Among the younger writers one must mention Aaron Appelfeld (b. 1932), whose stories ("Smoke," 1962; "In the Fertile Valley," 1963) evoke with eerie lucidity the world of survivors of the Holocaust, whose cruel memories burden them with guilt and terror. The sustained spiritual suffering in the books of Pinhas Sadeh (b. 1929; *Life as a Parable*, an autobiography, 1958; *Notes on Man's Condition*, 1967) is interlaced with melancholic beauty. Yoram Kaniuk and Abraham B. Yehoshua (b. 1937) also stand out among the younger writers.

In the 1930's and 1940's the poetry of Avraham Shlonsky and Nathan Alterman introduced European modernism into the mainstream of Hebrew poetry. Their flexible idiom and bold imagery had a great impact on the younger generation of poets. The poems of Alterman, with their more enigmatic imagery and sprightly fancy, had less ideological commitment and were a more direct influence.

Alterman (1910-1970) created a private modern vision of a stylized urban world of medieval cities, roads, squares, inns, and lanterns. An abundance of figure, metaphor, and color produced brilliant fantasy. Motifs of fable and ballad form situations that Alterman infuses with symbolic dimension.

The situation of *The Joy of the Poor* (1941) is characteristically oxymoronic. The living/dead man haunts the woman he loves, seeking on his macabre visits to continue a tenacious, posthumous love that transcends death and offers a refuge from time and change.

In *City of Oppression* (1957) Alterman celebrates the new Jewish state. He leaves his imaginary cities and chronicles the return of exiles. His conception of history is more optimistic. Time and change not only bring intimations of death, they also justify suffering and hope.

The most extreme manifestation of secularization in Israeli culture, the Canaanite movement, has rejected the heritage of Judaism and envisaged the creation of a new Hebrew nation. This ideology aims to integrate the Hebrew nation into the Near East by the creation of a common culture with other peoples of the area. Yonatan Ratosh (b. 1908) is the foremost ideologue of the group as well as one of the most original Hebrew poets. His poems and ideas have common roots.

In his early poems, Ratosh draws on a pagan, pre-Israelite past of myth and culture for a symbolic structure that is highly intellectual and complex. Out of early biblical Hebrew and Canaanite sources he fashions language and imagery that are deliberately archaic; he evokes ancient liturgy and magic and peoples his poems with biblical figures and Canaanite gods. His incantatory rhythms and cultic situations give his poetry sureness of form. The remarkable versatility of structural dialectic and alliterative combinations unite his poems with precise ambiguity.

In the distant past Ratosh finds the formal, impersonal situations that teach modern man he is living in a closed system, that there are no breakthroughs of redemption. Man must accept the harsh conditions of life with courage. Only a brave posture in the precarious present can give life some meaning.

Aaron Amir (b. 1923) shares Ratosh's ideology and mythic materials. With the same inclination to dialectic symmetry, alliteration, and mannered erotic motifs, he has written impressive pagan litanies.

The early poems of both Alterman and Ratosh gain depth by their comprehensive vision, coherent universe of symbol and image, and distinctiveness of style.

Amir Gilboa (b. 1917) belongs to a new generation. He set an original course, abandoning mechanical meters for powerful rhythms. Biblical motifs and personal metaphor mix in vital, surrealistic visions. The fervor of his surging long lines and deeprooted symbolism sometimes reminds one of U. Z. Greenberg.

Under the influence of Shlonsky and Alterman, Russian poetics prevailed. In the 1950's there was a conscious departure from this tradition. English and American poetry influenced many of the younger writers to discard the old rhetoric. There was a new irony in their poetry, a restraint, a matter-of-fact tone which guarded emotions in disillusion. They endeavored to shape a more subtle poetry to express the dissonance of the times, for the development of contemporary poetry falls into the same pattern as contemporary prose. David Avidan (b. 1934) expressed the loss of ideals: "What justifies most / the loneliness of the great despair . . . / is the simple, decisive fact / that we don't have anywhere to go" (*Interim Report*, 1960). Binyamin Galai (b. 1921) mutters, "no more! Now I don't want to hear / words more lofty than supper" (*On the Shore of Mercy*, 1958).

The new rhetoric begins with the loss of ideals. The poems of Haïm Guri (b. 1922) reflect a turn from the certainty of public values to fragmented visions of personal anxiety.The ambiance of camaraderie in battle, the feeling of the "first person plural" (*Flowers of Fire*, 1949; *Poems of Seal*, 1953), dissipates in a decade, and in his later work (*The Rose of the Winds*, 1960) Guri undergoes the travail of his generation. Personal style relaxes structure, syntax, rhyme, and meter. The course of Guri's work is a dramatic record of the spiritual crisis of his generation.

The work of T. Carmi (b. 1925) is characteristic of the new quality in poetry. His poems have a laconic integrity that gives added resonance to his symbols. In his poems there is the subtle inner tension of silence instead of the earlier fullness of rhythm and imagery.

Yehuda Amihai (b. 1924) expresses best the posture of resignation and irony of the past two decades. Amihai uses imagery of the technological present. Machines, garages, buses, and telephones are the *realia* which feed his imagination; they are transformed into a rich system of metaphor. "God lies on His back under the world—always busy fixing, something always going wrong," is typical of the range of Amihai's metaphorical in-

ventiveness, of the aptness with which his unexpected metaphors capture human situations. His startling juxtapositions become revelations
of despair and guilt. Phrases of liturgy, contracts, questionnaires, and children's songs are interpreted to yield a distortion of innocence and faith.
Biblical associations abound in his work, not to introduce the past but to
measure ironically its distance from us.

Tuvya Ruebner (b. 1921) seeks to capture the present. His poems
(*Poems to Find Time*, 1960) strive to hold the ephemeral experience. Dan
Pagis (b. 1930) has written poems of richer texture than most of the young
poets. The density of *Shadow Dial* (1959) is relaxed in *Late Leisure*
(1964). The poems of Nathan Sach (b. 1930) tend to be prose-like, colloquial, repetitious, and ironic. The later poetry of Yonatan Ratosh, Amir
Gilboa, and David Avidan also blends lexical bareness and incantatory
repetition into internal rhythms that shape ironic structures of verbal experiment.

BIBLIOGRAPHY

A

Special studies of distinct periods or authors

BAND, ARNOLD J., *Nostalgia and Nightmare: A Study in the Fiction of S. Y.
    Agnon*. Berkeley and Los Angeles, 1968.
PATTERSON, DAVID, *Abraham Mapu*. London, 1964.
———, *The Hebrew Novel in Czarist Russia*. Edinburgh, 1964.
UMEN, SAMUEL, *The World of Isaac Lamdan*. New York, 1961.

B

Translations

AGNON, S. Y., *A Guest for the Night*. Translated by Misha Louvish. New York,
    1968.
———, *Twenty-One Stories*. Edited by Nahum N. Glatzer. New York, 1970.
———, *Two Tales*. Translated by Walter Lever. New York, 1966.
BEN YITZHAK, AVRAHAM, *Poems*. Translated by I. M. Lask. Jerusalem, 1957.
CARMI, T., *The Brass Serpent*. Translated by Dom Moraes. London, 1964.
GOLDBERG, LEA, *Lady of the Manor*. Translated by T. Carmi. Jerusalem,
    1967.

C

Anthologies: Translations of modern short stores

Ariel, a Quarterly Review of the Arts and Sciences in Israel. Published in Jeru-
    salem since 1962.

BLOCKER, J. (ed.), *Israeli Stories*. New York, 1962.
KAHN, S. J. (ed.), *A Whole Loaf*. Tel-Aviv, 1957.
PENUELI, S. Y., and UKHMANI, A. (eds.), *Hebrew Short Stories*. 2 vols. Tel-
Aviv, 1965.

D

Anthologies: Translations of modern poems

AUSUBEL, NATHAN and MARYNN (eds.), *A Treasury of Jewish Poetry*.
New York, 1957.
BURNSHAW, S., CARMI, T., and SPICEHANDLER, E. (eds.), *The Modern He-
brew Poem Itself*. New York, Chicago, San Francisco, 1965.
MINTZ, RUTH FINER (ed. and trans.), *Modern Hebrew Poetry—A Bilingual
Anthology*. Berkeley and Los Angeles, 1966.
PENUELI, S. Y., and UKHMANI, A. (eds.), *Anthology of Modern Hebrew
Poetry*. 2 vols. Jerusalem, 1966.

E

Bibliography

A bibliography of Ch. N. Bialik's works in English translation, by Jacob
Kabakoff, appears in *Jewish Book Annual*, XVII (1959-1960).
A bibliography of S. Y. Agnon's tales in English translation appears in *Ariel*,
No. 17 (1966/67).
GOELL, YOCHAI, *Bibliography of Modern Hebrew Literature in English
Translation*. Contains 3300 references. New York, 1969.

CHAPTER 8

JEWISH RELIGIOUS LIFE AND INSTITUTIONS IN AMERICA

(A Historical Study)

By Moshe Davis

INTRODUCTION

The essential factor in American history was the migration of some sixty million Europeans to the Western Hemisphere during the past four centuries. The meaning of American civilization lies in the ideals and motivations which prompted these immigrants to come to the New World, the influences of the American natural environment upon them, and the adjustment of their traditions and culture to the new way of life. The history of the Jews in the United States, like that of any other group in America, must be studied in the light of the forces that molded the character and civilization of the American people.

The Jews, like their fellow immigrants, sought complete integration into the American pattern. They contributed freely and fully to the American enterprise; they benefited greatly. In one major respect, however, the Jews were different from the other peoples of European origins. They insisted not only on maintaining and practicing their religious tradition, but they also continued to maintain a special relationship to their fellow Jews throughout the world. Although the Jews identified their future and the future of their children with that of America, they were also part of *Kelal Israel*, or Catholic Israel, and therefore shared in the destiny of the Jewish people and its faith.

This striving for social integration and religio-cultural identity within the framework of American democratic society is the unique quality of American Jewish history and its central theme. It can be traced most effectively in the history of Jewish religious life and institutions in the United States.

Ever since the earliest settlements of Jews on this continent, one question concerned them as a religious group more than any other: what shall be the nature of Judaism in America? In colonial times, when there were in the United States but a handful of congregations, similar in design and

274

purpose, the answer seemed comparatively clear and simple. During the nineteenth century and until World War I, as American Jewry increased greatly, and as the patterns of belief and observance varied in the widest degrees, contradictions and confusions multiplied. Religious leaders proposed conflicting formulas of social and religious adaptation and created movements to implement their views. These movements vied with one another for the support of American Jewry—this against a background of continuing waves of immigration and unprecedented changes on the American and Jewish scenes.

Yet, early in the twentieth century, despite the inner contradictions and confusions, American Judaism began to take distinctive shape and form. After World War I, international responsibilities hastened the process of maturity. American Jewry rose to world Jewish leadership. In May, 1948, the historic declaration of independence proclaiming the republic of Israel brought into sharper focus the need to define the character of American Judaism and, more specifically, the exact relationship between American Jewry and Jewry in the new state. The religious groups had an answer which was deeply rooted in Jewish tradition. This answer emphasized American Jewry's undivided allegiance to the United States, its duty to sustain maximum Jewish life and expression in this country, as well as its obligation to help build the republic of Israel as the vital spiritual center of Judaism.

This essay surveys the history of Jewish religious life, thought, and institutions in the United States in relation to the American Jewish experience as a whole.

I

Jewish Religious Life in Colonial Times, 1654-1800

Already during the colonial period steps were being taken and thoughts expressed which were to have a singular effect on American Jews and Judaism. It is significant that all kinds of people—fundamentalist and separatist, deist and theist—searched the Bible for guidance in their daily lives; that in Massachusetts was a town called Salem (*Shalom*, peace); that a Pennsylvania Quaker went by the name of Israel Israel; that William Bradford, colonial governor of Plymouth Colony, should manifest an abiding love for the Hebrew language in his *History of Plymouth Plantation*. Even more significant, perhaps, was the proposal by Benjamin Franklin, Thomas Jefferson, and John Adams, that the theme of the Exodus be adopted for the seal of the United States of America. It seems as though these men hoped to engrave on the minds of every American in every generation the scene of "Pharaoh sitting in an open chariot, a crown on his head and a sword in his hand, passing through the dividing waters of the Red Sea in pursuit of the Israelites; with rays from a pillar of fire beaming on Moses, who is represented as standing on the shore extending his hand over the sea . . ." The legend on the seal reads: "Rebellion to tyrants is obedience to God." The statute of Jacob was to feed the spirit of the law of the American people.[1]

The character of the religious life of American Jewry in the pre- and post-Revolutionary years can best be portrayed by a description of the leading religious personality of the period, Gershom Mendez Seixas, and of Jewish synagogal life in the Sephardic community of his time.

Seixas was the first native American *hazzan*. He was born in New York in 1745. In 1768, at the age of twenty-three, when Congregation Shearith Israel issued its call for a new *hazzan*, Seixas was elected for the period of his "Decent and Good Behavior" at a salary of eighty pounds per year, in addition to firewood and other perquisites.[2] His task, as was the wont in those days, was all inclusive. He was preacher, reader, teacher, and community servant. The pedagogic assignments were carefully detailed by his congregation. He was to teach his students to read Hebrew, and enable them to translate portions of the prayer book and Bible; moreover, he was to furnish convenient quarters for a classroom, and assume final responsibility at the religious services for the conduct of lads under the age of thirteen.

On the outbreak of the War for Independence, Jews like others in the country were divided over the issue of rebellion. In Shearith Israel one could meet Tory, as well as patriot. But Seixas used every influence he had to win his congregation's sympathy and support for the American cause. When Lord Howe brought his British army to Long Island and was about to approach New York, Seixas chose to shut down the synagogue rather than serve under occupation. Immediately prior to the capture of the city, he gathered his flock and held a farewell service. He thought this was perhaps the last service before the Ark in the Mill Street synagogue. Every object of worship in the synagogue, the scrolls of the Law, the tablets, the prayer books, and the candlesticks, he took with him, and fled to Stratford, Connecticut, to the safety of the American lines. The synagogue, barren of its appurtenances, was used on occasion by the Tories, and its sanctity was carefully guarded by the British.

The stream of American refugees wound its way to Philadelphia. Many of the former Shearith Israel congregants settled in the mother city of the Revolution. The handful of original Philadelphia Jewish residents grew to a considerable number, as the Jews of all occupied cities, including Newport and Savannah, arrived. Mikveh Israel, the congregation that was formerly without a home of its own, soon had a reader and a building. The dedication ceremonies, held in 1782, just before the end of the Revolutionary War, were attended by many distinguished Christian patriots; special prayers were offered on behalf of the Continental Congress and the commander in chief, George Washington.

Seixas became famous as the patriot Jewish minister of the Revolution. His zeal for the revolutionary cause was expressed in prayer, in sermon, and in action. The *Pennsylvania Gazette* of July 9, 1788, carries an account of the extraordinary demonstration in Philadelphia to celebrate the ratification of the Federal Constitution. In the parade, the correspondent writes, marched "the clergy of different Christian denominations with the rabbi of the Jews walking arm in arm." American legend tells of fourteen ministers invited to attend the inauguration of Washington, and Seixas is said to have been one of them.

In 1784, after the evacuation of New York by the British, Seixas and the Congregation Shearith Israel were reunited, the synagogue rededicated, and his former activities resumed. He continued to serve his congregation until his death in 1816. He introduced Pinto's translation of the Hebrew prayer book,[3] published in 1766, the first work of its kind ever issued in America, and containing the prayers for the Sabbath and High Holy Days, in order to meet the need of the members of the congregation who lacked a Jewish education. As Pastor, Seixas felt the need for a special society to aid in the relief of the sick and the burial of the dead. He therefore founded the Hebra Hesed v'Emet (Society of Loving-kindness and Truth) in 1802.

Seixas was one of the first American preachers to deliver regular Thanksgiving sermons. As spokesman of the Jewish community and as an American patriot, he was invited to preach in the churches of the city. One of his most important addresses was delivered in historic St. Paul's Church in 1800. Special honor came to him when he was appointed a member of the board of trustees of Columbia College, and his name is in its charter as one of the original incorporators. Through the War of 1812 and until his death, Seixas continued his fervent work in the vineyard of the Lord. He was the forerunner of a new type of spiritual leader, created by the needs of American Jewish life—student, preacher, teacher, pastor, and community servant.

Six Jewish congregations sent greetings to President George Washington. They were, in the order of their establishment: New York (1655); Newport, Rhode Island (1658); Savannah, Georgia (1733); Philadelphia, Pennsylvania (1740); Charleston, South Carolina (1749); and Richmond, Virginia (1790).[4] Though the Jews were primarily settled in seaport cities and busily engaged in commerce and trade, Jewish life maintained its traditional character. Religious life and practices were traditional in every respect. The house of worship was a house of assembly and also a school; the order of the service was in accordance with the ancient Spanish *minhag* and was observed in all of its minutiae; members of the congregation were subject to community opinion; community sanction derived from a central authority.

The Jewish population is variously estimated as having reached between twenty-five hundred and three thousand in the first decade of the nineteenth century. The majority were of Sephardic stock: Spanish, Portuguese, and Dutch. The number of German Jews, however, was considerable, far larger than the impression given us by historians of the past generation, who enjoyed dividing American Jewish history into three sharply defined periods of immigration.

The chief of the community, in law and in substance, was the *parnas*. He and his associates supervised every aspect of congregational life. Their control was supreme and autocratic. The *parnas* set the schedule of hours for the services, distributed the "honors," and authorized the performance of wedding ceremonies. This prerogative, preserved in many Sephardic congregations to this day, was accepted also by most of the Ashkenazic synagogues in the nineteenth century. As late as 1862, Dr. Morris Raphall, the rabbi of Congregation B'nai Jeshurun, was compelled, in accordance with his congregation's ruling, to request permission from the *parnas* to officiate at the wedding of his own daughter! The *parnas's* duties included rendering opinions on ritual law and supervising all congregational needs. For Passover, matzot were prepared under the auspices of the congregation and the price was set sufficiently above cost to ensure adequate income for free distribution of matzot to the needy. The *shohet* was engaged by the congregation, and all kosher food was issued under synagogue supervision and sanction. Unlimited authority was granted to the *parnas* in the punishment of the unaffiliated and religiously wayward. The files of Rodeph Shalom Congregation, Philadelphia, for 1810 (first congregation of German Jews, established in 1802) state:

This Committee, after much deliberation, found it advisable, that when a married Yahudi, with family, comes to live in the State of Pennsylvania, such Yahudi be allowed to remain in this state 6 mos. and should during this time declare himself willing to join Rodeph Shalom. When such a family has in the eyes of the cong. been found well behaving and when it should, may God forbid, be in need or trouble, then the cong. should come to its help. But in case the family has not declared itself as desiring to affiliate itself with us, no help should be forthcoming to it.[5]

Shearith Israel warned transgressors that

whosoever . . . continues to act contrary to our Holy Law by breaking any of the principles command will not be deem'd a member of our Congregation, have none of the Mitzote of the Sinagoge Conferred on him & when Dead will not be buried according to the manner of our breathren.[6]

These stringent regulations already indicate the beginnings of community disintegration and laxity in observance. This became more serious as the Jewish community spread beyond the confines of its original small area of settlement. Demographic change was the barometer of the weakening of religious influence. In the early period, however, major offenses were rare. There were no doubt many minor infractions, the penalty for which was a petty fine. But there was no redress for one who intermarried and thus deserted Judaism.

Except for Seixas, the *hazzan* was most often a lay member of the congregation, a man with a pleasant voice and smattering acquaintance with Hebrew, who served as reader and teacher to the young. On occasion he would preach. Most frequently a distinguished member of the congregation assumed the responsibilities of preaching or delivering the address. Second to the *hazzan* was a *shammash*, who served as a combination superintendent, secretary, and beadle: it was his duty to "call the Yechidimz that they may assemble togeathere at the usuall hours."[7]

Frequently Christian members of the community visited at Jewish services. Ezra Stiles (1727-1795), later president of Yale, was a frequent visitor at the Newport synagogue in the days of his own ministry in that city. Another visitor, the Swedish traveler Peter Kalm (1716-1779) who came to America in 1748, offers us a description of a Jewish community in action as seen through Christian eyes:

During my residence at *New York,* this time and in the next two years, I was frequently in company with Jews. I was informed among other things, that these people never boiled any meat for themselves on Saturday, but that they always did it the day before; and that in winter they kept a fire during the whole Saturday. They commonly eat no pork; yet I have been told by several men of credit, that many of them (especially among the young Jews) when traveling, did not make the least difficulty about eating this, or any other meat that was put before them; even though they were in company with Christians. I was in their synagogue last evening for the first time, and this day at noon I visited it again, and each time I was put in a particular seat which was set apart for strangers or Christians. A young *Rabbi* read the divine service, which was partly in Hebrew, and partly in the Rabinical dialect. Both men and women were dressed entirely in the *English* fashion; the former had all of them their hats on, and did not once take them off during service. The galleries, I observed, were appropriated to the ladies, while the men sat below. During prayers the men spread a white cloth over their heads; which perhaps is to represent sackcloth. But I observed that the wealthier sort of people had a much richer cloth than the poorer ones. Many of the men had Hebrew books, in which they sang and read alternately. The *Rabbi* stood in the middle of the synagogue, and read with his face turned towards the east; he spoke however so fast as to make it almost impossible for anyone to understand what he said.[8]

That not all young Jewish men when away from home transgressed the religious precepts may be adduced from extant letters and records. One, for example, records that

Hart Jacobs, of the Jewish Religion, having signified to this Committee that it is inconsistent with his religious profession to perform military duty on Friday nights, being part of the Jewish Sabbath, it is

Ordered, That he be exempted from Military duty on that night of the week, to be subject, nevertheless, to the performance of his full tour of duty on other nights.[9]

The architecture of the colonial synagogue was in a style typical of the period. The first New York synagogue, which was built on Mill Street in 1730, and remained the center of worship for all New York Jewry until 1825, was a structure but thirty-five feet square and twenty-one feet high. The oldest example of colonial synagogal architecture, still in existence, is the Jeshuat Israel Synagogue at Newport, Rhode Island. (On March 5, 1946, this was declared a national American shrine.) Newport was visited by George Washington on August 17, 1790. At this time the congregation sent him greetings, and his reply is the oft-quoted historic letter which, among other things declares, "It is now no more that toleration is spoken of as if it was by the indulgence of one class of people that another enjoyed the exercise of their inherent natural rights. For happily the Government of the United States, which gives to bigotry no sanction, to persecution no assistance, requires only that they who live under its protection, should demean themselves as good citizens, in giving it on all occasions their effectual support."[10] The cornerstone of the synagogue was laid on August 1, 1759. On December 2, 1763, corresponding to the first day of Hanukkah of the year 5523, the synagogue was dedicated, as Ezra Stiles says in his *Diary,* "in a Edifice, the most perfect of the Temple kind perhaps in America, & splendidly illuminated, could not but raise in the Mind a faint Idea of the Majesty & Grandeur of the Ancient Jewish Worship mentioned in Scripture."[11]

In traditional Jewish manner, great attention was devoted to the education of the young. The school was the core of society. In the years prior to the advent of public education, those children who had any schooling at all received both their general and their religious education from private tutors. The congregations realized the need for a more effective educational system. The most advanced school, the Yeshibat Minhat Areb, was conducted under the auspices of Congregation Shearith Israel. From its beginnings in 1731 until 1800, it was run along lines characteristic of all other schools within the colonial educational system. Full and final responsibility for the school was vested in the congregational board. They arranged curricular standards and requirements. In addition to English and Hebrew, students were taught Spanish; general courses were given in arithmetic, spelling, and literature. Classes were conducted the year round, daily from nine to five with an intermission period of two hours. The cost of maintenance was covered by tuition fees and community subvention. The children of the poor were admitted without charge. At the beginning of the nineteenth century the school was given the same grant-in-aid that the state advanced to religious schools of other denominations. The affluent retained private instructors or sent their children to private schools, conducted by Christian teachers; others sent their children abroad.[12]

Social service aid also was controlled by the religious authorities. The conditions of the Dutch West India Company, qualifying the admission of the Jews to New Amsterdam, "provided, that the indigent among them shall not become a burthen on the Company or the public, but maintain'd at the expense of the Jewish nation."[13] This promise was zealously fulfilled even beyond the expectation of Peter Stuyvesant and others of his ilk. The widow and the orphan, the halt and the blind, the feeble and the indigent found their source of relief in the synagogue.

The minute books of Congregation Shearith Israel fully reveal how taxing *"Sedaca"* was. Records of specific cases spanning the full range of social disabilities are included. Itinerants were aided in their journey; "sufficiencies for lodging and boarding the sick" were dispensed; the poor were not denied their daily bread; ". . . if application be again made for Moses Hart to allow him a Loaf of Bread per day if he wants it." The constitution of the congregation required the reading of its section on charity procedures twice a year both in Portuguese and in English:

If any poor person should happen to come to this place and should want the assistance of the Sinagog the Parnaz is hereby impowered to allow every poor person for his maintainance the sum of Eight Shillings pr Week and no more Not Exceeding the term of twelve weeks. And the Parnaz is also to use his utmost endeavours to despatch them to sum othere place as soon as Possible assisting them with necessarys, for their Voyage, that is for a single person fourty Shillings, but if it be a family then the parnaz shall call his assistance and consult with them both for their maintainance whilst ashore and also for their necessarys when they depart; those poor of this Congregation that shall apply for Sedaca [charity] shall be assisted with as much as the Parnaz and his assistants shall think fitt.[14]

At the close of the colonial period there was a small, compact and united Jewish community, firm in the tradition of their fathers, at home in the land of their adoption, and partners in the creation of its greatness.

2

Growth of the Jewish Community, 1800-1840

The first German Jewish congregation was organized in 1802. And in the hundred years which followed, American Jewry grew from a comparatively simple congregation of some 2,500 concentrated on the Atlantic seaboard to a complex community of approximately 1,050,000 reaching to the farthermost points on the continent.

Every sign in the American adventure pointed westward: the Louisiana Purchase, expansion beyond the Mississippi basin, the conquest of the west. In his book, *The Epic of America*, James Truslow Adams appropriately entitles the chapter on the twenties and thirties of the nineteenth century, "The Sun Rises in the West." By 1830 the "men of the western waters" beyond the Alleghenies constituted one-third of the American population. The imprint of settlers' boots paved new roads. American industrialists in the east attempted to stop the exodus. They failed.

During the first four decades of the nineteenth century the Jewish population multiplied fivefold. Isaac Harby writing in the *North American Review*, placed the number at 6,000 in 1826. In 1840, the *American Almanac* raised the figure to 15,000. The *Publications of the American Jewish Historical Society* are sprinkled with accounts of plans for local colonization. The motives of the initiators were varied; they included speculation, promotion, and even conversion. In one superdramatic incident —the dream of bringing Noah's Ark to an American Ararat—its impresario, the dreamer, journalist, and alcalde, Mordecai Manuel Noah, claimed that the future of the entire Jewish people was at stake. These plans to colonize the Jews in America, heralded by advertisements, pamphlets, and European agents, lured many an innocent soul in quest of the "golden bough." The European unrest caused by the Napoleonic Wars was a further incentive to the emigration of Jews from Central Europe.

The new arrivals moved westward in the American train; Gratzburg and Aaronsburgh were two stopovers on the western route. Jewish communities were slowly formed along a typical pattern; the steps in the operation became almost mechanical. A concrete example is Cincinnati, the city that was destined to play a leading role in the history of American Judaism.

Joseph Jonas of Exeter, England, arrived in Cincinnati in 1817. Among his other gifts, Jonas evidently possessed a keen sense of history, for he bequeathed to posterity his memoirs, replete with important historical information. The economic potentialities of the Ohio Valley attracted Jonas. He traveled westward, against all sound advice, the first Jew to be seen in those parts. People traveled many miles to view this object of curiosity. One old Quaker woman said to him: "Art Thou a Jew? Thou art one of God's chosen people. Wilt thou let me examine thee?" As she turned him round about, she remarked, "Well, thou art no different to other people."[15]

In 1819 a trio of English Jews joined him; then came another handful. Within five years, in 1824, a congregation was established and named, simply, Bene Israel. The synagogue required assistance. Letters were dispatched to England, Barbados, and older sister congregations in America: ". . . a few years before nothing was heard but the howling of wild beasts and the more hideous cry of savage man. It is worthy of remark that there is not a congregation within 500 miles of this city . . . and we are well informed that had we a Synagogue here, hundreds from that City who now know nothing of their religion would frequently attend here during holidays." Until 1830 only English Jews resided in Cincinnati. Then the German Jews poured in. In 1836, the Bene Israel dedicated their house of God.[16]

In short, the record of American Jewish history in these early years of the nineteenth century not only indicates that the Ashkenazic Jews fanned out into the American hinterland; but, more profoundly, the record reflects how deeply American Israel was involved in the expansion of America. From these two primary forces—the westward expansion of America and the German Jewish immigration—there emerged several ancillary factors which slowly weakened the uniform congregational structure. They are, in order: the preponderance of Ashkenazic over Sephardic Jewry,[17] the waning of synagogal authority, and the beginnings of Reform.

The problem of "authority" has always constituted one of the most fascinating and complicated chapters in the Jewish spiritual odyssey. In America the problem was all the more interesting because the two contesting mother countries, England and Holland, exerted a powerful influence on American culture. During the greater part of the nineteenth century, America was firmly tied to the skirts of the mother continent. One lived in America but Europe was "home." In each important legal question, the congregations referred to their chief rabbi, for American Jewry lacked qualified scholars and rabbis who could interpret ritual law. The authority sitting in London was accepted as the final word by all English Ashkenazic synagogues in America. As late as 1837, Congregation B'nai Jeshurun, for example, paid an annual half shekel to the chief rabbi, as the minutes of the congregation reveal.[18]

While in such matters as the pronunciation of Hebrew there may have been differences, and the minor details of custom and ceremony were performed with varying emphases, the forms of synagogal organization were not altered. In this respect, the American Sephardic congregational tradition prevailed. Shearith Israel was the model for the new Ashkenazic synagogues. The *parnas* retained all his powers, synagogue attendance was declared compulsory, the recalcitrant and obstreperous were duly fined. Once the new congregations were established and the stringencies of personal feuds reduced, the most amicable relations existed between them. A helping hand was extended in times of need. Properly enough, Harmon

Hendricks, then *parnas* of Shearith Israel, contributed generously to the seceding congregation, B'nai Jeshurun. The respective Sephardic and Ashkenazic synagogues continued to accept members of the other group into their fold.

This relationship was more than an expression of amenities. In the deeper realm of religious life, in theology and in fundamental practice, the Sephardim and Ashkenazim were of one thought. The shade of difference was infinitesimal in comparison with the wide area of common interest. Both Sephardim and Ashkenazim sought to uphold the Torah through the institution of the synagogue. All hands were joined to ward off the onrushing forces of assimilation and communal disintegration. With one voice they proclaimed the inviolability of the Sabbath. With equal determination they joined to ban the faithless. They were also pained when they saw that the synagogue was slowly but surely being dislodged from its central position in Jewish life.

The battle over the centrality of the synagogue was not lost without a serious attempt to meet the growing needs of the expanding community. In 1828, Shearith Israel established a Hebrew Benevolent Society as part of the congregation's functions. However, as the push toward decentralization became stronger, the synagogue simply could not meet the pressing social needs of the heterogeneous and undisciplined community. Sixteen years later, when German Jews were to establish a social agency, they organized the German Hebrew Benevolent Society apart from the synagogue. That very decade saw the founding of the largest international Jewish order, B'nai B'rith (1843), to be followed by the orders B'nai Israel (1853) and B'nai Abraham (1859). Slowly the Jews were weaned away from the synagogue as their central communal institution. The fraternal orders, which began as supplementary agencies to the synagogue, were to become their chief competitors.

The school, the very heart of the congregational system, also spread its wings in trial flight. The first Sunday school, which was organized in Philadelphia in 1838 by Rebecca Gratz (1781-1869), assumed a communal rather than a congregational character. Similar schools were shortly introduced in Charleston, Richmond, Cincinnati, and New York.

The real challenge to the uniformity which characterized the synagogue came from a totally unanticipated source: the challenge came from within. The first signs of Reform Judaism appeared in Charleston in 1824. After a brief period of existence, this attempt disappeared and seemingly left no trace. Twenty years later, however, Reform flowered once again; this time to remain permanently in the garden of American Judaism.

History cannot be controlled by logic. It was in a sedate Sephardic congregation, Beth Elohim, not a German synagogue, that Reform Judaism was first planted in America. A group of forty-seven members, led by Isaac Harby (1788-1828) and David N. Carvalho (1784-1860), influenced by the developments in Hamburg and repelled by the perfunctory order of their own congregational affairs, appealed for a modification of their service. They asked what seems in retrospect to be very little: a shorter, more intelligible, and more decorous service. They requested that some prayers be read in English as well as in Hebrew and that the rabbi offer a commentary on the portion of the week. The heads of the community refused to depart from their accustomed practice. In protest, twelve of the more determined members in the group resigned and established the Reformed Society of Israelites. Within the short space of two years their number grew to fifty. Their long range purpose soon became apparent. They published a new prayer book, introduced the organ, and announced reforms in Jewish practice in order to adapt Judaism to the "situation of an enlightened world." Despite these serious preparations, the project failed and the money that had been donated for the proposed building was returned to the contributors. This sudden dissolution was not the last chapter in the story of Charleston Reform. It was but the first attempt. As a footnote to the development of Reform in Charleston, it is interesting to observe with David Philipson that the practice of establishing "Reform-Vereine" for the purpose of propagating Reform sentiment in the community and then organizing a congregation was adopted by other groups as well. Such societies served as the basic units of congregations Har Sinai in Baltimore, Emanu-El in New York, Keneseth Israel in Philadelphia, and Sinai in Chicago.

At the end of this period, in 1840, American Jewry entered a new stage in its development. The dynamism of American life had released powerful forces. America and its Jews were on the move. Now centrifugal forces gained sway. The older methods of fines and bans lost their punitive powers. Disaffection and spiritual corrosion could not be met with declarations and resolutions. Intermarriage, Jewish ignorance, and above all, the paralyzing indifference to the destiny of Judaism thoroughly upset Jewish religious institutional life. In the Colonial period, a Jew was zealously controlled from birth to death by the synagogue. Now a Jew could live or die as a Jew without regard for that control.

3

New Jewish Religious Trends, 1840-1869

The hundred years from 1840 to 1940 marked the greatest period of migration in all human history. The political, social, and industrial revolutions in Germany, and the resultant agrarian crisis in the forties of the nineteenth century, compelled large portions of the population to emigrate to western countries, particularly the United States. The appeal of Leopold

Kompert (1822-1886), the German Jewish novelist and political writer, that all Jews of Central Europe emigrate to America, was answered in deed by tens of thousands of his fellow religionists. In eight years (1840-1848), the estimated Jewish population figures in America jumped from fifteen to fifty thousand.

These statistics of Jewish increase serve but as an index to the formidable spiritual complications that now beset American Judaism. Fortunately, the enveloping crisis brought forth elements for its own cure. Fresh forces arose. They injected a vitalism which gave the sagging religious life a new spirit and a new heart. The most prominent participants in this revival were Isaac Leeser and Isaac Mayer Wise.

"To learn and to teach, to observe, and to do." This is the legend Isaac Leeser (1806-1868) selected for the masthead of his new magazine, the *Occident and American Jewish Advocate*. It serves as a clue to the life, character, and activities of this pioneer in Jewish religious life in America.[19]

Leeser pioneered in every conceivable field of Jewish endeavor. He is credited with being the first *hazzan* to introduce the English sermon as a permanent part of the Sabbath service. He translated the Sephardic and Ashkenazic prayer books into English. In the field of publications his name is imprinted on the flyleaf of virtually every important Jewish religious text that appeared in his generation, including children's spelling books, catechisms, and supplementary liturgical volumes. He was the first to produce a volume on Eretz Yisrael, the English translation of the famous geography of Rabbi Joseph Schwarz, *A Descriptive Geography and Brief Historical Sketch of Palestine*. The climax of his literary career was his translation of the Bible into English, a translation which for the first time replaced the King James version in Jewish schools and homes. Until the appearance of the Jewish Publication Society translation in 1917, Leeser's edition served as the Jewish home Bible in all English-speaking countries in the world.

Isaac Mayer Wise (1819-1900) was rabbi, student, editor and administrator *par excellence*. The history of American Judaism will ever remember him as master architect of Reform religious institutions. In his autobiography, Isaac Mayer Wise, the man with the penetrating eyes and the spectacles on his forehead (whose portrait is fixed in the heart and imagination of American Israel), wrote: "The reforming spirit was innate in me; it was my foremost characteristic."[20]

Wise the reformer was not an iconoclast. He had many orthodoxies. Denying the central position of Eretz Yisrael in the future of world Israel, he substituted America in its place; declaring modernism as his child, he insisted that biblical critics keep hands off the sacred and ancient text; rejecting talmudic authority, he nevertheless created a new authority of rabbis; rejecting aspects of ceremonial law, he believed with a firm faith that Judaism was the theosophy of mankind; disgruntled with the absence of lay leadership in religious life, he created the Union of American Hebrew Congregations. Wise's successes were unquestionably due to his accent on the positive task. As Professor Samuel S. Cohon chooses to describe him, Wise was the "foremost leader of Constructive Reform in America."

Leeser and Wise, who were to join forces only to separate, were the respective founders of the two contending movements in American Judaism in the nineteenth century—Historical, or Conservative Judaism; and Progressive, or Reform Judaism. Both men attracted to themselves devoted associates who helped establish their policies of action. The goal was the same: the adjustment of Jews and Judaism to the American scene. The anarchy in American Jewish religious life was inherent in its very system of organization. Throughout the Western Hemisphere, from Canada to the West Indies, congregational independence held sway. The principle of the separatists, who abandoned Elizabethan England because they repudiated the idea of a national church, was the rule in America; and, thought Leeser, this system as it applied to Jewish life could serve only further to decentralize the synagogue. Congregational absolutism led to dishonorable competition and stubborn isolationism even between sister congregations in one city. Leeser began to speak of *Kelal Israel*—the United Synagogue. He was the first to use the idiom "Catholic Israel" in the exact connotation and frame of reference that Schechter so effectively employed in the twentieth century.

Leeser formulated a program of action. Citizen of the United States and ardent advocate of its democratic principles, he thought along American constitutional lines. He devised a federated synagogue plan which would guarantee congregational autonomy. The proposed union was to deal with transcongregational problems: religious issues, education, publications, community representation, etc. The union would not seek to interfere in any manner with the local *minhag*, order of service, or language of prayer. As early as 1841, Leeser met with Louis Salomon, *hazzan* of the Rodeph Shalom Congregation, and together they issued a joint proposal. The full details of this program, as elaborated by the leaders of the three Philadelphia congregations—Mikveh Israel, Rodeph Shalom, and Beth Israel—and published in the *Occident*, make up a document of historic importance in the development of American Jewish communal organization.[21] A call was issued for a national assembly. Leeser was rebuffed. Union was declared unfeasible. The plan was premature.

Leeser turned to other tactics. If the solution to congregational anarchy was not to come from reorganization, why not reform from within? With careful and self-critical step, he outlined the procedures: pruning the service of unnecessary encumbrances, introduction of novel ceremonies, incorporation of English readings, and production of a religious literature.

To the reformers these efforts seemed trivial. The American synagogue, they insisted, would not fulfil its potentialities unless a more radical revision of the traditional service were instituted. Reform forces were growing in number and their program of action began to take shape.

In November, 1845, Max Lilienthal (1815-1882), then just thirty, arrived in the United States. Though a young man, his fame preceded him, for he came from Russia where for five years he had served on the staff of Count Uwaroff, imperial minister of education. This newcomer to the ranks of American Reform played a leading role in the growth of that movement. Although in his introductory sermons Lilienthal declared himself to be a traditionalist, he later veered to the moderate reformism of Isaac Mayer Wise.

It was Max Lilienthal who introduced the custom of confirmation into the United States. The festival of Shabuot, 1846, is the date of the first ceremony of confirmation, which later came to be observed in Orthodox and Conservative, as well as Reform, synagogues. Lilienthal carries the additional distinction of being the president of the first rabbinical association in America. Wise had been in Albany scarcely a month when he joined with Lilienthal, Dr. Hermann Felsenheld and Rabbi Kohlmeyer to organize an ecclesiastical court, a *Bet Din*. Lilienthal was chosen president and Wise served as secretary. But three rabbis gathered at the initial meeting held April 18, 1847. Nevertheless, the small gathering had a lasting effect. They declared their purpose was to offer "beneficial service to the Jewish congregations of America," and "not to assume any hierarchical authority, but to act only in advisory capacity." The agenda of the conference called for preparation of a catechism and biblical history for Jewish schools. These plans did not materialize.

The more important assignment given at that time to Wise was ultimately accomplished. It was at this meeting that Wise proposed his *Minhag America*. The very name is indicative of the spirit with which Wise and his associates conceived the future of American Judaism. They (like the traditional groups) declared their faith in America as a permanent home for Israel. However, in place of the prevailing liturgies in American congregations, the Sephardic and Ashkenazic *minhagim*, they intended to substitute an American rite. Characteristic of Wise's approach was his insistence that the new prayer book be issued under the imprimatur of an accredited rabbinical body. He prepared his manuscript subject to its being considered at the following meeting. That meeting was never held. He placed the text aside until a proper authority of rabbis would be constituted.[22]

The service book could wait, but other synagogal reforms could not. Upon his return to Albany, Wise set to work. As yet no one, either in

Europe or in America, had ventured to impose the reforms proposed by Abraham Geiger, as early as 1837, for the "religious emancipation of the Jewish woman." Geiger's important essay *"Die Stellung des weiblichen Geschlechtes in dem Judenthume unserer Zeit"* (The Position of Woman in the Judaism of our Time),[23] remained a theoretical statement as far as European Judaism was concerned. It was Wise who initiated the practice of mixed choir and family pews in American Jewish religious life. Then came the issue over the use of an organ at religious services. In 1846, the organ dispute reached the Court of Errors and Appeals in the state of South Carolina. In time organ music was to be heard in all Reform congregations throughout the land and in many Conservative congregations.

These differences of opinion did not sever the bond between the men of the Historical and Reform schools. Differences existed, but lines of opposition were not yet formed. On the contrary, the growing differences made both groups ever more anxious to seek an area of compromise. The amorphous mass of indifferent Jews concerned them more than rabbinical polemics. Reform was moderate and Historical Judaism alert. All minds searched for a formula.

Suddenly Isaac Mayer Wise wrote to Leeser. He prepared an article for publication in the *Occident* in which he endorsed Leeser's activities on behalf of a national religious federation. The two captains rallied their parties and issued a call of assembly for 1849. Eight congregations responded favorably. Nevertheless, they sought a large representation of at least twenty participants. Once again New York City was the determining factor. Wise took the organizing lead. Temple Emanu-El, fearful lest common effort with the traditionalists would impede the growth of Reform, demurred. Wise lashed out in characteristic manner. He challenged Emanu-El's integrity. Not the greater interests of Judaism, but autocratic congregational independence compelled Emanu-El's refusal to co-operate, he wrote. Recriminations only aggravated difficulties. The lone New York support of Shaaray Tefila, synagogue of Samuel Myer Isaacs (1804-1878), stanch friend of Leeser, was small consolation. The champions laid down their arms for a brief respite before they began the next round in the battle for unity.

A third impassioned attempt was made. In 1855, largely through the tireless efforts of Isaac M. Wise, a gathering predominantly of Reform elements was assembled in Cleveland with the symbolic motto *Shalom al Yisroel* (Peace in Israel). Leeser, who was apprised of the constituent delegates, was wary of participating unless his condition, that all discussions be premised on the authority of tradition, be accepted. The eastern contingent of reformers absented themselves for a contrary reason. They were unhappy with the moderation of Wise and Lilienthal. Thus, it was largely a midwestern moderate Reform-oriented group that convened in Cleveland. Wise was so concerned with "Union in Israel" that he was prepared to meet Leeser more than half way. He was convinced, as his later writings reveal, that once all the elements in Judaism would function co-operatively, Reform, which in his opinion was weighted with truth, would inevitably triumph.

Leeser returned from the meeting in Cleveland with the wreath of victory. Even the rightists in the Historical school, those who had counseled abstention, agreed that Leeser had been vindicated. What lasting good might have come to American Judaism had Leeser and Wise stood firmly together! But they did not remain united. The wind of wrath blew strongest from the eastern Reform camp. David Einhorn led the opposition. "Who authorized you," the reformers scorned, "to make alliances with the Orthodox and their talmudic ideas?"[24] Further rebuke came from the house of Reform in Germany. Rabbis Ludwig Philippson (1811-1889) and Leopold Stein (1810-1882) admonished their former *Liebling*, Wise, for his treachery, and gave full support to Einhorn. Wise was bitterly discouraged by this opposition. The simmerings of doubt and challenge directed against his leadership now developed into a full-fledged revolt. New personalities had emerged on the Reform scene in America. They were to be reckoned with.

Foremost among the eastern Reform wing was David Einhorn (1809-1879), who came to America in 1855. Einhorn had already benefited from his experience in the German Reform movement. His native talents and especially his oratorical ability won him an established place on the central dais of American Reform. Einhorn summarized his philosophy of Judaism in one sentence: "Like man himself, the child of God, the divine law has a perishable body and imperishable spirit." Idealistic German philosophy was at the root of his thinking. He was convinced that the permanent ideas of Judaism could find their truest expression only in the German language. Second only to the doctrine of God, Einhorn stressed the priestly mission of Israel as the hope of humanity's salvation. He published the magazine "Sinai" a monthly in German, from 1856 to 1862.

Bernhard Felsenthal (1822-1908), who arrived in America in 1854, was known for his independent views and scholarly attainments. Later he was to be one of the founders of the American Zionist movement. From 1858 on, even before he became rabbi, first of Sinai Congregation and later of Zion Congregation in Chicago, he was a leading spokesman for congregational union, but urged that individual synagogues maintain their autonomy. In March, 1859, the pamphlet, *Kol Kore Bamidbar, ueber juedische Reform* (A Voice in the Wilderness), in which he preached his doctrine, established the new arrival as an important and dominating spirit.

Following Einhorn and Felsenthal came Samuel Adler (1809-1891) who arrived from Alzey in 1857. He, too, had participated in the early deliberations of the German Reform movement. Adler served at Temple Emanu-El in New York for nineteen years and consistently called for a crystallized Reform position.

In 1866, Samuel Hirsch (1815-1889) assumed the Keneseth Israel pulpit in Philadelphia. He was soon recognized as the philosopher of extreme Reform. Hirsch's wide influence had been felt even earlier from abroad. Now his scholarly support in America was added to the struggle for theological reorientation. Hirsch was bound to the Hegelian system and regarded history as the divine process of revelation. Differing from his master, however, he developed the conception of Judaism as *Lehre*. Torah is not "law" but *Lehre*, doctrine. These doctrines were revealed to Israel through the prophets, and Israel was chosen to exemplify *Lehre* before the entire world.

Wise read the handwriting clearly. American Judaism was in a state of confusion. His dream of an all inclusive synod had to be postponed, if not forgotten. The reality of the moment required a stabilization of the Reform position. There were two groups in Reform, fairly well distributed in the East and the West. The well defined program of the German school was transplanted to America, while the more moderate and adaptable program of pragmatic Reform was losing its hold. Strategy called for concentration on the advancement of the Reform position and co-ordination of its high command.

In the ranks of the Historical school, the identical cell splitting took place. Only the reasons and personalities varied. The rightists in the group were soon aided by Wise himself. The *Minhag America* appeared, and it reflected his writing and thinking. Prayers for the return to Eretz Yisrael, the rebuilding of the Temple in Jerusalem, the restoration of the sacrificial system and the restoration of the Davidic dynasty were all eliminated. Bernard Illowy (1814-1871) submitted a bill of particulars explaining why he, Wise, should be placed under ban.[25]

Leeser was stunned. The appearance of the *Minhag America* completely shattered his hopes. It demonstrated the true position of Wise, Lilienthal, and their like minded associates. The Cleveland Conference was wasted. Disappointment was transmuted to open warfare. Reform, Leeser claimed, was bankrupt. Its synagogues were empty, its memberships static, and the religious feeling of its congregants dissipated. So-called Reform was only a paring of the candle ends.

Leeser then reached the very conclusions for the Historical school that Wise had formulated for Reform Judaism. If an all-inclusive synod was impossible, the obvious alternative was a union of traditionalists.

But as in the case of Reform, immediate unification of the Historical school was frustrated from within. The Historical school in America included a number of adherents who were as estranged from the rightist elements in the traditionalist grouping as they were from the extreme of German Reform. They had greatest affinity with the moderate reformism of Wise and Lilienthal and actually went beyond them in proposals to modify Jewish practice. The chief exponents of moderate reformism in the ranks of the Historical school were Benjamin Szold and Marcus Jastrow.

Benjamin Szold (1829-1902) received his advanced Jewish training at the Breslau Juedisch-Theologisches Seminar, where, under the influence of Zacharias Frankel (1801-1875), Heinrich Graetz (1817-1891), and Jacob Bernays (1824-1881), he prepared for his calling as rabbi and teacher in Israel. In 1859, Szold settled in Baltimore, serving Congregation Oheb Shalom for forty-seven years with distinction, integrity and affection.

Marcus Jastrow (1829-1903) was dedicated to the rabbinical service in his early youth. He received an excellent training in Rabbinics. Under the influence of Professor Graetz, Jastrow assumed a post in Warsaw, where his modernism and liberalism combined with his traditional bearing, reflected much credit on the young rabbi. In 1866 he accepted the call of Congregation Rodeph Shalom in Philadelphia. Jastrow's arrival in the United States was marked with pomp and circumstance. The rabbis of the city readily deferred to his learning and scholarship, and turned to him in all matters of interpretation of Jewish law. Jastrow soon discovered a kindred soul in Szold, with whom he shared a common platform of thought and action. Szold and Jastrow attempted to clarify their position which, despite their reforming practice and their interest in Wise's work, kept them well within the ranks of Historical Judaism when the final test came.

"Judaism," Szold wrote to Wise in German, "has two fundamental principles; one is mobile, the other is static. Only through the fusion of both elements will we discover the golden mean."[26] The purpose of Reform is to vitalize the precepts, not to force their abrogation. Development does not come in spurts through radical change in the elimination of ancient usage, but rather in adapting the *Mitzvot* to the spirit of the times.

As early as 1864, Szold prepared the original edition of the *Abodat Israel* in Hebrew with German translation for use in his congregation. The following year he found it necessary to issue a Hebrew and English edition. In 1871 a second edition of the Hebrew and German prayer book appeared, revised by Marcus Jastrow and Henry Hochheimer (1818-1912). The latter was a left wing colleague of Szold and Jastrow in the Historical school, an authority on classical German literature, and rabbi of the Nidche Israel Congregation in Baltimore. The prayer book became exceedingly popular in many of the German congregations. In 1873

Jastrow published his Hebrew and English edition of the *Abodat Israel*, which subsequently gained popularity as the *Minhag Jastrow.*

Despite many theological disagreements, all the rabbis, Reform or Conservative or Orthodox, felt strongly that Judaism represented more than worship and ritual practice. In the nineteenth century it was the recognized duty of the rabbi to function as a *religious* leader in every area of Jewish service, despite the specialized nonreligious auspices under which he served. In this manner the rabbis endowed with religious spirit and instruction all communal agencies in which they served. The foundation stones of Jewish institutional life—education, social service, defense of Jewish rights, overseas relief, Palestine aid, and democratic action—were hewn from the quarry of religious inspiration and leadership.

In the field of education, the Jews had a special stake in the victory of the free public school system in American education, for the private schools were pervaded by Christian belief and practice. Even the most punctilious religious care of the Jewish child at home could not weather the emotional associations and habits imbibed in a strong Christian religious culture and environment. Until the complete acceptance of the public school, there was but one corrective to the existing Christian private schools—Jewish private schools. An example of the type of school established in this period was the boarding school opened by Max Lilienthal in 1849. He had the undivided support of all Jewish religious groups. The full curriculum, as announced in the *Occident,* included both religious and secular studies.[27]

The advocates of public education, led by Henry Barnard (1811-1900) and Horace Mann (1796-1859), triumphed. State after state adopted formal laws. In the wake of this important change in the texture of American life, for which they, too, had labored, Jewish religious leaders were compelled to build a new structure of Jewish education. All day schools were on the wane. As a result, the supplementary Jewish school system for Sunday and weekday afternoons was created.

The Sunday school rapidly became part of the American Jewish way of life. However, as time went by, the hollowness of a curriculum based on a one-hour instruction period per week became shockingly apparent. Rote recitation of catechisms was not Jewish education. And what of Bible, Hebrew, and prayers? That which ostensibly seemed so excellent a contribution to Jewish life (was it not created in the image of the Protestant Sunday-school system and as such integral to the American pattern?), became a sham and delusion which undermined any possible effort for intensive Jewish living. A flickering effort was made by the leaders of the Historical School in the direction of building a congregational supplementary school system. In word, Leeser, Szold, and Jastrow stressed the inadequacy of Sunday-school education. However, their action was not equal to their promises and the results were unrewarding.

However, in the realm of higher Jewish education their approach was more vigorous. Although the obstacles were overwhelming, the initiators brooked no compromise, accepted their several defeats with equanimity, and ultimately emerged victorious. In a series of leading articles entitled "Education for the Ministry," published in the *Occident* in 1847, Isaac Leeser projected a plan for the training of a native ministry and teachers' corps in a higher school of general and Jewish education. The Hebrew Education Society of Philadelphia responded to his appeal, applied for a charter, and received permission to create such an institution in the state of Pennsylvania. Isaac Mayer Wise echoed Leeser's call with a proposal to establish the Zion Collegiate Institute. After announcing his plan in 1854 in the *Asmonean*, a New York Anglo-Jewish weekly, Wise launched a series of supporting societies in several cities on behalf of his new venture. For a variety of reasons, chiefly indifference and petty jealousies, Wise's project was rejected after a brief and dismal start.

The next to raise the theme of higher Jewish education was a group of young men in Baltimore. Banded together in an association of Hebrew literary societies, they called for the establishment of a National Hebrew College. In 1866, Benjamin Franklin Peixotto (1834-1890), grand master of the B'nai B'rith, proposed the establishment of an American Jewish university. He planned to finance the school through a per capita volunteer tax of ten dollars from the general membership. The heavy response of silence crushed his high hopes.

A final drive was made to overcome indifference. In 1864, toward the end of his days, Isaac Leeser rallied the forces of Historical Judaism and established the Maimonides College in Philadelphia—on the strength of the original charter granted to the Hebrew Education Society authorizing the granting of degrees "in divinity and other subjects." The Board of Delegates of American Israelites agreed to support the new institution. Marcus Jastrow and Sabato Morais, among the rabbis, and Mayer Sulzberger (1843-1923) and Moses A. Dropsie (1821-1905), representing the laity, supported Leeser's noble attempt. A curriculum including all the subjects necessary to a college of Jewish studies was published. The opening of classes was announced for October, 1867.

The college constantly faced a struggle to exist. Until his dying day, Leeser held the reins. He was replaced by Marcus Jastrow. Matters went from bad to worse. The Board of Delegates slowly withdrew support. In 1873, after a valiant struggle, the doors of Maimonides College were closed. Four students had been graduated, the first four men in America to receive specialized training for Jewish service.

The cause of Jewish education was advanced further by the establishment of the first Jewish publication society. The agency through which

Leeser hoped to solve the problem of an acute shortage of literary material, was born quite by accident. Two friends of Leeser turned to him for a rare book. They were prepared to spend a goodly sum to acquire the volume. Leeser nonchalantly suggested that they reprint the edition. They agreed. Thus in 1845 a new organization came into being.[28] Leeser issued a prospectus which included a plan for publications, memberships, and distribution. Gathering its funds, penny by penny, the American Jewish Publication Society managed to maintain itself for five years until a fire broke out in the buildings where the plates and stocks of books were stored. The flames consumed the books and the society. A score of years were to pass before Isaac M. Wise gathered the courage to propose the re-establishment of this vital organization. The second American Jewish Publication Society was incorporated in 1872, but it, too, had a short life, ceasing publication in 1875.

As the Jewish population grew in numbers, specialized social agencies were required to meet the problems of the sick, the infirm and the aged. The first philanthropic institution, the orphan house in Charleston, had been established in 1801. Here and there, as the need arose, additional homes were built. The German inflow accelerated the process and provided, as in the case of education, a compelling challenge to social initiative. In this program of social work, the role of the religious institutions and personnel was paradoxical. While the human and material resources for the development of Jewish social agencies came in greatest measure from the synagogue, corporate control was vested in a nonsynagogal body which ultimately divested itself of the compelling influence of the synagogue. This was a departure of great consequence.

Jewish hospitals were a primary concern. In many cases the dying were furtively baptized by hyperzealous nuns in order "to save them from the hands of Satan and to assure them a place in Paradise." Missionizing Christianity was the reason given for the establishment of the first Jewish hospitals in Cincinnati, Philadelphia and Baltimore, respectively.

As regards the organization of charity service, the rabbis quickly realized that direct personal gifts compromised both donor and recipient. Isaac Leeser called attention to flagrant iniquities and urged the formation of a central agency which could regulate and report income and disbursements to the entire community and which would be subject to community surveillance and counsel. Out of this idea the United Hebrew Charities of Philadelphia was formed in 1869.

Aid to European Jews was restricted in these years to those who sought the haven of American shores. The Jewish communities on the mother continent were self-sufficient. From time to time reports were received from distant places—from China, India and North Africa—concerning the activities of Christian missionaries among the impoverished Jewish

communities. Very little, however, was done by the organized American
Jewish community to act on these reports.

Support of Eretz Yisrael was always forthcoming. In 1832 a Hebrah
Terumat ha-Kodesh (Society for Offerings of the Sanctuary) was formed
under the chairmanship of Israel Baer Kursheedt (1766-1852) with the
specific purpose of collecting annual membership contributions for Palestine Jewry. The revolutions of 1848-1849, which unbalanced community
life in Europe and consequently forced European Jews to curtail their
support to Eretz Yisrael, compelled the Jews in Palestine to cast about
for alternative sources of income. They turned to American Jewry. A
thorough housecleaning was necessary in the affairs of Eretz Yisrael philanthropic effort. Samuel Myer Isaacs assumed the task. In 1853 the North
American Relief Society for the indigent Jews in Jerusalem, Palestine,
was organized with Isaacs as treasurer. To this association, Judah Touro
(1775-1854) left a bequest of $10,000 with an annual income of $700.
The pages of Isaacs' *Jewish Messenger* are replete with information about
the cause and continued appeals for community support. While he did
not wish to withhold aid when needed, Isaacs protested against useless
and demoralizing charities. He called for a working community in Palestine. Leeser went further. He spoke of the possibilities of an agricultural
economy. In 1853 Leeser upheld the hands of Moses Sachs of Palestine to
found such a settlement in Jaffa and accepted the chairmanship of the
American committee. In addition, Isaacs appeared before the Board of
Delegates and prevailed upon them to grant an extensive subsidy to the
new agricultural school established in Jaffa by the Alliance Israélite
Universelle.[29]

In the mid-nineteenth century, the central issue of group discrimination
was not based on racial or national differences but on specious religious
argument. To speak of nineteenth century America as a secular country is
a myth. Church and state were perhaps constitutionally divided, but the
Christian spirit penetrated deep into the character of the American people
and into every phase of American social life. One of the sharply debated
questions that reflected itself in the public mind and deed was: Is the
United States a Christian country? The Jews had to face the question and
its implications. The influences of this continued belief that America was
a Christian nation were exceedingly subtle. This was particularly important
in so far as both the general and the Jewish educational systems were
affected. The question of Bible teaching in the public school (in its Christian translation and commentary) has recurred again and again in American
educational theory, but at no time before had the problem been so acute
as in the period under discussion.

A second area in which the Jews had to overcome discrimination was
that of Sunday law legislation. Every piece of discriminatory legislation

had to be pulled up root and branch. Slowly, but steadily, the legislatures of New York, Maine, New Hampshire and Vermont granted to Jews who "keep the seventh day as the holy day" the right to engage in business on the "Christian Sabbath." The change in law as regards Jewish rights was but one aspect of the general trend toward greater religious freedom and understanding among the various faiths. It became increasingly apparent that restrictive religious laws had no place in the democratic tradition.

Other illustrations of the overbearing influence of the dominant faiths on American life were the official public statements, particularly the Thanksgiving proclamations. It had become good American political practice for the governors and President of the United States to issue annual declarations announcing the Thanksgiving festival. These proclamations most of them unwittingly, yet others with deliberate denominational conviction, were couched in Christian religious phraseology. On one occasion, in 1849, when Hamilton Fish, the governor of New York State, confused his private Christian belief with his public office, ten Jewish congregations in New York called off the specially announced Thanksgiving service in protest.

If the Jews were successful in combatting discrimination in the United States, it was primarily due to the fundamental democratic precepts of the country. In Europe, and in North Africa, the tradition of universal freedom did not prevail. Prejudice and bigotry reared their heads in a series of three international incidents: the Damascus, Swiss, and Mortara affairs. The Damascus blood libel (1840) brought American Jewry to its feet; it was the beginning of the organizational awakening of American Israel. The Swiss regulations (1855) were even more humiliating, for in a proposed commercial treaty the attempt was made to draw the line between American citizens of the Christian faith and those of Jewish origin. The third incident that inflamed American Jewry was the kidnaping of the Mortara child in 1858, and his enforced conversion to Catholicism.[29a]

The troubles of the hour produced a formula of hope. The Board of Delegates of American Israelites was brought into being by the spontaneous combustion of the Mortara incident, although in a profound sense, the board was the capstone of congregational, lay, and rabbinic efforts over the hardworking decades. It was the first attempt to organize American Israel on a congregational basis for the total interests of American Jewry. Apart from the later attempt by Isaac M. Wise through the formation of the Union of American Hebrew Congregations, religiously oriented Jewry was never again in the position to assemble a supervisory body of such proportions and design for the affairs of American and world Israel. The Board of Delegates had no intention of creating a hierarchy or of interfering in the affairs of local congregations. Its areas of action were sevenfold: education, statistics, Jewish law court, strengthening of charity organizations, information exchange, relations with international Jewry, and defense of Jewish rights. This was an ambitious program; and though little was achieved toward its realization, some lasting contributions were made.

One of the important acts of the Board was the influence it exerted to establish a Jewish chaplaincy in the armed forces of the United States. The Acts of Congress approved July 21 and August 3, 1861, calling for the chaplaincy in the Union Army, read: "The chaplain appointed by the vote of the field officers and company commanders, must be a regular ordained minister of some Christian denomination." As a result of continued effort on the part of the Board, the section II regulation was amended to read:

. . . That no person shall be appointed a chaplain in the United States army who is not a regularly ordained minister of some religious denomination, and who does not present testimonials of his present good standing as such minister, with a recommendation for his appointment as an army chaplain from some authorized ecclesiastical body, or not less than five accredited ministers belonging to said religious denomination.[30]

The precedent for the Jewish Chaplaincy was firmly established.

The picture of American Jewish religious thought and action in the formative period would be incomplete without understanding the contemporary Jewish religious view of American society and destiny. To these immigrants, America was not a haven, but a hope; not a refuge, but a dream. Even the traditionalists, who did not equate America with Zion, and Washington with Jerusalem (as did Wise, Einhorn, and the Reform leaders), felt that America was the land where justice and righteousness would emerge triumphant. The profound identification with the American spirit was reflected in the concentrated, almost wearying efforts, emotionally and linguistically, on Americanization. For the Jews, the transfer was more than a change in geography. The entire Western European experience was to be exchanged for the spiritual climate of the Anglo-Saxon world, and the religious tradition of the Orient was to be merged with Occidental values.

4

DIVISION IN AMERICAN JUDAISM, 1869-1886

The year 1869 was the beginning of the great divide in American Jewish religious history. Philadelphia was the scene of the first independent Reform conference. During the two preceding years, the pages of the *Israelite* regularly carried Wise's refrain for a meeting. Eighteen congregations had responded to the call, when David Einhorn and

Samuel Hirsch stole a march upon Wise and called a conference in Philadelphia. Wise participated; Hirsch was host and chairman of the sessions; but the spirit of Einhorn permeated the resolutions. Wise's star dimmed at this conference. His *magnum opus*, the *Minhag America*, was not accepted as the American prayer book. The personal opposition to him was formidable. Ignoring the expressed agreement to convene the following assembly in Philadelphia, Wise called the convention to Cleveland in 1870, with the avowed purpose of considering suggestions for, and modifications of, his prayer book. Thirteen rabbis constituted the western wing of the Reform camp. Their final resolutions differed from that of the eastern segment only in the names of the signers. Being unified in counsel, the western rabbis were better prepared to meet their eastern colleagues. They returned for further deliberations. Einhorn avoided the contest of strength. Wise, anxious to seal the final decision in his favor, called a third conference in Cincinnati in 1871. Twenty-seven delegates appeared, the majority of them representing western congregations. The agenda included discussions on education, publications, and itinerant preachers. The most important decision was the confirmation of Wise's proposals to found the Union of American Hebrew Congregations and the Hebrew Union College. In 1873, this Union was organized by Wise with an initial membership of twenty-eight congregations located in the Midwest and South. The first president was Moritz Loth. Its purposes were to establish a seminary, to stimulate popular Jewish education, to organize new congregations, and to provide such other institutions as Judaism would require.

Despite the inevitable clash of personalities, the paltry differences in emphasis, and the underdeveloped organizational structure, Reform Judaism was the foremost movement on the American Jewish horizon. In contrast, the forces of Historical Judaism were anemic. Leeser's sharp and clear voice was silenced forever. Szold, Jastrow, and Hochheimer were straddling, so to speak. The numbers dwindled. Sabato Morais (1823-1897) and Samuel M. Isaacs held the fort alone.

Had this weakness of the Historical school continued but a few years more, the very nature of American Judaism would probably have been formed, unalterably, in the mold of Reform. A series of external and internal factors prevented this from happening: the return of Szold and Jastrow to the group now rallying about Morais and Isaacs, the enlistment of younger men in the ranks, the steady trickle of Eastern European immigration, and the establishment of the *American Hebrew*.

Szold, Jastrow, and Hochheimer found increasing reason to be disappointed with the extremism of many Reformers. The irresponsible slurs upon basic Jewish precepts, such as those on the Sabbath and *kashrut*, violated their beliefs. They proclaimed publicly their disavowal.

The newer spirits who served to refresh the Historical school were

Frederick de Sola Mendes (1850-1927), who served first as assistant and later as successor to S. M. Isaacs in the Congregation Shaaray Tefila of New York; Aaron Wise (1844-1896), who was called originally to Congregation Beth Elohim in Brooklyn and then, after two years, succeeded to the post of rabbi at Congregation Rodeph Shalom in New York; Henry Pereira Mendes (1852-1937), younger brother of Frederick de Sola Mendes, who was invited to the pulpit of Congregation Shearith Israel and remained its *hazzan* until his retirement in 1927. These men not only contributed their own powers, but also brought the added strength of their important congregations.

The Russian-Polish immigration that began to be significant in the seventies gave increased strength to the Historical school. In time, these immigrants formed a separate Orthodox movement. At first, however, they served as opponents of the reformists and provided a wider base for the Historical school. An Orthodox congregation had been established in Buffalo as early as 1848. The first synagogue of Russo-Polish extraction formed in New York in 1852, was the Beth Hamidrash; in Boston, the first Russo-Polish synagogue was Beth Abraham, established in 1873. The largest settlements were in New York. It is estimated that as early as 1872 there existed twenty-nine synagogues of the Orthodox Eastern European *minhag* in New York City. However, fair sized representations were soon to be found in Philadelphia, Boston, and Baltimore, on the east coast; in Chicago, and in dozens of other cities as far west as California. In 1874 an Orthodox weekly, *Die Yiddishe Gazette*, began to appear, and in 1885 its founder, Kasriel H. Sarasohn (1835-1905), commenced the publication of the first Yiddish daily in New York, the *Yiddishes Tageblatt*.

The establishment of the *American Hebrew* in 1879 as a weekly was a fourth factor in the revival of the Historical school. The initiator and leading spirit behind the magazine was Frederick de Sola Mendes, who had formerly been the editor of the short lived *Independent Hebrew*. Although the news was impartially presented, the editorial policy was clearly that of Historical Judaism. This was reflected not only in the leading articles and editorial statements but even in the advertisements; the sponsors of *trefa* food or restaurants were not permitted advertising space.

In aggregate, these compelling factors reduced the fears of extinction from the Historical school and induced that group to co-operate as equal partners with the reformists in all community efforts. During the period 1840-1870 co-operation between the two contending religious factions had been based on the hope of each that the other would be *ideologically* absorbed in an eventual all American-Jewish organization. On the other hand, co-operation in the years 1870-1886 was based on the recognition that opposition was permanent. At the same time, each group hoped that the other would be organizationally absorbed in some future congregational union.

The communal structure of American Israel was undergoing rapid change. The census of 1870 reported a count of 189 Jewish religious organizations, 152 edifices, and 73,265 sittings, an increase from 77 synagogues with a total seating capacity of 34,412 as calculated in the 1860 census. For an understanding of the extent of Jewish settlement, it is important to note that, in the 1870 tally, the states of Arkansas, Colorado, Iowa, Kansas, Maine, Michigan, North Carolina, Tennessee, Texas and West Virginia reported congregations for the first time. Religious statistics under governmental auspices were gathered in 1880. Unfortunately, they were never published. However, a census was made of the Jews under the jurisdiction of the Union of American Hebrew Congregations and the Board of Delegates of American Israelites during the years 1875-1878. The totals indicated increases to 270 congregations and 50,000 communicants.[31]

Co-operation was manifest in every phase of communal endeavor, while the field of education preoccupied the religious leadership. The communal Sunday school gave way to the congregational Sunday school. Each synagogue developed its own unit. The midweek supplementary school system continued its slow growth. The strongest support for the "Hebrew Free School" movement which started in 1872 in New York came from the traditionalists. The reformists looked askance at this type of Jewish education. All hands, however, joined in the establishment of several Jewish vocational schools for orphans and immigrant children. The serious lack of proper Jewish school texts continued to plague the authorities. In order to meet the requirement for printed matter, teachers would use Christian textbooks replacing the name of the central figure in the Christian faith, with that of God. Even foremost scholars, recognizing this serious need for proper material, took time to prepare educational texts for children.

The greatest educational lack was qualified teachers. Strenuous efforts were made to establish the indispensable training school for teachers. Two projects were in progress simultaneously, in the East and in the West, both under Reform auspices. The trustees of Temple Emanu-El had provided ample funds for such a purpose. They elaborated their original plan of creating an "Emanu-El Theological Seminary Society," as it was known two decades earlier, and sought to establish an "American Hebrew College" in New York. Their brochure announced both secular and Jewish courses on a college level. Rabbis Samuel Adler and David Einhorn supported this plan. The school was actually launched, increased funds were made available, and a preparatory department begun. Unfortunately, the energies soon gave out and the venture lapsed. In lieu of the total program, a portion of the funds was allocated to send gifted students abroad. Two of these young men were Felix Adler (1851-1933) and Bernard Drachman (1861-1945), neither of whom returned to the fold of Reform Judaism.

The first permanent rabbinic institution was the Hebrew Union College established by Isaac M. Wise in Cincinnati in 1875. He had almost given up all hope of seeing his dream come true. In 1873, dejected at his failure in Cincinnati, he agreed to accept the call of Congregation Anshe Chesed in New York. His Cincinnati congregants were appalled. They succeeded in retaining him, only after a promise that they would support his school. The institution, as conceived by the founders, was not to be narrow or limited in outlook; it was to serve the total needs of American Israel. From its very inception, the catholicity of Jewish interests was stressed. Indeed, in the first announcement of Moritz Loth (1832-1913), president of Wise's congregation, the traditionalists were conscientiously considered. The eastern congregations were not invited to the founding sessions. The Historical school was adequately represented. Marcus Jastrow participated in the deliberations; Lewis N. Dembitz (1833-1907), a leading lawyer and protagonist of Historical Judaism in the Middle West, was elected secretary of the sessions; Sabato Morais was a member of the committee of examiners.

October 3, 1875, was the historic day of opening. The rabbinic motto, "the study of Torah is equivalent to all other duties," was adopted by the institution. Work at the school began in earnest. In 1875 the library, apart from a few textbooks, contained but a set of the Talmud and Midrash Rabbah. One year later, Wise reported, the library contained 154 volumes. The house of books had to be built. A faculty had to be created. A student body had to be enlisted. And all this Wise accomplished with prodigious effort and perspicacity. In 1883 the first class was graduated. They were four: Israel Aaron (1859-1912), Henry Berkowitz (1857-1924), Joseph Krauskopf (1858-1923), and David Philipson.

The Board of Delegates played a progressively diminishing role. Marcus Jastrow, sensing that in the decline of the Board's power the Historical school would suffer further loss of influence, devoted himself for a time to its reorganization. Mayer Sulzberger (1843-1923) proposed a new constitution for the Board which was as ingenious as it was impractical. The attempt at an artificial revival of the organization was reminiscent of Herbert Spencer's warning that "a government agency originally formed to discharge a function is apt to reach a stage at which its self-sustention becomes the primary thing and the function to be performed by it, the secondary thing." Sulzberger soon realized the artificiality of his program, and became the chief proponent for the absorption of the Board into the Union of American Hebrew Congregations, particularly since the Reform group now controlled the policies of the Board as well. In 1876 two subcommittees representing the Board and Union, respectively, were appointed to consider possibilities. In 1879 the merger was consummated and the Board became a standing committee of the Union. A gala conference was called in which 118 congregations (of an estimated 200 invited) participated. The all American-Jewish congregational organization was in the hands of Reform leadership.

Along with all other American theologians, Jewish religious thinkers had to face the challenge of the new and revolutionary theories in science, philosophy and religion. Fundamental tenets of supernaturally revealed religion were shaken. The writings and speeches of Asa Gray (1810-1888) at Harvard and of John Fiske's (1842-1901) *Outlines of Cosmic Philosophy*, were but the frontal assault in America on the certainties of the age. The universities became the centers of the new thought. One of the foremost thinkers of the period, William T. Harris (1835-1909), who founded the *Journal of Speculative Philosophy* in 1867 in St. Louis, encouraged a younger group of American scholars including Josiah Royce (1855-1916), Charles S. Peirce (1839-1914), and William James (1842-1910). Everyone was intent on finding the solution to the riddle of the universe; philosopher, scientist and religionist in turn each insisted that his was the only solution.

Skepticism had its effect on Jewish institutional life, too. In 1873, Felix Adler (son of Rabbi Samuel Adler) who had originally been trained for the rabbinate, returned from his studies at Heidelberg, found his philosophic ideal in conflict with the Jewish faith, and established in 1876 the Society for Ethical Culture. In this movement moral and ethical purposes were considered independent of all religious orientation or ritualistic practice. Adler did not conceive his group to be a talking society. He proposed the creation of institutions, particularly of an educational character. The movement spread throughout the United States and even abroad.

The inner need to defend the faith and the sincere desire to discuss that which united them, brought the rabbinic leaders together in newly formed ministers' associations. It was Dr. Gustav Gottheil (1827-1903) who inspired the formation of the first New York Local Board of Jewish Ministers, or as it was good humoredly titled, "The Big Six"—Gottheil, Kohler, Adolph Huebsch (1830-1884), Henry S. Jacobs (1827-1893), and the two Mendes brothers. Soon the New York group was expanded to include the Jewish ministers of the Atlantic seaboard. Semiannual conferences were held. Of these Gottheil said, paraphrasing the familiar verse in Psalms: "Behold how goodly and how pleasant it is if we can get the brethren merely to sit together."

Despite such meetings, the real lines of division between the Reform and Historical schools remained. They were drawn largely in the areas of Jewish practice. The groups were inexorably divided on questions of

synagogue ritual, Eretz Yisrael, Sunday or Historical Sabbath, Hebrew
and *kashrut*. However, in certain areas of ritual practice, the Historical
school incorporated various moderate reforms. The Western European
concept of synagogue decorum became normative in all their congregations. Special instructions were issued on the method of folding the *tallit*
after services, uninhibited frivolity on Simhat Torah was condemned,
many prayers were read rather than chanted, the *piyuttim* were deleted,
the names of those called up to the Torah were not announced by the
baal kore, and sections of the service were read in English. The left-wing
congregations of the Historical school went further. They introduced
mixed pews and the organ. The *American Hebrew* was neutral on the
organ question, for within the Historical school opinion was divided. There
was no equivocation as to the mixed choir. The Reform group was chastised. It was an effrontery to the spirit of worship, the *American Hebrew*
wrote, to select Christians as leaders of the service.

As a result of the Russian pogroms, the ancient hope for Zion took on
fresh meaning. The Historical school's ardent devotion to Eretz Yisrael in
contradistinction to Reform's negativism was a second factor of division
between two groups. The Reform position was on record in the Philadelphia conference of 1869.[32] With minor exceptions, the entire Reform
rabbinate and laity continued to maintain this position.

The third issue between Reform and the Historical school arose over the
Sabbath. The issue was not a result of the conflict of tradition with
scientific thought; it was the result of other circumstances, essentially
practical and not speculative. The majority of Jews, particularly the
younger generation, were above all preoccupied with the pressure for a
livelihood; and it was not an easy matter to find employment and at the
same time refrain from work on Saturday, the traditional Sabbath day.
No wonder then that Synagogues on the Sabbath were soon empty and
that observances continued to decline. It may be said that the traditionalists
took the view that while the Sabbath was made for man, Israel was made
for the Sabbath—in other words, that the Jewish Sabbath could not be
shifted to another day. The reformists on the other hand were prepared
to make some accommodations.

One fact is highlighted in the speeches, articles, and papers on the Sabbath question. The reformists were not, as they are so often accused of
being, committed to the elimination of the historical Sabbath. The responsible leadership was appalled at the radical twist that fate and time forced
upon their ideas. Their error was grievous only in their unrealistic compromise, not in the sincerity of their motives. The Historical school was
prepared to suffer temporary failure and unpopularity, but refused to
yield on fundamental tenets.

Said the Reform leaders: men need a living religion and to get this they need "a living day of worship." Einhorn's unsuccessful attempt in 1854 to establish a Sunday service was recalled. The leaders of the movement for the Sunday service were Kaufmann Kohler, then of Sinai Congregation in Chicago, and Samuel Hirsch of Philadelphia. Isaac M. Wise was unalterably opposed to any compromise with the biblical Sabbath. Under the impress of Kohler's inaugural Sunday sermon, *Das neue Wissen und der alte Glaube* (The New Knowledge and the Old Faith), delivered January 18, 1874, the Sinai Congregation made the radical departure from Jewish tradition which, it is true, had been advocated by such Reform leaders abroad as Holdheim, Formstrecher, Philippson, and Geiger for some forty years, but was first translated into practice in America.

Samuel Hirsch represented the extreme view. He proposed that Sunday, the civil day of rest, should be Judaized as a real Sabbath day. Kohler's approach was of another character. In a sermon entitled "Sabbath Observance and Sunday Lectures" delivered December 27, 1879, he set forth his views:

> I sincerely and heartily support all efforts in behalf of restoring our Sabbath to its pristine glory, and wish I could prevail on all the members of my congregation to join the Sabbath Observance Association just now started. But I think the only successful beginning can alone be made at home. *The Jewish household must have the Sabbath revived in all its attractive lustre and sweetness. The Friday evening family reunions with all their melodious strains of song and joy must be restored as means of cultivating piety and devotion....*
> ... And if, thus, the Friday evening will sound the silver trumpet of liberty and joy to herald the day of God, while Jewish Sunday lessons will work like scouts and skirmishers in disarming and routing rampant atheism all along the line, the walls of Jericho will fall, the victory will be ours.

It was during these years that the practice of convening the congregation for late services on Friday was instituted in many Reform congregations. Congregation Adath Jeshurun in Philadelphia, which was slowly moving into the Reform camp, instituted late Friday evening services in 1883, thus becoming the first congregation in Philadelphia to hold such services. Of the two attempts, the Friday and Sunday services, the latter won immediate popularity. Yet gradually the former, by virtue of its relation in time and spirit to the Sabbath day, has pre-empted the position of the Sunday Sabbath even in Reform congregations.

This very truth the Historical school felt instinctively. It was to be expected that the right wing of the Historical school would be outraged by this new phase of Reform. It was unanticipated, however, that a left-winger such as Szold would come to the forefront and assume command of the counter-Reform battle on this very issue. In a passionate address,

Der Sabbat, he ruled that all who violated the Sabbath profaned the entire Torah.

The attitude toward the Hebrew language in America (as in every country in every generation) was a further token of devotion to traditional values. Einhorn's *siddur*, the *Olat Tamid*, ignored the Hebrew text almost entirely; the text indeed, symbolically enough, was laid out to be read from left to right.

But the breaking point in Reform-Traditionalist relations came over *kashrut*. For the Reformists *kashrut* was a primitive barbarism and its upholders "kitchen Jews." Isaac M. Wise heaped derision upon the heads of those who would maintain the laws and practices of *kashrut*.

Jastrow challenged Wise's authority. He precipitated a series of resignations from the Union by influencing his congregation, Rodeph Shalom of Philadelphia, to withdraw from the Union. De Sola Mendes's congregation Shaaray Tefila, resigned from the Union. Szold, although he petitioned his Baltimore Synagogue to take similar action, was not successful in his endeavor.

The year 1885 may be taken as the date when the hope to unite American Israel was definitely abandoned and separate groups—Reform, Conservative, and Orthodox—came into being. Three events tell the tale. In the spring, the Historical group hailed Alexander Kohut as its leader; in the fall, Kaufmann Kohler convened the Pittsburgh conference; and in the winter, Sabato Morais became president of the Jewish Theological Seminary Association.

Alexander Kohut (1842-1894), surnamed "the Mighty Hammer," combined in himself a passion for scholarship and community action. His record of achievement in Hungary included important scholarly works, exciting rabbinical experience, and participation in liberal movements. No sooner had he arrived in New York as successor to Dr. Huebsch at Congregation Ahavath Chesed, than he declared his full alliance with the Historical school.

The Kohut-Kohler controversy, which soon broke out, became the "talk of the town." The phrases were chiseled, the ideas clear, the tones gentlemanly but none the less firm. And the antagonists were worthy of each other. Kohler presented his philosophy of Judaism in a series of six lectures which he called "Backwards or Forward." He regarded Mosaic-Rabbinical Judaism as retrospective and backwards; Reform Judaism as prospective and forward looking. He contested Kohut's belief in revelation as well as his emphasis on the observance of all the ceremonies of Judaism, and he vehemently opposed the restoration of the Jewish state with its sacrificial institutions. The Kohut-Kohler debate accelerated the final development of a specifically Reform group. After consultations with Isaac

M. Wise and Samuel Hirsch, Kohler issued a call for a conference to be held in Pittsburgh from November 16-18, 1885, "for the purpose of discussing the present state of American Judaism, its pending issues and its requirements, and of uniting upon such plans and practical measures as seem demanded by the hour."[33]

Nineteen rabbis met in Pittsburgh. Wise was elected chairman, but Kohler was the leading militant spirit behind the sessions. He had prepared the draft of a statement which, edited and modified, was to become the famous Pittsburgh Platform—the standard document of classic American Reform. In eight paragraphs, the current Reform theology—on the God-idea, Bible, Mosaic legislation, *kashrut* and priesthood, nationalism, Jewish mission, immortality, and social justice—was succinctly formulated.

Over every one of the statements there was violent debate. Kohler declared the platform to be the "declaration of Jewish independence." His critics rhetorically asked, "Independence from what?" and answered, "Independence from Judaism." Ismar Elbogen (1874-1943) in his analysis of the Pittsburgh statement, described it as "a peculiar document which can only be understood on the basis of contemporary intellectual currents. Nothing was said of faith or piety; the advantages of Judaism over other religions were mentioned, but not clarified. It was not a *Confessio Judaica* but a homage to the latest European school of thought in science, in the history of religion and particularly of the religious evolution of Israel. The laymen did not get much out of this platform; they did not learn what to believe and what to do, but only what not to believe and not to do."[34]

Not only the later historian, but even devoted contemporary reformists, did not consider the declaration binding. Dr. Gottheil castigated the platform. The program as such was never endorsed by the Central Conference of American Rabbis organized four years later; Isaac M. Wise, in defense of his college and its curriculum, forthrightly stated that the platform, the Union, and the College were not of one mind. In a straightforward disavowal he wrote in the *American Israelite* of December 4, 1885:

But who can tell what that Pittsburgh Conference had to do with the Union of American Hebrew Congregations? . . . The Union consists of congregations and their elected representatives, and the Conference consisted of Rabbis who went there voluntarily and without the advice or appointment of their respective congregations. That Union, according to its Constitution, is entirely secular, takes no cognizance whatever of theological questions, and the Conference discussed theological questions exclusively. That Union consists of a hundred and odd congregations, while in Pittsburgh only eighteen Rabbis were present, not all of whom are at the head of congregations belonging to that Union.

Two weeks later he wrote in the same publication:

The enactments, resolutions or proceedings of the Pittsburgh Rabbinical Conference, or of any other Conference, except the Council of the Union of American Hebrew Congregations, have nothing in the world to do with the course of studies or the methods of teaching adopted in the Hebrew Union College. The Hebrew Union College . . . remains the honest seat of Jewish learning—and no drilling institution for opinionated candidates—to educate competent scholars of free and unbiased minds . . . men who can draw their information from the original Jewish sources and think for themselves.

Nevertheless, the alarm had been sounded. Sabato Morais turned to his associates in the Historical school—left, center, and right—and urged that the reply to the Pittsburgh platform be delivered in action, not words. What had been in his mind since the closing of Maimonides College, and had been postponed because of the united attitude toward the Hebrew Union College, now emerged in specific form. Morais wrote to Congregation Shearith Israel in New York calling upon its board to take the lead in the establishment of a new seminary actively counter-Reform and dedicated to the "knowledge and practice of historical Judaism."

Morais was a pillar of strength and determination. He urged, cajoled, disturbed, encouraged, and inspired his coworkers in the building of the Seminary. He referred to the Seminary as "my Benjamin—the son of my old age." Alexander Kohut and State Senator Joseph Blumenthal (1834-1901) upheld his hands. It was Kohut who influenced his friend to name the new institution The Jewish Theological Seminary rather than the Orthodox Seminary as Morais proposed. Kohut's intuition was correct, for in the name, as in the development of the institution, Kohut sought to establish the tradition of historic Judaism, rejecting denominationalism and partisanship and embracing *Kelal Yisrael*. Historical Judaism, he maintained, is not a movement or a party—it is Judaism. This thought was knit into the fabric of the constitution and by-laws of the Jewish Theological Seminary Association, which states in article II:

The purpose of this Association being the preservation in America of the knowledge and practice of historical Judaism as ordained in the Law of Moses (*Torat Moshe*) and expounded by the prophets (*Nebiim*) and sages (*Hakamim*) of Israel in Biblical and Talmudical writings, it proposes in furtherance of its general aim the following specific objects:
1. The establishment and maintenance of a Jewish Theological Seminary for the training of Rabbis and teachers.
2. The attainment of such cognate purposes as may upon occasion be deemed appropriate.

The dedication exercises were held in Lyric Hall, January 2, 1887, after a year of preparation and planning. That very week an advertisement appeared in the newspapers with the single-line announcement that preparatory classes were being conducted at the Congregation Shearith Israel. Eight students were registered in the first class, one of whom, Joseph H. Hertz (1872-1946), rose to international prominence as chief rabbi of the British Empire.

With the dedication speeches over, the struggle for survival began in earnest. The faculty was selected, the student body was increased, and classes were moved to larger quarters in Cooper Union. Historical Judaism had permanently launched its first independent institution in America.

5
THREE JEWISH RELIGIOUS GROUPS:
REFORM, CONSERVATIVE, ORTHODOX, 1886-1902

The years until the turn of the century were devoted by both Reform and Historical Judaism to clarification, intensification, and expansion of their respective emphases and institutions. Each group sought to erect its citadel on three pillars: a rabbinical school, a union of congregations, and a conference of rabbis. First to achieve this triad was the Reform movement.

The organization of the Central Conference of American Rabbis in Detroit on July 9, 1889, celebrated Isaac M. Wise's seventieth birthday year. The purpose of the new organization was to maintain and perpetuate a union of all American rabbis, to publish a yearbook of proceedings, and to establish a fund for the support of superannuated ministers. Perhaps the most important declaration made at the conference, which linked the new organization to the Reform movement in Europe, was "That the proceedings of all the modern Rabbinical Conferences from that held in Braunschweig in 1844, and including all like assemblages held since, shall be taken as a basis for the work of this Conference." The Conference instantly became the legislative body of Reform Judaism, for it was resolved that at its annual meetings decisions would be taken in "all matters appertaining to Judaism, its literature and its welfare."[35] Nineteen members were present in Pittsburgh; one hundred joined the Conference. Isaac M. Wise served as president until his death.

The Historical school was faced with the additional task of creating a congregational base and an assembly of rabbis. The leaders attempted to solve their problem indirectly. Hoping to gain a large mass following by a coalition with the Orthodox, who showed vital signs of organization, a movement was encouraged, led by H. Pereira Mendes and Bernard Drachman of the Seminary and supported by Cyrus Adler (1863-1940) and Max Cohen (1853-1941). They wished to create a union of Orthodox congregations which would accept the Seminary as its own rabbinical school and the rabbis associated with it as coworkers in a traditional federation. An orthodox union would probably have been established in the normal course of events. The attempted alliance, however, was premature and had two major effects on Jewish religious history in America: the more rapid development of official Orthodoxy and the diversion of effort from Historical or Conservative, Judaism's immediate object of creating its own institutions.

Chaos and confusion prevailed in the internal life of American Orthodoxy. Small celled congregations came into existence suddenly and in almost as short a time split up. This seemed to go on endlessly. The chief attraction of the Orthodox synagogue was its cantor, and only in rare cases the spiritual leader; the Hebrew classes were conducted in dingy unsanitary stores and cellars; the sale of religious objects was abused; *kashrut* was mismanaged.

The first attempt at formal organization of the Orthodox congregations had taken place in 1879. Representatives of twenty-six congregations met to found a Board of Delegates of Orthodox Hebrew Congregations. They planned to invite a chief rabbi from abroad who would set their house in order. The attempt failed for want of a proper candidate. Nine years were to pass before further action was initiated. Chief Rabbi Jacob Joseph (1848-1902), distinguished scholar of Vilna, consented to come to America. The tragedy that befell him and the shame and disgrace that resulted to the community were a painful reflection of the scandalous state of affairs. The salary of the rabbi was to be gathered from the tax that was attached to kosher meat. Despite severe warnings by friends among the Reformists and Conservatives, not to finance the office of the rabbinate through kosher food income, the Orthodox association insisted on its plan. The direst predictions were unhappily realized; the association was dissolved and the idea of an Orthodox chief rabbinate shattered on the rocks of irresponsibility.

Other Orthodox ventures had more fortunate results. The aspiration to establish a higher institution of learning in keeping with the high traditions of the European *yeshibot*, became a reality. The development and progress of Yeshiva University is a wholesome chapter in American education. The Rabbi Isaac Elchanan Theological Seminary, known by its Hebrew name, *Yeshivat Rabbenu Yitzchak Elchanan*, was founded in 1896. The new Orthodox seminary was named in memory of Rabbi Isaac Elchanan Spektor (1817-1896), the Lithuanian scholar and saint, who had passed away in the months preceding the founding of the institution. Its patrons properly claimed the distinction for their school as being the first higher Yeshiva to be established on the continent of North America.

The purpose of the Yeshiva differed from that of the other two seminaries in that it did not consider the training of students for the rabbinical calling its primary task. *Torah Lishmah* was its object—the study of Torah for its own sake. In the miniature *Bet Ha-Midrash* at 156 Henry Street,

New York, was a group of young men who had already begun their Talmud studies in Europe. They were supported by a weekly stipend ranging from $2.50 to $4; the "supervisor," or one-man faculty, was Rabbi Benjamin Aronowitz (1864-1945); the course of study consisted exclusively of the Talmud and related rabbinic literature. Such were the Yeshiva's beginnings. Today it is a university, in addition to a school of rabbinic studies.

A call for an Orthodox Jewish Congregational Union was issued in Hebrew and in English. Of the thirteen signers to this document only two were of the official Orthodox camp; the other eleven were members of the Jewish Theological Seminary's faculty and board. The address was also that of the Seminary. One hundred delegates attended the founding convention on June 8, 1898. H. Pereira Mendes was elected president.

Steps were taken to implement the new program. At the second biennial convention, Mendes, as president, was in a position to render a favorable report. It was soon obvious, however, that Conservative Judaism's major purpose in helping to found the federation was to be vitiated. If any group was to capture the Orthodox Union, the West European faction would be the last. The clash was not in religious orientation; it was in spiritual backgrounds and cultural proclivities. A variety of obstacles, seemingly conquerable in individual relations, but impassable in the aggregate, separated the two groups: the differing attitudes toward form and behavior during the service; the latent "snobbism" of the *Westjuden*, the insular attitude of the Russian Jew toward the American environment; the deep love of the East European Jew for Yiddish, and the manifest disdain of Yiddish by the others. These deeper and virtually unexpressed disparities were symbolized in two words which the respective groups used for Jewish study: *Lernen* (learning) and *Juedische Wissenschaft* (the science of Judaism). The East Europeans scorned the baggage of Western civilization; the Western oriented Jews considered such knowledge their passport to civilization.

Antipathies, suspicions and basic differences came to the fore. The Jewish Theological Seminary was the target. At first, in deference to the respected H. Pereira Mendes, a resolution was passed in support of both the Conservative and the Orthodox Seminaries. At a later assembly, a resolution was passed with Mendes himself in the chair, to repudiate the authority of The Jewish Theological Seminary's graduates as rabbis in Israel. Inevitably, the Conservative group returned to its own needs and responsibilities. Yet, out of the unsuccessful effort at union a strong third party in American Judaism was born.

The immediate requirements of American Jewry in the religious and educational realms brought co-operation between the three parties on limited objectives. The nonexistence of a teaching profession was the result, not the cause, of the infantilism in Jewish educational efforts. Adolescents and other volunteers taught in the Sunday schools; few professional teachers were qualified either pedagogically or temperamentally to educate the American school child. A minority voice in Jewish institutional life had always proclaimed the high priority of teacher-training institutions. It may be recalled that the Hebrew Union College proposed to establish such a department. Kohut, in his early conversations with Morais, attempted to persuade him that the teachers' college should take precedence over other departments in the order of Conservative institutions.

In 1893, Congregation Mikveh Israel fell heir to a bequest from Hyman Gratz (1776-1857). The will stipulated that an institution be established "for the education of Jews residing in the city and country of Philadelphia." Subject to legal sanction, Gratz Mordecai (1849-1902), a grandnephew of Hyman Gratz, hoped to establish a Jewish university in America. He corresponded with the presidents of Columbia, Harvard, and Cornell. The exchange of letters to be found in the unpublished correspondence of Sabato Morais at Dropsie College is in itself an interesting commentary on the prevailing attitudes of American college presidents toward Jewish universities. In brief, Mordecai was counseled that the results would not be advantageous to the Jewish position. Sabato Morais, rabbi of the congregation, was violently opposed to the inquiry and the trend of thought it reflected. He wished to establish the long awaited teacher training school. In a series of communications to Doctor Solomon Solis-Cohen (1857-1948) he expressed these views candidly. Morais's position won out. Classes at Gratz College began in 1897. Rabbi Henry M. Speaker (1868-1935) was principal; Arthur A. Dembitz (1870-1940), instructor in history; and Isaac Husik (1876-1939), instructor in Hebrew and Bible. Moses A. Dropsie (1821-1905) served as chairman of the Board of Trustees. Gratz College was established as the first American Jewish teachers' college.

The settlement activities in Eretz Yisrael continued apace. Conservative and Orthodox circles supported every wholesome venture in the Holy Land; the reformists continued to echo Gustavus Poznanski's refrain, "America is our Zion, Washington our Jerusalem." Orthodoxy supplied the mass following to the "Lovers of Zion" and the "Seekers of Zion" movements; the Conservatives contributed active leaders such as Jastrow, Szold, H. Pereira Mendes, Solomon Solis-Cohen and Lewis N. Dembitz. In 1894, Szold was instrumental in founding in his home city of Baltimore the first Zionist group in America.

Then came the book that shook the Jewish world. Theodor Herzl's (1860-1904) *Der Judenstaat* (1896). *Hibbat Zion* became political Zionism. American Judaism was drawn into international Jewish affairs. And the reformists decided to attack. Emil G. Hirsch (1851-1923) made invidious comparisons between the ancient Temple sacrifices and the Chicago slaughterhouses. Kaufmann Kohler wrote that "The Zionists cry: 'Back to Judea!' shows a degeneracy, a demoralization, a Katzenjammer sentiment . . ."; Wise termed the dream of ages Ziomania. For half a century, the philosophy of Reform, as expressed in the creeds of Philadelphia and Pittsburgh, had devastating effect on the development of Zionism.

Not all reformists were in the anti-Zionist camp. Bernhard Felsenthal, Maximilian Heller (1860-1929), Gustav Gottheil, and the younger men, Stephen S. Wise and Richard Gottheil (1862-1936), helped establish the American Federation of Zionists. But, for the while, anti-Zionism remained the most prominent note in Reform circles.

The Conservatives, despite their wariness as to the impact of a purely political movement on Judaism, rallied about the Zionists' banner. They, too, had their surprising exceptions. Frederick de Sola Mendes stressed the impracticability of colonizing a country which included the holy places of three contending faiths. Sabato Morais expounded against the secularist antireligious Zionist spokesmen and leaders. Both men, however, supported every activity of a constructive nature in Eretz Yisrael. Most of the Conservatives saw in political Zionism a means to an end: not only the reclamation of the Jewish people, but, in the spirit of Herzl's classic formulation, the return of the Jews to Judaism.

The census of 1890 established for the first and only time the existence of two bodies within what the officials termed the "Jewish Church." They divided all their information into two sections: Orthodox and Reform. The more strictly religious problems that confronted American Israel in the years 1886-1902 were in a sense variations on a familiar theme. Debate continued on *kashrut* control, "mushroom" synagogues, the use of English in the service, Reform-Traditionalist relationships, religious activities among the immigrant groups, and the problem of the unaffiliated. And in smaller circles arguments flew pro and con over the Sunday service and prayer book proposals (in the Reform ranks) and on the synod question (among the Conservatives).

With the establishment of the creedal principle in Reform Judaism all barriers of ceremonial law had disappeared; the phrase "eternal truths" had sanctioned all excesses made in its name—even the transfer of the Sabbath to Sunday. Now for the first time such radicalism became less self-confident. The very holiday celebration which was called at the Chicago Sinai Congregation to commemorate the introduction of Sunday services twenty-five years earlier offered evidence of the serious misgivings of even such intrepid reformers as Hirsch and Kohler. At these exercises, Rabbi Moses J. Gries (1868-1918), reiterated the Sunday-Sabbath plea:

"This is the evil of two Sabbaths, blessed with two we are cursed with having none." Hirsch had other things to say to a congregation which ignored the Sunday service as they had formerly ignored the Sabbath service.

I can understand the difficulties which beset congregational participation in the services on the traditional Sabbath, and if I had the fortune of being the minister of a congregation with a Saturday service, never would my lips open to chide the members for their indifference manifested by their non-attendance ... but a congregation that has a Sunday service has no excuse for empty pews. Every empty pew is a monument to hypocrisy. It points to a pretense, and it calls as such for a rebuke. . . .

I plead for honesty to the cause. You have chosen Sunday; not I. You proclaimed it the day of our worship, not I. Therefore we must show by the deed that it is our day. Prove that you are in terrible earnest. There can be no excuse for absence from the self-appointed service hour. Charity meetings are no excuse. Other business is no excuse . . .

We must have a temple filled with our own members unless we wish to stand before the world as pretenders . . . Empty pews do not spread the message; neither do the wooden backs and all the beautifully upholstered seats.

It was Kaufmann Kohler, however, chief advocate of the Sunday service and the initiator of the idea in that very Sinai Congregation, who suggested that the attempt to shift the Jewish Sabbath day to Sunday was unwarranted.

During these years, the Reform movement succeeded in publishing a uniform prayer book for its constituency. This was the climax of Wise's importuning since his first call for a *Minhag America*. At the organizational session of the Central Conference of American Rabbis in 1889, Wise had urged the immediate establishment of a committee to prepare a uniform prayer book. He deemed it a vital necessity in order to end the uninhibited individual prayer book production that catered to a wide variety of congregational tastes. Two years later, the subject was formally considered. A committee prepared a text. In 1894 the volume was ratified. The completed version of the Union Prayer Book was satisfactory to all shades of Reform opinion and represented the consummation of Reform thought on synagogue ritual and practice. After Part II was adopted, Kohler could proudly state that in the new ritual Einhorn and Wise dwell together in the historical past and the living present.[36]

The synod proposal was to be debated furiously twice more in American religious life before it was to be abandoned, by the Conservative school in the fading nineties and by the Reform wing in the early years of the new century. Two new forces were represented in the discussion among the Conservatives: Solomon Schechter (1847-1915) and the young Henrietta Szold (1860-1945). Writing from England on December 26, 1898, Schechter said:

On the whole, I think, Synods, unless confined to purely administrative affairs, are useless and even harmful . . .

Besides that, I think no man is capable of representing other men in matters spiritual.

Synods have also a tendency to create among us certain sacerdotalism which is quite foreign to the Jewish spirit.[37]

Borrowing her title "Catholic Israel," a term which Schechter had popularized, Miss Szold subjected the synod proposal to a thorough-searching analysis in an essay which identified her in thought as in action with the Conservative movement.[38]

As the American Jewish community continued to grow, cultural institutions of great importance were developed in which the religious leadership served on the strength of individual gifts rather than as representatives of organized religious groups. These developments included the incipient Hebrew and Yiddish literary movements, the permanent establishment of the Jewish Publication Society of America (1888), the founding of the American Jewish Historical Society (1892), and the recognized participation of the Jews in the World's Columbian Exposition at Chicago (1893). Last in order but perhaps foremost in significance came the rooting of Jewish scholarship on the American continent.

Until the mid-nineteenth century there was no American Jewish scholarship to speak of; in the second part of the century, such scholarship was to be found only among the learned rabbis who came from abroad. Benjamin Szold published his *Hebrew Commentary to the Book of Job* (1886), and occasional articles on the Bible; much of this work remained in manuscript form. Marcus Jastrow might be said to have benefited from his ill health, for he thus found the leisure from other duties to prepare his *magnum opus, A Dictionary of the Targumin, the Talmud Babli and Yerushalmi, and the Midrashic Literature* (1903), the first important rabbinic work in English. Alexander Kohut completed his monumental *Aruch Completum* (1889), which is so dramatically described by Rebekah Kohut.[39]

Jewish scholarship was firmly established in American soil through the various seminaries. These became, in addition to training schools for rabbis, citadels of learning and centers of study for scholars. The rabbinical schools attracted men of international standing who magnetically opened new frontiers for American Judaism. The Hebrew Union College in its formative years included Moses Mielziner (1828-1903), first full time professor at the College, whose special field was Talmud. He wrote an *Introduction to the Talmud,* in which he included a section on "Outlines of Talmudical Ethics" (1894). At the College were also Gotthard Deutsch (1859-1921), gifted student of Heinrich Graetz, whose archives of rare history sources in the Hebrew Union College Library contain a veritable mine of information; Max Leopold Margolis (1866-1932), philologist and Bible student, later to become the editor of the Jewish Publication Society translation of the Bible; Casper Levias (1860-1934), Semitist; Moses Buttenwieser (1862-1939), Bible scholar and critic; and, at the end of the century, Henry Malter (*c.* 1864-1925), leading scholar of Judeo-Arabic literature and medieval philosophy. At first the Hebrew Union College had an advantage over the later organized Jewish Theological Seminary and Yeshiva. Soon, however, the two younger institutions, had no less distinguished men on their respective faculties.

In these years, too, still another opportunity began to present itself to scholars of Judaism. American universities began to invite them to their Semitic, religion and history departments. In 1886 a chair in Semitics was endowed at Columbia University, and was filled by Richard J. H. Gottheil (1862-1936); Cyrus Adler, the first student in America to receive a higher degree in Semitics, was appointed to that department at the Johns Hopkins University in 1887; in 1892, Morris Jastrow, Jr. (1861-1921), began to teach Semitic languages at the University of Pennsylvania; in the same year Emil G. Hirsch was called to the chair of Rabbinic literature and Jewish philosophy at the University of Chicago; in 1902, William Rosenau (1865-1943) was appointed to the Johns Hopkins University department of Semitics.

This was a beginning—admittedly belated and faltering, but a beginning nonetheless. Two new plans for the rapid development of scholarship in America were proposed by Isidore Singer (1859-1939), later editor of the *Jewish Encyclopedia*, and the resourceful Cyrus Adler. Dr. Singer suggested a Jewish University of Theology, History and Literature. Dr. Adler had another plan. "We have Mss. and some books at Columbia College, the Library of the Jewish Theological Seminary, the Leeser Library in Philadelphia, the Cohen Library in Baltimore, the Library of the Hebrew Union College, and the Sutro Library in California. But," he pleaded, "who would think of comparing all of them together with any of the better libraries in England, Germany, Italy or Austria?"[40] In his limpid mind, Adler charted a course of action. He proposed therefore the establishment of a Jewish academy in America for the advancement of scholarship. This academy was to collect a great library, publish the fruits of scientific research, arrange meetings of learned societies, and above all encourage, stimulate and support young and gifted scholars to devote of their time and talent to Jewish research. Adler suggested that a fund of a half million dollars (an enormous sum for those times) would be required to launch this venture. But neither an individual nor a communal Maecenas appeared to support his project. Adler's suggestion, though enthusiastically received in limited circles, was premature. Once again scholarship was being treated as though it were a luxury and not a prime necessity of Judaism.

As the liberal and expansive nineteenth century gave way to the new era, America looked forward to the literal fulfillment of Isaiah's prophecy, "That the government may be increased, And of peace there be no end" (Is. 9:6). All the inhabitants of the great American continent shared in the dream of such a future; and the Jews were no exception. Internally American Judaism was faced with division of opinion. Despite mutual reproach, fundamentally the religious groupings were in search of the same solution. As Mayer Sulzberger wrote to Schechter, "Orthodoxy, reform, conservatism, all have been found to be names, and it is no bad thing to be uncomprehended in or by any of them. He who has scholarship, talent, and enthusiasm may be more appreciated for the first time in our history than he who leads a party."[41]

Organizational impasses were surmounted. Isaac M. Wise was succeeded by Kaufmann Kohler at the Hebrew Union College. The Seminary, after some years of extremely doubtful prospects, suddenly took on new life. Both schools had spurned a suggested amalgamation; each group had confidence in its own future. Orthodoxy, too, supplied with an ever-flowing stream of immigrants, felt secure and hopeful. As in the dream which Joseph interpreted, religious life and institutions became a vine of three branches, and, as it was budding, its blossoms shot forth. Would the clusters bring forth ripe grapes? That was the question.

6

Ideological Clarification and Emphasis on Learning, 1902-1919

In the very developments of the new century were concealed those events that, in their unfolding, brought to American Jewry the material, numerical and, in the dream of a few, the spiritual hegemony of world Israel. From 1900 to 1912 ten million immigrants came to the shores of the United States, of whom approximately one million were Jews. The centrality of America in the orbit of Jewish world affairs, first perceived by the historically sensitive and confirmed by events, strengthened the hands of religious leaders as they prepared for American Judaism's great role. On the horizon, new leaders appeared, each devoted to the fulfillment of the philosophy of life for which he stood. Their achievements are organically incorporated in the institutions they helped to create. Such was the case with Jacob H. Schiff (1847-1920). He was the unelected head of his people, respected by all alike—religious and secularist, learned and illiterate, fourth- or first-generation American—for he transcended all party lines. As Jacob Schiff grew older in the service of American Israel, two younger men, Louis Marshall (1856-1929) and Felix M. Warburg (1871-1937), continued his tradition.

Reform's first major decision was the selection of its new leader. After

Wise's death, Professors Mielziner and Deutsch served as acting presidents
of the Hebrew Union College. It was, however, the devout and scholarly
Kaufmann Kohler who was called to the presidency. At the age of sixty,
when most men place their mantle on younger shoulders, Koehler, fondly
named "the Battler," began to build the College on the three-pillared
philosophy of Revelation, Reform, and America, or God, Progress, and
the Democratic Spirit.

Scholarship was the nerve center of the College. Kohler fashioned the
faculty and the student body in his own image. With the twofold purpose
of raising the teaching standards and encouraging academic pursuits,
Kohler added to the faculty Julian Morgenstern, gifted Bible scholar and
later his successor in the presidency of the College; Jacob Z. Lauterbach
(1873-1942), talmudic scholar and associate of Kohler in the *Jewish
Encyclopedia;* and David Neumark (1866-1924), philosopher and Hebraist, who despite Kohler's earlier objections succeeded in introducing the
techniques of modern Hebrew into the curriculum.

Kohler was the exemplar of industry. He continued to work for the
Jewish Encyclopedia, producing in total some three hundred articles; his
Jewish Theology, originally published in German in 1910, appeared in
English translation in 1918; during his retirement he published a volume
Heaven and Hell in Comparative Religion on the occasion of the Dante
anniversary in 1923; *The Origins of the Synagogue and the Church*
appeared posthumously in 1929. The latter two books represented the
fruits of his labors during the busy presidential years.

Physical growth accompanied scholarly development. The movement to
acquire a new home for the Hebrew Union College began in 1905, and
in 1913 the college and library buildings were dedicated on their present
site. The library is a monument to the foresight and assiduity of Adolph
S. Oko (1883-1944), who served as its director from 1905 to 1938.

In 1909, as a direct result of the establishment by Jacob H. Schiff of a
fund of $100,000, the interest of which was to be equally divided between
the Hebrew Union College and the Seminary for use of their respective
teachers' institutes, a teacher-training department was established at the
College. Because there was no significant Reform congregational school
system, students could not be developed for the institute, and those who
might have chosen teaching as a calling saw in it no future. In lieu of
formal classes, extension lectures for Sunday-school teachers and limited-
period institutes were arranged, particularly in the smaller cities of the
country.

The Union of American Hebrew Congregations continued to expand its
program. A department on circuit preaching was established to provide
opportunities for religious instruction and service to the smaller communities. Holiday sermons were published for congregations without

rabbis. In 1905 this committee was expanded into a full Department of Synagogue and School Extension. In 1913 the Union merged the local sisterhoods into a national women's auxiliary under the name of National Federation of Temple Sisterhoods with an initial charter membership of forty-nine groups.

Despite these externals of organizational expansion, the Reform movement was stunted in its growth: and this for a variety of reasons. Numbers were not in its favor. The mass of Jewish immigrants were East European. In the first decade of the century eighty-seven per cent of the recent arrivals settled in the east, while only eight per cent moved on to the central states. The center of Reform, being located in a midwestern city, was thus far away from the heart of the American Jewish community. Then again, socially, the membership of Reform congregations was comfortable and staid, having little in common with the recent immigrants. Nor did Reform theology respond to the needs or idioms of the large masses of Jews. Reform did not reckon with traditional associations, the deep and ancient love for Eretz Yisrael, the ceremonial of home and synagogue. The carefully documented records of the annual conventions of the Central Conference reveal how, consistently, the choice was always on the side of classic Reform doctrine. Nationalists and ceremonialists were quickly outvoted; the overwhelming majority sought to fulfill the prophecies and declarations of Reform. It must be emphasized, however, that despite the fervent antitraditionalism and antinationalism, the intention was not to break away from the main stream of Judaism; a party, yes; but not a schism. The specific cases in point are those of creed, synod, Zionism, and religious ceremonialism.

In 1903, Max L. Margolis (1866-1932), under the distinct influence of Protestant theology and higher criticism, attempted to influence the Reform movement to accept a formal creed on an ecclesiastical basis. His report to the Central Conference, "The Theological Aspect of Reformed Judaism"[42] was a departure from classic Reform lines and included his suggested creed under the four headings of Theology (and Cosmology), Anthropology, Psychology, and Ecclesiology. Margolis's plea for an ecclesia was rejected on the basis of counterreports submitted by Rabbis Felsenthal, Marcus Friedlander (1866-1944), Max Heller (1860-1929), and Kohler. The principle of the opposition was Reform's determination to disagree with Orthodoxy, but not to dissociate Reform from the Synagogue of Israel. As Kohler stated: ". . . nor will it [Reform] be checked by the champions of conservatism whose power appears to be in the ascendancy at present, but we shall ever insist on being in full continuity with the Judaism of the past."[43]

Zionism almost proved to be the splintering rod of Reform Judaism at all times. The old guard repeated the standard clichés and fulminated vociferously at any suggested watering down of the universalistic mission of Reform. Against this position two valiant spirits arose and contributed to the reshaping of Reform Judaism. These were Stephen S. Wise and Judah L. Magnes. The young Wise had been one of the first to answer Herzl's call. He became, as it were, Zionism incarnate, everywhere in America, troubling the placid and self-confident souls. Wise, Magnes, Richard Gottheil, and their elders—Gustav Gottheil, Felsenthal, and Heller—were the *Nachshonites* of an imposing movement against a well nigh overwhelming opposition.

Stephen Wise was also critical of the congregational structure of Reform Judaism. In 1906, after a spirited exchange of letters with the board of Temple Emanu-El, which had invited him to become its rabbi, he spurned their invitation on the issue of a free pulpit. He came to New York and established the Free Synagogue, in which the pulpit was to be free of all restraint. The congregation was to be supported by voluntary contributions; both the pew system and class distinctions were abolished, and greater democracy was introduced in synagogue organization.

Judah Magnes had additional charges against Reform. He found its doctrine and ritual to be a spiritual wasteland. Magnes had accepted the call to Emanu-El only to quit its pulpit and that of Reform Judaism altogether on the Passover of 1910. His dramatic plea for a "return to the sources of Judaism" was but the climax of a long bill of particulars which he had expressed earlier both publicly and privately. Magnes urged that Reform Judaism could be saved from oblivion only if there were a reformation of Reform Judaism. He sought contact with the living Jewish people—its Torah, language, custom, ceremony, and observance. He demanded a proper Jewish educational system, adult classes, the return to the *Bar Mitzva*, the reduction of congregational dues so that the lower income groups could afford to join a congregation, and the use of the traditional *siddur*.

In the stability and security of Reform Judaism, these gusts of wind did not affect the main line of its action. On the Zionist issue antinationalism held sway. And so, too, Reform stood pat on ceremonial and ritual issues, apparently unaware that its classical position was no longer adequate.

Waves of immigration, the ascendancy of the Conservative movement, the emptying of pews and the consequent de-Judaization of the young, the Balfour Declaration and a cataclysmic war—these historic factors seemingly did not affect the official Reform position. Toward the end of the period, after World War I, the first signs of Reform's response to the changing times became noticeable.

The Conservative movement and the Seminary had the unparalleled opportunity of undergoing a complete metamorphosis. The positive historical tradition was promulgated and the counter-Reform program de-emphasized; the limited faculty was replaced by a unique group of scholars; the financial structure was thoroughly rebuilt through the creation of a new board of directors, including Jacob H. Schiff, Louis Marshall, Mayer Sulzberger, and Leonard Lewisohn (1847-1902); the new head of the institution was the peerless Solomon Schechter. Chiefly responsible for the entire reorganization was Cyrus Adler, devoted student of Sabato Morais, who would not permit his master's foremost contribution to American Judaism to disintegrate. The uniqueness of Adler's achievement was the alliance he formed between a board almost completely Reform and a faculty unswervingly devoted to traditional Judaism. This was possible because of the extraordinary caliber of the lay leaders who felt that only a traditional school could function effectively among the new immigrants.

Center of all eyes and hope of all hearts was the Rumanian-born, German-trained, British professor, American-destined Shneur Zalman Schechter. Virtually every person of importance claimed some influence on Schechter's decision to come to America; he was the most wooed Jewish scholar in modern times. Dramatized by his fortunate Genizah find, *hasid*, Zionist, and anti-reformist, master of style and gifted scholar, Schechter was what Conservative Judaism needed as a leader and a symbol.

In his inaugural address, delivered on November 20, 1902, Schechter proclaimed the goals of the re-created Seminary. Unity must be forged out of the diversities in Jewish community life; such unity would be realized through the training of a native ministry; Jewish scholarship was to be the chief altar in the temple of Judaism. "Judaism is absolutely incompatible with the abandonment of the Torah"; the Seminary stands for historical and traditional Judaism, for, "we cannot create halting places at will. We must either remain faithful to history or go the way of all flesh . . ."[44]

Schechter's first and most formidable task was to create a faculty worthy of his dream and representative of his thought. The ultimate success with which his efforts were crowned is represented not only in the rare individuals whom he brought to the Seminary, but in their collective strength. The faculty selected by Schechter is perhaps his greatest contribution to American Judaism, for as a body they were unrivaled. Their international standing established the Seminary as a central pillar of Jewish scholarship in America.

Louis Ginzberg, dean of Jewish scholars and pathfinder in every field of Judaica, was considered by Schechter even prior to his arrival in America. Professor Ginzberg's extraordinary learning, catholicity of knowledge and unswerving devotion to scholarly pursuits, quickly established him as, next to Schechter, the central figure of the faculty. After a thorough search in Europe in the summer of 1903, Schechter announced his selection of Dr. Alexander Marx for the chair of history and Dr. Israel Friedlaender (1876-1920) as professor of biblical literature and exegesis. Little did he suspect that in Dr. Marx he had invited not only a historian and bibliographer who was to achieve distinction second to none, but also the builder of the world's greatest Jewish library. Dr. Friedlaender, promising young docent at the University of Strasbourg, became in his short span of years a brilliant teacher, an exponent of Zionism, and the leader of American Jewish youth. In his martyr death, American Judaism lost one of its leading spokesmen.

Joseph Mayer Asher (1872-1909), English-born rabbi of Congregation B'nai Jeshurun, was appointed professor of homiletics. The faculty was completed with the addition of the gifted Israel Davidson (1870-1939), who rapidly rose to prominence as the world authority in medieval Hebrew literature.

The second department to be launched was the library. Mayer Sulzberger, to whom Professor Ginzberg repeatedly refers as the "outstanding Jew produced in America," was the library's greatest benefactor. It was Sulzberger's unique collection that served as the nucleus of the new library. "To compass the high ends for which we strive, the library must satisfy the needs of the few choice spirits as abundantly as it provides for those of ordinary scholars," Mayer Sulzberger said at the dedication of the Seminary library in 1902. By identifying himself completely and overwhelmingly with this purpose, Professor Marx, at once master and servant, has created what the men assembled at the opening ceremonies could neither anticipate nor dream of.

The Teachers Institute, which was to inaugurate a religious educational movement, was the third link in the chain of Seminary institutions. The young Mordecai M. Kaplan, European-born and American-trained graduate of the Seminary in whom Schechter had detected "a power so inspiring and stimulating," was invited to become the principal of the new institution. Kaplan threw himself into the task with originality of approach and breadth of action. The growth of the Institute and of its later auxiliary, the Seminary College of Jewish Studies (for the training of lay leaders), to the status of the foremost Jewish collegiate institution in the country was due to the efforts and amazing vision of Dr. Kaplan and the faculty he later assembled: Joseph Bragin (1875-1932), principal of the Hebrew High School of New York; Professor Zevi Scharfstein, leading American Jewish pedagogue, distinguished Hebraist and author of pedagogic textbooks used throughout the world, and Professor Morris D. Levine, who wrote his enduring volumes on the tablets of his students' hearts.

These institutions under way, Schechter and his colleagues turned to the task of developing a conservative movement in American Judaism. This was manifest in their attitudes toward scholarship; Torah and *mitzvot*, Zionism, and the American center. Schechter's favorite plea was that a community as practical as America stood in dire need of a few men who had the courage to be impractical—impractical in the material sense of the word. For scholarship was not divorced from life; it was the only force that could save American Judaism.

In contrast with the majority of the board, the Seminary faculty represented a united force of active Zionists. The adherence of the Conservative wing of Judaism to the official Zionist movement, as opposed to the antizionism of the Reform rabbinate and as differentiated from the Orthodox Mizrachi position, gave to the center Zionist Organization of America its greatest strength. Schechter's decisive statement of 1906, coming at a time when it meant a public debate in the *New York Times* with Jacob H. Schiff, was an extraordinary declaration. In his Zionism, Schechter repeated the Jewish pledge of ages: "Zionism was, and still is, the most cherished dream I was worthy of having." However, the Zionism of the Conservative movement, while it stressed the national factor in Israel's history, did not relegate the religious character of that history to a secondary position. Louis Ginzberg who had identified himself immediately with Herzl's call and had written one of his first essays, *Het Zionisme*, in Dutch, and who together with Friedlaender had voted "no" on the Uganda proposal while all other Americans had voted favorably, stressed the great danger that faced Judaism if its religious elements were ignored. Foreseeing the possibilities of a later development of a philosophy negating the Diaspora, he warned that an exclusive nationalist Zionist viewpoint would cut Diaspora Judaism off from its future. If Judaism is equivalent to nationalism, then only those who will reside in the Jewish state will be Jews. Moreover, he held that Jewish nationalism is not an abstract concept; its very essence is religious. "For us who adhere to historical Judaism, Jewish nationalism without religion would be a tree without fruit, Jewish religion without Jewish nationalism would be a tree without roots."[45]

This point of view expressed itself in a new formula: Diaspora plus Palestine. Granted that a wholesome Jewish life could be obtained in Eretz Yisrael by the Jewish resettlement of the Holy Land, could, however, a wholesome Jewish life be established in America? Conservatives responded with an unqualified, Yes. The building in America of a dominant center of Judaism was a cardinal plank in the program of Conservative Judaism. This was especially well expressed by Israel Friedlaender in his remarkable essay, "The Problems of Judaism in America."[46]

With scholarship, Torah and *mitzvot*, Zionist-Hebraism, and the American center as the dynamic constants of the Conservative movement, it became necessary to find a task force which, in addition to the Seminary, could make these ideals active in the life of the Jews in America. A younger generation of graduates had grown up. They rallied about their teachers; they brought their own congregants and students in February, 1913, to New York. This was the founding assembly of the United Synagogue of America.

The purpose of the new organization was defined as follows:

The advancement of the cause of Judaism in America and the maintenance of Jewish tradition in its historical continuity; to assert and establish loyalty to the Torah and its historical exposition; to further the observance of the Sabbath and the Dietary Laws; to preserve in the service the reference to Israel's past and the hopes for Israel's restoration; to maintain the traditional character of the liturgy, with Hebrew as the language of prayer; to foster Jewish religious life in the home, as expressed in traditional observances; to encourage the establishment of Jewish religious schools, in the curricula of which the study of the Hebrew language and literature shall be given a prominent place, both as the key to the true understanding of Judaism, and as a bond holding together the scattered communities of Israel throughout the world. It shall be the aim of the United Synagogue of America, while not indorsing the innovations introduced by any of its constituent bodies, to embrace all elements essentially loyal to traditional Judaism and in sympathy with the purposes outlined above.[47]

The Seminary and the Rabbinical Assembly had co-operated in the establishment of its action group. Under a joint committee, the Central Administrative Committee, representing the three branches of the organized movement, and under the presidency first of Schechter and then of Adler, Conservative Judaism went out among the people. In November, 1915, Solomon Schechter passed away in the midst of his labors.

Cyrus Adler became acting president of the Seminary and, in time, president. He had already become the head of the United Synagogue. Professor Louis Ginzberg became the scholarly leader of the movement. Both men had serious problems to cope with, for the inner perplexities and inconsistencies that had been passed over in the rush of organization and expansion now were increasing rather than disappearing. An umbrella ideology was agreeable in the abstract; in its application to contemporary problems and events interpretations varied. A definitive stand had to be taken on the approach to Jewish law and *mitzvot*, the Jewish Homeland, and the American Jewish Congress. The last two issues were hammered out to majority satisfaction. A definite position on the adjustment of Jewish law and observance has yet to be taken.

The major characteristics of Orthodoxy in America during the early part of the twentieth century were these: transplantation of type, decentralization, and spiritual insulation. Nor could the characteristics have been otherwise. Groups of immigrants, establishing miniatures of their old country in some corner of a metropolis, huddled together into *hebrot*, painted a sign, and organized themselves as a congregation in exile—exile from Kasrilevke. Shortly thereafter their religious functionaries, the *rabbonim, melamdim, shohetim,* and *mohalim,* arrived with the training, viewpoint and spiritual armor of East European Judaism. This was in full effect a transplantation of culture.

If energies were squandered and hopes dashed in the effort to implant Orthodox belief and practice in America, it was due in additional measure to the stubborn refusal of Orthodoxy to reckon with the facts of American life and thought in the twentieth century—the very life indeed of their children born and raised in the new world. Orthodox parents still liked to pretend that the East European pattern of culture could be native to America, too. And when the rabbi of Slusk came to America and appeared at a public meeting of the Union of Orthodox Jewish Congregations, he chastised the assemblage for having emigrated to this *trefa* land.

The history of Orthodoxy in America since 1900 is the development of an Orthodox rabbinate and laity who were as anxious as their predecessors to transmit the ancient heritage but who proceeded in a spirit and language which took the contemporary American trends and ideals into account. This transfer of leadership from the Agudath Ha-Rabbanim to the Rabbinical Council of America, from the basement synagogues to Young Israel and to Hapoel Hamizrachi, from the "rented store" schools to the United Yeshivot, did not happen overnight. Three decades were to pass before it became clear that Orthodoxy could flourish on American soil.

The patterns of Reform and Conservative religious institutional life had their counterpart in the Orthodox party: higher institutions of learning, a lay organization, and a rabbinical association. Latest in formation (1902), the Union of Orthodox Rabbis of the United States and Canada (the Agudath Ha-Rabbanim) was first in strength.

The initial call came from the West. The former plan to establish an American *Bet Din* of three learned Russian rabbis, was found to be impractical. Rabbis Judah Leib Levin (1862-1926) of Detroit and Asher Lippman Zarchy (1862-1932) of Louisville sent a circular letter to ten of their colleagues in Cincinnati, Chicago, St. Louis, New York, Boston, Pittsburgh, Philadelphia, Omaha, and Denver, under the title *Et La-asot* (Time for Action). The second step was taken in Boston when a group of Orthodox rabbis attending the Zionist convention gathered to prepare a tentative constitution. The leaders of the group were the veteran Rabbi Moses Z. (Ramaz) Margolies (1851-1936), chief rabbi of Boston and later rabbi of Congregation Kehilath Jeshurun of New York City, who had come to America in 1889, and Rabbi Bernard Louis Levinthal (1864-1952), who arrived in America in 1891 and resided in Philadelphia during his long and fruitful career as the revered head of Orthodoxy in that city.

The newly formed union was short lived. After four years of disappointment a second call was issued, once again from the western Orthodox rabbis: Rabbis Abraham Lesser (1834-1925) and Sander Lifshitz (1846-1915) of Cincinnati, Rabbi Zarchy of Louisville and Rabbi Isaac E. Neustadt (1869-1913) of Indianapolis. Was it due to the fact that these men, situated in the nest of Reform Judaism, were disturbed by the heavy inroads which Reform had made among their people? A guide to the promptings of this western group may be discovered in their heartrending appeal for the slumberers to awaken, urging as the prerequisite of an active Orthodoxy "the training of ordained rabbis, teachers and preachers who have mastered the English language and who will be fit to wage combat against the forces of reform."[48]

At the seventh convention, Rabbi Levinthal, in his opening address, pleaded that the organization "take to heart the needs of the Yeshivat Rabbenu Yitzchak Elchanan, from which Judaism may be rebuilt in America." The Agudath Ha-Rabbanim did intensify its efforts on behalf of the Yeshiva. A double purpose was served. Not only was the Yeshiva reinforced as a nursery for future teachers of Orthodoxy, but, in the concrete and constructive effort to build institutions, the Agudath Ha-Rabbanim itself took on life.

The recognition that the older, European way of Jewish life was not the path to the future, first came to the students of the Yeshiva. They sought to prepare themselves more effectively for service in the American scene, and therefore arranged their secular studies in local colleges. The directors of the Yeshiva violently opposed this practice. In 1908, an assembly of rabbis met to adjudicate the difference between the authorities and the students. The students won. They were granted permission to continue with their general studies until such time as the Yeshiva itself could organize courses under its own administration. The acceptance of higher education as compatible with rabbinic integrity was the first important step that American Orthodoxy took toward winning a position of equality with the other religious parties in American Judaism. In addition, the Yeshiva, unlike the other rabbinical seminaries and in keeping with the tradition of European *yeshibot*, did not limit its student body to those preparing for the rabbinate, but rather encouraged students who might later pursue other professions, including business careers, to master Jewish knowledge. This change of approach placed the Yeshiva in an advantageous position, for it made possible the training of an intensely devoted Orthodox lay leadership. Amalgamation between the Rabbi Isaac Elchanan Theological Seminary and the Yeshiva Etz Chaim in 1915 led to greater strength. To cap these constructive factors, the new institution elected Dr. Bernard Revel (1885-1940) as *Rosh Ha-Yeshiva* and president of the combined institutions. Thus was inaugurated an era of consolidation and expansion which was climaxed by the incorporation of Yeshiva University as the first Jewish university in America.

Dr. Revel was born in Kovno in 1885. After his arrival in America in 1906, Dr. Revel pursued studies at Dropsie College, where he received his Ph.D. degree. He keenly understood the need for relating the Jewish tradition to American community life. His firm organizing hand was felt immediately. Through the establishment in 1915 of the first Yeshiva high school, the Etz Chaim Talmudical Academy, where both secular and general studies were taught under the same roof, he blazed a new trail in Orthodox education. As the First World War came to a close, Orthodoxy had laid the foundation for a higher educational institution of historic proportions.

A second Orthodox rabbinical school, which was in its infancy at the turn of the century, was organized in the Midwest in 1916, the Beth Midrash Le Rabbonim of Chicago. This seminary grew out of a small group of students who were taught Talmud in a private *heder* in 1895, later called the Yeshiva Etz Chaim. The student body consisted in the main of young immigrants who received regular weekly stipends (as was customary in European *yeshibot*) in order to be free to continue their full-time talmudic studies.

The activities of the Orthodox group were based on the opposing premises of negation and affirmation. The Reform, Conservative, and secularist theories of survival were vigorously condemned; the fields of education, ceremonial, and ritual observance, European aid, and Zionism were actively cultivated. Greater rewards accompanied the constructive efforts. First and foremost was the precept "And thou shalt teach them diligently." The schools were in a sorry state. At an early convention of the Union of Orthodox Jewish Congregations, it was stated that the Christian mission schools on the East Side "take the place of those schools which we have neglected to provide." In the first decade of the century, matters took a turn for the better. Communal Talmud Torahs were built and supported largely by local Orthodox parents. These schools offered a condensed version of the subjects of the European *heder*. The schools prospered and were effective in attracting devoted and gifted teachers. Children of the poor were given free instruction. In 1903 the Yeshivat Jacob Joseph on the lower East Side of New York was founded with facilities for one thousand children. The Agudath Ha-Rabbanim called for the rapid multiplication of such effort. They were anxious to found adequate elementary schools in the rural areas and to conduct classes in Talmud and Midrash for the adolescents. The national Yeshiva Ketanah movement for the establishment of all day schools, as the effective solution to the problems of Jewish education, was not yet in existence. In 1918 there were only four such schools in New York City.

Most effort was concentrated on ritual and ceremonial matters, particularly Sabbath observance and *kashrut*. One of the first and most important
achievements of the Union of Orthodox Jewish Congregations was the
establishment in 1905 of the Jewish Sabbath Alliance of America, whose
object was to promote "the observance of the Holy Sabbath in every
possible way." Recognizing that Sabbath observance has "in many places ...
become the exception rather than the rule," the Alliance endeavored to
restore the sanctity of the traditional holy day in a variety of ways—by
means of propaganda, political or legislative activity, securing employment
service for Sabbath observers, and so on. For several years, a monthly
organ, the *Sabbath Journal*, was published in English, Yiddish, and
Hebrew. The Alliance frequently appeared in the legislative halls of many
states to secure desired legislation; it was instrumental in defeating a bill
in the New York state legislature which would have prohibited the sale
of all articles of food on Sunday. Some seventy thousand Sabbath observers,
including grocers, butchers, clothiers, tailors, laundrymen, watch repairers,
shoemakers, standkeepers, pushcart peddlers, and other merchants, arrested for work done on Sunday, were defended in the courts; Alliance
representatives appeared before Christian Sunday Associations explaining
the Jewish Sabbath view; an employment bureau was opened to bring
together Sabbath-observing employer and employee; successful intercession
on behalf of public service employees gave them the opportunity to observe
Saturdays and holy days. In these efforts the Alliance was aided by many
individuals, primarily among the Orthodox, but also from the Conservative
and Reform ranks. Louis Marshall was one of their most active counselors.
An interesting development occurred in labor circles when, in 1910, a
special section of the cloak and skirts union formed a Sabbath observing
chapter. They appealed to the Agudath Ha-Rabbanim to help them enlarge
their membership.

The control of *kashrut* fell into the domain of the Orthodox. For some
unknown reason, certainly not because they were less concerned, the Conservatives defaulted completely. The results, though not entirely due to
the inadequacies of the Orthodox, were truly discouraging. New York
State aid, for example, was forthcoming, and the Agudath Ha-Rabbanim
were effective in gaining that aid. Nevertheless, the variety of excesses
against the law and spirit of Judaism rendered the observance of *kashrut*
a challenge to the basic fidelity of many observant Jews.

The supervision of *mohalim* was another illustration of how the
maladministration of religious duties ofttimes drives even its most ardent
devotees away from observance. In this case, the state medical laws took
control of the situation. The Orthodox were keenly aware of these
indignities to religious life; the proceedings of their conferences include
unabashed statements of the repugnant state of affairs. Fundamentally, the

evil arose from the fragmentization of Jewish religious life. The Reform paid no heed; the Conservatives defaulted; the Orthodox alone were helpless.

In the area of overseas relief Orthodoxy displayed superior imagination and originality. Impatient with the general relief agencies because of their neglect of religious institutions, the Central Jewish Relief Committee and Ezrath Torah Fund were organized. The original purpose of the Committee was to bring aid and succor to the European *yeshivot*, their rabbis and students, as well as to all religious functionaries during World War I. But because of the great need for relief for all Jewish sufferers from affliction, the Committee's plans were expanded to meet developing emergencies. The Ezrath Torah Fund fulfilled the original functions of the Committee. Some of the world famous *yeshivot*—Mir, Slobodka, Lomza, Telz and Slonim—were saved from total extinction through the efforts of this fund. The work that was executed under the chairmanship of Rabbi Israel Rosenberg was not limited to European *yeshiva* relief but was also extended to the religious institutions in Eretz Yisrael.

The separation of American Jewry's communal, social and cultural affairs from the control of organized religious bodies, was complete early in the new century. The last effort to bring together an American Jewish Congress under religious auspices was the attempt of the Union of American Hebrew Congregations. It did not succeed. Henceforth religious organizations were reduced to the same status as all other national organizations in the representative councils of American Israel. The responsibilities for world Israel suddenly became so heavy, the activities so intensified, and the need for leadership so urgent, that the religious parties welcomed the new alignment.

The Kishinev pogroms shook American Jewry out of its parochialism. Emil G. Hirsch, rabid antinationalist, cried out under the stress and agony of the pogroms, "I am now a Zionist." American Jews, who had not sent one dollar to aid their distressed brethren overseas in any nationally organized manner until 1905, hastily dispatched $1,250,000 through the office of the National Committee for the Relief of Sufferers by Russian Massacres. The Galveston movement expended a million dollars for the more effective settlement of immigrants in the American hinterland; national Jewish agitation started for the organization of an American Jewish congress or assembly; in November, 1906, the American Jewish Committee was founded "to prevent the infraction of the civil and religious rights of Jews, in any part of the world . . . [to] alleviate the consequences of persecution and to afford relief from calamities affecting Jews, wherever they may occur . . ."

In its attempt to effect a better internal organization of American Jewry, the Jewish community of New York City tried the experiment of establishing a Kehilla which would not merely represent one party in Judaism, but include all Jews who believed in a Jewish future, even though they differed considerably as to what form that future should take. The Kehilla was started because of false allegations regarding the percentage of criminality among Jews, but it did not succeed. Some of its branches, such as the Bureau of Jewish Education and the Federation of Jewish Philanthropies, survived as independent agencies. Nevertheless the Kehilla was a sign of the times. An advisory council of seventy, representing every walk of Jewish life—religion, *Landsmannschaften,* philanthropy, and labor, etc.—began to learn how to work together.

The Americanization of the immigrants was a serious problem, although not half so serious as was the social maladjustment of their children. This was true for all ethnic groups. The children lived in two worlds, at home in a world of their parents, and outside in an American universe of discourse. The Jewish parents worked out their own salvation. Yiddish cultural activities enjoyed extraordinary developments. Channels of communication such as the press, stage and club organizations, served as instruments for Americanization. But neither the synagogue nor Yiddish culture seemed to be the way to the heart of Jewish youth. To solve the cultural, social and recreational problems of the juvenile, the Young Men's Hebrew Association was reconstructed. The model "Y" was the famous 92nd Street building which was established in 1900 by Jacob H. Schiff. In 1905, the Center movement was given financial stability when it was granted full community support, through the intercession of Schiff, who contended that "there is absolutely no reason . . . why larger provision should be made for the orphan than for the religious education and moral care of the juvenile." The movement expanded rapidly. In 1910 five regional Y.M.H.A.'s were in existence; in 1913, at a special conference, the Council of Young Men's Hebrew Associations and Kindred Associations was created.

The organization was founded, the need was great, but the specific program for the "religious education and moral care" of Jewish youth was wanting. Although the Y.M.H.A. called itself by a name adapted from the existing Christian organization, it did not adopt the same purpose. The Y.M.C.A. was a religious movement among the unchurched with the avowed purpose of propagandizing for Christian religious interests. The Y.M.H.A. was recreational, social, and at best, cultural—certainly not religious. This problem of Jewish program content plagued the sponsors since the earliest days. Professor Mordecai M. Kaplan, who among the religious leaders is probably the foremost protagonist of the Center movement, wrote to Felix M. Warburg, then president of the Y.M.H.A. Council, on November 1, 1913:

In my opinion, all Young Men's Hebrew Association work, which at present is still to a large extent a mere fumbling in the dark, would be rendered more definite and effective, if ranged about a religious, rather than a purely social or philanthropic ideal. By this I mean, that, instead of confining ourselves to holding out such distractions as might compete successfully with the dangerous distractions that tempt young men, we should seek to stimulate in them a positive enthusiasm for Judaism. Entertainments, the pool room and the gymnasium may serve as a temporary means of keeping young men away from the gambling dens and worse places. But a Young Men's Hebrew Association should not content itself with evoking anything less than the very highest manhood of which the young men are capable. The fact is that ignorance due to a lack of youthful training has been the cause for religion appearing to many of our young men a negligible factor in their lives. It is this very defect in their training that a Young Men's Hebrew Association should strive to eliminate . . .

It must be borne in mind, however, that it is futile to expect Young Men's Hebrew Associations to adopt this course without leaders who unite in themselves the qualifications of social worker as well as those of the religious worker. That there are no such leaders at the present time is due to the fact that the Young Men's Hebrew Association movement has only begun to assume the proportions necessary to call them forth. Instead, however, of leaving it to chance for these leaders to arise, it were advisable that the National Young Men's Hebrew Association get into touch with the two Seminaries in this country, which prepare men for the ministry, and urge them to encourage some of their students to prepare themselves for a career of Y.M.H.A. leadership. This might be brought about by having those students who have a leaning for social work, take up in addition to their regular Rabbinic course, such post-graduate studies in the University as have a bearing upon practical social work. With the problem of leaders solved the rest would be sure to follow.

Had this sound advice not been neglected in practice by both Synagogue and Center authorities, Jewish religious life would have benefited exceedingly, the Center movement might not have been regarded as a competitor of the Synagogue and, most important, we probably would have gained a generation which would have been trained in the moral and religious spirit envisaged by the founders of the Center movement and their successors.

A new type of institution of higher Jewish learning, the first post-graduate Jewish institution in the world devoted exclusively to scientific research, was created in 1907 through the bequest of Moses Aaron Dropsie. He directed in his will that "there be established and maintained in the City of Philadelphia, a college for the promotion of and instruction in the Hebrew and cognate languages and their respective literatures and in the Rabbinical learning and literature." According to Cyrus Adler, the first president of the Dropsie College for Hebrew and Cognate Learning, the idea occurred independently to the boards of the Seminary and of the Dropsie College that the cause of Jewish learning might be best served if a consolidation could be effected. A plan was considered for the establishment of a Jewish university which would combine the faculties and facilities of the Seminary, the Gratz College, and the new foundation. However, the time was not propitious, and instead the first nonsectarian higher academy of learning was brought into being. The original faculty included Henry Malter and Max L. Margolis, who left their posts at the Hebrew Union College; Jacob Hoschander (1874-1933) was added a year later; and, in 1913, Benzion Halper (1884-1924). In the same year, a history department was established and Abraham A. Neuman, who was later to become the president of the college, was chosen as professor of history. The *Jewish Quarterly Review*, which had been issued in England for twenty years under the editorship of Israel Abrahams and Claude G. Montefiore, was re-established at Dropsie College in 1910 by Dr. Adler in association with Schechter. After Schechter's death, Adler continued the editorial responsibilities alone.

Learning was a great cohesive force. Men of all schools of thought worked together to produce major contributions which could only have been made collectively. The *Jewish Encyclopedia* (1901-1906) was a landmark of scholarship. Under the leadership of Isidore Singer and the editorship of Joseph Jacobs a whole array of pre-eminent figures in Jewish learning combined to produce a twelve-volume work which has until this date (1948) remained unrivaled. In 1917 the long awaited authoritative Jewish translation of the Bible into English was presented to the American public. This first American Jewish edition of the Bible since Leeser's translation was supervised by an editorial board including Adler, Jacobs, Kohler, David Philipson, Schechter and Dr. Samuel Shulman, with Dr. Margolis as editor in chief.

The Orthodox rabbis and scholars continued in their tradition of publishing commentaries and insights on talmudic texts. In 1919, after years of patient effort, the full text of the Talmud Babli was issued for the first time in America under the vigilant auspices of the Agudath Ha-Rabbanim. Through this effort they were enabled partly to repay their martyr teachers and dispersed fellow students of the European *yeshibot*. Hundreds of sets were sent as gifts to the *yeshibot* in Lithuania, Poland and other places, where the centers of learning had been destroyed and the holy texts consumed by the ravages of war.

World War I was the first great test of American Israel's strength and mercy. The Joint Distribution Committee combined the efforts of the Central Jewish Relief Committee (organized by the Orthodox), the American Jewish Relief Committee (organized by the American Jewish Committee), and the People's Relief Committee (organized by labor groups). The new agency brought comfort and aid to millions of Jews caught in the net of devastation.

On April 6, 1917, America declared war. On April 9, 1917, seven national Jewish organizations convened and called for the creation of the Jewish Welfare Board. Before the war was ended, nine additional organizations had joined the Jewish Welfare Board. The newly created instrument was to serve as the organized Jewish voice to the men in service and as the official representative to the government on behalf of Jewish religious activities; moreover, the Board was to provide for the social and religious needs of the men in the armed forces of the United States at training base, military front or hospital. The responsibilities were overwhelming, for there was no precedent to guide Jewish action.

During the Civil War, four Jewish hospital chaplains had been appointed. Army organization did not call for Jewish regimental chaplains to serve with the battle troops. Consequently, at the outbreak of World War I, the legal question of chaplaincy appointments in other areas of service was not clear. Dr. Cyrus Adler, the first chairman of the Committee on Chaplains, met with Secretary Newton D. Baker to draft the legal formula that would qualify appointment of chaplains of denominations not represented at that time in the armed forces. The first Jewish chaplain to be appointed was Rabbi Elkan C. Voorsanger. He had enlisted in the service, was sent overseas, became a sergeant in the Medical Corps, and then, when the law was changed to allow the appointment of Jewish chaplains, was commissioned by appointment of General Pershing overseas. Twenty-three Jewish chaplains served during the war; twenty-two in the army and one in the navy. Dr. David de Sola Pool, then president of the New York Board of Jewish Ministers, became active aide to Dr. Adler and finally succeeded him as chairman of the committee. There were very special problems to solve. One of these had to do with the insigne, which in the army was the shepherd's crook. A special Jewish insigne was authorized in Washington. When Chaplain David Goldberg, the only Jewish naval chaplain in World War I, requested the authorities to change the insigne from the shepherd's crook to the star of David, he was informed by the Bureau of Navigation that "this star constitutes part of an insignia used by the Army" (the Sixth Army used it). Other problems which had to be faced were the preparation of an abridged Bible and a prayer book. Edited by Adler, Drachman, and Rosenau, the prayer book was published as an abridged traditional *siddur* with footnotes indicating the Union Prayer Book variations.

The war had taken a heavy toll of Jewish lives. European Jewish communities were in shambles. Yet out of the horror came a promise, the promise of the Balfour Declaration. American Israel, having suddenly grown into the responsibility of leadership, began its role in the rebuilding of the mother communities overseas, and in helping to establish Eretz Yisrael as the Jewish homeland.

7
AMERICA, A CENTER OF WORLD JUDAISM, 1919-1939

World War I altered the face of Europe; it changed the heart of America. In a series of laws passed during the years 1921, 1924, and 1929, America ended her former liberal immigration policy. President Wilson, who vetoed two restrictive immigration bills, asked of the American conscience: "Has not every ship that has pointed her prow westward borne hither the hopes of generation after generation of the oppressed of other lands?" The legislative voice in Washington responded in effect: America is no longer the Promised Land. It is the land of splendid isolation.

The changes in the immigration policy of the United States transformed the internal structure of the American Jewish community. Within two decades, American Jewry was preponderantly native ·American. The children of former immigrants rose to affluence and station in the rapidly expanding economy. A survey of Jewish occupational distribution shows that the white collar workers among the Jews exceeded the number in manual trades. In the natural course of events, these special and economic factors reflected themselves in Jewish communal life.

As the period of immigration came to an abrupt close, second generation American Jews became predominant in the leadership of all religious groups. Ever since the days of Leeser and Wise, progressive Jewish leadership had urged the training of a native ministry and teaching service. With immigration arrested, it became difficult to import rabbis and teachers.[49] A native born rabbinate therefore assumed religious responsibilities of the hour. Symbolically, the two new appointees to the presidencies of the Jewish Theological Seminary and the Hebrew Union College—Cyrus Adler and Julian Morgenstern—were both born and educated in America.

The emergence of an American trained and American centered religious leadership brought with it the development of new outlooks on Judaism and different interpretations of the special tasks which confronted the religious groups. While the leaders of the former generation saw as their central objective the building of strong and well knit independent religious parties and institutions, the leadership of the new generation sought, in addition, spiritual hegemony over all American Israel. This desire to create an indigenous American pattern for all American Jewry which would be predominantly Reform, Orthodox, or Conservative (depending on the particular designer of the pattern) is the special characteristic of

American Jewish religious history in the decades between the two world wars. Each group shaped its thought and action toward the ultimate goal of becoming, not as formerly, the major party in American Judaism, but American Judaism itself; the others ultimately would be assimilated into the new and main stream of American Judaism.

The desire to influence the religious character of American Judaism is reflected in the dissatisfaction of the rising generation with the adjectives of their respective group names. Reform Judaism at varying times called itself Progressive Judaism, Historical Judaism, and Liberal Judaism.[50] Orthodox Jewry was also unhappy with that description. For a period, the term "Torah-true Judaism," based on the Germanic compound *Torah-treu*, gained wide popularity; the official statements of the Yeshiva College and its authorities preferred the name, Traditional Judaism. The Conservatives were dissatisfied with their name (except for the active anti-Reform period in their history), and they used terms like Historical, Traditional, and Conservative interchangeably. Many preferred to drop the adjective altogether.

A second characteristic of this period was the refusal of the religious leadership to confine its role to that of the pastorate in American Jewish life. Reform leaders began to speak of relating their movement to the totality of American Jewish life; Orthodoxy sought to place all communal enterprises under the influence of Torah ideals; Conservative Judaism proclaimed that the synagogue should be the center of all Jewish activities.

This striving for an all embracing program was expressed in the first instance through an intensification of congregational activities and efforts. Memberships were increased, new departments established, personnel augmented. It was soon apparent, however, that the religiously unaffiliated were eagerly courted by each of the organized Jewish religious groups. The drive for possession was on. Each religious group planned to capture larger numbers for its special platform, and soon discovered that theological arguments and sectarian philosophies seemed irrelevant in broad areas of the Jewish community. Rivalry for primacy only led to further misunderstanding and confusion, particularly on the local scene. The American Jew did not comprehend the ideological differences which divided religious spokesmen. Native Jewish community life was primitive; a generation of de-Judaized Jews had grown up on American soil; to children, who did not learn about Judaism in Jewish schools, was presented a Judaism based on misconceptions and misinterpretations from the general world. Consequently, even when many Jews later did return to Jewish life, as a result of the Hitler catastrophe, they identified themselves principally with Jews, rather than with Judaism. This fact had to be faced by all Jewish religious groups. In the early years of the century, Jewish leaders had to meet the problem of Americanization; now it was the opposite problem: assimilation.

In their competition with each other all the religious groups soon discovered that each was emphasizing the same ideals for a healthy Jewish life in America: learning, scholarship, traditional values and ceremonials, the influence of Eretz Yisrael, ethical and social objectives.

The chapter heading for the history of Reform Judaism in these decades may well be entitled *Heshbon Ha-Nefesh* (Spiritual Re-evaluation). Reform had drifted from the people. The events that led to the Columbus platform in 1937 were signs of the return.

Julian Morgenstern was elected president of the Hebrew Union College in 1921. Under his direction, the school grew in strength and scope. Intensely engaged in biblical scholarship all the days of his busy presidential years, Morgenstern came to symbolize the combination of modern American Jewish scholar-administrator. He conceived the Hebrew Union College to be the focal institution in American Judaism and consecrated himself to this purpose. New faculty appointments were made.[51] Courses were added to the curriculum: religious education, pastoral psychology, Jewish music, and American Jewish history. A younger group of scholars, many of them graduates of the college, were invited to join the faculty.[52] Qualified students were encouraged to pursue postgraduate research work in international capitals of learning, and exchange lectureships with Christian theological seminaries were established. In 1924 the college began the publication of the *Hebrew Union College Annual*, the only scholarly publication of its kind in America. It has appeared regularly since the first issue.

During these years the library of the college grew to magnificent proportions including some 125,000 books and pamphlets, 3,000 manuscripts, 10,000 Jewish art and ceremonial objects, and about 130 incunabula. The Teachers Institute, after conducting summer sessions from 1926 to 1936, resumed its earlier practice of arranging special seminar meetings in local cities.[53] One of Morgenstern's most significant contributions was the establishment of a college-in-exile during the years of the Hitler regime. Foremost scholars, who might otherwise never have survived the world cataclysm, were saved to continue in Cincinnati their fruitful work.

Morgenstern always possessed a passionate faith in American Reform Judaism as the only philosophy of Judaism which adjusted itself consciously and sympathetically to modern life. As he continued in office, he came to believe that all three religious groups in America would ultimately be one, and in the final union, he foresaw the principles of American Reform as dominant. The differentia between Judaism and other American social units, he predicted, would be essentially theological. National elements in Judaism would be reduced to a minimum, but a consciousness of membership in the world Jewish community would prevail. The Jewish people will think of itself as a distinct, chosen people with a destiny to fulfil God's revelation, and American Israel would then be the *Ebed Adonai*, the servant of the Almighty.

To the ranks of Reform Judaism was added a second higher institution of learning when the Jewish Institute of Religion was established in New York in 1922. The new rabbinical school was a symbol of the bold and free spirit which America and the world came to know in the personality of Stephen S. Wise. From the very beginning, both in the selection of faculty and student body, the Institute fully lived up to its declared purpose of creating a school where "the different constructions of Judaism and of Jewish life, orthodox, conservative, liberal, radical Zionist, and non-Zionist, are expounded to the students in courses given by men representing different points of view." A four story building was erected by the Free Synagogue for the combined use of the Synagogue and the Institute. Originally the faculty consisted of Jewish and Christian guest lecturers. Dr. Wise soon succeeded in creating a permanent faculty.[54] In a brief span of years, largely through the indomitable efforts of its president, the Institute rose to an important position in higher Jewish academic circles through its library, lectureships, publications, and scores of graduates prepared for leadership in the rabbinate, Jewish education, and other areas of community service.

Wise's attempt to bring greater unity into American Judaism by training a rabbinate at a common center, despite individual differences in religious orientation, did not materialize in practice. Dedicated as "the only inter-denominational school for the training of rabbis in America," the Institute virtually became a New York Reform college, for most of the graduates, inspired by the thought and deed of the founder-president, affiliated themselves with the Central Conference of American Rabbis. Only a small group later chose to join the Rabbinical Assembly of America. As the work of the Institute progressed, and as the thesis of its trans-sectarianism proved untenable in the pattern of American Jewish religious life, a merger between the Cincinnati and New York schools became eminently desirable for both institutions.[55] In the full score of Reform Judaism's development, the Jewish Institute of Religion represents the accents of community, international Jewish solidarity, and Zionism-Hebraism, so sadly lacking in classic Reform's formulation.

In the meantime, the work of the Union of American Hebrew Congregations continued apace. The National Federation of Temple Sisterhoods had been organized in 1913; ten years later the National Federation of Temple Brotherhoods was created "to stimulate interest in Jewish worship, Jewish studies, social service and other kindred activities." The work of the Jewish Chautauqua Society advanced considerably. Lectures on Judaism and Jewish problems were assigned to hundreds of colleges throughout the United States and Canada. A union of temple youth groups, the National Federation of Temple Youth, was established in 1939. Regional departments of the Union were organized in 1931 to secure greater co-operation between the isolated settlements and the larger communities, as well as to raise the standards of Jewish education in the smaller towns. The Union functioned through a series of commissions, most of them in co-operation with the Central Conference of American Rabbis. The former Tract Commission became the Commission on Information about Judaism. It published a series of studies on a wide variety of historical and contemporary subjects. The reorganized Commission on Jewish Education (1923) and the newly created Joint Committee on Ceremonies (1936) represented revolutionary departures in Reform activities. In 1926, the Union, wishing to extend the influence of Reform Judaism to other countries, founded the World Union for Progressive Judaism. The new organization, however, was seriously resisted in Europe and therefore made little headway.

The beginning of ideological evaluation is stocktaking. In 1931 the Commission on Research of the Union, under the directorship of Abraham N. Franzblau, supervised "a survey of the homes of members of Reform Congregations affiliated with the Union of American Hebrew Congregations in the eleven cities of the United States which have a Jewish population of over fifty thousand."[56] This study disclosed the great lag between the *avant garde* leaders and their congregational constituents. It did indicate, however, the loyalties and attachments to Judaism of the affiliated membership, and the basis upon which a convinced leadership could build a more intensive synagogue program.

The forum and the tribunal for the developing Reform movement were the annual conventions of the Central Conference of American Rabbis. The volumes of proceedings of the Conference include symposia, scholarly papers, and resolutions reflecting the profound changes that came over Reform Judaism. Reform leaders must recognize, Dr. Samuel Schulman once said, that Reform was a revolutionary movement and, like all revolutionary movements, it went too far. "Reform Congregations continue the process of reforming," Dr. Solomon B. Freehof wrote in a similar vein, "They do not hesitate to change not only the practices of Orthodoxy but even the earlier practices of Reform itself." Thus did the highest and most effective form of criticism, self-criticism, emanate from the leadership. Retreat from earlier Reform attitudes toward education, worship, Jewish practice and ceremony, and Eretz Yisrael was demanded. It was a battle in which the very foundations of the movement rocked. After steady and unceasing struggle, the intensivists emerged victorious.

In 1923 the Commission on Education brought Emanuel Gamoran to

Cincinnati. Within two decades, Gamoran, a Zionist and Hebraist, who fully understood the inherent values of Jewish ceremony and observance in Jewish tradition, helped chart a new approach to the education of the young. His program of educational action included the intensification of Jewish life, the introduction of Jewish practice into the home, straightforward propaganda for the increased use of Hebrew in the curriculum, the development of weekday instruction in the Reform school system and the higher priority rating of Jewish education in the schedule of Reform organizational activities. These views were slowly and democratically impressed on the main line of rabbinic and lay Reform leaders. In time, because of the high caliber of his work and extraordinary standards of book production, the texts that Gamoran prepared were used in many Orthodox and Conservative schools. History texts, for example, were produced under the guiding principle that no religious party should be offended by their contents. In such progressive manner did Reform educational methodology reflect the deeper stirrings in the movement.

The accepted forms of the Reform prayer service were more emotionally rooted. Little was done until the criticism against the Union Prayer Book became an organized and formal complaint. In a special symposium held in 1930, the inadequacies of the Union Prayer Book were scored. Professor Bettan warned that "The Jew does not pray philosophy"; Professor Cohon stressed that the prayer book must speak to the hearts of all worshippers; Dr. Freehof called for a Union Prayer Anthology. Some asked for more Hebrew in the services; others for the re-identification of American Israel with the dream of Eretz Yisrael. Everyone urged greater congregational participation in the service.[57] Out of the welter of criticism and suggestions, another committee was appointed to prepare a basic revision of the prayer book.[58]

The Committee on Ceremonies was more practical. It embarked upon a program of Jewish ceremonial revival. The *kiddush*, the lighting of the candles, the traditional Sabbath melodies were reinstated; Hanukkah and Purim, virtually nonexistent in Reform practice, were introduced; the public *Seder* gave new communal meaning to the Passover; the *Shofar* was heard again at the High Holy Day service; Sukkot was re-established as a consecration festival.

From synagogue, to school, to home. The following quotation from an official report by Rabbi Jacob D. Schwarz reflects the complete turnabout from the earlier days of deceremonialization in Reform practice:

If, as we believe, the perpetuation and advancement of Judaism depend on the cultivation of Jewish life, the revival of ceremonies cannot stop with synagogue and school. It must penetrate the home, to make the home again the sanctuary of Jewish faith and practice. The traditional home was made Jewish by a regimen of prayer and song and ceremony and consecrated living. It will become Jewish again when Jewish observance, nurtured in synagogue and in Religious School, takes root and flourishes there within the family circle. When the rabbis took steps to replace, through the medium of the synagogue and all its agencies, ceremonies discarded in the home, their ultimate objective was a revival in the home. By teaching the children and by presenting ceremonial object lessons, as it were, in the synagogue, they hoped to restore the spirit of knowledge and understanding that was so woefully lacking and to create an appreciation of symbolism and a desire for ceremony that would make home observance not only possible but also devoutly wished.

Some results are already apparent. Through the children the Jewish holidays have become more intimate and are being brought back in some measure to the home. Hanukkah candles put in the hands of the children have kept the home lights burning; the school Seder has encouraged the restoration of the home Seder, as has the public Seder in general. The introduction of Sabbath songs and ceremonies in the synagogue has brought closer their revival in the home. Sukkot symbolism, exemplified by the table Sukkah and other decorative motifs, is adapting itself anew to the home. Congregations are beginning officially to urge upon their congregants the restoration of the Jewish home observance and are furnishing suggestions and materials to that end. Thus, the synagogue has become the instrument and the home the objective for the revival of ceremonies in these modern days.[59]

The road to unity on the Palestine issue was paved on the floor of the annual conventions. In 1935 the classic anti-Zionist formula was discarded and the famous neutrality clause adopted in its stead. The final reading was as follows:

Whereas, at certain foregoing conventions of the Central Conference of American Rabbis, resolutions have been adopted in opposition to Zionism, and. . . .

Whereas, we are persuaded that acceptance or rejection of the Zionist program should be left to the determination of the individual members of the Conference themselves, therefore

Be It Resolved, That the Central Conference of American Rabbis takes no official stand on the subject of Zionism, and be it further

Resolved, That in keeping with its oft-announced intentions, the Central Conference of American Rabbis will continue to co-operate in the upbuilding of Palestine, and in the economic, cultural, and particularly spiritual tasks confronting the growing and evolving Jewish community there.[60]

The time had come for a new official platform. At Columbus, Ohio, on May 27, 1937, fifty-two years after the Pittsburgh platform had been adopted, a new set of guiding principles of Reform Judaism was formulated. Under three main divisions—Judaism and its foundations, ethics, and religious practice—the debates and discussions of two decades were crystallized into a compromise program.[61]

There was much unhappiness on the right and on the left with the

Columbus declaration.[61a] To those who now became an organized minority, this was the beginning of the end; to the victors, it was but a temporary respite in the battle for greater intensification of Judaism. During the following decade, the intensivists achieved victory. Reform Judaism redefined its entire program in accordance with the objectives foreshadowed in the period of *Heshbon Ha-Nefesh*.

Orthodoxy in this period in America was passing through a stage of transition—transition in methodology and techniques, not in basic belief or ritual practice. The European-trained, Yiddish-speaking rabbinate and their American-schooled, English-speaking associates worked in separate camps, but preached the same doctrine of the supernatural revelation of the written and oral law and the scrupulous observance of the commandments of the Torah, as interpreted in the Talmud and codified in the *Shulhan Aruk*. In the course of events, disagreements developed in substance as well as in form.

For Orthodox Jews the Rabbi Isaac Elchanan Theological Seminary met the demands of the modern American scene with creative force. In 1928 the pathfinding decision to incorporate a fully equipped American college under Orthodox auspices, was carried through. The establishment of the Yeshiva College was duly authorized by an amendment in the charter of the Rabbi Isaac Elchanan Theological Seminary, and in September, 1928, the college was opened in temporary quarters at the Jewish Center in New York with a mixed faculty of Jewish and Christian scholars. It fulfilled the dual purpose of raising a Jewishly trained laity in America and offering Orthodox rabbis a fine secular education.

The entrance of the Yeshiva into the field of general education was but one of the important tasks which this pioneering institution had assumed for itself under the presidency of Dr. Revel. In 1921 the Teachers Institute, which had been founded four years earlier by the Mizrachi Organization of America as the first teacher training institution established under Orthodox auspices in the world, was incorporated as a regular department of the Yeshiva. Pinkhas Churgin became dean of the Institute. In 1937 as an outgrowth of graduate courses first offered in 1935, the Yeshiva Graduate School was formally opened. Eminent Jewish scholars were brought to these faculties.[62]

The financing of this program was a tremendous undertaking for the modest means of Orthodox Jewry and its constituencies. Not only were funds unavailable; the entire project was jeered at in many sanctimonious quarters. Promises of aid were no sooner made than they were promptly forgotten. Dr. Revel and his associates continued in a spirit of enthusiasm and courage. In December, 1924, a building fund for the Yeshiva College was launched; in May, 1927, the cornerstone of the new institution was laid on a site at Amsterdam Avenue and 186th Street; in December, 1928, the new structure which had been reared was finally dedicated.[63]

The Yeshiva soon embarked upon a series of scholarly publications. The *Scripta Mathematica*, a quarterly journal devoted to the philosophy, history, and expository treatment of mathematics, appeared in September, 1932, and has subsequently earned an international reputation for its excellence. In 1934 Dr. Churgin founded the semiannual *Horeb*, a magazine devoted to Jewish history and Hebrew literature.[64]

Higher Jewish education made further headway under Orthodox auspices in the Midwest. After much struggle and indecision, the Beth Ha-Medrash La-Torah, the Hebrew Theological College, was established in Chicago in 1921 for the purpose of preparing Orthodox rabbis, teachers, and lay leaders. The curriculum provided a four year prerabbinical (high school) course to be followed by a seven-year rabbinical training course. While attending the rabbinical school, the student was required to take general studies leading to a college degree. The final three years were to be devoted entirely to rabbinic studies. In 1922 Rabbi Saul Silber (1881-1946), spiritual leader of the Anshe Sholom Congregation in Chicago, was elected president, an office he held until the time of his death; Rabbi Jacob Greenberg became the dean.[65] The college attracted a student body primarily from Chicago and the Midwest, but included young scholars from other parts of the country as well. Scholarships and dormitory facilities were provided. Within a decade the school population grew to some 450 students, of whom 125 prepared for the rabbinate. The others were registered in preparatory or teachers' courses. The first class was graduated in 1925; in 1938 a library fund drive was completed; in September, 1940, the Teachers' Institute of the College was officially established. As the graduates of the high school and college entered into the many walks of Jewish lay and professional service throughout the country, it was demonstrated that Orthodoxy had established a firm center of higher Jewish learning in the Midwest.[66] Shortly, the young American-trained graduates of both the eastern and midwestern Orthodox rabbinical schools, were to join hands and bring their two alumni associations into one national rabbinic body. Other alumni, who preferred to associate themselves with the Conservative movement, entered the ranks of the Rabbinical Assembly of America.

The lay organization from which Orthodoxy in America derived its chief strength remained the Union of Orthodox Jewish Congregations of America. A chain of affiliates was soon established corresponding to the varying age levels and interest groups of the movement. The Women's Branch (founded 1923), consisting of the sisterhoods of the congregations, organized and sponsored a Hebrew teachers' training school for girls, the Ha-Banot clubs for adolescent girls and the Jewish University Club, for

Orthodox college youth. The National Union of Orthodox Jewish Youth completed the organizational framework.

The Union and its agencies embarked on a program of expansion and intensification. The established forms of American organizational procedure were adopted. However, one of the singular attempts of the Union which transcended strict religious party lines was the effort to standardize *kashrut* endorsement and supervision. The conflict over *kashrut* was so uncontrolled that the Union felt compelled to enter the field officially in order to protect the interests and good name of Judaism. A special Rabbinical Council was appointed with Dr. Leo Jung as chairman. In its capacity of rabbinic advisory board to the Union, it was the Council's duty to render decisions upon questions of Jewish law and to raise the standards of *kashrut* enforcement throughout the country. The Union established a policy of limiting the costs of rabbinic supervision to a minimum.[67] One of the most important acts passed by the Rabbinical Council under the administration of Dr. Jung was the condemnation of *heksherim* (endorsements) granted by individuals without regard for the social consequences involved. Vested interests were fought off. In many instances, these questions were brought before the bar of legal state opinion The Council even appeared before the Supreme Court of Ottawa in an important decision. In 1934 as part of this trend, Governor Herbert H. Lehman established the Division of Kosher Law Enforcement as a section of the Bureau of Food Control under the New York State Department of Agriculture and Markets. It was in this year that the New York legislature first appropriated funds for the implementation of the law which had been on the books since 1922. These efforts on the part of the Union while extremely worthy in each individual case, did not succeed in solving the profounder problems of *kashrut* observance in America. But they did establish a precedent of communal interest, control and sanction.

The Union was not the only lay organization that functioned on behalf of Orthodox Jewry. Orthodoxy in America had segments of rightists, centrists and liberals. In the thirties, for example, largely as a result of increased immigration from Poland, Germany and Central Europe, the neo-Hasidic, Agudas Israel, and German congregational movements found new sources of strength. The Hasidic movement was considered a strange plant in American soil even by many of its own most ardent devotees. While its numbers increased slightly, it did not show signs of becoming part of the American Jewish milieu. Among the first of the Hasidic rabbis to establish the order and service of the Hasidic movement in America after World War I was Rabbi Joshua Heschel Rabinowitz (1860-1938), known as the Monastrishtcher Rabbi, and author of numerous works on Hasidism. He was one of the founders of the Union of Grand Rabbis of the United States and Canada (organized in 1928). The influence of these men was confined and limited to special small coteries. In March, 1940, the Lubavitcher Rabbi, Joseph Isaac Schneersohn, came to America with his family and entourage. The impact of this personality on the educational system of the Orthodox was phenomenal. Day schools and *yeshibot* were established in sections of the land where such efforts were formerly inconceivable. It is interesting to note that many of the Yiddishist and Hebraist culturalists found an intrinsic emotional and aesthetic appeal in this Hasidic movement.

A more remarkable resurgence in the ranks of Orthodox Jewry was the growth of the Sephardic community in America. Although many a nineteenth century writer predicted their extinction, the Sephardic Jews have recently come into a new pulsating community life. At the turn of the century, a trickle of immigration, chiefly from the Middle East and the Balkans, forecast the renewal of Sephardic congregational life in the United States. The majority of Sephardim settled in New York City; others dispersed among the larger cities of the country. In New York they found the lower East Side and Harlem most congenial, for they shared the limited economic lot of other immigrant groups. In religious life they were completely isolated from their Ashkenazic brethren, speaking neither English nor Yiddish. During this period the Sephardic newcomers were as disorganized on their limited scale as were their East European brethren on a larger one. The basis of organization was the city of origin. In 1912 the first attempt to organize the various groups resulted in the formation of the Federation of Oriental Jews of America, whose purpose was the creation of "a forum where communal problems are discussed and presented to the Oriental Community for solution." These problems related to Americanization, immigration, employment, and social welfare. But the Federation ultimately ceased functioning because of the indifference of its members.

A second attempt at organization was made in 1924. Almost all the Ladino-speaking groups were united into the Sephardic Jewish community of New York. The organization conducted a community center in Harlem which included a synagogue, a Talmud Torah, a youth program, and adult social services. It also sponsored two schools in the Bronx where the Sephardim were beginning to settle, and a Talmud Torah on the East Side. The depression wiped out all these centralized efforts and the community was dissolved once again. But the groundwork had been laid for a renewal of activity which took place on an unprecedented scale after the arrival, during World War II, of Dr. Nissim J. Ovadia (1890-1942), former chief rabbi of the Sephardic community of Vienna and Paris.[68]

Far more indicative of the fundamental transformation which American Orthodoxy was undergoing, was the growth of the Young Israel movement, which in its act of incorporation in 1926 declared as its purpose, "To awaken a love for orthodox Judaism and the Jewish people within the hearts of American Jewish youth." The Young Israel movement began in 1912 as an effort on the part of young people to establish, within traditional Judaism, surroundings where the disheartening aspects of the East Side synagogues would be eliminated. The movement was inspired and activated by Israel Friedlaender, Judah Magnes and Mordecai M. Kaplan. At first the group was gathered together for Friday night lectures. Then, in 1915, it established a model synagogue in one of the rooms of the Educational Alliance. Religious services were held "with the dignified practice of proper decorum, and with the added interests of congregational singing, abolition of commercialism, delivery of sermons in English, and a synopsis of the weekly portion or *sidra*." Social activities for youth were an important part of their program. In a very short time, as the original membership began to move away from the lower East Side, similar organizations were formed in other sections of the city. Before long an important national movement was under way. In 1922 a Council of Young Israel was formed to centralize the various activities and to serve as the authoritative body of the entire movement. At this meeting, the bond of relationship with the founding leaders was broken and the Young Israel identified itself completely with the Orthodox group. In 1939 about thirty-five synagogues were associated in the National Council. The well rounded program of Young Israel's activities in the fields of Sabbath observance, Zionism, youth and adult education, defense of Jewish rights, synagogal activities, *kashrut* enforcement, and social activities, fully reflects the efforts made by the organization to bring the older and newer generations of Orthodoxy together and to create an indigenous American Orthodoxy for the youth of America.

The gradual replacement of the European *rabbanim* with an American-trained rabbinate, completed the cycle of change in American Orthodoxy. A new type of Orthodox rabbi grew out of the American experience. While the younger men sought a unified front with the Agudath Ha-Rabbanim in questions of Jewish ideology and national Jewish policy, they found it impossible to work within the ranks of the older group. They therefore determined to form a separate organization. The Rabbinical Council of America grew out of a union in 1935 between the original Council (which was organized in 1923 as the advisory arm of the Union of Orthodox Jewish Congregations) and the Rabbinical Association of the Rabbi Isaac Elchanan Theological Seminary, the alumni body of the Yeshiva. The new organization opened its membership rolls to all duly ordained Orthodox rabbis who had *Semika* from a recognized Yeshiva or from two recognized authoritative Orthodox rabbis, in addition to one year of service in the active Orthodox rabbinate. In 1936 the graduates of the Hebrew Theological College in Chicago organized their own alumni association. Further consolidation was thought desirable, and the amalgamation between the eastern and western rabbinical bodies was arranged in 1942.[69] With the establishment of an authorized American trained, national Orthodox rabbinical association, native American Orthodoxy came of age.

The records of the Agudath Ha-Rabbanim reveal how little the group understood the social forces that were radically changing the American scene. Nevertheless the efforts of this group produced excellent results (considering its limited energies) in matters relating to European relief and intercession. The *yeshivot* and religious institutions in Europe were its special interest. In 1924 when word came from Lithuania that the government had passed discriminatory legislation against the Jews which resulted in the enforced closing of religious institutions, the Agudath Ha-Rabbanim influenced important political action in Washington. With the beginning of the Nazi regime and the conquest of Europe, the specially created Vaad Ha-Hatzala (Committee for Rescue) carried on vigorous and, in many cases, highly successful, efforts for immediate relief, escape, and support of Jewish victims. This aspect of Orthodoxy's history is a noble and as yet unwritten chapter of devotion and sacrifice.[70]

In the overall picture of Orthodox influence and achievement, the Mizrachi Organization of America has a special place. The Zionist members of the Reform movement joined either the centrist Zionist Organization of America or the Poale Zion (Workers of Zion). The Conservatives in largest numbers entered the Zionist Organization of America; some of their members joined the Poale Zion or the Mizrachi Organization. The Orthodox, however, built their own movement which organically represented both their religious and Zionist beliefs. The Mizrachi Organization was supported and financed almost exclusively by the various Orthodox agencies. The Orthodox rabbis and lay leaders formed the parent organization; the sisterhood members joined the Mizrachi Women's Organization; and the young people became affiliated with the junior groups. Several delegations of the antipolitical-Zionist Agudat Israel movement visited the United States. They founded an American wing of the movement, with their established purpose: "To solve in the spirit of the Torah all problems which confront Jewry from time to time in Eretz Yisrael and the Diaspora." But they made small impression on the broad masses of American Orthodoxy.[71] From the very beginning, in order to avoid an internal rift, the Agudath Ha-Rabbanim officially endorsed both the Agudat Israel and Mizrachi organizations. The heart of the people, however, was with political Zionist action. Thus the work of Mizrachi flourished.[72] The organic relationship between Mizrachi and American Orthodoxy had beneficial results on American Jewish life, particularly in Jewish education. Unlike the other political Zionist parties, Mizrachi embarked on an intensive program of educational effort in America, in addition to its propaganda and fund-raising work for Palestine.

In 1938 the Orthodox movement developed the United Yeshivos Foundation which, in the light of subsequent events, played a telling role in the advancement of Orthodox life and institutions. In very short time the educational structures of the Conservative and Reform movements also felt the impact of this intensive educational system. The Foundation was organized in the midst of the most depressing crisis in the history of the *yeshiva* movement. After a long list of failures in the attempt to coordinate *yeshiva* schools, a Central Board of Yeshiva Education was formed. This board concentrated on the raising of standards and unification of curricula in the *yeshiva* schools. Then a secular Yeshiva Board of Education was organized which served as liaison with the New York State Board of Regents in Albany. Within a comparatively brief period of eight years (1938-1946), the *yeshiva* parochial school movement grew from fourteen schools with an approximate enrollment of 4,000 students to eighty-four day schools with an enrollment of 17,500. These figures of increase do not represent the profounder development. As one of their spokesmen put it: "One of the main aims of the United Yeshivos Foundation was to bring out the *yeshiva* movement from the ghetto to the broad American avenue. This we achieved fully. The idea of the *yeshiva* parochial school has taken root in American soil. . . ."[73]

As the younger American Orthodox elements assumed control and responsibility for the destiny of American Orthodoxy, they began to appraise their problem realistically. Could they arrest the progressive dwindling of their numbers? Could they create an "Orthodox Jewish Front" which could speak authoritatively on behalf of a united and integrated American Orthodoxy? Could they meet the challenge of other Jewish religious groups who had formulated a program of adjustment to modern conditions and particularly to the American scene? Could they train the coming generation in the belief and practice of the ritual laws, as expressly formulated in the legal codes? These were the crucial questions which the new Orthodox rabbinic, lay and congregational leadership had to answer as a new era in Jewish history dawned upon American Jewry. Despite the imperfections they knew had to be reckoned with in their movement and approach, the Orthodox leaders believed that the survival of American Judaism depended on unification in the spirit of Orthodoxy.

During this period, the Conservative movement was the most rapidly developing religious group in American Judaism. Scores of new congregations affiliated with the United Synagogue; a constant stream of students turned from the Orthodox preparatory *yeshibot* to study at the Seminary's rabbinical school. American Israel clearly required a synagogue program which was traditional in thought and practice, modern in its recognition of the validity of change, Zionist in orientation, and Hebraic in spirit.

Cyrus Adler, who became acting president of the Seminary after the death of Schechter, was elected president in 1924. He served in office until his death in 1940. In his interpretation of Conservative Judaism, Adler reasserted the Leeser formula of an adjectiveless Judaism; in community relationships, he endeavored to transcend all factionalism; although he was head of two higher institutions of learning and many kindred societies he nevertheless refused to use his vast influence in other associations for his own institutional purposes. As a leader and administrator of rare gifts, Adler's guidance was sought by American Israel in many official capacities. But his outlook was fundamentally spiritual and his conception of Judaism essentially religious. Adler's doctrine of active faith, stated as early as 1894, helped him remain staunch in his views even when he stood as a minority of one:

I will continue to hold my banner aloft. I find myself born—aye, born—into a people and a religion. The preservation of my people must be for a purpose, for God does nothing without a purpose. His reasons are unfathomable to me, but on my own reason I place little dependence; test it where I will it fails me. The simple, the ultimate in every direction is sealed to me. It is as difficult to understand matter as mind. The courses of the planets are no harder to explain than the growth of a blade of grass. Therefore am I willing to remain a link in the great chain. What has been preserved for four thousand years was not saved that I should overthrow it. My people have survived the prehistoric paganism, the Babylonian polytheism, the aesthetic Hellenism, the sagacious Romanism, at once the blandishments and persecutions of the Church; and it will survive the modern dilettantism and the current materialism, holding aloft the traditional Jewish ideals inflexibly until the world shall become capable of recognizing their worth.[73]*

During Adler's incumbency, the Seminary continued to maintain the scholarly integrity for which it had already gained international renown. Additional faculty members were required to teach the expanding student body.[74] The Seminary Library, containing about 117,000 printed books and pamphlets, and about 7,800 manuscripts, became the largest and finest collection of Hebraica and Judaica in the world. Because of its growing importance and the need for a special board to manage its treasures, the library was chartered in 1924 as a separate corporation.

The Museum of Jewish Ceremonial Objects of the Seminary was opened in 1931 as an adjunct to the library, under the direction of Professor Alexander Marx. Its growth was enhanced in 1939 through the addition of the notable collection of Dr. H. G. Friedman. Later, through the gift of Mrs. Warburg, the Museum became a separate department of the Seminary and moved to expansive quarters in the former home of Mr. and

Mrs. Felix M. (Frieda Schiff) Warburg at 92nd Street and Fifth Avenue.[75]

The Teachers Institute expanded considerably. In response to the petition of the Jewish youth educational institutions in New York, the extension department of the Institute was formed in 1921, called the Israel Friedlaender Classes, with the purpose of offering Jewish youth nonprofessional Jewish training. The motto selected for the Friedlaender Classes was *Torah Lishmah* (study for its own sake). Under the direction of its founder and guiding spirit, Israel S. Chipkin, the school soon became a model for similar ventures in adult Jewish education throughout the country.[76] In 1929 the Seminary College of Jewish Studies was created as the academic department of the Teachers Institute. The Seminary outgrew the Schiff building on 123rd Street, and moved to its present quarters at 122nd Street and Broadway. It was the climax of a half century of vision, tireless effort, and devotion.

In this period the Conservative movement also enlarged the scope of its activities in the congregations. The United Synagogue was considered by Dr. Schechter as "the greatest bequest that I shall leave to American Israel." Without a strong and vibrant congregational base, Conservatism would have remained an academy, not a movement. Within two decades, some 400 congregations were affiliated with the national organization; the National Women's League had been established in 1917; the Young People's League in 1921; the National Federation of Jewish Men's Clubs in 1929. In addition to these strictly organizational activities, the United Synagogue pioneered in religious educational programs for Boy Scout camps, in cultural centers at universities, and in pedagogic curricula for the congregational school.[77]

One of the most significant trends in the Conservative congregational system was the development of the synagogue-center movement. Professor Kaplan had inspired and founded the first such institution in New York City in 1918. "The Jewish Center" as developed by Kaplan, represented the institutional integration of religion, education, and recreation based on the traditional threefold function of the synagogue as a place of worship, study, and fellowship.[78] The second synagogue-center was the Brooklyn Jewish Center, of which Israel H. Levinthal became the spiritual leader. "Institutional synagogues" with the similar purpose of providing a full and varied program of Jewish activities under congregational auspices, were later developed by the Orthodox. In line with its effort to develop this type of synagogue movement as the pattern for the future, the magazine established by the United Synagogue in 1940 was named *The Synagogue Center*.

An important undertaking of the United Synagogue, was the building and support of a synagogue-center in Jerusalem. This project was designed to render for the Jews of Jerusalem the same services as those of the synagogue-center in America. Moreover, it was intended as a vital bridge between Conservative Jewry in the United States and the rapidly growing Yishuv. The Jerusalem Center was auspiciously dedicated by Dr. Levinthal in 1926, in the presence of Chief Rabbi Kook, Nahum Sokolow, Menahem M. Ussishkin, and other Eretz Yisrael leaders. Unfortunately, the plans were not completed, and the deed to the land was given to the Jewish National Fund. The lapse of the United Synagogue's interest in this center project is all the more lamented, for the Yishuv in Eretz Yisrael had no notion of Jewish traditional religious life other than East European Orthodoxy, and the Center would have given Conservative Judaism an opportunity to be of great service to the developing spiritual life of Eretz Yisrael.

The third sphere of expansion in the Conservative movement was the Rabbinical Assembly of The Jewish Theological Seminary, originally organized as an alumni body of the Seminary. In 1919 it changed its name to the Rabbinical Assembly of America, and in so doing, it also redefined its scope and purpose. Membership was opened to graduates of other rabbinical seminaries in America and abroad, who wished to identify themselves with the Conservative group. In the threefold division of responsibilities within the movement, the Rabbinical Assembly became, in consultation with the other two agencies, the legislative body. The Assembly was described as the motive power of Conservative Judaism. In its attempt to evolve a specific program of action, the Assembly was perforce required to come to grips with its philosophy of Judaism in relation to the daily problems of Jewish life in America and most particularly, with those in the field of Jewish ritual and practice.

The unresolved, recurring question at every convention was: what is Conservative Judaism? Many, like Cyrus Adler and Louis Ginzberg, contended that the adjective "Conservative" should be eliminated; some leading alumni, including Solomon Goldman and David Aronson, maintained that the term should be more specific and definitive. All Conservative Jews accepted the formula that Judaism is a changing and developing religion. The difference of opinion revolved about the procedures for implementing "the changing and developing" aspects of Judaism. The advocates of the theory of obsolescence argued that Catholic Israel will itself determine what laws are to be abrogated and what laws retained in the permanent system of Judaism. Others, who could not suffer the steady disintegration of Jewish legal sanction, proposed immediate collective revision of the ritual law. A third group counseled that both these viewpoints be incorporated into an organic Judaism, for "these and these are the words of the living God."

The predominant group in the Rabbinical Assembly shared the views of Professor Ginzberg. The Committee on Jewish Law was especially influenced by his learning and advice. Ginzberg's attitude toward the interpretation of Jewish practice was fully expressed on many occasions. In an address delivered at the United Synagogue convention on the theme of "Judaism and Modern Thought," Professor Ginzberg stressed the view that private judgment cannot be held up against the collective judgment of *Kelal Israel*. He was not unaware of the gravity of the problems that confronted modern congregations, including: the organ question, seating of men and women together, the use of electricity on the Sabbath, membership rights for a Jew married out of the faith. Nevertheless, he warned:

Tampering with the laws and regulations of the Talmud harbors great danger. It is very easy to discard them but extremely difficult to put something better, yes, something else, in their place. And who are the men today that could take the place of the great saints and religious geniuses of the Talmudic times? They may have had their shortcomings, but they were those of their times while their virtues were their own; our shortcomings are our own; our virtues those of our times. . . .

. . . It is, however, the Synagogue one and indivisible from which we may hope for the solution of our difficulties, but not the synagogues.

The Synagogue is the essential, but the synagogues are accidental. It is one of the most grievous misfortunes of modern Jewry that many are found who are willing to sacrifice the essentials for the sake of the accidental. If, indeed, the Synagogue is to remain a genteel and fashionable communion for the rich and happy, as it has been in some measure in modern times, then it may indulge in any incongruity or monstrosity for any length of time; but if the Synagogue is to be as it has been in our glorious past; if it is to be real and to encounter the realities of human life; need, sickness, pain, affliction, sin, doubt, despair; if it is to match the great ills, which it was sent to the world to overcome; it must express the religious soul of Israel and not the vagaries of those who are tossed about with every wind of thought that may chance to blow from the cave of Aeolus.[79]

Although the law committee of the Rabbinical Assembly deliberated and voted its decisions in the spirit of this judgment, in effect every effort was made to keep congregations within the Conservative fold, even if they deviated in individual practices. This precedent had been established by Schechter. Inquiring congregants were told that the law did not sanction instituting mixed pews or an organ, yet those changes alone were not sufficient reason for any individual to withdraw from the congregation. A festival prayer book was issued by the United Synagogue in two versions. One was prepared for those congregations wishing to change the traditional petition for the return of the sacrificial order; the official version, on the other hand, retained the historical prayer service in every detail. Thorough study was made by Louis M. Epstein (1887-1949) of the *Agunah* problem, and a procedure completely within the legal tradition was adopted by the Rabbinical Assembly in regard to this vexing problem.[80] However, because of the outcry which was raised by the Orthodox rabbinate against this procedure, the Rabbinical Assembly withdrew from its established position.

In opposition to this prevailing school of thought in Conservative Judaism, there developed another school of opinion, of which Professor Kaplan was the focal personality. As early as 1915, Kaplan had launched an attack on the working hypothesis of the Conservative movement and its arch concept, Historical Judaism. Subsequently, other independent forces rose to challenge the official majority viewpoint. Chief among them was Solomon Goldman, rabbi of the Anshe Emet Congregation in Chicago, who formulated his interpretation in a series of addresses and articles later published in his volume, *A Rabbi Takes Stock*. He felt that "Jewish laws, customs and ceremonies must be searchingly studied. Many of them we will find obsolete—these we must lose no time in discarding if we hope to continue Jewish communal life. Many practices, however, we will have to retain because of their group binding value."[81]

It was Dr. Kaplan, however, who succeeded in consolidating the opposing forces into an organized group. He attracted to himself disciples and supporters for whom he became spokesman and ideologist. His closest associates among the members of the Assembly in this effort were Ira Eisenstein, Eugene Kohn, and Milton Steinberg (1903-1950). Kaplan presented his philosophy in his *Judaism As A Civilization* (1934), and became the founder of the Reconstructionist movement. Within a few years, he and his associates produced many volumes and brochures explaining the theory of their movement. The program of Reconstructionism was later graphically represented in a seal on the cover of the Reconstructionist magazine (established 1935). The explanation of the seal follows:

The form is that of a wheel. The hub of the wheel is Palestine, the center of Jewish civilization from which all the dynamic forces of Judaism radiate. Religion, culture and ethics are the spokes by which the vital influence of Palestine affects and stimulates Jewish life everywhere and enables it to make its contribution to the civilization of mankind. The wheel has an inner and an outer rim. The inner rim represents the Jewish community that even in the dispersion, maintains its contact with the Jewish civilization rooted in Palestine, by the spiritual bonds of religion, ethics and culture. The outer rim is the general community, for us the community of America, with which the Jewish civilization as lived by the Jewish community maintains contact at every point. The seal thus symbolizes the whole philosophy of the Reconstructionist movement.[82]

As regards Jewish practice, Kaplan was prepared, if necessary, to depart from traditional observances. He urged the development of new ceremonial patterns in keeping with the facts of Jewish living in modern times. He did not seek to freeze Jewish practice into a new code. Rather did he hope for the development of guides for ritual practice which would release new creative forces in the entire realm of religious life and experience.

During the early years of the movement, the Reconstructionists had to determine whether they would become a separate religious party or serve as a catalytic school of thought in American Judaism, permitting the individual Reconstructionist members to maintain their former institutional affiliations. They chose to remain a transparty school of thought. This decision became confused in the public mind as the Reconstructionist Foundation continued to publish religious works of a distinctive theology by the foremost exponents of the movement.[83] They are, therefore, frequently referred to as a fourth religious party in American Judaism. The example set by the Reconstructionist members of the Rabbinical Assembly, continuing to work within the framework of Conservative Judaism, had a salutary effect on the entire movement. It revealed the great wisdom of the minority in not confusing the part for the whole; it also revealed the commensurate wisdom of the majority in not using numbers to crush opposition and eliminate differences. Professor Kaplan, granted freedom to continue with his independent thinking, teaching and studies at the Seminary, even by those who disagreed most radically with him, devoted his talents, in collaboration with his colleagues, to the further intensification and consolidation of the Conservative movement and its institutions. As a result of this reintegration with the Seminary, there later developed the concept of expanding the Seminary into a University of Judaism.

Many of the younger alumni, while they were deeply impressed by Kaplan's analyses and interpretation, could not accept his whole program of Reconstruction. Many strenuously objected, for instance, to his ideas about ritual. Two groups were in the process of crystallization in the late thirties. The first group was led by a succession of presidents of the Rabbinical Assembly, Louis M. Levitsky, Robert Gordis and Israel M. Goldman. They demanded unequivocal formulation of Conservative Judaism vis-à-vis Reform and Orthodox Judaism, the adaptation of Jewish law to contemporary needs within the legal framework of traditional Judaism, and the development of a philosophy and literature which would establish Conservative Judaism as an aggressive ideological movement in American Israel. While they thoroughly disapproved of the radical changes of the Reconstructionists in the area of ritual practice, they were also unhappy with the temper of inaction represented in the Seminary faculty. They prodded the Rabbinical Assembly into decisive action. This group soon became the predominant voice in the counsels of the Rabbinical Assembly.[84] The chief exponents of the second group were Max Kadushin and Simon

Greenberg. They consistently underplayed the adjective, Conservative, and opposed all trends leading to the definitive reformulation of Conservative Judaism. In taking this position, they did not regard themselves as evading the problems of modern Judaism. Quite the contrary. They were most emphatic that the complexity, the fluidity, the organic character of life, and the imponderables of human affairs, defy in the present state of the Jewish world, any specific pattern of formal legislation. Any formulation of new guides could not possibly include the variety of practices which mark the lives of individual Jews and congregations. What then is their program for Conservative Judaism? To interpret the specific situation in Jewish life in terms of its organic relationship to the totality of the Jewish tradition, with a sympathetic understanding of the needs and demands of the changing times. This was what Schechter meant by the "positive-historic" approach of Catholic Israel. This point of view was developed in the writings of Dr. Kadushin; it was further extended and propounded in the councils of the Rabbinical Assembly by Dr. Greenberg.[85]

These deep stirrings within the Conservative movement did not lead to a splintering of forces, as was originally feared. While the points of difference were noted, the comprehensive body of common belief was also clarified. As early as 1927, when the first signs of the intellectual ferment began to take shape, Dr. Finkelstein, in a symposium called, "The Things That Unite Us," analyzed the cohesive elements of Conservative Judaism: the conception of God; the attitude toward the Torah; the attitude toward change in ceremonial; the attitudes toward Israel, Palestine and the Hebrew language; the Seminary.[86] In his discussion of the crucial question in Conservative Judaism, the attitude toward change in ceremonial law, Dr. Finkelstein wrote:

. . . the purpose that fills the minds of all of us is to maintain the Torah. None proposes to yield the marriage law or the Sabbath; the most rash among us have suggested only the abrogation of some customs, ceremonies and prohibitions that have arisen in the course of time, and of which the value is no longer evident to all. After all, Resh Lakish did say "Sometimes the transgression of part of the law is the saving of the whole of it." There is all the difference in the world between proposing a change in a single law for the sake of saving the Torah and disregarding the whole of the Torah.

Still, it cannot be denied that the attitude of permitting changes in the usage of Israel by individual congregations and rabbis is untraditional and revolutionary. . . .

As to the proposed innovations and new interpretations, there is none of us so bigoted as to refuse to cooperate with those who are attempting them, provided always that the ultimate purpose of the change is to strengthen the attachment of Israel to the whole of the Torah, and that it does not defeat its own end by striking at the fundamentals of Judaism.[87]

While the interpretations of each particular element in Dr. Finkelstein's analysis of Conservative Judaism's "consciousness of unity" may have varied, the constellation as a whole was overwhelmingly accepted by the entire movement. This was the uniqueness and underlying unity of Conservative Judaism as interpreted and bequeathed by Schechter, advanced by Adler and intensified by Finkelstein. As the Conservative movement rapidly expanded under the unifying influence and guidance of Dr. Finkelstein, the newly elected head of the Seminary, it demonstrated that the broad base of Conservative Judaism had within itself the power to build constructively while adjusting at the same time to the diversities within its ranks.

In addition to the Reform, Orthodox and Conservative movements, in the post World War I period other agencies developed whose contributions to the spiritual welfare of American Jewry were of lasting benefit. As the Jews became rooted in the large American cities, they had need for organized citywide sponsorship and supervision of their educational and cultural activities. The national religious institutions were neither prepared nor disposed to establish the necessary boards of Jewish education, libraries and colleges of Jewish studies, so vital to local Jewish life; while the local congregations of the various groups could not find a basis for co-operative effort. For a time a cultural vacuum was created. Soon community organization on a trans-religious-cultural basis began to fill the void. A new trend was discerned: the growth and subsequent communalization of educational institutions under metropolitan auspices.

Boards or bureaus of Jewish Education were established in Pittsburgh, Boston, Detroit, New York, Baltimore, and Chicago. Teacher training institutions were created under Educational Bureau auspices in Baltimore (Baltimore Hebrew College and Teachers Training School founded 1918), Chicago (College of Jewish Studies organized in 1924), and Boston (Hebrew Teachers College chartered in 1927). The Herzliah Hebrew Teachers Institute in New York City began to function in 1921.

In the area of elementary Jewish education, metropolitan boards of education went beyond their administrative and supervisory functions and assumed responsibility for the operation and direction of a communal Talmud Torah school system. For a time, this system seemed destined to become the established pattern throughout the country. Before long, however, the place and purpose of the communal Talmud Torah system was contested by a rapidly developing congregational school system. The individual congregation was zealous for the loyalty of its children; the rabbi and the congregational board refused to relinquish their privilege to train the children of their members. They further insisted on the right of direct religious indoctrination.

The conflict between the congregational and communal education viewpoints halted the progress of the Bureau of Jewish Education movement. Indeed, for a considerable time, the entire field of Jewish education was injured, for the roof of one educational system was taken off, before the foundations of another system had been built. In the premature transition from a communal to congregational school program, many losses were suffered. The enrollment fell, the cost per child increased, classes were smaller, the teaching less proficient, and supervision not as readily available. The leaders of both opinions searched for a solution. The rabbis and congregations recognized their educational shortcomings. They were ready to participate in a communal board of education with the provision that they could be free to conduct their schools in accordance with their own interpretations of Jewish life. The educators also were prepared to revamp their program. They reckoned with the changes which had come over Jewish life. They realized that the congregation would probably be the basic educational unit in the future Jewish educational structure. It would therefore be the function of the communal agency to advise, counsel and aid the congregational school to realize its own objectives.

Another indication of the general trend to develop local foci of culture and scholarship in the major cities of America and to spread Jewish education into the broader reaches of the community, was the establishment of chairs of Jewish learning and special collections of Judaica in the great universities. Jewish scholarship in America, with the outstanding exception of the Dropsie College, seemed heretofore to be the exclusive concern of the various national rabbinical seminaries. Now it was slowly being spread into the broader reaches of the community through independent and specially created agencies. The Nathan Littauer chair in Jewish literature and philosophy was endowed at Harvard in 1925 and the Miller Foundation for Jewish history, literature and institutions was endowed at Columbia in 1929. Notable collections of Judaica and Hebraica had already found their way into the Jewish Division of the New York Public Library and the Semitic Division of the Library of Congress. Famous collections of Jewish scholars were acquired by the libraries of Harvard University, the University of Texas, Columbia University, and the College of the City of New York, while the Sutro Library in San Francisco opened a valuable collection on the west coast. The Alexander Kohut Memorial Foundation created a large Jewish scientific library at Yale University and published a considerable number of scholarly works. The American Academy for Jewish Research was organized in 1920, providing opportunities for scholarly discussion and publication. The Yiddish Scientific Institute (YIVO) established in 1925 with its center in Vilna, Poland, transferred its possessions and center of activity to New York City in 1940.

On the campus proper, in addition to the effective work of the Menorah Society (founded 1906) and Avukah (founded 1925), the National Hillel

Foundation movement was launched under the sponsorship of B'nai B'rith. It is of especial interest that the Hillel movement, although supported by a national fraternal organization, adopted the techniques of student organization devised by various Christian denominations. It therefore assumed a religio-cultural-social character. From the very beginning, the Hillel Foundations were led by rabbis and scholars. The first Foundation was established at the University of Illinois in 1923, by a newly ordained rabbi, Benjamin Frankel. In 1933 Dr. Abram L. Sachar became director of the national Hillel Foundations. Under his brilliant organizational hand, Hillel became a part of the American university tradition and, in association with the names of Wesley and Newman, the spiritual values of the historic Western religions were integrated into American university life.

The steady growth of opportunity for intensifying Jewish religious life in America and the rapid advance of the organized religious groups called for the creation of an agency where matters of common interest could be considered and clarified. This purpose was already accomplished on the local level through the extension of the various boards of Jewish ministers in every major city or region of the United States. Reform, Conservative and Orthodox colleagues met to discuss the questions of common concern and action. On the national level, the Synagogue Council of America was organized in 1926. It included representation from the three unions of congregations and the three rabbinic bodies for the purpose of "speaking and acting unitedly in furthering such religious interests as the constituent organizations in the Council have in common."

The declared primary purpose of the Synagogue Council was to strengthen Judaism in America by making the Synagogue "the center of Jewish spiritual influence." Unfortunately, the Council was not very successful in achieving this aim. Technically, this failure might be explained by the veto agreement which nullified any decision that did not receive unanimous support. But the fundamental reason was the fact that the major areas of Jewish activity in cultural and spiritual affairs were pre-empted by communal and national nonsynagogal and religious bodies—all were jealous of their prior jurisdictional rights. The Synagogue Council was therefore compelled to develop only those projects that would neither duplicate nor conflict with the older established institutions. However, some significant steps were taken. In 1929 the Council issued a pronouncement and joined with other groups in opposing the adoption of any system of calendar reform that would interfere with the fixity of the Sabbath. The Council was responsible for arranging the Jewish exhibits at the Sesquicentennial Exhibition in Philadelphia (1926), at the Chicago World's Fair (1936), and at the New York World's Fair (1939-1940); it became the representative of the Jewish religious group in the interfaith

program of the National Conference of Christians and Jews, and co-operated in similar interfaith projects with the Federal Council of the Churches
of Christ in America and the National Catholic Welfare Conference.
Surveys were made of Jewish and Christian religious textbooks for suggested revision of those portions not consonant with proper respect for
other faiths. Other studies were made of proselyting activities among Jews,
and representation was made before the appropriate Christian bodies.

One of the most important and fruitful areas of religious activity developed during this period by all the groups was in the realm of social
action. In the latter part of the nineteenth and early twentieth centuries,
the American religious groups were compelled to face the issues of the
changing economic order particularly as it affected the conflict between
capital and labor. The religious ethic had to be translated into action;
social justice meant nothing if it did not mean social reform. In the
struggle for these reforms, labor found strong friends not only among
the social workers and intellectuals, but also among the clergy.

The American rabbinate responded to the social challenge with understanding and vigor. The Reform rabbis especially applied themselves to
a constructive evaluation of religious social vision in the machine age. The
religious lay and rabbinic associations expressed themselves on social issues
in a variety of ways: committee reports and official resolutions adopted
at conventions; social justice platforms or "creeds" summarizing agreements reached over a period of years; prayers and devotions, either as
regular or supplementary readings in the prayer book; special services,
appeals and public meetings for the underprivileged and victims of social
unrighteousness; investigations and impartial arbitration in industrial
conflicts; intercession with employers and government officials. In the
action phase of this work, the rabbinate usually participated jointly with
Catholic and Protestant welfare and social groups.[88]

The determination of the American rabbinate to become involved in
the immediate problems of minimum wage, working hours, rights to
organize, unemployment insurance and other contemporary social issues,
strengthened the position of religion and religious leadership in their
constant struggle for the betterment of mankind.[89]

With the outbreak of World War II the Jewish religious community
was united as never before. A half million young Jewish men and women
were destined to serve in the armed forces of the United States all over
the globe. Their spiritual needs had to be taken care of. This was the task
of the American rabbinate. The National Jewish Welfare Board was
once again authorized by the War and Navy Departments to endorse
Jewish chaplains. A Special Committee on Army and Navy Religious
Activities (CANRA) was organized on which all the Jewish religious

groups were represented.[90] The rabbinical groups immediately recognized the full authority of the Jewish Welfare Board, although they reserved judgment as to the wisdom of the initial decision to place the control of chaplaincy endorsements and religious program in the agency of a non-synagogal body.[91] Each rabbinical organization supervised the work within its own group. More than half the rabbis of the country volunteered for service. The seminaries, like the other professional schools in American university life, accelerated their classes and virtually became, on a volunteer basis, schools for the training of chaplains. The new young wartime graduates, if eligible, enlisted in the service, and if ineligible, replaced older graduates who were thus freed to leave their congregations for the duration of the war to serve as chaplains. By September 2, 1945, when the Japanese surrendered, 309 rabbis had been commissioned chaplains. According to Philip Bernstein, wartime director of CANRA, these constituted two-thirds of the eligible qualified rabbis of the country and probably the highest percentage of any religious group in the land to be commissioned chaplains.[92] A model of working harmony was achieved. Liturgical materials, literature and responsa were created for all Jewish personnel in service.[93] It was agreed that no material would be used which might influence religious practice in the postwar period. The individual chaplains were free to work out their own solutions to special problems. Yet most of the chaplains, irrespective of group affiliation, arrived at the same conclusions. The accepted decision that the denominational loyalties and personal religious predilections of the chaplains must be subordinated to the needs of the Jewish G.I., "led to more observance of tradition by the Reform, a liberalization of the Orthodox and an expansion of Conservatism, which seemed to characterize the general pattern that evolved under military conditions."[94] Out of the meetings and deliberations on behalf of a common objective during the critical war period a mood of co-operation was created and a desire for even greater association of interests in other areas of Jewish religious endeavor. This feeling was shared by rabbis in the field, congregations in the community, and national officers and seminary authorities.[95] Joint meetings of rabbinic bodies were considered. The Reform and Conservative groups had set the pace. They conducted a joint convention in 1943. A joint committee, composed of the representatives of all the rabbinical bodies, lay organizations, and seminaries, was convened in 1946 to work out a standard for relationship between rabbi and congregation. The Synagogue Council of America was reinforced in scope and administration, and embarked on an expanded program as the co-ordinate agency and spokesman of the religious groups.

The war had compelled amalgamated religious activity. Other forces operative in general and Jewish life, also were leading to collaborative effort. It is premature to attempt a systematic description and appraisal of these forces. At most, they may be considered as trends which are helping to create a basic and underlying unity in American Judaism. The most significant are: the identification of the religious groups in a new conception of higher Jewish education; their firm desire to remain rooted in American society and, in co-operation with other faiths and intellectual forces, to strengthen the spiritual foundations of American tradition and experience; their complete and fervent enlistment in the struggle to establish the Republic of Israel.

The tendency of the theological schools to expand into universities was not accidental; it was the natural culmination of their earlier decision to serve the totality of Jewish interests. American life and the Jewish community within it had changed radically since 1920. The temper of the time called for new techniques to introduce Jewish ideals and values into the stream of Jewish consciousness. Interpretation of Judaism on both the highest intellectual and popular mass levels was of vital importance.

Scholars, rabbis and teachers were not the only individuals who could influence Jewish life. Social workers, communal workers, artists and lay leaders trained in Judaism, were other key people who could exercise decisive influence upon American Jewry. A chasm of disregard, born out of unfamiliarity, separated the two groups of social engineers. A program of joint training and collective undertakings, could bring the two separate camps together. Moreover, if all these powerful forces could be coalesced into a religious leadership dedicated to the conservation and advancement of Jewish life itself, then a new future would await the Jewish community in America.

The Yeshiva, Hebrew Union College and Seminary almost simultaneously launched a series of new schools in these various fields of endeavor, each developing differently in accordance with its special emphases.[96] In every instance the rabbinical school was to remain the heart and core of the expanded institution. The very plan of including schools of education, community service, social work, and creative arts as co-ordinate schools of a theological seminary, although it intensified institutional loyalties, broadened the horizons of the religious groups, lessened the tensions of denominationalism and helped bring them closer to one another in thought and spirit.

A second major influence for basic unity among the religious groups was their shared determination to go beyond the realms of Jewish activity and to participate actively in interdenominational efforts for the solution of problems of group tension and group adjustments in America. In the local communities, the rabbinate participated with the ministers of other faiths as co-sponsors of significant undertakings, such as Thanksgiving celebrations and other national observances. The goodwill movement soon became part of local American community vernacular. In an effort to transpose the formalistic expression of pious intentions between the various American faiths into a positive program of religious fellowship and understanding, the National Conference of Christians and Jews (organized in 1928), engaged in a series of important projects. One of its chief contributions was the annual celebration of Brotherhood Week which promises to become a national institution, between the anniversaries of Lincoln and Washington in February. In order to create an academic center for authoritative dissemination of information about the Jewish faith, the Hebrew Union College called together Institutes on Judaism in various cities throughout the country for the clarification of Jewish thought and practices.

The very need which gave rise to these activities reflected the basic weaknesses in the American democratic structure. The American dream, conceived by the Founding Fathers, of establishing a society in which the human being could achieve full emancipation, was vanishing. The profound religious precepts which were the very essence of the American society-in-creation were being slowly disassociated from American society-in-action. The growing cynicism and amorality of government was the unhappy result. American religious leaders began to probe the root evil, and the Jewish religious groups wished to contribute to the reintegration of religious ideas into the thought-fabric of American democracy. The seminaries planned their specific programs in the areas of learning and scholarship; the rabbinical and lay associations in social action. Dr. Finkelstein evolved a pattern of action as a possible solution to this vexing problem. In 1939, speaking at the founding meeting of the Conference on Science, Philosophy and Religion (organized in 1940), he urged American scholars of all disciplines to attempt a new form of intellectual integration. He stressed that, "the true relation of democratic ideas and institutions to religious traditions, the historical indebtedness of science to monastic and rabbinical schools, and the vindication of traditional ethics in our growing economic and political confusion have been consistently overlooked. The various religious traditions may, without sacrifice of their integrity, recognize analogous values in their faiths. The totality of science, philosophy and religion can become a pluralistic but well regulated universe of thought."[97] In the spirit of this interpretation of the deeper issues in American democracy, the Seminary established its Institute for Religious Studies (later called The Institute for Religious and Social Studies) in 1938. In the very same spirit, Dr. Nelson Glueck, as he discussed his plans for a far reaching expansion program at the Hebrew Union College, declared that "the universal spiritual values of religion must be made a part of our higher education." He felt that if America is to solve its deepest spiritual problems, then teacher and educator must stand shoulder to shoulder with men of religion working together toward the achievement of humanity's highest ideals.[98] The ever widening perspective of the Jewish religious groups with regard to their responsibilities in America's spiritual crisis, enlarged the area of the shared common problem and opened new vistas for collaborative efforts in the strengthening of the foundations of American democracy.

A third overwhelmingly vital force for the consolidation of Jewish life in America, was the historic effort on behalf of Eretz Yisrael leading to the United Nations decision of November 29, 1947, and the declaration of Jewish independence in the new born State of Israel on May 15, 1948. The interrelationship between American Jewry and the Yishuv in Eretz Yisrael since the earliest days of Haim Carregal's visit to America, is one of the most interesting chapters in modern Jewish history. American Jewry, destined to become one of the greatest and most influential Jewish communities in all history, never forgot Jerusalem. The prayer for the rebuilding of the Holy Land, though for a time and in limited circles removed from its lips, was never removed from its heart. The martyrdom in death of six million Jews during the war and the martyrdom in life, after the war, of the remnant that was saved, made the immediate realization of the Zionist program for Jewish independence a crucial necessity. During the most intensive and difficult phases of the struggle for international recognition, the organized congregations in American Israel were completely and readily available for any action on behalf of the Yishuv. As an increasing majority of the Reform rabbinate and congregations joined with the other Zionist forces, the American Synagogue stood in the vanguard of the supreme effort to redeem Zion.

Perhaps necessarily, the birth of the new state was accompanied with great travail. Although recognized as a *de facto* state by the enlightened nations of the world, including the United States, the new Republic of Israel was forced to wage war for its right to freedom and independence.

A century ago, in September, 1848, Isaac Leeser, in a dream of Zion established, described the vision of the ages to which the contemporary Israel stands consecrated:

If our religion flourishes, if our state is triumphant, it need not be at the expense and tears of others; we hope for a kingdom of peace, for a spread of divine truth, to be accomplished without the agency of the sword, or political tyranny. It is mercy which is to rule; it is blissful peace which is to conquer. We are to be the pioneers of the regeneration of man. . . .[99]

Whether these forces are the precursors to a greater unity in American Judaism or whether they are the temporary aftergrowth of a war and enforced co-operation, is a query which will only be answered in the fullness of time. There are many unresolved questions, within and without the religious community structure, which will have a decisive influence on the specific directions of religious life in the second half of the twentieth century. Will the vigorous leadership now at the head of the religious groups, while pursuing a program of expansion and intensification of their own institutions, seek isolation, co-operation or integration among themselves? Will the rabbinate in the cities and smaller communities insist on increased denominationalism in the accepted pattern of three distinct party and organizational divisions in American Judaism? Is a federated synagogue plan feasible in America? If so, will it permit of a variety of religious expression while amalgamating the separate national bodies? What will be the influence of the newly conceived Jewish center program on the synagogue? What will be the future of the American Zionist movements as they necessarily abandon political activity and seek an intrinsic Hebraic centered program of activity? Will the immediate relationships between the non-synagogal national movements (Zionist, philanthropic, fraternal, and defense) be complementary to or competitive with the synagogue? Can American Jewry be trained to respond as graciously and liberally to long range religious and cultural enterprises as it has responded in the past to the demands of philanthropic, relief and Zionist activity? What will be the permanent influences of the Republic of Israel on the religious life and practice of American Judaism?

These are the questions and counter-questions, the doubts and the hopes of the great Jewish settlement in America as it stands on the threshold of its newest and most important test of world Jewish leadership. In the chronicle of human events, America has become the greatest center of Diaspora Jewry, the partner with Eretz Yisrael in the rebuilding of world Judaism. As, in the years to come, the cultivation of the Holy Land and its spirit will be the sacred task of the people in Israel, so will it be the consecrated duty of American Jewry to nurture the spirit and practice of Judaism in America. This is the promise of our generation.

8

The Mid-Century Decades

The post-World War II period in American Jewish life was marked by the most pronounced surge of religious affiliation in its three-century history. Religion, the feeling ran, was at the core of American civilization; and the Protestant-Catholic-Jew triad constituted an indigenous quality of American society. To be Jewish was to be American; and to be American was to be religious.[100]

Jewish religious institutional increase, supported by a growing native community, seemed to imply a synagogue revival. Available figures since 1945, both of synagogues and members of rabbinical associations affiliated with the three major Jewish religious groups, suggest that religious institutions and personnel have virtually trebled: from about 1000 to about 3000 synagogues; and from about 1200 to 3500 rabbis.[101] In addition, the respective groups reported a total of several hundred unfilled rabbinic posts. Furthermore, of some seventy-five new national Jewish organizations or units of institutions established in the United States since 1949 (in the broad categories of religion, education, culture, community relations, overseas aid, social welfare, social and mutual benefit, Zionism, and pro-Israel organizations), about half were of religious sponsorship or motivation.[102]

This growth was not unique among American religious groups. Synagogue identification followed general American religious interest and movement: westward across the continent, and to suburbia from the metropolitan centers. Synagogue attendance, though not as high as Catholic and Protestant participation in churches, rose with the religious curve. Religious activity in general was found to be greatest among the more Americanized and urbanized segments of population; and the demographic characteristics of the Jews were a striking illustration of these social processes.

Jewish congregational life flourished substantively as well as numerically, as is borne out by its diversified institutional forms and content. Among these were the originality and creativity expressed in the several thousand physical structures which arose in town, country, and city; the proliferation of educational adjuncts to the synagogue enterprise; the emergent leadership role of women; and the enormous emphasis on "civic religion" and interreligious thought and action.

American synagogue architecture uniquely reflected the totality of formal and informal Jewish community needs. Assuming as never before in American Jewish life its traditional threefold function as House of Study, Prayer, and Assembly, the synagogue has also become a surrogate collective home, an all-purpose educational, recreational, social and communal center.[103]

Jewish educational intensification was related to synagogue expansion. Already in the early sixties, over ninety percent of Jewish school enrollment was under synagogue auspices, branching out to preschool and adult classes, day camps and weekend institutes.[104] National educational agencies became permanent features of the respective religious groups, establishing publishing houses and producing extensive informational literature. As mass media opened new avenues for education, religious institutions eagerly seized upon the unprecedented opportunity to present the image of Jews and Judaism to the American public mind. In 1953 synagogues for the first time permitted telecasts of actual services. Henceforth, even if one had never met a Jew, by the turn of a dial, one could see and hear him.

A most remarkable achievement was the continued development of the respective rabbinical schools. Reaping the fruits of earlier plantings, American Jewry was the only Diaspora community to prepare its own rabbis and scholars, directors of religious activities for hundreds of campuses, and academicians in Judaic studies to cope with expanding needs of American universities.[105] Indeed, most replacements on Jewish seminary faculties now come from the ranks of their own graduates.

The vital position achieved by women in all branches of American Judaism strengthened the American synagogue considerably. Their participation at services, involvement in parent-teacher groups and adult study circles, not to speak of the local, regional, and national sisterhood organizations, heightened the family spirit in American Jewish synagogue experience. This correlative development—a part of the general American societal tendency—profoundly influenced Jewish religious continuity, as it augured further departures from historic synagogue organization.

The trend toward interreligious thought and action which originated in previous decades sharply accelerated in the postwar years. Conceptually set in the framework of American religious pluralism, interfaith amity and action soared during the sessions of the Ecumenical Council (Vatican II, 1962-1965) and regressed in the aftermath of the Six Day War (June 1967). Yet the profound basis of continuing Christian-Jewish interchange was firmly established. Inevitable failures and disappointments did not alter the common need to meet the challenge of an essentially secular Western world. While forms of cooperation varied, the keystone was compatibility within difference. Programs on local, national, and institutional levels multiplied in two main directions: joint action for civic enhancement and theological-philosophical exchange around a corpus of contemporary human and societal problems. A landmark of "civic religion" was the Religion and Race Conference in 1963, through which the organized religions of America collectively affirmed the bettering of race relations as a moral imperative. An outstanding example of basic "dialogue" is the literature created by The Institute for Religious and Social Studies of The Jewish Theological Seminary of America and the associated Conference on Philosophy, Science and Religion.

The scales of American Jewish religious achievement registered prestige, power, and optimism. But they also held in balance the inestimable weight of what was lost in American Judaism. Reflective literature of the period argued that the supremacy of association over commitment had created a kind of spiritual schizoid within religion itself. Quantitative intensification created qualitative disorder.

The two main defeats suffered by American Judaism, cultural absorption into the environment and the virtual disappearance of the "learning" Jew, derived from the very gift of America. Jews had become fully American. Sociological evidence, particularly on the vexing mixed-marriage phenomenon, pointed to progressively attenuated involvement with Judaism as the native population became more distant from immigrant origins. In the educational perspective, the American Jewish community experienced a strange paradox. Its children achieved a level of education in which some eighty percent were college-trained; at the same time, they were virtually illiterate in Judaism. A new class of Jews arose—"the indifferent"—who related to the fellowship of "Jewishness" but not to the traditional values of Judaism.[106] In effect, then, the present community is living on the capital of the past. Hence the question most frequently asked in thoughtful circles: Can Judaism survive in freedom?

Other unresolved problems on the continuing agenda of American Jewry became more persistent and vigorous in the early 1960's. On the international and national fronts, the dilemma of the American ethos in a period of world disarray brought moral challenges for American religion generally, engaging the Jewish religious groups to their very depths.

The movements of aggiornamento and ecumenism in world Christianity also had an impact on American Judaism. As these trends intensified, the Christian-Jewish encounter assumed a new appearance, requiring a different type of confrontation between religious Jewry and their ecumenical-minded Protestant-Catholic neighbors. Would America revert to its nineteenth-century position as "a Christian country," rather than uphold the pluralistic religious ideal of the present century?

Finally, the permanent relationship with the State and *Yishuv* in Eretz Yisrael required reformulation. From the establishment of the State, religious Jewry in America, as American Jewry generally, accepted in theory, though not in practice, the centrality of the State in world Judaism. Although crises affecting Israel always elevated it to a principal concern, a consensus had not been reached about the accommodation between the State as the center of Jewish political sovereignty and the American Jewish community living in freedom virtually unparalleled in Jewish history. The Six Day War, the most concentrated focus of American Jewry's identification with Israel, intensified fundamental questions both in America and in Israel about the actual relative position of the American Jewish community vis-à-vis the *Yishuv*. Even the broader American Jewish leadership now began to think of the State as a primary need for American Jewry's future. For Israel might conceivably become an instrumentality to strengthen the Jewish identity of the ethnic and nonreligious elements of the Jewish group, through their sense of Jewish brotherhood attracting them to Jewish learning and religion.[107] In other words, in their grasp of "the corporate reality of the Jewish People," to use Professor Mordecai M. Kaplan's formulation, the nonreligiously identified elements might be led to reidentification with Judaism as a Covenant Faith and People.

Judaism in America, like America itself, is future-directed. If its history is an indication, Jewish religious institutional life, now entering the final third of the century, will grapple with its problems and dilemmas with seriousness and self-criticism. Mindful of its responsibility to account for the greater part of the Diaspora in the free world, it will aspire, as always, to create a spiritual as well as a physical home for the Jews of America.

Notes

¹ Oscar S. Straus, *The Origin of Republican Form of Government in the United States of America* (2nd ed., rev.; New York and London, 1926), p. 140. See also Abraham A. Neuman, *Relation of the Hebrew Scriptures to American Institutions* (New York, [1938]), especially pp. 11-16, where his interpretation and parallels of Puritan institutions and the community organization of the Jewish *kahal* are particularly interesting.

² *Publications of the American Jewish Historical Society* [PAJHS] *(The Lyons Collection,* I), No. 21 (1913), p. 101.

³ *Prayers for Shabbath, Rosh-Hashanah, and Kippur, or the Sabbath, the beginning of the Year, and the Day of Atonement; with the Amidah and Musaph of the Moadim, or Solemn Seasons, according to the Order of the Spanish and Portuguese Jews,* translated by Isaac Pinto (New York, 5526 [1766]).

⁴ Joshua Trachtenberg, *Consider the Years* (Easton, Pa., 1944), p. 317, n. 1. See also Rudolf Glanz, "The First Twenty-five Jewish Communities in the United States," *YIVO Bleter,* XXVI (September-October, 1945), pp. 37-49.

⁵ Edward Davis, *The History of Rodeph Shalom Congregation, Philadelphia, 1802-1926* (Philadelphia, 1926), pp. 27-28.

⁶ PAJHS, No. 21, p. 74.

⁷ *Ibid.,* p. 4.

⁸ Peter Kalm, *Travels into North America,* translated into English by John Reinhold Forster (Warrington, England, 1770), I, pp. 245-246.

⁹ PAJHS, No. 10 (1902), p. 163.

¹⁰ Morris A. Gutstein, *The Story of the Jews of Newport* (New York, 1936), pp. 212-213.

¹¹ Franklin Bowditch Dexter, ed., *The Literary Diary of Ezra Stiles* (New York, 1901), I, p. 6. n.

¹² PAJHS, No. 21, p. 14; Alexander M. Dushkin, *Jewish Education in New York City* (New York, 1918), pp. 40 ff., 449 ff.; Hyman B. Grinstein, "Studies in the History of Jewish Education in New York City (1728-1860)," *The Jewish Review,* II, No. 1 (April 1, 1944), pp. 41-42. See also Hyman B. Grinstein, *The Rise of the Jewish Community of New York, 1654-1860* (Philadelphia, 1945), pp. 228-230.

¹³ PAJHS, No. 21, p. 180.

¹⁴ *Ibid.,* pp. 2-3.

¹⁵ David Philipson, "The Jewish Pioneers of the Ohio Valley," PAJHS, No. 8, p. 45.

[16] *The Occident and American Jewish Advocate,* I, No. 11 (February, 1844), pp. 547-550; II, No. 1 (April, 1844), pp. 29-31. See also Anita Libman Lebeson, *Jewish Pioneers in America, 1492-1848* (New York, 1931), pp. 263-264.

[17] Jacques J. Lyons and Abraham de Sola, *A Jewish Calendar for Fifty Years* (Montreal, 1854), pp. 148-165. This list of new congregations strikingly demonstrates the shift from Sephardic to Ashkenazic influence.

[18] Israel Goldstein, *A Century of Judaism in New York* (New York, 1930), p. 77.

[19] The most comprehensive essay is that of Henry Englander, "Isaac Leeser," *Yearbook, Central Conference of American Rabbis,* XXVIII (1918), pp. 213-252. See also Moshe Davis, "Isaac Leeser, Builder of American Judaism," *Hadoar,* XXI, Nos. 7 and 8 (December 13 and 20, 1940) (in Hebrew).

[20] Isaac Mayer Wise has been well served by a virtual library of biographies, essays, and evaluations. The best single volume is his autobiography, *Reminiscences,* translated from the German and edited by David Philipson (Cincinnati, 1901).

[21] *Occident,* III, No. 4 (July, 1845), pp. 169-176; No. 5 (August, 1845), pp. 217-227.

[22] David Philipson, *Max Lilienthal* (New York, 1915), pp. 54-56; *Occident,* IV, No. 11 (February, 1847), pp. 554-555; V, No. 2 (May, 1847), pp. 109-111.

[23] *Wissenschaftliche Zeitschrift fuer juedische Theologie,* III (1837), pp. 1-14.

[24] Philipson, *op. cit.,* pp. 76-78; *Occident,* XIII, No. 8 (November, 1855), pp. 407-414.

[25] *Occident,* XIII, No. 8 (November, 1855), pp. 414-417.

[26] *Israelite,* VI, No. 21 (November 25, 1859), p. 165.

[27] *Occident,* VIII, No. 8 (November, 1850), pp. 424-426; IX, No. 2 (May, 1851), pp. 104-105. See also Grinstein, "Studies in the History of Jewish Education in New York City (1728-1860)," *The Jewish Review,* pp. 47 ff.

[28] *Constitution and By-laws of the American Jewish Publication Society* (founded on the 9th of Heshvan, 5606), adopted at Philadelphia, on Sunday, November, 30, 1845, Kislev 1, 5606.

[29] See Salo W. Baron and Jeanette Baron, "Palestinian Messengers in America, 1849-1879," *Jewish Social Studies,* V, No. 2, pp. 115-162; No. 3, pp. 225-292.

[29a Cf. Cecil Roth, "The Jews of Western Europe (from 1648)," this work, Vol. I, p. 280.]

[30] *Occident,* XX, No. 5 (August, 1862), pp. 212-215. See also Bertram W. Korn, "Jewish Chaplains During the Civil War," *American Jewish Archives,* I, No. 1 (June, 1948), pp. 6-22.

[31] Uriah Z. Engelman, "Jewish Statistics in the U.S. Census of Religious Bodies (1850-1936)," *Jewish Social Studies,* IX, No. 2 (April, 1947), pp. 130-134.

[32] See Joseph Krauskopf, "Fifty Years of Judaism in America," *American Jews' Annual,* IV (Cincinnati, 1888), pp. 65-95.

33 *American Israelite*, XXXII, No. 19 (November 6, 1885), p. 4.

34 Ismar Elbogen, *A Century of Jewish Life* (Philadelphia, 1944), pp. 344-345.

35 *Yearbook of the Central Conference of American Rabbis, 5651—1890-91,* I (Cincinnati, 1891), pp. 4-5.

36 *Ibid.*, IV (1895), p. 87.

37 *American Hebrew*, LXIV, No. 11 (January 13, 1899), p. 372.

38 *Ibid.*, LXV, No. 1 (May 5, 1899), pp. 9-11; No. 2 (May 12, 1899), pp. 45-49.

39 Rebekah Kohut, *My Portion* (New York, 1925), pp. 91-92, 126-127, 135-139, 143-145, 160-165.

40 *American Hebrew* LVI, No. 6 (December 14, 1894), p. 181.

41 Norman Bentwich, *Solomon Schechter* (Philadelphia, 1938), p. 169.

42 *Yearbook*, CCAR, XIII (1904), pp. 185-308.

43 *Ibid.*, XV (1905), p. 101.

44 Solomon Schechter, "The Charter of the Seminary," *Seminary Addresses and Other Papers* (Cincinnati, 1915), pp. 9-33.

45 *The United Synagogue of America, Sixth Annual Report* (New York, 1919), p. 21.

46 *Jewish Comment*, XXVIII, No. 2 (December 25, 1908), pp. 193-195, 204-205; No. 13 (January 1, 1909), pp. 219-220, 223.

47 *The United Synagogue of America, Fourth Annual Report* (New York, 1917), pp. 9-10.

48 *The Jubilee Volume of the Union of Orthodox Rabbis of the United States and Canada* [in Hebrew], (New York, 1928), pp. 134-136.

49 In 1937 the number of Jewish congregations in the country was about 3,700: approximately 3,000 Orthodox congregations with a membership of about 250,000; approximately 350 Conservative congregations with a membership of about 75,000; approximately 300 Reform synagogues with a membership of about 65,000. A closer analysis of these statistics reveals that the greatest number of Orthodox congregations were tiny units, a fraction of which was served by rabbis. In sum, the total estimated congregational membership based on family affiliations was about 1,500,000 individual Jews which represented less than one-third of the Jews in the United States at the estimated 1937 calculation of 4,770,647. The statistics are based on the United States Census of Religious Bodies report of 1937.

50 The latter description seemed to have the widest acceptance. In 1943 the official magazine established by the Union of American Hebrew Congregations and the Central Conference of American Rabbis was called *Liberal Judaism*.

51 Jacob Mann (1888-1940), historian and scholar of the Genizah; Zevi H. W. Diesendruck (1890-1940), philosopher and Hebraist; Abraham Z. Idelsohn (1882-1938), musicologist. Jacob R. Marcus, who had been an instructor in Bible and Rabbinics, was appointed assistant professor (and later, professor) of Jewish history.

52 Israel Bettan, homiletics and Midrash; Samuel S. Cohon, Jewish theology; Abraham Cronbach, Jewish social studies; Sheldon H. Blank, Bible;

Nelson Glueck, Bible and archaeology. In 1947, Dr. Glueck succeeded Dr. Morgenstern as president of the College.

[53] In 1946 the College decided to establish a School of Religious Education in New York City. The Union of American Hebrew Congregations joined in the support and administration of the school, and in January, 1947, classes were held for the first time at the Community House of Congregation Emanu-El. Abraham N. Franzblau was named dean.

[54] Among the scholars who served on the faculty were: Salo W. Baron, history; Sidney E. Goldstein, social studies; Julian J. Obermann, Bible and Semitic philosophy; Ralph Marcus (1900-1957), Bible and Hellenistic literature; Henry Slonimsky, philosophy; Shalom Spiegel, Hebrew language and literature; Nisson Touroff (1877-1953), psychology and education; Chaim Tchernowitz (1870-1949), Talmud; Harry A. Wolfson, Jewish philosophy.

[55] This merger was formally consummated in June, 1948, and the combined institution was called the Hebrew Union College-Institute of Religion.

[56] *Reform Judaism in the Large Cities* (1931).

[57] *Yearbook,* CCAR, XL (1930), pp. 251-303.

[58] Vol. I of the newly revised edition of *The Union Prayerbook,* was published in 1940; vol. II in 1945.

[59] "From the Synagogue" (issued in mimeographed form by the Union of American Hebrew Congregations, April, 1937).

[60] *Yearbook,* CCAR, XLV (1935), p. 103.

[61] Guiding Principles of Reform Judaism (adopted by the Central Conference of American Rabbis, at Columbus, Ohio, May 27, 1937).

[[61a] For full text, cf. below, Louis Finkelstein, "The Jewish Religion: Its Beliefs and Practices," pp. 486 ff.]

[62] Solomon Polachek (1877-1928), Moses Soloveitchik (1877-1941) and Julius Kaplan (1884-1939), in Talmud Solomon Zeitlin, in history; Pinkhas Churgin, in Bible and history; Joshua Finkel, in Semitic languages; Jekuthiel Ginsburg (1889-1957), in mathematics; Samuel K. Mirsky, in Rabbinics; Samuel Belkin, in Hellenistic literature; Leo Jung, in ethics; Joseph H. Lookstein, in sociology, and Joseph Soloveitchik in philosophy. In June, 1943, Dr. Belkin was elected president of the Yeshiva. For a statement of his views on the role of Yeshiva University, see *The Inauguration of Samuel Belkin* (New York, 1944), pp. 31-37.

[63] For a survey treatment of the history of Yeshiva College, see Jacob I. Hartstein, "Yeshiva University: Growth of Rabbi Isaac Elchanan Theological Seminary," *American Jewish Year Book,* 5707 (1946-1947), XLVIII (Philadelphia, 1946), pp. 73-84.

[64] *Talpioth,* a quarterly in Hebrew dedicated to Jewish law and ethics, began publication in September, 1943, under the editorship of Samuel K. Mirsky.

[65] The faculty included such figures as Meyer Waxman, author of the four volume, *A History of Jewish Literature,* and Samuel I. Feigin (1893-1950), orientalist.

[66] Other *yeshibot* for higher learning were established. The most important were the Mesifta Torah Va-Daat, the Mesifta Chaim Berlin, the Yeshiva

Rabbi Israel Meir Ha-Cohen, the Mesifta Tifferes Yerushalaim, and the Yeshiva of the Lubavitscher Rabbi. *Yeshibot* in other parts of the country were: the Yeshiva Ner Israel in Baltimore and the Rabbinical College of Telshe, in Cleveland. Famous European *yeshibot* which established schools in America were the Mirer Yeshiva and the Lomze Yeshiva; schools for exiled scholars were also established in Spring Valley, New York, and Lakewood, New Jersey.

[67] The nationally known Ⓤ symbol soon offered the food manufacturer a regular method of indicating to the consumer that the product had rabbinic endorsement.

[68] The new organization, named the Central Sephardic Jewish Community of America, was organized in 1941. It issues a quarterly bulletin called *The Sephardi*, the first number of which appeared in September, 1943. The Union of Sephardic Congregations (organized in 1929, David de Sola Pool, president) did not confine its interests to the needs of the Sephardim in the United States. It serves the world Sephardic community and co-operates in America with the Central Sephardic Jewish Community.

[69] *Proceedings of the Seventh Annual Convention of the Rabbinical Council of America* (1942), pp. 46-47.

[70] After World War II, the special status of the Union of Orthodox Rabbis in this field of endeavor was officially recognized by the American Jewish Joint Distribution Committee. An agreement was signed in July, 1947, between Rabbi Israel Rosenberg, chairman of the presidium of the Union, and Edward M. M. Warburg, J. D. C. Chairman, which provided "that those programs of the J. D. C. specifically devoted to the rehabilitation and advancement of Orthodox Jewish life in Europe will be conducted with the advice and counsel of the chief elements of Jewish Orthodoxy in America."

[71] For a statement of the Agudas Israel program, see *Agudist Essays* (London, 1944); and Jacob Rosenheim, *Agudist World Problems,* an address delivered to the convention of Agudas Israel of America, in Baltimore on August 23, 1941.

[72] In 1922 Hapoel Ha-Mizrachi was founded as a worldwide religious labor movement, as an affiliate of the Mizrachi, with the motto of *Torah Va-Avodah* (Torah and Labor). In America, Hapoel Ha-Mizrachi is the senior organization of the Torah Va-Avodah movement, with branches in various cities. Its Halutz department is known as the Halutz Ha-Mizrachi, and its youth movement is known as Zeirei Ha-Mizrachi. An independent youth organization, Ha-Shomer Ha-Dati, was also organized (1934) with the specific aim of *Kibbutziut* (collectivization). In July, 1947, the first religious collective of American halutzim was established at Ein Hanatziv in the valley of Bet Shaan, by this group.

[73] For a fuller statement of the growth of the *yeshiva* parochial movement, see *Yeshiva Review* (April, 1941), published by the United Yeshivos Foundation. For a rationale of the all-day school, see Jacob I. Hartstein, "The Yeshivah as an American Institution," *Jewish Education,* XVIII, No. 2, (March, 1947), pp. 26-29. Other national Orthodox agencies who are determined to introduce the *yeshiva* movement, through their financial aid, into

every community with a sizable Jewish population, are the Yeshivah Tomchei Temimim, the Mizrachi, and the Torah Umesorah Organizations.

[73*] Joseph H. Hertz, (ed.), *A Book of Jewish Thoughts* (London, 1920), p. 4.

[74] Jacob Hoschander (1874-1933), Bible; Louis Finkelstein, theology; Boaz Cohen, Talmud; Alexander Sperber, H. L. Ginsberg, Robert Gordis, Bible; Simon Greenberg, education; Max Arzt, practical theology. At the beginning of World War II, as the lanes to and from Palestine were being closed, Saul Lieberman, world renowned Talmudist, began his association with the Seminary as professor of Palestinian literature and institutions. In 1937 Dr. Finkelstein was appointed Provost of the Seminary, and in 1940 he succeeded Dr. Adler as president of the institution. In 1947 Dr. Greenberg became Provost.

[75] At that time, 1947, Stephen S. Kayser was appointed Curator.

[76] In 1942 the name of the Classes was changed to the Seminary School of Jewish Studies and Dr. Louis M. Levitsky was appointed Director.

[77] Samuel M. Cohen (1886-1945) was the first Executive Director of the United Synagogue. He served from 1917-1945. In 1946 Albert I. Gordon was appointed as Director.

[78] "The Jewish Center," *American Hebrew*, LI, No. 20 (March 22, 1918), pp. 529-531.

[79] "Judaism and Modern Thought," *United Synagogue Recorder*, 11, No. 4 (October, 1922), pp. 2-4.

[80] *The Problem of the Agunah*, A Statement by the Rabbinical Assembly of the Jewish Theological Seminary of America (New York, 1936).

[81] Solomon Goldman, *A Rabbi Takes Stock* (New York, 1931), p. 19.

[82] *The Reconstructionist*, XI, No. 1 (February 23, 1945), p. 15.

[83] See *Sabbath Prayer Book* (New York, 1945), especially the Introduction, xvii-xxx.

[84] The most important expression of their point of view is the publication of an official Prayer Book under the joint sponsorship of the Rabbinical Assembly and the United Synagogue, *Sabbath and Festival Prayer Book* (New York, 1946). Also see, Robert Gordis, "A Jewish Prayer Book for the Modern Age," *Conservative Judaism* II, No. 1 (October, 1945), and "The Tasks Before Us," *ibid.*, I, No. 1 (January, 1945).

[85] For Dr. Kadushin, see *Organic Judaism* (New York, 1938). For Dr. Greenberg, see "Evaluating the Mitzvot," *Bulletin of the Rabbinical Assembly*, V, No. 1, (New York, June, 1942), pp. 9-18.

[86] *Proceedings of the Twenty-Seventh Annual Conference of the Rabbinical Assembly of the Jewish Theological Seminary of America* (1927), pp. 42-66.

[87] *Ibid.*, pp. 48-49.

[88] See Abraham Cronbach, "The Social Outlook of Modern Judaism," *Popular Studies in Judaism*, No. 25, published by The Union of American Hebrew Congregations.

[89] See *Yearbook* CCAR, XXVIII (1918), pp. 101-104; XXXVIII (1928), pp. 73-97; XLVII (1937), pp. 114-125; "Pronouncement of the Rabbinical Assembly of America on Social Justice," adopted July 5, 1934, *Proceedings of*

the Rabbinical Assembly, V (1939), pp. 156-164; the Union of Orthodox Jewish Congregations of America, at a conference in New York in April, 1936, set up a permanent committee for social justice.

[90] David de Sola Pool was Chairman, Barnett P. Brickner (Reform), Chairman of the Administrative Committee, Louis M. Levitsky (Conservative), Chairman of the Executive Committee, and Joseph H. Lookstein (Orthodox), Vice-Chairman of the Executive Committee.

[91] All considerations of the change of auspices were postponed until the end of the war. In 1947 as an act of deference to the will of the Association of Jewish Chaplains, the Jewish Welfare Board created a Division of Religious Activities under its general supervision and administrative control. All the religious groups are represented, and they have full authority in the determination and implementation of policy. Solomon S. Freehof was appointed chairman; Aryeh Lev, director.

[92] "Jewish Chaplains in World War II," *American Jewish Year Book,* 5706, (1945-1946), vol. 47 (Philadelphia, 1945), pp. 173-178.

[93] See *Responsa in War Time* (New York, 1947), published by the Division of Religious Activities, National Jewish Welfare Board.

[94] Philip Bernstein, *op. cit.,* pp. 174-175.

[95] At the first national convention of the chaplains' association, the following resolution was unanimously passed:

"We Chaplains who served in this last war, alumni of the three major rabbinic seminaries, and representative of the Orthodox, Conservative and Reform religious ideologies within American Judaism unanimously affirm that the mutuality, fellowship, and conradeship which united us in our common service of God and country proved a most enriching spiritual experience which we aim to apply in our civilian ministry. To expand and extend the blessings of this creative fellowship so that it may embrace other facets of Jewish life, we urge upon the three rabbinic bodies to project plans for their respective national conventions in a manner that would provide, once every three years, a simultaneous session for the three bodies."

Proceedings of the First National Convention (New York, 1947), p. 26.

[96] In February, 1945, Dr. Kaplan, speaking at a convocation of the Seminary, called for its development into a university of Judaism; the following year the Seminary did establish a University of Judaism in Los Angeles as its West Coast Branch. In November, 1945, the Yeshiva announced its change to university status. See Samuel Belkin, *Yeshiva University—Its Purpose and Philosophy* (New York, 1948). While the Hebrew Union College did not announce a formal change of name, its plan of growth as outlined by Dr. Glueck in his inaugural year, 1947-1948, probably will bring the college into a similar scheme.

[97] "The Aims of the Conference," *Science, Philosophy and Religion* (New York, 1941), pp. 11-19.

[98] *New York Times* (March 14, 1948).

[99] "The Past and Future," *Occident,* VI, No. 6 (September, 1848), pp. 275-285.

[100] See Gerhard Lenski, "Religious Pluralism in Theoretical Perspective,"

International Yearbook for the Sociology of Religion (Koeln and Opladen, 1965), I, 25-41; David O. Moberg, "Religious Pluralism in the United States of America," *op. cit.*, I, 69–107.

[101] It need hardly be repeated that these figures are only estimates, for accurate statistics were not kept by the respective organizations. The best available comparative figures are as follows:

SYNAGOGUES OF THE THREE MAJOR TRENDS

Year	U.A.H.C. (Reform)	Un. Syn. (Conservative)	U.O.J.C. (Orthodox)
1949	392	365	500 plus unaffiliated
1965	660	800	ca. 607 " "

MEMBERS OF RABBINICAL GROUPS

Year	C.C.A.R. (Reform)	R.A. (Conservative)	R. Alliance / R.C.A. (Orthodox)	
1945	540	376	?	279
1967	944	950	324	857

(*American Jewish Year Book*, LI [1950], p. 154; LXVI [1965], p. 25; LXVII [1966], p. 182).

[102] Directory of National Jewish Organizations in *American Jewish Year Book*, LXVIII (1967), pp. 473-498.

[103] Descriptive analyses and illustrations of this evolution can be found in Peter Blake, ed., *An American Synagogue for Today and Tomorrow* (New York, 1954); Rachel Wischnitzer, *Synagogue Architecture in the United States* (Philadelphia, 1955); The Jewish Museum, *Recent American Synagogue Architecture* (New York, 1963); Avram Kampf, *Contemporary Synagogue Art* (Philadelphia, 1966).

[104] See Oscar Janowsky, "Jewish Education: Problems and Needs," *The American Jew: A Reappraisal* (Philadelphia, 1964), Chap. 6, pt. 2, pp. 157-159.

[105] Arnold Band, "Jewish Studies in American Liberal-Arts Colleges and Universities," *American Jewish Year Book*, LXVII (1966), pp. 3-30.

[106] Moshe Davis, "Centres of Jewry in the Western Hemisphere: A Comparative Approach," *Jewish Journal of Sociology*, V (June, 1963), pp. 4-26.

[107] Eli Ginzberg, *Agenda for American Jews*. Unpublished Foreword to forthcoming edition.

SELECTED BIBLIOGRAPHY

ADLER, CYRUS, *I Have Considered the Days*. Philadelphia, 1943.
———, *Jacob H. Schiff. His Life and Letters*. 2 vols. New York, 1928.
———, *Lectures, Selected Papers, Addresses*. Philadelphia, 1933.
———, "Louis Marshall: A Biographical Sketch." Reprinted from *American Jewish Year Book*, Vol. 42. New York, 1931.

———, (ed.), *The Jewish Theological Seminary of America.* Semicentennial Volume. New York, 1939.

———, (ed.), and MARGALITH, AARON M., *With Firmness in the Right: American Diplomatic Action Affecting Jews, 1840-1945.* New York, 1946.

ADLER, SAMUEL (Chairman of the Editorial Committee), *Protokolle der Rabbiner-Conferenz abgehalten zu Philadelphia vom 3. bis 6. November 1869.* New York, 1870.

BARON, SALO W., *A Social and Religious History of the Jews.* Vol. II., pp. 164-462. New York, 1937.

———, and Baron, Jeanette, "Palestinian Messengers in America, 1849-1879," in *Jewish Social Studies,* V, Nos. 2 and 3, April and July, 1943.

BENTWICH, NORMAN, *Solomon Schechter.* Philadelphia, 1938.

COHON, SAMUEL S., "The Theology of the Union Prayer Book." Reprinted from *Central Conference of American Rabbis Yearbook.* Vol. XXXVIII, p. 245. Cincinnati, 1928.

———, *What We Jews Believe.* Department of Synagogue and School Extension of the Union of American Hebrew Congregations. Cincinnati, 1931.

COWEN, PHILIP, *Memories of an American Jew.* New York, 1932.

DALY, CHARLES P. (M. J. Kohler, ed.), *The Settlement of the Jews in North America.* New York, 1893.

DAVIDSON, GABRIEL, *Our Jewish Farmers.* New York, 1943.

DRACHMAN, BERNARD, *The Unfailing Light.* Rabbinical Council of America. New York, 1948.

DUSHKIN, ALEXANDER M., *Jewish Education in New York City.* New York, 1918.

EINHORN, DAVID, *Selected Sermons and Addresses.* New York, 1911.

David Einhorn Memorial Volume, ed. by Kaufmann Kohler. New York, 1914

EISENSTEIN, J. D., "The History of the First Russian-American Jewish Congregation." *Publications of the American Jewish Historical Society,* No. 9, pp. 63-74. Baltimore, 1901.

ELBOGEN, ISMAR, "Alexander Kohut," *American Jewish Year Book.* XLIV, pp. 73-80. Philadelphia, 1942-1943.

———, *American Jewish Scholarship: A Survey.* New York, 1943.

———, *A Century of Jewish Life.* (Translated by Moses Hadas.) Philadelphia, 1944.

ELIASSOF, HERMAN, *German American Jews.* 1915.

ELZAS, BARNETT A., *The Jews of South Carolina* (From Earliest Times to the Present Day). Philadelphia, 1905.

FELSENTHAL, EMMA, *Bernard Felsenthal, Teacher in Israel.* London and New York, 1944.

Fifty Years of Social Service. The History of the United Hebrew Charities of the City of New York (Jewish Social Service Association). New York, 1926.

(Editors of) Fortune Magazine. *Jews in America.* New York, 1936.

FINK, REUBEN (ed.), *America and Palestine.* New York, 1945.

FREEHOF, SOLOMON B., *Reform Jewish Practice and Its Rabbinic Background.* Cincinnati, 1944.

FRIEDLAENDER, ISRAEL, *Past and Present.* Cincinnati, 1919.

FRIEDMAN, LEE M., *Jewish Pioneers and Patriots.* Philadelphia, 1942.

GAMORAN, EMANUEL, *Changing Conceptions in Jewish Education.* New York, 1924.

GINZBERG, LOUIS, *Students, Scholars and Saints.* Philadelphia, 1928.

GOLDSTEIN, ISRAEL, *A Century of Judaism in New York.* New York, 1930.

GORDIS, ROBERT, *Conservative Judaism.* New York, 1945.

GRINSTEIN, HYMAN B., *The Rise of the Jewish Community in New York 1654-1860.* Philadelphia, 1945.

GUTSTEIN, MORRIS A., *The Story of the Jews of Newport: 1658-1908.* New York, 1936.

HELLER, JAMES G., *As Yesterday When it is Past.* Cincinnati, 1942.

HIRSCH, EMIL G., *My Religion.* New York, 1925.

———, *Twenty Discourses.* Reprinted from Reform Advocate. New York, n.d.

JANOWSKY, OSCAR I. (ed.), *The American Jew.* New York, 1942.

———, *The J.W.B. Survey.* New York, 1948.

JUNG, LEO (ed.), *The Jewish Library.* First Series. New York, 1928.

———, *The Jewish Library.* Second Series. New York, 1930.

———, *The Jewish Library.* Third Series. New York, 1934.

KALLEN, HORACE M., *Judaism At Bay.* New York, 1932.

KAPLAN, MORDECAI M. (ed.), *The Jewish Reconstructionist Papers.* New York, 1936.

———, *Judaism as a Civilization.* New York, 1934.

———, *Judaism in Transition.* New York, 1936.

———, *The Future of the American Jew.* New York, 1948.

KARPF, HYMAN J., *Jewish Community Organization in the United States.* New York, 1939.

KOHLER, KAUFMANN, *Backwards or Forward?* New York, 1885.

———, *Hebrew Union College and Other Addresses.* Cincinnati, 1916.

———, *Jewish Theology.* New York, 1918.

———, "Personal Reminiscences of My Early Life." Reprinted from *Hebrew Union College Monthly*, May, 1918. Cincinnati, 1918.

———, *Studies, Addresses and Personal Papers.* New York, 1931.

KOHN, EUGENE, *The Future of Judaism in America.* New York, 1934.

KOHUT, ALEXANDER, *Ethics of the Fathers.* (Translated into English by Max Cohen and edited by B. Elzas). New York, 1920.

KOHUT, REBEKAH, *My Portion.* New York, 1925.

LEBESON, ANITA L., *Jewish Pioneers in America: 1492-1848.* New York, 1931.

LEVINGER, LEE J., *A Jewish Chaplain in France.* New York, 1921.

LEVINTHAL, ISRAEL HERBERT, *Judaism, An Analysis and An Interpretation.* New York, 1935.

LEVY, BERYL H., *Reform Judaism in America.* New York, 1933.

LIPSKY, LOUIS, *Thirty Years of American Zionism.* (Vol. I. of *Selected Works*) New York, 1927.

Marcus, Jacob R., *The Americanization of Isaac Mayer Wise*. Cincinnati, 1931.

Marx, Alexander, *Essays in Jewish Biography*. Philadelphia, 1947, pp. 223-298.

Mielziner, Ella M. F., *Moses Mielziner* (1828-1903). With a reprint of his *Slavery among the Ancient Hebrews and Other Works*. New York, 1931.

Moise, L. C., *Biography of Isaac Harby*. Sumter, S.C., 1931.

Morais, Henry Samuel, *Eminent Israelites of the Nineteenth Century*. Philadelphia, 1880.

——, *The Jews of Philadelphia*. Philadelphia, 1894.

Neuman, Abraham A., *Cyrus Adler*. New York, 1942.

Philipson, David, *Max Lilienthal, American Rabbi: Life and Writings*. New York, 1915.

——, *My Life as an American Jew*. Cincinnati, 1937-1938.

——, *The Reform Movement in Judaism*. New York, 1931; rev. ed., with an Introduction by Solomon B. Freehof, New York, 1967.

Reform Judaism in the Large Cities, A Survey. Union of American Hebrew Congregations. Cincinnati, 1931.

Rosenau, William, *Benjamin Szold*. Baltimore, 1902.

Schachner, Nathan, *The Price of Liberty*. New York, 1948.

Schechter, Solomon, *Seminary Addresses and other Papers*. Cincinnati, 1915.

——, *Studies in Judaism*. First Series. Philadelphia, 1896.

——, *Studies in Judaism*. Second Series. Philadelphia, 1908.

——, (Alexander Marx and Frank I. Schechter, eds.), *Studies in Judaism*. Third Series. Philadelphia, 1924.

Solis-Cohen, Solomon, *Judaism and Science, with Other Addresses and Papers*. Philadelphia, 1940.

——, "Mayer Sulzberger." In *Addresses Delivered in Memory of Mayer Sulzberger*. Pp. 24-55. Philadelphia, 1924.

Steinberg, Milton, *A Partisan Guide to the Jewish Problem*. New York, 1945.

Stiles, Ezra, *The Literary Diary of Ezra Stiles*. (ed. by F. B. Dexter). New York, 1901.

Straus, Oscar, *The Origin of Republican Form of Government in the United States*. New York, 1901.

Trachtenberg, Joshua, *Consider the Years*. Easton, Pa., 1944.

Tscherikower, E., *History of the Jewish Labor Movement in the United States* (Yiddish). 2 vols. New York, 1943, 1945.

Wise, Isaac Mayer (David Philipson, ed.), *Reminiscences*, Cincinnati, 1901.

——, (David Philipson and Louis Grossman, eds.), *Selected Writings*.

Wise, Stephen S., *As I See It*. New York, 1945.

Wolf, Simon, *The American Jew as Patriot, Soldier and Citizen*. Philadelphia, 1895.

ADDENDUM

BELKIN, SAMUEL, *In His Image*. London, New York, Toronto, 1960.

BENJAMIN, I. J., *Three Years in America*. Vol. II. Edited by Charles Rezni-koff. Philadelphia, 1956.

BLAU, JOSEPH, and BARON, SALO W. (eds.), *The Jews of the United States, 1790-1840—A Documentary History*. 3 vols. New York and Phila-delphia, 1963.

CAHNMAN, WERNER J. (ed.), *Intermarriage and Jewish Life*. New York, 1963.

COHEN, JACK J., *Jewish Education in Democratic Society*. New York, 1964.

DAVIS, MOSHE, *The Emergence of Conservative Judaism*. Philadelphia, 1963.

———, "America: Its Role in Civilization," Davis (ed.), *America and Israel*, pt. 4. New York, 1956.

DUSHKIN, ALEXANDER M., and ENGELMAN, URIAH Z., *Jewish Education in the United States*. New York, 1959.

EISENDRATH, MAURICE N., *Can Faith Survive?* New York, 1964.

EISENSTEIN, IRA, *Varieties of Jewish Belief*. New York, 1966.

FEINSTEIN, MARVIN, *American Zionism, 1884-1904*. New York, 1965.

FREEHOF, SOLOMON B., *Reform Responsa*. Cincinnati, 1960.

———, *Recent Reform Responsa*. Cincinnati, 1963.

FRIEDMAN, THEODORE, and GORDIS, ROBERT (eds.), *Jewish Life in America*. New York, 1955.

GINZBERG, ELI, *Agenda for American Jews*. New York, 1964.

HALPERIN, SAMUEL, *The Political World of American Zionism*. Detroit, 1961.

HELLER, JAMES G., *Isaac Mayer Wise*. New York, 1965.

HERBERG, WILL, *Protestant-Catholic-Jew*. New York, 1960.

HESCHEL, ABRAHAM J., *The Insecurity of Freedom*. Philadelphia, 1966.

JANOWSKY, OSCAR I. (ed.), *The American Jew: A Reappraisal*. Philadelphia, 1964.

KALLEN, HORACE M., "Of Them Which Say They Are Jews," Judah Pilch (ed.), *The Jewish Struggle for Survival*. New York, 1954.

KAMPF, AVRAM, *Contemporary Synagogue Art*. Philadelphia, 1966.

KAPLAN, MORDECAI M., *A New Zionism*. New York, 1965.

———, *The Greater Judaism in the Making*. New York, 1960.

KARP, ABRAHAM J., "New York Chooses a Chief Rabbi," *Publication of the American Jewish Historical Society*, XLIV, March, 1955.

———, *The United Synagogue of America, 1913-1963*. New York, 1964.

KORN, BERTRAM W., *Eventful Years and Experiences*. Cincinnati, 1954.

——— (ed.), *Retrospect and Prospect* (Essays in Commemoration of the 75th Anniversary of the Central Conference of American Rabbis, 1889-1964). New York, 1965.

KRAMER, JUDITH R., and LEVENTMAN, SEYMOUR, *Children of the Gilded Ghetto*. New Haven and London, 1961.

KRANZLER, GEORGE, *Williamsburg: A Jewish Community in Transition.* New York, 1961.

LENSKI, GERHARD, *The Religious Factor.* New York, 1961.

LIEBMAN, CHARLES S., "Orthodoxy in American Jewish Life," *American Jewish Year Book,* LXVI. New York and Philadelphia, 1965.

LURIE, HARRY L., *A Heritage Affirmed.* Philadelphia, 1961.

MARCUS, JACOB R., *Early American Jewry.* 2 vols. Philadelphia, 1951, 1953.

———, *Memoirs of American Jews.* 3 vols. Philadelphia, 1955, 1956.

MORGENSTERN, JULIAN, *As a Mighty Stream.* Philadelphia, 1949.

"Organized Religion in the United States," *The Annals,* CCLVI, March, 1948.

PLAUT, W. GUNTHER, *The Growth of Reform Judaism.* New York, 1965.

POLL, SOLOMON, *The Hasidic Community of Williamsburg.* Glencoe, Ill., 1962; reissued New York, 1969.

"Religion in America," *Daedalus,* Winter, 1967.

"Religion in American Society," *The Annals,* CCCXXXII, November, 1960.

RINGER, BENJAMIN B., "The Edge of Friendliness," *The Lakeville Studies,* II. New York, London, 1967.

RISCHIN, MOSES, *The Promised City: New York's Jews.* Cambridge, Mass., 1962.

SCHIFF, ALVIN I., *The Jewish Day School in the United States.* New York, 1966.

SHERMAN, C. BEZALEL, *The Jew Within American Society.* Detroit, 1961.

SKLARE, MARSHALL, *Conservative Judaism.* Glencoe, Ill., 1955.

———, (ed.), *The Jews: Social Patterns of an American Group.* Glencoe, Ill., 1958.

———, and GREENBLUM, JOSEPH, "Jewish Identity on the Suburban Frontier," *The Lakeville Studies,* I. New York, London, 1967.

SMITH, JAMES WARD, and JAMISON, A. LELAND (eds.), "The Shaping of American Religion," *Religion in American Life Series,* I. Princeton, 1961.

STEMBER, CHARLES H., and others, *Jews in the Mind of America.* New York, 1966.

WAXMAN, MORDECAI, *Tradition and Change.* New York, 1958.

WISCHNITZER, RACHEL, *Synagogue Architecture in the United States.* Philadelphia, 1955.

CHAPTER 9

JEWISH EDUCATIONAL INSTITUTIONS

By Simon Greenberg

I. INTRODUCTION

Educational activity performs two functions. It broadens the range of man's knowledge and skills, and transmits this knowledge and these skills from one generation to another, or from one man to his fellow.

Educational activity is inherent in human societies on all levels of development. One society is distinguished from another, however, not merely by the quality of its intellectual inquisitiveness and the character of its accumulated knowledge and skills. Intellectual and spiritual progress are equally reflected by the institutions a society creates or adapts in order consciously to increase its knowledge and skills, consciously to transmit them to the group as a whole.

Until comparatively recent times the educational institutions of all peoples of the world were each concerned almost exclusively with the transmission of the skills, the knowledge and the traditions of its own particular group. Educational institutions were not expected to be centers for the discovery of new knowledge or channels for the transmission of truth and beauty and wisdom, regardless of their source of origin.

In the following pages we shall attempt to sketch only in briefest outline the history of the main types of educational institutions created by the Jewish people from the earliest times to the present. Another chapter in the work is devoted to the educational philosophy underlying the work of these institutions, and to the pedagogic principles adopted to achieve their goal. While a certain amount of duplication is inevitable, because it is virtually impossible to discuss any aspect of an educational institution without some reference to its philosophy and curriculum, this chapter will seek to limit itself primarily to the external history of the institutions, to the occasions that brought them into being, and to the conditions that enabled them to function.

The recorded history of the Jewish people extends over a period exceeding three thousand years and is divided into rather well-defined eras. Moreover, Jewish life took on differing forms in the various countries in which it existed. We might, therefore, treat our theme either chronologically or geographically. However, since many of the educational institutions existed during more than one era and in more than one land, we chose to present chronologically the story of the individual institution as it developed and changed from one era to another and from country to country.

II. THE HOME

The home is mankind's universal educational agency. It was but natural that within the family fathers should transmit a knowledge of their occupations to the sons and mothers teach their daughters the skills required for homebuilding. Thus, while there are no specific references in the Bible to this particular matter, we have every reason to assume that Jewish sons learned from their fathers how to plow, plant, care for vineyards, tend sheep, the art of the potter and the warrior and the other arts in ancient Israel.

But the home was not used by all groups with equal awareness and effectiveness for transmitting the spiritual and ethical teachings and the treasured historic memories of the group. The biblical record clearly indicates that among the Jews the home was at a very early period *consciously* employed for such educational purposes. Responsibility for transmitting the group's spiritual heritage to one's children is specifically enjoined upon parents, particularly the father. Abraham is known "of the Lord" in order that "he may command his children and his household after him, that they may keep the way of the Lord, to do righteousness and justice" (Gen. 18:19). A well-defined body of instruction is to be transmitted. "And these words which I command thee shall be upon thine heart and thou shalt teach them diligently unto thy children." The family is commanded to practice prescribed ceremonies for the express purpose of perpetuating the knowledge of great historic events and for stimulating the inquisitive mind of the child. His questions provide a natural setting for the father to explain and emphasize some precious traditions of the group. "And it shall come to pass, when your children shall say unto you: What mean ye by this service? that ye shall say: It is the sacrifice of the Lord's passover, for that He passed over the houses of the children of Israel in Egypt, when He smote the Egyptians and delivered our houses" (Ex. 12:26-27). In the same spirit every Jewish family was commanded to dwell in booths for seven days "that your generations may know that I made the children of Israel to dwell in booths, when I brought them out of the land of Egypt" (Lev. 23:43). The festivals and ceremonies were not and are not merely means of worshiping the Lord. They were and are the re-enactments of great historic moments in the people's past, not only to stimulate appropriate religious sentiments but also to preserve and transmit precious group memories. While the parents are commanded consciously to teach their children, the children are urged to take to heart the instructions of their parents. They are not only to "honor thy father and thy mother" (Ex. 20:12) but also to obey the instruction of the father and not to reject or neglect the teaching of the mother (Pr. 1:8).

The records do not indicate the extent to which parents gave formal instruction at regular intervals to their children. But it seems fair to imply that in the case of intellectually and spiritually alert parents that type of instruction was not entirely lacking. Hannah's relation to her son Samuel, the careful training given to Samson by his parents, a mother's recorded instruction to her son (Pr. 31:1-9), the care with which Job is reported to have supervised the religious life of his children (Job 1:5)—these and other indications justify the assumption that there were parents in early Israel who performed their duties as teachers with a high degree of seriousness.

During the days of the Second Temple, when Judaism, under the leadership of the scribes and Sages, acquired the traditional forms associated with Rabbinic or normative Judaism, the home became a far more effective educational agency. From the moment the child learned how to speak the father recited the morning and evening prayers with him; and as the child developed the father trained him in the performance of the mitzvot. Even though elementary schools were plentiful, the Rabbis stressed the father's duty that he himself teach his son, for a "child's true father is he who teaches him Torah." In addition, it was incumbent upon the father to teach his son a trade or profession, even how to swim, for lack of a trade may lead him to a life of violence and inability to swim may endanger his life.

In observing how the mother conducted the household, children learned the detailed dietary laws and the manner of daily Jewish living. They saw her welcoming the Sabbath every week not only by numerous and arduous labors in the kitchen; they also saw her dressing her home, herself and her children with particular attention, and kindling the Sabbath lights. The father's *kiddush*, recited over a cup of wine or two loaves of bread to usher in the Sabbath or the festival meal, the washing of the hands before meals, the grace after meals, the celebrations of holidays, major and minor festivals, particularly the unique and remarkable Passover eve Seder service, the fast days of the Jewish year—these and a host of other religious observances inculcated piety and faith in the growing child's heart, and acquainted him with the noblest spiritual and historical experiences of his people.

If the Jewish girl until very recent days was most often not sent to receive formal instruction in a school, it was not merely because of a widespread attitude that a girl needed no formal education. It was due rather to the feeling that her mother and home training could provide her with all the instruction she needed to live a good and pious Jewish life. Until very recent times, the expectation was, by and large, fully realized. And because the Jewish home was so effective an educational institution, the Jewish school could devote itself exclusively to the formal teaching of the sacred texts, leaving instruction in personal religious matters to the home.

For two thousand years and more, the Jewish home continued to be the most effective institution for educating the Jewish child. The social and economic forces that, after the French Revolution, tended to minimize family and home influence among Western peoples, had even more disastrous effects upon Jewish life. In addition, the vast migrations of millions of East European Jews to the West severed Jewish family life from its moorings in a well-organized community with an established public opinion. Today in America and throughout the Western world, therefore, the home as a Jewish educational institution, though still important, does not approach in effectiveness the Jewish home of Eastern Europe before World War I, or of any part of Europe before the French Revolution.

The breakdown of the Jewish home as an effective, primary Jewish educational agency in the Western world has placed enormous responsibilities upon the other educational agencies of the Jewish community. All educators are agreed, however, that the best school cannot possibly substitute for the home. At present, particularly in America, the reconstitution of the Jewish home as an effective educational agency for rich religious life represents one of the greatest challenges to Jewish educators and religious leaders.

III. THE SYNAGOGUE

Next to the home the synagogue was and is the most democratic and universal Jewish educational institution affecting the lives of old and young, men and women.[1a] Our records give us no clear picture of the place, the age or the circumstances under which it came into being. But it is safe to say that the element of instruction played at least as great a part in the founding of the synagogue as did prayer. Many unique and specifically educational features were combined in the synagogue almost from its very inception; these have remained an integral part of it to our own day.

The first and probably the oldest of these is the reading from the Scriptures. The Bible relates that Moses, after having written the Torah, commanded the priests, the Levites and all the elders that "when all Israel is come to appear before the Lord thy God in the place which He shall choose, thou shalt read this law before all Israel in their hearing. Assemble the people, the men and the women and the little ones, and thy stranger that is within thy gates, that they may hear, and that they may learn, and fear the Lord your God" (Deut. 31:11-12). While this reading was to take place on Sukkot, it was apparently to be held in every community throughout the land and not only in Jerusalem, for the women, children and strangers were not commanded to make the pilgrimage to Jerusalem, but they were commanded to hear the reading. Such a reading of Scripture before a vast throng is recorded as having taken place on various occasions before the establishment of the Second Temple.

The revolution introduced by Ezra into the religious life of the post-exilic Jewish community made the Torah at once the core and the foundation of the community's spiritual life. Scripture readings gradually became a fixed feature of the gatherings on the Sabbath and on Monday and Thursday, the two market days when the peasants came into town. Reading Scripture in itself, however, could not serve the educational purpose adequately. Hence, there was added either a translation into the vernacular or a religious message based upon the passage that was read. In time, the Five Books of Moses were divided into sections, so that the whole Pentateuch might be read from beginning to end on the Sabbaths once in three years or once every year. To the readings from the Penta-teuch, passages from the Prophets were later added. Today in every traditional synagogue the Pentateuch is completed once a year through weekly Sabbath readings. The portion read is no longer orally translated into the vernacular, for in most synagogues the congregation is provided with a printed text and translation. This scriptural reading is still the central feature of the traditional Sabbath synagogue service. Many have objected to it because of the time it requires and its noninspirational quality as read in many synagogues today. Nevertheless, it continues to hold its place in the vast majority of the synagogues of the world; and it continues to exercise, though far less effectively than it might, the educa-tional function of instructing the congregation in the contents of the Pentateuch.

In addition to the Scripture reading the synagogue became the center where spiritual leaders of the people regularly delivered their message of inspiration or information. In biblical days the prophet addressed the people in the courtyard of the Temple. On various occasions the prophet would be visited at home by his followers in order to be blessed or in-structed by him. In Babylonia Ezekiel's home was apparently the ren-dezvous for the pious who wanted to hear a Divine message. Ezekiel's complaint that many of his listeners came to be entertained rather than instructed, sounds very modern indeed.

When a knowledge of the Torah became the *sine qua non* for spiritual leadership among the Jews, it was but natural that the message of the leader should become associated with the Torah and more particularly with the portions read on any given occasion. Until modern times that message would most often be delivered in the synagogue on the Sabbath afternoon immediately preceding the afternoon service. In more recent times a message or sermon in the vernacular based on the weekly pentateuchal portion has become a permanent feature of the Sabbath morning service in well-nigh all synagogues, particularly in America. This message is inspirational and informative and serves as a significant educational medium.

But the sermon and the Scripture readings are not the only direct educational features of the synagogue service. The traditional prayer book itself contains many educational features ordinarily not associated with a liturgy. In the first place, Judaism considers study as being superior even to prayer as a means of worshiping God. Hence passages of an ethical and historical nature from the Talmud are incorporated into the prayer book. The prayers are modified for various occasions of the year, so that the festival celebrated, or the historic occasion remembered, is given its meaning and interpretation. The synagogue liturgy does not stress merely the *individual's* relation to God, the *individual's* needs and hopes, and the *individual's* longing for Divine salvation. Equal emphasis is placed upon the *group's* relation to God, upon the *group's* needs and hopes, upon the *group's* yearning for collective salvation.

Moreover, the synagogue by its organization and form of worship has been a mighty force making for democracy within the Jewish community. Any ten male adults may conduct a regular service. Anyone among them may be their reader or preacher. There is a complete absence of anything like a clerical hierarchy. Knowledge and piety alone are the paths to leadership. Where a congregation diverges from these principles, it does so not because of the requirements of ritual or liturgy. On the contrary, it does so in violation of those requirements and merely as a concession to the human limitations of those who compose that particular congregation.

The synagogue's role as a Jewish educational agency is by no means exhausted by the above-mentioned activities. The synagogue building has always been a center of study for either children or adults. But that aspect of the synagogue's contribution to Jewish education we shall discuss later under the general subject of schools.

Thus, through its liturgy, scriptural reading, sermon and organization, the synagogue was, next to the home, the most significant educational agency in the life of the Jewish people. Together with all other religious institutions throughout the world, the synagogue's influence as a house of prayer has perceptibly waned in modern times. Other aspects of it have, however, taken on new vitality in our day. More-over, among the Jews no other institution has as yet been created to take its place, nor to approach it even in its present weakened condition, as an influence for the moral, ethical and religious education of the people.

IV. THE ELEMENTARY AND SECONDARY SCHOOL

A. IN BIBLE TIMES

The Bible contains no direct reference to the existence of schools for either children or adults. But there can be little doubt that educational activity in biblical times was not limited exclusively to the home. There undoubtedly were men who taught children other than their own either as pupils or as apprentices. Bezalel and Oholeav, the artists who built the Tabernacle and all its vessels, were endowed by the Lord not only with the skill of their own hands, but also with the ability "to teach" others. The children of the royal family most likely had their own private teachers. The elders of Samaria seem to have trained Ahab's seventy sons. Moreover, members of the court apparently studied the dominant language of the age, as well as the Hebrew language. The ability to write—no mean achievement in ancient times—was apparently quite prevalent among Israelite children.

Priests and Levites are spoken of most frequently as the teachers of the people. King Jehoash was instructed by the priest Johoiada, Jehoshaphat, King of Judah, sent officers, together with priests and Levites, to teach throughout the Land of Judah. The Bible refers to "teacher," "instructors" and "wise men," who acted as teachers. These presumably had some fixed place and time for teaching. That the priests and Levites received some kind of systematic and formal instruction must be taken for granted. The priest had to be thoroughly acquainted not only with an elaborate and complicated sacrificial system but with the equally intricate laws of Levitical purity and physical health. The Levites had to be proficient as assistants to the priests and as members of the Temple choir. They could not possibly enter upon their duties without thorough previous instruction. The advanced age at which they started to perform their duties in the Temple, the priest at thirty and the Levite at twenty-five, probably reflects the extended period of training they had to undergo.

The early prophets appear also to have had schools or at least groups within which they trained the novitiates and developed their own spiritual powers.

However, the elementary school for the education of all Jewish children did not come into its own until well toward the end of the Second Commonwealth.

B. FROM THE SECOND COMMONWEALTH TO MODERN TIMES

The following short talmudic passage gives us the most significant information available regarding the establishment of Jewish elementary schools:

However, that man is to be remembered for good, and his name is Joshua ben Gemala [c. 64 c.e.]; for were it not for him Torah would have been forgotten in Israel. For at first he who had a father was taught Torah by him, and he who had no father did not study Torah. It was then decreed that teachers of children should be appointed in Jerusalem. However, he who had a father, the father would bring him to Jerusalem and have him taught, while he who had no father, would not come to Jerusalem to study. It was then decreed that teachers of the young should be appointed in every district throughout the land. But the boys would be entered in the school at the age of sixteen and seventeen and if the teacher would rebuke one of them, he would resent it and leave. Thus it was until Joshua ben Gemala decreed that teachers of children should be appointed in every district and every city and that boys of the age of six and seven should be entered.[2]

It is obvious from the above passage that the elementary school had a very long development behind it by the time Joshua ben Gemala instituted his reform. Simeon ben Shatah (first century B.C.E.)[3a] is credited with the decree requiring children to go to a *Bet Sefer*, a school, while another passage has it that Ezra was the one who sought to "set a scribe next to a scribe," that is, to multiply the number of schools in the community. The chief educational contribution of Jewish religious leaders of the Second Commonwealth was the principle that a basic elementary Jewish education must be provided by the community for every Jewish boy regardless of his social or economic status. The goal thus set was probably never fully attained, no more than any modern society with laws for universal compulsory elementary education has attained its goal. But it can be said without fear of serious contradiction that except for periods of communal disintegration or impoverishment following mass persecutions and plagues, or accompanying the pioneer efforts of recently established Jewish settlements, universal elementary education for boys was more fully attained among Jews up to the end of the eighteenth century than among any other contemporary group. The Rabbis forbade a Jew to live in a community which had no elementary school teacher. Every community having at least ten Jewish families could be compelled by law to maintain a teacher in its midst although not all of the ten families may have had pupils for him. It was, moreover, a widespread practice during these centuries for a family living in isolation to invite a teacher to become a part of the household in order to teach the children. An authority of the fourth century suggests that only if a Jewish child were captured as an infant and raised among non-Jews could he grow up without an elementary

Jewish education. This is most likely an exaggeration, as are the traditions about the hundreds of elementary schools in Jerusalem before its destruction in 70 C.E.,[4a] and the thousands of elementary schools in Bethar before the failure of the revolt of Bar Kokbah (*c.* 135 C.E.).[5a] But none can gainsay the fact that the elementary Jewish school in which Jewish children learned how to read Hebrew and translate the Pentateuch has been the most widespread institution of the Jewish community for the past two thousand years.

I. THE BET HA-SEFER AND THE BET HA-KENESET

From the very beginning there was a very close relationship between the school and the synagogue. The synagogue premises were the meeting place of the school, and synagogue functionaries very often acted as teachers. The elementary school was referred to in talmudic times as a *Bet Ha-Sefer* (Aramaic—*Bet Sifra* or *Bet Mikra*), House of the Book, or *Bet Ha-Keneset* (Aramaic—*Be Kenishta*), the House of Gathering. The second name is most likely derived from the place where the school met. The first name may indicate the subject matter taught, namely, the Bible, or perhaps the fact that instead of meeting in the synagogue the school met in a special community building or in a private home, and was the private enterprise of the teacher.

2. THE BET TALMUD

Secondary education, which consisted in study of Rabbinic texts—particularly the Mishna—and in an introduction to the method by which the Oral Law was discussed and developed, was provided by the *Bet Talmud*, and Talmud school. The relationship between it and the *Bet Sefer* is indicated by the Rabbinic dictum that a boy should start to study Bible at five, Mishna at ten and Talmud at fifteen, and by the remark that out of every thousand pupils who started to study Bible only one hundred continued with the study of the Mishna.

3. THE HEDER AND THE TALMUD TORAH

The twofold aspect, private and communal, of the Jewish elementary school has characterized it throughout the centuries. The duty to educate the Jewish child never became the exclusive responsibility either of the community or of the father. Circumstances determined which of the two assumed the responsibility in any particular instance. The average Jewish parent made great sacrifices to pay for his child's education. Together with other parents he could make his own arrangements with a private teacher. But when a child had no parents or when the parents were too poor to pay, the community would step in and either pay all or part of the child's tuition to a private teacher or else, where the number of indigent children warranted it, a community school supported by voluntary contributions and self-taxation would be established.

Among the Jews of Eastern Europe the private elementary school for children was called a "heder" (a room). It took its name from the fact that it usually met in one of the rooms of the teacher's home. There a group of fifteen to twenty-five children of varying ages, usually below thirteen, would meet during the whole day. Within each heder there was a minimum of gradation. But there was gradation among the various hedarim serving a community. The most elementary heder catered to children who were beginning to read and write Hebrew and to translate sentences from the Pentateuch. Above that was the heder supervised by a rabbi who taught only those prepared to master the translation of the Pentateuch and selected passages from Rashi's Commentary. The highest Heder introduced the student to the Talmud and prepared him to go on to the *Yeshiva*.

The curriculum, the school year, the financial arrangements varied but little from community to community. They were governed by the prevailing cultural standards, by well-established traditions or by special communal enactments.

The communally supported school was called the Talmud Torah, a house for the study of the Torah. It offered the same opportunities to the children of the poor as the heder did to the others. In rare instances, as in the case of the Amsterdam Talmud Torah of the seventeenth century, it was by far superior to the private heder, having a comparatively rich, graded curriculum, a staff of well-equipped teachers, and catering to all children of the community, not merely to the poor. The Talmud Torah often occupied a structure of its own, though just as often it would meet on the synagogue premises.

Both of these educational institutions continued to flourish in Eastern European Jewish communities as late as the twentieth century. They disappeared in Russia only with the Russian Revolution and continued among the Jews of Poland until the 1939 debacle, which overwhelmed Polish Jewry.

4. MODERN JEWISH SCHOOLS AND THE RISE OF SECULAR EDUCATION AMONG JEWS

The heder and the Talmud Torah held undisputed sway in Jewish communities throughout the world until the end of the eighteenth century. These schools, though they taught some elementary arithmetic and the reading and writing of Judeo-German, were otherwise devoted exclusively to religious subject matter. Whatever secular education was attained by

Jewish individuals here and there was the result of private instruction or personal initiative and persistence. Moreover, all government schools were either closed to Jews or were boycotted by them. In the second half of the eighteenth century a perceptible change occurred. The activities of Moses Mendelssohn (1729-1786)[6a] and his colleagues resulted in the organization (1778) in Berlin of the first Jewish free school which included German and French, as well as Hebrew, in its curriculum. The Edict of Toleration issued by Emperor Joseph II of Austria in 1781 was enthusiastically greeted by German Jewish intellectuals, and elaborate programs for the reform of Jewish education were proposed by them. Modern Jewish schools, sponsored by the government and supported by special taxes levied upon the Jewish community, were established particularly among the Jews of Galicia. While Jewish intellectuals welcomed the schools, the Jewish masses rightly suspected that the schools intended not merely to impart information but also to wean Jewish children away from Judaism and the Jewish people. Though a Jew was appointed inspector, and though some hundred such schools were opened after 1790, resistance of the Jewish masses and other factors led to their close in 1806.

Somewhat the same situation was repeated in Russia, where in 1844 a special decree permitted Jews to open their own modern schools to be supported by special taxes upon the Jewish community. The Russification and proselytizing aspect of these schools was so pronounced, however, that after ten years of functioning only a little more than three thousand Jewish pupils were attracted by them. A change in the Russian government's attitude in 1857 eliminated the element of religious proselytization from these schools, and Jews flocked to them in large numbers. But such was the zeal for Russification, which inspired even the Jewish supervisors of the schools, that before long the distinctly Jewish subjects were practically excluded from the curriculum. By that time Jewish students and parents could discern little or no difference between these Jewish government schools and the general government schools. As a result, Jewish youth turned to the general school, which had been open to them since 1804 but had been almost unanimously boycotted by Jews heretofore. By 1873 it became apparent that, from the government's point of view, the special Jewish elementary and secondary schools were no longer necessary, and they, plus the two government-sponsored rabbinical seminaries, were closed. Jewish youth was coming in increasing numbers to the general Russian government schools; within twenty years, from 1853 to 1873, the percentage of Jews in the total student body rose from 1.25 to 13.2. By 1880 Russian educators started to advocate and apply a *numerus clausus.*

a. The "Heder Metukan" and Modern Jewish School Systems in Eastern Europe

Until the last quarter of the nineteenth century all efforts to bring secular education to the Jews, whether sponsored by Jews themselves or by non-Jews, were inspired primarily by the desire to assimilate the Jew into the general population. By about 1885 a change of attitude became discernible in the ranks of Jewish intellectuals. The high hopes entertained by Jews that complete civil and social emancipation would automatically follow the secularization and modernization of Jewish life, were rudely shattered by one unhappy event after another. At the same time, a renewed spirit of self-respect was awakened within the ranks of those Westernized or modernized Jews who were deeply and irrevocably attached to Judaism and to the Hebrew language and literature. Zionism and modern Hebrew literature made remarkable headway among all classes of the Jewish community. The Yiddish language and literature simultaneously experienced an unprecedented development. All this inner cultural revival was bound before long to be reflected in the community's educational activities. A new modern Jewish school appeared, the Heder Metukan, the modern progressive heder. The language of instruction was Hebrew. There was less emphasis on religious piety and on Rabbinic literature, but there was a positive attitude toward the Jewish religion and toward all the spiritual and cultural treasures of the Jewish people. The hope for a re-established Jewish state in Palestine was at the heart of this educational activity.

Though these new schools increased in number and flourished, they never replaced the heder and the Talmud Torah, which remained predominant within Eastern European Jewry until 1914.

5. ELEMENTARY AND SECONDARY JEWISH EDUCATION IN SOVIET RUSSIA

The Soviet government soon after it was firmly established effectively outlawed the heder, the Talmud Torah and every other Jewish educational institution devoted to the preservation of the Jewish religious heritage or of the Hebrew language and culture. In their place, regular government supported schools using the Yiddish language as a medium of instruction were established in neighborhoods with preponderantly Jewish populations. The curriculum in these schools followed the curriculum of all other government schools of similar grade, except that Yiddish literature and some elements of Jewish history were taught. Since Jewish children had the choice of attending either these schools or other government schools, the percentage of the Jewish children in the Ukraine and White Russia attending Jewish schools rose to the high point of sixty-four per cent in 1932 but declined steadily since then.

Moreover, Jewish citizens of the Soviet Union today may not and do not maintain supplementary schools in which their young children can legally and systematically achieve some knowledge of the tenets of Judaism, or of the grammar and literature of the Hebrew language. No official information is at present available regarding the number of Jewish children attending Yiddish-language schools, and consequently receiving some instruction in Jewish history and Yiddish literature. We do know, however, that, with the exception of a Yiddish daily which is reputedly appearing in Biro-Bidjan, no other Yiddish periodical is now being published in all of the Soviet Union. We know, too, that so basic and elementary a religious need as a Jewish calendar indicating the religious holy days and festivals, is not available to Jews in Soviet Russia at the present time.

6. ELEMENTARY AND SECONDARY JEWISH EDUCATION IN POLAND BETWEEN THE TWO WORLD WARS

Despite the depressed economic position of Polish Jewry between the two World Wars and the patent anti-Semitic policies of the government, elementary and secondary Jewish education achieved much during those hard years. The minority rights granted to Polish Jewry by the Treaty of Versailles included the power of self-taxation for educational purposes. Funds thus made available were in themselves not sufficient to maintain the schools. Tuition fees, voluntary contributions and help from abroad supplemented government funds. Unfortunately, Polish Jewry could not unite on any one educational program. Three main national groups competed for the child. These schools paralleled the regular Polish government school in hours of sessions and in general subject matter. However, they added distinctly Jewish subjects to their curricula. The largest unit consisted of the Jabne-Mizrachi religiously and Zionistically oriented schools, claiming some fifty-six thousand pupils in 1936. Next to them came the Tarbut schools, with Hebrew as their language of instruction and Zionism as their chief ideological orientation. In 1938 forty thousand pupils attended three hundred Tarbut schools. The smallest of the three groups consisted of the Yiddish-language schools with their antireligious and antinational, or anti-Zionist, approach. In 1934-1935, some sixteen thousand pupils were registered in their classes. Obviously, a very large percentage of the Jewish children of Poland's prewar 3,300,000 was not found in any of these school systems. Many of them preferred to attend the regular Polish government schools and get their Jewish education either in a heder or from a private teacher. Horeb, a non-Zionist fundamentalist religious group, claimed in 1934-1935 to have sixty-one thousand boys in the hedarim and Talmud Torahs affiliated with it, and twenty thousand Jewish girls in its Bet Jacob schools. In addition, there undoubtedly were many private hedarim and local Talmud Torahs independent of all nationally organized groups. The heder and Talmud Torah thus continued to play an important role in Polish Jewry up to 1939.

7. ELEMENTARY AND SECONDARY JEWISH EDUCATION IN THE UNITED STATES

a. The Heder in the United States

The heder and the Talmud Torah were brought to this country by Jewish immigrants from Eastern Europe. The heder, however, deteriorated rapidly in America. Without a well-formulated and clearly articulated public opinion to supervise it, the heder became the happy hunting ground of numerous ill-prepared, maladjusted individuals who brought it into disrepute despite many self-sacrificing and noble private teachers who established hedarim a generation ago in American Jewish communities. While some thirty years ago a majority of Jewish boys in America were still receiving their religious education in such private "rooms," the number attending them today is well-nigh negligible.

b. The Talmud Torah in the United States

The Talmud Torah followed a unique course of development in this country. Since, in the beginning, American Jewry almost unanimously gave wholehearted and enthusiastic support to the American public school system, Jewish education was conceived as being supplementary to it both in curriculum and in hours of instruction. Schools maintained by the Jewish community were to limit themselves exclusively to distinctly Jewish content and were to meet during hours other than those when the public school was in session. The Talmud Torah, therefore, started its sessions at four o'clock in the afternoon on weekdays and nine o'clock on Sunday mornings. The pupil was expected to attend five two-hour sessions. Moreover, influenced by the example of the American public school, builders of the American Jewish community of the first two decades of this century sought to make the Talmud Torah the communally supported Jewish elementary school for all Jewish children, boys as well as girls, rich as well as poor. Organizationally and physically it was to be completely dissociated from the synagogue. Many imposing Talmud Torah structures were built by Jewish communities throughout the land in the first quarter of the twentieth century. Graded courses of instruction were developed by well-trained modern pedagogues. Central bureaus of education attempted to guide and co-ordinate the activities of the schools and tens of thousands of Jewish children flocked to their classes.

But Jewish life in the United States was destined soon to take a course which halted the growth of the Talmud Torah along the lines originally anticipated. As the wealthier and more Americanized Jewish families moved out of the congested areas to new neighborhoods, they organized their Jewish communal life around the synagogue. The school in which their children were to receive a Jewish education was an integral part of the synagogue and the congregation. In addition, the conflict among the religious and social ideologies struggling for supremacy within the Jewish community resulted in the establishment of a variety of weekday afternoon school systems. Finally, the number of parents willing to subject their children to ten hours of weekly afternoon or evening instruction steadily diminished. The Talmud Torah, therefore, was not able to fulfill the role originally conceived for it by American Jewish educators. It is still an extremely important educational factor, but it no longer dominates the scene as it did a generation ago. The bureaus of Jewish education of the larger Jewish communities of the land no longer give their exclusive attention to it. The leaders of these bureaus strive incessantly to make the bureaus serve all Jewish schools regardless of their religious or social ideologies.

c. The Congregational Schools

1. The Sunday School

Jewish elementary education in the United States has in the past two decades shown a definite tendency to come under congregational auspices. It was thus at the beginning of American Jewish history.[7a] The first communal Jewish school was organized in America by Congregation Shearith Israel in New York (1731). Since no other schools were then available to Jewish children, the Shearith Israel school taught secular as well as Jewish religious subjects. The following century witnessed attempts by other congregations, individually or in co-operation with one another, to establish similar day schools. All these attempts came to an abrupt end with the rise of the American public school. At first these congregations made efforts to maintain weekday afternoon schools for Jewish instruction. But, following the dominant tendency of American Protestantism at the time, most of the congregations soon limited the religious instruction of their children to Sunday morning. Since not all Jewish families were affiliated with synagogues, communally sponsored Jewish Sunday schools were also organized for the children of the poor and the unaffiliated. The Philadelphia Sunday School Society organized by Rebecca Gratz in 1838 was the most effective and proved to be the most long-lived of such communally maintained Jewish Sunday schools. It celebrated the centenary of its existence in 1938 and is still functioning vigorously. The overwhelming number of Sunday schools today are, however, integral parts of well-established synagogues. Every synagogue organized by American-born or Americanized Jews considers an elementary school to be an indispensable part of its function. Most Reform congregations consider their responsibilities for the Jewish education of their children fulfilled by maintaining a Sunday school only. But even the Orthodox and Conservative congregations, which usually strive for a more intensive elementary Jewish education, maintain Sunday departments meeting from one and a half to two and a half hours each Sunday morning. These departments are intended for children who cannot or will not take more intensive instruction, or for boys and girls still too young to carry the more exacting curriculum.

2. The Congregational Weekday School

Many Reform Jewish congregations, all Conservative, and the comparatively small number of Orthodox congregations that sponsor elementary schools have found Sunday morning instruction completely inadequate for the transmission of the Jewish religious and cultural heritage. Many of the members of the present Conservative congregations were formerly the main supporters of the communal Talmud Torah. Hence, these congregations have organized weekday afternoon schools, and require their children to attend from four and a half to six and a half hours per week divided into three to five sessions including Sunday morning. The curriculum of these schools is very similar to that of the communal Talmud Torah, the chief emphasis being upon the study of Hebrew, primarily for the sake of understanding the prayers and the Pentateuch. Jewish history and the Jewish religious calendar are the other principal subjects of instruction.

Each of these congregational schools is in theory and can in fact be a law unto itself. However, national organizations with which the individual congregation is affiliated maintain commissions on education which publish textbooks and suggest curricula. The same is done by various local congregational organizations and city bureaus of Jewish education. It is but natural for the individual congregation to seek help and guidance from these central bodies. Some measure of uniformity in educational goals and procedures has thus been attained.

While many of the congregational schools are open only to children of members of the congregation, there is a tendency to depart from this unhappy procedure and to admit any child on the payment of a fixed tuition fee ranging from ten dollars per year up. Most congregations also admit at reduced rates or free of charge those children whose parents cannot afford to pay the regular rates.

3. Other Jewish Weekday Afternoon Schools

Religious, national and social ideologies have given rise to other types of Jewish weekday afternoon schools, which appeal to a comparatively small group within the Jewish community. Though these schools differ among themselves in ideological minutiae relating to attitudes on general social problems and Zionist aspirations, by and large they agree on two basic matters. The first has to do with the Yiddish language. All schools previously discussed adopt a neutral or negative attitude toward the preservation of the Yiddish language in America. These schools, on the other hand, have a positive attitude toward the Yiddish language and make it the chief subject of instruction. Some have a positive attitude toward the Hebrew language also. But most of them have a neutral and some a definitely negative attitude toward it. Secondly, the curricula of all these schools display a neutral or definitely negative attitude toward all religious instruction. Recently a marked change has become evident in the attitude toward the Jewish religion, and particularly toward Jewish customs, holidays and festivals. Ways are being sought to reintroduce these into the school curriculum as "folk ways" and Jewish cultural values rather than as religious observances. But some seek to go further than that and are rethinking their attitude toward religion itself.

4. The Jewish Day School in the United States

We noted above that the rise of the American public school found practically the whole of American Israel committed to it. In more recent years various factors have modified that unanimity. In the first place, the expectation that Sundays and weekday afternoons would offer ample opportunity for adequate instruction in Jewish religious and cultural subjects has by and large not been realized. These schools have not produced men and women thoroughly at home in the Hebrew language and familiar with even a considerable portion of the Hebrew Scriptures, of Rabbinic literature and of modern Hebrew literature. Though there are those who maintain that this failure is to be attributed to factors other than the hours of instruction, others consider the time element the root of the evil. Hence, they seek to create schools in which a greater number of hours during the morning and early afternoon can be devoted to Jewish studies. The proponents of the Jewish day school also find that the separation of church and state is not as complete in the public schools as it should be. Not only are Christian religious festivals such as Christmas and Easter celebrated with great impressiveness in most public schools, but attendance on Jewish religious holidays is very often definitely encouraged.

Moreover, among a group of progressively minded Jewish parents there is the desire to effect a more complete integration between the general and the Jewish education of their children than that which attendance at two separate schools makes possible. Thus there have come into being all-day Jewish elementary and secondary schools providing a rich curriculum of Jewish subjects in addition to the regular school curriculum. The distribution of the hours of study devoted to the various subjects differs from school to school.

The schools organized by the progressively minded parents, usually called academies, are maintained completely out of the tuition fees or special additional contributions made by the parents, though in all instances the meeting place of the school is provided free or for a minimum rental by a congregation. These schools also give the fewest number of hours weekly to Jewish subjects, though even this minimum is more than the maximum offered by the weekday congregational school. They have the further obvious advantage of preferred hours and highly trained teachers.

Most of the other all-day schools, usually referred to as *Yeshibot Ketanot*, junior *Yeshibot*, started with devoting the whole of the morning and most of the afternoon to Jewish religious studies. General studies were taught only after public school hours, so that the services of public school teachers might be obtained at a minimum expense. The law and the parents compelled most of the schools to shorten their teaching day and to distribute their time more judiciously among the various subjects. The average all-day school now meets practically during the same hours as the public school and divides its time about evenly between Hebrew and secular subjects. Financially, the schools are maintained only in part by tuition fees. The balance of the budget is met by special campaigns conducted by the individual schools and by one national campaign whose proceeds are shared by the co-operating schools in proportion to their efforts. Many of these schools have well-equipped dormitories to accommodate numerous out-of-town students. In 1945 there were approximately nine thousand Jewish children attending sixty-five all-day schools, concentrated mostly in New York City but found also in twenty-five other Jewish communities. But the number of all-day schools has been steadily increasing as the smaller Jewish communities throughout the country are being stirred to organize such schools.

8. JEWISH ELEMENTARY AND SECONDARY EDUCATION IN PALESTINE

a. Introduction

The Jewish population of Palestine assumed significant proportions numerically and spiritually soon after the expulsion of the Jews from Spain. It declined, however, in both respects during the eighteenth and the first half of the nineteenth century. The Damascus blood libel of 1840 and Sir Moses Montefiore's repeated visits to the Holy Land brought Palestine,[8a] as well as all of Oriental and Turkish-governed Balkan Jewry, into the orbit of general Jewish interest. The awakened concern of the emancipated Western European Jewries of France and England in their brethren of the Orient was reflected also in educational endeavors in their behalf. Heretofore, the heder and the Talmud Torah were alone in the field of Jewish educational activity throughout these regions. Nor were these institutions in too flourishing a state. In 1867 through the initiative of the *Alliance Israélite Universelle*, the first modern school for Jewish children in the Balkans was opened in Adrianople. In 1937 ninety-five schools with a reported pupil enrollment of 47,822 were maintained and subsidized by the *Alliance* in the Balkans, North Africa and the Near East. Of these, five were in Palestine, among them the outstanding agricultural school at Mikveh Israel, founded in 1870. English Jewry followed some time later with the organization of a few modern schools in Palestine and the Orient. At the beginning of the Twentieth century, German Jewry through the *Hilfsverein der Deutschen Juden* also entered the field and by 1914 had established or aided some fifty schools catering to about seven thousand pupils. Each one of these groups did worthy work.

b. Effects of the Zionist Movement

However, the remarkable revolutionary change in Jewish education in Palestine resulted wholly from the activities of the Zionist movement and its national and international agencies. Impressive beginnings were made even before World War I in establishing the Herzliah Gymnasium in Tel-Aviv, the Bet Sefer Reali, Hebrew Secondary School, in Haifa, and the schools in the small and struggling Jewish settlements of that era. By 1914 there was no longer any doubt that Hebrew was to be the language of the modern Jewish community of Palestine and of its school system. When after World War I the Palestinian Jewish community reorganized itself within the political framework of the Balfour Declaration and the League of Nations mandate, one of its first and chief concerns was the creation of a national system of Jewish education, which should reflect not the economic impoverishment and cultural backwardness characteristic of 1920 Palestine as a whole but the high cultural aspirations and the rich spiritual history of the Jewish pioneers who came to rebuild Jewish life in the land of their fathers. The Jewish community in Palestine resolved on complete autonomy in its educational work. The lure of larger government educational subsidies did not succeed in breaking this resolution. Since the resources of the Jews of Palestine were at the time extremely limited, and since the Palestine government appropriated only a small percentage of its meager budget for educational purposes and out of that gave a ludicrously small subsidy to Jewish education, the bulk of the educational budget of the modern Jewish schools in Palestine up to 1927 was met by the Zionist Organization. The Vaad Leumi, the nationally and democratically elected, politically recognized, represent-

JEWISH EDUCATIONAL INSTITUTIONS 399

ative body of Palestine Jewry then assumed sole responsibility for the educational budget of the schools affiliated with it. The government subsidy was gradually increased though never represented more than about twenty-two per cent of the total educational budget. Nor did the sum granted by the government to Jewish schools represent a percentage of the total educational budget of the government equal to the percentage paid in taxes by the Jews of Palestine or to the percentage of the Jewish school population within the total school population of the country. Furthermore, the authority of the Vaad Leumi was not complete, for Jews could choose to remain outside its authority and organize separate Jewish communities. Despite these legal and financial handicaps, the Education Department of the Vaad Leumi dominated elementary and secondary education in Palestine. The budget for the schools under its supervision was met out of the parents' tuition fees and special educational taxes wherever the community had the legal right to levy them, the government subsidy, and the general funds made available to the Vaad Leumi by the Zionist movement through the Jewish Agency for Palestine.

Three distinct educational systems were united under the Vaad Leumi's supervision. The largest of these was composed of the schools organized, directed and completely controlled by the Educational Department of the Vaad Leumi itself. These were usually referred to as the General Zionist Schools. They corresponded very closely to the American public schools in philosophy and curriculum. Religion as such was not formally taught in them. The Bible and Rabbinic literature formed part of the curriculum and Jewish national and religious holidays were observed and celebrated. In 1943 there were 181 such schools with a pupil population of 38,936.

The second group of schools were under the direct supervision of the Mizrachi, the Orthodox branch of the World Zionist Organization. The curriculum of these schools and the general atmosphere pervading their classrooms and administration represented the intense religious interests of their sponsors. Much more time was given to Rabbinic literature and to Bible study in their curriculum. In 1943 there were 84 such schools with an enrollment of 14,486.

The third group was composed of the schools organized and sponsored by the Palestine Labor and the left-wing Zionist groups. They were found chiefly in the communal or co-operative colonies founded in the last quarter of a century, and in urban centers occupied by members of these groups. While the Bible was taught and Jewish holidays were celebrated, Rabbinic legal literature was hardly touched. A neutral or negative attitude toward religion pervaded the ideology and the pedagogy of these schools. Their outstanding characteristic was an emphasis upon vocational training, upon the history of the labor movement throughout the world and upon the most progressive pedagogic methods. The 218 schools of this group taught 14,561 students in 1943.

The 65,983 pupils of the schools thus united in the Education Department of the Vaad Leumi represented approximately two-thirds of the total Palestine Jewish child population of school age. Of the remainder a goodly number of girls of the Oriental or older Jewish communities in the country received no formal education of any kind, some 24,000 attended either a heder, a modern private school, or a school sponsored by some other Jewish body, while some 1,200 were in the schools of the Christian missionaries. It is a strange fact that many a poor pious Jewish parent did not hesitate to send a daughter to acquire a general elementary education in a Christian missionary school, where no tuition fee was required and where occasionally some article of clothing or other assistance was given.

Judged by modern standards, the schools of the Vaad Leumi undoubtedly represented the best organized, most adequately financed and staffed, most efficiently supervised, best housed, pedagogically and educationally best planned elementary and secondary school system ever maintained by any Jewish community in all of Jewish history. The schools formerly under the supervision of the Vaad Leumi are now, 1949, part of the Education Department of the State of Israel. The rapid expansion, transformation, and modernization of the schools within Israel are keeping pace with the many other extraordinary events that have taken place there in so kaleidoscopic a manner since the State came into being on May 14, 1948.

c. Elementary and Secondary Schools for Vocational Training

The vocational and technical school was the last to appear within all modern school systems. Among the Jews agitation for such schools first appeared at the beginning of the nineteenth century. But no practical step was taken to create such schools until the late sixties and early seventies in Russia. Because of the government's attitude, these sporadic attempts soon petered out. In 1880 the ORT, an organization for advancing trades and agriculture among Jews, was established. Its chief aim was to support existing handicraft schools, establish additional ones, and subsidize those seeking vocational training in a school or as apprentices. But all ORT's efforts were impeded by government restrictions. Only in 1905 was a charter finally granted, after which its activities among the Jews of Russia rapidly advanced. Since then ORT has been functioning on a world-wide scale, helping the Russian Jews after the revolution to retrain themselves within the new economic framework of Soviet Russia, creating retraining opportunities for victims of the Nazi persecutions, whether in concentration camps or as refugees, and establishing schools in Poland, in the Near East and in other Jewish communities for vocational training of their youth.

In Palestine the vocational and technical school has been assuming increasing importance within the Jewish educational system. The Mikveh Israel Agricultural School, established in 1870, proved to be the most successful institution of its type. In 1943 there were seven well-established agricultural schools, in addition to a number of girls' training farms and the agricultural courses given to refugee youth in labor co-operative and collective settlements. Since 1932 there has been a marked increase in the attention given to industrial education. The report of the survey of the Vocational Training Committee of the Jewish Agency for 1943 listed ten such schools including a nautical school with a total enrollment of 1,105 pupils.

V. JEWISH INSTITUTIONS OF HIGHER LEARNING

A. BIBLE TIMES

Just as poetry preceded prose in the history of literature, so organized institutions for higher learning preceded elementary and secondary schools. This was true in Israel, as well as among other peoples. We noted above that, though the Bible makes no mention whatsoever of elementary schools, it does speak of "schools" of prophets. Moreover, the Bible's reference to the manner in which people came to listen to Solomon's wisdom, which surpassed that of all the other wise men of old, would indicate that these wise men had schools very much like those of the Greek philosophers of later generations. King Hezekiah's men who copied the proverbs of Solomon (Pr. 25:1) were most likely members of some kind of academy of the learned maintained by the royal house, in order to preserve the cultural treasures of the people. The scribes and secretaries of the government,[9a] the Levites and priests of the Temple, surely had to be trained somewhere for their work.

B. THE SECOND COMMONWEALTH

For a period of some 150 years, very little is known of the inner or outer life of the Jewish community that re-established itself in Palestine after the activities of Ezra and Nehemiah.[10a] But when with Alexander's conquest of Palestine the Jewish community of the Holy Land reappears in the light of history, it seems to possess a well-established and well-organized authoritative religious body. This was the *Keneset Ha-Gedolah*, the Great Synagogue. Scholars differ on the exact nature of this body, its composition, its function, and its history. We do know, however, that one of its guiding principles was "to increase the number of students." The reference is obviously not only to children but also to adults. From what we know of the character of this body, it may be safe to assume that the *Keneset Ha-Gedolah* exercised the threefold functions of court, legislature and center of higher learning and research.

The *Keneset Ha-Gedolah* was superseded by the Sanhedrin. Considerable controversy and conjecture also surround every aspect of the history, the composition and the functioning of the Sanhedrin. But all agree that in one manner or another it, too, functioned as a legislative, judicial and educational institution. The various parties and schools of thought which multiplied in the Jewish community during the century immediately preceding the destruction of the Temple (70 C.E.) had their own centers of discussion and learning. But the conflicting viewpoints were all reflected in the seventy-one elders who composed the Sanhedrin.

C. THE ACADEMY AND THE BET MIDRASH

When the Temple was destroyed by the Romans, the authority formerly lodged in the Sanhedrin was transferred by the towering personality of Johanan ben Zakkai to the academy he founded at Jabneh.[11a] This academy, and the others which succeeded it in Palestine, continued to exercise the function of courts, legislatures and universities. They administered the law, they amended it when necessary, legislated when necessary, and continued ceaselessly to explore the hidden recesses of the Torah, in order to bring to light some previously unnoticed moral or legal implication. The Talmud records indicate that the question, "What new thought was expressed at the session of the academy today?" was frequently asked by members who had been absent. The intimate contact maintained by the academy, by virtue of its judicial and legislative functions, with the daily life of the members of the community kept its purely intellectual pursuits from departing too far into the realms of the impractical and theoretical.

The members of these academies most often supported themselves. But many were maintained out of the treasury of the patriarchate or through the generosity of individuals.

As the body of knowledge and tradition increased, various schools of interpretation and of methods of study inevitably appeared. It was but natural that similarly minded scholars should have a common meeting place for study and discussion. Moreover, outstanding teachers and scholars attracted younger men seeking knowledge of the Torah. The most natural place for such gatherings of scholars or of teachers and pupils was some room in the local synagogue, though a special structure for such purposes, usually near the synagogue, was undoubtedly frequently used. The place where these scholars, individually or in groups, pursued their studies was called a Bet Midrash, a house for studying and interpreting the Torah, to distinguish it from the Bet Tefilah, the room used primarily for prayer, or the *Bet Sefer,* the place used for instructing the young. One room could at various times of the day be used for any one of the three purposes. Apparently, however, in the early days of the Bet Ha-Midrash, scholars would not use it for prayer, but would leave off their studies and join the congregation in the synagogue. The stress laid upon study by the rabbis is perhaps best reflected in the law that a synagogue structure may be turned into a Bet Ha-Midrash but a Bet Ha-Midrash may not be sold for exclusive synagogue use, for one is permitted to elevate an object from a lower to a higher state of sanctity, but not to reduce it from a higher to a lower state.

The Bet Ha-Midrash required practically no financing. Its meeting place was supplied either by the synagogue or by voluntary contributions for the erection of a special structure. Its teacher was not a paid officer, its students were self-supporting adults, and its curriculum of studies was determined completely by the interests and desires of the participants.

The Bet Ha-Midrash remained an integral part of the synagogue throughout the ages. Practically every synagogue had a room, usually the basement, containing a library of Hebrew books including the Bible and its commentaries, the various Midrashim—homiletic interpretations of Sacred Scripture—and the Talmud and its commentaries. In the long-established communities of Eastern Europe this room would buzz with activity from early morning till late at night. Busy laymen would meet here daily in the morning or the afternoon to spend a fixed period in study either by themselves or with a companion, or with a larger group under the leadership of the rabbi or of one of their own more learned lay companions. The most advanced studied the Talmud, others studied the Mishna, while the less learned devoted themselves to the Midrashim or the Pentateuch with its commentators, especially Rashi.

American synagogues, by and large, still have a library of Hebrew books, but the men to study them are unfortunately no longer available, except in very rare instances. The modern Bible class, or study circle, meeting usually about fifteen to twenty times during the year under the leadership of the rabbi, is a very pale reflection of the intense advanced Jewish studies carried on in the Bet Ha-Midrash of some of the smallest Jewish communities of Eastern Europe up to 1939.

The discussions that took place in the academies and the Bate Midrashim until about the middle of the second century c.e. developed the vast storehouse of law and tradition that Judah the Nasi drew upon when in the second half of the second century he edited the Mishna. His compilation did not include everything that was said and taught. What he had omitted, others collected and edited. But his work, because of its intrinsic excellence and his own great personality, became almost immediately popular and authoritative, and formed the chief text for the studies in the academies of the following centuries. The Palestinian academies continued to exist and to exercise great influence throughout the Jewish world until about the fifth century. The discussions and decisions of the last two hundred years of their existence were included in the Palestinian Talmud.

D. THE BABYLONIAN ACADEMIES

With the beginning of the third century, Babylonian academies started to challenge the schools of Palestine in erudition, in creativity, and later even in authority.[12a] The greatest of the Babylonian academies was founded by Rav in Sura about the year 219. It continued to function with only brief occasional interruptions until approximately the thirteenth century. The second academy founded at about the same time by Samuel at Nahardea, was transferred by Judah ben Ezekiel in 260 to Pumbedita. There it also continued to flourish with some intermission for about eight hundred years. These two academies were the recognized leaders of Jewish religious and cultural life throughout the world from the fifth to the eleventh century. The discussions, opinions and reflections of the members and the leaders of these academies during the first three centuries of their existence form the contents of the vast treasure trove of law, history, morals, ethics and folklore, known as the Babylonian Talmud. The heads of each of these two academies from the end of the sixth century on bore the title of Gaon. Jewish communities throughout the world turned to successive Geonim for religious guidance and leadership and students came to them from great distances to study. In the beginning, the Babylonian Jewish community itself was in a position to maintain these academies through taxation and voluntary contributions. But with the deterioration of the Jewish position in the eastern Mohammedan world, the academies found it necessary to send messengers to Jewish communities throughout the Diaspora for additional support.

E. THE KALLA

A unique feature of the activities of these academies was the *Kalla*. Twice a year during the month of Ellul, the month preceding Rosh Ha-Shanah and the High Holy Day season, and during the month of Adar, preceding the Passover festival, thousands of students and scholars would come to the academies from all parts of the Diaspora and spend the month in study and discussion. The talmudic tractate analyzed during the month's session of the *Kalla* was one which had been announced at the end of the previous *Kalla* gathering and had thus been studied by the participants during the preceding five months. During the *Kalla* sessions difficult passages in the tractate would be explained, the text corrected, the diligence of the students tested, important legal decisions' rendered and the subject to be studied in preparation for the next session announced. Little imagination is required to recognize the tremendous influence such semi-annual gatherings of large numbers must have had in stimulating and directing scholarly pursuits and thus influencing the spiritual and intellectual life of Jews in the remotest communities.

F. THE TARBITZA

In connection with the *Kalla* sources frequently mention the *Tarbitza*. The exact nature of this institution has not been established. Some are of the opinion that the *Tarbitza* was for those who were not sufficiently well-prepared to attend the *Kalla* sessions. At the *Tarbitza* gathering each student studied whatever tractate he preferred.

G. THE YESHIVA

The most widespread institution for higher Jewish learning developed by the Jews on the European continent was the *Yeshiva*. It was a natural outgrowth of the Babylonian academy and the Bet Ha-Midrash. No European *Yeshiva* ever attained the stature of any of the Babylonian or Palestinian academies. The European *Yeshibot* did not prove to be intellectually as bold and as creative as their predecessors, nor did they enjoy the same authority either within the Jewish community or in relation to the non-Jewish authorities. However, their outstanding leaders and students equaled their predecessors in mental acumen, in depth and breadth of erudition, in piety, and in lives of exemplary holiness and singleness of devotion to the study of Torah.

The only requirement for entrance into a *Yeshiva* was talmudic knowledge and the ability to follow the more involved talmudic debates. Exceptionally brilliant youngsters of ten or twelve could, therefore, sit side by side with men twice and three times their age to listen to the lecture and participate in the debate that followed. The Talmud and all its commentaries constituted practically the exclusive subject of study, though in some *Yeshibot*, moral and ethical texts also were read and discussed for brief periods weekly or daily. Every sizable Jewish community sought to have a *Yeshiva* in its midst and every rabbi coveted the honor of having a *Yeshiva* under his guidance. A description of the Jewish community in Poland before the massacres of 1648 relates that there was not a Jewish community of fifty families or more which did not have at least one *Yeshiva* with some thirty students.

After the Chmielnicki massacre of 1648, a period of intellectual deterioration set in for almost a century. By the middle of the eighteenth century, Polish Jewry had recovered from the disastrous effects of the massacres. There was a great revival of higher learning, particularly in Lithuania. It reached its high-water mark in the personality of the Gaon, Elijah of Vilna (1720-1797), intellectually a giant and spiritually a saint. In 1803 his student, Hayim of Volozhin, organized the *Yeshiva* of Volozhin, which for over a century exercised considerable influence on Jewish life. Other outstanding *Yeshibot* arose in impressive numbers during the subsequent century and a half until 1939. These *Yeshibot* attracted thousands upon thousands of students. As long as the Jewish communities had the legal right to impose and collect taxes, *Yeshibot* received their support, at least in part, from such taxes and from the billeting of some of their students in local Jewish homes. For the past hundred and fifty years, they were maintained exclusively by self-imposed meat or slaughtering taxes and by additional voluntary contributions, not only of money but of meals and lodging for students.

The East European *Yeshiva* devoted itself exclusively to Jewish studies. Because of the weakening of the religious bonds evident among those Jews who had acquired a secular education, secular studies, even the reading of modern secular Hebrew literature, were excluded from and forbidden by the *Yeshiva*.

The *Yeshiva* consisted most often of little more than one or two large rooms with tables at which the students sat, or with individual lecterns at which the student stood while studying his text. Except for the hour or two each day when the headmaster or other teacher gave his lecture, examined the students or discussed the text with them, each student studied aloud by himself or with a companion. Because most students at a *Yeshiva* came from a distance and dormitories and dining rooms were provided by only a few of the larger and more adequately supported modern *Yeshibot*, sleeping quarters and food were frequently arranged for in the homes of local families. Poor students were often supported by meager grants from the treasury of the *Yeshiva* or the community. Householders, however, considered it a great deed of piety to offer one daily meal or more to a *Yeshiva* student or a bed in which he could spend the night. As a result, a student frequently ate his meals each day at a different home and had various sleeping quarters for his use, including the bench in the *Yeshiva* on which he sat and studied during the day. The privations under which the average *Yeshiva* student pursued his studies are thus easily imagined and have been frequently described. Nor did the *Yeshiva* grant a rabbinic title or degree to all its students. Comparatively few desired or attained this distinction. The primary aim of the *Yeshiva* was to produce *Talmide Hakamim*, Disciples of the Wise, learned Jews who would live their lives in accordance with the laws of the Torah and set aside daily periods for its study all the days of their lives. Such was the intensity of the thirst for knowledge and such the devotion to Torah that despite the hardships the *Yeshibot* never lacked students. They produced a veritable galaxy of exceptionally learned and saintly rabbis and of highly erudite laymen for the Jewish communities of Eastern Europe.

H. THE YESHIVA IN THE UNITED STATES

Until very recently the traditional *Yeshiva*, which proscribed all secular knowledge and concentrated all its attention on talmudic studies, was nonexistent in the United States. The American Jewish day school which called itself a *Yeshiva* and is now spoken of as a *Yeshiva Ketana*, a junior *Yeshiva* (because it caters to boys of elementary and high school age), of necessity included the American public school curriculum in its studies. It never directly or indirectly discouraged or prohibited its students from pursuing further studies at a college or a university. As a matter of fact, the Isaac Elchanan Yeshiva founded in 1896,[13a] one of the oldest and today the best known of the *Yeshibot* in America, was the first to add the regular high school to its curriculum (in 1919) and hoped from the very beginning to be able to grant the regular bachelor's degree to its qualified students. That hope became a reality when in 1928 the Yeshiva College was organized, and in 1948 it was granted university status, thus becoming the first *Yeshiva* in Jewish history to make the regular college and secular post-graduate studies an integral part of its program. Nor is there a ban on modern secular Hebrew literature. Indeed, in the Teachers' Institute which was incorporated into the over-all organizational structure of the Isaac Elchanan Yeshiva in 1921, Hebrew is the primary language of instruction and modern Hebrew literature one of the main subjects of study. While many American *Yeshibot* do not consider the college degree a prerequisite to the granting of a rabbinic degree and ordain men as rabbis only on the basis of their talmudic and general Jewish knowledge, the attitude toward secular studies reflected in the American *Yeshiva* is a far cry from what it was in the East European *Yeshiva*.

We noted above the increased number of Jewish all-day schools on the elementary and secondary level in America within the past two decades. The unparalleled catastrophes which in five years' time completely destroyed Polish Jewry and every one of its educational centers brought many of the deans, faculty members and students of the Polish *Yeshibot* to this country. They at once set about with their customary energy and self-sacrifice to organize *Yeshibot* here. Their labors have not been unproductive. The *Yeshibot* thus far established have had no lack of students. Moreover, there is little likelihood that the attitude of the *Yeshiva* leaders in America toward secular studies will be what it was in Eastern Europe a generation and more ago.

I. RABBINICAL SEMINARIES

Until the middle of the nineteenth century, the *Yeshibot* produced the men who were called to rabbinical leadership of Jewish communities. But Jews who had themselves acquired secular knowledge and who were culturally part of the Western world required differently trained men as their religious leaders. Hence, for the first time in Jewish history there were established schools whose express purpose was to prepare men for the modern rabbinate. The seminaries of necessity reflected the theological views of the groups who organized and maintained them. During the past hundred and fifty years Western Jewry divided itself religiously into three main groups, usually distinguished as the Orthodox, the Conservative, and the Reform. Seminaries to serve the needs of each of them were first founded in Germany. In 1854 the Conservative Jewish Theological Seminary of Breslau was founded by Zechariah Frankel. In 1872 two seminaries were opened in Berlin, the Reform *Hochschule fuer die Wissenschaft des Judentums* and the Orthodox Rabbinical Seminary in Berlin.

No seminary for the training of modern rabbis was opened by the Jews of Eastern Europe. Between 1844 and 1873 there were two rabbinical schools sponsored by the Russian government. Their graduates, known as "government rabbis," were never regarded by the Jews as religious leaders. Jews in Eastern Europe by and large either remained orthodox in their religious outlook or became agnostics or nonbelievers.

In the United States the first rabbinical school, the Hebrew Union College, was opened by Reform Jews in 1875 under the leadership of Isaac M. Wise.[14a] During its seventy-five years of existence, the school has graduated some five hundred rabbis. It maintains a large library, has a distinguished faculty, and has published many scholarly volumes. The well-equipped and spacious buildings include a dormitory for students. A bachelor's degree is a prerequisite for entering upon the rabbinic course. The college is maintained by income from an endowment fund, supplemented by contributions from individuals, Reform congregations and community chests.

In 1886 The Jewish Theological Seminary of America[15a] was founded in New York City by Sabato Morais, rabbi of Congregation Mikveh Israel of Philadelphia. In 1902, it was reorganized under the presidency of Solomon Schechter. Though the Seminary as such consistently refuses to identify itself as a school for the training of rabbis for any one group or party in Israel, nevertheless, because of the character of its faculty and its avowed traditional leanings, it is generally referred to as the school of the Conservative, or Historical, party. Since its reorganization the seminary has graduated some four hundred rabbis. A bachelor's degree is a prerequisite to its four-year rabbinical course. The seminary's scope of activities has steadily broadened. Its imposing buildings erected in 1930 in the Morningside Heights educational center, include the Jacob H. Schiff Library building housing the largest collection of Judaica ever gathered by Jews; the Unterberg building with quarters for the Teachers Institute of the Jewish Theological Seminary, organized in 1909, and the Seminary

College of Jewish Studies. In addition, the Brush Dormitory building, including a spacious lounge and dining hall, offers dormitory quarters for the students.

The Jewish Museum, housed in the former home of Mr. and Mrs. Felix M. Warburg, at Ninety-second Street and Fifth Avenue, is an integral part of the Seminary. So is the University of Judaism in Los Angeles, whose classes began in the autumn of 1947.[16a]

The Seminary's budget is met by income from endowments and by special annual contributions from individuals, Conservative congregations and community welfare chests.

The Isaac Elchanan Yeshiva described above is the best known institution preparing rabbis for modern American Orthodox congregations. It, too, is housed in a spacious building with dormitories and library and has a Teachers' College affiliated with it.

In 1922 the Hebrew Theological College of Chicago was founded. Its graduates are prepared to serve Orthodox communities. The other *Yeshibot* also qualify their graduates to lead this type of congregation.

In 1922 Dr. Stephen S. Wise founded the Jewish Institute of Religion in New York to train rabbis for any of the religious groups in Israel. The Institute permits complete freedom to its faculty and student body in all theological and ideological matters. Its students and graduates choose whatever Jewish theology or ideology appeals most to them and seek to serve congregations most congenial to their point of view. The Institute also requires a bachelor's degree of those applying for matriculation. Its financial support comes from contributions of individuals and of community welfare funds and of congregations served by its graduates. In 1948, the Jewish Institute of Religion and the Hebrew Union College merged under the name of Hebrew Union College-Jewish Institute of Religion.

At the present time (1948) the United States is the only country with modern seminaries training rabbis for groups other than those who are orthodox in the traditional sense of that word.

Jewish teachers' training schools also first appeared in the nineteenth century in Germany. The Kassel community opened such a school in 1810, Muenster in 1827, Berlin and Hanover in 1859, and Wuerzburg in 1864. The last of these was the only one which continued after 1926.

In Russia the first teachers' school was opened in Grodno in 1907. Other similar schools were founded later, particularly in Poland, to serve the needs of the various school systems existing there between 1920 and 1939. The Soviet government also provided teachers' training schools to prepare teachers for its Yiddish-language schools.

The first modern teachers' training school was opened in Palestine in

Jerusalem by the Ezra Verein in 1905. Similar institutions were organized by the various groups affiliated with the Education Department of the Vaad Leumi. The development of teachers' training schools is one of the most pressing problems facing the Education Department of Israel.

In the United States the first teachers' training school, Gratz College, was opened in Philadelphia in 1895. Its establishment was made possible by a bequest of Simon Gratz. The school has been functioning uninterruptedly since it was opened. In 1909, the Teachers Institute of the Jewish Theological Seminary was organized and since 1931 has been permitted to grant the graduates of its regular department the degree of Bachelor of Jewish Pedagogy. By special arrangement, its students take some of their courses at Columbia's Teachers College. In 1921, the Teachers' College formerly maintained by the American Mizrachi organization became a part of the Yeshiva College. Other teachers' training colleges were founded in various communities, such as the Baltimore Jewish College, the Chicago School of Jewish Studies, the Boston Jewish College and others. Few of these schools limit themselves exclusively to the training of teachers for the Sunday or weekday schools. They have extension departments for the education of adults and some have high school departments to prepare students for the more advanced studies.

J. Dropsie College

Unique among Jewish institutions of higher learning is Dropsie College,[17a] founded in 1907 in Philadelphia with funds bequeathed by a Philadelphia lawyer, Moses Aaron Dropsie. Under the presidency of Cyrus Adler the college was organized as a postgraduate institution granting only the Ph.D. degree in the field of Hebrew and Cognate Studies. It occupies attractive quarters, has an excellent working and reference library and a distinguished faculty. In its student body and among its graduates, Jew and Christian, men and women, are represented. More recently the college has expanded its program to include a postgraduate department in Jewish Education and an Institute on the Near East.

K. The Hebrew Institute of Technology

In 1912 a Russian Zionist, Wolf Wissotzky, with the help of Jacob H. Schiff, the Jewish National Fund and the Hilfsverein established the Hebrew Institute of Technology in Haifa. It was at this school that the language question came to a head. Many of the school's supporters wanted German to be the language of the institution. After a long and bitter struggle, the pupils, teachers and the Palestine Jewish community succeeded in making Hebrew the official language of the school. After World War I the institution was taken over by the Zionist Organization and reopened with increased facilities in 1925. Today it is the most advanced school for the training of engineers of all types found in the whole Near East. In its field it occupies relatively the same position that the Hebrew University occupies in the field of the humanities, sciences and free professions.

L. THE HEBREW UNIVERSITY IN JERUSALEM

The most rapidly developing Jewish institution of higher learning of our day is perhaps the Hebrew University in Jerusalem. Its organization was suggested at the first Zionist World Congress in 1897. Its cornerstone was laid by Dr. Chaim Weizmann in the presence of Lord Allenby, conqueror of Jerusalem, in July, 1918, while the din of battle still clearly resounded on Judea's hills. In December, 1924, the first regular classes of the university's Institute of Jewish Studies began their sessions and on April 1, 1925, Sir Arthur James Balfour in the presence of Sir Herbert Samuel, the British High Commissioner of Palestine, Dr. Chaim Weizmann, and Dr. Judah Magnes, first president of the university, officially opened and dedicated this new center of Jewish and universal learning.

The university began as a research institution. The first undergraduate department was opened in 1928 with a four-year course given by the faculty of Humanities and leading to the degree of Master of Arts. Since then the faculty of Natural Sciences has been offering a four-year course leading to the degree of Master of Science. Courses qualifying graduates of the Hebrew University or other universities for the degree of Doctor of Philosophy have also been arranged.

Since its opening, the university has become the greatest modern institution of higher learning throughout the Near East. Some fifteen different departments and institutes now exist. The foundations have been laid for a first-rate modern medical center. During the war the various scientific laboratories maintained by the university made invaluable contributions to the welfare of the fighting forces of the United Nations stationed throughout the Near East.

The student body of the university now numbers over a thousand men and women of all creeds and races, and the faculty includes some of the best known names in all fields of study. Many of them, forced out of European universities by the Nazi regime, have found in the center of learning on Mt. Scopus an opportunity to continue their teaching and research.

Given an extended period of peaceful development, the Hebrew University is destined to exert tremendous influence upon the cultural life of the whole of the Near East as well as upon the cultural life of the Jews of Palestine and the Diaspora.

NOTES

[¹ᵃ Cf. below, Louis Finkelstein, "The Jewish Religion: Its Beliefs and Practices," pp. 496 ff.]

² Baba Batra 21a.

[³ᵃ Cf. Judah Goldin, "The Period of the Talmud (135 B.C.E.-1035 C.E.)," this work, Vol. I, pp. 124-125.]

[⁴ᵃ Cf. *ibid.*, pp. 145 ff.]

[⁵ᵃ Cf. *ibid.*, pp. 157-159.]

[⁶ᵃ Cf. Cecil Roth, "The Jews of Western Europe (from 1648)," this work, Vol. I, pp. 270-271.]

[⁷ᵃ Cf. above, Moshe Davis, "Jewish Religious Life and Institutions in America (A Historical Study)," pp. 277 ff.]

[⁸ᵃ Cf. Roth, *op. cit.*, pp. 280-281.]

[⁹ᵃ Cf. Elias J. Bickerman, "The Historical Foundations of Postbiblical Judaism," this work, Vol. I, pp. 99-101.]

[¹⁰ᵃ Cf. William Foxwell Albright, "The Biblical Period," this work, Vol. I, pp. 52 ff., and Bickerman, *op. cit., passim.*]

[¹¹ᵃ Cf. Goldin, *op. cit.*, pp. 150-153.]

[¹²ᵃ Cf. *ibid.*, pp. 181 ff.]

[¹³ᵃ Cf. Davis, *op. cit.*, p. 310.]

[¹⁴ᵃ Cf. *ibid.*, pp. 302-303, 318-319, and on Isaac M. Wise, pp. 286 f.]

[¹⁵ᵃ Cf. *ibid.*, pp. 308-309, 320-323.]

[¹⁶ᵃ Cf. *ibid.*, pp. 348-349.]

[¹⁷ᵃ Cf. *ibid.*, pp. 331-332.]

BIBLIOGRAPHY

CHIPKIN, ISRAEL, *Twenty-five years of Jewish Education in the United States.* New York, 1937. Reprint from American Jewish Symposium of the Jewish Day School.

DRAZIN, NATHAN, *History of Jewish Education from 515 B.C.E. to 220 C.E.* Baltimore, 1940.

DUSHKIN, ALEXANDER, M., *Jewish Education in New York City.* New York, 1918.

GAMORAN, EMANUEL, *Changing Conceptions in Jewish Education.* New York, 1924.

GREENBERG, LOUIS, *The Jews in Russia.* New Haven and London, 1944. I, Chs. IV-VII.

KAPLAN, MORDECAI M., *The Future of the American Jew.* New York, 1948. Chapter XXVI.

MORRIS, NATHAN, *The Jewish School—an Introduction to the History of Jewish Education.* London, 1937.

NARDI, NOAH, *Education in Palestine.* New York, 1945.

SCHARFSTEIN, ZEVI, *The History of Jewish Education in Modern Times* (Hebrew) (*Toldot Hahinuch Beyisrael bedorot haachronim*). New York, 1945. I.

SHERRILL, LEWIS JOSEPH, *The Rise of Christian Education.* New York, 1944. Chs. I-IV.

TSCHARNO, Y., *Education Among the Jews*. (Hebrew) Jerusalem, 1939.
(*Toldot Hahinuch Beyisrael*).

POSTSCRIPT

The vast, multifaceted educational structure which had served the Jewish communities of Central and Eastern Europe before the Second World War was completely destroyed by the Nazis, together with the men, women, and children who had built and used it. The approximately 3,000,-000 Jews of Soviet Russia have, since 1945, not been permitted to establish a single educational institution for the teaching of any subject of distinctly Jewish content, whether it be religious or cultural-secular in nature. Only in two Jewish communities, the one in the State of Israel and the other in the United States, have new educational institutions of considerable significance and effectiveness been created or expanded in the past two decades.

A. IN THE STATE OF ISRAEL

Whether we define a Jewish educational institution as one administered by Jews, regardless of the subject matter taught, or as one in which distinctly Jewish subject matter is taught, the greatest advances in the past twenty years were made in the State of Israel. "An estimated 740,000 children and students were enrolled in Israel's educational institutions at the beginning of the 1966-67 school year. Of these 120,000 were in post-primary schools. . . . Fifty-five percent of the pupils in primary schools (up to the age of 14) attended State schools (without special emphasis on religious education); twenty percent went to State religious schools, and seven percent studied in 'recognized' schools (run by the Orthodox Agudat Israel). . . . An estimated 28,000 students were matriculated in Israel's institutes of higher Jewish learning, 14,000 of them in the Hebrew University in Jerusalem . . . 2,700 in Bar-Ilan (religious) University (founded in 1955) . . . 5,000 in the Technion-Israel Institute of Technology (formerly The Hebrew Institute of Technology) . . . 6,700 in Tel-Aviv University. . . . The Weizmann Institute of Science at Rehovot (a post-graduate science research center) had a staff of 280 scientists, with 280 students preparing for the MS and Ph.D. degrees." (*American Jewish Year Book*, 1967, pp. 435-436.) These bare figures are but a pale reflection of the great variety of modern secular educational institutions of higher learning now serving the citizens of the State of Israel. At the same time, there has been a marked growth in the number and enrollment of *yeshivot* (talmudic academies) in Israel.

B. THE UNITED STATES

In the United States greatest progress has been made in two types of educational institution, the Jewish day school and the educational summer camp. In 1940-1941 there were 35 day schools with some 7,700 pupils in the entire country. In 1967 there were 339 such schools with some 70,000 pupils in the United States, and another 38 schools with some 10,000 pupils in Canada. Until 1958 the day schools were identified almost exclusively with the Orthodox group. Since then the Conservative Movement has developed a chain of Solomon Schechter Day Schools, which in 1967 had 25 units with some 4,400 pupils. More recently some leaders of Reform Judaism and of the secular Jewish community have expressed interest in establishing day schools.

The first attempts to establish summer camps with a specifically Jewish educational orientation were made in the twenties. However, it was only after the Second World War that summer camping as a significant Jewish educational institution came into its own with the founding of Masad in 1941 and Ramah in 1947, of the Zionist-oriented camps, and of special educational camps organized and administered by the local Bureaus of Jewish Education of the larger Jewish communities.

In some of these camps Hebrew is the official camp language, and daily attendance at organized classes during a period of eight weeks of residence at the camp are part of an overall camping program, which, whenever possible, is educationally oriented toward Judaism. Some of these camps provide an intensive course of Hebraic and Jewish studies for specially chosen young people preparing to be camp counselors, group leaders, or teachers. It is estimated that approximately 20,000 campers attended such camps in the summer of 1967, for periods of two to eight weeks.

An unexpected phenomenon of great significance was the remarkable increase in the number of American liberal-arts colleges and universities offering courses given by full-time faculty that deal with "the historical experiences in the intellectual, religious and social spheres of the Jewish people in all centuries and countries." In 1945 there were about ten universities offering such courses. In 1965 there were ninety-two, of which thirty-four were listed among the top fifty colleges and universities of the country. In 1945 there were about twelve full-time faculty positions in the field of Jewish studies. In 1965 there were well over sixty, with indications that this number would continue to grow annually by two or three for the foreseeable future.

Significant advances have also taken place in the realm of Jewish institutions of higher learning. Each of the three main rabbinical seminaries mentioned previously has expanded its facilities and programs. In 1947-1948, The Jewish Theological Seminary of America established the University of Judaism in Los Angeles. The University does not ordain rabbis. It has an undergraduate College of Jewish Studies, a Teachers Institute, a School of the Fine Arts, a rapidly expanding library, and a large department for adult extension classes. At about the same time, the Hebrew Union

College-Jewish Institute of Religion opened a branch in Los Angeles where students can complete the first two years of their rabbinic training. The Isaac Elchanan Yeshiva in New York, which heretofore had only an undergraduate college associated with it, transformed itself into Yeshiva University, adding a number of graduate schools (in education, social work, mathematics) and the Einstein School of Medicine. The three seminaries also added schools of Jewish music for the training of cantors.

New among Jewish educational institutions are The Melton Research Center, established in 1960 at The Jewish Theological Seminary of America and devoted to advancing elementary and secondary Jewish education by research in the areas of curriculum, of preparation of pedagogic materials for pupils and teachers, and of providing for the professional growth of teachers; and the National Curriculum Research Institute, established in 1960 by the American Association for Jewish Education, whose purpose is "to further the effectiveness of Jewish schooling by concerning itself with the components that make for effective education, realizable goals, proper materials and tools, qualified and dedicated personnel."

C. BRANDEIS UNIVERSITY

Also new in the history of Diaspora Jewry was the founding in 1948 of Brandeis University in Massachusetts as a completely nonsectarian school conceived as a Jewish-sponsored contribution to higher education in the United States. Although it includes the Philip W. Lown School of Near Eastern and Judaic Studies (undergraduate and graduate departments) and the Philip W. Lown Graduate Center for Contemporary Jewish Studies, Brandeis' main emphasis is on general secular subjects.

D. OTHER COUNTRIES

The Jewish communities of Western Europe have only partially recovered from the trauma of the Second World War. There, too, the Jewish day school is becoming an ever more prevalent institution. In 1965 there were forty day schools with about 8,200 pupils, constituting a little less than one-third of the total enrollment in all types of Jewish schools. In Canada and Latin America, Jewish day schools enroll a far higher proportion of the children receiving some kind of Jewish education at any one time than they do in the United States. However, the Jewish component in the curricula of these schools varies greatly, so that graduates of secular-oriented Jewish day schools have "only scant knowledge of Jewish subjects." This is true not only because of the amount of time devoted to these subjects but also because of the scarcity of adequately trained teachers.

In 1962 the Seminario Rabinico Latinamericano was founded in Buenos

Aires by Rabbi Marshall T. Meyer, as the first non-Orthodox school in Latin America to train students for rabbinical studies.

E. CONCLUSION

The overall conditions prevailing in Jewish education leave much to be desired and give cause for great concern. The number of Jewish children throughout the world between the ages of sixteen and seventeen receiving any kind of Jewish education, even excluding the Jews of the Soviet Union, probably constitutes only 45-50 percent of the total. Nor can we derive much satisfaction from the quality and quantity of education the vast majority of these are receiving. Yet considering the overwhelming tragedies inflicted upon the body of the Jewish people since 1934, it is heartening to note that the number of pupils enrolled in the schools has in the past two decades been steadily increasing and the percentage of those receiving an intensive Jewish education is slowly but steadily rising. The established schools of Jewish higher learning have been expanding, new elementary and secondary schools are being established, and new kinds of educational institutions are being created to meet the ever-changing needs of an ever-changing society.

CHAPTER 10

YIDDISH LITERATURE

By Yudel Mark

The Five Periods in the History of Yiddish Literature

Language is one of the principal elements distinguishing the Ashkenazic Jews from the Sephardic. The language of the Ashkenazim is Yiddish; that of the Sephardim, Judesmo (Ladino). Prior to World War II more than 10,000,000 persons, about two-thirds of all the Jews in the world, spoke or at least understood Yiddish.

Yiddish was born when emigrants from northern France, who spoke their own variation of old French, settled in a number of cities on the Rhine (later moving eastward) and adopted the German dialects of the area. In adopting these dialects, they adapted the new language to their old speech patterns and created a unique mixture of German dialects, caused by their wandering from one town to another. In addition, Hebrew had a continuing influence on the new dialect from the very beginning, because it (together with Aramaic) was the language of religion and scholarship. As a result, lexical, syntactical, and even morphological elements of Hebrew-Aramaic were amalgamated into Yiddish. This process of language formation began almost a thousand years ago. Later, the Slavic tongues (Czech, Polish, Ukrainian, Russian) exerted an influence on Yiddish. Thus Yiddish has to be considered a result of a fusion of the above-mentioned linguistic elements. It developed many unique characteristics due to the cultural isolation of the Jews.

Yiddish literature is only slightly younger than the Yiddish language and accompanied Ashkenazic Jewry wherever it moved. When Ashkenazic Jews arrived in sixteenth-century Italy, it became, for a short time, a center of Yiddish literary work. When an Ashkenazic community flourished in seventeenth-century Amsterdam, it became a center for the printing of Jewish books; there theatrical art in Yiddish was developed and the first Yiddish newspaper founded. When the focus of Jewish life shifted to the Slavic countries, they in turn became centers of Yiddish literature. Yiddish literature came to the United States of America with the East European immigrant masses, and the same is true in the Argentine, South Africa, and

Australia. Yiddish literature will be found on all the continents, wherever there are Ashkenazic, Yiddish-speaking Jews.

The history of Yiddish literature, which is almost eight hundred years old, may be divided conveniently into five periods:

I. The period of oral and manuscript literature—from the beginning to the close of the fifteenth century.

II. The folk book period—the sixteenth and the first half of the seventeenth century.

III. The period of relative decline—the latter half of the seventeenth and first half of the eighteenth century.

IV. The latter half of the eighteenth century to 1864 (the year Mendele Moicher Sforim began writing in Yiddish).

V. The past hundred years (1970).

The first three stages, up to the middle of the eighteenth century, represent the period of old Yiddish literature, reflecting as they do a life governed by tradition, stable, and relatively distinct from the surrounding Christian community, despite ever-present influence from the outside. The past hundred years may also be further subdivided into two periods: the first fifty years, to World War I, and thereafter to the present.

1. THE PERIOD OF ORAL AND MANUSCRIPT LITERATURE

A. THE OLD YIDDISH LITERATURE

From the outset, Yiddish literature was limited to a modest role. It was not meant to serve as the vehicle for scholarship; that was the prerogative of Hebrew. Yiddish was to provide recreational, light reading matter for the people of all social strata. At the same time however, it became a means of instructing those who had no access to Hebrew literature—women and the barely literate men. For hundreds of years the title pages of Yiddish works often carried this note: "Beautiful and instructive for Women and Girls" (for it would not have done to advertise that it was for the untutored!). Women were thus the avowed readers of Yiddish literature. A serious and scholarly man was often ashamed to be discovered frittering away his time with a work meant only to entertain.

It would be a mistake to compare the relationship between the literature in Yiddish and Hebrew with that between the vernacular and Latin literatures of Europe. For among the Jews almost every man was literate and the number who understood Hebrew was always incomparably greater than the number of educated medieval Christians who knew Latin. There was another significant difference: all didactic literature in Yiddish was either a direct outgrowth of Hebrew literature or influenced by it. Until very recent times the bond between the two literatures was so strong that one may justifiably speak of one literature in two languages (this, incidentally, was the view of Mendele Moicher Sforim, Baal-Machshoves, and Samuel Niger).

Yiddish literature, like many another, is related to folk lore, in this instance the folk lore of an ancient and sorely tried people. This folk lore is, on the one hand, didactic, full of tales of holy men, religious parables, and scholarly aphorisms and, on the other, recreational, full of general human themes. The didactic literature is based on traditional elements; the recreational works drew on the German heroic epic, chivalric tales, European folk songs and folk plays. For a short time there was a direct influence on Yiddish literature from Italian; indirectly there was influence even from Provençal.

While all the works based on general literature were often popular they were never held in high esteem by the people. Pious folk disparaged this literature, permitting its use only at celebrations, weddings, feasts. There were also periods when some rabbis expressly opposed the literature, because of its alien themes. This opposition stimulated the creation of devotional works which would be as absorbing as the secular adventure stories. As a result, the quality of the didactic literature improved.

B. THE SCRIBES AND THE SINGERS

There are extant some one hundred manuscripts containing about 150 works. Most of the manuscripts were lost as a result of the many expulsions and persecutions, and therefore our picture of the first period of Yiddish literary history is necessarily incomplete. Either the earliest manuscripts are concerned with popular medicine or they are translations of prayers and parts of the Bible.

Because handwritten works were expensive, only wealthy women could afford them. They would order scribes to prepare little anthologies for specific occasions. These scribes were not always mere copyists; they were also translators, adaptors, and even authors of original material. The scribes—or "servants of pious wives," as they called themselves—were often supported by their patronesses. These anthologies were conglomerations of songs, stories, amusing sketches, translations or new renditions of Biblical passages, important religious rules to be observed by women, and sundry helpful hints on proper conduct.

The principal disseminators of old Yiddish literature were the bards (singers) and jesters (fools), the comedians of their day. The bards sang ballads and selections from long metrical works or gave readings. Like the German *Spielmann*, or minstrel, they recounted sagas of heroism and of unusual events. The whole technique of the Yiddish bard—the tunes and stunts and terms—as well as a considerable portion of his repertoire, was adopted from the German minstrel. Almost all the better known works of the *Spielmann* reached the Jewish audiences, generally in some modified form. For example, passages referring to Christianity were either eliminated or replaced by Jewish allusions; the original work was abridged and thus made more compact; brutal scenes were somewhat humanized and made less offensive; chivalric details were omitted. Sometimes the changes were even more profound: Jewish motifs and details would be introduced and the elements of tragedy might be heightened the more effectively to arouse sympathy.

The oldest known documents of Yiddish literature stem from the four-teenth century. In 1953 Leo Fuks discovered at the Cambridge University Library a manuscript which Solomon Schechter brought from the Genizah of Fostat. The manuscript, which is heavily damaged, is clearly dated 1382. The manuscript was probably written in Egypt, presumably for the Ashkenazic Jews who found there a haven from persecution in the Ger-manic lands. It contains a long (more than a thousand lines) epic poem, *Ducus horant;* a new version of the *Hildesaga;* four poems from Jewish sources—*Our Rabbi Moses, The Paradise, Patriarch Abraham,* and *The Pious Joseph;* and a new version of the fable of the sick lion. We now possess unquestionable evidence that as far back as the fourteenth cen-tury, a flourishing Yiddish literature had developed a variety of motifs and forms.

Much more interesting than the variations on foreign themes are the romances based on Jewish sources: generally, biblical stories adorned with midrashic and fanciful detail. The principal work of this genre is the *Shmuel-Bukh* (fifteenth century), a work of almost 1800 four-line stanzas, by a learned and highly talented author named Moshe Esrim Vearba. We know nothing of his life. However, the Bible, together with midrashic tales, is the basis of the work. The author created a literary school. Lesser talents followed him with *Melokim-Bukh, Daniel-Bukh, The Book of the Judges,* and others. No work was as popular as Moshe Esrim Vearba's, which was recited in song with a special *Shmuel-Bukh* tune. Another such popular work was the eighty-stanza poem called *Akeydas Yitskhok,* or *Yiddisher Shtam* (*The Sacrifice of Isaac, or Jewish Descent*). With delicate lyricism and religious pathos it tells of Abraham's struggle with Satan as Isaac was being led to the sacrifice.

Not many lyrics have survived from this early period—and these only of the professional scribes and troubadours. Of the lyrics extant we find three types: (1) religious songs in praise of God and in honor of the Sabbath and the holidays; (2) didactic poems underscoring the Jewish view of life; (3) poems on general moral and folk-loristic themes.

This lyric material is also closely connected with the beginnings of Jewish drama, the humorous skits and didactic monologues and dialogues performed for the most part in the homes of the wealthy on festive occasions and during the Purim or Hanukkah holidays. Such a work was the popular *Dance of Death*; it may date back to the Spanish-Jewish period. Apparently the *Purimshpil* was already developing during this period; those we know, however, have come down to us from a later period.

C. THE RELIGIOUS POPULAR TALES

In the period between the Crusades and the sixteenth century many new legends were developed. New tales were told of the lives of great personalities. There are whole cycles of legends on men like Rabbenu Gershom, Rashi, and Rabbi Judah Hasid. Every community had its local tales. These folk stories reflect life under constant threat of expulsion, the blood libel, the pogrom, and, withal, the faith that all these dangers will be surmounted. Irrespective of the language in which they were first recorded, all these stories were developed in Yiddish.

2. THE PERIOD OF THE FOLK BOOK

A. LITERARY UPSWING IN THE SIXTEENTH AND THE FIRST HALF OF THE SEVENTEENTH CENTURY

1. Elijah Bochur and the Bouva Story (Bova Bukh)

The invention of printing gradually made the scribe superfluous and diminished the importance of the bard and the jester. Their tales could now be read and they had hundreds of thousands of readers. Unlike the previous period whose figures are anonymous, the great writers and folk teachers are distinct personalities. By far the most interesting figure of the first half of the sixteenth century is Elijah Bochur (1468?-1549).

Elijah Bochur's fame rests principally on his Hebrew scholarship; but he was interested in Yiddish too, and his poetic works were written exclusively in this language. His two great Yiddish novels are the *Bova Bukh* and *Paris un Viene*[1] (the latter never became popular). Both works are free adaptations of Italian romances and both are written in the Italian *ottava rima* stanza. The *Bova Bukh* became a most popular parody of the troubadour romances. Its author is playful, ironic; his jumbling of elements of Jewish folkways with stories of knightly exploits is grotesque. In short, he makes merry with the old claptrap of the troubadour's art.

The popular, short fantastic tale gave rise to a rich repository of novelle, legends and prose versions of the poetic works of the preceding period. The *packn-treger* (book peddler) who bore his library upon his back was the special agent who disseminated this literature, trudging all the way into the twentieth century with his bag of diverting merchandise.

Typical of the sixteenth century is the brief prose tale or novella based usually upon folk lore, Hebrew literature or foreign themes. Yet there were also some completely original works, the pearl among these being the anonymous *A Tale of Brie and Zimre*,[2] a glorification of that abiding love which is stronger than death.

2. *The Story Book and the Moralistic Tracts*

The story book (*Maase-Bukh*) of the latter sixteenth century (the oldest printed edition extant is dated 1602) is a compilation of the earlier *belles-lettres* and the cradle of later folk tales. This *Maase-Bukh*, which exerted a powerful influence on the style and content of Yiddish prose tales up to the modern period, is a collection of talmudic legends and medieval folk tales embellished with new particulars. If the *Maase-Bukh*, blending naiveté and deep faith with color, fantasy, and dramatic suspense, may be classified as didactic literature, it is the gem of that literary genre, displacing such frivolous works as the *Cow Book* (*Kuh Bukh*) and the earlier items in the bard's repertoire.

Although glossaries, like the *Mirkeves Hamishne* (Cracow, 1534), by Reb Asher Anshil, and translations of the Pentateuch, intended as aids to the teacher (*melamed*), never became folk books, they did start a trend which led to the *Woman's Pentateuch*. The so-called morality books, which showed great development during this period, applied the ethical principles of Judaism to everyday life. Whereas its prototype, the Hebrew morality book, is briefly formulary, severe and dryly apropos, the Yiddish version is more picturesque in style and less moralizing in tone. Aimed at the two-fold audience of the untutored man and the woman reader, it contains a parable at every step, illustrates the moral by an epigram and arouses interest by means of a story. Although the goal is to influence the conduct of the reader, the method is nevertheless to entertain him. The oldest Yiddish moralistic work handed down to us is the *Seyfer Mides* (*Book on Behavior*, Izni, 1542). Some morality books were meant only for the female reader, such as *Brantshpigl* (*Burning Mirror*, Basle, 1602). Later the most popular of these works was the *Lev Tov* (*Good Heart*), by Reb Isaac ben Elyokum of Posen (Prague, 1620), which was addressed to both men and women and is fervently religious.

3. *The Woman's Pentateuch and the Special Prayers*

Literal translations of the books of the Bible, removed as they were from the sphere of everyday life, failed to gain especial favor, and it was not until several efforts, such as the translation of the Pentateuch by Reb Isaac ben Samson, had been made that the most widely read and influential work of all Yiddish literature, the *Tseno-Ureno* (*Go Out and See*) by the Polish Jew, Jacob ben Isaac Ashkenazi (1550-1623?), appeared. Ostensibly a translation of the Pentateuch, the *Haftoros* and the Five Scrolls, it is actually a unique mosaic of commentary, legend, allegory, epigram and ethical observation. The author drew upon the entire popular literary heritage from the canonization of the Bible to his own day, choosing those stories which related to the passages of the Pentateuch he was paraphrasing. Directed to the feminine reader, the work became a kind of woman's Bible which has been the source of Jewish knowledge for generations of mothers, who, Sabbath after Sabbath, have absorbed its Cabbala-flavored philosophy of life.

The *Tseno-Ureno*, reflecting the triumph of individual interpretation over literal translation, the prominence of the woman's role in everyday Jewish life and the paramount influence of Polish ritual over the more worldly Germanic, overshadowed all previous works in Yiddish and affected the life of the general population more deeply and more lastingly than any other.

Although Yiddish, like Aramaic before it, had become the language of the Jewish religion, the attempt (characteristic of the Reformation era), such as that of Joseph Bar Yokor (1544) to inaugurate a Yiddish prayer book, was not successful. However, the prayers of entreaty called the *tkhines* voluntarily added to the canonized Hebrew prayer did become popular. This supplementary prayer is concrete, speaks for a single individual and concerns a specific situation. Humbly pious and for the most part femininely delicate, many of these prayers were composed by women. The oldest collections we know are dated 1590 and 1599, while others were composed as late as the middle of the nineteenth century.

This special prayer, in reality a prose poem, expresses the religious lyricism so strongly developed in this period. A number of these Yiddish religious poems were incorporated into the Hebrew religious ceremonial. Of the numerous poets mention is made of "the pious Reb Jacob" of Teplitz and the poetesses Rebecca Tiktiner and Toïbe Pan of Prague.

Some secular works were invested with a religious quality, such as the biting epigrams and doggerel of the misogynist Seligman Ulma, *Tsukht-spigl* (*Mirror of Manners*, Hanau, 1610). Although less completely developed, "wine, women, and song" poetry did make its appearance—the collection of Isaac, son of Moses Wallich of Worms (end of sixteenth century).

During the latter half of the sixteenth century Prague was the center of Yiddish poetry and the home of the most popular poet of the time, Solomon Zinger. He was famous for his wit and the few of his lyrics that are known today are distinguished for their humor and forcefulness.

The outstanding poetic form was the historical epic, describing and commemorating some important occurrence in the life of the community such as a pogrom, a fire or an epidemic. The historic poem followed a set pattern, opening with a passage in praise of God, recounting the main events in considerable detail, and ending with a prayer for the speedy advent of the Messiah. An example of such a poem is the *Vints-Hans-Song* by Elchanan, son of Abraham Heln (Frankfort on the Main, 1616), describing the anti-Semitic attack organized by Vincent Fettmilch, the expulsion of the Jewish community and its return. This scroll of Vints was read every year in Frankfort during observance of the local Purim.

The historical works in prose, of which the most popular was the *Yosifon* (Zurich, 1546) an adaptation of Josephus's *Antiquities,* followed the pattern of the earlier didactic morality books which did not separate fact from legend. Banishment and persecution are the principal themes of these historical works, such as the Yiddish translation of the *Tribe of Judah,* which recounts the expulsions from Spain and Portugal.

Descriptions of journeys are similar to the story books. Most popular and most fantastic of these travelogues was *The Regions of Eretz Israel* (Lublin, 1635), which was publicly burned by Jesuits in Warsaw. This book later was republished under the title *Path of Holiness.*

Although the stories and legends of the time were rich in dramatic detail, they did not become the bases for dramatic works. For this period we know only of Purim plays and of a rollicking comedy called *A Play About Deaf Yeklein, His Wife Kendlein and His Two Sons Fine* (end of sixteenth century).

3. THE LATTER HALF OF THE SEVENTEENTH AND FIRST HALF OF THE EIGHTEENTH CENTURY

The Sabbatai Zevi movement[3a] gave a kind of ascetic and mystical overtone to Jewish life in eastern Europe, which also became increasingly conservative. While these tendencies are reflected in the literature, no new forms were evolved or great works written to supplant the old favorites. The only center of a freer life was Amsterdam.[4a] There during the 1680's two antihomiletic translations of the Bible were made (by Blitz and Witzenhausen), entirely contrary to the spirit of the times.

However, the focal book of the period was not the Bible but the *Zohar,* the holy book of the Cabbala.[5a] Indicative of the interest in Jewish mysticism is *The Work of the Lord* (Frankfort on the Main, 1691), a collection of fifty stories about its heroes from the founder (?) Reb Simon ben Jochai to Reb Isaac Luria. The morality book *Nakhlas Tsvi,* known as "*Taytsh Zohar*" (Frankfort, 1711), by the Cracow Cabbalist Zevi Hirsh Chotscz also became popular. In the main the Cabbalists addressed themselves to the male reader, appealing to the emotions of the ordinary man of the people, and in doing so took a strong stand against the intellectual aristocracy of the talmudic scholars. Zevi Hirsh Koidanover, in his *Kav Hayosher* (Frankfort, 1705) inspires pious fear in the hearts of his readers, threatening them with punishment for their sins in the hereafter. Closely akin to the spirit of this stern work are the translations from the Hebrew of the early morality books, of which one of the best known is the gentler and more mystical Khoives Halvoves (*Duties of the Heart*, 1716). A work of this period, which foreshadowed the Hasidism of a later era, was Elchanan Kirkhhan's *Simkhas Hanefesh* (*Soul's Delight*, Frankfort, 1707).

A. POETIC AND NARRATIVE WORKS OF THE PERIOD

Laments over proscriptions and expulsions, usually entitled "new" (e.g., *A New Lament upon the Destruction in Worms; A New Lament over the Expulsion from Tannhausen*) were the most important poetic works. Their titles are ironic, for their themes are as old as the Diaspora, the form set by tradition and the only changes, those of place, year and detail of horror.

The tradition of "Sacred Poems" continued, as exemplified by Aaron ben Samuel of Eggershausen's collection entitled *Gentle Prayer or Powerful Medicine for Body and Soul* (Fuerth, 1709). Containing poetic variations of the traditional prayers along with new and original songs of praise, the work was printed in square letters like those of the authorized prayer book, instead of in "woman's script" used for Yiddish translations of Hebrew books, and consequently was banned by the rabbis.

Folk songs were the source for much vibrant poetry, such as numerous lyrics of the "one kid" variety and paraphrases of the "Who Knows One?" verses. The most important piece of satiric expression of the times is the anonymous *Description of Ashkenaz and Pole* in which Polish, German and Czech (Prague) Jews are compared. Motifs of social protest also occur in some of the laments.

The narratives, such as the humorous story about the bigamist, *A Nice New Song About What Happened in Hamburg* (Amsterdam, 1675), still follow the verse form of the "singer" or "bard." However, the "story book" pattern is used with increasing frequency, as in *The Story of Miracles*, a collection of twenty-five popular legends of Worms, by the sexton of the community, Jeptha Yuspa ben Naftoli. A curious work is the *Story of West India* in which the new and foreign literature of adventure is combined with the old fount of Jewish legend. Quite characteristically Jewish is the travel romance entitled *Amsterdam Story* which describes the experiences of a rabbi who set out to comb distant lands in search of the Lost Ten Tribes of Israel.

The best prose work of this period, however, remained in manuscript. The splendid memoirs of Glikl Hamil (of Hameln, near Hamburg) written between 1691 and 1719, tell the life story of a prominent woman, well acquainted with old Yiddish literature. The work gives an account of the contemporary way of life, of family and economic affairs, of important historical events, and of private joys and sorrows. In her entries Glikl revealed a gift for accurately observing life and still greater facility for narration.

The great events of the period aroused an interest in history manifested by a Yiddish translation of *Yeveyn-Metsule*, an account of the holocaust of 1648-1649. Menachem ben Solomon Amelander's original historical work, *Remnants of Israel* (Amsterdam, 1741), an account of Jewish history from the destruction of the Second Temple to the author's own time, enjoyed great popularity.

Of the travelogues worthy of note is the early eighteenth-century work *A Description of the Travels of Abraham Levi*. Sabbatai Bass's geographical work, *Ways of the World*, contains, in addition to directions for reaching a number of large cities, prayers to be said en route. This period also witnessed the appearance of many popular medical works, account books and collections of model letters.

Amsterdam, center of Yiddish book production, was also the home of the first Yiddish newspaper, *Di Dinstogshe Kurantn* and *Fraytogshe Kurantn* (*Tuesday and Friday Courant*), a semiweekly publication which compared favorably with contemporary Dutch papers. It appeared from 1686 to 1687.

Despite the growth of religious feeling during this period and despite the Jews' seclusion from the rest of the world, the Yiddish theater was well liked both as a temporary stage for Purim players and *yeshiva* students and as the theater of professional actors. A number of plays from the first half of the eighteenth century have come down to us, such as *The Sale of Joseph, The Sacrifice of Isaac, David and Goliath, The Exodus from Egypt, King Solomon's Verdict, Sodom and Gomorrah*.

4. THE SECOND HALF OF THE EIGHTEENTH AND THE FIRST HALF OF THE NINETEENTH CENTURY

A. THE DECLINE OF YIDDISH LITERATURE IN WESTERN EUROPE

Yiddish literature, like the Yiddish language, had its beginnings in Western Europe. For hundreds of years there had been a lively interchange of books and authors between West and East, when, at about the middle of the eighteenth century, a cleavage became apparent.

The period began with the abandonment of the spiritual Ghetto by the Yiddish intelligentsia of the West and its involvement in the capitalist system, which Jews helped to erect. In contradiction to its intended function, the Enlightenment movement became one of increasing assimilation, as evidenced by the use of the derogatory term "jargon" to describe the Yiddish language. For the first time Jewish scholars took pains to disparage their own language in the eyes of their people. Thus literary art in Yiddish declined rapidly; it was, however, preserved in Eastern Europe, where it later came to fruition.

In the West we find only epigonian works in the spirit and style of the foregoing period: historical poetry, chronicles, memoirs (such as the recollections of Aaron Isaacs, the first Jew in Sweden), translations of world literature (like that of *Robinson Crusoe* published in Metz in 1764). A unique work that attempted a compromise between tradition and Enlightenment, but which remained in manuscript, was *Love Letters* by Itsik Vetslar. We have only two plays of the Enlightenment school in Yiddish, both belonging to the late eighteenth century and both excellent literary creations in the style of the bourgeois drama—*Reb Hennach* or *What's to Be Done with It*, by Isaac Eiche, and Aaron Wolfson's *Frivolity and False Piousness*. The final remnants of Western Yiddish literature in the nineteenth century are the dialect parodies of Joseph Herts and the lampoonery and playlets of Morits Gotlib Saffir.

Of the many periodical publications not one was long-lived. The *Dirnfurter Privilegirte Tseytung*, a semiweekly (1771-1772), was directed primarily to the Jews of Poland. In Amsterdam the new scholarly community of the Enlightenment and followers of the revolutionary movement published the periodical *Diskurs* (*Discourse*, 1797-1798). Amsterdam, the most stable center of Yiddish literature in the West, was also the birthplace (1784-1802) of the Yiddish operatic theater of Jacob Dessoier, himself the author of various *Zingshpiln*. Amsterdam is the setting for a comedy (*Az der sof is gut iz ales gut*, *All's Well That Ends Well*) about a cheat who runs away from his wife and collects money for nonexistent charities. It was written about 1800 by an unknown author. In Vienna the musical comedies of David Leib Biderman were produced during the 1830's and 1840's.

B. HASIDIC LITERATURE

Hasidism, which brought a stream of joyousness and exaltation into the life of the ordinary man, made greater use of Yiddish than had earlier religious movements. Famous Hasidic rabbis frequently prayed in Yiddish and gave expression to their teachings in that tongue, thus enriching and refining the language. The Hasidic movement also gave impetus to a renascence of popular creativity: stories, poetry, parable, apothegms, and adages. The popular tale acquired a new hero, the Hasidic rabbi, while the former hero, the *Lamed Vov*, took on new importance. Thus inspired,

Jewish popular fancy expressed itself in a whole series of marvelous tales which became part of the "literature of praise" of the Hasidic rabbis, the most popular being *Shivkhey Besht* (*Praises of the Besht*, 1815). In this manner a new holiday spirit entered the soul of the people and the heavens moved a little closer to earth.

The allegories and stories of the Baal Shem Tob (the Besht) himself gave the impetus to Hasidic literature. His skill in relating these tales raised them to the level of recited Torah. His disciples, in retelling these anecdotes, always added embellishments of their own, thus laying the foundation for a new and widespread oral tradition among the less educated and even the untutored Jews. The courts of some Hasidic rabbis became centers of artistic creativity in poetry, music, and the dance. The Maggid of Mezeritsh was a fine fabulist. Reb Levi Yitzkhok Barditshever was an outstanding allegorical poet. His prayers reveal the rather unusual union of exalted pantheism, a sense of intimacy with the Creator, and a feeling of the importance of the individual.

One of the greatest Jewish narrators of all time was the mystic dreamer Reb Nachman Brahtslever (1772-1810). A great-grandson of the Besht, rocked in the cradle of Hasidism, he lived more in a visionary realm than in his actual environment, against which he rebelled. While some of the elements of his fantasies are taken from the folk tale, and even from universal motifs, the essential construction, the winged scope, the delicate form, and the ethical-mystical ideas are all completely original. His romanticism, so characteristic of the period, is deeper and more revealing than the vague longings of the *Weltschmerzler*, imbued as it is with the fervor for serving God.

One group of his stories is realistic, containing details of everyday life, while the majority of his tales are of the cloth of free fantasy interwoven with lyricism. After Reb Nachman's death, his colleague and pupil, Nosn Nemirover, published the stories (which his disciples believed disclosed the secrets of the Torah and of life) in a collection entitled *Sipurey Maasiyes* (*Narrative Tales*, 1815). The disciple recorded the sayings of his master verbatim, regarding every word as a holy utterance. Thus we have an accurate picture of the style of Reb Nachman, whose wonderful personality left so deep an impression upon his followers that they never acknowledged another leader—they remained the "dead Hasidim." Up until the outbreak of World War II, they made annual pilgrimages to his grave in Uman and always conducted themselves differently from all other Hasidim.

In the *Narrative Tales* we see a link in the chain of the centuries-old narrative tradition begun with the *Maase-Bukh* and to be continued in the works of Isaac Leibush Peretz.

At the same time that the West European Jew was beginning to assimilate and cease creating anything in Yiddish, East European Jewry was being influenced by the Hasidic movement to delve deeper into itself, to amass new vitality, and to bring to the fore new works of art in Yiddish letters, music and dance.

C. THE LITERATURE OF THE ENLIGHTENMENT, TO THE MIDDLE OF THE NINETEENTH CENTURY

The movement for enlightenment (*Haskala*) followed two roads from West to East: the principal one, through Galicia to southern Russia and Poland; the other, directly to Lithuania. The *Haskala*, embracing the intelligentsia and the merchant class, aimed to free the individual from the restraints of tradition by educating him and by remodeling Jewish life on a freer foundation so that he might deserve and achieve emancipation.[6a] But the *Haskala* also brought with it from Germany the desire to forget Yiddish and adopt the language of the land. However, the more realistic of the enlightened readily realized that they had to make use of Yiddish in order to spread their beliefs. Another point of difference, and a more fundamental one, was the clash (which continued throughout the nineteenth century) between the elements opposed to Yiddish and those cultured East European Jews who loved the rejected masses and were devoted to their language. Two closely related trends are characteristic for the *Haskala* literature in Yiddish. One is indicated by works designed to instruct and propagate the ideas of the *Maskilim* (followers of *Haskala*), and the other by polemic works which were critical of the old way of life. The instructive works were a modern continuation of the morality books, while the polemic works consisted almost entirely of satires. The dramatic form was used by the *Maskilim* only as a means of faithfully recording daily events and for the purpose of debate. The narrative form is also rich in realistic detail but it is often exaggerated and interrupted by journalistic digressions.

Oddly enough it was a Geman Jew, Moses Markuse, a physician in the small towns of Poland and Lithuania where he was stranded, who wrote a most unusual book, *Seyfer Refues* (*The Book of Remedies*), highlighting the differences between the *Haskala* of the East and that of the West. The work, a mixture of popular medicinal practice and Enlightenment ideology, reveals a great love for the common man. At the same time, *Maskilim* made new translations into Germanized Yiddish of works from other languages, such as Kampe's *Discovery of America*, with a view toward contributing to the education of the people. This version by the Lithuanian *Maskil*, Mordecai Aaron Ginsburg, was not particularly successful but that of an Uman merchant, Chaim Chaikl Hurvits, *Tsofnas Paneach* (1817), was immensely popular. The language of this work, based as it was upon spoken Yiddish, represents a definite departure from the old literary language, which had become too archaic and Germanic.

The theoretician and chief protagonist of this new trend, which was making rapid headway, especially among the *Maskilim* of Galicia and Podolia, who used it in revising earlier Yiddish works, was Mendl Leffin, or Mendl Satanover (1749-1826), as he was known, a dominant figure in the Enlightenment and a link between the Berlin *Haskala* and that of Galicia and southern Russia. He proposed to translate the Bible into the idiomatic Yiddish of his Ukrainian dialect, intending, as did Moses Mendelssohn,[7a] to turn the people toward the Bible. Satanover hoped to do this by relating the Scriptures to Yiddish in contradiction to the endeavors of Mendelssohn. Satanover's plan was not realized because of disputes which arose concerning it, and only the Book of Proverbs was published (1814), several other sections circulating in manuscript. The whole project was not completed until the twentieth century through the translation by Yehoash in the United States. However, the new Yiddish literary language, based upon everyday spoken vernacular, was strengthened. Satanover affected two generations of writers who made use of their local dialects. At approximately the same time the practice was established of using square characters for printed Yiddish instead of the cursive "woman's script."

At the beginning of the nineteenth century the new forms and ideas worked their way into the model-letter pamphlets which for generations had served as texts for learning Yiddish style, as well as the writing of the language itself. Illustrative is Levin Lion D'Or's *Nayer Kinstlecher Brivnshteller* (*New Artistic Letter Writer*, Vilna, 1825), which went through ten editions.

The *Maskilim* directed their sharpest satire against the Hasidim and the courts of their rabbis. In 1815 the rabbinical judges of Lemberg excommunicated the local *Maskilim* and by way of comment there appeared the excellent anonymous *The Duped World*, a Tartuffian comedy of much wit. Undoubtedly the author belonged to the circle of Mendl Satanover, as did Joseph Perl, wealthy merchant of Tarnopol, who authored in Hebrew and in Yiddish the satiric *Megale Tmirin*. Consisting of 151 letters of twenty-six correspondents, this work is an imitation of the humanist *Epistolae Obscurorum Virorum*. Another author of the same circle wrote the satirical story, *The Greatness of Reb Volf of Charni-Ostrow*.

The ill and poverty-stricken Isaac Baer Levinson, known as the "Philosopher of Kremenetz" and the "Mendelssohn of Russian Jewry," wrote a social satire attacking the injustice of the community to the poor masses. Entitled *Hefker Velt* (*Heedless World*), this work marks the beginning of the militant social writing of the nineteenth century. "Rivol," as he was known, also wrote a satirical poem, *Purim Play*. The Polish *Maskil*, Efraim

Fishlzon, composed a three-act comedy, *Theater of Hasidim,* an anti-Hasidic satire in the form of arguments. The anonymous derisive poem, *Troubles of the Teachers,* gives a sad picture of traditional education. The above-mentioned works are important for their social message rather than for their artistic merit.

In addition to the hindrances imposed by the Russian government, the fact that they were but scattered groups, prevented the *Maskilim* from developing a journalistic press. In 1823-1824 the weekly *Observer on the Vistula* was published in Warsaw; its language being quite Germanic, the publication did not long survive. It was not until the revolution of 1848 that a Yiddish weekly, called *Zeitung,* made its appearance in Lvov, Galicia; it was published again in 1863 as the *Yudishe Zeitung.*

D. ISRAEL AXENFELD AND SOLOMON ETTINGER

Almost all the *Haskala* writers mentioned thus far also wrote in Hebrew and regarded their Hebrew works as the more important. Now we turn to two writers of the first half of the nineteenth century who wrote exclusively in Yiddish.

Israel Axenfeld (1787-1866), an Odessa lawyer, was the first great storyteller of the Enlightenment. Although as a youth he had been a Hasid, indeed a colleague of Reb Nosn Nemirover, he devoted all his literary talents to combating "Baal-Shemism" and Hasidism. In the main, the naturalist in him triumphed over the satirist, and his characterizations, patterned as they were after actual persons, are vital if primitive. Yet he lacked the power for synthesis so necessary in a truly great realistic writer. The *Maskilim* read his many novels and stories in the manuscript form used in the days before the invention of printing. He was more fortunate in getting his dramatic works published and his play, *The First Jewish Recruit,* was performed with evident success on the Yiddish stage of the 1920's and 1930's. Axenfeld's sketches of milieu are still interesting today as source materials.

Although Galicia and southern Russia produced most of the writers of this period, the most important talent came from Poland. Solomon Ettinger (1800-1856), who has been called "the great-grandfather of modern Yiddish literature," wrote in Yiddish not for the purpose of spreading cultural or social ideas but for art's own sake. He was the first to attempt to refine Yiddish, to create new words and polish his style. The first lyricist per se, he described nature and his own moods even though they were subjective and pointed no moral. His clever allegories and good-humored epigrams are lively and witty; the poetic descriptions of character types lack the sharpness of the *Haskala* satire. Ettinger pioneered in the kind of literature that focuses upon the individual and his feelings rather than upon the group and its problems, and widened the scope of Yiddish literature, linking it with that of Europe.

Ettinger's masterpiece is the dramatic comedy *Serkele* (*Little Sarah*), a story of character and environment in which the central figure is a capable woman who dominates her household and is unscrupulous in her drive for wealth and power. Although Ettinger did borrow a few secondary details from the militant comedies of David Eiche and Aaron Wolfson, his plot, technique, and characters were his own and became the prototypes for later works, such as Jacob Gordin's *Mirrele Efros* (see below) and the plays of Abraham Goldfaden. Ettinger's works, censored by the czarist regime, did not appear until after his death.

E. THE FIFTIES AND SIXTIES OF THE NINETEENTH CENTURY

The first nineteenth-century Yiddish author to enjoy a reading public numbering in the tens of thousands was the Vilna *Maskil*, Isaac Meir Dyk (1814-1893). His hundreds of realistic short stories and more romantic novels were especially popular in Lithuania and were always to be found in the itinerant peddler's pack. His intention was to enlighten and instruct the people, refine their ways, and teach them German by using many German expressions in his writings, translating them into pure Yiddish. Dyk's style often reminds us of that of the morality book. He addresses himself to the "dear lady reader" and discourses with her about child education, the dangers of luxurious living, purity in family life, the value of living off the soil and of educating oneself. Isaac Meir Dyk is a combination of the maggid and the modern storyteller, embodying the old tradition and at the same time foreshadowing the realistic literature of a later period.

The theoretician among the conservatives of the *Haskala* was Eliezer Tsvi Tsveifl, whose aim it was to combine the positive elements of Orthodoxy and Hasidism with the newer teachings of the Enlightenment. He not only sought to interest his colleagues and disciples at the rabbinical school of Zhitomir in writing in Yiddish, but was the author of some good stories himself, such as *The Fortunate Maftir* and the half-literary, half-journalistic *Life's Punishments*. Influenced by Mendl Satanover, he in turn affected Mendele Moicher Sforim and was the first to give impetus to the Neo-Hasidism of the late nineteenth and the early twentieth century.

The radical wing of the *Haskala* was distinguished by the fighting spirit of Abraham Gotlober, who had led the difficult life of a wanderer. His comedy, *The Veil, or Two Weddings in One Night*, shows the influence of Ettinger's *Serkele*. Of principal importance to Yiddish literature are his poems, such as *The Poor Yisroilik*, which was exceedingly popular and topically characteristic of the Enlightenment. His humorous Yiddish version of Schiller's *Song of the Bell* became the *Song of the Sabbath Pudding*. Incidentally, Schiller was the German writer most popular with the *Maskilim*, and there are several curious versions in Yiddish of his aforementioned *Song of the Bell*, the most felicitous of which is Hirsh Reitman's *The Kittel (The White Prayer Mantle)*.

Alongside the poetry of the more intelligent *Maskilim* there existed the folk lyrics in the old tradition of the bards. During the middle years of the nineteenth century there were two great poets of the people: the wandering, bohemian Berl Margolies, known as Berl Broder, and the more colorful and refined Wolf Ehrenkrants, who went by the name of Velvl Zbarzher.

In the city of Brody, the center of trade and of the *Haskala*, Berl Broder established a cabaret troupe for which he created the repertory. These "Singers of Brody" became very popular and made guest appearances all over Galicia, southern Russia, and Poland, spreading Broder's merry yet melancholy songs of the fate of the common man as well as his lyrical nature poems. The collection, entitled *Shirey Zimro (Song Poems)*, was published in 1860.

Velvl Zbarzher sang of wine and love, of the eternal yearning for peace, and of the pettiness of life in the wine cellars of Rumania and Bessarabia, in Vienna and Constantinople. Motifs of the intellectual *Haskala*, the mundane details of everyday life, old lyric balladry, and modern writing— all were interwoven in the works of these two poets, the last in the many generations of bardic singers.

With the exception of the little-theater performances by the Singers of Brody and by sporadic companies in Warsaw (1838-1839; 1866-1870), there had not developed a permanent professional Yiddish theater. However, this did not prevent the writing of a number of dramatic works, some of them rather effective, such as *The Town Community*, by Wolf Kamrash; Joel Berish Falkovitch's *Reb Chaim the Rich* and *Little Rachel, the Singer*; *Heaven-Made Match* by Hirsh Reitman; Isaiah Gutman's *The Three Cousins* and *Kolboynik (The Rascal)*. Such works were read aloud at small gatherings and performed by amateurs.

By the middle of the nineteenth century there was a large reading public thirsty for new books. The lack of a Yiddish press, barred by the Russian government, retarded the development of Yiddish literature. In 1862, however, the *Koil Mevasser (The Voice of the Messenger)* appeared in Odessa, and from that time forward Yiddish journalism developed very rapidly. Many talented new writers appeared and the earlier authors became more strongly established as their works were reprinted.

At about this time important changes occurred in Jewish life, with the emancipation of the Russian peasant in 1861, the migration from the small towns to the big cities, the development of commerce and trade in which the Jews took a more active part, and the rise of the working class, struggling for a freer and a better life—all related to the rapid advance of Yiddish literature.

5. THE NEW YIDDISH LITERATURE

A. MENDELE MOICHER SFORIM, HIS CONTEMPORARIES AND DISCIPLES

The central figure in Yiddish literature in the last three decades of the nineteenth century is Mendele Moicher Sforim. The major trend is his trend: the realistic. The major achievement is his, too: the establishment of form, style, technique, and modern literary language. All the literati may be grouped about him: those who walked with him and those who followed, the ones who opposed him and the ones who wrote during his time but belonged to that of his predecessors. We begin with the last mentioned.

The most important in the line of Yiddish authors linking the folk song with individual poetry is the Vilna-born Michl Gordon (1823-1892), who criticized the traditional way of life in his works. In a rhythmic and lucid style he created ballads of milieu such as *The Divorce, The Beard, After the Wedding*. And in pained elegiacs he bemoaned his impoverished life (*My Years, My Lifetime, My Last Day*). His brother-in-law, the great Hebrew poet, Yehuda Leib Gordon, touched upon social themes of the Enlightenment in his Yiddish poems collected under the title *Sikhas Khulin* (*Commonplace Talk*, 1886). The Vilna poet, S. Y. Katsenelenbogen, treated of the most diverse topics with delicate lyricism which revealed the influence of Heine and the Russian poets, and paved the way for the poetry of Frug.

The most popular song writer was the last bard of Yiddish poetry, Eliokum Tsunzer (1835-1913). Didactic and moralizing, Tsunzer propagandized for the Enlightenment and later for Zionism. In his ballads, as in those of the bards, personification is common (*The Ferryboat*). Sung first at celebrations in well-to-do homes, his songs found their way to the masses and *The Plow, The Aristocrat, The Nineteenth Century* became extremely popular. More polished and more individual is the poetry of Abraham Goldfaden (1840-1908), author of romantically nationalistic poems and skilled in the art of versification. (On his operettas, see below.) There also belong in this line of writers Samuel Bernstein, poet and writer of comedies, and Ludwig Levinson, author of the very comical *Vaybershe Kniplekh* (*Women's Savings*).

We may now turn to the central figure, the grandfather of modern Yiddish literature. Sholem Jacob Abramowitz (1834-1917) was born in the small town of Kapulye in the province of Minsk. After several years of the hard life of a *yeshiva* student, he became the companion of a wandering beggar. But in Kamenets Podolsk he met Abraham Gotlober, who influenced him to take up cultural pursuits. For a time he lived in Barditchev, but was obliged to leave because of his work *Die Takse* (*The Meat Tax*) in which he exposed the local clique of "do-gooders." He struggled in Zhitomir and finally settled in Odessa, where he became the director of a Talmud Torah. When he began writing in Yiddish (1864) he took the name Mendele Moicher Sforim, which is more than just a pseudonym: through his works there passes the figure of an elderly Jew who rides about with his wagonful of books providing the people with prayers of supplication and lament, all the time smiling good-naturedly as he observes life around him. This figure helped to narrow the distance between the author and his readers. Mendele Moicher Sforim, inspiring love and admiration, was the first to establish a really intimate relationship between the Yiddish writer and his public.

During the first twenty years of his creative life, Mendele was a fighting satirist. Becoming more tranquil with the passage of time, he turned from satire to humor, from social crusading to memorializing a bygone way of life. True to the teachings of Eliezer Tsvi Tsveifl, he did not oppose Hasidism and never wounded the religious feeling but directed his social satire against those in power who wrong the people (*The Little Man*, *Die Takse*), against economic injustice (*The Wishing Ring, Fishke the Lame*), against the helplessness of the small town and its ignorance of the world (*The Travels of Benjamin the Third*).

The motifs of the *Haskala* gain depth in his work, personified as they are by a gallery of realistic figures. Mendele is a perfectionist and does not hesitate to rewrite his works, improving and adding to them. In *Die Takse* (see above) he not only mentions the clique of exploiting benefactors, but also gives us the autobiographical figure of Shloime Wekker, forerunner of the revolutionary movement among the Jews of Russia.

In the symbolic *Klyatshe* (*The Nag*, 1873) we have, ten years before its active acceptance, the manifestation of a national idea which did not become current until the eighties, as well as a penetrating socioeconomic critique of the *Haskala*. Thus the author also occupies an outstanding place in the history of Jewish social consciousness. This parallel development of literary art and social awareness is a fundamental characteristic of the years between 1864 and 1914, the period of the greatest advance in Yiddish literature.

In making Kabtsansk (*kabtsen*-Hebrew: poor man) his typical town and Gloopsk (*gloop*-Slavic: foolish) his typical city, Mendele is a synthesist. His broad canvases depict the most ordinary small-town happenings and present the house of study and the house of the poor, the home and the public bath, the weekday and the Sabbath, the philosophy of life and the merest grimace. It is curious, however, that this richly detailed picture of Jewish life has a definite limit in time. Anything later than the 1880's escapes Mendele's brush. In the main he relies upon his memory, so that it is not surprising that his autobiography, *Schloime, Son of Reb Chaim*, is also a splendid objective novel.

Since Mendele is extremely exacting in his realistic portrayals of a rather static life, his plot structure suffers. This careless attitude toward plot development became characteristic of the entire realistic school in Yiddish literature. (Is this perhaps due to the influence of the Russians?) But his masterful descriptions of various ordinary types, specifically Jewish in flavor, and his wonderful pictures of nature have a beauty which has never been surpassed.

Mendele is primarily responsible for the standardization of modern literary Yiddish. Eschewing the use of his own dialect, he was the first to strive consciously toward a synthesis of the Lithuanian and Ukrainian dialects and to include words and usages from earlier works. Mendele is the hub of the whole nineteenth century: as a social satirist, as the creator of a plastic yet statically synthetic realism, as the molder of a new style, he embodies the sum total of the Enlightenment movement. His antecedents, Mendl Satanover and his circle, lived at the beginning of the nineteenth century and his influence extends far beyond its close.

Appearing at the same time as Mendele's writings in the *Voice of the Messenger,* was *The Polish Boy* (in the second edition, *The Hasidic Boy*), a satirically biting autobiographical novel by Isaac Joel Linetski (1839-1916), whose indictment of Hasidic practices was the strongest ever written. The work created a great furor, but Linetski showed no further development and accomplished nothing with his anti-Mendele position.

Temporary success was enjoyed by *The Dark Young Fellow,* a sensational, melodramatic novel by Jacob Dinnezon (1856-1919). At first Dinnezon was opposed to Mendele in principle, claiming that the latter was too refined and too indifferent to the receptive capacity of the mass of Jewish readers. Although Dinnezon's themes are inclined to be those of primitive folk lore, the triumph of Mendele's artistic approach is apparent. In *Hershele* and *Yossele,* which appeared in the nineties, Dinnezon did preserve his sentimentalism, but it is subtler, revealing the influence of Mendele.

The less educated reader, in particular the women of the lower social strata, could not enjoy the Mendele literature. To fill the need of this audience, there appeared during the seventies and eighties colorful and unrealistic novels of improbable romances between a *yeshiva* student and a princess or a count and a servant maid, with detailed descriptions of their misfortunes, thus affording the reader a chance for a good cry.

Dozens of such novels were written by Shomer (pseudonym of Nokhem Meyer Shaykevitch), founder of a whole school of hack writers (Blohstein, Buchbinder, èt al.). These Shomerians challenged, so to speak, the disciples of Mendele Moicher Sforim: There, let us see you create artistic works that will be intelligible as well as entertaining to all. Sholem Aleichem quite consciously took up the gauntlet and emerged the victor.

B. PIONEERS IN POETRY, DRAMA, CRITICISM

Before proceeding to Mendele's disciples, we pause for those who performed his task, that of laying the foundation for future development, in the fields of poetry and drama. Among the poets, there were Simeon Frug (1860-1916) in Russia and Morris Rosenfeld (1862-1923) in the United States.

Brought up on Russian poetry and himself a recognized Russian-Jewish poet, Simeon Frug achieved mastery in fashioning facile, rhythmic Yiddish verse despite his complaint about the crudity of the underdeveloped language. Raised in a Jewish colony in southern Russia, he was close to the land and his lyrical descriptions of nature have a directness and matter-of-factness quite foreign to Yiddish poetry. A Zionist, Frug lamented the bitterness of the Dispersal and dreamed in his poetry of the happy future when everyone would sit under his own fig tree. He made many paraphrases of the Bible and drew upon folk lore in his ballads. Nor is social pathos foreign to him. He is many-faceted but none of his faces is really distinct.

Immeasurably more profound and more effective is Morris Rosenfeld. He lifted social poetry to new heights. The socialist Morris Vintshefski (1856-1932), the anarchists David Edelstadt (1866-1892) and Joseph Bovshover (1872-1915), and many other poets of lesser stature had depicted the difficult life of the workingman. But theirs was a poetry aimed at arousing its readers to the social struggle and only indirectly expressed deeply personal experiences. However, in Morris Rosenfeld's social poetry are the very sighs and pain of the worker.

Himself a sweatshop slave, Rosenfeld went through the many metamorphoses of the Jewish immigrant in England and the United States. He portrays the worker lashed to the sewing machine, spending his strength without any brighter prospects for the morrow, crying out his protest in anguish and despair. National motifs of Jewish homelessness and the dream of deliverance also are prominent in his rough-hewn, glowing verses. The breadth and depth of his poetic creativeness, the range and frequent unexpectedness of his imagery, more than compensate for certain roughnesses of diction. Rosenfeld was the first Yiddish poet to attract foreign readers and to have his works translated into many languages.

Both Frug and Rosenfeld, pioneers in Yiddish poetry, so different in expression, paved the way for later poets who drew upon the formal elements of the one and the sincerity of the other.

Abraham Goldfaden, the founder of the first modern professional Yiddish theater, was at the same time its manager, director, composer, and playwright. He had evinced all these talents as early as 1876, in Jassy where he laid the cornerstone for the rapid development of the theater. His operettas, setting a pattern for the Yiddish theater, which aims primarily to entertain and only secondarily to educate its audience, were of two types: comedies which make sport of the negative elements in Jewish life (e.g., *Di tsvey kunelemlekh, The Two Simpletons,* and *Di kishef-makherin, The Sorceress*) and nationalistic-romantic plays (e.g., *Shulamis, Bar-Kokbha*).

The comedies contain grotesque and entertaining exaggerations and are in the tradition of the Purim play and the wine cellar art of the Singers of Brody, but also include themes of the Enlightenment and telling portrayals of mores. The dramas are melodramatically sentimental interpretations of Jewish history, combining elements of heroism and buffoonery. Tuneful melodies played no small part in making Goldfaden's operettas great favorites. The negation of Mendele's realistic approach and the catering to the popular taste, first evident in Goldfaden's works, opened the way to the banalization of his own method by such hacks as Joseph Lateiner, "Professor" Hurwitz, Shomer, and others who, in the United States particularly, brought empty melodrama and quite vulgar operetta to the theater.

The early nineteenth-century Yiddish movement is linked with Mendl Satanover; but after the pogroms in Russia during the eighties, came the upheaval in social ideology and men turned from the Enlightenment to Zionism and nationalism. Part of the Jewish intelligentsia turned "homeward" and became more interested in the life of the masses, allying themselves more closely with those leaders of popular thought who had never strayed. At that time there were those, called the "Jargonists," who quite consciously wanted to strengthen the position of Yiddish. Thanks to this movement, such writers as I. L. Peretz, David Frishman, Simeon Frug, *et al.*, were attracted from the Hebrew and Russian literatures to the Yiddish. Simultaneously, interest in folklore increased, attempts were made to set up a uniform orthography and works of previous years were reprinted.

A number of new writers appeared on the scene: Moishe Aron Shatskes, with his excellent, mildly satirical *Before the Jewish Passover;* Paltiel Zamoshin, author of the short verses *Pictures of Life;* and "Yaknehoz," with his pleasant descriptions of small-town life. In almanacs such as the *Yiddishe Folks-Bibliotek (Jewish People's Library)* by Sholem Aleichem and Mordecai Spector's *Der Hoyzfraynd* (*Home Companion*), literary criticism first appeared. The young Sholem Aleichem wrote a very keen and witty critique of Shomer's novels; Joshua Honon Ravnitsky analyzed literary works instead of merely judging them; Joseph Judah Lerner introduced the positivist approach.

C. SHOLEM ALEICHEM AND ISAAC LEIBUSH PERETZ

Mordecai Spector (1858-1925) and Sholem Aleichem made their literary debuts at the same time and in the same weekly publication, the *Yiddishe Folksblat* (*Yiddish Folk Paper*) of 1883. Spector was faithful to Mendele's technique of detailed description, but his style is almost as colorless as the lives of his poor characters. His novels (*The Jewish Peasant, The Humble and the Needy, Reb Traytl*) and numerous stories are humorous and sentimental. With calm resignation and great insight he portrays the fate of the downtrodden. There is in Spector's work a deep sympathy for the poor man but no indication of any way out of his lot nor of any spiritual elation.

Sholem Rabinovitch (1859-1916), who took the pen name Sholem Aleichem, was born in the warm and fertile Ukraine. A difficult adolescence followed his idyllic childhood and it was not until he became private tutor in the home of a Jewish landowner, whose daughter he later married, that things began to go well for him. For a short time after the death of his father-in-law he conducted a successful business but subsequently lost his fortune and began to live by his writing. Illness sent him to Switzerland and Italy. Whenever he came to a "Jewish city" to deliver readings of his works, he received a great ovation, for he was the most popular of all Yiddish writers. The final years of his life were spent in New York City.

Sholem Aleichem began by writing realistic short stories and novels (*Stempenyu, Yossele Solvey*). In these early works he stood, so to speak, on the shoulders of Mendele, from whom he adopted many qualities of language and style. His originality came to the fore in *Kleine Mentshelekh mit Kleine Hasoges* (*Little People with Little Ideas*), where he first portrayed Kasrilevke, the composite town of poor but cheerful Jews with its happy-go-lucky Kasrillik. Later on, in *Menakhem Mendl*, his Kasrillik begins to wander, lands on the exchange and becomes a "speculator." Sholem Aleichem's vocabulary contains the wealth of idiom and the picturesqueness of expression found in spoken Yiddish, and his style ceases to be that of Mendele but becomes nervously dynamic. Instead of dwelling upon every detail, he sketches only a few particulars, usually the most humorous. At times he tends to become grotesque, but at his best he is a master of characterization.

Sholem Aleichem writes with especial tenderness of simple folk and of children. In the series of sketches, *Tevye the Dairyman*, we have the naïve yet deeply philosophical laborer who has intuitively absorbed the Jewish faith and its unshakable affirmation of life. In the children's stories, such as the *Song of Songs*, there is an additional individual lyricism which gives them much charm. In *Motl Peysi, The Cantor's Son*, a bright child gives an account of the life of a group of immigrants across the sea "in the golden land." The longer novels that first appeared as newspaper serials (*Wandering Stars, The Bloody Joke*) show only in part the excellence of his pen. And in the autobiographical novel *From the Fair* the writer abandons his favorite monologue form and writes in the third person. Of his dramatic works, the most performed were *Tsezeyt un Tseshpreyt* (*Scattered Far and Wide*), concerning the life of a Jewish family about the year 1905, and *Dos Groise Gevins* (*The Great Winnings*), where Shimmele Soroker, the main character, is a simplified Tevye the Dairyman.

Sholem Aleichem's genius has both breadth and depth. His characters are drawn from every class, although the background is always characteristically Jewish, whether it be Kasrilevke or the Lower East Side of New York. While writing of spiritual and emotional experiences in a seemingly cursory fashion, he is in reality plumbing the depths of an inward struggle. Thus Sholem Aleichem is interesting not only to the folk-lorist or the ethnographer, but also to the psychologist. His writing gives pleasure to the simplest reader who relishes the aphorisms and the humorous situations, while the most discriminating will find a philosophical depth and a symbolism of character rare in the works of other writers.

Everyone who read Yiddish at the turn of the century read Sholem Aleichem and even those who could not read knew of him, as it was customary to read his works aloud at celebrations and family gatherings. His unrivaled popularity is due largely to his humor, a humor which is many-sided: fresh, carefree laughter, tearful smiles, subtle wit, and grotesque exaggeration. Particularly characteristic of Sholem Aleichem is his treatment of sad and even tragic events with a kind of levity which springs from the faith that man can overcome any adversity. He gives us the comfort of a laughter which does not belittle the values of life but rather serves to emphasize them.

The genius for humor of the sorely tried Jewish people, formerly manifested in jest and epigram, shone in Sholem Aleichem's works through hundreds of characters, four of which are outstanding: Kasrillik, Menakhem Mendl, Tevye the Dairyman, and Motl, the Cantor's Son. These figures came to be regarded almost as members of the reader's own family. Indeed, the extent of the influence of Sholem Aleichem upon the daily life of the East European Jew can hardly be exaggerated.

The third member of this trio of classicists, Isaac Leibush Peretz (1852-

1915), affected his readers and society in quite another manner. Born in the Polish city of Zamość, Peretz showed great intellectual ability as a youth. To earn his livelihood, he first practiced law and then worked for the Warsaw Jewish community. By his own efforts he became thoroughly versed in European literature. He was past middle age and had already written many Hebrew verses before his writings appeared in Yiddish.

At first there were succinct, realistic short stories and during the period of the *Yontev Bletlekh* (*Holiday Folios*), he devoted himself to works of the Enlightenment and to the popularization of scientific material. His poetry is strongly influenced by that of Heine and Chamisso; his *Haskala* motifs are sarcastic and militant; his portrayal of the lot of women and children, sentimental and romantic.

However, it was not until the nineties, when he took up Hasidic themes, that Peretz reached the height of his career. His Hasidic stories in which he idealized the rabbis, painting them as the model men of the future, helped initiate a neo-Hasidic trend in Yiddish and Hebrew literature. But Peretz did not seek the "Sabbath and the Holy-day" Jew only among the great. He wrote the series *Silent Souls* and other tales of the "thirty-six saintly Jews" where the hero—a woodcutter, a water carrier, or a confused youth—plumbs the profoundest depths of the soul. Thus Peretz went from the realistic to the romantic, from the romantic to the symbolic. His drama *The Golden Chain* embodies the basic process of development of every religion and stresses the continuity of the age-old chain of Jewish culture. His last symbolic drama, *A Night at the Old Marketplace*, is a pessimistic summation of his own achievements, for Peretz was not satisfied to create a work of art for its own sake, but wanted to use his talents to refine the soul of his generation.

The conflict between the way of life of the Jewish radical and that of the towering personalities of the traditional past is revealed in Peretz's works. In feverishly sharp and impressionistic *feuilletons*, he champions true freedom of thought and at the same time stresses the traditional quest for God and the belief in the chosenness of the Jewish people—tenets which found new strength in the years bridging the nineteenth and twentieth centuries. While Peretz's literary technique is West European, it also stems from the folk tale and there is a direct line from the stories of Nachman Brahtslever with their romantic symbolism to the works of Peretz.

During the last fifteen years of his life, Peretz was not only the dominant literary figure of the great center in Warsaw but was also the leader of those who hoped to modernize Jewish life through the use of Yiddish and to effect a national cultural renaissance in all the lands of the dispersion. He was one of the leaders at the language conference at Czernowitz (1908), where Yiddish was proclaimed "a national language." Near the end of his life he helped establish Jewish schools for refugee children and died while composing a poem for a children's home.

Almost all the young authors whose writings appeared in Peretz's publications or who made their debuts in the early years of the twentieth century were influenced by Peretz, whose attitude toward them was fatherly and encouraging. When the younger writers bestowed upon him the honorary title of "Father of Modern Yiddish Literature," they were expressing their esteem and affection for him.

The constellation of Mendele, Sholem Aleichem, and Peretz is a happy combination of mutually complementary temperaments. Mendele criticizes yet memorializes what is characteristic and typical of his age; Sholem Aleichem brings us the comical and the humorous with no apparent motive; Peretz evokes the exotic past as a model for the future. Mendele is static, the other two are dynamic. Sholem Aleichem definitely draws upon Mendele, while Peretz is tangential. Mendele and Peretz demand concentration from the reader; Sholem Aleichem is universally familiar and satisfying. All three created a new centripetal force linking, through literature, the present and the past, the intellectual and the untutored, the Jew of one region and the Jew of another.

D. THE EXPANSION OF YIDDISH LITERATURE TO 1914

Until 1914 the whole of Yiddish literature in Russia reflected the influence of Mendele, Sholem Aleichem, and Peretz.

In the United States other forces were at work: (1) The "green" immigrant needed to become organized and literature took on the character of propaganda; (2) the low cultural status of the newcomers led to semiliterate writing which impeded the development of the artistic; (3) a great, new power arose in the form of a free Yiddish press.

It is curious that Russian literature exercised a lesser influence upon Yiddish literature in Russia than it did upon Yiddish writing in America. Some of the more important American prose writers are Z. Libin (pen name of Israel Hurwitz), who, with restrained warmth faithfully records the life of the Jewish worker; Leon Kobrin, who dwells upon the problems of the individual, particularly the sexual; Bernard Gorin, who, for the most part, portrays the old country; Abraham Cahan, whose stories are dominated by socialist propaganda; Tashrack (Israel Joseph Zevin), who depicts the difficulties in the adjustments the immigrant has to make to his new environment.

In addition to this socially aware writing, such as that of Morris Rosenfeld (see above), we have the popularly oriented songs of Joseph Jaffe, the tender, idyllic poesy of Jacob Adler, M. Sharkanski's fine rhythm. While the Yiddish theater had been banned in Russia in 1883, it developed rapidly in America. The Tolstoian Jacob Gordin raised the level of the theater, producing more than sixty plays, many of which were based on foreign themes, and others that were original plays of milieu which were extremely successful (*Mirrele Efros; God, Man and the Devil*).

In Europe the seventeen years from 1897 to 1914 saw remarkable social progress. The philosophies of Zionism, socialism, and autonomism were hotly debated; parties organized; new ideas on the march. Yet the Jewish press in Russia was banned until 1903 when *Fraynd* (*The Friend*) appeared in Petersburg, to be followed by Yiddish newspapers in Odessa, Warsaw and other provincial cities. Life was particularly stormy from 1904 to 1906. There was a temporary mood of despair immediately after the failure of the 1905 revolution, but hopes soon rose and the Yiddish movement was strengthened.

The most important literary publications were *Literary Monthlies* (1908), edited by Samuel Niger, Shmaryohu Gorelik and A. Vayter (pen name of Meyer Davenishsky); *Der Pinkes, Yearbook of the History of the Yiddish Literature and Language, Folklore, Criticism and Bibliography* (1913); and the monthly magazine, *Jewish World*, also edited by Samuel Niger. Most of these publications appeared in Vilna, seat of the modern Kletskin Publishing House. The Warsaw publishing firms were modernized as well, and the output of books was great.

Again during this period a group of Hebrew writers were attracted to Yiddish literature: Hayyim Nachman Bialik translated his *Poems of Grief and Wrath* into Yiddish and wrote directly in that language; Jacob Fichman composed delightful children's songs; Judah Steinberg painted idyllic pictures of Hasidic life; Miche Yosef Berdichevsky wrote of ordinary people. Zalman Itzkhok Onoikhi, who created the character of the philosophizing Hasid in his *Reb Abbo*, was one of the many new writers.

Folk lore was very popular and Sholem Aleichem discovered a Jewish Beranger in a Kiev lawyer, Mark Varshavski (1848-1907), whose *Genuine Folksongs* are so widely sung that many are amazed to learn that *Oif'n pripetchok brennt a fayerl* comes from his pen. The most prominent of the folk-lorists was Shloime Anski (1863-1920). His *Dybbuk* became popular in a later period and influenced both the Yiddish and Hebrew theaters. The work of Reb Mordkhele (Chaim Tschemerinski, 1862-1917), with its diverting allegories and satirical poetry, is also based upon an unusual familiarity with the popular idiom.

The career of Abraham Reisen (1874-1953), who wrote both poetry and prose, illustrates the fact that the influence of the folk song is more lasting than that of the folk tale. His poetry shows the impact of the folk song while his short stories have a European and Peretz-like flavor. Reisen's poems are short, unaffected melodic revelations of mood with distant echoings of *Weltschmerz*, filled with great sympathy for the lonely and the oppressed. His lucid style found great favor and Reisen early became one of the most popular poets.

Abraham Liesin (1872-1938), who was a contemporary of Reisen, individualized social-revolutionary poetry. Yehoash (pen name of Jehoash Shloime Blumgarten, 1871-1927) began with romantic nationalistic ballads, fables and lyrics. Both these poets reached their peak in later years and we shall return to them.

The Lithuanian-born David Einhorn wrote with resignation of the decline of the small town in *Quiet Songs,* while his *Jewish Daughters* introduced idyllic love motifs. His work has unusual individuality of tone and pleasant rhythm. The work of the Galician Shmuel Yakov Imber is more turbulent, more erotic.

Although the development of poetry during this period was rapid, the principal advance took place in narrative prose. In this field we have a threesome to start: Abraham Reisen, Sholem Asch, and Hersh David Nomberg. Reisen's short stories deal with daily problems and simple spiritual conflicts. They are often just barely humorous, often lyrical with compassion for man who, after all, is not so highly developed as is sometimes believed.

The perennially enamored Sholem Asch is quite different; he began by singing the praises of the small town. (Samuel Niger has called him the "Prophet of the Soil.") But he soon turned to the problems of the big city, to the life of the new immigrant in America, and to the underworld, creating a series of interesting novels. We shall return to him.

Hersh David Nomberg (1876-1927) introduced psychological analysis in portraying the dissatisfied, introverted intellectual. The clarity of style and masterly construction of his stories give him a prominent place in Yiddish literature, although he wrote little and in a single vein.

The earthiness of the writings of Itshe Meyer Vaysnberg (1881-1937) is in direct contrast to Sholem Asch's idyll of the small town. Veisnberg, himself a workingman, describes the worker's life with unrelenting realism, stressing the crude and the brutal. Jonah Rosenfeld (1880-1944), also a laborer, began with realistic stories but went on to psychological analysis. Lamed Shapiro painted impressionistic portraits of nature and his powerful stories of pogroms are impregnated with the spirit of vengeance. Itzkhok Doiv Berkowitz, son-in-law of Sholem Aleichem and his splendid translator into Hebrew, portrayed ordinary people in extraordinary circumstances. Toward the end of the period appeared David Bergelson, delineating moods and highlighting the tragedy of the young woman in *Nokh Ale-men* (*It's All Over*).

The drama developed much more slowly than *belles-lettres*. David Pinski, who began in the nineties with stories of the laboring classes, is the author of plays which demonstrate the conflicts arising out of the breakup of the patriarchal-religious family relationship. Sholem Asch created a sensation with his *God of Vengeance*. He also attempted historical drama and contemporary comedy. Peretz Hirshbein (1880-1948), himself the organizer of a dramatic troupe, first wrote realistic plays, turned to Maeterlinckian dramas of mood, and finally found himself among simple country folk and their rustic surroundings. There is less continuity in Yiddish drama than there is in poetry and prose. The thread Goldfaden had spun was broken, and a definite rift between the professional theater and the literary drama became apparent. The devotees of this more cultivated theater (including the semisymbolic plays of A. Vayter) are definitely characteristic of the Yiddish cultural life of this period.

Literary criticism was especially popular and was written not only by the editors of periodicals, but also by many literary minded people. Yet there was no outstanding literary critic before Baal-Makhshoves (Isidor Eliashev, 1873-1924). With strict aesthetic standards he became the servant of Jewish letters, giving encouragement to almost every beginner. A follower, in principle, of the school of Hippolyte Taine, Baal-Makhshoves nevertheless employed the environmental method, especially in the interpretation of realistic works. From Yiddishist circles emerged Samuel Niger, who early proved a talented critic. His work is characterized by detailed analysis particularly of the relationship of the writer to his surroundings. (More of him later.)

After 1905 the stream of immigration brought to America many authors who had already won fame in the old country, as well as young writers who had taken their first steps in the literary field. In 1908 there evolved from among these the group known as "the Young," militant beginners dissatisfied with the status of literature on the Continent, and calling for its independence of social ideologies. They published collected *Writings* (edited by David Ignatoff), in which they followed the course and even anticipated the literary development in Eastern Europe. The principal works of these "Young" were not to appear until 1914.

In summary, the fifty years between 1864 and 1914 witnessed the development of a worldly, many-sided Yiddish literature; principally realistic yet with more than a tinge of romanticism, it showed tendencies toward modern symbolism as well. Although centered in Russian Jewry, there was a parallel development of Yiddish literature in America. With its unshakable affirmation of life and its intimate family spirit, this literature was an instrument of social progress and a mighty force for unifying the scattered Jewish people.

E. YIDDISH LITERATURE IN AMERICA, 1916-1956

World War I rent asunder Russia's Jewish community of 6,000,000. The settlements in the Soviet Union, in Poland, and the small center of the Baltic countries and Rumania became completely distinct. The hegemony of Jewish life was transferred to the American center.

A kaleidoscope of literary groups, trends and forms, such as had never been known before, developed in New York, and to a lesser extent in other North American cities such as Montreal, Chicago, and Los Angeles. While social motifs were characteristic of literary endeavors of the late nineteenth and the early twentieth centuries, national consciousness has marked the writings since the First World War. Negative traits, however, also became apparent such as the rift between the reader and the ultra-modern author, the language assimilation of the younger generation, the halting of immigration, thus raising the average age of the reading public with little prospect of building for the future. All these factors could not help but influence the writer and his work.

Especially important was the development in the field of poetry with the appearance of a variety of temperaments, styles and themes. The two elder poets, Yehoash and Liesin, renewed their creative activities. The imagery of Yehoash became richer and more satisfying, Apollonian in its lyrical restraint. Abraham Liesin, the most nationalistic of Yiddish poets, is inspired by the *Kiddush ha-Shem* motif and relives his youth in mystical songs of remembrance. Younger than these two were the ever-changing and very prolific Hayim Rosenblat (1883-1956) and the constant, introspective Joseph Rolnick (1878-1955). The poetry of Nokhum Yood is clear and musical.

Theoretically, Zisha Landau (1889-1937) is an antisocial aesthete but actually he celebrates the joys of everyday life in his delicate, mildly imagist songs. Mani Leib (1883-1953), influenced by the Russian poets, particularly Fett and Alexander Block, writes tender, romantic lyrics, as well as charming children's poems and ballads based on folk motifs. Israel Jacob Schwartz is equally fond of the European background of his pious rabbi father and the American environment of his children. He introduced American themes in his long poem *Kentucky*, as well as in a number of shorter works. He is also an untiring translator of both old and new Hebrew poetry.

Most impassioned of the modern Yiddish poets is Moishe Leib Halperin (1886-1932). Torn between an inborn romanticism and the cynicism of a chaotic world, he incorporates the disillusionment of the postwar generation and the spiritual "otherness" of the immigrant, who, to the very end, is unable to come to terms with his environment. The feminine poetry of Anna Margolin was subtle and passionate. The poetry of Reuben Aizland was complacent and resigned.

Faithful to the teachings of Peretz, that ethics is the goal and aesthetics but the means, is H. Leivick,[8a] who voices the sorrow and the unrest of our generation. In his great symbolic dramas, *The Golem* and *The Comedy of Redemption*, are unfolded the problems of world deliverance and the struggle for progress. During long years of serious illness his poems dealt with death and destruction, but his *Songs of Paradise* are touched with the joy of life. In these last years he expresses deep wrath and sorrow over the devastation of Europe. He became one of the principal poets of lamentation after the Hitler holocaust (in his volume *In Treblinke Bin Ikh Nit Geven* and in scores of later poems). A prolific poet, despite his limited themes he is outstanding because of the nuances and inferences that create variety in his leitmotiv. His last volume of poems is called *A Leaf On An Apple Tree*. Leivick is the most honored Yiddish poet of our century.

Ten years after "the Young" came the group known as *Inzikhistn*, "the Introspectionists" (after their magazine, *In Zikh, Within Oneself*). Urbane intellectuals, they espoused free verse, abstraction, allusion and metaphor. Aaron Leyeles (Aaron Glanz), N. B. Minkoff, and Jacob Glatstein headed this group. Mark Schweid introduced modern poetry in difficult verse. Jacob Glatstein was an ultramodern bold experimenter with language in the first period of his poetic creativity; of late his poetry has been less revolutionary in form and more profound in spirit, as witnessed by the book *Shtralndike Yidn*. The poetry of Leyeles also became more profound (*A Yid Oifn Yam*).

Quite distinct was the realistic "Proletpen" group, whose spiritual home was the Soviet Union. Only the capricious, bitterly sarcastic poems of Moishe Nadir (1885-1943) rose above the average monotony of their writings.

The feeling of instability, the anxiety about the course of the development of Jewish life in America, Hitler's persecutions and devastation of Europe—all these factors had the effect of strengthening traditionalism. Poetic form acquired simplicity and purity and ever recurrent were themes from the Old World. This traditionalism is apparent in the works of almost all the Yiddish-American poets, one of the outstanding being Menakhem Boraisho (1888-1949), whose face turned toward the past in his great work *Der Geyer* (1943), one of the outstanding creations in Yiddish poetry. In Jacob Itzkhok Segal's (1896-1954) mellow lyrics we hear the echoes of one's grandmother's *Tkhines* (prayers). Ephraim Auerbach concludes that *The Old Spring Is Pure;* he drinks from it and dwells in *The Tents of Jacob*. Benjamin Jacob Bialostotzki and Naftoli Gross (1895-1956) also are part of this trend.

The versatile L. Feinberg is facile in his prolific verse both in describing his own *Doomed Generation* and when he glorifies the Tannaim. B. Lapin (1887-1953), a painstaking translator of poetry, earned recognition through the last collection of his original poems, *The Full Jug*. We must also mention the unique A. Lutzky, the intellectual Eliezer Greenberg, the imaginative Aleph Katz, and the younger Berish Weinstein who depicts his old home town Reishe and his American environment in epic verse.

Yiddish poetry in America for the past forty years presented a multicolored gallery of temperaments, a symphony of different tones, and a richness of themes. (Scores of names have been omitted for lack of space.)

Many stories and novels were serialized in the Yiddish press. Undoubtedly the most popular narrative writer was Sholem Asch, whose particular strength lies in the scope of his canvas and in his vivid mass scenes. He is guided by a deep faith in man and by real affection for his characters. His trilogy *Three Cities: Petersburg, Warsaw, Moscow*, depicting scenes of Jewish life before, during, and after World War I, enjoyed great success. His finest talents came to the fore in *Salvation*. Asch's *The Nazarene* and *The Apostle* gave rise to considerable controversy. The American scene is represented in many of his novels, beginning with *Uncle Moses* and concluding with *Grossman and Son*. His last historical novels were *Moses* and *The Prophet*.

Israel Joshua Zynger (1893-1944) limited his subject matter to life in Poland in the recent past. Like Balzac, he portrayed the bitterness of the "Human Comedy," but even more coldly and more naturalistically than did the French master. His principal novels are *Yoshe the Calf*, *The Brothers Ashkenazi, Comrade Nachman,* and *The Karnovski Family*.

Zalman Shneour (1887-1959), Hebrew poet and Yiddish author, became known largely by way of the New York newspaper *Forward*, and is therefore included among the American writers, although it is difficult to ascribe him to any one country. In his stories he delights in physical prowess and is prone to linger over erotic passages. Shneour's series *Jews of Shklov* was very popular and his favorite hero is the young butcher, Noah Pandre. Among his numerous novels the outstanding is the historical *Napoleon and the Rabbi.*

Master of the short story is Joseph Opatoshu (1887-1954), who has a special affinity for the physical. In his trilogy (*In Polish Woods, 1863, Alone*), which treats of Jewish life in Poland in the mid-nineteenth century, there is an added romantic undertone. He turns easily from Old World themes to both Jewish and Christian life on the American continent. He wrote historical novels and novelettes (*A Day In Regensburg, The Last Insurrection*). His diction is scrupulously refined. More the painter than the storyteller was Issac Raboi (1882-1948), who introduced both the Far West (*Mr. Goldenberg*) and New England (*A Strip of the Sea*) to Yiddish literature; Samuel Niger described Raboi's novels as "masses of arrested lyricism."

The playwrights David Pinski and Peretz Hirshbein wrote a number of novels. David Ignatov (1885-1954) attempted to record the history of the

American Jewish intelligentsia in his novels. Boruch Glassman (1893-1945) dwelt on the psychology of the lonely and the maladjusted; Shin Miller depicts the disintegration of Jewish life in America and in the Soviet Union. B. Demblin is one of the few Yiddish writers who protrays non-Jewish types as well (*West Side*). Although the skeptical Moishe Nadir undertook to "de-create" the silly world and "disenchant" foolish man, an unexpected warmth is to be found in his stories. The previously mentioned Jonah Rosenfeld and Lamed Shapiro (1878-1948) continued and refined their techniques of short-story telling, enriching their themes with American subjects. Jacob Glatstein combined creative writing and factual reporting in his *When Yash Went Away* and *When Yash Returned*. The charming Leon Elbe excelled in the field of literature for children. I. Metzker, who started out as a children's writer, gave us the idyllic *Grandfather's Fields*. We conclude this brief review of *belles-lettres* by mentioning the names of N. Brusiloff (*Shtile Erd, Quiet Earth*), M. Y. Shelubsky, and the younger M. Dluzhnovsky.

In America as in Europe, the drama does not keep pace with poetry and prose. In this field, David Pinski tends to be symbolic and abstract; Peretz Hirshbein refined his idyllic folkplays (*Green Fields*); Hersh Sackler found his characters in the romantic popular tale. Leon Kobrin (1873-1946) wrote dramas of everyday life (*The Country Fellow* from the old country, *Riverside Drive* in the New World). H. Leivick's *Rags* represents the real drama of the immigrant; *When the Poet Became Blind* relates the tragedy of a Yiddish poet in America. More recently he dramatized the revolt of the Warsaw ghetto (*The Miracle of the Ghetto*), then turned to the afflictions of the post-Hitler era in *The Wedding at Fernwald*, and finally returned to his previous symbolic style in *In The Days of Job*.

In America, too, almost all poets and publicists engaged in literary criticism but none of them approximated the influence exerted by Samuel Niger (1883-1955), whose diligence and sincerity made him the guardian as well as the judge of Yiddish literature. Of the multitude of critics, we mention Alexander Mukdoni, impressionistic and discerning; Borukh Rivkin, obscure and casuistical; Joel Enteen, warm and straightforward; Abraham Cahan, for many years the very influential editor of the *Forward;* Hillel Rogoff, now the editor of this sixty-year-old newspaper; Jacob Glatstein, who writes pointed weekly reviews in *Yiddisher Kempfer;* the connoisseur of poetry, A. Tabachnik; and the expert of character depiction, Shloime Bickel of the *Day-Morning Journal*. The literary historian, the late N. B. Minkoff, was secretary of the *Zukunft* editorial collegium. (Other members: H. Leivick, A. Meness, and Jacob Pat.)

In the broad field of the essay, distinction has been won by Chaim Zhitlovsky, leader of the nationalistic-socialist intelligentsia; Abraham Coralnik, sensitive aesthete; Chayim Greenberg, editor of *Yiddisher Kempfer;* and Abraham Liesin, for many years editor of the *Zukunft.*

What makes Yiddish literature in America American? Much more fundamental than the subject matter is the influence of life in the New World upon the writer who began to see the old country in a different light, and to interpret the problems of the Jew in a way which stamps his work as peculiarly American.

F. YIDDISH LITERATURE IN POLAND BETWEEN THE TWO WORLD WARS

The second most important center of Yiddish literature was Poland, whose 3,500,000 Jews had been rooted in Polish soil for some 800 years. Geographically close to Russia, Polish-Yiddish literature was separated as by a wall from that of the Soviet Union. Of the two, it was the Polish center that was in contact with America.

In Poland, Yiddish literature was closely connected with the diversified communal activities and the firmly patterned everyday life. Yet it also reflected the dissensions and the gnawing uncertainty about the future. World War I destroyed the established order; the older generation of writers died out; the younger men, who had come to Warsaw from the provinces and felt insecure in their new environment, were caught up in the crosscurrents of a belated *Haskala,* radicalism, and nationalism. This milieu gave rise to an antiaesthetic and antisocial expressionism particularly among those poets of the magazine *Khalastre (The Bunch)*. To this group belong the prose writers Ozer Varshavski, who, in his *Smugglers,* gave an angry picture of wantonness during the war period, and Avrom Moishe Fuchs, who skillfully portrayed shady characters from the dregs of humanity.

The leader of a group of poets from Lodz was Moishe Broderzon, whose rhythmic poetry illustrated his primary interest in form; but underneath his playfulness there lurked a corroding pessimism. Two Lithuanian poets introduced a fresh, youthful romanticism: Leib Neidus (1890-1918), who was a master at versification, and Moishe Kulbak, who wrote impetuous, unaffected, and somewhat modernistic poetry.

The strongest and most enduring poetic stream was fed by tradition, by a pessimistic sentimentalism, and by a universal yet specifically Jewish restlessness. Some sought solace in mysticism and a fancied traditionalism.

The traditional and the mystical are basic qualities of the creative works of Aaron Zeitlin, son of the God-seeking publicist Hillel Zeitlin, who was put to death by the Nazis. The mystic and moralist, Israel Shtern, always had a premonition of martyrdom and actually perished with those martyred by Hitler.

The well of folk lore is mirrored in the lucid, prayerlike poems of Miriam Ulinover, who drew all *From Grandmother's Treasure,* as she called one of her poetry collections. An original combination of the grotesque and the

romantic is found in the bohemian carelessness and the anguished senti-
mentality of the poems by Itsik Manger. The poetess Kadya Molodovski
found herself in singing of the lives of the poor. Just before the war, Yechiel
Lehrer, also one of the martyred, produced the long poem of day-to-day
life, *My Home*. The "Young Vilna" group was very much under American influence. Outstanding are both Chaim Grade and Abraham Sutzkever, who were able to save themselves only to lament the devastation
of Vilna, but not of Vilna alone. To the same group belonged the energetic
Shmerke Kocherginski (who met an accidental death in Argentina in 1954)
and the very young Hirsh Glick, author of the inspirational "Hymn of the
Partisans."

Of the multitude of talented writers, the poetess Rokhl Korn, the poets
Joseph Rubinstein and Nokhum Bomse (d. 1954), and literary critic Rokhl
Auerbach survived. The elder Yitskhok Katzenelson, who died a martyr's
death, left for posterity the unforgettable *Song of the Slaughtered Jewish
People.*

Mention has already been made of the narrative writers who left Poland for America. Among those remaining in Poland were Zusman Segalovitch, who depicted either capricious female characters or himself in his
popular novels; Joshua Perle, who had a great love for the land of the
Vistula; Efraim Kaganovski, who portrayed the poverty-stricken and the
underworld of Warsaw; the tragically fated Simeon Horontchik (1889-
1939), whose long novels deal with the lives of working people. In the
works of Isaac Bashevis (brother of Israel Joshua) Singer are to be found
purity of form and vividness of imagery. His *Satan of Gorei* depicts the
aftermath of the Sabbatai Zevi movement. Just prior to World War II
there appeared some powerful young writers of small-town life.

In general the drama (*Dybbuk* has already been mentioned) departed
from gray reality. Jacob Pregger builds upon the folk tale (*The Temptation, Simkho Plakhte*), as does Aaron Zeitlin; Alter Kacyzne uses the story
of the "true proselyte" of Vilna in *The Duke;* Jekheskal Moishe Neiman
gives us the idyll of *The Sabbath Fruit,* while Fishel Bimko's *Thieves*
dramatizes the exotic underworld.

Of the more than one hundred periodicals flourishing at that time, *Book
World, Jewish World, Art and Life, Literary Leaves,* and *Weekly* were
among those devoted to literature. Some of the many critics and essayists
were Nakhman Mayzil, editor of *Literary Leaves;* the philosophizing Yekhiel Yeshaye Trunk and Leon Finkelstein; the enthusiastic Zalmen Reyzen,
compiler of the four-volume *Lexicon of Yiddish Literature, Press and
Philology;* the historian Isaac Shipper and the philologist Noah Prilutsky.

With the advent of Hitler, the deeply rooted Polish Jewish community
faced extermination. Yet its spiritual strength was inexhaustible and in
the Ghettos of Vilna and Warsaw, in the shadow of the concentration

camps, Jews conducted literary meetings and celebrated the anniversaries of famous authors. Some writers fled to the Soviet Union, others came to the United States, but a painfully large number perished with their readers.

In 1915 the Czarist regime forbade the use of the Yiddish alphabet in the printing of any periodicals. But immediately following the March Revolution of 1917 and during the first years of the October Revolution (1917-1921), literary creation was relatively unhampered. Gradually the situation changed: one had to become "proletarian" or remain silent.

Yiddish literature in the Soviet Union became a "Soviet" literature and no longer regarded itself as part of world Yiddish literature. Quite deliberately the leaders of this controlled Jewish life did everything possible to separate the Jews of the Soviet Union from the Jews of the rest of the world. Even the orthography was changed radically and Yiddish writers avoided phrases and expressions which stemmed from the *heder* or were associated with religious Judaism. It was not until the Popular Front of the thirties that this isolationist policy began to weaken.

In addition to the geographical isolation there was a spiritual departure from the earlier literature. A writer who walked *In Step* (a typical name for a literary collection) received greater material compensation than did the average Yiddish writer elsewhere. He also had an audience, for the reading and discussion of literary works became a routine part of club activities. However, the writer always had to fulfill a "social assignment": to defend one point of view, to oppose another. Thus he felt that his writing filled a definite need. It is impossible to understand the fluctuations of Yiddish literature in the Soviet Union without taking into consideration the constant political changes.

Even more so than elsewhere, poetry in the Soviet Union is the most important form of expression. An example of the revolutionary romanticism of the civil war period is the work of Osher Shvartsman (1890-1919). The deeply nationalistic David Hofstein influenced almost all Soviet-Yiddish poets with respect to poetic form. Peretz Markish, in his long, versified novels, depicted the struggle against the vestiges of the old order. Leib Kvitko is modest and refined. Somewhat younger than those mentioned are Itsik Feffer and Izzi Kharik; the former, faithful to the Soviet regime, earned official recognition while the latter was a victim of the purges. Yet both sing with joy of the new life and glorify the fatherland.

Yiddish prose in the Soviet Union has developed much more slowly. The novels and stories dealing with the revolution are, to quote David Bergelson, "scarcely finished literary works with their roughness of style and characterization." In the twenties social progress was the principal theme; later it was praise of the champions of production and of the victory over saboteurs. In addition to following the "party line," Yiddish writers glorified the establishment of new Jewish colonies and the development of Biro-Bidjan.

David Bergelson stands head and shoulders above his Soviet colleagues. One of the finest stylists in Yiddish literature, his chief power lies in describing environment and mood. At first he saw the revolution as *A Measure of the Law* and later accepted it fully; his characters conform to the new order. In his great autobiographical novel, *Beside the Dnieper*, he gives a graphic account of his childhood and youth. The novelist *Der Nistor* (the Anonymous) (Froyim Kahanovitch), who stood apart from the others, won renown with his novel, *The Mashber Family*. A return to classicism is found in the stories of Itsik Kipnis, whose idyllic *Months and Days* aroused much controversy. Moishe Kulbak painted a pleasantly humorous portrait of a lower-class family in his *Zelmenians*. The Yiddish theater was well developed in the Soviet Union, but not the art of the drama.

No field of letters was so completely under the influence of Soviet dogma as that of literary criticism. Moishe Litvakov, editor of *Emes* (Truth), was the overseer of political *kashrut* (yet he died in prison). The excellent analyst, Nochum Oislender, was the freest and the most interesting of his colleagues. Israel Tsinberg spent many years on his ten-volume *History of Literature Among the Jews*, which was being printed in Poland but remained unfinished. The author is presumed to have died in a Soviet prison.

Western Russia with its dense Jewish population was the first to suffer Nazi attack. Most of the writers of Minsk and Kiev fled deep into Russia, thus avoiding the fate of their fellow Jews. During World War II, the restrictions on Soviet writers were eased, and they were permitted to deviate from the previously imposed limitations as to how and what they could write. As a result, the Yiddish writers began to write on Jewish themes. Even Itsik Feffer, whose poetry was a paean of praise to Stalin, published material on Jewish national themes. During this period Jewish national trends were evident in the works of both Peretz Markish and David Bergelson, as well as in the works of the writers from Poland which were published in the U.S.S.R. Literary activity was centered in the Jewish Anti-Fascist Committee, which published the Yiddish periodical *Eynikeyt*.

The end of the war saw a change in government policy which dealt a death blow to Yiddish literature in the Soviet Union. In 1948, almost all the Yiddish writers—there were at least 200 of them—were arrested, accused of treason, and sentenced to long terms of servitude in the Siberian slave labor camps. In 1952, Stalin ordered the execution of the most important writers. Of those who were not executed the vast majority died in prison. Only a few could survive the hardships of the labor camps, and these remained prisoners until Khrushchev repudiated Stalin and his policy.

These survivors, however, were not permitted to return to literary activity after their liberation. Nothing has been published in Yiddish in the Soviet Union for many years.

Such is the tragic end of that part of Yiddish literature which sought in vain to adapt itself to a tryannical political order. Its writers died martyrs' deaths.

H. THE UNIVERSALITY OF YIDDISH LITERATURE (TO 1956)

The past forty years saw such a rapid development of Yiddish literature, and the emergence of so many colorful writers, that in order to survey it, it was necessary to divide it geographically into the three major centers. Actually, however, it remained a single integrated literature, just as it had been in the past.

We dealt first with the most important center—America—and then with Poland. To complete the picture of America we now report on the writers from Poland who escaped just before, during, and after the war.

After years spent in Eretz Yisrael, Z. Segalovitch, the most embittered poetic lamenter of the Hitler holocaust, came to the United States, where he died in 1949. Aaron Zeitlin, whom we have already mentioned, wrote more profound Jewish poetry. The destruction of the whole Zeitlin family affected the work of this outstanding Yiddish and Hebrew poet, and he, now in America, seeks to understand the religious and moral significance of the great tragedy. I. Bashevis became one of the most important novelists. His novel *The Family Moskat*, the series of short stories *In My Father's Court*, and other works give evidence of further development of Singer's scope and his talent. J. J. Trunk published a multivolume work on Poland which gives a picture of the lives of two generations, based on a background of his own life and family. After years in London, the poet Itsik Manger settled in America. The poetess Kadia Molodovski achieved maturity and tragic profundity. Chaim Grade, who was productive during the years of war and wanderings, published his volume of poems entitled *My Mother's Will*, and wrote other poems which describe life among the religious Jews in his old home. Recently, he has become a respected writer of prose. *My Mother's Sabbaths* received great recognition. Mordecai Shtrigler wrote a number of novels dealing with the horrors of Hitler's extermination camps.

Generally it must be kept in mind that since the forties, in all Yiddish literature, and poetry particularly, there has been one basic theme—the terrible destruction of European Jewry. Both those who barely survived and those who lived in safety created a whole literature based on this unprecedented tragedy of the Jewish people. In this respect no other literature, including the Hebrew, can compare with the Yiddish literature of the past fifteen years.

Yiddish literature was never limited to the three great centers of America, Poland, and the Soviet Union. Wherever there were Yiddish-speaking settlements there appeared literary works of all kinds to meet the great demand of the large reading public.

In Rumania between the two World Wars there was a Jewish population of about 1,000,000. Despite persecution which obstructed the development of the Yiddish press and the expansion of cultural societies, a number of vigorous talents appeared. The best allegorist is Eliezer Steinbarg (1880-1932), who introduced social motifs into the fable, giving them, a witty, typical Jewish flavor. The refined and cultured Moishe Altman created a unique novel, *Medresh Pinkhos,* and wrote interesting short stories (*Blendenish*). The stage director Jacob Shternberg was a modernistic poet. Beside the authors already mentioned from Bessarabia, we must single out the poet Jacob Gropher, a native of Moldavia.

Lithuania, with Kuanas as the principal center, teemed with young poets and authors. Outstanding was the poet Jacob Gotlieb. There were literary groups in Latvia, too, and even in the small settlement of Estonia.

The Argentine, with its 400,000 Jews, is the second largest Jewish community in the New World. With its great daily newspapers and a flourishing cultural life, it has distinguished itself in the short fifty years of its history by an unusual interest in *belles-lettres.* In his truly artistic memoirs, Mordecai Alperson has told of the hardships of thirty years of Jewish colonization. Moishe Pintshevski was the first to write Yiddish poetry in which the South American landscape is described. Berl Greenberg (1906-1961) is a talented storyteller. The energetic Jacob Botashanski (1895-1964) is prominent in the field of the essay, the memoir, and literary criticism. Jacob Rollanski is one of the prominent journalists. The most important poet is Kehos Kliger. Argentina is the only country where a Yiddish magazine devoted to philosophy is published. It is called *Davke* and is edited by Shloyme Suskovitch. During the past ten years Argentina has become the center of Yiddish publishing activities, and hundreds of volumes by Yiddish writers the world over have been published there. The most active publishing group has been the Central Association of Polish Jews.

Other Jewish communities in Latin America publish various periodicals to which local writers contribute; most prominent among these communities are Uruguay and Mexico. The relatively new Mexican Jewish community also engages in the publication of books, and has a number of groups interested in Yiddish literature and literary activities. Among the Mexican Yiddish writers Jacob Glantz is the most prominent poet and Meir Corona the local novelist.

In Palestine, where Hebrew is the official language, there was an energetic group of Yiddish poets and narrative writers who gave expression to the joys and sorrows of the pioneers. In 1937 the collection entitled

Writings of Eretz Israel, appeared in Tel-Aviv. During this period the prominent poet was Israel Papernikov. After the holocaust and the establishment of Israel, many Yiddish writers settled in the new Jewish state. This led to the rise of a considerable center of Yiddish literature in Israel. The works of poets and prose writers are often published there. Some writers concentrate around the Yiddish newspaper in Tel-Aviv. The most important literary journal is the quarterly, *The Golden Chain,* edited by Abraham Sutzkever, who has excelled in his poetry of the holocaust and in his newer poems which extol the land, the people, and the events of the State of Israel. The fine narrative writer Joshua Shpigl; the enterprising Moishe Grossman, who publishes a new magazine *Heimish;* the prose writer Mendl Mann; and many other young writers now live in Israel.

The other continents, too, are represented in Yiddish literature. The community in South Africa has its publications and literati, among them the novelist I. M. Sherman, and the poets David Fram and David Volpe. Before World War II, Australia had a very small Jewish community, but despite this it added new names to the field of Yiddish letters, as noted in the *Australian Yiddish Almanac* (Melbourne, 1937). After the war, many refugees emigrated to Australia, and two newspapers are now published there. Among those active in Yiddish literature is the exacting literary critic, I. Rappaport. Even in Paris, where the Yiddish-speaking community did not take root, there is energetic publishing activity. The unique multivolumed novel of a Russian-born Orthodox Jew, Sambatien, appeared there, among many books of poetry and *belles-lettres.*

It has not always been easy to describe a roving writer as belonging to a particular country, and in the case of the following men it is impossible: Leib Malakh, author, among others, of the sensational drama *Ibergus,* of *Don Domingo's Crossroad,* a novel of South America, and of highly literary travel reports; Melakh Ravich, wandering ambassador of Yiddish poetry (now in Montreal), whose *Continents and Oceans* embraces most of the world, and whose *Poems and Ballads* displays a great variety of subject matter; Daniel Charney (of Vilno, Berlin, Paris, and since 1940 in hospitals and sanitariums of this country), whose penetrating memoirs are distinguished by humor. These three prove that Yiddish literature transcends all boundaries.

Despite the geographical dispersion, one sees a similarity of literary development linking one land to another and the present with the past. Although weakened by language assimilation, Yiddish literature has, nevertheless, revealed in recent times a breadth of vision and a sense of responsibility for the course of development of the whole Jewish people, which is striving to clarify for itself and for the world its spiritual physiognomy.

I. MODERN YIDDISH LITERATURE (TO THE PRESENT)

In recent years Yiddish literature evinced its earlier vitality, its universality and its dispersion all over the world. Themes and motifs remained similar to those prevalent in the years following the Holocaust. The writers already mentioned refined and developed their talents and, as a result, these years have been fruitful. However, very few new names of younger writers were added to the list of Yiddish authors. The single exception is in Israel, where a significant number of able young poets and writers of fiction are publishing their work. Israel has become an important center of Yiddish literature.

Yiddish literature continues to bear the mark of the Holocaust. In large measure, Yiddish poetry continues to mourn for the victims of Nazi genocide, and to view the Eastern European Jew in a bright light, crowned with the aureole of a life sanctified by death *al Kiddush ha-Shem* (for sanctification of the Name of God). The older poets return more and more to their childhood experiences, to the warmth of the old family life. Short stories and novels reflect a strong nostalgia for a life that no longer exists. There is a compulsion to reflect the wholeness of Jewish life in the past and contrast it with the disintegration and the new problems in the lives of those who were saved, with the general fragmentation of Jewish life in the Diaspora, and with the inner confusion of individuals whose Jewish supports had been removed. The whole gamut of thought and emotion concerning the relationships between Jews and the world vibrates in both poetry and fiction.

It is characteristic of the time that so many memoirs which deal with childhood and adolescence in the old country and the difficult life of early immigrant years have been published. There are also many eyewitness accounts of terrible torture under the Nazis and of the road to the crematoria from which the writer was miraculously saved. There is also a series of descriptions of wartime experiences in the Soviet Union, in the prisons and forced labor camps in the "wondrous land of the legendary 'Dzugashvii-Stalin.'" The series of books about destroyed Jewish communities is being continued.

There are very few books that describe the transplantation of Jews to new homes, but there is almost nothing describing the life of the second and third generation in lands of resettlement. In conformity with the mood of much current world literature, Yiddish literature is generally permeated with a spirit of gloom. There are also some specific Jewish reasons: echoes of the Holocaust, bitter memories, fear that future generations will be less Jewish, and the responsibility felt by the creative Jew for the continued existence of his people. On the whole, there is a trend toward nationalism and the search for merit in the beauties of the past, in the consistency and persistence of the Jew in his struggle with the most difficult conditions, and in the light of great and lasting Jewish values.

A unique historicism reigns in and around the world of Yiddish literature. It expresses itself in various ways—in turning to both the recent and more distant past and also in the desire to seek and find commemorative dates, anniversaries of births and deaths. In 1959 the one hundredth anniversary of Sholem Aleichem's birth was celebrated, and 1965 was a Sholem Aleichem year (the fiftieth anniversary of his death); 1966 was a Peretz year (for the same reason), and 1967 was a Mendele year. These observances were proclaimed by the Congress for Jewish Culture, which guards and encourages Yiddish literature. In previous years there were fewer and less varied literary prizes. The Congress for Jewish Culture is currently publishing a new *Great Lexicon of Yiddish Literature* (six volumes have been published thus far). A series called *Masterworks of Yiddish Literature*, edited by Shmuel Rozhanski, is being published in Buenos Aires. Israel Tsinberg's *History of Literature Among the Jews* was also being reprinted there (1967). The history of literature now has greater interest than before. There is a characteristic evaluation and reevaluation of the writers who have passed on.

By and large, we see in recent Yiddish literature the general literary characteristics and trends of the whole postwar period. We find the same good traits and the same weaknesses and omissions. Thus poetry dominates fiction. Dramatic writing has almost entirely disappeared. Literary criticism plays a noticeable role. The close bonds between Yiddish readers and their poets and writers remain. It is now hard to speak about differences in various countries and centers. The only exception is Yiddish literature in Israel.

J. IMPORTANT RECENT YIDDISH WORKS

In 1959 H. Leivick's last book, *Lider tsum Eybikn* (*Songs to the Eternal*), the great poet seeks peace with the eternal. Subsequent to a long illness which began soon after the publication of this volume, Leivick died in 1962. On the first anniversary of his death, a collection of his essays and speeches appeared. The Congress for Jewish Culture awards the Leivick prize annually. (Among the winners are Itsik Manger, I. J. Schwartz, Aaron Leyeles, Jacob Glatstein, Ephraim Auerbach, Melakh Ravich.) In his last years, the late A. Leyeles remained prolific: in 1957 he published *Baym fus fun barg* (*At the Foot of the Mountain*) and in 1963, *Amerike un Ikh* (*America and I*). In 1957 Jacob Glatstein published a selection of his poetry, *Fun mayn ganster mi* (*Of All My Labor*), which was followed by *Di freyd fun yiddishn vort* (*The Joy of the Yiddish*

Word) and *A Yid fun Lublin* (*A Jew from Lublin*). In addition Glatstein is an energetic critic, essayist, and journalist.

To the books by Ephraim Auerbach already mentioned, we add *Di vayse shtot* (*The White City*), which describes Tel-Aviv on Israeli Independence Day, *Gildene shkie* (*The Golden Sunset*), *Der step vakht* (*The Steppe Is Awake*), and in 1968, *A lebn tsvishn tovlen* (*A Life Between Covers*).

Kadya Molodovski's *Likht fun dornboym* (*Light from the Thorn Tree*) gives evidence of her increased profundity and decreased bitterness. Among other poets, the already-mentioned Rokhl Korn, as well as Reyzl Zhikhlinski, Malke Lee, Rose Gutman, Khave Rosenfarb, and Bessie Herschfield are active.

Aaron Zeitlin, who wrote much Hebrew poetry, published the third volume of his collected poems. Chaim Grade found new and deeper expression of his haunting memories and his burning conscience in the excellent collection of poems *Der mentsh fun fayer* (*The Man of Fire*). Joseph Rubinstein expressed fear and desolation in his epic *Megilas Rusland* (*The Scroll of Russia*) and in *Khurbn poyln* (*Polish Jewry: A Lament*). L. Feinberg gave us the poetic history of his generation, with all its going astray. Berish Weinstein came from Reishe and America to dwell in *Dovid hameylekhs giter* (*In the Estates of King David*) and then to return to his previous motifs. Aleph Katz, in his symbolic manner, continues to utilize the depth and wisdom of Yiddish words and idioms in *Kholem aleykhem* (*A Dream upon You*) and *Di emese khasene* (*Quite a Wedding*). M. Z. Tkatch wrote his transparent poetry. Meyer Shtiker experimented in search of his own genre. Israel Emiot, after many years of silence in the Soviet Union, returned to poetry in Israel. M. Frid-Vayninger sings of many lands. Gabriel Preil, the Hebrew poet, saved a book of Yiddish poems. Israel Goichberg and M. Olitsky wrote children's poems. Leib Wasserman tried to find the connection between himself and the world.

Yiddish poetry in the United States and Canada is still rich and colorful. The poets of America, Canada, Israel, and other lands constitute a pool of talent of which any other literature could be proud.

With the passing of Sholem Asch, Israel Joshua Zynger, Zalman Shneour, Joseph Opatoshu, and other narrative writers and novelists, Yiddish fiction is poorer now than in previous decades. Yet, as some poets turned to prose and the prose writers already mentioned in this survey developed further, Yiddish fiction remains impressive. The poet Chaim Grade became a first-rate novelist. After the lyrical *Der mames shabosim* (*Mother's Sabbath*), *Der shulhoyf* (*The Synagogue Courtyard*), *Di agune* (*The Deserted Wife*), and many other newspaper serials, the great novel *Zemach Atlas* (2 vols., 1967-1968) won critical acclaim and first prize for a Yiddish

THE JEWS

work from the American Academy for Jewish Research. Grade's fictional writings depict the life of his native Vilna in the years before World War II, and in *Zemach Atlas* he tells the story of a Yeshiva of the moralistic movement (*Musornikes*). This fills a void by picturing a stratum of Jewish society not adequately described before.

Melakh Ravich wrote a charming *Storybook of My Life*. His *Mayn lexicon* portrays many Yiddish writers. Rokhl Korn appeared as a seasoned storyteller in her *Nayn dertseylungen* (*Nine Stories*). Kadya Molodovski wrote a few novels.

Among the novelists already mentioned, B. Demblin wrote *Tzankendike likht* (*Flickering Lights*), *Oyf eygenem barot* (*On His Own*), the third volume of an autobiographical novel, and *Oyf dray kontinentn* (*On Three Continents*), from the viewpoint of the American Jewish scene. The prolific M. Dluznovsky published several novels, among them *Vintmiln* (*Windmills*), about the life of the Jews in Moroccan *Mellahs*. He is also a playwright. I. Metzker's collection of animal stories, *Gots bashefenishn* (*God's Çreatures*), is most charming.

Among the writers not mentioned before, Khonon Ayalti has a *sui generis* light and humorous tone. He depicts the American Jewish scene in *Vaiter fun Bruklin* (*No Escape from Brooklyn*) and in other stories. The milieu of the New York garment industry is mirrored in Samson Apter's *The Prayzingers*. Rakhmil Bryks keeps alive the memories of the ghetto of Lodz in *A Cat in Ghetto* and *Der Keyzer fun geto*. Ezekiel Keitelman writes moving stories on the Holocaust. Solomon Simon, as many others, turns to autobiography in *Vortslen* (*My Jewish Roots*) and *Tsvaygn* (*In the Thicket*). Shmuel Izban and Shloyme Roznberg try the historical novel: the former, in *The Queen Jezebel and Jericho*; the latter, in *The Khazers* and *Sabbatai Zev*. Schloime Bickel wrote an interesting book on his native *Rumania*.

The central figure of recent Yiddish fiction is Isaac Bashevis Singer. He is very popular, especially among the English-reading public, as witnessed by the following translations: *The Magician of Lublin, The Family Moskat, The Slave, In My Father's Court, Gimpel the Fool, The Spinoza of Market Street, Short Friday*, and *The Manor*. Bashevis Singer is an excellent storyteller whose characters are gripped in the claws of fate.

One of the basic characteristics of Yiddish literature has been its universality. We find literary activity in all the Latin American countries where there is a viable Jewish settlement. The most active country is Argentina, where the following poets and prose writers are publishing their work: Avrom Zak, Moyshe Knapheys, the novelists J. Okrutni and B. Epshteyn, the Freudian critic Gershon Sapozhnikov, the journalist I. Yanasovich, as well as a number of others. In Brazil there are some excellent storytellers: Hersh Shvarts, Rose Palatnik, and Mayer Kuchinski. Mexico and Uruguay also have their own Yiddish press, staffed by local literati.

In Johannesburg the monthly journal *Dorem Afrike* (*South Africa*) has rich literary content (editors, Zalman Levy and David Volpe). In Australia Herts Bergner was writing short stories, and in 1965 a literary magazine called *Sidneyer yidish-indzl* (*Sydney Yiddish Island*) began to appear at irregular intervals. In 1967 the third *Australish-yidisher almanakh* (456 pages long) was published in Melbourne.

In Western Europe there is one Yiddish literary center—Paris. There the late Efraim Kaganovski wrote many short stories, and the novelist Mendel Mann (author of a trilogy whose last volume is called *Dos faln fun Berlin, The Fall of Berlin*) went to Paris from Israel. The poet M. Shulshteyn has contributed his beautiful *Blumen fun badoyer* (*Flowers of Sorrow*) and a collection of modern fables. L. Domankevich is a unique essayist. Menukha Ram published a collection of stories *Vintn* (*Winds*). The second almanac of Yiddish writers in France was published in 1960 (the first one was in 1955).

In Poland, a monthly *Yidishe shriftn* (*Yiddish Writings*) is published, in which stories and poems of local writers are appearing. The most talented of these is David Sfard (*A zegl in vint, A Sail in the Wind*).

The first book to appear in the Soviet Union after Stalin's liquidation of Yiddish culture was a modest selection of Sholem Aleichem's short stories in 1959. In 1961 the first issue of the magazine edited by Aron Vergelis, *Sovetish heymland* (*Soviet Father Land*), was published. It is superfluous to point out that this magazine hews religiously to the party line on Jews. The survivors among the Soviet Yiddish writers publish in *Sovetish heymland*. There are some new names. In 1965 Eli Shekhtman's *Erev* (*On the Eve*) appeared. Sometime later there appeared another novel by Note Lurye, *Himl un erd* (*Heaven and Earth*), some poems by Moyshe Tayf, a prose anthology, a poetry anthology, and that is all.

What is most remarkable and encouraging in recent years is the flowering of the Yiddish literary center in Israel. Both the writers who live in Israel and many prominent writers all over the world are grouped around the quarterly *Di goldene keyt* (*The Golden Chain*), edited by the poet Abraham Sutzkever. On his fiftieth birthday his *Poetishe verk* (*Poetic Works*) was published in two volumes. Sutzkever is a master of language and various poetic forms who wrote some very moving Holocaust poetry. In recent years he has turned to the beauties of the Land of Israel, to the might of its protectors, and to a profound symbolism. There is a whole group of younger poets in Israel. The most important of this group is Yakov Fridman, who has mystic neo-Hassidic inclinations. Also noteworthy are M. Yungman, A. Shamri, Moses Gurin, Rivke Basman, Rokhl Fishman. Also productive are the "first Yiddish poet" in Israel, Israel Papernikov, and the immigrant poet from Poland, Bunim Heller.

The prose is equally rich. Joshua Shpigl's last novel, *A Ladder to Heaven,* describes the world of a Jewish child. Yekhiel Hofer is a prolific writer. It is interesting to note that the intimate life of a *kibbutz* is described in a Yiddish novel *Oyf shmole trotuarn (On Narrow Sidewalks),* by Yosl Birshteyn. Avrom Moishe Fuchs retains the power of his youth in *Di nakht un der tog (The Night and the Day).* Ka. Tsetnik's *Der zeyger vos ibern kop (The Clock Overhead)* is like a nightmare. L. Kheyn-Shimoni, in *Bazalt,* describes life in Palestine between the World Wars. Israel Kaplan in *Veg un umveg (Road and Byroad)* provides us with episodes of human cruelty. A. Karpinovich returns to the Vilna underworld in his book of stories, *Baym vilner durkh-hoyf.* We can do little more than mention some of the prose of recent years, but it is enough to indicate how varied are the themes, the styles, and moods of the Yiddish prose writers of Israel.

Essayists are represented by M. Gros-Tsimerman, Rokhl Auerbach, and others. M. Tzanin, the editor of the daily *Letste nayes,* is also concerned with the essay form.

In Tel-Aviv the Peretz Publishing Company was developed, and it now publishes works of Yiddish writers all over the world.

To sum up, Yiddish literature today is impressive, variegated, interesting, and it is no wonder that translations from Yiddish constantly appear in many languages.

NOTES

[1] These are names of individuals, not cities.

[2] These are names of individuals.

[3a] Cf. Cecil Roth, "The Jews of Western Europe (from 1648)," this work, Vol. I, p. 269.]

[4a] Cf. Roth, *ibid.,* pp. 262-263.]

[5a] Cf. above, Chap. 5, Abraham J. Heschel, "The Mystical Element in Judaism."]

[6a] Cf. above, Chap. 7, Hillel Bavli, "The Modern Renaissance of Hebrew Literature."]

[7a] Cf. Roth, *op. cit.,* pp. 270-271.]

[8a] H. Leivick's first name was Leivick, and his second name was Halper, but he has become known as H. Leivick.]

ADDENDUM

The following is a partial list of birth and death dates for Yiddish writers mentioned in the text:

Aizland, Reuben (1884-1955)
Alperson, Mordecai (1860-1947)
Asch, Sholem (1880-1957)

Bergelson, David (1884-1952)
Berkowitz, Doiv (1885-1967)
Bialostotzki, Jacob (1893-1962)
Bimko, Fishel (1890-1965)
Botashanski, Jacob (1895-1964)
Broder, Berl (1815-1868)
Broderzon, Moishe (1890-1956)

Charney, Daniel (1888-1959)
Coralnik, Abraham (1883-1937)

Feffer, Itsik (1900-1952)

Glanz, Aaron (1889-1966)
Gordin, Jacob (1853-1909)
Gorin, Bernard (1868-1925)
Gotlieb, Jacob (1911-1945)
Gotlober, Abraham (1811-1899)
Greenberg, Chayim (1889-1953)
Gropher, Jacob (1890-1966)
Grossman, Moishe (1904-1961)

Hofstein, David (1889-1951?)
Hurwitz, Israel (1872-1955)

Imber, Shmuel Yakov (1889-1942)

Kacyzne, Alter (1886-1944)
Kaganovski, Efraim (1893-1958)
Kahanovitch, Froyim (1884-1950)
Katzenelson, Yitskhok (1886-1944)
Kharik, Izzi (1898-1937)
Kobrin, Leon (1872-1946)
Kulbak, Moishe (1896-1940)
Kvitko, Leib (1893-1952)

Lehrer, Yechiel (1910-1943)
Leivick, H. (1888-1962)
Lutzky, A. (1894-1957)

Malakh, Leib (1894-1936)
Margolin, Anna (1887-1952)
Markish, Peretz (1895-1952)
Mayzil, Nakhman (1887-1966)
Miller, Shin (1895-1958)
Minkoff, N. B. (1893-1958)
Mukdoni, Alexander (1878-1958)

Perle, Joshua (1893-1958)
Pinski, David (1872-1959)
Pintshevski, Moishe (1894-1955)
Prilutsky, Noah (1889-1941)

Reyzen, Zalmen (1887-1941)

Segalovitch, Zusman (1884-1949)
Shapiro, Lamed (1878-1948)
Shaykevitch, Nokhem Meyer (1849-1905)
Sherman, I. M. (1885-1958)
Shipper, Isaac (1884-1943)
Shtern, Israel (1894-1940?)

Tsinberg, Israel (1873-1937)
Tsveifl, Eliezer Tsvi (1815-1888)

Ulinover, Miriam (1890-1944)

Varshavski, Ozer (1898-1944)
Vaysnberg, Itshe Meyer (1881-1937)

Weinstein, Berish (1905-1967)

Yood, Nokhum (1888-1966)

Zbarzher, Velvl (1826-1883)
Zhitlovsky, Chayim (1865-1943)

BIBLIOGRAPHY

SELECTED WORKS IN ENGLISH AND OTHER LANGUAGES

ABRAMOWICZ, DINA, *Yiddish Literature in English Translation*. New York, 1967.

AUSUBEL, NATHAN, and AUSUBEL, M. O., *A Treasury of Jewish Poetry*. New York, 1957.

BELLOW, SAUL (ed.), *Great Jewish Short Stories*. New York, 1966.

BIRNBAUM, SOLOMON A., "Literature, Yiddish" (except pt. B, sec. III), in *The Universal Jewish Encyclopedia*, Vol. VII. New York, 1942. A very brief account of the history of Yiddish literature to the end of the nineteenth century; however, the discussion is merely of types of works, so the development of the literature as a whole is lost sight of.

CITRON, SAMUEL J., "Yiddish and Hebrew Drama," in *A History of Modern Drama*. New York, 1947.

COOPERMAN, J. B. and S. H., *America in Yiddish Poetry: An Anthology*. New York, 1967.

FALK, FELIX, and FUKS, L., *Das Schemuelbuch des Moshe Esrim Wearba*. Assen, The Netherlands, 1961.

FUKS, L., *The Oldest Known Literary Documents of Yiddish Literature (c. 1382)*. Leiden, 1957.

GASTER, MOSES, "Yiddish Literature in the Middle Ages," in *Essays by Diverse Hands*. London, 1927.

GOLDBERG, FRED (ed.), *The Jewish Mirror*, Vol. I, nos. 1-4. Chicago, 1963-1964.

GOLDENTHAL, LEON, *Toil and Triumph: Life of Morris Rosenfeld*. New York, 1960.

HOWE, IRVING, and GREENBERG, ELIEZER, *Treasury of Yiddish Stories*. New York, 1954.

JACOB BEN ISAAC OF JANOW, *Tzeenah u-reena, a Jewish Commentary of the Book of Exodus*. Translated by Norman C. Gore. New York, 1965.

JEWISH BOOK COUNCIL OF AMERICA, *Jewish Book Annual*, Vols. I-XXV. New York, 1942-1968.

LANDIS, JOSEPH C. (ed. and tr.), *The Dubbuk and Other Great Yiddish Plays*. New York, 1966.

LEFTWICH, JOSEPH, *The Golden Peacock, an Anthology of Yiddish Poetry*. Cambridge, Mass., 1939.

—— (comp., tr., and ed.), *The Golden Peacock; a Worldwide Treasury of Yiddish Poetry*. 2d, rev. ed. New York, 1961.

LIPTZIN, SOL, *The Flowering of Yiddish Literature*. New York, 1963.

——, *Eliakum Zunzer; Poet of His People*. New York, 1950.

MARK, YUDEL, "Yiddish Literature," in *Encyclopedia of Literature* (J. Shipley, ed.), Vol. II. New York, 1946.

——, *I. L. Peretz, His Life and Works*. New York, 1952.

MINKOFF, NOKHUM BORUKH, "Literature, Yiddish" (pt. B, sec. III), in

The Universal Jewish Encyclopedia, Vol. VII. New York, 1942. Formal-istically schematizes the twentieth-century literature into three schools: impressionism, expressionism, traditionalism. For this reason the distinct-ness of the three principal centers (America, Poland, Russia) is not recognizable.

————, in collaboration with Judah A. Joffe, "Old Yiddish Literature," in *The Jewish People Past and Present,* Vol. III (New York, 1952), 145-164.

NIGER, SAMUEL, "Yiddish Literature in the Past Two Hundred Years," in *The Jewish People Past and Present,* Vol. III (New York, 1952), 165-219.

————, "Yiddish Culture in the United States," in *The Jewish People Past and Present,* Vol. IV (New York, 1955), 264-307.

————, "New Trends in Postwar Yiddish Literature," in *Jewish Social Studies,* Vol. I, no. 3 (New York, July 1939), 337-358.

PINES, M., *Histoire de la littérature judeo-allemande.* Paris, 1911. This work is based mainly on that by L. Wiener, below.

ROBACK, ABRAHAM A., *The Story of Yiddish Literature.* New York, 1940. With a great deal of love for Yiddish literature and with a tendency to engage in apologetics, this book gives a brief picture of ancient and later Yiddish literature and dwells principally on the contemporary; it presents many facts (not always accurately) but without a clear scheme. The bibliographical notes on pp. 403-420 are valuable.

————, *I. L. Peretz, Psychologist of Literature.* Cambridge, Mass., 1935.

————, *Curiosities of Yiddish Literature.* Cambridge, Mass., 1933.

SAMUEL, MAURICE, *The World of Sholem Aleichem.* New York, 1943. An excellent introduction to East European Jewish life.

————, *I. L. Peretz, Prince of the Ghetto.* New York, 1948.

SCHWARZ, LEO (ed.), *Feast of Leviathan: Tales of Adventure, Faith and Love from Jewish Literature.* New York and Toronto, 1956.

————, *The Jewish Caravan: Great Stories of Twenty-Five Centuries,* rev. ed. New York, 1965.

WAXMAN, MEYER, *A History of Jewish Literature from the Close of the Bible to Our Own Days.* 4 vols. (New York, 1930-1941), see II, 613-615; IV, 463-566, 996-1047. The author provides many facts, but the material appears to be foreign to him, and it is not free of inac-curacies.

WIENER, LEO, *The History of the Yiddish Literature of the 19th Century.* New York, 1899. Written with a love for Yiddish literature but with-out a thorough knowledge of its history to the middle of the nineteenth century, this book is interesting only when treating the middle and the second half of the century; unfortunately, there are a number of inac-curacies.

SELECTED WORKS IN YIDDISH

BASIN, M., *Antologye—finf hundert yor yidishe poezye,* Vols. I-II. Introduction and linguistic remarks by Ben Borokhov. New York, 1917.

————, *Amerikaner yidishe poezye.* New York, 1940.

BIALOSTOTZKY, B. I. (ed.), *Dovid Edelshtat gedenk-bukh tsum zekhtsikstn yortseit*. New York, 1953.

BICKEL, SHLOMO, *Shrayber fun mayn dor*, Vol. I, New York, 1958. Vol. II, Tel-Aviv, 1965. Collection of essays on contemporary poets, novelists, essayists.

BOROKHOV, BEN, *"Di bibliotek fun yiddishn filolog"—400 yor yiddisher shprakhforshung, Pinkes*. Vilna, 1913.

CONGRESS FOR JEWISH CULTURE, *Lexikon fun der nayer yidisher literatur*. New York, 1956. Bibliographical dictionary of modern Yiddish literature.

ERIK, MAX, *Vegn alt-yiddishn roman un novele*. Warsaw, 1926.

———, *Die geschichte fun der yiddisher literatur fun die aeltste zeiten bis Haskala-Tekufa*. Warsaw, 1928. A very valuable book for the older literature but exaggerates the importance of the "bardic" period.

GLATSTEIN, JACOB, *In tokh genumen*. 2 vols. New York, 1947-1956.

GROSS-TSIMERMAN et al., *Almanakh fun di yidishe shrayber in Yisroel* (Tel-Aviv, 1967), 359 ff. An almanac containing poetry, short stories, and essays by Yiddish writers in Israel.

HRUSHOVSKI, B., SUTSKEVER, A., and SHMERUK, Kh., *A shpigl oyf a shteyn*. Introduction by Kh. Shmeruk. Tel-Aviv, 1964. A lengthy (812 pp.) anthology of poetry and prose by twelve martyred Yiddish writers of the Soviet Union.

JOFFE, JUDAH A., *Elia Bokhur*, Vol. I. New York, 1949.

MAYZIL, NAKHMAN (ed.), *Amerike in yidish vort*. New York, 1955. Yiddish poetry about America.

———, *Forgeyer un Mittsaitler*. New York, 1946.

———, *Noente un eygene*. New York, 1957.

———, *Dos yidishe shafu un der yidisher shrayber in Sovetufarband*. New York, 1959.

MINKOFF, N. B., *Elias Bokhur un zain bovo-bukh*. New York, 1950.

———, *Glikl Hamil*. New York, 1952.

———, *Zeks yiddishe kritiker*. Buenos Aires, 1954.

———, *Pionern fun yiddisher poezye in Amerike*. 3 vols. New York, 1956.

———, and NIGER, SAMUEL, "Literatur bei Yiden," in *Algemeine Enziklopedie*, Vol. III, cols. 1-174. New York, 1942.

MOLODOVSKI, KADYA, *Lider fun Khurbn*. Tel-Aviv, 1962. Anthology containing poems on the Holocaust.

NIGER, SAMUEL, *Geklibene shriftn*, Vol. III. New York, 1928.

———, *Sholem Aleichem*. New York, 1928.

———, *Mendele Moicher Sforim*. Chicago, 1936.

———, *Dertseylers un romanistn*. New York, 1946.

———, *H. Leivick, 1888-1948*. Toronto, 1951.

———, *I. L. Peretz, zain lebn, zain firndike perzenlekhheit*. Buenos Aires, 1952.

———, *Yidishe shrayber in Sovet-Rusland*. New York, 1958. Posthumous collection of the author's articles on the most prominent Yiddish writers in Soviet Russia.

———, *Bleter geshikhte fun der yidisher literatur*. New York, 1959. Posthumous edition of the author's studies "Yiddish Literature and Its Women Readers," "Reb Nachman Brahtzlever," "Beginning of the New Yiddish Literature," and "On the Old and New Yiddish Literature."

POMERANTZ, ALEXANDER, *Di sovetishe harugey malkhus*. Buenos Aires, 1962. The Jewish writers martyred by the Soviets.

RAIZEN, ZALMEN, *Fun Mendelssohn bis Mendele*. Warsaw, 1923. An anthology, with introductory articles, of a number of writers of the second half of the eighteenth and the first half of the nineteenth centuries.

————, *Lexicon fun yiddisher literatur, presse un philologie*. 4 vols. Vilna, 1926-1929. A very good, almost always trustworthy source of information; fairly long accounts of all the more important writers.

RAVICH, M. (ed.), *Dos amolike yidishe varshe biz der shvel fun dritn Khurbn* (Montreal, 1966), 914 ff. Selection of works dealing with Jewish life in Warsaw prior to 1939.

RIVKIN, B., *Grunt-tendentsn fun der yiddisher literatur in Amerike*. New York, 1948.

SAPOZNIKOW, GERSHON, *Fun di tifenishn*. Buenos Aires, 1958. Essays on Lamed Shapiro, Jonah Rosenfeld, Sholem Asch, I. L. Peretz.

SHAMRI, ARYE, *Vortslen, antologye fun yidish-shafn in Yisroel* (Tel-Aviv, 1966), 413 ff.

SHATZKY, JACOB, *Elia Bokhur*. Buenos Aires, 1949.

————, *Simkhas Hanefesh*. New York, 1926.

SHIPPER, ISAAC, *Geschichte fun yiddishe-kunst un drama fun die aeltste zeiten bis 1750*. 2 vols. Warsaw, 1923-1925. A very valuable monograph.

SHTIF, NOKHUM, *Die aeltere yiddishe literatur*. Kiev, 1929. An anthology with brief biographies and characterizations of the writers.

SHULMAN, ELIAS (ELIJAH), *Geshikhte fun der yiddisher literatur in Amerike, 1870-1900*. New York, 1943.

SHULMAN, ELIEZER, *Sefat yehudit-ashkenazit vesifrata*. Riga, 1913. A good, brief review of the old and the Haskala literature without, of course, any of the related facts that have accrued during the past fifty years.

TABACHNIK, A., *Dikhter un dikhtung*. New York, 1965. Essays on fifteen poets, on a few storytellers and literary critics.

TRUNK, J. J., and ZEITLIN, A., *Antologye fun der yidisher proze in Poyln tsvishn beyde velt-milhomes* (New York, 1946), 637 ff.

TSINBERG, ISRAEL, *Di geshikhte fun literatur bay Yidn*. Vilna, 1935-1937; reprinted New York, 1943; Buenos Aires, 1964; Vol. VI and parts of Vols. VII-IX, New York, 1967. Very good, informative studies concerning the ancient and later literature, with many details of the lives of the writers and of their times.

WEINREICH, MAX, *Bilder fun der yiddisher literatur-geshikhte, fun di onheybn biz Mendele Moicher Sforim*. Vilna, 1928. Excellent; detailed studies of the older literature.

WIENER, M., *Tsu der geshikhte fun der yidisher literatur in 19th yorhundert*, Vols. I-II. New York, 1945-1946. Studies on Axenfeld, Ettinger, Mendele Moicher Sforim, and Sholom Aleichem.

YANASOVICH, ISAAC, *Mit yidishe shrayber in Rusland*. Buenos Aires, 1959.

Essays on David Hofshtein, Itzik Fefer, Leib Kvitko, David Bergelson, and Paretz Markish.

YOFE, MORDECAI, *Erets-Yisroel in der yidisher literatur*, Vol. I: *Poezye*. Tel-Aviv, 1961. Anthology of poems on the land and State of Israel.

CHAPTER II

THE JEWISH RELIGION: ITS BELIEFS AND PRACTICES

By Louis Finkelstein

INTRODUCTION

Judaism is a way of life that endeavors to transform virtually every human action into a means of communion with God. Through this communion with God, the Jew is enabled to make his contribution to the establishment of the Kingdom of God and the brotherhood of men on earth. So far as its adherents are concerned, Judaism seeks to extend the concept of right and wrong to every aspect of their behavior. Jewish rules of conduct apply not merely to worship, ceremonial, and justice between man and man, but also to such matters as philanthropy, personal friendships and kindnesses, intellectual pursuits, artistic creation, courtesy, the preservation of health, and the care of diet.[1]

So rigorous is this discipline, as ideally conceived in Jewish writings, that it may be compared to those specified for members of religious orders in other faiths. A casual conversation or a thoughtless remark may, for instance, be considered a grave violation of Jewish Law. It is forbidden, as a matter not merely of good form but of religious law, to use obscene language, to rouse a person to anger, or to display unusual ability in the presence of the handicapped. The ceremonial observances are equally detailed. The ceremonial Law expects each Jew to pray thrice every day, if possible at the synagogue; to recite a blessing before and after each meal; to thank God for any special pleasure, such as a curious sight, the perfume of a flower, or the receipt of good news; to wear a fringed garment about his body; to recite certain passages from Scripture each day; and to don *tephillin* (cubical receptacles containing certain biblical passages) during the morning prayers.

Decisions regarding right and wrong under given conditions are not left for the moment, but are formulated with great care in the vast literature created by the Jewish religious teachers. At the heart of this literature are the Hebrew Scriptures, usually described as the Old Testament, consisting of the Five Books of Moses (usually called the *Torah*), the Prophets and the Hagiographa. These works, particularly the Five Books of Moses, contain the prescriptions for human conduct composed under

Divine inspiration. The ultimate purpose of Jewish religious study is the application of the principles enunciated in the Scriptures, to cases and circumstances the principles do not explicitly cover.

Because Judaism is a way of life, no confession of faith can by itself make one a Jew. Belief in the dogmas of Judaism must be expressed in the acceptance of its discipline rather than in the repetition of a verbal formula. But no failure either to accept the beliefs of Judaism or to follow its prescriptions is sufficient to exclude from the fold a member of the Jewish faith. According to Jewish tradition, the covenant between God and Moses on Mt. Sinai included all those who were present and also all their descendants. This covenant was reaffirmed in the days of Ezra and Nehemiah, when the people together with their leaders made "a sure covenant to walk in God's law, which was given to Moses the servant of God, and to observe and do all the commandments of the Lord our Lord, and His ordinances and His statutes" (Neh. 10:30). To apply the words used by Scripture in another connection, this covenant has thus been made binding upon the Jews, "and upon their seed, and upon all such as joined themselves unto them" (Esth. 9:27). There is therefore no need for any ceremony to admit a Jewish child into the faith of Judaism. Born in a Jewish household, he becomes at once "a child of the covenant." The fact that the child has Jewish parents involves the assumption of the obligations that God has placed on these parents and their descendants.

This concept of the inheritance of religious traditions does not imply any sense of racial differentiation. The concept derives simply from the belief that a person may assume binding obligations not only for himself, but also for his descendants. Thus anyone who is converted to Judaism assumes the obligation to observe its discipline, and makes this obligation binding on his descendants forever, precisely as if he had been an Israelite, standing with Moses, before Mt. Sinai on the day of the Revelation.

The ancestry of the proselyte, and therefore his "race," are quite irrelevant. Whether he be of Arabic background like Queen Helene, or Roman like Aquila, or Khazar like the members of the south Russian kingdom that became converted to Judaism in the eighth century of the Common Era, or like Obadiah, the well-known Moslem who became a proselyte, or Polish like the famous Count Valentine Potocki of the eighteenth century, his descendants, from the point of view of Judaism, would all be bound by his obligation to follow the laws and customs of Judaism.

On the other hand, in view of the Jewish attitude toward other monotheistic faiths, it is considered improper for a Jew to urge a member of another faith to become a Jew. Indeed, a person who desires to adopt Judaism must be told of all the difficulties inherent in affiliation with the faith. Only a person who persists in his desire to become a Jew, and demonstrates that his desire is based on no mundane motive, may be accepted into the Jewish fold.

Because of the special place that the home occupies in Judaism as a center of religious life and worship, almost co-ordinate with the synagogue itself, Judaism holds it essential that both parties to a Jewish marriage be members of the Jewish faith. There is, of course, no objection to marriage with a sincere convert to Judaism. But it is not possible for the home to function in the manner prescribed by Jewish law unless both husband and wife are of the Jewish faith.

In the case of a mixed marriage, the status of the children is determined by the faith of the mother, as the greatest influence in their lives. The children of a Christian mother are considered Christians; the children of a Jewish mother are considered Jews. The Jewish partner in such a mixed marriage is considered living in continual transgression of Jewish law, but remains, like those who deviate from the Law in other respects, within the fold of Judaism, entirely subject to the duties and obligations placed on other Jews.

While no one outside of the Jewish faith is bound by the rules of Jewish ceremonial discipline, Judaism draws a distinction between the adherents of monotheistic faiths—including Christianity and Islam, which are recognized as each making a distinctive contribution to the realization of the Kingdom of God on earth—and nonmonotheistic faiths. The various regulations Judaism, like early Christianity, established to prevent reversion to paganism, obviously have no application to the relationship between Jews and their neighbors in either Christian or Muslim countries. A Jew may not enter a building dedicated to idol-worship even to protect himself from inclement weather; and of course he cannot participate in any festivity dedicated to any form of idol-worship.

These ceremonial rules are intended to register a protest against paganism; they do not place the pagan in any inferior position with regard to Jewish law or ethic. According to Philo and Josephus, it is a violation of Jewish law for a Jew to speak with disrespect of the gods of any people, for the verse "Thou shalt not revile God" (Ex. 22:27) is interpreted as applying to all gods. While this interpretation is not accepted in the Rabbinic tradition, it does express the spirit with which Judaism approaches all systems of belief, regardless of the extent of their difference from itself.

This spirit is expressed in the principle that every rule of moral conduct a Jew must observe toward another Jew applies also to relations with persons of other faiths. The laws of justice, kindness, and charity, as well as the obligation to visit the sick, bury the dead, support the needy, must be assumed for all people.

Like other religions, Judaism can be, and indeed has been, practiced under various forms of civil government: monarchical, semimonarchical, feudal, democratic, and totalitarian. Adherents of the Jewish faith, like those of other religions, regard themselves as citizens or subjects of their respective states. In every synagogue prayers are offered for the safety of the government of the country of its location; and in the ancient Temple of Jerusalem daily sacrifices were offered on behalf of the imperial Roman government, as long as Palestine remained under its dominion. This patriotic loyalty to the state has often persisted in the face of cruel persecution. The principle followed has been that formulated by the ancient teacher, Rabbi Haninah: "Pray for the welfare of the government; for without fear of the government, men would have swallowed each other up alive."

Despite this ability to adjust itself to the exigencies of any form of temporal government, Judaism, like other faiths derived from the Prophets, has always upheld the principles of the Fatherhood of God and the dignity and worth of man as the child and creature of God; and its ideals are more consistent with those of democracy than any other system of government.

The most vigorous and consistent effort to formulate the discipline of Judaism in terms of daily life was that made in ancient Palestine and Babylonia. The Palestinian schools devoted to this purpose were founded in the second or third century before the Common Era, and flourished in their original form for six centuries and in a somewhat altered form until the Crusades. The Babylonian schools were founded in the third century of the Common Era and ended the first and most significant phase of their activity about three hundred years later.[2a]

The rules of conduct worked out in the discussion of these academies form the substance of Jewish Law. In arriving at these precepts, the ancient teachers were guided by their desire to know the Will of God. So far as possible they sought to discover His will through an intensive study of the Scriptures. Where Scripture offered no clear guidance, they tried to ascertain His will by applying its general principles of moral right. In addition, they had a number of oral traditions, going back to antiquity, which they regarded as supplementary to the written Law, and equal to it in authority and inspiration.

The high purpose of the discussions made them of monumental importance to Judaism. As a result, they were committed to memory by eager and faithful disciples, until the memorized material grew to such proportions that it had to be reduced to writing. The work in which the discussions were thus preserved is known as the Talmud. As there were two groups of academies, differing slightly from each other in their interpretation of the Law, and widely in their manner of approach to the subject, we have two Talmudim, that of Palestine and that of Babylonia. Both are considered authoritative guides for Jewish Law. Where they disagree, the Babylonian Talmud is, for historical reasons, considered the more authoritative.

THE PLACE OF STUDY IN JUDAISM

It is impossible to understand Judaism without an appreciation of the place it assigns to the study and practice of the talmudic Law. Doing the Will of God is the primary spiritual concern of the Jew. Therefore, to this day, he must devote considerable time not merely to the mastery of the content of the Talmud, but also to training in its method of reasoning. The study of the Bible and the Talmud is thus far more than a pleasing intellectual exercise, and is itself a means of communion with God. According to some teachers, this study is the highest form of such communion imaginable.[3]

Because the preservation of the Divine will regarding human conduct is basic to all civilization, none of the commandments is more important than that of studying and teaching the Law. The most sacred object in Judaism is the Scroll containing the Five Books of Moses. Every synagogue must contain at least one copy of it. The Scroll must be placed in a separate Ark, before which burns an eternal light. The position of this Ark in the synagogue is in the direction of Jerusalem; everyone turns toward the Ark in prayer. When the Scroll is taken from the Ark for the purpose of reading, all those present must rise. No irreverent or profane action may be performed in a room which contains a Scroll, nor may a Scroll be moved from place to place except for the performance of religious rites. From time to time the Scroll must be examined to ascertain that its writing is intact.

The preparation of the Scroll is a task requiring much care, erudition, and labor. It is usually done by a professional copyist called a *sofer* (scribe). The text is written on sheets of parchment, especially prepared for the purpose. Only skins of animals permitted for food, in accordance with Lev. 11:1-9 and Deut. 14:3-9, are used. The whole work is then attached at the beginning and at the end to wooden rods, so that it can be rolled in the form of a scroll.

The ink used in writing must be black, and should be indelible. Before beginning to copy the text, the scribe must say, "I am about to write this book as a sacred Scroll of the Law." He must repeat a similar formula every time he is about to copy the Divine Name, saying, "I am writing this word as the sacred Name."

Like other Semitic languages, Hebrew requires only a consonantal text for reading: the vowels are omitted in classical texts. Hence the Scroll of the Five Books of Moses contains only the consonantal text. This text is

fixed by tradition, almost to the last detail. Even such matters as division
into paragraphs and sections, and the special size of certain letters, which
are particularly large or particularly small, is determined. The texts of all
the extant Scrolls are thus virtually identical. Any significant deviation
from the traditional text makes a Scroll unfit for use, and must be corrected
as soon as it is discovered. No decorations or illuminations are permitted in
the Scrolls intended for the public service. Tradition prescribes, however,
that certain poetic portions are to be written in verse form and that certain
letters shall have little coronets adorning them.

No less important than this homage paid to the Scroll as symbol of the
Law, is that paid to the living Law itself. Fully three-fourths of the Hebrew literature produced within the first nineteen centuries of the Common Era, is devoted to the elucidation of the Law. Many of the best
minds in Judaism have been devoted to its study. Every parent is required
to teach his child its basic elements. Its study is considered vital not only
for the guidance it offers in the practice of Judaism, but for liberation from
the burden of secular ambition and anxieties. The study of the Law is
believed to be a foretaste of the immortal life, for the Sages of the Talmud
believed that Paradise itself could offer men no nearer communion with
God than the opportunity of discovering His will in the study of the Law.

The Talmud derives its authority from the position held by the ancient
academies. The teachers of those academies, both of Babylonia and of
Palestine, were considered the rightful successors of the older *Sanhedrin*,
or Supreme Court, which before the destruction of Jerusalem (in the year
70 of the Common Era) was the arbiter of Jewish Law and custom. The
Sanhedrin derived its authority from the statement in Deut. 17:8-13, that
whenever a question of interpretation of the Law arises, it is to be finally
decided by the Sages and priests in Jerusalem.

At the present time, the Jewish people have no living central authority
comparable in status to the ancient Sanhedrin or the later academies.
Therefore any decision regarding the Jewish religion must be based on the
Talmud, as the final résumé of the teachings of those authorities when
they existed. The right of an individual to decide questions of religious
Law depends entirely on his knowledge of the Bible, the Talmud, and
the later manuals based on them, and upon his fidelity to their teachings.
Those who have acquired this knowledge are called *rabbis*. There is no
sharp distinction in religious status between the rabbi and the layman in
Judaism. The rabbi is simply a layman especially learned in Scripture
and Talmud. Nor is there any hierarchical organization or government
among the rabbis of the world. Yet some rabbis, by virtue of their special
distinction in learning, by common consent come to be regarded as superior
authorities on questions of Jewish Law. Difficult and complicated issues are
referred to them for clarification.

To be recognized as a rabbi, a talmudic student customarily is ordained.

Traditionally, the authority to act as rabbi may be conferred by any other rabbi. It is usual, however, for students at various theological schools to receive this authority from their teachers. In America, there are several rabbinical schools, each of which ordains its graduates in the manner in which degrees are conferred on graduates of other institutions of learning. At present (1958) the best known of these schools are:

The Hebrew Union College—Jewish Institute of Religion, Cincinnati, New York City and Los Angeles

The Jewish Theological Seminary of America, New York City

Jewish University of America, formerly the Hebrew Theological College, Chicago[4]

Yeshiva University, New York City.[5a]

There is considerable variation among the interpretations of Judaism taught at these seminaries, and consequently there is a considerable difference in emphasis on the subjects included in their respective curricula. This has resulted from the fact that during the second half of the nineteenth century various groups of rabbis, primarily in Germany and America, claimed authority not merely to interpret but also to amend talmudic, and even biblical Law. These rabbis are known as Reform rabbis, and their congregations as Reform congregations. Of the rabbis who adhere to traditional Judaism, some reject any significant innovations from customary practice; these rabbis are called Orthodox. Others maintain that Jewish law is a living tradition, subject to change, but they insist that such changes must be made in accordance with traditional canons for the interpretation and development of Rabbinic law. These rabbis are usually called Conservative.[6a]

The differences between the various groups of American rabbis have not led to any sectarian schism. Although the difference in practice between the traditional and Reform groups is considerable, each accepts the other as being within the fold of Judaism. It is possible for them to do so, because of the principle that even an unobservant or a heretical Jew does not cease to be a member of the covenant made between God and Israel at the time of the Revelation. Only actual rejection of Judaism, by affiliation with another faith, is recognized as separating one from the Jewish community.[7] So long as a follower of the Jewish faith has not by overt act or word and of his own free will declared himself a member of another religion, other Jews are bound to regard him as one of their own faith, and to seek his return to its practice and beliefs.

THE PLACE OF ETHICS IN JUDAISM

The ceremonial discipline is considered obligatory only for members of the Jewish faith, but the ethical element in Judaism is universal in scope.[8a] The commandment against murder is explicitly stated in Scripture to have been revealed to Noah (Gen. 9:5); and therefore applies to all human-kind. By analogy, the commandments against theft, cruelty to animals, sexual license, blasphemy, idol-worship, and the violation of civil justice are considered to be universal. Those who observe these fundamental laws are considered "the righteous of the peoples of the world," who will par-take in the resurrection and in immortality.

One further distinction is made between the ethical and the ceremonial content of Judaism. When faced with the danger of death, one may violate any of the commandments, save only those against murder, sexual license, and idolatry. This rule does not apply in the event of a religious persecution. When a government undertakes to suppress the observance of Judaism, it becomes the duty of the Jew to submit to martyrdom rather than deviate from his faith in even a slight matter.

The duty of accepting martyrdom, either for the ethical Law in the normal course of events or for the whole of the Law in times of persecu-tion, is called *Kiddush ha-Shem* (sanctification of the Name of God). Any violation of this duty is called profanation of the Name of God, *Hillul ha-Shem*. These terms may also be applied to situations that do not call for martyrdom, but where it is possible to increase or lessen respect for religious faith through action. Anyone who through sacrifice and saint-liness brings others to more profound recognition of God "sanctifies" the Name of God. But anyone whose actions bring religion generally and Judaism in particular into disrespect is guilty of *Hillul ha-Shem*. Because of this principle, religious leaders are expected to be particularly careful of their ethical conduct, for even the slightest deviation from propriety on their part naturally casts aspersion on the whole faith. Similarly, any impropriety on the part of a Jew in his relations with members of other faiths tends to decrease respect for Judaism as a faith, and is therefore a "profanation of the Name of God."

The application of the ethical teachings of Judaism to every aspect of daily life has necessarily involved the creation and development of a system of civil law. Like contemporary Christians, the Jews of the talmudic period believed it wrong to resort to the pagan courts of their time for adjudication of civil differences. Not only did the Jewish conception of justice frequently differ from that of the pagans, but the pagan courts were often corrupt, and almost always cruel. The tradition opposing the use of civil courts for adjudication of civil disputes persisted during the Middle Ages. For many centuries secular courts were few and inaccessible, and even in later periods their judgments were generally considered unfair. Only with the enlightenment of the eighteenth and nineteenth century, and the disappearance of the ghettos, have Jews become ac-customed to apply to secular courts of justice for settlement of litigation. However, it is a fundamental principle of talmudic Law that the civil law of a country is binding there, and a Jewish court would necessarily have to take cognizance of the civil law on any disputed point.

The necessity of dealing with civil litigation compelled the talmudic Sages and their medieval successors to give much attention to this aspect of the Jewish Law. Hence, about one-fourth of the Babylonian Talmud, and a proportionate share of later Rabbinic literature, is devoted to questions of civil law. The latest compilation of this law is to be found in the *Hoshen Mishpat*, the fourth volume of Rabbi Joseph Caro's famous code, the *Shulhan Aruk*.

The Jewish civil law is frequently applied even today in the adjudication of disputes arising among religious functionaries, and is sometimes used as a basis for arbitration agreements.

But the Jewish conception of justice transcends the realm of civil law. Justice includes all ethical conduct, as well as philanthropy. Indeed, the word for charity in Rabbinic Hebrew is *zedakah*, or righteousness. Under certain circumstances, talmudic Law actually permits courts to compel a man to do his duty by the community or by individuals, beyond the letter of the law.

As a rule, a Jew is expected to give between one-tenth and one-fifth of his income to charitable purposes. To give less than one-tenth is to fail in duty to the community; to give more than a fifth may involve injustice to his own immediate family. Beyond provision of material assistance for the needy and suffering lies the duty of encouraging them with personal attention and kind words, of recognizing them as personal friends, and above all enabling them to help themselves. In his Code, Maimonides recognizes eight types of philanthropy, arranged according to their merit, as follows: (1) helping the needy to be independent by providing opportunity for work; (2) giving charity to the poor in such a way that neither the donor nor the recipient knows the other; (3) giving charity in such a way that the donor can identify the recipient but the recipient cannot identify the donor; (4) giving in such a way that the recipient can identify the donor but the donor cannot identify the recipient; (5) giving in such a way that the donor and recipient know each other, provided the gift is made before it is requested; (6) giving after a request is made, provided the amount is sufficient to meet the need; (7) giving less than is needed, but with a kindly countenance; (8) giving less than is needed, and without a kindly countenance.

Judaism lays great stress on the importance of personal ethical relations between friends. The last of the Ten Commandments is a prohibition against "coveting" the blessings of a neighbor. Other regulations warn against talebearing, gossip, envy, and dislike of a neighbor. Any form of vengeance also is prohibited. If a persons says to another, "Lend me your hatchet," and the second replies, "I will not lend you my hatchet today, because yesterday you refused to lend me your sickle," the second transgresses the commandment, "Thou shalt not take vengeance" (Lev. 19:18). If the second replies, "I will lend you my hatchet, despite the fact that yesterday you refused to lend me your sickle," he transgresses the second half of the verse, "nor bear any grudge." The importance of these commandments in Judaism is such that one of the most distinguished Jewish scholars of the eleventh century, Bahya ibn Pakudah, devoted a whole book to their analysis, the *Book of the Duties of the Heart*.[9a] In our own generation, the famous Rabbi Israel Meir Kahan (better known by the title of his book, *Chofetz Chayyim*, first published anonymously) devoted his life to warning against the transgression of these laws of ethical conduct. During the nineteenth century, there developed under the influence of Rabbi Israel Salanter (1810-1883) a whole group of students who refrained from conversation over long periods, in order to discipline themselves against the sin of "evil speech."

In accordance with the precept of Lev. 19:17, Judaism considers every member of the faith responsible for the moral conduct of those neighbors over whom he is able to exert influence. To see injustice done without protesting against it is to participate in the injustice. To provoke a man to anger is to partake of the sin of unjust anger. To permit an opposing litigant to take a false oath is to share in the transgression of perjury; just as to listen to blasphemy, gossip, or talebearing is to be a party to them. The concept is summarized in the teaching of Rabbi Jacob that "a person, on whose account God has to inflict punishment on another, will not be admitted into the presence of God" (*Shabbat* 149b). The underlying principle of this teaching is the doctrine that a victim of injustice falls short of the ideal of Judaism to the extent that he fails to obtain Divine forgiveness for the person who acted unjustly toward him.

The public confession of sins prescribed for the Day of Atonement reflects this consciousness that every member of the community is to some extent responsible for the sins of every other member. The confession lists not only the sins the average man is liable to commit through oversight, but also such sins as theft, unchastity and rendering false judgment, of which the vast majority are usually innocent.

THE BASIC CONCEPTS OF JUDAISM

The central doctrine of Judaism is the belief in the One God, the Father of all mankind. The first Hebrew words a Jewish child learns are the confession of faith contained in the verse "Hear, O Israel, the Lord is our God, the Lord is One," and every believing Jew hopes that as he approaches his end in the fullness of time he will be sufficiently conscious to repeat this same confession. This monotheistic belief is subject to no qualification or compromise.

We owe this monotheism to some of the earliest teachers of Israel who, having discovered that the Lord is One and His name One, devoted their lives to the propagation of this teaching. But the prophets proceeded a step further. To whom shall you compare God, they exclaimed, and what manner of likeness shall you set up alongside Him? This served as a cue to sages and philosophers who pondered over the meaning of God. Through their insight the Jew learned that at most every description of God was a metaphor, due to the limited idiom of man. God is not to be compressed into physical form (He is incorporeal), He is not subject to the boundaries of time, of beginning and end (He is eternal), He cannot be confined by space (He is omnipresent). As one of the talmudic Sages put it, "In God is the universe fixed, not He in it."

True enough, not only the simple but the learned, not only the average but the saintly, have described God as wise, just, long-suffering, merciful; and, depending on the occasion, have appealed to Him because pre-eminently these attributes are His. When our motives are questioned we call upon Him for support, for in His wisdom He knows the deepest stirrings of our hearts. When we suffer, we invoke His justice. When in haste we sin, we plead for sufferance on His part. Where we have been exacting or rebellious, we cry for His mercy. What, however, does such language suggest? That man in his dependence and helplessness employs as best he may, to the stretching point if necessary, the sounds and vocabulary at his disposal. These terms, and others like them, are the finest human beings have developed. But even at their finest they will not do; they cannot be precise; they are a stammering to which we have simply grown accustomed. God, the nature of God, rises higher than our discourse. As He is the source of wisdom, we call Him wise; as He is the fullness of mercy, we call Him merciful. But the words fall short of His being.

Put thus, monotheism may strike us with the chill of an intellectual premise, necessary for an adequate interpretation of the universe but inaccessible to man, who is matter, transient and earth-bound. Indeed, these are the qualities that forever interfere with our ambition to understand the meaning of God in full. Fragments, approximations of this understanding, have been the privilege of the saintly in every age. Yet the more they beheld the more they saw that their ignorance was endless. It was as though one filled his cup once and again and once more and still again with water from the ocean; the sea was not diminished.

God's uniqueness and transcendence, however, have not discouraged the Jew from the effort to understand Him and cleave to His ways, for Judaism has also told him that the Lord is near unto them that call upon Him; to all that call upon Him in truth, God's proximity and majesty form a speculative paradox only if they are regarded as categories unrelated to man's own awareness of his shortcomings, to his perennial urge to supersede his *status quo* of deed and thought. To the self-satisfied, it is probably true, God is not nigh; otherwise, how could such a one be content? His charity is niggardly, his justice expedient, his patience mannered, when weighed against Him Whose qualities are a contradiction of the imperfect.

The very surpassing nature of God has taught the Jew that God is not only to be revered, but loved, that the Creator of the heavens and earth, and all that in them is, is also his Rock, his Father, his Shepherd, his Beloved. And in order to escape being remote from God he utilizes every phenomenon and occasion to remind him of the Creator and Father of all. This his prayers accomplish for him. A new morning begins; God has created this light, his morning liturgy reminds him. An evening arrives; and the prayers force upon him the realization that God's activity is once more manifest. For every occasion, experience, event, the Rabbis declared, man ought to pray. The sight of the rainbow, the new moon, a shooting star, the sea, a wise man; deliverance from peril; a visit to historic scenes, particularly those related to biblical history; good fortune, tragedy—each has its proper blessing, and these Rabbinic formulations are the Jew's memoranda. Nothing happens but that his thoughts are at once directed to God. Nothing is taken for granted, nothing is ordinary. Everything is alive with the reality of God, at once man's support and dwelling on high.

Man differs from all other creatures in that he is made "in the image of God." Because Judaism denies that God has any physical form, the image of God in this passage refers to man's mind, unduplicated self, individuality. Created in the image of God, all persons must be accorded the respect due to this dignity which the Divine grace has accorded them. There can, therefore, be no differentiation between various human personalities in their status before God. From the time when the prophet Amos declared, "Are ye not as the children of Ethiopians unto Me, O children of Israel" (9:7), until this day, Jewish religious teachers have continuously emphasized this doctrine. To Ben Azzai, the great teacher of the second century, the most inclusive principle of the whole Law is to be found in the verse "In the day that God created man, in the likeness of God made He him, male and female created He them" (Gen. 5:1-2). He considered this verse uniquely important because it expresses unequivocally the equality and dignity of all human beings, irrespective of nationality, sex, color, creed, or genealogical origin.

The discovery of self, of that element in each of us which is absolutely and unmitigatedly singular, is undated, never complete, and the most momentous experience of life. There are men who may recall that as children they never grasped or gave thought to phenomena of their individuality. Who can, however, recall the instant when that knowledge first pressed itself upon him? Dates, let us grant, are sometimes dispensable, and it may not be necessary to recall that exact instant. It is enough that the mature person recognizes the reality of that self. But even in maturity the recognition is only partial, not altogether clear. Though we find it impossible to picture ourselves disembodied, we know that our self is more than our body. That self is not merely our rational being, for this often may withdraw or fail—in sleep or in delirium—while the self, the "I," has not vanished. Yet awareness of our individuality, incomplete as that awareness may be, constitutes the final appeal and justification for our value. It cannot be exchanged.

Again, it is the prophets of Israel whom we must thank for the most vigorous emphasis on the supreme value of each soul *qua* its individuality. They, not alone but most clearly, saw that the classification of men according to color, the accident of ancestry or purely material condition was never more than secondary; and they, too, perceived that the relation of body to self was not definitive and exclusive.

To the prophets and later the Rabbis, the self therefore appeared so precious that they could not believe that it was coterminous with body. Man's body cannot be proxy for his personality; how then can the body determine life span? Even as self is something more than body, so its survival need not depend on body. Bearing in himself the image of God, man is also—Jewish doctrine insists—endowed with immortality. As conceived by most Jewish theologians, immortality implies the endless persistence of the human personality. This personality is believed to find its consummate expression in the ultimate reunion with God, and to lose all concern with the divisions, rivalries and antagonisms characteristic of physical life.

Attainment of this endless communion with God is the highest reward reserved for man, and its loss the greatest punishment he can suffer. The evil of wickedness consists, therefore, not merely in the harm it does a man in his mundane life, but in the fact that it deprives him of immortal existence. There are many Rabbinic authorities who believe, as do members of other faiths, that certain sinful people may attain immortal life, after having undergone temporary suffering after death. It is held in the Talmud that "the punishment of the wicked in Gehenna does not exceed twelve months." According to Maimonides, this punishment consists of the keen awareness by the soul of its failure to utilize its opportunities for the service of God, and is analogous to the shame sometimes felt by adults for unwise and unkind acts in their youth. We might almost say, the "righteous" is he who has refined and perfected his own self (and obviously other selves along with his own) so that there is an entity capable of reuniting with God; there is the "reward." The "wicked" is he who has neglected and demolished his self so that nothing survives the death of his body and there is an emptiness incapable of reunion with anything; God abhors a vacuum, and there is the "punishment." Be that as it may, a fundamental principle in Judaism, formulated as an ethical norm by Antigonus of Socho, one of the founders of Rabbinic Judaism, declares that men "should not be as servants, who serve their Master with the expectation of receiving reward, but rather as servants who serve their Master, without expectation of receiving reward." In other words, the belief in immortal life is accepted as a metaphysical and theological truth. But it is not to be considered a motive for proper conduct. Proper conduct should be based simply on love of God and the desire to see His Will performed in the world.

That the principle of "reward and punishment" cannot be translated into commercial or nursery terms was already demonstrated by the superb author of Job. In what sense the principle is to be understood remains a mystery, and man repeatedly collides with righteous who suffer and wicked who prosper. Unlike Job, most of us are not even granted the dramatic rejoinder that silences without answering all protest. But in some measure we escape utter confusion if we perceive that "reward" and "punishment" are terms often equatable with *result*. Rebellion against the Will of God, contempt for moral law, perversion of personality, cannot have peace, friendship or love as a consequence. These are the harvest, if harvest there is to be, of submission to God's Will, obedience to the demands of morality and integrity. The lines of the philosopher-poet Rab Saadia (882-942 c.e.) express this thought beautifully: "Not Thee, O Lord, have I injured, but myself. For if man sin, wherein doth that affect Thee? And if his transgressions be multiplied, how doth that harm Thee? But alas for the men who have sinned against Thee, and alas for their souls, for they have brought evil on themselves."

The mystery of reward and punishment remains a mystery; its truth is but too often vindicated; and for all that Judaism insists that conduct must be motivated by that love of God the fullest satisfaction of which is found when His Will is done. Many Rabbinic Sages endured personal affliction without murmur, but suffered anguish at the frustration of God's Will in the world through human sin and waywardness.

Because of God's love for men, He has made it possible for them to escape some of the consequences of error and sinful conduct. Most errors can be rectified through earnest repentance. Indeed, repentance sometimes makes it possible for the experience of error itself to become a virtue. The fact that a person has not lived in accordance with the discipline of religion does not, therefore, condemn him to suffering. It merely places on him the obligation to repent of his error and return to God. In this return to God he obtains the same measure of happiness awarded to the "righteous." Repentance, however, cannot always be achieved. If a man injures his neighbor, he will not be able to repent completely or win peace of mind until he has won the forgiveness of his neighbor. Rulers who mislead their people, causing whole nations and races to indulge in wrongdoing, and to that extent deflecting the development of human civilization, cannot repent.

To be effective, repentance must be more than sorrow or remorse; it must include a determination never again to commit the transgression, and a rearrangement of one's way of life so as to avoid the temptation to fall into the transgression. Thus, for example, if a person has been guilty of theft, repentance requires not merely restitution of the stolen article and a determination never to steal again, but also a study of the motives that led to the theft, and an endeavor to prevent them from being effective in the future.

One of the most important stimulants to the good life is the companionship of well chosen friends. It is a duty to select friends with a view to their probable influence on character. But the greatest possible deterrent from evil deeds or evil thoughts, the greatest stimulant to good, is the study of the Torah. It removes from man the temptation to infringe on the rights of others or the commandments of God. "He who faces temptation should diligently study Torah."

It is through the Law, the prophets, and the Holy Writings that God's Will was revealed to man. Literary excellence and wisdom do not belong to Scripture alone and the riches, artistic or intellectual or scientific, available in the world's classics are not to be minimized without grave sacrifice to civilization. But there is an excellence to Scripture which these other works do not share, for in Scripture came the expression of those truths whose nature has and will admit further elucidations, finer expansion, and interpretation—but never displacement. "It hath been told thee, O man, what the Lord doth require of thee: but to do justly, love mercy, and walk humbly with thy God." Time and discipline may teach us profound meanings of these ideals, meanings perhaps unknown to our predecessors. Dynamically, we may discover implications to these commandments which are thus far unsuspected. But that justice, mercy, humility, and other ideals fixed for man's destiny by Scripture are makeshift standards or temporary hypotheses, Judaism has never been even tempted to accept. There is a finality to these ideals, which does not mean that we know everything there is to know; what it does mean is that these ideals do represent the ends of being and ideal grace and that their removal from life is nothing less than blasphemy. Man is eternally obliged to discover fresh possibilities inherent in these ideals, to extend their applicability, and to be their recurrent expositor.

That is why, though other writings may share with Scripture properties of merit in one thing or another, Scripture is unique in its holiness. And that is why works devoted to the analysis and interpretation of Scripture, to its greater fulfillment, that were developed in its spirit, share in a degree its sacredness. Through the insight of the Talmud—the discussions of Scripture in the Palestinian and Babylonian academies, the commentaries on the Talmud, the codes based on these, and all instruction clarifying Scripture—we see light.

This is what Jews mean when they say the Law is immutable. The statement is not intended as a denial of progressive knowledge or illumination, or to affirm that everything had been discovered in antiquity. Much indeed is new under the sun. But the ultimate imperatives of the Holy Scriptures are absolute. They are not prudential or conditional.

The people to whom this revelation was made was the people of Israel, of which only a remnant now survives, known as the Jewish people. The fact that the people of Israel received the Law and heard the prophets does not, according to Jewish teaching, endow them with any exclusive privileges. But it does place upon them special responsibilities. "You only have I known of all the families of the earth," the first literary prophet (Amos) exclaimed, "therefore I shall visit all your iniquities upon you." These responsibilities—to observe the Law, to study it, to explain it, and to be its unwavering exponents—are expressed in the term "The Chosen People." For similar reasons the Hebrew language, in which these permanent ideals were articulated and recorded, is the holy language; and Palestine, the country where the prophets lived and whence spring so many discoveries of these extraordinary men, is the Holy Land.

Virtually every prophet in Scripture has predicted that in the fullness of time man will gain a more complete understanding of God and a reign of justice and peace on earth will be inaugurated. According to the interpretation of this prophecy in the Talmud and later writers, this age of universal peace will be established by a great, but humble teacher of the lineage of David: the Messiah. Reform and many Conservative Jews expect that the Messianic age will come about through the gradual enlightenment of men and through the work of many thinkers and teachers. All agree that the age will be one of profound and universal faith in God, recognition of human brotherhood, and an unprecedented knowledge of the universe. There will be no discrimination between persons because of sex, origin, faith, occupation, nationality, or any other reason. The evils of human origin will have been overcome; those inherent in nature will be mitigated through further knowledge and increased piety. In this world of brotherly love there will be no room for pride in achievement, nor for memories of past bitterness and oppression.

The prophetic tradition, originating in the teachings of Moses, may be considered a continuous endeavor, looking to the fulfillment of this vision. Together with other faiths derived from Scripture, Judaism has a unique contribution to make to the enlightenment of the world. Its special gift consists, in part, in the preservation of the Hebrew language and the original form of the Hebrew Scriptures, as well as in the transmission unchanged of the ethical ceremonial and intellectual disciplines that were native to the prophets and the later Sages.

The increased hatreds and persecution of our day do not weaken the Jew's faith in God and in His prophets, or his conviction that ultimately the age of universal human brotherhood will be established on earth. In the most trying moments of his own and world history, the Jew repeats with assurance the ancient declaration: "Thou are faithful, O Lord our God, and Thy words are faithful. And not one word of Thine shall ultimately remain unfulfilled; for Thou art a great, holy, Divine King."

There is a wide variety of interpretation among Rabbinical scholars, both ancient and modern, with regard to the concepts of Judaism. In some instances, the differences of interpretation are so great that it is difficult to speak of a concept as being basically or universally Jewish or Rabbinic. There are thus a number of concepts, each having its own limited authority and following.

This applies also to a degree to the fundamental beliefs which have been brought together in the best known Jewish creed, that of Maimonides. According to this creed, there are thirteen basic dogmas in Judaism. They are as follows:

1. The belief in God's existence.
2. The belief in His unity.
3. The belief in His incorporeality.
4. The belief in His timelessness.
5. The belief that He is approachable through prayer.
6. The belief in prophecy.
7. The belief in the superiority of Moses to all other prophets.
8. The belief in the revelation of the Law, and that the Law as contained in the Pentateuch is that revealed to Moses.
9. The belief in the immutability of the Law.
10. The belief in Divine providence.
11. The belief in Divine justice.
12. The belief in the coming of the Messiah.
13. The belief in the resurrection and human immortality.

This creed has been incorporated in the Jewish liturgy, in the famous hymn *Yigdal*. Nevertheless, various distinguished authorities, including such teachers as Hasdai Crescas[10a] and Joseph Albo, rejected the classification of the doctrines, and even denied the basic character of some of the doctrines themselves. Because of this divergence of opinion among the most eminent authorities on the subject, traditional Judaism cannot be described as having a universally accepted creed or formulation of its dogmas. This has led to the assertion that "Judaism has no dogmas." The assertion is true only to the extent already indicated. On the other hand, as Rabbi Albo pointed out, the requirement that Jews observe the discipline of the Law implies the belief in God, in Revelation, and in Divine providence.

Orthodox and Conservative Jews have in general followed the example of the ancient and medieval teachers in avoiding any effort to formulate a generally adopted Jewish creed, beyond the informal consensus of opinion found in traditional writings. As a result, there is still wide latitude of interpretation of Judaism among both Orthodox and Conservative Jews.

Reform Jews have tried to formulate a definite platform outlining the principles on which they agree, and which they believe basic to Judaism. The most recent platform is that adopted at a meeting of the Central Conference of American Rabbis (the organization of American Reform rabbis) in 1937. In this platform no effort is made to indicate the way Reform Judaism deviates from the Orthodox or Conservative interpretation of Judaism. And, indeed, the platform does not contain much to which Orthodox and Conservative groups can take exception. It is rather in its implications than by its direct statements that it deviates from tradition.

Known as the Columbus Platform from the Ohio city in which the meeting was held, the statement reads as follows:

In view of the changes that have taken place in the modern world and the consequent need of stating anew the teachings of Reform Judaism, the Central Conference of American Rabbis makes the following declaration of principles. It presents them not as a fixed creed but as a guide for the progressive elements of Jewry.

I. JUDAISM AND ITS FOUNDATIONS.

1. NATURE OF JUDAISM. Judaism is the historical religious experience of the Jewish people. Though growing out of Jewish life, its message is universal, aiming at the union and perfection of mankind under the sovereignty of God. Reform Judaism recognizes the principle of progressive development in religion and consciously applies this principle to spiritual as well as to cultural and social life.

Judaism welcomes all truth, whether written in the pages of Scripture or deciphered from the records of nature. The new discoveries of science, while replacing the older scientific views underlying our sacred literature, do not conflict with the essential spirit of religion as manifested in the consecration of man's will, heart and mind to the service of God and of humanity.

2. GOD. The heart of Judaism and its chief contribution to religion is the doctrine of the One, living God, Who rules the world through law and love. In Him all existence has its creative source and mankind its ideal of conduct. Though transcending time and space, He is the in-dwelling Presence of the world. We worship Him as the Lord of the universe and as our merciful Father.

3. MAN. Judaism affirms that man is created in the Divine image. His spirit is immortal. He is an active co-worker with God. As a child of God, he is endowed with moral freedom and is charged with the responsibility of overcoming evil and striving after ideal ends.

4. TORAH. God reveals Himself not only in the majesty, beauty and orderliness of nature, but also in the vision and moral striving of the human spirit. Revelation is a continuous process, confined to no one group and to no one age. Yet the people of Israel, through its prophets and sages, achieved unique insight in the realm of religious truth. The Torah, both written and oral, enshrines Israel's ever-growing consciousness of God and of the moral law. It preserves the historical precedents, sanctions and norms of Jewish life, and seeks to mold it in the patterns of goodness and of holiness. Being products of historical processes, certain of its laws have lost their binding force with the passing of the conditions that called them forth. But as a depository of permanent spiritual ideals, the Torah remains the dynamic source of the life of Israel. Each age has the obligation to adapt the teachings of the Torah to its basic needs in consonance with the genius of Judaism.

5. ISRAEL. Judaism is the soul of which Israel is the body. Living in all parts of the world, Israel has been held together by the ties of common history, and above all, by the heritage of faith. Though we recognize in the group loyalty of Jews who have become estranged from our religious tradition, a bond which still unites them with us, we maintain that it is by its religion and for its religion that the Jewish people has lived. The non-Jew who accepts our faith is welcomed as a full member of the Jewish community.

In all lands where our people live, they assume and seek to share loyally the full duties and responsibilities of citizenship and to create seats of Jewish knowledge and religion. In the rehabilitation of Palestine, the land hallowed by memories and hopes, we behold the promise of renewed life for many of our brethren. We affirm the obligation of all Jewry to aid in its upbuilding as a Jewish homeland by endeavoring to make it not only a haven of refuge for the oppressed but also a center of Jewish culture and spiritual life.

Throughout the ages it has been Israel's mission to witness to the Divine in the face of every form of paganism and materialism. We regard it as our historic task to co-operate with all men in the establishment of the kingdom of God, of universal brotherhood, justice, truth and peace on earth. This is our Messianic goal.

II. Ethics.

6. ETHICS AND RELIGION. In Judaism religion and morality blend into an indissoluble unity. Seeking God means to strive after holiness, righteousness and goodness. The love of God is incomplete without the love of one's fellowmen. Judaism emphasizes the kinship of the human race, the sanctity and worth of human life and personality and the right of the individual to freedom and to the pursuit of his chosen vocation. Justice to all, irrespective of race, sect or class is the inalienable right and the inescapable obligation of all. The state and organized government exist in order to further these ends.

7. SOCIAL JUSTICE. Judaism seeks the attainment of a just society by the application of its teachings to the economic order, to industry and commerce, and to national and international affairs. It aims at the elimination of man-made misery and suffering, of poverty and degradation, of tyranny and slavery, of social inequality and prejudice, of ill-will and strife. It advocates the promotion of harmonious relations between warring classes on the basis of equity and justice, and the creation of conditions under which human personality may flourish. It pleads for the safeguarding of childhood against exploitation. It champions the cause of all who work and of their right to an adequate standard of living, as prior to the rights of property. Judaism emphasizes the duty of charity, and strives for a social order which will protect men against the material disabilities of old age, sickness and unemployment.

8. PEACE. Judaism, from the days of the prophets, has proclaimed to mankind the ideal of universal peace. The spiritual and physical disarmament of all nations has been one of its essential teachings. It abhors all violence and relies upon moral education, love and sympathy to secure human progress. It regards justice as the foundation of the well-being of nations and the condition of enduring peace. It urges organized international action for disarmament, collective security and world peace.

III. RELIGIOUS PRACTICE.

9. THE RELIGIOUS LIFE. Jewish life is marked by consecration to these ideals of Judaism. It calls for faithful participation in the life of the Jewish community as it finds expression in home, synagogue and school and in all other agencies that enrich Jewish life and promote its welfare.

The Home has been and must continue to be a stronghold of Jewish life, hallowed by the spirit of love and reverence, by moral discipline and religious observance and worship.

The Synagogue is the oldest and most democratic institution in Jewish life. It is the prime communal agency by which Judaism is fostered and preserved. It links the Jews of each community and unites them with all Israel.

The perpetuation of Judaism as a living force depends upon religious knowledge and upon the education of each new generation in our rich cultural and spiritual heritage.

Prayer is the voice of religion, the language of faith and aspiration. It directs man's heart and mind Godward, voices the needs and hopes of the community, and reaches out after goals which invest life with supreme value. To deepen the spiritual life of our people, we must cultivate the traditional habit of communion with God through prayer in both home and synagogue.

Judaism as a way of life requires in addition to its moral and spiritual demands, the preservation of the Sabbath, festivals and Holy Days, the retention and development of such customs, symbols and ceremonies as possess inspirational value, the cultivation of distinctive forms of religious art and music and the use of Hebrew, together with the vernacular, in our worship and instruction.

These timeless aims and ideals of our faith we present anew to a confused and troubled world. We call upon our fellow Jews to rededicate themselves to them, and, in harmony with all men, hopefully and courageously to continue Israel's eternal quest after God and His kingdom.

None of the basic doctrines of Judaism deals expressly with the teachings, principles or leading personalities of the younger religions derived from it. As Judaism antedates the origin of both Christianity and Islam, its views regarding both of these faiths are simply negative: it has not accepted their teachings. This attitude does not, however, prevent Judaism from endeavoring to appraise the significance and value of other faiths as spiritual and moral phenomena. Rabbi Jacob Emden (1697-1776), one of the foremost teachers in the history of Judaism, summarized the general Jewish view regarding Christianity in the following words:

It is, therefore, a customary observation with me that the man of Nazareth wrought a double kindness to the world: On the one hand he fully supported the Torah of Moses, as already shown, for not one of our Sages spoke more fervently about the eternal duty to fulfill the Law. On the other hand he brought much good to the Gentiles (if only they do not overturn his noble intention for them, as certain stupid people, who did not grasp the ultimate purpose of the New Testament have done; in fact, just recently I saw a book from the press whose author did not know himself what he had written; because, had he known what he had written, then his silence would have been more becoming than his speaking, and he would not have wasted his money nor spoiled the paper and the ink uselessly; just as among us are to be found stupid scholars who know not between their right hand and their left in the written, nor in the oral law, but deceive the world with a tongue that speaks arrogantly; but there are highly educated men of intelligence among the Christians, even as there are among the students of our Torah a few outstanding individuals, men of lofty erudition). For he (the man of Nazareth) forbade idol-worship and removed the image-deities, and he held the people responsible for the seven commandments, lest they be like the animals of the field; he sought to perfect them with ethical qualities that are much more rigorous even than those of the Law of Moses (as is well known), a policy that was surely just for its own sake, since that is the most direct way to acquire good traits. . . .[11]

None of the articles of faith in the creed of Maimonides deals with the holiness of Jerusalem, as the Holy City, or Palestine; yet the concept that Jerusalem, as the Holy City, and Palestine, as the Holy Land, have a special relation to the Jews and its religion is fundamental to all Judaism. Every service contains a petition for the welfare of the Holy City and the Holy Land, and it is a basic principle in Judaism that to provide for the settlement of the land of Israel is to fulfill one of the biblical commandments. A Jew seeing a city of Israel in ruins must recite the benediction of bereavement, for every member of the Jewish faith is expected to regard the desolation of the Holy Land as a personal loss.

In the centuries since the destruction of the Second Temple by Titus in 70 C.E. and the gradual diminution of the Jewish population of the Holy Land, many efforts were made to resettle the country, to reclaim its arable soil, to restore its ancient forests and rebuild its cities. The persecution of Jews in Russia and other East European countries toward the end of the nineteenth century gave new impetus to this movement (described elsewhere in this work[12a]). The whole endeavor culminated in the establishment of the State of Israel on the 5th of Iyyar, 5708 (May 14, 1948).

The problems of the new State, political, social, economic, and spiritual are enormous. As an independent State Israel claims allegiance only of its own nationals and inhabitants. But it also had declared that any Jew settling in Israel will be welcomed as a brother and become an Israeli citizen. Established in the Holy Land, the State under Jewish law is entitled to economic support from Jews everywhere. As the first State in almost 2,000 years in which the Jewish Sabbath and festivals are national holidays, and the Hebrew language an official tongue, its establishment clearly opened a new chapter in the history of Judaism and of the Jews. How the discussions of human relations in the Talmud and medieval Jewish writings will be translated into concrete policies, to what extent the solution of internal and external problems of the State of Israel will be affected by the tradition in which it is rooted, whether the civilization fostered in the State of Israel will in any wise differ from that of purely secular countries, how far the very soil of the Holy Land will determine the character of the community, are issues still unresolved.

As a modern republic, the State of Israel grants freedom of worship to all its inhabitants. However, the manner in which the State will approach deviations within Judaism itself is as yet not clearly defined. After bitter debate permission was granted to establish in Jerusalem a synagogue modeled after American Reform temples; and there are several synagogues in Israel which follow the ways of American Conservative Jews. Nevertheless, the authoritative spokesmen for the Jewish religion in Israel are all committed in different degrees to what is in America called Orthodox Judaism.

The vast influx of Jews from North Africa, from Iraq, from Yemen, have brought to the State new problems of group relations and of accommodation among differences of traditional practice. Leading Israeli citizens and thinkers hope that the educational system, far more effective in Israel than in most other lands, will ultimately lead to a solution of the problems created by the new situations.

One of the remarkable developments following the emergence of the State was the renewed study of Scripture. Biblical archaeology has a fol-

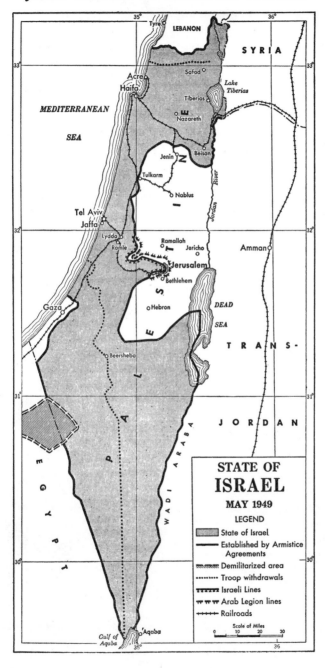

STATE OF
ISRAEL
MAY 1949

LEGEND

State of Israel

Established by Armistice Agreements

Demilitarized area

Troop withdrawals

Israeli Lines

Arab Legion lines

Railroads

Scale of Miles
0 10 20 30

lowing, both professional and amateur, of truly astonishing proportions. The country is studded with talmudic academies. The discovery of the Dead Sea Scrolls has aroused new interest and concern with the development of ancient Jewish sects. Many of these studies are fostered with special vigor at the Hebrew University in Jerusalem.

ELEMENTS OF UNITY AND DISUNITY IN JUDAISM

From what has been said, it is clear that Judaism is not a unit in any organizational or institutionalized form. There is no person or group of persons to whom the Jewish people everywhere owe obedience, or whose views must be accepted by all Jews as authoritative and binding. The principle set down in Deut. 17, ff., making the Sanhedrin at the Temple in Jerusalem the final authority in the interpretation of Jewish law, lost some of its effectiveness when the Temple was destroyed by the Romans in the year 70, and became completely inoperative as the talmudic academies in Palestine lost their vigor. For a time the successive schools of Jabneh, Usha and Tiberias claimed this authority, but ultimately it ceased to be recognized. Every effort since that time to re-establish some center of authority has failed. At times local groups and even countrywide communities have agreed to recognize rabbinic or lay councils or individuals as their guides. During some periods, scholars and groups of scholars have been accepted over far wider areas. The views of the Geonim (the heads of the Babylonian academies from the seventh to the eleventh century C.E.) were considered binding on most Jewish communities of the Diaspora during that period. Ashkenazic Jews, in general, still follow the ordinances established by Rabbenu Gershom, the Light of the Exile, in the eleventh century, and by "the communities" of the Rhineland in succeeding centuries. Toward the end of the nineteenth century, Rabbi Isaac Elchanan Spektor, the Rabbi of Kovno, won recognition first as the leading guide in Jewish Law in his own country of Lithuania, and then throughout Russia and a large part of the Western world.

While there is thus no central Jewish religious organization, there have been various attempts to create worldwide organizations of Jews for special purposes. The most effective of these was the World Zionist Organization, which was expanded in 1929 through the addition of Jewish non-Zionists, and became the Jewish Agency for Palestine. But even the Jewish Agency did not include representatives of all Jewry, and claimed authority to act on behalf of the Jewish people only in connection with the establishment of a Jewish community and state in Palestine.

Organizations like the American Jewish Committee, the Order B'nai B'rith, the American Jewish Congress (part of the World Jewish Congress) and similar agencies in lands other than America, have arisen to make articulate special requests and wants of the Jewish community. The American Jewish Joint Distribution Committee has become a nationwide effort to provide assistance to Jews in distress abroad. The National Council of Federations and Welfare Funds represents virtually every large fund-raising committee in the cities of the United States outside New York and Chicago, and has been constituted by philanthropic agencies throughout the country for mutual discussion of joint problems.

But Judaism seems to resist organization as a denominational group, and preserves the independence of its many diverse elements, despite the common bond of tradition and history. It does not seem likely that in any foreseeable time, any organization will be established approaching the strength and comprehensiveness of Judaism in the times of the Temple. Yet the ties of history make for consciousness of a *Keneset Yisrael* (the congregation of Israel) which Solomon Schechter translated into "Catholic Israel." This mystic, abstract entity existing without organization, power or authority, is the only bond that can be described as uniting the Jewish people.

THE SYSTEM OF BLESSINGS

The fundamental concept of the Jewish ceremonial system is that God continually reveals Himself in nature, in history, and in man's daily life. Each ceremony seeks to emphasize some aspect of this Divine revelation, and thus becomes a special means for communion between man and God. By stressing the common dependence of all men on God, ceremonies strengthen the sense of human kinship. By drawing attention to the phenomena of nature, they help develop man's sense of the aesthetic and increase his joy in the contemplation of beauty. By opening vistas of achievement and satisfaction, they help free him from subjection to material needs and desires, and enable him to fulfill his higher potentialities.

Jewish tradition has evolved the system of ritual blessings as an effective means for achieving continual realization of God's manifestation in the world. According to Rabbinic Law, a Jew is expected to recite a blessing whenever he enjoys any particular aspect of the world.

When he awakes, he thanks God for having created the day, for having granted him the power of sight, for the creation of the earth, for the gift of clothes, for the power to walk, and for the renewal of his strength in sleep. He also thanks God that he is not an idolator nor a slave. Mindful of the severity of woman's lot in the world, and her consequent inability to fulfill some of the rituals, the man recites a benediction that he is male, rather than female; while a woman thanks God that He "has created her according to His Will." The observant Jew also recites some verses from Scripture and a passage from the Talmud. Before doing so, he thanks God for the revelation through the Law, and for the commandment to study the Law.

Before sitting down to his morning meal, he is expected to recite special prayers. At the meal itself, both before and after eating, he recites prescribed blessings. These blessings are repeated at every meal. The blessing at the beginning of the meal is the simple benediction, "Blessed art Thou, O Lord, our God, King of the Universe, Who dost bring bread out of the ground." The blessing after the meal consists of four paragraphs. The first is devoted to thanks to God for supplying all men and indeed all living things with their daily needs. The second is an expression of gratitude for His having caused ancient Israel to inherit the Holy Land. The third is a prayer for the restoration of Jerusalem. The fourth paragraph is a blessing of God for His continued goodness to all men.

When three people eat together, the blessing after the meal is recited in unison. Such a group is popularly called *mezuman* (prepared), because before he begins the person reciting the grace asks whether all are prepared for it. If there is a guest at the table, the recital of the grace is assigned to him. If there are several guests, the most learned is expected to recite it. At the end of the grace, the person reciting it invokes a blessing on his host and the hostess: "May the All-merciful bless the master and mistress of this house, them, and their house, and their children, and all that is theirs; us, and all that is ours, as our ancestors, Abraham, Isaac, and Jacob were blessed."

At every meal attended by three or more persons "words of the Torah" should be spoken. If this is done, the meal becomes sanctified, and "it is as though they have partaken of the table of the Lord," i.e., of a sacrificial meal. In order to fulfill this requirement, it is customary to recite a psalm at every meal. Psalm 137 is recited on weekdays, and Psalm 126 on Sabbaths, festivals, and half-holidays. On festival occasions, and other occasions when it is possible, the recital of these psalms is supplemented by discussions of questions related to religious or spiritual life. To emphasize the sacred character of the meal, one's hands should be washed both before and after it, just as was done at sacrificial meals in the Temple.

In addition to these blessings which are recited virtually every day, there are special blessings to be repeated, such as those for the sight of the trees in the spring, a view of the ocean, a meeting with a friend after a long absence, the appearance of meteors, lightning, the rainbow, the new moon, the sight of strange creatures, the acquisition of new clothes[13] or new possessions, and the reception of good news. On hearing bad news, a special benediction must be recited, accepting the Divine judgment. This benediction, "Blessed art Thou, O Lord our God, King of the Universe, the true Judge," is also recited on the occasion of any bereavement. Finally, there are prayers prescribed for the afternoon and the evening and a concluding prayer at bedtime.

THE SYNAGOGUE AND THE PRAYERS

In ancient times, the center of Jewish worship was the Temple in Jerusalem, where sacrifices were offered in accordance with the prescriptions of the Law. But there were prophets in Israel even in the days of priests, and the prophets frequently organized prayer meetings at which people assembled for devotion and religious exhortation. From these meetings eventually the synagogue was to develop; and subsequently the church and the mosque. As the chief element in the Temple service was sacrifice, so that of the synagogue was prayer. The precedent for prayer was, of course, ancient. Abraham interceded with God on behalf of the people of Sodom. Fearing attack, Jacob uttered the beautiful prayer that contains the memorable words, "I am not worthy of all the mercies, and of all the truth, which Thou hast shown Thy servant; for with my staff I passed this Jordan, and now I am become two camps" (Gen. 32:11). Hannah came to the Temple to petition and praise the Lord. Indeed, Solomon in his dedication service referred to the Temple essentially as a house of prayer in which men would supplicate the Lord.

Even before the Exile, gatherings for prayer were to be found among the people. The Babylonian Exile and the return to Palestine,[14a] however, were especially instrumental in strengthening the synagogue. The institution offered an opportunity not only for pious devotion but for study as well, for it was at these assemblies that Scripture was read and explained. The assembly for worship, which proved of such importance in Palestine while the Temple at Jerusalem still endured, became indispensable when the Temple was destroyed. Since that time, the synagogue has been the sole sanctuary of the Jewish people.

The architecture of the synagogue varies according to country and age. The essential elements of the institution are the Ark containing the Scroll of the Law, a stand for the reader of the service who faces the Ark, and in most traditional synagogues a second stand in the middle of the gathering for the reading of the Law. In a large number of American synagogues, no provision is made for this second stand.

In accordance with the tradition derived from the Temple in Jerusalem, the "court of women" is separated from that of the men in traditional synagogues. It is either marked off by a partition or is situated in a gallery. Again, a considerable number of American synagogues, including most of the Conservative synagogues and all the Reform synagogues, have deviated from tradition in this respect, and permit men and women to sit together.

No human figures may be used in the decoration of the synagogue. However, it is permitted, and has even become customary, to depict on the Ark and elsewhere in the building a lion or an eagle, suggesting the latter half of the Rabbinical injunction: "Be bold as the leopard, fleet as the deer, light as the eagle, and strong as the lion, to do the will of thy Father Who is in Heaven." In many synagogues, the passage is inscribed over the reader's stand. It is also usual to place over the Ark a symbolic representation of the two tablets containing the Ten Commandments. Generally, only the first words of each of the commandments is inscribed on the tablets. The so-called Shield (or Star) of David found in many synagogue buildings, and otherwise in Jewish symbolism, is of unknown origin. But its use can be traced back to Rabbinic times.

In many synagogues, there is to be found over the reader's desk a candelabrum, or two candelabra, symbolic of that which stood in the Temple of Jerusalem. But because it is forbidden to set up in a synagogue an exact replica of the utensils used in the ancient Temple, such candelabra have, instead of seven, eight or nine, sometimes fourteen branches.[15a]

In further deference to the unique sanctity of the Temple, kneeling or prostrating oneself in the synagogue worship is forbidden, except on certain occasions in the services of the New Year's Day and the Day of Atonement. Prayers are said either standing or sitting. It is customary to bow one's head on entering the synagogue and while reciting certain portions of the prayers. In Orthodox and Conservative synagogues, men pray with covered heads. It is considered a violation of custom to perform any act of worship, including study of the Scripture or the Talmud, with uncovered head. This custom derives from that prescribed for the priests of the Temple in Ex. 28:40-42. The custom has been abandoned in most American Reform synagogues.

It has become customary to speak of Reform synagogues and Conservative synagogues, as temples. This change of name does not imply any difference other than those already indicated.

The essential element in the synagogue is, of course, not the building, but the community. Public worship may be conducted in a building or out of doors. But it can be held only in the presence of a congregation, which theoretically consists of a minimum of ten heads of households. For the purpose of prayer, and because of the difficulty in finding ten heads of households in very small communities, ten males (over thirteen years of age) are considered heads of households. The assembly of ten such people is called a *minyan* (quorum) sufficient for public service.

The group that habitually prays together each day develops an astonishing community of interest and personal friendship. It is the experience of many who attend synagogue services regularly that the ties of association between the members of a *minyan* is a source of especial delight. Because the daily attendance at prayer is usually small, each person counts; the failure of anyone to come, because of illness or for any other reason, may disrupt the services. Perhaps in no other relationship of life is the personal worth of the individual—no matter how humble his status—so unmistakable as in this religious worship, which requires ten adult Jews and cannot be performed with a lesser number, no matter how learned, how pious, or how distinguished.

Any adult male Jew may lead the congregation in public prayers. The rabbi participates simply as a member of the congregation. It has become usual in large congregations to appoint a special official to read the prayers, especially those of the Sabbaths and festivals. Such a reader is called a *hazzan*. In some congregations the *hazzan* has a choir to assist him. In Orthodox congregations, this choir consists only of men; in some Conservative and in all Reform congregations, women are also admitted to the choir. A number of passages in the service are traditionally sung by the whole congregation in unison. The tendency of modern Orthodox and Conservative synagogues is to extend this practice to include a much larger part of the service.

In addition to the *hazzan*, the congregation may require the services of a special reader for the Scriptures. He must be able not only to read the consonantal text of the Scroll without the aid of vowels, but must be expert in the traditional system of cantillation of the Scriptures. This system of chanting is of great historical interest, because at least certain parts of it, particularly that prescribed for use on the High Holy Days, are of great antiquity.

The duty of looking after the arrangements for the service, that is, seeing that the Scrolls are prepared for reading, that the prayer books are available for the worshipers, and that the members having special duties during the service know their assignments, devolves generally on a functionary called the *shammash* (sexton).

In addition to these officials, who generally are remunerated for their duties, American Jewish congregations usually have lay officers, a president, one or more vice-presidents, a secretary, a treasurer, and board of directors, upon whom devolves the responsibility for the material well-being of the congregation.

As already indicated, tradition expects every member of the Jewish faith to pray at least three times a day: in the morning, *shaharit*; in the afternoon, *minhah*; and in the evening, *maarib*. On Sabbaths and festivals, an additional prayer is assigned for morning service, called *musaf* (addition), to commemorate the special sacrifices offered on such days at the Temple in Jerusalem. On the Day of Atonement, a fifth prayer is recited at sunset. This prayer, in some respects the most solemn of the year, is called *neilah* (closing), and commemorates the service held at the Temple when its gates were closed at the end of the sacred day.

All these prayers should, so far as possible, be recited at a public service. But if it is difficult to arrange to participate in a public service, they can be recited in private (with omissions of certain portions which belong only to the public service). Most observant Jews attend synagogue services at least on the Sabbaths and holidays; every Orthodox and Conservative synagogue endeavors to arrange for public services also on weekdays.

The essential element in all these services is the prayer called *amidah* (literally, standing, so called because one must rise to recite it). The weekday version of this prayer consists of nineteen paragraphs. But in the original Palestinian form, given it by Rabban Gamaliel II eighteen centuries ago, it contained only eighteen paragraphs; and the prayer is therefore frequently called *shemoneh esreh* (eighteen).

At all services, except the evening service, this prayer is recited twice. It is first recited in an undertone by each individual in the congregation; and then aloud by the reader, on behalf of the congregation. The first and last three paragraphs of the *amidah* are identical for all the services. The first paragraphs consist of confessions of faith in God as the God of the Patriarchs, Abraham, Isaac, and Jacob; as the One Who gives strength to the living and new life to the dead; and as the Holy One, Who has no equal. The final paragraphs include a prayer for the return of God's presence to Jerusalem; an expression of gratitude for all the goodness God has shown; and a prayer for peace.

On the festivals, it is the rule in all Orthodox and in many Conservative synagogues, that the descendants of the ancient Aaronid priests bless the people before the final paragraphs of the public reading of the *musaf amidah*. The formula used in this blessing is that prescribed in Num. 6:22-27, "May the Lord bless thee and keep thee; may the Lord cause His countenance to shine upon thee and be gracious unto thee; may the Lord lift His countenance upon thee and give thee peace."

Before reciting this blessing, the descendants of Aaron who are in the synagogue remove their shoes (as was the custom in the Temple in Jerusalem). The Levites who are present in the synagogue then wash the hands of the Aaronids, who thereupon step forward, face the congregation, and recite the ancient blessing.

The middle paragraphs of the daily *amidah* contain petitions for the fulfillment of various needs for the granting of wisdom, repentance, and forgiveness, for the redemption of Israel, for the healing of the sick, for prosperous years, for the gathering of the dispersed, for the restoration of the Sanhedrin, for the suppression of tyranny, for the protection of the righteous, for the rebuilding of Jerusalem, for the coming of the Messiah, and for the acceptance of prayer.

All the prayers are for the good of the whole community. Petitions for private needs may be inserted in their appropriate place. For example, the prayer for a sick person may be included in the general prayer for the sick of the world.

On Sabbaths and festivals, these petitions for the satisfaction of material wants are omitted; for it is forbidden to consider material needs on such days. On these occasions there is a single prayer for a complete rest on the Sabbath, and for happiness on the festival.

At every service the silent reading of the *amidah* ends with the prayer which begins: "O my God! Guard my tongue from evil, and my lips from speaking guile. To such as curse me, let me be dumb. Let me, indeed, be as dust unto all. . . . If any design evil against me, speedily make their counsel of no effect, and frustrate their intentions."

At the morning and evening services the *amidah* is preceded by the recital of the *Shema* and the various benedictions with it. The *Shema* begins with the verse, "Hear, O Israel, the Lord is our God, the Lord is One" (Deut. 6:4), and includes Deut. 6:5-9, 11:13-21, and Num. 15:37-41. In all services the recital of the *Shema* is preceded by a blessing of God for His revelation in the Law, and is followed by a blessing for His redemption of Israel from Egypt. In the morning, there is also a blessing for the light, in the evening a blessing for the darkness.

Each of the services begins and ends with the recital of the *Kaddish*, an Aramaic prayer for the coming of the Kingdom of God. It is, in effect, a prayer on behalf of the congregation by the reader before he enters on his service and after he ends it. Its essential element is its first section, reading: "May the great Name of God be exalted and sanctified in the world which He created according to His will, and may He cause His Kingdom to come, in your lives and in your days, and in the lives of all the House of Israel; speedily, and in a short time. Amen."

In the course of time, it has become customary to recite this prayer at other parts of the service. Since the Middle Ages, it has been usual also for the observant Jew to recite it at services during the year of a bereavement, and on the anniversary of the death of his parents.

In the morning services held on Mondays and Thursdays (the market days of ancient Palestine, when a larger congregation would be available than on other weekdays), as well as on Sabbaths, festivals, new moons, and fast days, portions of the Five Books of Moses are read from the sacred Scrolls. The readings are so arranged that the whole of the Pentateuch is covered within a year. On Sabbath and festival mornings, as well as at the afternoon services on fast days, selections from the Books of the Prophets are read in addition to those from the Torah. Such a portion is called the *haftarah*, and the person reading it is called the *maftir*.

As stated above, the reading from the Torah is now assigned to a special functionary. In ancient times, the members of the congregation would each in turn perform this duty. In deference to this tradition, it is still customary to call various individuals to read special portions of the Torah, though they merely repeat the words *sotto voce,* while the reading aloud is the duty of the professional reader. There are seven such participants in the Sabbath morning reading of the Torah; six in that of the Day of Atonement, five in those of the festivals; four in those of new moons and the festival weeks; and three at all other services when the Torah is read. Whenever the Torah is read, the first person to be called must be a descendant of Aaron, if there is any in the synagogue. The second to be called must be a Levite, and the others are chosen from the remainder of the congregation. When the prophetic portions are read at the morning services of the Sabbaths and festivals, an additional person is called for that purpose. He may be either an Aaronid, a Levite, or any other Israelite.

There are certain occasions when it is considered an especial obligation to participate in the public reading of the Torah. The most important of these are the Sabbath succeeding a boy's thirteenth birthday; the Sabbath preceding one's marriage; the anniversaries of the death of one's parents; and the Sabbath following one's recovery from illness or escape from danger. It is usual for persons who are thus required to participate in the reading of the Scriptures to be assigned to the *haftarah.* A person recovering from illness or escaping from danger recites a special blessing on the occasion, saying: "Blessed be Thou, O Lord, our God, King of the Universe, Who dost grant kindness to the undeserving, and Who has granted me every good." The congregation, hearing the blessing, responds, "He Who has granted thee kindness, may He ever continue to grant thee kindness." This ceremony is usually performed when such a person is called to read from the Torah in synagogue. But the blessing may be recited, if necessary, simply in the presence of the congregation. Thus a woman after childbirth should, on her first appearance in the synagogue, recite this blessing and receive in return the good wishes of the congregation.

The language of the prayers of the traditional service is for the most part Hebrew. However, a number of prayers are in Aramaic, the vernacular of the Jews in the first centuries of the Common Era in Palestine and Babylonia. At the present time the proportion of Hebrew to some other language (in America, for example, English) will vary with the individual congregation. But everywhere some portions of the public service are read in Hebrew.

According to Rabbinic tradition, it is customary for men to wear a prayer shawl called the *tallit* (garment) during the morning prayers. This prayer shawl is a square or oblong woolen cloth, with fringe at each of its four corners. It is a very ancient garment, probably worn in antiquity as a cloak. The purpose of the fringe (*sisit*) at the four corners is explained in the Bible: "That ye may look upon it and remember all the commandments of the Lord and do them . . . and be holy unto the Lord your God" (Num. 15:39-40). In addition, it is customary for men to don the *tephillin* (phylacteries) during the morning services on weekdays. These *tephillin* consist of two boxes of parchment to which are attached long leather straps. In the boxes are deposited little strips of parchment with the contents of Ex. 11:16, 13:1-10; Deut. 6:4-9, 11:13-21. The Bible also gives the meaning of this symbol: "And it shall be for a sign unto thee upon thy hand, and for a memorial between thine eyes, that the Law of the Lord may be in thy mouth; for with a strong hand hath the Lord brought thee out of Egypt" (Ex. 13:9). To the ancient Rabbis the *tephillin* on the head, and on the left arm close to the heart, represented the concentration of the intellect and the emotion on the Divine. As Maimonides subsequently expressed it: "As long as the *tephillin* are on the head and on the arm of a man, he is modest and God-fearing; he will not be attracted by hilarity or idle talk, and will have no evil thoughts, but will devote all his thoughts to truth and righteousness."

Two of these biblical sections, namely, Deut. 6:4-9 and 11:13-21, are also inscribed on pieces of parchment which are placed in receptacles, attached by the observant Jew to the doorposts of every room. Such receptacles are called *mezuzot* (literally, doorposts). These inscriptions are intended to remind man, as he enters home or leaves it, of the unity of God and of the duty of loving Him.

THE SABBATH AND THE FESTIVALS

While according to the Jewish faith God's presence can be felt at any time and place, there are times, just as there are places, which through their associations have come to lead especially to communion with God. Of these the most important are the Holy Days and the fast days. The Holy Days, according to the Jewish ritual, are the *Shabbat* or Sabbath, celebrated on the seventh day of each week, *Pesach* (Passover), *Shabuot* (Pentecost), *Rosh Ha-Shanah* (the Jewish religious New Year's Day), *Yom Kippur* (Day of Atonement), and *Sukkot* (Tabernacles).

In order that these days may be devoted as completely as possible to the spiritual life, work is forbidden on them. This prohibition includes not only all gainful occupation, but also household tasks.

As a result of these various prohibitions, the Sabbath and festivals become virtually periods of cessation of all labor on the part of observant Jews. Because of the difficulties involved in maintaining this rigid discipline in an industrial society, many Jews otherwise very observant do not refrain from all labor on the Sabbath. Nevertheless, even among these a large number set aside the free hours of the day for spiritual contemplation and for prayer, and mark the Sabbath with the ceremonials devoted to it.

Theoretically, observant Jews should not benefit from the willingness of members of other faiths to perform tasks for them on the Sabbath day. But because of the severity of the winters in northern and central Europe, and the consequent danger of disease, it became customary in the Middle Ages to permit people who were not Jews to kindle the fire for the Jews on the Sabbath. As a result, in time Christian and Moslem boys came to look after the heating of Jewish homes on the Sabbath. In recent centuries, people of other faiths also extinguish lights for Jews on the Sabbath, on the theory that rest is as imperative for health as warmth.

In the Jewish religious calendar, the observance of festivals begins a little before sunset on the preceding day. Because no fire is kindled on the Sabbath, it has been customary from time immemorial for Jewish house-wives to conclude all their household arrangements for the day of rest by preparing the lights, which have therefore become known as the "Sab-bath lights." The great antiquity of this usage, and the significance that came to be attached to it, have sanctified it, and consequently in modern Jewish homes the Sabbath candles are lit, even though other means of illumination are available and are in use. Many a Jew has tender memories of his mother lighting the Sabbath candles. As their light is not to be enjoyed by her before the blessing, the Jewish mother with her hands over her eyes recites, "Blessed art Thou, O Lord our God, King of the Uni-verse, Who has sanctified us with Thy commandments, and commanded us to kindle the Sabbath lights."

In the absence of the mother of the household, the lights are kindled by someone acting for her. If by chance the lights have not been kindled on a Sabbath, it is customary for her to kindle an additional light before every Sabbath afterward throughout her life.

The beauty and impressiveness of the custom of the Sabbath lights has caused it to be extended, so that similar lights are now kindled also on festivals for which the use of fire is permitted, and when therefore there is no special reason for lighting candles before dark. In kindling the lights on the seasonal festivals the mother recites the special prayer of thanks for life called *sheheheyanu* (Who has kept us alive), "Blessed art Thou, O Lord our God, King of the Universe, Who hast caused us to live, and attain this day."

Evening services are held in the synagogue on the eve of festivals and Sabbaths at dusk. After the services, the members of the family return home for the Sabbath meal. On the table are placed a flask of wine and two loaves of bread. The Sabbath loaf of bread is called by its Hebrew name, *hallah* (plural, *hallot*, or as popularly pronounced, *hallos*). The two loaves of bread are said to symbolize the double share of manna God granted the Israelites in the wilderness on Fridays to provide for the Sabbath (Ex. 16:5). It is customary in many localities to prepare these loaves in an especially attractive form, made of twisted strands of dough. On festivals, the bread is further enriched by a plentiful supply of raisins. (On Passover the bread is replaced by unleavened cakes.) Recalling the ancient Rabbinic custom of setting the table only after the Sabbath or festival has been ushered in, the loaves of bread are covered with a napkin, and remain concealed, while the head of the household takes a cup of wine, and recites over it the blessing called the *kiddush,* or sanctification of the day. This blessing consists of a prayer of thanks to God for the gift of the wine, and then for the gift of the special festival. The head of the household drinks some of the wine, and distributes the rest among the others present. On seasonal festivals, the *kiddush* also includes the blessing *sheheheyanu,* mentioned above. Then follows the ritual washing of the hands, the blessing for the bread, the breaking of the bread, the meal itself, the special hymns of the Sabbath or festival meal, and the blessing after the meal.

In many Conservative and Reform congregations, special services on Sabbath eve are held after the Sabbath meal. These services are intended to enable those men and women who because of modern industrial conditions do not attend the traditional service at dusk to commune with God during the course of the holy day. The ritual used at these services varies considerably. In some congregations it is the usual Sabbath eve service. In others it consists of the hymns sung at the Sabbath evening meal. In virtually all congregations where such services are held it is customary to include a sermon by the rabbi.

The Sabbath and festival morning service are longer than those of the weekdays, and occupy most of the morning hours. As it is considered improper to eat before prayers, traditional Jewish homes do not provide any breakfast on Sabbaths or festivals. The ritual of the noon meal is similar to that of the evening. It includes a blessing over the cup of wine, the blessing for the bread, the breaking and distribution of the bread, the meal itself, and the blessing after the meal.

In observant homes it is customary to arrange for another meal to be served in the late afternoon of the Sabbath day, so as to complete three Sabbath meals. This third meal is called *seudah shelishit* (third meal) or, more popularly and less correctly, *shalosh seudot* (three meals). No wine need be drunk before the third meal, but the blessing for the bread is recited as usual.

In Israel it has become customary within the past generation, as a result of the influence of the famous Hebrew poet, Hayyim Nahman Bialik,[16a] to substitute for the third meal a public gathering, preferably one at which refreshments are served, called *oneg shabbat* (the delight of the Sabbath). The practice of holding such gatherings has become an institution in other parts of the world, and is rapidly being adopted by congregations in the

United States. It is an effort to bring people together on the Sabbath afternoon for a discussion of religious, literary, or ethical problems, while participating in a symbolic Sabbath meal.

The Sabbath is concluded about half an hour after sunset with a blessing called *habdalah* (division, that is, marking the division between the Sabbath and the weekdays). A flask of wine and a box of incense are set on the table, and a light is struck. It seems appropriate that the workaday week should begin with the taste of the wine, the odor of the incense, and the appearance of the light, which, satisfying three different senses, increase man's awareness of his dependence on God for all his needs. The blessing consists, therefore, of thanks to God for the gift of the wine, of the incense, and of the light; and ends with further thanks for the division between the Sabbath and the weekdays. It is customary to let the cup of wine for *habdalah* overflow, as a symbol that the happiness of the week may likewise overflow. It is also customary to use a candle with three or four wicks (resembling an ancient torch) for the light of the *habdalah*.

The same ritual of *habdalah* is recited in the synagogue, in order to provide for those who cannot observe it in their homes. It also concludes the Day of Atonement and, with the exception of the blessing for the incense and the light, all the other festivals.

The rigid prohibition of work on the Sabbath does not, as is frequently believed, make it a day of gloom for the observant Jew. On the contrary, the complete release from all mundane concern, the concentration on the study of the Torah, and the joy in the sense of communion with God, make it a day of great, though perhaps indescribable, delight. To participate in the observance of the Sabbath gives such happiness that one of the prayers added to the blessing after the meal on the day asks that Paradise may be one long Sabbath. As twilight descends on Sabbath afternoon, some feel an ineffable sense of yearning and loneliness, which the mystics among the Jews have characterized as the loss of part of one's soul.

Aside from the Sabbath, the major Jewish festivals are Passover, Pentecost, New Year's Day, the Day of Atonement, and the Feast of the Tabernacles. Each of these is, according to tradition, a day of judgment for all mankind. "On Passover the world is judged regarding its grain; on Pentecost regarding the fruits of the tree; on New Year's Day [and also on the Day of Atonement] all creatures pass before God in review; and on Tabernacles they are judged concerning the rain."

While this consciousness of judgment gives an air of solemnity to all the festivals, the three festivals of the ancient pilgrimages, Passover, Pentecost, and Tabernacles, are primarily periods of joy. The manner in which the joy of the festival is combined with the sense of solemnity and judgment before God is difficult to explain to the uninitiate. The festival prayers, as well as the special melodies which in certain rituals accompany them, reflect a feeling of awe, arising from the sense of communion with God as Judge and Ruler of the universe; yet united with this feeling and permeating it is a sense of confidence that His judgment will be one of mercy rather than severity, as that of a father upon his child. The joy of the festival is thus prevented from becoming one of physical pleasure or self-indulgence. Ideally conceived, it is a joy arising largely from participation in synagogue and home rituals, that bring about a closer communion with God.

The significance of each festival is enhanced through the natural and historical interpretations associated with it. All are intended to increase man's faith in God by reference to His revelation in the natural order and also in the succession of human events. Their symbols are particularly significant in an industrial and commercial civilization, where man tends to be separated from nature; and their reflection of the Divine purpose in history gives one strength in times of international crisis, and fills one with humility in moments of peace and prosperity. The purpose of the festivals may thus be said to place human life in both its cosmic and historical perspectives. They enable man to see himself both as part of nature and as distinguished through the providence of God. Passover, occurring on the full moon of the first month of spring (toward the end of March or the beginning of April), is the great festival of the rebirth of nature, and also commemorates historically the Exodus from Egypt. The concentration of Jews in the cities during past centuries has tended to minimize the agricultural aspect of the Passover. Nevertheless, certain ancient customs emphasizing the seasonal character of the festival are still observed. The first month of spring in Palestine marks the end of the rainy season and the beginning of the dry season. In this dry season the crops are saved from destruction by a heavy dew each night. Hence Passover became a festival of prayer for the dew, and the *musaf* (additional) prayer of the first day of Passover is dedicated to petition for copious dew on the earth. The second night of Passover was celebrated in ancient Palestine as the beginning of the barley harvest. In accordance with Lev. 23:14, no part of the new crop might be eaten before that night, when the first sheaf (the *omer*) was harvested and prepared as a sacrifice to God. While the observance of the sacrifice is impossible today, it is still customary for men of great piety in European communities to avoid eating new grain before the second night of Passover. All traditional Jewish communities mark the second night of Passover as the beginning of the barley harvest in ancient Palestine; and, following a literal interpretation of Lev. 23:15-16, include in the daily evening service an enumeration of the forty-nine days from that night until Pentecost, the festival of the wheat harvest.

But the historical significance of Passover as commemorating the Exodus and the promulgation of the idea of freedom in the world has far overshadowed the agricultural phase of the festival. The ceremonies prescribed for the festival in Scripture and the additional rules established by the Rabbis have as their purpose emphasis on the idea of human liberty and equality. The most obvious characteristic of the festival is the use of the unleavened bread (called *massah*, pronounced *matzah*), the bread of affliction (Deut. 16:3), recalling to each Jew the bondage of his ancestry in Egypt, and emphasizing by inference his equality with the humblest and most oppressed of men. The significance of the custom has become such that it is observed with greater precision than almost any other law in Scripture. Observant Jews abstain on the festival from eating not only any leavened bread but even any food which might conceivably have a taste or trace of leaven. The grain used for *massah* is carefully examined to see whether any of it has become leaven. The examination is usually performed by a rabbi, who takes a sampling. If he finds that none in his sample has become leaven, the contents of that granary may be used for Passover. After the examination, the grain must be carefully guarded against moistening that might cause it to leaven. The mills in which it is ground are carefully scoured and purified from all leaven. The flour is then again guarded from moisture, until it is brought to the bakery. In the bakery, expert mechanics and especially devised machines make it possible to prepare the dough and bake it with such speed that no leavening can take place. No salt and of course no yeast or any material other than flour and water enter into the making of the *massah*. After the *massah* has been baked, it may be ground again into flour (*matzah* meal), which can then be used for making pastries and other dishes for consumption on the Passover.

Traditional observance of the Passover requires that no prepared food such as dried fruits or vegetables shall be used, unless it has been made certain that not a speck of flour attaches to them. For this reason, raisins, prunes, coffee, pepper, and similar foods are used by observant Jews during the Passover only if they are prepared under the supervision of a rabbi. Dried peas or beans may not be eaten under any circumstances. Ashkenazic Jews do not eat rice on Passover, though following the tradition of their ancestors, Jews of Sephardic descent consider it permitted.

Special cooking utensils and dishes are set aside for the Passover week, so that no utensils or dishes which have contained leaven will come in contact with the Passover food. Families which cannot afford a complete set of special dishes may cleanse their metal utensils and certain types of glassware for use during the Passover week. Such cleansing must follow the ritual prescriptions, and should be done only after consultation with a rabbi.

To purify the home from all leaven before the Passover, it is customary on the night before the festival eve to "search the house" for any bread or leaven. In earlier ages, this searching had the practical purpose of discovering such leaven, for in the simple one-room homes of the ancient East it was possible to delay the removal of leaven until the night before the festival. In modern homes, this cleaning naturally occupies several days or even weeks, and the ritual searching for the leaven has become almost a formal custom. Nevertheless, it is observed in most Orthodox and Conservative homes. The head of the household searches for the leaven, removes all he finds, and puts it aside until the next morning, when it must be burned during the first quarter of the day, that is, around 9:00 A.M. After that hour it is forbidden to eat or to own leavened food. As it is usually difficult to destroy all the leavened food in a home and impossible to dispose of all the dishes used for leavened food, many groups of observant Jews transfer the title of their leavened food to the rabbi of the community during the Passover week. The rabbi in turn technically transfers the title to a member of another faith.

On the first and second nights of Passover there is celebrated a unique home service called the *seder* (order), because the whole meal follows a prescribed ritual order. In addition to a festive gathering of the whole family in each household, strangers separated from their families are invited as guests. In communities where the number of strangers is considerable, provision is frequently made for a group *seder* at a public institution.

The poignant beauty of the *seder* service leaves an indelible impression on every Jewish child who participates in it. It is in effect a pageant in which ancient Palestinian life is re-created in as detailed and precise a form as possible. The head of the household (or, at a public celebration, the leader of the service) is provided with a divan on which after the fashion of the ancients he may recline during the meal and the celebration. According to some rituals, he is expected to don a *kittel*, a white linen garment worn in ancient Jerusalem on festive days.

The service followed at the *seder* is described in a special prayer book, the *Passover Haggada*. This book contains directions for arranging the Passover dish to be placed before the master of the house, and detailed instructions for the procedure during the service.

One of the most significant elements in the *seder* is its highly developed pedagogical technique. In order to impress the child, he is urged to observe the various ceremonies and to ask for their explanation. As the service is recited it thus becomes fundamentally a reply to these questions. The child is informed that the celebration is in memory of the Exodus from Egypt; he is told the story of the Israelite bondage; of the redemption of the people through the mercy of God; and is taught to respect the liberty he has inherited through this redemption.

At the end of the Passover meal, which is eaten in the course of the *seder*, the door is opened as a symbol of the entry of Elijah the Prophet. A cup of wine, "the cup of Elijah," is filled, the whole company rise, and cry, "Blessed is he who has come!" The concept that Elijah, the immortal prophet, visits every Jewish home on the Passover eve emphasizes the significance of the festival as a symbol of eternal freedom, as well as memorial of a past emancipation; for Elijah is the prophet who, according to the words of Malachi, will be the precursor of God's establishing His Kingdom on earth, at the end of days.

The *seder* ends with the recital of various psalms, the tasting of a fourth and final cup of wine, the singing of various hymns, and finally with popular songs dating from medieval times. In many communities the head of the household concludes the whole service by reading Canticles (The Song of Songs). The joyful spirit of youth, which permeates that portion of the Bible, seems appropriate for the spring festival; and its allegorical meaning as an epic of God's relation to Israel is particularly fitting for recollection on the festival of the Exodus.

The period between Passover and Pentecost is now observed in many Jewish communities as one of partial mourning, because it is traditionally described as the time when the disciples of Rabbi Akiba, one of the foremost teachers of the Talmud,[17a] died. Except for certain special days within the period, no weddings are celebrated by observant Jews; and they also abstain from listening to music, attending the theater, or other pleasures.

The thirty-third day of this period, called *Lag Ba'Omer* (literally, the thirty-third day of the *Omer*), is a half-holiday, devoted to the celebration of weddings and other festivities. It is sometimes said to be the anniversary of the death of Rabbi Simeon ben Yohai, the foremost disciple of Rabbi Akiba, which is marked in this way as the occasion of his translation to the Heavenly Academy. To this time it is therefore customary in Israel to mark the day with a festive pilgrimage to the supposed grave of Rabbi Simeon in Meron, a village of Galilee.

Pentecost, or *Shabuot* (occurring toward the end of May or the beginning of June), is described in Scripture primarily as the festival of the wheat harvest (Ex. 23:16). But it also commemorates the Revelation on Mt. Sinai, and is therefore the festival of the Ten Commandments. The reading of the Law assigned to it covers the chapter telling the story of the Revelation (Ex. 19:20); the liturgy of the day is also dedicated in part to commemorating this incident. In many Orthodox congregations, the evening of the first night of Pentecost is spent in reading Scriptural passages. Among some especially pious Jews, it is customary to remain awake all night, reading the Bible and the Talmud. In many modern congregations, the first day of Pentecost is celebrated by the confirmation of boys and girls.

The third of the great joyous festivals is that of Tabernacles, or *Sukkot*, marking the coming of the autumn and the late harvests (some time in October), and also commemorating God's protection during the period when Israel dwelt in the wilderness (Lev. 23:43).

Both the seasonal and the historical aspects of the festival are symbolized in the *sukkah,* the booth in which observant Jews eat their meals during the holiday week. This booth is essentially a rustic cabin, with improvised walls, and a covering of leafy branches and twigs instead of a solid roof or ceiling. Both the covering and the walls are usually adorned with vegetables and fruits, in order to emphasize the harvest rusticity of the surroundings.

The festival is celebrated further by the ceremonial of the *lulab,* a cluster of a palm branch, three myrtle twigs, and two willow sprigs. During the recital of the *hallel* (i.e., Ps. 113-118) in the morning service of the festival, the *lulab,* together with a citron, is taken in hand, and at certain portions of the prayer, they are moved to and fro, eastward, southward, westward, northward, upward, and downward, to indicate that God, Who is being thanked for His gifts, is to be found everywhere. At the end of the service, a Scroll is taken out of the Ark, and each of those having a *lulab* marches about the Scroll in a festive procession, commemorating the similar procession about the altar in Jerusalem in the days of the Temple. On the seventh day of *Sukkot* (*Hoshanna Rabba*) there is a special service of prayer for abundant rains. After the usual service of the day, the palm branches are put down, and the willow (symbolic of abundance of rain, because it grows by the river) taken up. With these willow sprigs in hand, the congregation recites various hymns having the refrain *hoshanna* (or, as it was frequently pronounced in ancient times, *hosanna*), meaning "Help, we pray Thee." At the end of these hymns, the willows are beaten against the floor of the synagogue.

Following *Hoshanna Rabba* is the "eighth day of solemn assembly" or, as it is called in Hebrew, *Shemini Azeret.* This festival is intended as a climax for the joyful season, which begins with *Sukkot.* The festival is marked especially by the prayer for rain in the additional (*musaf*) service, which is therefore called *tephillat geshem* (the prayer for rain).

The final, or ninth, day of the autumn celebration (properly the second day of the *Shemini Azeret* festival) is popularly called *Simhat Torah* (the day of rejoicing in the Law). On this day, the last section of the Five Books of Moses, *viz.,* Deuteronomy 34, and the first section of Genesis are read. In celebration of the annual completion and fresh beginning of the reading of the Pentateuch, all the Scrolls of the Law are taken from the Ark and carried about the synagogue in a procession. To enable every member of the congregation to participate in this ceremonial, the procession moves about the synagogue hall at least seven times in the evening, and then seven times more at the morning service. It is also customary in certain rituals for each member of the congregation to participate in the public reading of the Pentateuch on *Simhat Torah*. Immediately before the reading of the last section of the Pentateuch, it is customary in most congregations to call to read from the Torah one of the distinguished members of the congregation together "with all the children" (Hebrew, *kol ha-nearim*), so that even minors may participate in the reading on this occasion.

The person called to complete the reading of the Pentateuch on *Simhat Torah* is called *hatan ha-torah* (bridegroom of the Law, popularly pronounced, *hoson torah*). The person called to read the first chapter in Genesis on that day is called *hatan bereshit* (the bridegroom of the beginning, popularly pronounced, *hoson bereshis*). These offices are usually bestowed on men of especial piety or learning, and are among the highest honors that can be given in the synagogue service.

While on these festivals communion with God is sought through joy, on *Rosh Ha-Shanah* and *Yom Kippur* it is sought through solemnity. They are described as Days of Judgment when all living things pass before God, to stand in judgment for their deeds during the past year. During the month before *Rosh Ha-Shanah* (which usually occurs during the last three weeks of September or the beginning of October) preparation is made for the festival by sounding a ram's horn, or *shofar*, at the synagogue service each morning, and reciting Psalm 27 each morning and evening. Beginning with the Sunday preceding *Rosh Ha-Shanah* (if *Rosh Ha-Shanah* occurs on Monday or Tuesday, beginning with the Sunday of the preceding week), special prayers (called *sel:hot*) are recited at dawn of each day, beseeching Divine forgiveness for man's transgressions. While only the most pious assemble at the synagogue to recite these prayers each day, many recite them on the first day, and on the day before *Rosh Ha-Shanah*. In some congregations, these prayers are recited at midnight rather than at dawn, to make possible a larger attendance.

The festival of *Rosh Ha-Shanah* itself is particularly devoted to prayers for peace and prosperity for all mankind, and for life and happiness for individual human beings. It also emphasizes the recognition of God as King of the Universe. This phase of the festival is reflected not only in the prayers of the day, but in several of the ceremonials. The *shofar* is sounded before, during, and after the additional morning prayer. The notes sounded by the *shofar* tend to arouse the people to repentance, reminding them that the Kingdom of God can be realized in our hearts and in our personal lives, even in the world in which we live. In the afternoon of the first day of the festival it is customary in many communities to walk to a river bank, as was sometimes done in ancient times at the anointing of a king. This custom is called *tashlik* (throwing), because of the popular belief that it is intended to cast off one's sins into the river.

On the evening of the first day of *Rosh Ha-Shanah* it is customary to eat apples and other fruits, dipped in honey, saying, "May it be Thy will that this year shall be happy and sweet for us." In many localities bread is dipped in honey at all the meals eaten on *Rosh Ha-Shanah,* and during the days following it until the Day of Atonement. On the second evening of *Rosh Ha-Shanah* it is customary to eat new fruit, over which the blessing *sheheheyanu* (Who has kept us alive) is recited.

The ten days beginning with the first days of *Rosh Ha-Shanah* and ending with *Yom Kippur,* are called the "Ten Days of Penitence." It is expected that everyone will observe particularly high standards of ethical and ceremonial conduct during these days. There are special prayers assigned for the period, beseeching continuance of life and peace, and the *selihot* are recited on them as on the days preceding *Rosh Ha-Shanah.*

On the day preceding *Yom Kippur* (the ninth of Tishri) tradition prescribes festive meals. The final meal of the day, eaten before the sundown that ushers in *Yom Kippur,* thus is marked by a peculiar combination of joy and solemnity. Before eating this meal, an oral confession of sins is recited by each person as part of the afternoon prayer. It is also customary during the day to distribute money for charitable purposes. After the meal the head of the household kindles a lamp or candle to burn for twenty-four hours, that is, until the end of the day. The mother kindles the usual festival lights, and the family proceeds to the synagogue.

The Day of Atonement is a season not only for repentance for trespasses against the ceremonial law but more especially for trespasses committed against ethical conduct in relations between men. Forgiveness for these trespasses can be obtained only when the man who suffered wrong pardons the injustice. It is therefore customary for anyone who is conscious of having injured a neighbor to obtain forgiveness before the Day of Atonement.

Men and women may unwittingly injure even those dear to them, including members of their families. Such thoughtlessness may raise a barrier to friendship and love. The eve of the Day of Atonement is considered an appropriate time to remove these barriers; relatives and friends call upon each other or write, offering good wishes for the coming year and either directly or indirectly asking forgiveness for any misunderstanding. Parents and grandparents bless their children and grandchildren. The moving prayer which is recited just before the evening service closes with the words: "I completely forgive anyone who has committed a trespass against me, whether against my person or against my property. . . . May no man suffer punishment because of me. And may it be Thy will, that just as I offer my forgiveness to all my fellows, that I may find grace in their eyes, so that they, too, will forgive my trespasses against them."

The Day of Atonement thus becomes a day for the renewal of bonds of affection and friendship.

The evening service in the synagogue, which must be recited before dark, is called *kol nidre* from its first words (meaning all vows), and is a service of absolution for ceremonial vows. This ceremony is made necessary by the rule of Jewish Law requiring fulfillment of every vow, even at great sacrifice. The vows that the ceremony of *kol nidre* releases are of course only those relating to ritual and custom. Without the consent of his neighbor, no ceremony can release anyone from a vow or promise made to his neighbor.

Because the *kol nidre* opens the service of the Day of Atonement, it is a particularly solemn ceremony. Its melody is probably the best known of all those associated with synagogue services.

The Day of Atonement is the major fast in the Jewish calendar, a day on which all principal sensual pleasures are interdicted. Men of piety also avoid wearing shoes made of leather on this day, particularly in the home or in the synagogue.[18]

The prayers of *Yom Kippur* are so arranged that they continue uninterruptedly from their beginning in the morning until their end in the *neilah* service after sunset. At each service, there is a confession of sin and a prayer for forgiveness. During the additional prayer of the morning (*musaf*) there is a re-enactment of part of the ancient service at the Temple. In its course, the members or at least the elders of the congregation prostrate themselves four times, just as the community gathered in the ancient Temple prostrated itself whenever the Divine Name was pronounced in the service.

The melodies of each of the *Yom Kippur* services follow definite traditions, and are reflective of the mood in which the service is expected to be pronounced. In the course of these services (as well as in those of *Rosh Ha-Shanah*) the Ark is frequently opened for the recital of especially impressive hymns and poems. The service of the Day of Atonement ends with the sounding of the ram's horn, and the joint cry by all of the congregation, "Hear, O Israel, the Lord is our God, the Lord is One."

There is a curious difference between Israel and other countries with regard to the observance of the Jewish festivals. In Israel Passover is observed for seven days, in accordance with the rule set down in Ex. 12:15; outside Israel it is observed for eight days. Similarly Pentecost and *Shemini Azeret* are each observed for one day in Israel, but for two days elsewhere. Moreover, in Israel work is forbidden only on the first and seventh days of Passover, and on the first day of *Sukkot*; outside Israel it is forbidden also on the second and on the eighth day of Passover, and on the second day of *Sukkot*.

The reason for this variation of custom is historical. In ancient times the beginning of the Jewish month was fixed when the authorities of the Temple in Jerusalem observed the new moon. As the lunar month had been accurately measured in antiquity, it was comparatively easy to foretell when the moon ought to appear in Jerusalem. But the first crescent of the new moon was frequently so thin and set so soon after the sun, that it was impossible to be certain that it had actually been observed. Therefore, those away from Jerusalem always had some doubt as to whether the Temple authorities had proclaimed one day or the next as the beginning of the calendar month.

To meet this difficulty, Temple authorities would send out messengers informing distant communities of the precise day they had fixed as that of the new moon. These messengers were able to reach all parts of Palestine in a comparatively short time, but they could not reach the distant communities of Babylonia. Hence the Babylonian Jews were always in doubt as to whether the month had begun on the precise day of the new moon, or the day following. This put them in doubt regarding the exact day of all the festivals. Therefore, in order to avoid any possible violation of a holy day, they observed all the customs relating to each festival for an additional day. In the fifth century of the Common Era, the Jewish calendar was reduced to a fixed computative system, and thereafter no one could be in doubt with regard to the time of a festival. Nevertheless, the Jews outside Israel continued to observe their ancient custom. In Israel, uncertainty regarding the precise period of the festival could occur only with regard to *Rosh Ha-Shanah*, which occurs on the first day of the month. Hence, *Rosh Ha-Shanah* is observed for two days in Israel as well as in other countries. It is not customary to observe the Day of Atonement for two days because it is considered impossible to impose the severity of two successive days of fasting on the whole community. Reform Jews have, in general, abandoned the observance of the second day of the holidays.

In addition to these major festivals, whose celebration is commanded in the Law of Moses, there are two lesser festivals in Judaism, which are occasions of great religious joy and sense of communion with God: *Purim*, the Feast of Esther, and *Hanukkah*, the feast commemorating the rededication of the Temple during the time of the Maccabees.

In accordance with the prescription of the Book of Esther, *Purim* (occurring in the first half of March) is celebrated as a day of rejoicing and thanksgiving, with the exchange of gifts between friends, and charity to the poor. The Book of Esther is read publicly both at the evening and at the morning service. In the late afternoon, a family festival, second in importance only to that of the *seder* service, is usually held. This festive dinner is called the *seudat purim* (*Purim* meal).

Hanukkah (the midwinter festival that occurs in the month of December) is celebrated in commemoration of the purification of the Temple by the Maccabees, after it had been defiled by the Syrian king, Antiochus IV, in the year 168 before the Common Era. Led by Judas the Maccabee, the Jews won amazing victories over outnumbering Syrian armies, and finally reconquered Jerusalem, drove the pagans out of the Temple, and re-established it as a place for the worship of God. The day of the rededication of the Temple was the third anniversary of its first defilement, the twenty-fifth of Kislev, and that day, together with seven succeeding days, is observed as *Hanukkah* (the feast of dedication).

On the first night of *Hanukkah* a candle is lit, and on each succeeding night of the eight-day festival an additional candle is lit, in celebration of the holiday. It is also customary to mark the festival with family meals, games, and the exchange of gifts, particularly within the family.

Besides *Yom Kippur*, there are several lesser fasts in the Jewish calendar. Of these the most important is *Tisha B'ab* (popularly pronounced *Tishoh B'ov*), the ninth day of the month of Ab, the anniversary of the burning of the first and also of the second Temple. In memory of these catastrophes, it is the rule to fast from sunset on the evening before this day until the sunset of the day itself. The Book of Lamentations is recited in the evening, and in the morning a number of dirges record ancient and medieval sufferings of the Jewish people. To increase a sense of bereavement it is customary in many communities to spend the afternoon of *Tisha B'ab* visiting the graves of relatives.

There are several other fasts, less commonly observed, during which food is forbidden only during the day. These are the fast of *Gedaliah* (on the day following *Rosh Ha-Shanah*); the tenth day of the month of Tebet; and the seventeenth day of the month of Tammuz. All these fasts are mentioned in Zech. 8:19. The fast of *Gedaliah* commemorates the murder of the last governor of Judah in the year 586 before the Common Era (Jer. 41:2). The fast of Tebet commemorates the beginning of the siege of Jerusalem by the Babylonians (Ez. 24:1-2). The seventeenth day of Tammuz is the anniversary of the breach in the wall of Jerusalem by the Romans in the year 70.

Partial mourning is still observed during the three weeks between the seventeenth day of Tammuz and the ninth of Ab, the period when Jerusalem was pillaged by the victorious Roman soldiery. No weddings are performed; other festivities and the wearing of new clothes are considered inappropriate. During the last nine days of this period it is customary for many Jews to abstain from meat and wine (except on the Sabbath day).

The Jewish religious calendar begins in the autumn with *Rosh Ha-Shanah*, the festival of the New Year. The names of the months were adopted from the Babylonian calendar and are as follows: Tishri, Marchesvan (frequently called Heshvan), Kislev, Tebet, Shebat, Adar, Nisan, Iyyar, Sivan, Tammuz, Ab, Elul.

The length of the month is fixed by the lunar cycle of twenty-nine and a half days and therefore is alternately twenty-nine and thirty days. The length of the year of twelve months is thus 354 days, though under special circumstances it may be 353 or 355 days. To make up the difference between this period and that of the solar year of 365¼ days, an additional month is added to the year, seven times in a cycle of nineteen years. This additional month is added immediately before Nisan (the month of the Passover) and is called the Second Adar. The additional month is added on the third, sixth, eighth, eleventh, fourteenth, seventeenth, and nineteenth years of the cycle.

Because of the character of the Jewish calendar, the beginning of each month coincides with the new moon, and the first days of the festivals of Passover and *Sukkot* (falling on the fifteenth day of their respective months) occur at the full moon.

Rabbi José ben Halafta, a great scholar who lived in Palestine in the first half of the second century c.e., compiled a history of the Jews, which, following the example of Scripture, opened with the Creation. This book is called *Seder Olam* (The History of the World). Utilizing the chronology of Scripture for its time, and reconstructing postbiblical history as well as he could, Rabbi José arrived at the conclusion that the world was created in the year 3828 before the destruction of the Temple at the hands of the Romans. As by Rabbinic tradition the date of the destruction was placed in the year 67-68 c.e., the Creation according to his calculation occurred in the year 3761-3760 b.c.e., or to be more nearly exact, in September or October, 3761 b.c.e.

The most significant confusion in Rabbi José's calculation was that reducing the whole period from the rebuilding of the Temple by Zerubabel in 516 b.c.e. to the conquest of Persia by Alexander (which he dates 318 b.c.e.) to no more than thirty-four years. Like other Rabbinic scholars he believed that Zerubabel (sixth century b.c.e.), Malachi, Ezra, Nehemiah (all fifth century b.c.e.) and Simeon the Righteous (third century b.c.e.) were all contemporaries.

For many centuries this calculation by Rabbi José was of interest only to talmudic students, who also tried to satisfy a curiosity for historical reconstruction. The usual calculation adopted by Jews in Rabbinic and even post-talmudic times, was that of the Seleucid monarchy, that assumed rule over Syria and Palestine in the year 312 b.c.e. This era is in Jewish literature usually referred to as that of "legal documents," for it was in dating such documents that it generally occurred.

Only when the center of Jewish life was moved from Babylonia to Europe, and the era calculation based on the rule of the Seleucids seemed anachronistic and became meaningless, was it replaced by that based on the calculations of Rabbi José ben Halafta. Though this calculation (making

5719 the equivalent of 1958-1959) is now in universal use among Jews, it has no dogmatic sanction and is in effect simply an arbitrary figure used for convenience and uniformity.[19]

SPECIAL OCCASIONS IN THE COURSE OF LIFE

The occasions of special joy or sadness in human life are, in Judaism, surrounded with ceremonials intended to make them means for closer communion with God. These ceremonials aid the Jew to temper joy with solemnity and sorrow with resignation. When he is happy, the Jew is instructed to think with gratitude of God, Who is the source of happiness; and when he is in grief, he is likewise instructed to look to God, as the source of consolation. Birth, marriage, and death are thus more than incidents in temporal and sensual existence. They are the occasions for thinking more deeply than usual about the meaning of existence, and the relation of man to God.

Every person born of Jewish parents is considered bound to observe the covenant of Sinai, and therefore subject to the observance of Jewish ceremonial. Although mixed marriages are prohibited, the child of a Jewish mother is regarded as a Jew and need undergo no ceremony of conversion to be admitted to the Jewish faith. A member of another faith who desires to be converted to Judaism must (according to traditional ritual) appear before a rabbi and state his desire to be converted. The rabbi will then provide for his instruction in the elements of Jewish law, belief, and practice. Before admitting him to the Jewish fold, the rabbi must warn him of the severe discipline of Judaism and the difficulties involved in adherence to the Jewish faith. If the applicant persists in his desire to enter the Jewish faith, the rabbi will arrange for the ceremony of proselytization. A male applicant must be circumcised. According to the traditional ritual followed by Orthodox and Conservative Jews, both male and female applicants become proselytes by immersion in a pool of running water, declaring that they are performing the ceremony in order to be admitted into the Jewish faith, and reciting as they emerge from the water the benediction, "Blessed art Thou, O Lord, our God, King of the Universe, Who didst sanctify us with Thy commandments, and hast commanded us regarding the ceremonial immersion of the proselyte." Reform rabbis do not include this ritual immersion in their ceremony of proselytization.

In accordance with the prescriptions of Gen. 17:9-14, the son of Jewish parents is circumcised on the eighth day of his life. (The ceremony may be postponed for reasons of health.) Because the ritual of circumcision involves at once a knowledge of surgery and of traditional customs, it is performed by a man especially trained for the purpose, called a *mohel* (one who circumcises). At the circumcision, the father recites the benediction, "Blessed art Thou, O Lord, our God, King of the Universe, Who didst consecrate us with Thy commandments, and hast commanded us to bring this child into the covenant of our ancestor, Abraham." All those present respond, "Just as he has entered the covenant of Abraham, may he also enter into the study of the Law, into marriage, and into good deeds!" The *mohel* or some other person present, then prays for the child's future piety and welfare and that of his mother, and announces his name.

A girl is named at the service in the synagogue on the Sabbath (or any other day when the Torah is read) following her birth, when the father is called to participate in the reading of the Torah. One of those present then prays for the health of the mother of the child, and for the health of the child, and announces its name.

Boys under thirteen and girls under twelve years of age are theoretically not obligated to observe the discipline of the ritual Law. In order to be trained in the Law, they are expected to observe such parts of it as they can without impairing their health. As soon as a child can speak, he is taught to recite simple evening and morning prayers, consisting primarily of the first verse of the *Shema*. When the child reaches school age, he is taught the Hebrew language, the Bible and, as he grows older, advanced Jewish studies. The instruction is given the child by his parents, by a private teacher, or in a religious school. The traditional school devoted to this purpose is called a *Talmud Torah* (the place of the study of the Law). In America, these institutions usually provide instruction for children for either three or five (in some instances, seven or ten) hours per week, after the regular secular school hours on weekdays, and on Sunday mornings. There are also Jewish day schools established in some communities, providing both secular and religious education. These are sometimes called *yeshibot* (singular, *yeshiba* or *yeshiva*, academy). The name *yeshiba* or *yeshiva* is also used for traditional schools of advanced talmudic study in Europe and for similar institutions in America.[20a]

A month before a boy has reached his thirteenth birthday he is expected to begin to don the *tephillin* each morning. On the Sabbath following his thirteenth birthday, he is called to participate in the formal reading of the Torah at the usual synagogue service. The ceremony of which this is part is popularly called *bar mitzva* (son of the commandment, in reference to his obligation to perform the commandments thereafter). Parents frequently arrange a celebration in honor of this occasion.

In many American synagogues similar note is taken when a girl attains the age of twelve, and therefore becomes subject to the commandments. The ceremony which is called *bat mitzva* (daughter of the commandment, popularly pronounced *bas mitzva*) is variously observed in different communities. In some, the girl is permitted to read the prophetic portion in the vernacular. In others, there is simply a family festivity.

Many Conservative and Reform congregations have established, either in lieu of these *bar mitzva* and *bat mitzva* ceremonies or in addition to them, that of confirmation. This ritual is usually observed on Pentecost. Boys and girls from fourteen to sixteen are taught the elements of Jewish faith and history in preconfirmation classes, and are then called to announce their devotion to the faith at a public synagogue ceremonial.

In the traditional marriage service, the ceremony takes place under a canopy (*huppah*), which symbolizes the home established through the marriage.

Judaism regards complete mutual understanding and trust between the bride and the bridegroom as a basic requirement for a valid marriage. A number of ceremonies have been established to give expression to this conception, and there are even several legal forms which emphasize it.

Before the wedding, the rabbi or other person in charge of the ceremony asks the bridegroom whether he undertakes to fulfill all the traditional obligations of a Jewish husband to his wife. These include various provisions for the maintenance of the wife, both during married life and, if the occasion should arise, during her widowhood. As these are civil obligations, a formal agreement must be made to provide for them. On the bridegroom's assenting, the ceremony of *kinyan* (agreement) is performed. This consists of the rabbi's handing the bridegroom an object of value, usually a handkerchief, as a symbolic consideration, to make the bridegroom's acceptance of the conditions of the marriage valid. The rabbi then draws up a document called a *ketubah* (writ, popularly pronounced *kesubah*) detailing these obligations as well as those of the wife. This *ketubah* is witnessed by two observant Jews, neither of whom may be related to the bride or bridegroom. The officiating rabbi, if not a relation, may act as one of these witnesses.

The language of the *ketubah* is Aramaic, the vernacular of the Jews of Palestine during the period when the present text was composed. The document is sometimes artistically decorated; and a number of the *ketubot* preserved in various museums of Jewish antiquities are of great interest to the student of art.

The wedding ceremony itself consists of a series of benedictions, having for their purpose the expression of thanks to God for the institution of marriage and the family, for having implanted His image on the human race, and for the joy of the wedding, and including prayers for the happiness of the bride and bridegroom and for the restoration of Jerusalem. After the first of these benedictions, the bridegroom hands the bride a ring, and says to her in Hebrew, "Thou art sanctified unto me, with this ring, in accordance with the Law of Moses and of Israel." At the end of the ceremony a glass is broken to commemorate the destruction of Jerusalem.

There is a considerable difference between the marriage customs of traditional and Reform Jews. In the marriage service of the Reform group, the canopy and the *ketubah* are generally omitted. The wedding is usually celebrated in the synagogue. The special prayer for the restoration of Jerusalem is omitted. On the other hand, several prayers in English on behalf of the bride and the bridegroom are added. The service ends with the recitation of the priestly blessing (Num. 6:24-26) by the rabbi.[21]

Jewish Law forbids husband and wife to cohabit or to come into physical contact during the period of menstruation or for seven days afterward. At the end of the period the wife is required to take a ritual bath in a pool of running water, or one especially built for the purpose (*mikveh*). A bride also bathes in such a *mikveh* before her wedding. The value of these regulations in preserving Jewish family life and in the prevention of certain diseases has been recognized by various Christian and Jewish writers on genetics.[22]

In Jewish Law marriage can be terminated by a religious divorce (called *get*).[22a] In practice such a divorce is granted by a rabbi only if both parties consent, and have already been divorced in the civil courts. The ritual of divorce is extremely complicated, and is performed only by specially trained scholars. Reform rabbis generally recognize a civil divorce as terminating a Jewish marriage from a religious as well as from the secular point of view, and therefore do not insist on a religious divorce as prerequisite for remarriage of either husband or wife.

There is one instance in traditional Jewish Law in which the death of the husband does not completely break the marriage bond; that is the case of a childless widow, described in Deut. 25:5-10. Biblical Law, as stated in Deuteronomy, requires such a childless widow to marry her husband's brother, so that her first-born son, by the second marriage, may "succeed in the name of the brother which is dead, that his name be not put out of Israel." Later Rabbinic ordinances forbade the performance of such a Levirate marriage, but nevertheless insisted that the widow may not remarry without performing the ceremony of *halitzah*, ordained in Deuteronomy, as alternative to such a marriage.

When a Jew feels that the end of his life is approaching he should confess his sins in accordance with the fixed ritual, making special mention, however, of any sin which he is conscious of having committed, and which is not mentioned in the traditional formula. In his last conscious moments he recites the traditional confession of faith, "Hear, O Israel, the Lord is our God, the Lord is One." Those about him may help him recite the formula by repeating it with him.

According to Rabbinic tradition, the body should be washed after death and dressed in linen shrouds. The universal use of linen shrouds dates back to the beginning of the second century of the Common Era. Rabban Gamaliel II, the head of the Academy of Jabneh and one of the most distinguished scholars and communal leaders of his time,[23a] specifically requested that no elaborate provision such as was then customary be made for his burial, but that he be interred in a shroud like those used for the poor. The custom has been universally adopted by observant Jews to stress further the equality of all men.

The body must be interred in the ground, as soon after death as possible. Cremation is forbidden, as being an implicit denial of the Resurrection.

The funeral service is usually recited in the home of the deceased, though in the case of a person of special piety it may be recited in the synagogue. Because of the conditions of modern urban life, funeral services are sometimes held in rooms especially devoted to that purpose, so-called funeral chapels. The purpose of the service and the ceremonies associated with it is to give expression to the natural grief of the bereaved, and at the same time to inculcate in the bereaved resignation to the Will of God.

The service consists of the recital of one or more psalms and selections of appropriate verses from other psalms. Usually Psalm 16, 23, 90, or 91 is recited. The reading of the psalm may be followed by an address; and the service closes with a prayer for the peace of the soul of the deceased. This prayer is repeated at the grave, and a second psalm is recited, after which the bereaved recite the *kaddish*. Either during the funeral services or immediately before the burial, the person officiating at the ceremonies asks the near relatives of the deceased (husband, wife, son, daughter, father, mother, brother, or sister) each to cut one of his garments. This ceremony is called *keriah* (tearing the garment) and is reminiscent of the ancient Jewish usage of tearing one's clothes in bereavement (see II Sam. 1:11). After tearing the garment, each of the bereaved recites the blessing of resignation to the justice of God: "Blessed art Thou, O Lord, our God, King of the Universe, the true Judge."

During the week after the burial of a relative, near relatives, including husband, wife, children, brothers, sisters, and parents, remain at home. They must not engage in any gainful occupation, unless the income is vital to their subsistence, or unless they will otherwise forfeit their employment. It is customary for friends to visit the mourners to console them, and to arrange community prayers in the house of the deceased. During the whole week of mourning (called *shiva*, seven, i.e., the seven days of mourning) a lamp is kept burning in the house of the deceased. None of the mourners wears any jewels, and mirrors, considered a luxury, are covered. The mourners sit on low stools instead of chairs; they do not study the Law or the Scriptures, save such solemn works as the Books of Job and Lamentations, the dire prophecies in Jeremiah, and the laws of mourning in the Talmud and Codes; and they are forbidden to wear shoes made of leather.

After the completion of the *shiva*, the relatives observe partial mourning for the remainder of the month. They do not don new clothes, and avoid taking part in festivities, or listening to music. On the death of a parent, this partial mourning is observed for a whole year. In order to make grief itself a means for closer communion with God, the bereaved children are expected, during this year of mourning, to be particularly mindful of religious observances, to attend synagogue service regularly, and to recite the *kaddish* at each prayer. Whenever possible, a bereaved son serves as reader of the public prayers on weekdays during this year of mourning. These customs are also observed on the anniversary of the death of one's parents. Such an anniversary is called *yahrzeit* (a German name, because the custom assumed its present form among the German Jews). It is customary, also, to have a light burning at home during the day marking the anniversary of the death of a near relative. This light symbolizes the belief in human immortality, in accordance with the Rabbinic interpretation of the verse (Pr. 20:27), "The spirit of man is the lamp of God, searching all the inward parts." About a year after the death of a relative, the mourners set up a monument marking the place of the grave. At the unveiling of this monument called *massebah* (pillar, popularly pronounced *matzevah*), psalms are read, prayers are recited for the peace of the soul of the deceased, and the *kaddish* is repeated.

THE JEWISH HOME AND THE DIETARY LAWS

Like every other authentic experience, piety cannot stop short of the home. If religion were to be merely ecclesiastical, it would soon cease to be that too. The Psalmist who was told "Let us go up to the house of the Lord" rejoiced because in his own house the reality of God was never forgotten. Throughout Jewish history the attempt to reproduce in the home the order and mood of the place of worship has never been relaxed.

The interrelationship of sanctuary and home has been responsible for at least two significant results. On the one hand, the Jew did not remain a stranger to the ceremonial and purpose of his sacred institutions. On the other hand, his home and home life were transfigured. His residence became a habitation of God.

This sanctification of the home was achieved by a religious discipline whose purpose was constantly to prompt a remembrance of God. The Jew who visited the ancient Temple, for example, readily understood that the elaborate rites, precautions, exactitudes and purifications were the appropriate expressions of the beauty of holiness. "If you were to serve a king of flesh and blood," the saintly Hillel once reminded a guest, "would you not have to learn how to make your entrances and exits and obeisances? How much more so in the service of the King of kings!"

That such fastidiousness was therefore required in God's House the

Jew accepted unquestioningly. The forms reminded him of God. And because they did, and because Israel's teachers tried to prevent the Jew from forgetting God even when he was away from the Sanctuary, corresponding rituals and attitudes were introduced into the Jewish home. Thus the Jewish home became a sanctuary in miniature, its table an altar, its furnishings instruments for sanctity.

In a sense, every detail of home life is an expression of the pattern of sanctity. Jewish homes, for example, are generally expected to contain basic religious texts such as the Bible, usually accompanied at least by the commentary of Rashi, the Talmud, perhaps an abbreviated code (the short *Shulhan Aruk*), some of the magnificent moralistic works, and of course the prayer book—actually one of the most extraordinary anthologies of Jewish classical literature. It is not uncommon to find in a Jewish home an excellent library with volumes handed down from father to son, volumes which reveal constant use.

Similarly, the various family festival celebrations with their rituals constitute activities that bring the Divine message very close to the Jew. It is an insensitive Jewish child who forgets the beauty of the *seder* at Passover, or the kindling of the lights during *Hanukkah*, or the sight of his mother kindling the Sabbath lamps at dusk. These and like activities collaborate to make holiness a familiar emphasis and delight.

Part of the daily pattern of sanctity is formed by the so-called dietary laws. As is well known, Jewish law prohibits the eating of certain foods. These prohibitions are enumerated essentially in Lev. 11, and again in Deut. 14. No vegetable growths are prohibited; but of animal life the Law permits fish having scales and fins, certain types of fowl, and only those quadrupeds that chew their cud and have cloven hoofs. Among the domestic quadrupeds this includes only oxen, sheep, and goats.

According to traditional Judaism, warm-blooded animals may be eaten only if they are ritually slaughtered, i.e., if they are slaughtered in the manner used in the Temple for sacrificial purposes. The knife used in slaughtering must be sharp, and must be examined both before and after slaughtering to be certain that its edge contains no notch, which by tearing the animal's throat might give it unnecessary pain. The animal must not, however, be stunned before slaughtering, for stunning prevents the free flow of the blood, and the absorption of the blood in the meat makes the food prohibited. To ensure the animal's speedy death, the person who slays it must be trained for the work. He must know enough of the diseases of animals to be able to examine the body and to make certain that it was suffering from no serious disease. A person so trained is called a *shohet* (slaughterer). In order to be allowed to perform his duties, he must receive authorization from a rabbi.

After an animal is slaughtered, its lungs are examined to guard against symptoms of various communicable diseases, mainly tuberculosis. The Talmud, its commentaries, and the later codes, contain an impressive amount of veterinary information regarding the symptoms of disease in animals, so that an examination based on this information is a valuable means of detecting disease.

If an animal has been found to be free from serious disease, its meat is declared *kasher* (fit, popularly pronounced *kosher*).

The meat must not, however, remain unwashed for three days. If it does, the surface blood is believed to be absorbed in the tissues, and the food becomes prohibited. After the meat is cut, the various parts are placed in a container of water for half an hour to be cleansed of surface blood. Thereafter the meat is covered with salt, to draw out the blood further, and remains in the salt for at least an hour. The salt is then washed off, and the meat may be boiled. Meat which is to be roasted on a spit need not be soaked in water or salted. Meat from the udder or the liver may be prepared only by roasting.

In addition to the various laws prohibiting certain types of food, there is a rule mentioned thrice in Scripture against seething a kid in its mother's milk (Ex. 23:19 and 34:26; Deut. 14:21). This rule was originally intended, according to Maimonides, to extirpate an idolatrous practice. It is interpreted as prohibiting the cooking or eating the meat of any warm-blooded animal with milk, or a derivative of milk. Hence to serve meat and milk or butter or cheese at the same meal is prohibited. In order to avoid any possibility of a mixture of meat and milk, observant Jews provide themselves with two types of plates, one of which is used only for meat foods, the other only for milk foods. Further, it is customary in many countries not to eat milk dishes for six hours after a meat meal.

THE STATUS OF WOMAN IN JEWISH LAW AND RITUAL

From its beginnings, Judaism has consistently endeavored to proclaim and effectuate the equality of the sexes before God and in society. The first chapter of Genesis describes Adam as created "male and female" (v. 27), and continues to narrate how "God blessed them, and God said unto them, Be fruitful and multiply and replenish the earth and subdue it. And have dominion over the fish of the sea, and over the fowl of the air, and over every living thing that creepeth upon the earth." This description emphasizing the equality of woman and man, is repeated at the beginning of the fifth chapter of the Book.

Though in the general pattern of Mediterranean society, in which Judaism originated, the status of women was definitely inferior to that of men, Jewish law in its biblical and particularly in its postbiblical stages endeavored to overcome this differentiation between the rights of the sexes.

Among the most significant reforms introduced by the talmudic Sages was that providing for the inheritance by orphan daughters, even when they had brothers.

Plural marriage had become virtually obsolete for Jews in Rabbinic times. It was formally interdicted by Rabbenu Gershom who lived in Germany in the eleventh century. As the foremost Rabbinic scholar in the Europe of his day, he issued a decree of excommunication against any Jew who would practice plural marriage (except under a dispensation to be granted by one hundred Rabbis, in cases other systems of law would regard as justifying divorce or annulment of marriage). He also declared an excommunication against anyone who would divorce his wife against her will. With these measures, and those of older times that permitted a wife to apply to a Jewish court for a writ of divorcement under certain circumstances, the status of husband and wife was practically equalized in regard to marriage law.

While formal education in Rabbinics was generally limited to men, provision was often made also for the education of women. During Rabbinic times, and even more frequently in the Middle Ages, some women achieved high distinction in scholarship. In later ages, books were written in Yiddish for the edification and instruction of women; and many achieved an astonishing degree of erudition simply through listening to the learned disquisitions of rabbis on the Sabbaths.

While the service at the synagogue, like that of the priests in the Temple, is conducted by men, what might be called worship at home is largely the prerogative of the wife and mother. Kindling of the Sabbath lights, supervision of the child's education, maintenance of the food laws, and preparation for the festivals are considered especially part of woman's share in Divine worship.

In the latter part of the nineteenth and in the twentieth century Reform Jews and many Conservative Jews abolished the separation of the sexes in the synagogue. In all groups, there is in modern days far greater participation of women in synagogue work and administration, growing provision for the education of girls, and increasing opportunities for women to serve as teachers and school executives. In many congregations, Orthodox as well as Conservative and Reform, women serve on the lay boards of the synagogues and of synagogue organizations. They serve as members of faculties of teachers institutes, and have been known to be admitted as students in rabbinical schools.

PROHIBITIONS OR NEGATIVE COMMANDMENTS

Most of the laws so far described are affirmative commandments. They tell the Jew what he is expected to do on particular occasions. But according to Rabbinical calculation, the greater part of the biblical Law consists of negative regulations or prohibitions. In fact, a Palestinian scholar of the third century maintained that Scripture contains no less than three hundred and sixty-five prohibitions but only two hundred and forty-eight positive injunctions. Since his time these have been variously enumerated; the most important codification being that of Maimonides, in his Book of the Commandments and in the introduction to his Code.

The system of negative commandments is as vital to Judaism as are its positive ceremonials. Some of the prohibitions have been discussed in preceding sections, and are associated with the ceremonial observances themselves. Thus the observance of Passover includes not only eating *matzah*, but also abstention from leaven. Worship of God involves rejection of all idolatry, including rituals which were part of ancient pagan faiths no longer in existence.

Whatever may be the significance of a particular rule—whether personal hygiene, the extirpation of idolatry, the inculcation of gentleness—the whole system of prohibitions has a common goal. It is to make the awareness of God a continuous, uninterrupted experience. Affirmative actions and gestures are, by their nature, limited to stated occasions. Negations are timeless. The positive ceremonial is intended to arouse man's spirit to particular heights; the prohibition prevents him from forgetting God at any time. There is never a time or place when, to quote the Rabbinic phrase, "a person is naked of the commandments." He is always on the alert against possible violation of the Law. He has more prohibitions to guard against on the Day of Atonement than on the Sabbath; and on the Sabbath than on weekdays. But he is never without the possibility of falling into error, and therefore never free from the responsibility of avoiding sin.

It is in his relations with fellow men that a person becomes especially aware of the presence of God; love for them inevitably develops into love for Him. Jews are therefore warned in their Law to beware any infringement of the rights and privileges of others. "What is distasteful to thee, do not to thy neighbor" was the summary of the Law made by the great talmudic teacher Hillel. To develop such sensitivity to others' feelings as to avoid what may give them pain, and to concentrate on what will cause pleasure, is a discipline demanded by Judaism not simply as courtesy and politeness but as the Law of God. It was the apparent purpose of the Lawgiver and his disciples to create a group for whom the service of God would be the principal vocation of life, and all earthly interests an avocation; for whom the presence of God would be so manifest that the trivialities and temptations of mundane existence would appear unimportant.

The very incongruity between the traditional Jewish system of life and one which lays great stress on efficiency, productivity, and abundance is a basic, implicit idea of the faith. The first premise of the Torah is that "man doth not live by bread alone," and that there are joys in the sense of communion with God, in the awareness of His being and His kingdom, of His love and of love for Him, so deep and all-pervading as to make all other experiences of life insignificant. As neither man as a whole nor Jews as a group have reached this stage of sensitivity to the Deity, the hastening of the process leading to it is a primary obligation. Life in accordance with Torah is a preparation for the detachment from material affairs, a means to attain absorption in spiritual ones. Without such absorption, man may seek compensation for his unhappiness and frustration in domination of his fellows; and his very search for earthly goods may become his undoing. Judaism assumes that there are many ways that man can learn to love God, so as to rise above interest in the physical world. But for its adherents, traditional Judaism prescribes the austerity of a system of conduct, involving not only ethics but ceremonial, which it regards as especially inconsistent with material ambition and especially conducive to spirituality.

LOVE FOR GOD

Love for God is thus both the beginning and the end of the Jewish way of life. Awareness of God's Being, the essence of this love, fosters the observance and study of the rituals and commandments, and is itself stimulated by them. The Torah draws Israel nearer to God; and God draws Israel nearer to the Torah. The greater man's love for God the easier his escape from the futilities of earthly temptation and ambition; the more complete his transcendence of his irrational and perverted hungers for immediate and transient goods the easier for him to attain preoccupation with God.

Absorption in God is man's perfection. As man tears himself free from the chains binding him to animal and less than animal existence, he finds himself contemplating the Eternal and the Spiritual; and conversely, as he, by an act of will, focuses his intellect on the transcendent, his reason allies itself with his good propensities to make him more nearly divine.

This interrelation of love for God and perfection of man is a basic postulate of Judaism. "And thou shalt love the Lord thy God with all thy heart and with all thy soul and with all thy might" is alpha, as well as omega of Judaism. That man is capable of loving God gives promise of his future; the future will be fulfilled as man attains increasing love for God and immersion in Him.

This doctrine teaches man humility, but denies his insignificance. He can escape frustration, and perhaps self-destruction, through the discovery that he is a mere incident in the Divine process of creation.

The recognition of that elemental relationship between him and God and the achievement of the humility indispensable to the service of God give him a unique role in the process of creation. "If I labor not to perfect myself, who will perfect me? Yet if I labor only for myself, what am I?" asked Hillel.

The triviality of man, both in his physical being and in his temporal aspirations, is in sharp contrast to the vastness about him. It is tempting to seek escape from responsibility as an instrument of Divine purpose through the illusion that the immensity of the universe and his own physical insignificance are a measure of relative value. Yet in view of the proverbial prodigality of nature no consideration could be more preposterous. Flowers produce millions of pollen grains, so that one may find its way to an ovule; trees bear fruit without number, so that the species may survive through a few. That galaxies and supergalaxies, numbering many millions and containing millions of suns, should derive meaning from the evolution on a minor planet in one of the less important systems, of a sentient creature knowing good and evil, is far from inconsistent with the usual procedures of Creation. If it be true that of all the conglomerations of atoms, man alone has the power to be like God, in his ability to choose his path, fulfilling or resisting the Will of his Maker, he is indeed the ultimate triumph of Creation. The universe as a whole proceeds according to its inexorable laws; in man God has created a being which can obey, because it can also defy; which can attain perfection, not through a process beyond its control, but through one which it itself directs.

Aware of the possibility that he has this unique role in existence, man will find its rejection for the sake of trifling advantages of power and luxury difficult indeed. To know God metaphysically may be consistent with rebellion against Him; but to know Him religiously is not. Men habituated to serve God, out of love for Him, will develop the calm detached resignation of the Stoic, and yet combine with it a passionate desire to see His Will done. They will not hate, but pity, those who have no share in this enterprise, or who, through ignorance or malice, impede it. They will not resent the painful and heart-rending tarriance; nor will they count the cost for themselves or for their fellows. Yet transcendence of life's vicissitudes will not harden their hearts and freeze their emotions. They will have faith in the ultimate fulfillment of the Divine purpose, and in man's proving himself worthy of his Maker. But they will wish to hasten the progress, and they will wish to share in it. They will want the Master to be pleased with their participation, though it is inconceivable that the effort as a whole should fail even without them.

In a world in which mankind as a whole achieved love of God, to live in accordance with Jewish ritual and morals and for the goals Judaism has set will not seem curious and awkward, but natural and rational. Such a world, still finite, still imperfect, still mortal, will yet be a Kingdom of God, because it will be comparatively free from the ills produced through the confusion of men. Those who bring it nearer may be said to accept the Kingdom of God, though its realization be in the distant future. The faith of Israel teaches that this Kingdom will come, in part through the observances and teachings of Judaism itself. Whatever else a Jew may be able to offer to the world, whether in science, art, philosophy, letters, or industry, his supreme contribution is, therefore, that which he can make through the fulfillment of his religious duties, his perfection as a human being, and his development of all-embracing love for God.

NOTES

1 Without desiring to ascribe to them any responsibility for this statement, the author records with deep gratitude the assistance in its preparation given by colleagues from different schools of Jewish thought. These include Rabbis Max Arzt, Ben Zion Bokser, Samuel S. Cohon, Judah Goldin, Israel M. Goldman, Simon Greenberg, David de Sola Pool, Samuel Schulman, and Aaron J. Tofield.

[2a Cf. Judah Goldin, "The Period of the Talmud (135 B.C.E.-1035 C.E.)," this work, Vol. I, Chap. 3, *passim.*]

3 Cf. the essay on "Study as a Mode of Worship," by Professor Nathan Isaacs, in *The Jewish Library*, edited by Rabbi Leo Jung, 1928, pp. 51-70.

4 Dr. Oscar Z. Fasman is now (spring, 1958) president of the Jewish University of America.

[5a Cf. above Moshe Davis, "Jewish Religious Life and Institutions in America (A Historical Study)," pp. 310 f., 326 f., and Simon Greenberg, "Jewish Educational Institutions," pp. 407-410.]

[6a For a survey of the Orthodox, Conservative and Reform movements in the United States, cf. above Moshe Davis, *op. cit.*]

7 The extent to which even conversion to another faith affects the status of an individual within Judaism is a subject of considerable discussion in Rabbinical literature. Many authorities consider such a person a Jew, despite his conversion.

[8a Cf. Mordecai M. Kaplan, "A Philosophy of Jewish Ethics," this work, Vol. III, Chap. 2.]

[9a Cf. Alexander Altmann, "Judaism and World Philosophy: From Philo to Spinoza," this work, Vol. III, p. 82.]

[10a Cf. *ibid.*, pp. 86-87.]

11 From Jacob Emden's Letter in his edition of *Seder Olam Rabba we-Sutta u-Megillath Taanit* (Hamburg, 1757). A translation of the whole text is given by Oscar Z. Fasman in "An Epistle on Tolerance by a 'Rabbinic Zealot,'" in *Judaism in a Changing World,* ed. Rabbi Leo Jung (New York, 1939), pp. 121-136.

[12a See Itzhak Ben-Zvi, "Eretz Yisrael Under Ottoman Rule, 1517-1917," this work, Vol. I, Chap. 8; Oscar I. Janowsky, "The Rise of the State of Israel," this work, Vol. III, Chap. 8.]

13 This blessing is not recited when wearing leather garments because it is not considered fitting to thank God for life when using material produced at the cost of life.

[14a Cf. William Foxwell Albright, "The Biblical Period," this work, Vol. I, pp. 47-52; and Elias J. Bickerman, "The Historical Foundations of Postbiblical Judaism," this work, Vol. I, pp. 72 f.]

[15a For further details on the decoration of synagogues throughout the ages, cf. Rachel Wischnitzer, "Judaism and Art," this work, Vol. III, Chap. 5, *passim*.]

[16a Cf. above, Hillel Bavli, "The Modern Renaissance of Hebrew Literature," pp. 242-244.]

[17a Cf. Goldin, *op. cit.*, pp. 160-162.]

18 Shoes or sandals were considered an object of luxury in the ancient Orient. It was therefore considered improper to wear them on days of fasting or mourning.

19 For further discussion of the chronology of R. José, cf. Professor Alexander Marx in the introduction to his edition of *Seder Olam* (Berlin, 1903), pp. viii ff. and the references there given.

[20a Cf. Greenberg, *op. cit.*, pp. 359-397 and 405-407.]

21 Rabbi's Manual, edited and published by the Central Conference of American Rabbis (Cincinnati, 1928), pp. 39 ff.

22 For a further discussion and bibliography, see Mrs. R. L. Jung, in *The Jewish Library*, edited by Rabbi Leo Jung, Third Series, pp. 355-365.

[22a Difficult problems—especially concerning remarriage—confront Jews divorced in civil courts who are unable to obtain a Jewish religious divorce. Therefore in 1952 the Rabbinical Assembly of America asked Professor Saul Lieberman for application of rabbinic scholarship to a serious contemporary ethical problem. He suggested a reformulated *ketubah*, which has been adopted by the Rabbinical Assembly. In this contract the bride and bridegroom undertake to bring any tensions which may arise in their marriage before a Beth Din (court) of the Rabbinical Assembly and The Faculty of the Jewish Theological Seminary of America, authorizing the Beth Din to impose penalties on either party who fails to respond to a summons issued at the request of the other, or to accept the decision of the Beth Din in regard to divorcement. For the new *ketubah* to be valid, both bride and bridegroom are thus required to accept its provisions.]

[23a Cf. Goldin, *op. cit.*, pp. 153-155.]

BIBLIOGRAPHY

EPSTEIN, I., *Judaism*. London, 1939.

FRIEDLAENDER, GERALD, *Laws and Customs*. London, 1921.

Friedlaender, Michael, *The Jewish Religion*. New York, 1923.
Greenstone, Julius, *The Jewish Religion*. Philadelphia, 1920.
Joseph, Morris, *Judaism as Creed and Life*. London, 1903.
Kaplan, M. M., *The Meaning of Modern Jewish Religion*. New York, 1937.
Philipson, David, *Reform Movement in Judaism*. New York, 1931.
Steinberg, Milton, *Basic Judaism*. New York, 1947.

Addendum

Bamberger, Bernard J., *The Story of Judaism*. New York, 1951; 3d, augmented ed., 1970.
Buber, Martin, *On Judaism*. Edited by Nahum N. Glatzer. New York, 1967.
Dresner, Samuel H., and Siegel, Seymour, *The Jewish Dietary Laws*. New York, 1962.
Epstein, Isidore, *Judaism; a Historical Presentation*. Baltimore, 1959.
Glatzer, Nahum N., *Franz Rosenzweig: His Life and Thought*. 2d, rev. ed. New York, 1961.
Gordis, Robert, *Judaism and the Modern Age*. New York, 1955.
Greenberg, Simon, *Foundations of a Faith*. New York, 1967.
Herberg, Will, *Judaism and Modern Man: An Interpretation of Jewish Religion*. Philadelphia, 1951.
Heschel, Abraham J., *God in Search of Man: A Philosophy of Judaism*. Philadelphia, 1956.
Jacobs, Louis, *Principles of the Jewish Faith*. New York, 1964.
Kadushin, Max, *Worship and Ethics*. Chicago, 1961.
Martin, Bernard, *Contemporary Reform Jewish Thought*. Chicago, 1968.
Roth, Leon, *Judaism: A Portrait*. New York, 1961.
Siegel, Seymour, "The Nature and Meaning of Jewish Law," in *Religion and Social Action*. New York, 1964.
Waxman, Mordecai (ed.), *Tradition and Change: The Development of Conservative Judaism*. New York, 1958.

I THE JEWS: THEIR HISTORY

III THE JEWS: THEIR ROLE IN CIVILIZATION

Introductory Note

LIST OF ABBREVIATIONS

Am. Jour. Sem. Lang.
   American Journal of Semitic Languages
Annual Am. Sch. Or. Res.
   Annual American Schools of Oriental Research
Antt.
   Antiquities, Josephus
Archiv f. Orientf.
   Archiv fuer Orientforschung
ARN
   Abot of Rabbi Nathan
AZA
   Ahavah Zedakah Ahdut (B'nai B'rith Youth Organization)
b.
   ben (son of)
B.
   Babylonian Talmud
B. B.
   Baba Batra
B. C. E.
   Before the Common Era
BEAS
   The Hebrew University, Jerusalem, *Bulletin (Louis M. Rabinowitz Fund) for the Exploration of Ancient Synagogues*
Beih. Zeits. Alttest. Wiss.
   Beihefte zur Zeitschrift fuer die Alttestamentliche Wissenschaft
Bell. Jud.
   De Bello Judaico, Josephus
Ber. Saechs. Akad. Wiss.
   Berichte ueber die Verhandlungen der saechsischen Akademie der Wissenschaften
Bull. Am. Sch. Or. Res.
   Bulletin American Schools of Oriental Research
Bull. de l'Inst. Français d'Archéol. Orient.
   Bulletin de l'Institut Français d'Archéologie Orientale

Bull. Jew. Pal. Explor. Soc.
 Bulletin of the Jewish Palestine Exploration Society

C. Ap.
 Contra Apionem, Josephus

C. E.
 Common Era

CCAR
 Central Conference of American Rabbis

CJFWF
 Council Jewish Federations and Welfare Funds

cod.
 codex

Comp. Rend. Acad. des Inscr.
 Comptes-Rendus de l'Académie des Inscriptions

De Abr.
 De Abrahamo, Philo

De Ant. Jud.
 Antiquitates Judaicae, Josephus

De Cher.
 De Cherubim, Philo

De Conf.
 De Confusione Linguarum, Philo

De Congr.
 De Congressu Eruditionis Gratia, Philo

De Dec.
 De Decalogo, Philo

De Ebr.
 De Ebrietate, Philo

De Fuga
 De Fuga et Inventione, Philo

De Gig.
 De Gigantibus, Philo

De Mig. or De Migr.
 De Migratione Abrahami, Philo

De Mut.
 De Mutatione Nominum, Philo

De Op.
 De Opificio Mundi, Philo

De Plant.
 De Plantatione, Philo

De Post.
 De Posteritate Caini, Philo

De Praem.
 De Praemiis et Poenis, Philo

De Sacr.
  De Sacrificiis Abelis et Caini, Philo
De Somn.
  De Somniis, Philo
De Vita Contempl.
  De Vita Contemplativa, Philo
Dion. Halic., *De. Thuc.*
  Dionysius of Halicarnassus, *On Thucydides*
Ec. Hist.
  Ecclesiastical History, Eusebius
Enn.
  Ennead, Plotinus
Ep.
  Epistulae Morales ad Lucilium, Seneca
Epist.
  Epistles, Horace
Eur.
  Euripides
Gen. R.
  Genesis Rabbah
Harv. Theo. Rev.
  Harvard Theological Review
Heracl.
  Heracles, Euripides
HIAS
  Hebrew Sheltering and Immigrant Aid Society
HICEM
  Combination of HIAS—Hebrew Sheltering and Immigrant Aid So-
  ciety ICA—Jewish Colonization Association, Emigdirect
HUCA
  Hebrew Union College Annual
ICA
  Jewish Colonization Association
JBL or *Jour. Bib. Lit.*
  Journal of Biblical Literature
J. D. C.
  American Jewish Joint Distribution Committee
JE
  Jewish Encyclopedia
JPOS
  Journal of the Palestine Oriental Society
JQR or *Jew. Quar. Rev.*
  Jewish Quarterly Review

JQR N.S. *Jewish Quar. Rev.* N.S.
   Jewish Quarterly Review New Series

JSS
   Jewish Social Studies

J. W. B.
   Jewish Welfare Board

Jour. Near East Stud.
   Journal of Near Eastern Studies
Jour. Pal. Or. Soc.
   Journal Palestine Oriental Society
Jour. of the Warburg Inst.
   Journal of the Warburg Institute

Ket.
   Ketubot
Lam. R.
   Lamentations Rabbah
Leg. All.
   Legum Allegoria, Philo
Lev. R.
   Leviticus Rabbah
Mas. Soferim
   Masseket Soferim
MGWJ
   Monatsschrift fuer Geschichte und Wissenschaft des Judenthums
n.d.
   no date
N.F.
   Neue Folge (new series)
N.S.
   New Series
n.s.D.
   new series, D.
ORT
   Organization for Rehabilitation and Training
OSE
   World Union for the Protection of the Health of the Jews
PAJHS
   Publication of the American Jewish Historical Society
Pal. Explor. Quar.
   Palestinian Exploration Fund Quarterly
Pal. Explor. Fund Quar. State.
   Palestinian Exploration Fund Quarterly Statement
Parm.
   Parmenides, Philo

Quis Rer.
> *Quis Rerum Divinarum Heres*, Philo

Quod Deus
> *Quod Deus Sit Immutabilis*, Philo

Quod Omn.
> *Quod Omnis Probus Liber Sit*, Philo

R.
> Rab or Rabbi

Rev. études juiv.
> *Revue des Etudes Juives*

R.S.P.C.A.
> Royal Society for the Prevention of Cruelty to Animals

s.a.
> sociedad anonima (corporation)

Shab.
> Shabbat

SI
> *Studies of the Research Institute for Hebrew Poetry* (Hebrew)

Sifre Deut.
> Sifre on Deuteronomy

Sifre Num.
> Sifre on Numbers

Sitz. Heidelberger Akad. Wissen.
> *Sitzungsberichte der Heidelberger Akademie der Wissenschaften*

Sitz. Preuss. Akad. Wissen.
> *Sitzungsberichte der Preussischen Akademie der Wissenschaften*

U.J.A.
> United Jewish Appeal

U.P.A.
> United Palestine Appeal

Yer.
> Yerushalmi

Zeit. Alttest. Wiss.
> *Zeitschrift fuer die Alttestamentliche Wissenschaft*

Zeit. Deutsch. Pal. Var.
> *Zeitschrift des Deutschen Palaestina Vereins*

Zeits. Deutsch. Morg. Ges.
> *Zeitschrift der Deutschen Morgenlaendischen Gesellschaft*

Zeits. Neutest. Wissen.
> *Zeitschrift fuer die Neutestamentliche Wissenschaft*

Z.O.A.
> Zionist Organization of America

INDEX

Persons, places, and subjects omitted from the index due to limitations of space may be located by reference to the main subject, *e.g.*, to locate a chemist, look under *Science*; an author, look under *Literature*. Publications are in general not indexed by title but by author. Names containing *bar, ben ibn, ha-,* etc., are indexed by the first word of the compound. Persons and publications cited in Notes or Bibliographies have not all been indexed. Before May, 1948, references are to *Palestine*; after that date to *Israel, State of*.